2006 Medicare Explained

CCH Editorial Staff Publication

CCH INCORPORATED
Chicago
A WoltersKluwer Company

Contributing Editors

Harold M. Bishop, J.D.
Paul Clark
Barbara Leopold, J.D., M.S.
Jay Nawrocki, M.A.
Susan Smith, M.A., J.D.
Nicole T. Stone, J.D.
Suzanne Szymonik, J.D.

Jenny M. Burke, J.D., M.S.
Anuradha Gupta, J.D.
Sheila Lynch-Afryl, J.D.
Michelle L. Oxman, J.D., LL.M.
Gene Stephens Connolly, J.D.
Geri Szuberla, J.D., LL.M..

Theresa J. Jensen
Production Specialist

This publication is designed to provide accurate and authoritative information in regard to the subject matter covered. It is sold with the understanding that the publisher is not engaged in rendering legal, accounting, or other professional service. If legal advice or other expert assistance is required, the services of a competent professional person should be sought.

ISBN 0-8080-1442-0

©2006, **CCH** INCORPORATED

4025 W. Peterson Ave.
Chicago, IL 60646-6085
1 800 248 3248
health.cch.com

No claim is made to original government works; however, the gathering, compilation, magnetic translation, digital conversion, and arrangement of such materials, the historical, statutory and other notes and referencesm, as well as commentary and materials in this Product or Publication, are subject to CCH's copyright.

All Rights Reserved

Printed in the United States of America

Foreword

This book has been prepared for Medicare beneficiaries and others who need a relatively thorough explanation of the Medicare program with particular emphasis on services covered in institutional settings and services provided by physicians and suppliers.

Published annually, this book includes changes made by law and regulation amendments and guidance in the form of updates to program manuals issued by the Centers for Medicare and Medicaid Services (CMS) during 2005.

The prescription drug benefit provided under Part D authorized by the Medicare Modernization Act of 2003 (MMA) (PubLNo 108-173) became available to beneficiaries for the first time on January 1, 2006. Beneficiaries may enroll with a benefit provider from November 15, 2005 to May 15, 2006. In 2006, Beneficiaries will pay a for the first $250 of drugs purchased. For drug costs between $251 and $2250, beneficiaries will pay 25 percent of the cost of each prescription. Beneficiaries will pay 100 percent for the cost of prescription drugs for amounts spent between $2251 and $5100 each year. At this point, beneficiaries will have spent $3600 out of their own pockets on the cost of prescription drugs. From this point forward, beneficiaries will pay $2 for generic drugs and $5 for nonpreferred drugs or 5 percent of the cost of the prescription medication, whichever is greater (see ¶ 500). These amounts will change in subsequent years.

The claims appeals process will be standardized in 2006. Part A and Part B claims appeals will have uniform procedures. The first level of appeal is a redetermination made by the contractor. The second administrative appeal, a "reconsideration," is conducted by a new entity, the qualified independent contractor (QIC). The third level of appeal is to an administrative law judge (ALJ) and the fourth is a review by the Medicare Appeals Council. All Intermediary redeterminations became subject to QIC reconsiderations beginning May 1, 2005. Beginning January 1, 2006, appeals of carrier redeterminations will be subject to QIC reconsiderations, which replace the carrier hearing. The new ALJ rules are in effect for all appeals that come through the QICs. The amount in controversy for appeals and the time frames for requesting appeals for both Parts A and B are now the same. Time frames for deciding appeals have been revised and appellants may escalate their cases to the next level of appeal if the reviewing entity cannot decide the appeal within the prescribed time frame.

A new process for admission of hospice patients will be implemented this year. A hospice physician may recommend a patient for admission as well as certifying terminal illness. Verbal certification of terminal illness will be needed within two days, with hard copy and supporting documentation needed with submission of claim. In addition, the election of hospice services is effective continuously until changed by revocation, choice of a new hospice or discharge. Finally, hospices may discharge patients for disruptive behavior by the patient or by family members.

In 2006, Medicare will cover only $1,740 per year for each beneficiary for outpatient physical therapy and speech language pathology services. A separate $1,740 limit applies to outpatient occupational therapy services furnished during 2006. Congress is considering repealing this cap for 2006 (see ¶ 100). Physical therapy services that are performed by chiropractors under the two-year demonstration project provided for in the MMA are included under this cap on therapy services because chiropractors are subject to the same rules as medical doctors for therapy services under the demonstration.

Effective January 1, 2006, the Medicare Part B annual deductible was increased from $110 to $124, as required by the MMA in conjunction with increases in growth in Part B expenditures.

Other CCH publications:

Further details on the topics covered in this book, together with the texts of pertinent laws, regulations, policy guidelines, court decisions, etc., may be found in **CCH** INCORPORATED's MEDICARE AND MEDICAID GUIDE. The GUIDE is available as a six-volume, loose-leaf print product as well as electronically on CD-ROM, online, and on the Internet. Other electronic databases, including the full text of the CMS Program Manuals and the codes and complete descriptions contained in the Physician Fee Schedule, are offered as part of CCH's electronic Health Law Library. In print form, CCH also has an easy-to-read, one-volume loose-leaf Reporter specializing in Part B issues entitled the PHYSICIANS' MEDICARE GUIDE.

Finally, CCH publishes the following related paperback books:

2006 Master Medicare Guide

Medicare Prescription Drug, Improvement, and Modernization Act of 2003—Law and Explanation

Medicare Part D: Medicare Prescription Drug Benefit

Medicare Part C: Medicare Advantage

2006 Medicare and Medicaid Benefits

2006 Social Security Benefits (Including Medicare)

2006 Social Security Explained

To find out more about these publications call 888 CCH REPS (888 224 7377) or visit health.cch.com.

A note about the citations in the text:

Throughout the text, statements are documented, when possible, by citations to the law, regulations, and program manuals issued by the federal government, etc. In the interests of simplicity and conservation of space, citations generally have been made only to the highest authority available for the statement in the text, although, where appropriate, multiple citations (*i.e.*, citations both to a law provision and its implementing regulation) are included. In some instances, when there is no clear ranking of authorities, only the most widely available source is cited.

January 2006

Table of Contents

Chapter		Page
	Detailed Table of Contents	7
1	Introduction	13
2	Medicare Part A—Hospital Insurance	15
3	Medicare Part B—Supplemental Insurance	81
4	Medicare Part C—Medicare Advantage	149
5	Medicare Part D—Prescription Drug Benefit	181
6	Exclusions from Coverage	227
7	Administrative Provisions	247
8	Payment Rules	281
9	Claims, Payments, and Appeals	335
	Topical Index	355

Detailed Table of Contents

Chapter 1—Introduction
¶ 100   Introduction to Medicare

Chapter 2—Medicare Part A—Hospital Insurance

Eligibility and Enrollment
¶ 200   Entitlement to Part A Hospital Insurance Benefits
¶ 203   Voluntary Enrollment in the Hospital Insurance Program
¶ 204   Disability Beneficiaries
¶ 205   End-Stage Renal Disease Beneficiaries
¶ 206   Government Employees
¶ 209   Geographic Limits

Inpatient Hospital Services
¶ 210   Inpatient Hospital Services: Coverage in General
¶ 211   Accommodations
¶ 212   Drugs and Biologicals
¶ 213   Supplies, Appliances, and Equipment
¶ 214   Diagnostic and Therapeutic Items and Services
¶ 215   Services of Interns, Residents-in-Training, and Teaching Physicians
¶ 217   Nursing and Related Services; Private-Duty Exclusion
¶ 218   Inpatient Services Connected with Dental Services
¶ 220   Inpatient Hospital Services: Limitations on Coverage
¶ 221   Inpatient Hospital Deductible
¶ 222   Inpatient Hospital Coinsurance
¶ 223   Whole Blood and Packed Red Blood Cells
¶ 224   Duration of Covered Inpatient Hospital Services
¶ 225   Psychiatric Hospital Restrictions
¶ 226   Physicians' Professional Services
¶ 227   Emergency Services
¶ 228   Religious Nonmedical Health Care Institutions
¶ 229   "Hospital" Defined—Qualified Hospitals

Nursing Home Services
¶ 230   Extended Care Services
¶ 231   "Skilled Nursing Facility"—Conditions of Participation
¶ 232   Accommodations
¶ 233   Physical, Occupational, and Speech Therapy
¶ 235   Drugs and Biologicals
¶ 236   Supplies, Appliances, and Equipment
¶ 237   Interns and Residents-in-Training
¶ 238   Whole Blood and Packed Red Blood Cells
¶ 239   Other Services
¶ 242   Skilled Nursing Facility Coinsurance
¶ 243   Duration of Covered SNF Services
¶ 244   Noncovered Levels of Care

¶ 248 Rights of SNF Residents

Home Health Services

¶ 250 Home Health Services: Qualifying Conditions for Coverage
¶ 251   Skilled Nursing Care
¶ 252   Physical and Occupational Therapy and Speech-Language Pathology Services
¶ 253   Medical Social Services
¶ 254   Home Health Aides
¶ 255   Medical Supplies and Durable Medical Equipment
¶ 256   Interns and Residents-in-Training
¶ 257   Outpatient Services
¶ 260   Care of a Physician
¶ 262   Establishment of a Plan of Care
¶ 264   Patient Confined to Home
¶ 266   Visits
¶ 267   Specific Exclusions from Coverage
¶ 268 "Home Health Agency" Defined—Qualified Home Health Agencies

Hospice Care

¶ 270 Hospice Care

Chapter 3—Medicare Part B—Supplemental Insurance

Eligibility and Enrollment

¶ 300 Eligibility for Part B Benefits
¶ 310 Enrollment in Part B
¶ 311   Enrollment Periods
¶ 312   Automatic Enrollment
¶ 313   Coverage Period
¶ 320 Premiums

Benefits

¶ 330 Part B Benefits: In General
¶ 335 Deductible and Coinsurance
¶ 340 Physicians' Services
¶ 350 Medical and Other Health Services
¶ 351   Services and Supplies Furnished Incident to Physicians' Services
¶ 352   Outpatient Hospital Services
¶ 353   Diagnostic X-Ray, Laboratory, and Other Diagnostic Tests
¶ 354   X-Ray, Radium, and Radioactive Isotope Therapy
¶ 355   Ambulance Services
¶ 356   Durable Medical Equipment
¶ 357   Prosthetic Devices
¶ 358   Braces, Artificial Limbs, Etc.
¶ 359   Surgical Dressings, Splints, Casts, Etc.
¶ 361   Inpatient Ancillary Services
¶ 362   Listed Drugs and Biologicals
¶ 366   Other Healthcare Practitioners
¶ 369   Prevention Services

Detailed Table of Contents

¶ 370 Therapeutic Shoes
¶ 381 Physical, Occupational, and Speech Therapy Services
¶ 382 Rural Health Clinics and Federally Qualified Health Centers
¶ 383 Home Health Services
¶ 385 Comprehensive Outpatient Rehabilitation Facility Services
¶ 386 Ambulatory Surgical Services
¶ 387 Mental Health Services
¶ 388 Telehealth Services
¶ 390 National and Local Coverage Decisions

Chapter 4—Medicare Part C—Medicare Advantage

¶ 400 Overview
¶ 401 Eligibility, Election, and Enrollment
¶ 402 Benefits and Beneficiary Protections
¶ 403 Beneficiary Grievances, Appeals, and Notifications
¶ 404 MA Regional Plans
¶ 405 Contracts with Medicare Advantage Organizations
¶ 406 Medicare Contract Determinations and Appeals
¶ 407 Bids, Negotiations and Premiums
¶ 408 Payments to Medicare Advantage Organizations
¶ 409 Marketing
¶ 410 Quality Improvement Programs
¶ 411 Relationships with Providers
¶ 412 Provider-Sponsored Organizations
¶ 415 Map of 2006 MA Regions

Chapter 5—Medicare Part D—Prescription Drug Benefit

¶ 500 Overview
¶ 505 Prescription Drug Benefit
¶ 506 Eligibility and Enrollment
¶ 508 Payment of Premiums
¶ 510 Benefits and Beneficiary Protections
¶ 515 Grievances, Coverage Determinations, and Appeals
¶ 520 Premiums and Cost-Sharing Subsidies for Low Income Individuals
¶ 525 Fallback Plans
¶ 530 Payments to Sponsors of Retiree Prescription Drug Plans
¶ 535 Prescription Drug Discount Card and Transitional Assistance Program
¶ 560 Map of 2006 PDP Regions

Chapter 6—Exclusions from Coverage

¶ 600 Exclusions Under Both Plans
¶ 601 Services Not Reasonable and Necessary
¶ 602 Experimental, Investigational and Other Excluded Procedures
¶ 604 No Legal Obligation to Pay
¶ 607 Services Paid for by Governmental Entity
¶ 610 Services Outside the United States
¶ 613 War Claims
¶ 616 Personal Comfort Items

¶ 619 Routine Checkups; Glasses; Eye Examinations; Immunizations
¶ 622 Foot Care and Orthopedic Shoes
¶ 625 Custodial Care
¶ 628 Cosmetic Surgery
¶ 630 Routine Costs in Clinical Trials
¶ 631 Charges by Relatives
¶ 634 Dental Services
¶ 635 Services Not Provided In-House
¶ 636 Medicare as Secondary Payer
¶ 637 Workers' Compensation
¶ 638 Automobile and Liability Insurance Coverage
¶ 639 Employer Group Health Plans
¶ 644 Limitation on Payments for Certain Drugs
¶ 646 Individuals and Entities Guilty of Program Abuses
¶ 654 Surgery Assistants in Cataract Operations

Chapter 7—Administrative Provisions

¶ 700 Medicare Organizational Structure
¶ 703 Role of the State and Local Agencies
¶ 705 Role of the Fiscal Intermediaries, Carriers, and Medicare Administrative Contractors
¶ 707 Role of Medicaid
¶ 710 Quality Improvement Organizations—QIOs
¶ 715 Privacy of Health Data
¶ 720 Fraud and Abuse Penalties
¶ 730 Provider Participation Agreements
¶ 740 "Medigap" Insurance

Chapter 8—Payment Rules

¶ 800 Introduction
¶ 810 Prospective Payment System for Inpatient Hospital Services
¶ 820 Physicians' Fee Schedule
¶ 821 Actual Charge Restrictions
¶ 826 Nonphysician Practitioners
¶ 827 Clinical Diagnostic Laboratory Tests
¶ 831 Assignment
¶ 833 Participation Program for Physicians and Suppliers
¶ 834 Private Non-Medicare Contracts with Healthcare Practitioners
¶ 835 Home Health Agencies
¶ 837 Hospital Outpatient Services
¶ 839 Skilled Nursing Facilities
¶ 841 Rehabilitation Hospitals
¶ 843 Long-Term Care Hospitals
¶ 845 Psychiatric Hospitals and Units
¶ 847 End-Stage Renal Disease

Chapter 9—Claims, Payments, and Appeals

¶ 900 Claims and Appeals
¶ 902   Part A Benefit Claims
¶ 903   Part B Benefit Claims
¶ 906 Overpayments and Underpayments
¶ 908 Waiver of Liability
¶ 920 Beneficiary Appeals
¶ 930 Provider Appeals

Topical Index (page 355)

Chapter 1—INTRODUCTION

[¶ 100] Introduction to Medicare

As part of the Social Security Amendments of 1965, Congress established two new programs to cover the cost of medical care for the elderly and disabled. The first of these programs, largely financed through the hospital insurance taxes, provides basic protection against the costs of inpatient hospital and other institutional provider care. Officially, this program is called "Hospital Insurance Benefits for the Aged and Disabled," although it includes much more than hospital benefits. Unofficially it is sometimes called "basic Medicare," "hospital insurance," or "Medicare Part A" (because the authorization for the program is Part A of Title XVIII of the Social Security Act).

The second of these programs is a voluntary program covering the costs of physician and other healthcare practitioner services and items and supplies not covered under the basic program. It is financed through monthly premiums from enrollees and contributions from the federal government. Officially, this program is called "Supplementary Medical Insurance Benefits for the Aged and Disabled," but unofficially it is called "supplementary Medicare," the "medical insurance program," or "Medicare Part B."

A third Medicare program that expands managed care options for beneficiaries who are entitled to Part A and enrolled in Part B was created under the Balanced Budget Act of 1997 (BBA) (PubLNo 105-33) and is called "Medicare Advantage." Formerly this had been known as "Medicare+Choice." The Medicare Prescription Drug, Improvement, and Modernization Act of 2003 (MMA) (PubLNo 108-173) changed the name and, to some degree, the structure of this part of Medicare. Since January 1, 1999, beneficiaries have had the option of choosing to receive their health benefits through the traditional Medicare "fee-for-service" program or to select a managed care plan certified under the Medicare+Choice and now the Medicare Advantage program. Payments Medicare makes to a Medicare Advantage plan replace the amounts Medicare otherwise would have paid under Parts A and B. This is also known as "Medicare Part C."

Most recently, the Medicare program has been expanded by the MMA to include a prescription drug benefit, under a new Part D of the Social Security Act. Beneficiaries entitled to Part A and enrolled in Part B, enrollees in Medicare Advantage private fee-for-service plans, and enrollees in Medicare Savings Account Plans will be eligible for the prescription drug benefit. The prescription drug benefit will be available to eligible individuals beginning January 1, 2006.

Together, the four programs are known officially as "Health Insurance for the Aged and Disabled," the name of Title XVIII of the Social Security Act, which contains the basic law governing the Medicare program.

Recent Legislation

As this book went to press, Congress was in the final stages of passing legislation that would impact both the Medicare and Medicaid programs. Both the House and the Senate have approved the conference report to "The Deficit Reduction Act of 2005." If adopted, this legislation would increase Part B premiums for more affluent seniors; reform payments for imaging and ambulatory surgical centers; tighten standards for repair and maintenance of durable medical equipment and shorten the rent-to-own period for such equipment; freeze the home health payment rate for 2006; and impose outpatient therapy caps. It also includes new quality reporting initiatives for hospitals and home health agencies; reduces the Medicare payment for care required because of hospital-acquired infections when the hospital failed to follow best evidence-based guidelines for prevention; phase out the budget

¶100

neutrality adjustment for Medicare Advantage plans; codifies the phase-in of the 75 percent rule for inpatient rehabilitation facilities; and provides additional funding for anti-fraud and abuse efforts. Beneficiary improvements include new preventative benefits; a one-year freeze for physician payments with an update for dialysis facilities; and improved access to diabetes self-management and nutrition therapy services in community health centers.

None of these changes are reflected in this book, because at press time they were not yet law, nor implemented. The House voted 212-206 on December 19, 2005, to approve the conference report; the Senate approved it on December 21, by a 51-50 vote, with Vice President Dick Cheney casting the deciding vote. Because of minor changes made in the legislation by the Senate, the House must approve it again. The date of that House vote is uncertain at the time of this writing, although it was likely to happen sometime in January 2006.

The last piece of major legislation was the MMA, which was enacted December 8, 2003, made significant changes to the Medicare program. In addition to the prescription drug benefit the legislation added a private fee-for-service coverage option, which will allow insurance companies to provide health care coverage to Medicare beneficiaries. The prescription drug discount card benefit became available to beneficiaries in the spring of 2004 and will end when the prescription drug benefit becomes available in 2006. Both drug plans provide for subsidies for eligible low-income individuals. The provision establishing the availability of health coverage through traditional fee-for-service or from a private insurance plan will become effective in 2010.

Contents of this Book

The hospital insurance program (Part A) is discussed in Chapter 2, and the supplementary medical insurance program (Part B) is discussed in Chapter 3. Medicare Advantage (Part C) is discussed in Chapter 4. The new prescription drug benefit (Part D) and the prescription drug discount card are discussed in Chapter 5. Certain items and services are specifically excluded from coverage under Part A and Part B—these are discussed in Chapter 6.

Chapter 7 contains a discussion of miscellaneous administrative features of the Medicare program, including quality control, privacy of health data, "Medigap" insurance, and initiatives to curb healthcare fraud and abuse. For information on how providers, physicians, and suppliers are paid by Medicare, see Chapter 8. Explanations about how claims are filed and how adverse determinations are appealed is provided in Chapter 9.

Rules concerning eligibility and applications for Medicare are discussed at the beginning of Chapter 2 in the case of Part A, and at the beginning of Chapter 3 in the case of Part B. Election and enrollment in Medicare Part C are discussed near the beginning of Chapter 4 (¶ 401). Eligibility and enrollment under Part D is discussed in Chapter 5 (¶ 506).

¶100

Chapter 2—MEDICARE PART A—HOSPITAL INSURANCE

Eligibility and Enrollment

[¶ 200] Entitlement to Part A Hospital Insurance Benefits

There are several ways of becoming entitled to hospital insurance benefits under Part A of the Medicare program. Most individuals become automatically entitled when they reach age 65 *if* they are eligible for monthly Social Security retirement or survivor benefits or railroad retirement benefits as "qualified railroad retirement beneficiaries." [Soc. Sec. Act § 1811; 42 C.F.R. §§ 406.5, 406.10.]

Entitlement to Medicare for the above individuals begins at age 65, *whether or not they have elected to receive Social Security (or other) retirement benefits*. Persons electing to receive Social Security benefits at age 65 or earlier need not file an application for Medicare—they will receive it automatically. Persons electing not to receive Social Security, however, will need to file an application for Medicare (see below under "Application Requirements").

Individuals under age 65 also are entitled to benefits under Part A if they are entitled to (1) Social Security or railroad retirement disability benefits (see ¶ 204), or (2) end-stage renal disease benefits (see ¶ 205). [42 C.F.R. §§ 406.5, 406.12, 406.13.]

Individuals age 65 or over who are not entitled to Part A benefits on one of the bases outlined above can enroll voluntarily in the Part A program by paying a monthly premium (see ¶ 203). [42 C.F.R. §§ 406.5, 406.20.]

Beginning January 1, 1999, individuals entitled to benefits under Part A (except persons with end-stage renal disease) and enrolled in the supplementary medical insurance program (Medicare Part B—see ¶ 300–¶ 320) may choose to receive benefits under these traditional fee-for-service programs or they may choose to enroll in a Medicare Advantage managed care plan, which offers additional benefits. [Soc. Sec. Act § 1851(a)(3).] The Medicare Advantage program, also called Medicare Part C, is discussed in detail in Chapter 4.

In addition, as mandated by § 101(a) of the Medicare Modernization Act of 2003 (MMA) (PubLNo 108-173), individuals entitled to benefits under Part A (except persons with end-stage renal disease) and enrolled in Part B may choose to enroll in the discount drug card benefit program under newly designated Part D (see ¶ 500). The prescription drug benefit will become available on January 1, 2006, and enrollment begins on November 15, 2005. [Soc. Sec. Act § 1860D-31.] Until enrollment is complete for the Medicare prescription drug benefit in 2006, a voluntary Medicare prescription drug discount card program will provide transitional coverage (see ¶ 535).

Coverage Period

As discussed above, Medicare entitlement usually begins when an individual reaches age 65. Benefits normally begin, however, on the first day of the month in which the individual's 65th birthday occurs. Thus, an individual whose 65th birthday is on July 6, 2004, would be eligible for benefits on July 1, 2004. [42 C.F.R. § 406.10(b)(1).]

The Social Security and Medicare programs follow the rule that a person reaches a given age on the day before the anniversary of birth. Thus, a person born on April 1, 1939, for example, will be considered to have reached age 65 on March 31, 2004. Medicare benefits in this case could begin March 1, 2004. [*Medicare General Information, Eligibility and Entitlement Manual*, Pub. 100-01, Ch. 2, § 10.2.]

A Social Security applicant who applies for monthly benefits after reaching age 65 can be entitled to Part A benefits retroactively beginning with the first day of the first month in which all the requirements for benefits otherwise are met, but not more than six months (12 months for disabled widow's or widower's benefits) before the month in which the application is filed. [42 C.F.R. § 406.6(d)(2), (4).]

Suspended Benefits of Aliens

An individual whose cash Social Security benefits have been suspended under § 202(t)(1) of the Social Security Act (relating to suspension of the benefits of certain aliens who are outside the United States) is not entitled to Part A benefits furnished in any month for which such a suspension is applicable. [Soc. Sec. Act § 202(t)(9).]

Conviction for Subversive Activities

The penalty that may be imposed under § 202(u) of the Social Security Act upon conviction for certain subversive activities (namely, the elimination of all Social Security earnings credits for the calendar quarter in which the conviction occurs and prior quarters) also applies to a determination of entitlement to Part A benefits. [Soc. Sec. Act § 202(u)(1).]

Application Requirements

A person age 65 or over who has filed an application and established entitlement to monthly Social Security benefits or who is a qualified railroad retirement beneficiary ordinarily does not need to file any additional application for Part A. It comes automatically with these other benefits.

An application for Medicare benefits *is* required, however, for such an individual who has not applied for Social Security benefits. An application also is required for an individual who seeks entitlement on the basis of (1) end-stage renal disease (¶ 205); (2) "Medicare-qualified government employment" (¶ 206); (3) deemed entitlement to disabled widow's or widower's benefits under certain circumstances; or (4) voluntary Part A enrollment (¶ 203). [42 C.F.R. § 406.6(c), (e).]

The form most people use to apply for Part A entitlement, which also may be used for enrollment in the Part B program (¶ 310), is Form CMS-18-F-5, "Application for Hospital Insurance Entitlement." End-stage renal disease applicants use Form CMS-43, "Application for Health Insurance Benefits Under Medicare for Individuals with End-Stage Renal Disease." [42 C.F.R. § 406.7.]

Except in the case of individuals seeking entitlement on the basis of end-stage renal disease, an application for Part A must be filed by an individual before death—a relative or legal representative may not file for retroactive entitlement after the individual has died. [42 C.F.R. §§ 406.10(b)(2), 406.13(d)(3).]

Filing claims for Medicare benefits by Medicare patients is discussed at ¶ 900 *et seq.*

Health Insurance Card

As evidence of entitlement to Medicare benefits, CMS issues each beneficiary a "Health Insurance Card," Form CMS-40 (in the case of railroad retirement beneficiaries, the Railroad Retirement Board issues the health insurance card). This card gives the name of the beneficiary, the claim number, sex of the beneficiary, the extent of entitlement, and the effective date(s) of that entitlement. The cardholder should show the card to the provider of services, doctor, etc., whenever covered services are required. [*Medicare General Information, Eligibility and Entitlement*, Pub. 100-01, Ch. 2, § 50.]

¶200

[¶ 203] Voluntary Enrollment in the Hospital Insurance Program

Hospital insurance (Part A) coverage is available on a voluntary basis to individuals 65 or over who are not entitled to Social Security (or other) Medicare-qualifying benefits (¶ 200).

An individual is eligible to enroll voluntarily in Part A if the individual:

1. has attained age 65;
2. is a resident of the United States and is either:
    a. a citizen of the United States; or
    b. an alien lawfully admitted for permanent residence who has continuously resided in the United States for not less than five years immediately before the month in which application for enrollment is made; and
3. is not otherwise entitled to Part A benefits.

In addition, the individual must enroll in the supplementary medical insurance program (Part B). [Soc. Sec. Act § 1818(a); 42 C.F.R. § 406.20.]

For purposes of determining U.S. residency, the term "United States" includes the Commonwealth of Puerto Rico, the Virgin Islands, Guam, American Samoa, and the Northern Mariana Islands. [Soc. Sec. Act §§ 210(i), 1861(x).]

Voluntary enrollment in Part A may be accomplished only during an "enrollment period." [Soc. Sec. Act § 1818(b); 42 C.F.R. § 406.21.] In general, the provisions governing enrollment (see ¶ 310, ¶ 311, and ¶ 312), coverage periods (see ¶ 313), and premiums (see ¶ 320) under Part B—excluding premium increases for late enrollment (see below)—also are applicable to voluntary enrollment in Part A.

An individual meeting the conditions for voluntary enrollment and paying the appropriate premium may elect coverage under a MedicareAdvantage managed care plan under Part C (see ¶ 401). [Soc. Sec. Act § 1851(a)(3).]

Payment of Premiums

Voluntary enrollees must pay a monthly premium based on the total cost of Part A protection for the enrolled group. The premium is updated annually according to a formula set out in the law. [Soc. Sec. Act § 1818(d)(2).] For 2006, the monthly premium is $393.00. [*Notice,* 70 FR 55896, Sept. 23, 2005.]

The following table shows the monthly premium rates in effect during the past five years:

Year	*$ Amount*
2000	301
2001	300
2002	319
2003	316
2004	343
2005	375

There is a reduced Part A premium for certain individuals with 30 or more quarters of Social Security coverage. An individual who has had at least 30 months of such coverage—or who was married to, widowed from, or divorced from such an individual for certain periods of time—is entitled to a 45 percent reduction in the Part A premium. [Soc. Sec. Act § 1818(d)(4)(A).] Accordingly, the reduced premium for eligible individuals in 2006 is $216. [*Notice,* 70 FR 55896, Sept. 23, 2005.]

¶203

Since January 1, 1998, the Part A premium has been reduced to zero for certain public retirees. [Soc. Sec. Act § 1818(d)(5).] Government employees are discussed in detail at ¶ 206.

Late Enrollment and Reenrollment Penalties

There is a 10-percent late enrollment penalty surcharge for individuals who enroll voluntarily in Part A 12 months or more after the expiration of the initial enrollment period, which is based on the date when an individual first meets the eligibility requirements for enrollment. The surcharge continues for twice the number of years (*i.e.*, full 12-month periods) that the enrollment was delayed. [Soc. Sec. Act § 1818(c)(6); 42 C.F.R. §§ 406.32(d), 406.33.]

If an individual drops out of the program and then reenrolls, the months during which the individual was out of the program are counted in determining the reenrollment penalty. [42 C.F.R. § 406.34.]

Example • • •

Agnes Williams was eligible to enroll during an initial enrollment period that ended May 31, 1997. She actually enrolled in the general enrollment period January 1, 2000—March 31, 2000. There are 34 months elapsing after the close of her initial enrollment period and before March 31, 2000, the close of the period in which she actually enrolled (delinquent enrollment is counted from the end of the initial enrollment period to the end of the enrollment period in which the individual actually enrolls—see ¶ 320). Thus, there are two 12-month periods during which she could have been, but was not, enrolled. She is assessed a 10-percent premium penalty, and that penalty expires after she has paid it for 48 months.

State and local government retirees who retired prior to January 1, 2002, can be exempt from the Part A delayed enrollment penalties, beginning in 2002. Their exemption depends on the total amount of payroll taxes paid by their employer or by themselves. [Soc. Sec. Act § 1818(d)(6).]

Group Premium Payments

A state or any other public or private organization can pay monthly premiums on a group basis for its retired or active employees age 65 and over. If group coverage is purchased, group premium payments are made under a contract or other arrangement entered into between the agency or organization and the Secretary. The Secretary may refuse to enter into a group premium payment contract if it is determined that payment of premiums under this type of contract is not administratively feasible. [Soc. Sec. Act § 1818(e).]

Termination

An individual's entitlement to the voluntary Part A program terminates if the individual (1) files a request for termination, (2) becomes entitled to regular Part A benefits in one of the ways described at ¶ 200, (3) terminates enrollment in Part B, or (4) fails to pay voluntary Part A premiums. [Soc. Sec. Act § 1818(c)(4), (5); 42 C.F.R. § 406.28.]

If the voluntary enrollee ceases to pay the premium, entitlement will end on the last day of the third month after the billing month. Entitlement will be reinstated, however, if the individual can show good cause for failing to pay the premiums on time, so long as all overdue premiums are paid within three calendar months after the date entitlement would have been terminated. [42 C.F.R. § 406.28(d).]

[¶ 204] Disability Beneficiaries

Qualified railroad retirement disability beneficiaries and the following categories of Social Security beneficiaries are entitled to Part A coverage:

- disabled workers;
- disabled widows and widowers between the ages of 50 and 65;
- certain men or women age 50 or older entitled to mother's or father's insurance benefits under § 202(g) of the Social Security Act; and
- persons age 18 and over who receive Social Security benefits because they became disabled before reaching age 22. [42 C.F.R. § 406.12.]

"Medicare-qualified government employment" is treated as Social Security qualifying employment for the purpose of the provision of Medicare disability benefits (see ¶ 206).

Disabled individuals described above may not receive Part A benefits, however, until they have satisfied a 24-month "waiting period" during which they have continuously been disabled. An exception to this rule is made for individuals with amyotrophic lateral sclerosis (ALS), who have no waiting period. [Soc. Sec. Act § 226(b), (h).]

Entitlement to benefits begins with the first day of the 25th month of disability and continues until the end of the month following the month in which notice of termination of disability status is mailed to the beneficiary or, if earlier, with the end of the month before the one in which age 65 is attained. [Soc. Sec. Act § 226(b).]

Returning to Work

Medicare benefits and entitlement are extended for disability beneficiaries who attempt to return to work or who give up or lose their disability benefits for other reasons. One provision continues Medicare coverage during a nine-month period of "trial work" and for up to 15 months thereafter. [42 C.F.R. § 406.12(e).] Other provisions allow beneficiaries who lose their disability eligibility, either because they return to work or for other reasons, to regain Medicare entitlement without being subject to the 24-month waiting period again so long as the second disability is the same as (or directly related to) the first disability. If the two disabilities are unrelated, the 24-month waiting period still can be avoided (1) in the case of workers who return to disability status within 60 months after the first disability, and (2) in the case of widows, widowers, and adults disabled since childhood who return to disability status within 84 months. [Soc. Sec. Act § 226(f); 42 C.F.R. § 406.12(b).]

Disabled beneficiaries who are not yet 65 and continue to be disabled, and who no longer are entitled to benefits solely because their earnings are in excess of the amount permitted, may purchase Part A coverage after they have worked for 48 months and have exhausted their extended period of Medicare eligibility. Enrollment can occur during special enrollment periods, as provided by law. Premiums will be similar to the premiums required for voluntary enrollees (see ¶ 203). [Soc. Sec. Act § 1818A.]

Upon reaching the age of 65, beneficiaries who are disabled can become eligible for Medicare as Social Security retirees if they satisfy the requirements for that status (see ¶ 200).

Note that Medicare would be the secondary payer for disability benefits in some cases—see ¶ 639.

[¶ 205] End-Stage Renal Disease Beneficiaries

Medicare covers individuals who have not reached age 65 and are suffering from end-stage renal (kidney) disease (ESRD) if they are (1) fully or currently insured for Social

Security or railroad retirement benefits (see ¶ 200), (2) are entitled either to monthly Social Security or railroad retirement benefits, or (3) are spouses or dependent children of individuals described in clause (2). The individual's dependents, unless they also have renal disease, are not entitled to Medicare. ESRD benefits are available only after an application for Medicare benefits is filed, and the application may be filed after the individual's death. [42 C.F.R. §§ 406.6(c), 406.13(c), (d).]

"End-stage renal disease" is defined by regulation as "that stage of kidney impairment that appears irreversible and permanent and requires a regular course of dialysis or kidney transplantation to maintain life." [42 C.F.R. § 406.13(b).] Payment for ESRD benefits is discussed at ¶ 847.

[¶ 206] Government Employees

Federal employees became eligible for coverage and were required to pay the hospital insurance portion of the Federal Insurance Contributions Act (FICA) tax beginning in 1983. State and local government employees hired after March 31, 1986, also are eligible for Medicare coverage and are required to pay the hospital insurance portion of the FICA tax. Not all federal employees or state and local government employees are included in Medicare coverage; their employment must be "Medicare-qualified government employment." [Soc. Sec. Act §§ 210(p), 226(a)(2)(C).] Medicare-qualified government employment is treated as Social Security qualifying employment for the purpose of the provision of Medicare disability benefits. In addition, it includes a spouse or dependent child of a Social Security or railroad retirement individual if the spouse or dependent child has end-stage renal disease and files an application for benefits. [Soc. Sec. Act § 226A.]

Individuals entitled to Medicare by virtue of their Medicare-qualified government employment also are entitled to Medicare disability benefits (¶ 204) and end-stage renal disease benefits (¶ 205). [Soc. Sec. Act §§ 226(b)(2)(C), 226A(a)(1).]

Government Employment Not "Medicare-Qualified"

Types of federal employment that are not considered "Medicare-qualified" include:

1. inmates in federal penal institutions;

2. interns (other than medical or dental interns or medical or dental residents in training) and student nurses employed by the federal government; and

3. employees serving on a temporary basis in case of fire, storm, earthquake, flood, or other similar emergency. [Soc. Sec. Act §§ 210(p)(1), 226(a)(2)(C).]

State and local government employment that is not "Medicare-qualified" includes that of:

1. individuals employed to relieve them from unemployment;

2. patients or inmates in a hospital, home, or other institution;

3. employees serving on a temporary basis in case of fire, storm, snow, earthquake, flood, or other similar emergency;

4. interns (other than medical or dental interns or medical or dental residents in training), student nurses, and other student employees of hospitals of the District of Columbia; and

5. an election official or election worker if the remuneration paid for services performed in a calendar year is less than $1,000. [Soc. Sec. Act § 210(p)(2).]

As noted above, state and local government employees hired before April 1, 1986, are exempt from the hospital portion of the FICA tax, and their employment, therefore, is not considered to be "Medicare-qualified." A state, however, may ask the Commissioner of Social Security to enter into an agreement whereby these employees also would have their employment treated as "Medicare-qualified." In such cases, only employment occurring after March 31, 1986, is considered "Medicare-qualified." [Soc. Sec. Act § 218(v).]

Voluntary Enrollment

Government employees who have retired but are unable to qualify for Medicare benefits in the manner described above are entitled to enroll voluntarily in the Part A program and pay the appropriate premium (see ¶ 203). Additionally, beginning January 1, 1998, public retirees meeting certain statutory conditions are entitled to avoid the payment of the monthly premium.

The methodology for determining whether a public retiree is exempt from Part A premium payment is similar in many respects to determining the reduced premium required of individuals having 30 or more quarters of Social Security coverage. (See "Payment of Premiums" at ¶ 203.) Specifically, the premium will be zero for any individual receiving cash benefits under a qualified state or local government retirement system on the basis of the individual's employment for at least 40 calendar quarters (or a combination of such quarters and Social Security-covered quarters totalling 40). As is the case with reduced premiums, individuals who have been married to, widowed from, or divorced from such an individual for certain periods of time also are entitled to a zero premium. [Soc. Sec. Act § 1818(d)(5)(B).] To be covered under this provision, however, two conditions must be met: (1) the individual's Part A premium may not be payable in whole or part by a state (including a state Medicaid program) or a political subdivision of a state; and (2) the individual must have been enrolled in Part B, and not have had the Part B premium paid in whole or part by any governmental entity described above for the preceding 84 months. [Soc. Sec. Act § 1818(d)(5)(A).]

The law defines a "qualified state or local government retirement system" as a system established or maintained by a state or political subdivision (or agency thereof) that covers positions of some or all employees of the governmental entity and that does not adjust cash benefits based on eligibility for the premium relief described above. [Soc. Sec. Act § 1818(d)(5)(C).]

[¶ 209] Geographic Limits

In general, payment will be made only for covered services furnished in the United States, which includes the 50 states, the District of Columbia, the Commonwealth of Puerto Rico, the Virgin Islands, Guam, American Samoa, the Northern Mariana Islands, and the territorial waters adjoining the land areas of the United States. For Medicare purposes, services rendered aboard a ship in an American port or within six hours of the time at which the ship arrives at, or departs from, that port will be considered to have been rendered in American waters. Services not meeting these criteria will be considered to have been furnished outside United States territorial waters even if the ship is of U.S. registry. [Soc. Sec. Act §§ 210(h), (i), 1862(a)(4); *Medicare Benefit Policy Manual*, Pub. 100-02, Ch. 16, § 60.]

The exceptions to this general rule are:

    1. certain inpatient hospital, physician, and ambulance services furnished outside the United States;

    2. emergency or nonemergency inpatient hospital furnished in Canada or Mexico when the hospital that has the most appropriate care is more accessible to the beneficiary than the closest United States hospital; and

3. emergency care when a beneficiary is injured in the United States or in Canada when the beneficiary is on his or her way to Alaska on the most direct route from another state. [Pub. 100-02, Ch. 16, § 60.]

Medicare may make payments to a foreign hospital for emergency inpatient services provided to a beneficiary when the beneficiary was present in the United States, as defined in Soc. Sec. Act § 1841(f), at the time the emergency that necessitated the inpatient hospital services occurred, and the hospital outside the United States was closer to, or substantially more accessible from, the place where the emergency arose than the nearest adequately equipped hospital within the United States. While typically the "foreign exclusion" exception involves hospital services that are furnished in Canada or Mexico, Soc. Sec. Act § 1841(f) provides that the United States includes the 50 states, the District of Columbia, Puerto Rico, the Virgin Islands, Guam, American Somoa, the Northern Mariana Islands, and, for purposes of services rendered on board a ship, the territorial waters adjoining the land areas of the United States. [*Medicare Benefit Policy Manual,* Pub. 100-02, Transmittal No. 38, Aug. 19, 2005.]

Inpatient Hospital Services

[¶ 210] Inpatient Hospital Services: Coverage in General

Medicare Part A covers services provided to beneficiaries who are patients in a qualified hospitals participating in the Medicare program for up to 90 days in any one "spell of illness." These services are defined as "inpatient" hospital services. In addition, each beneficiary has a lifetime reserve of 60 days that can be used after the 90 days have been exhausted (see ¶ 224). [Soc. Sec. Act § 1812(a)(1).]

Ordinarily, for hospital services to be covered under Part A, the hospital that provides the services must be *participating* in Medicare (to "participate" a hospital must have signed a Medicare participation agreement—see ¶ 730). In emergency situations, however, the services provided by a nonparticipating hospital also will be covered by Medicare (see ¶ 227). Nonemergency inpatient services furnished in accredited hospitals in Canada or Mexico also will be paid for under Part A if the beneficiary resides in the United States and the foreign hospital is closer to, or more accessible from, the beneficiary's home than the nearest adequately equipped hospital in the United States. [*Medicare Benefit Policy Manual*, Pub. 100-02, Ch. 16, § 60.]

Covered Inpatient Hospital Services

Specifically, the following services or supplies provided while the beneficiary is an inpatient in the hospital are covered [Soc. Sec. Act § 1861(b)]:

(1) *bed and board*;

(2) *nursing services* (other than the services of a private-duty nurse or attendant) and other related services that ordinarily are furnished by the hospital for the care and treatment of inpatients;

(3) *use of hospital facilities* and such medical social services as customarily are furnished by the hospital for the care and treatment of inpatients;

(4) *drugs, biologicals, supplies, appliances, and equipment* for use in the hospital that ordinarily are furnished by the hospital for the care and treatment of inpatients; and

(5) *diagnostic and therapeutic items and services* that ordinarily are furnished to inpatients.

To be covered, these services must be provided directly by the hospital or under an arrangement made by the hospital. Further, when payment can be made for an inpatient hospital stay under Part A, all Medicare-covered services furnished during that stay are paid under Part A. Covered services do not include (1) the services of physicians and certain other healthcare practitioners, and (2) pneumococcal and hepatitis B vaccine and their administration. [Soc. Sec. Act § 1861(b)(4); Pub. 100-02, Ch. 1, §§ 1–60; *Medicare Claims Processing Manual*, Pub. 100-04, Ch. 18, § 10.1.3.]

Limitations and exclusions related to inpatient hospital services.—The services of private-duty nurses are excluded from coverage (see ¶ 217) and physician services are covered under Part B, not under Part A (see ¶ 340). General exclusions from Medicare coverage can be found in Chapter 6, explanations of deductible and coinsurance limitations are at ¶ 221 and ¶ 222, coverage of services in a hospital after exhaustion of Part A benefits is discussed at ¶ 361, and the lifetime limit on inpatient psychiatric hospital services is explained at ¶ 225.

"Inpatient" Defined

An "inpatient" is a person who has been admitted to a hospital for bed occupancy for purposes of receiving inpatient hospital services. A person is considered an inpatient if formally admitted as an inpatient with the expectation of remaining at least overnight and occupying a bed, even if it later develops that discharge or transfer to another hospital is possible and a hospital bed actually is not used overnight. [Pub. 100-02, Ch. 1, § 10.]

When a patient with a known diagnosis enters a hospital for a specific minor surgical procedure that is expected to keep that individual in the hospital for only a few hours (fewer than 24), and this expectation is realized, the individual will be considered an outpatient regardless of the hour of admission, whether or not a bed is used or the hospital stay extends past midnight. [Pub. 100-02, Ch. 1, § 10.]

Special rules apply when a patient needs only extended care services but actually is placed in a hospital bed, including a "swing bed" (see ¶ 229).

"Spell of Illness" Defined

The duration of inpatient hospital services and post-hospital services in a skilled nursing facility (SNF) is limited according to the beginning and ending of a "spell of illness"—also commonly called a "benefit period."

Beginning a "spell."—A "spell of illness" is a period of consecutive days that begins with the first day (that is not included in a previous spell of illness) on which a patient is furnished inpatient hospital or SNF services by a "qualified" provider during a period in which the patient is entitled to Part A benefits. [Soc. Sec. Act § 1861(a)(1).]

A "qualified" provider is a hospital (including a psychiatric hospital) or SNF that has been certified as satisfying the requirements of the definition of such an institution (see ¶ 229 and ¶ 231). A hospital that meets the requirements related to emergency services, which are outlined at ¶ 227, is a qualified hospital for purposes of beginning a spell of illness when it furnishes the patient covered inpatient emergency services. [*Medicare General Information, Eligibility and Entitlement Manual,* Pub. 100-01, Ch. 3, § 10.4.1.]

Admission to a qualified SNF will begin a spell of illness even though payment for the services cannot be made because the prior hospitalization or transfer requirement has not been met (see ¶ 230).

Ending a "spell."—The spell of illness ends with the close of a period of 60 consecutive days during which the patient was neither an inpatient of a hospital nor an inpatient of a SNF. The 60-consecutive-day period begins with the day on which the individual is discharged. [Soc. Sec. Act § 1861(a)(2).]

It is important to note that a stay in a nonparticipating hospital will result in continuing a spell of illness even if the services received are not covered. For example, a stay in a nonparticipating hospital is counted as a qualified stay for purposes of determining whether a spell of illness has ended, even if the nonparticipating hospital did not furnish covered emergency services. A stay in a SNF does not continue a spell of illness unless the stay meets Medicare skilled nursing care requirements. Thus, a beneficiary who is transferred from a hospital to a SNF but receives only "custodial care" (see ¶ 244) at the SNF would begin counting the 60-consecutive-day period on the day of discharge from the hospital. [42 C.F.R. § 409.60(b); Pub. 100-01, Ch. 3, § 10.4.3.2.]

An individual may be discharged from and readmitted to a hospital or SNF several times during a spell of illness and still be in the same spell if 60 days have not elapsed between discharge and readmission. The stay need not be for related physical or mental conditions. [Pub. 100-01, Ch. 3, § 10.4.3.]

Example • • • _____

(1) John White was entitled to Part A benefits and was hospitalized in a participating general hospital on June 1. He previously had not established a spell of illness. He remained in the hospital for 30 days and then was transferred to a SNF for 50 days, after which he was discharged to his home on August 18. John's spell of illness began on June 1 and ended on October 17, the end of the 60-day period beginning with the date of his last discharge.

(2) Assume the same set of facts as above, except that John was rehospitalized after 50 days in the SNF and remained in the hospital for another 60 days, after which he was discharged to his home on October 17. John's spell of illness still began on June 1, but it ended on December 16, the end of the 60-day period beginning with the date of his last discharge.

(3) Assume the same set of facts as in example (2), except that John was required to enter the hospital for a third time, *before* exhaustion of the 60-day period following his last hospital discharge. Assume further, that he remained in the hospital until his death. No new spell of illness could begin regardless of how long John remained in the hospital during his terminal illness. The crossing from one calendar year to another does not end an ongoing spell of illness.

_____

Once a spell of illness has ended, the beneficiary's next admission to a qualified hospital or SNF will constitute the beginning of a new spell of illness. As long as a person continues to be entitled to Part A, there is no limit to the number of spells of illness covered. [42 C.F.R. § 409.60.]

Note that when a beneficiary begins a new spell of illness as a hospital inpatient, a new inpatient hospital deductible (see ¶ 221) must be paid, even if it is within the same calendar year.

Medicare deductible and coinsurance payments. Beneficiaries who use covered Part A services may be subject to deductible and coinsurance requirements. A beneficiary is responsible for an inpatient hospital deductible amount ($952 in 2006), which is deducted from the amount payable by the Medicare program to the hospital, for inpatient hospital services furnished during each spell of illness. When a beneficiary receives such services for more than 60 days during a spell of illness, he or she is responsible for a coinsurance amount equal to one-fourth of the inpatient hospital deductible per-day for the 61st/–90th/ day spent in the hospital ($238 in 2006). An individual has 60 lifetime reserve days of coverage, which they may elect to use after the 90th/ in a spell of illness. The coinsurance amount for these days is equal to one-half of the inpatient hospital deductible ($476 in 2006). A beneficiary is responsible for a coinsurance amount equal to one-eighth of the inpatient hospital deductible per day for the 21st/ through the 100th/ day of skilled nursing facility services furnished during a spell of illness ($119 in 2006). [*Medicare General Information, Eligibility, and Entitlement Manual,* Pub. 100-01, Ch. 3, § § 10.1, 10.3.]

[¶ 211] Accommodations

Part A generally will pay only for *semi-private* accommodations (rooms of two-four beds) or ward accommodations (five or more beds) in connection with inpatient hospital care or nursing care in a skilled nursing facility (see ¶ 232). [42 C.F.R. § 409.11; *Medicare Benefits Policy Manual* Pub. 100-02, Ch. 1, § 10.1.]

Private Rooms

Extra payment will be made for a private room or other accommodations more expensive than semi-private in a non-PPS hospital (see ¶ 810) only when such accommodations are *medically necessary*. Private rooms will be considered medically necessary in the following circumstances:

    1. the patient's condition requires isolation for the patient's health or that of others;

    2. the facility has no semi-private or less expensive accommodations; or

    3. all such accommodations are occupied, *and* the patient needs hospitalization *immediately*—that is, inpatient treatment cannot be deferred until less expensive accommodations become available. [Pub. 100-02, Ch. 1, §§ 10.1.1, 10.1.2, 10.1.3.]

Payment also will be made for intensive care facilities when medically indicated.

In a prospective payment system (PPS) hospital, no extra Medicare payment will be made for a patient staying in a more expensive private room because, under the applicable diagnosis-related group (DRG) rate, the hospital will be paid the same amount per discharge regardless of whether private or semi-private accommodations are provided. [Pub. 100-02, Ch. 1, § 10.1.4.]

PPS hospitals may charge the patient for the extra cost of the private room, however, if the private room is *requested by the patient* and the private room is *not medically necessary*. The hospital may charge the patient no more than the difference between the customary charge for the private room and the customary charge for a semi-private room at the most prevalent rate at the time of admission. The patient may not be charged, however, unless the more expensive accommodations were requested with the knowledge that the difference in costs would be charged.

Example • • • _____

At the time Mary Green is admitted to the hospital, she requests a private room. It is not medically necessary that she be in a private room, and she is told by the hospital that she will be charged the difference between its "customary charge" (see below) for a private room ($2,000 per day) and the customary charge for a semi-private room at the hospital's "most prevalent rate" (see below) at the time of admission ($1,300 per day). The hospital may charge Mary $700 per day for the private room, and the rest of her bill for bed and board—less any required deductible or coinsurance amount—is covered by Part A.

_____

"Customary charges" are the current amounts that the institution uniformly charges patients for specific services and accommodations. The "most prevalent rate" for semi-private accommodations is the rate that applies to the greatest number of semi-private beds. [Pub. 100-02, Ch. 1, §§ 10.1, 10.1.2, 10.1.3.]

Deluxe Private Rooms

A beneficiary in need of a private room (either because isolation is needed for medical reasons or because immediate admission is needed when no other accommodations are available) may be assigned to any private room in the hospital. Although the beneficiary does not have the right to insist on the private room of choice, the beneficiary's preference should be given the same consideration that would be given if the beneficiary were paying all hospital charges. The program does not, under any circumstances, pay for personal comfort

¶211

items (see ¶ 616). The program also does not pay for deluxe accommodations or services such as a suite or a room that is substantially more spacious than required for treatment, specially equipped or decorated, or serviced for the comfort and convenience of persons willing to pay a differential. If a beneficiary (or the beneficiary's representative) requests deluxe accommodations, the hospital should advise that there will be a charge, not covered by Medicare, of a specified amount per day and may charge that amount for each day the beneficiary occupies the deluxe accommodations. The maximum amount the beneficiary may be charged is the differential between the most prevalent private room rate at the time of admission and the customary charge for the room occupied.

The beneficiary may not be charged a differential in private room rates if that differential is based on factors other than personal comfort items. These factors might include, but are not limited to, differences between older and newer wings, proximity to a lounge, elevators or nursing stations, or a desirable view. [Pub. 100-02, Ch. 1, § 10.1.4.]

All-Private Room Hospitals

If the patient is admitted to a hospital that has only private rooms and no semi-private or ward accommodations, medical necessity will be deemed to exist for the accommodations furnished. Beneficiaries may not be subjected to an extra charge for a private room in an all-private room hospital. [Pub. 100-02, Ch. 1, § 10.1.5.]

Less Expensive Rooms

When accommodations *less expensive* than semi-private (for example, a ward) are furnished *at the patient's request or for a reason consistent with the purposes of the Medicare program,* payment will be made for the reasonable cost of the accommodations furnished. It is considered to be consistent with the program's purposes to furnish bed and board in less expensive accommodations when semi-private accommodations are not available. However, the patient must be moved to semi-private accommodations when they become available. [Pub. 100-02, Ch. 1, § 10.1.6.]

In some cases, a patient may be placed in accommodations less expensive than semi-private *neither at the patient's request nor for a reason consistent with the program's purposes.* The payment to be made to the provider for these services will be at a reduced rate—the lesser of either (a) the reasonable cost of the ward accommodations, or (b) the reasonable cost of semi-private accommodations minus the difference between the institution's customary charges for semi-private accommodations at the "most prevalent rate" at the time of the patient's admission and the charge customarily made for the accommodations furnished the patient by the institution. It is not consistent with the purposes of the law to assign a patient ward accommodations on the basis of social or economic status; national origin, race, or religion; entitlement to benefits as a Medicare patient; or any other discriminatory reason, when the patient has not requested such assignment. [Pub. 100-02, Ch. 1, § 10.1.6.]

[¶ 212] Drugs and Biologicals

Drugs and biologicals furnished to an inpatient for use in a hospital, that represent a cost to the hospital and ordinarily are furnished by the hospital for inpatient care and treatment, are covered under Part A. The drug or biological must be safe and effective and otherwise reasonable and necessary. The coverage rules outlined below are taken from the *Medicare Benefit Policy Manual,* Pub. 100-02, Ch. 1, § 30.

To be covered, drugs and biologicals must be (1) included or approved for inclusion in the latest official edition or revision of certain drug compendia (including the *United States Pharmacopoeia,* the *National Formulary,* the *United States Homeopathic Pharmacopoeia, AMA Drug Evaluations,* or *Accepted Dental Therapeutics* (except for any drugs or biologicals unfavorably evaluated); or (2) expressly approved by the pharmacy and drug therapeutics committee (or equivalent committee) of the medical staff of the hospital for use in the hospital (see ¶ 505). [Pub. 100-02, Ch. 1, § 30.1.]

Combination drugs are covered if the combination itself or all of the active ingredients are listed or approved for listing in any of the compendia named. Similarly, any combination drugs approved by the pharmacy and therapeutics committee for use in the hospital are covered.

Drugs and biologicals furnished by a hospital to an inpatient for use outside the hospital are, in general, not covered as inpatient hospital services. However, if the drug or biological is deemed medically necessary to permit or facilitate the patient's departure from the hospital, and a limited supply is required until the patient can obtain a continuing supply, the limited supply of the drug or biological is covered as an inpatient hospital service. [Pub. 100-02, Ch. 1, § 30.5.]

Coverage is not limited to drugs and biologicals routinely stocked by the hospital. A drug or biological not stocked by the hospital that the hospital obtains for the patient from an outside source, such as a community pharmacy, also is covered if the facility rather than the patient is responsible for making payment to the supplier. If the patient is responsible for making the payment, the drug or biological might be covered by Part B (see ¶ 351).

An investigational drug is not considered to meet the "reasonable and necessary" test that applies to all services (see ¶ 601) because its efficacy has not yet been established. The decisions of individual hospitals should not transcend the determinations of the Food and Drug Administration (FDA) and Public Health Service (PHS) with respect to the safety and effectiveness of drugs. Therefore, even if approved by an appropriate hospital committee, an investigational drug or biological cannot be reimbursed. [Pub. 100-02, Ch. 1, § 30.4.]

Beginning January 1, 2006, Medicare will cover the cost of prescription drugs for enrollees in the new Medicare Part D program. Beneficiaries entitled to Part A and enrolled in Part B, enrollees in Medicare Advantage plans, and enrollees in Medicare Savings Account plans will be eligible for the prescription drug benefit. From June 1, 2004, until enrollment is complete for the Medicare prescription drug benefit in 2006, a voluntary Medicare prescription drug discount card program provided transitional coverage.

The drug benefit will permit eligible individuals to choose from at least two prescription drug plans (PDPs) in their region, either a standard coverage plan or an alternative coverage plan with actuarially equivalent benefits (see ¶ 500). In 2006, standard coverage will have a $250 deductible and a 25 percent coinsurance for costs between $251 and $2250. Beneficiaries will pay 100 percent of prescription drugs costs between $2251 and $5100 for the year. At this point, beneficiaries will have spent $3600 out of their own pockets (see ¶ 500). Once the out-of-pocket threshold is met, beneficiaries will pay $2 for generic drugs and $5 for nonpreferred drugs or 5 percent of the cost of a drug, whichever is greater (see ¶ 500). Low-income individuals, those with incomes below 150 percent of the federal poverty line, will receive subsidies for deductibles, premiums, and cost-sharing amounts. Low-income eligibility determinations will be made by state Medicaid plans.

See chapter 5 for a complete description of the prescription drug coverage provided under Medicare Part D. Drugs and biologicals are further discussed at ¶ 362.

[¶ 213] Supplies, Appliances, and Equipment

Supplies, appliances, and equipment ordinarily furnished by the hospital for the care and treatment of the beneficiary during an inpatient stay in the hospital are covered inpatient hospital services. Under certain circumstances, supplies, appliances, and equipment used

¶213

during the beneficiary's stay are covered even when they leave the hospital with the patient at the time of discharge. There are circumstances in which it would be unreasonable or impossible from a medical standpoint to limit the beneficiary's use of the item to the period of the inpatient stay.

Examples of items covered under this rule are cardiac valves, cardiac pacemakers, and artificial limbs that are installed permanently in, or attached to, the patient's body while that patient is an inpatient; and items, such as tracheostomy or drainage tubes, that are installed temporarily in, or attached to, the patient's body while that patient is receiving treatment as an inpatient and which also are necessary to permit or facilitate the patient's release from the hospital. The reasonable cost of oxygen furnished to hospital inpatients also is covered as an inpatient supply. Coverage of oxygen and cardiac pacemakers are discussed further at ¶ 356 and ¶ 357.

Supplies, appliances, and equipment furnished to a patient for use *only* outside the hospital generally are not covered as an inpatient hospital service. However, a temporary or disposable item that is medically necessary to permit or facilitate the patient's release from the hospital and is required until the patient can obtain a continuing supply is covered. [42 C.F.R. § 409.14; *Medicare Benefit Policy Manual*, Pub. 100-02, Ch. 1, § 40.]

Routine Personal Hygiene Items and Services

Hospital "admission packs," containing primarily toilet articles (such as soap, toothbrushes, toothpaste, and combs), are covered if routinely furnished by the hospital to all of its inpatients. If not routinely furnished, the packs are not covered and the hospital may charge the beneficiary. The beneficiary may not be charged, however, unless the beneficiary requests the pack with the knowledge of what is requested and what will be charged. [Pub. 100-02, Ch. 1, § 40.]

[¶ 214] Diagnostic and Therapeutic Items and Services

Medicare covers "other diagnostic or therapeutic items or services" that ordinarily are furnished to inpatients by the hospital. [Soc. Sec. Act § 1861(b)(3).] The services must be furnished by the hospital or by others under arrangements made by the hospital. Billing for the services must be through the hospital. [42 C.F.R. § 409.16.]

Included in this benefit are diagnostic and therapeutic techniques too numerous to list (for example, blood tests, X-rays, etc.). Worth mentioning separately as covered services, in addition to those discussed below, are inpatient physical and occupational therapy and speech pathology (discussed as an outpatient benefit at ¶ 381).

Many diagnostic and therapeutic items and services also are covered when furnished as outpatient hospital services (see ¶ 352).

Psychologists and Physical Therapists

When a psychologist, clinical psychologist, or physical therapist is a salaried member of the staff of a hospital, that person's diagnostic or therapeutic services to inpatients of the hospital are covered in the same manner as the services of other nonphysician hospital employees. The services of psychologists, clinical psychologists, and physical therapists who are not salaried staff members are covered under Part A if furnished by the hospital as part of the services it ordinarily furnishes under arrangements that provide for billing to be handled by the hospital. [Pub. 100-02, Ch. 1, § 50.2.]

Rehabilitative Care

A patient may be eligible for Medicare inpatient hospital coverage solely on the basis of the need for rehabilitative services. A patient would be deemed to require a hospital level of care if requiring a relatively intense rehabilitation program necessitating a multidisciplinary coordinated team approach to upgrade the ability to function as independently as possible.

There are two basic requirements that must be met for inpatient hospital stays for rehabilitation care to be covered: (1) the services must be reasonable and necessary (in terms of efficacy, duration, frequency, and amount) for the treatment of the patient's condition; and (2) it must be reasonable and necessary to furnish the care on an inpatient hospital basis, rather than in a less intensive setting such as a skilled nursing facility or on an outpatient basis.

Determinations of whether hospital stays for rehabilitation services are reasonable and necessary must be based upon an assessment of each beneficiary's individual care needs. Services will not be denied based only on numerical utilization screens, diagnostic screens, diagnosis or specific treatment norms, "the three hour rule," or any other "rules of thumb." [Pub. 100-02, Ch. 1, § 110.1.]

An inpatient hospital program of this scope usually includes intensive skilled rehabilitation nursing care, physical therapy, occupational therapy, and, if needed, speech therapy and prosthetic-orthotic services. Coverage at the inpatient hospital level of care may continue until further progress toward the established rehabilitation goal is unlikely, or it is appropriate to assume it can be achieved in a less intensive setting. [Pub. 100-02, Ch. 1, § 110.5.]

Rehabilitation services also are discussed at ¶ 244. Cardiac rehabilitation programs provided on an outpatient basis are discussed at ¶ 352.

Respiratory Therapy

Respiratory or inhalation therapy is defined as those services that are prescribed by a physician for the assessment, diagnostic evaluation, treatment, management, and monitoring of patients with deficiencies and abnormalities of cardiopulmonary function. Respiratory therapy services include oxygenation and ventilation, medical gases, bronchial hygiene therapy, and pulmonary rehabilitation.

These services may be performed by respiratory therapists and technicians, physical therapists, nurses, and other qualified personnel. If they are reasonable and necessary, the services are covered regardless of where they are furnished in the hospital—for example, emergency room, intensive care unit, etc. [*Medicare National Coverage Determinations Manual*, Pub. 100-03, Ch. 1, § 240.].]

Independent Clinical Laboratory Services

Diagnostic services furnished to an inpatient by an independent clinical laboratory under arrangements with the hospital also are covered under Part A provided the lab is certified by Clinical Laboratory Improvement Amendments of 1988 (CLIA) to perform the services. An "independent laboratory" is independent of the attending or consulting physician's office and the hospital.

A "clinical laboratory" is where microbiological, serological, chemical, hematological, radiobioassay, cytological, immunohematological, or pathological examinations are performed on materials derived from the human body to provide information for the diagnosis, prevention, or treatment of a disease or assessment of a medical condition. [Pub. 100-02, Ch. 1, § 50.3.]

Alcoholism Treatments

Alcohol detoxification and rehabilitation services are covered by Medicare when furnished as inpatient hospital services under Part A and as physician services under Part B.

¶214

Inpatient hospital stays for alcohol detoxification are covered during the more acute stages of alcoholism or alcohol withdrawal when medical complications occur or are highly probable. Detoxification generally can be accomplished within two to three days, but this limit may be extended to five days or beyond if required by the patient's condition. Following detoxification, a patient may be transferred to an inpatient rehabilitation unit or discharged to a residential treatment program or outpatient treatment setting. [*Medicare National Coverage Determinations Manual*, Pub. 100-03, Ch. 1, §§ 130.1, 130.2.]

Inpatient hospital stays for alcohol rehabilitation are covered for treatment of chronic alcoholism. Because alcohol rehabilitation can be provided in a variety of settings, an inpatient hospital stay for alcohol rehabilitation will not be covered unless it is medically necessary that care be provided in an inpatient hospital setting, and not in a less costly setting or on an outpatient basis. Further, because alcoholism is classifiable as a psychiatric condition, the beneficiary must be receiving "active treatment." Generally, 16–19 days of rehabilitation services are considered sufficient prior to continuing care on a basis other than an inpatient hospital setting. [Pub. 100-03, Ch. 1, §§ 130.1, 130.2.]

Outpatient hospital coverage is provided for both diagnostic and therapeutic services furnished for the treatment of alcoholism. The same rules that apply to outpatient hospital services in general (see ¶ 352) also apply here. All services must be reasonable and necessary for diagnosis or treatment of the patient's condition. In addition, alcoholism treatment services such as drug therapy, psychotherapy, and patient education that are provided incident to a physician's services in a *freestanding clinic* are covered under the same rules as clinic services (see ¶ 351). The psychiatric services limitation discussed at ¶ 387 also applies to these services. [Pub. 100-03, Ch. 1, § 130.5.]

Chemical aversion therapy for the treatment of alcoholism is a covered service. Electrical aversion therapy is not covered, however, because it has not been shown to be safe and effective. [Pub. 100-03, Ch. 1, § 130.3.]

Treatment of Drug Abuse or Chemical Dependency

Treatment for drug abuse or other chemical dependency, when medically necessary, is covered by Medicare in all of the settings described above as long as the services provided are reasonable and necessary for the treatment of the patient's condition. [Pub. 100-03, Ch. 1, § 130.]

Smoking and Tobacco-Use Cessation Counseling Services

Smoking and tobacco use cessation counseling has been determined reasonable and necessary for certain individuals who: (1) use tobacco and have a disease or an adverse health effect that has been linked to tobacco use; or (2) who are taking a therapeutic agent whose metabolism or dosing is affected by tobacco use. These individuals are covered under Medicare Part B when certain conditions of coverage are met. Coverage of counseling for smoking cessation is available for two new levels, intermediate and intensive. Smoking and tobacco use cessation counseling services are limited to eight counseling sessions in a 12-month period. Additionally, Medicare's prescription drug benefit covers smoking and tobacco-use cessation agents prescribed by a physician beginning January 1, 2006. Coverage for smoking and tobacco use cessation counseling begins March 22, 2005. [Pub. 100-03, Ch. 1, § 210.4.]

Mental Health Benefits

Inpatient psychiatric hospital benefits are covered by Medicare, subject to some important limitations (see ¶ 225). Partial hospitalization services are covered under Part B when they would prevent the need for inpatient psychiatric care (see ¶ 387).

¶214

[¶ 215] Services of Interns, Residents-in-Training, and Teaching Physicians

Although the services of physicians furnished to inpatients generally are excluded under Part A (see ¶ 226), this portion of Medicare covers the services of interns and residents-in-training who participate in teaching programs approved by the appropriate accrediting associations. If the intern or resident is not providing services as part of an approved teaching program, those services are covered under Part B (see further ¶ 340). [Soc. Sec. Act § 1861(b)(6).]

The administrative and teaching services of teaching physicians are also covered under Part A. [42 C.F.R. § 415.55.] The services of teaching physicians to individual patients are covered under Part B (see ¶ 340 and ¶ 820).

[¶ 217] Nursing and Related Services; Private-Duty Exclusion

Nursing and other related services are covered as inpatient hospital services if ordinarily furnished by the hospital for the care and treatment of inpatients. The services of a private-duty nurse or other private-duty attendant are expressly excluded, however, from this coverage. [Soc. Sec. Act § 1861(b)(2), (5); 42 C.F.R. § 409.12.]

Private-duty nurses or private-duty attendants are registered professional nurses, licensed practical nurses, or any other trained attendants whose services ordinarily are rendered to, and restricted to, a particular patient by arrangement between the patient and the private-duty nurse or attendant. Private-duty services are engaged or paid by an individual patient or by someone acting on the patient's behalf, including a hospital that initially incurs the cost and looks to the patient for reimbursement of the noncovered services. When the hospital acts on behalf of a patient, the services of the private-duty nurse or other attendant are not inpatient hospital services regardless of the control the hospital may exercise over the services rendered by the private-duty nurse or attendant. [*Medicare Benefits Policy Manual*, Pub. 100-02, Ch. 1, § 20.]

[¶ 218] Inpatient Services Connected with Dental Services

Although the law contains a general exclusion of services performed in connection with the care, treatment, filling, removal, or replacement of teeth or structures directly supporting teeth (see ¶ 634), it permits payment for inpatient hospital services for dental procedures when the beneficiary, due to his or her underlying medical condition and clinical status or the severity of the dental procedure, requires hospitalization in connection with the provision of these services. [Soc. Sec. Act § 1862(a)(12).]

Thus, if a beneficiary is hospitalized for a noncovered dental procedure, but the hospitalization is required due to the severity of the procedure or to assure proper medical management, control, or treatment of a nondental impairment, the inpatient hospital services are covered. (An example is a beneficiary with a history of repeated heart attacks who must have all teeth extracted.) Similarly, when the beneficiary is hospitalized because of a nondental impairment and the need for the noncovered dental procedure is determined after admission (for example, a beneficiary requires hospitalization because of diabetes and after admission a decision is made to extract teeth), the inpatient hospital services also are covered. [Pub. 100-02, Ch. 1, § 70.]

Further, when a beneficiary has been admitted for a noncovered dental procedure and, during the stay, a non-dental condition develops or is discovered that necessitates inpatient hospital services to assure proper medical management, control, or treatment, then the inpatient services furnished subsequent to the development or discovery of the non-dental conditions are covered. For example, a beneficiary is admitted to the hospital for bilateral extraction of impacted wisdom teeth and develops a serious staphylococcus infection. The inpatient services furnished prior to the development of the infection are not covered. However, the inpatient services required for the medical management of the infection are covered.

When the hospital services are covered, then all ancillary services furnished by the hospital (such as X-rays, administration of anesthesia, use of the operating room) also are covered. [Pub. 100-02, Ch. 1, § 70.]

When a beneficiary is hospitalized for a covered dental procedure, the dentist's services are covered under Part B (see ¶ 340) and the inpatient hospital services furnished during the stay are covered under Part A. Thus, both the professional services of the dentist and the inpatient hospital expenses are covered when the dentist reduces a jaw fracture of a beneficiary who is an inpatient of a participating hospital. When a patient is hospitalized for a noncovered dental treatment, neither the professional services of the dentist nor the inpatient hospital services are covered. [Pub. 100-02, Ch. 1, § 70.]

A qualified dentist may certify, for purposes of inpatient hospital coverage in connection with a dental procedure, that the beneficiary suffers from impairments of such severity as to require hospitalization. See ¶ 340.

[¶ 220] Inpatient Hospital Services: Limitations on Coverage

Beneficiaries with hospital insurance coverage under Medicare Part A are entitled to have payment made on their behalf for up to 90 or more days of covered inpatient hospital services in each "spell of illness" (see ¶ 210). In addition, a beneficiary is entitled to a lifetime total of 60 days of inpatient hospital coverage after exhaustion of the 90 days of entitlement during a spell of illness—commonly called "lifetime reserve days." [Soc. Sec. Act §§ 1812(a)(1), 1821(b)(1).] (See ¶ 224 for a detailed discussion of lifetime reserve days.)

The amount payable by Part A is reduced by the deductible and coinsurances described in the table below.

Deductible and Coinsurance Amounts for Inpatient Hospital Services in 2006

Inpatient Hospital Deductible	$952
Inpatient Hospital Coinsurance	
1st through 60th days	$0
61st through 90th days	$238
91st through 150th days (lifetime reserve days)	$476

[*Notice*, 70 FR 55885, Sept. 23, 2005.]

See ¶ 221–¶ 223 for more detailed information on inpatient hospital deductible and coinsurance requirements.

[¶ 221] Inpatient Hospital Deductible

For inpatient hospital services furnished in each "spell of illness" (defined at ¶ 210), the patient is responsible for an inpatient hospital deductible. The amount of the deductible is determined by the year in which the patient's spell of illness begins. In 2006, the deductible is $952 *per spell of illness.* There can be more than one spell of illness, and thus more than one required deductible, in a calendar year. [*Notice*, 70 FR 55885, Sept. 23, 2005.]

The inpatient hospital deductible for each successive year is calculated by modifying the previous year's deductible by the same percentage used to determine Medicare payments to prospective payment system (PPS) hospitals. The amount calculated is rounded to the nearest multiple of $4 (an amount midway between two multiples is rounded up). The various coinsurance amounts listed at ¶ 220 are fractions of the deductible. Once the deductible is determined, the coinsurance amounts are adjusted accordingly. [Soc. Sec. Act § 1813(b)(1).]

If the hospital stay spans two calendar years, the deductible in effect on the first day of the hospitalization is applicable. The coinsurance, however, is based on the coinsurance in effect for the year in which the cost-sharing days are incurred. [Soc. Sec. Act § 1813(b)(3).]

The deductible is satisfied only by charges for *covered* services. Expenses for covered services count toward the deductible on an incurred, rather than a paid, basis, and expenses incurred during one spell of illness cannot be applied toward the deductible in a later spell of illness. The inpatient hospital deductible is imposed only once during a "spell of illness," even though the beneficiary may have been hospitalized more than once during that spell of illness (see the examples at ¶ 210). Neither expenses incurred in meeting the blood deductible (see ¶ 223) nor the monthly premiums paid by those voluntarily enrolled for hospital insurance coverage (see ¶ 203) count toward the inpatient hospital deductible. [Soc. Sec. Act § 1813(a)(1); *Medicare General Information, Eligibility and Entitlement Manual*, Pub. 100-01, Ch. 3, § 10.1.]

If the actual charges imposed for inpatient hospital services during a spell of illness are less than the deductible, then the amount creditable toward the deductible will be equal to the actual charges. Customary charges, however, are considered actual charges for purposes of this rule if they are greater than the actual charges. Thus, if the hospital's customary charges on an initial stay in a spell of illness are more than the actual charges to the patient, but neither of the charges exceeds the inpatient deductible, the customary charges will be used in computing the amount of the deductible met. [Pub. 100-01, Ch. 3, § 10.1.] ("Customary charges" are defined at ¶ 211.)

A reduction in benefit days resulting from the application of the psychiatric hospital carryover restriction, on and immediately preceding the date of entitlement, does not affect the amount of the deductible for which the patient is responsible. [Pub. 100-01, Ch. 3, § 10.1.] For a discussion of the psychiatric hospital carryover restriction, see ¶ 225.

[¶ 222] Inpatient Hospital Coinsurance

When inpatient hospital services are received for more than 60 days during a spell of illness, the patient is responsible for a coinsurance amount for each day after the 60th and through the 90th day on which these services are furnished. There also is a coinsurance amount for each day, after the 90th and through the 150th in any spell of illness, that is chargeable against the individual's 60-day lifetime reserve (see ¶ 224). [Soc. Sec. Act § 1813(a)(1).] (Information on applicable coinsurance rates per day is summarized at ¶ 220.)

The coinsurance amount for the 60th through 90th day is equal to one-fourth of the inpatient hospital deductible, as annually adjusted ($238 in 2006), and one-half of such deductible for lifetime reserve days ($476 in 2006). [Soc. Sec. Act § 1813(a)(1).] When a patient's hospitalization spans two calendar years, the coinsurance in effect for the year in which the cost sharing days are incurred applies. [Soc. Sec. Act § 1813(b)(3); *Final rule*, 70 FR 47278, Aug. 12, 2005.]

In determining the amount of the coinsurance met, the coinsurance charge for a day of inpatient hospital services may not exceed the charges imposed for that day with respect to the individual beneficiary. Customary charges are considered actual charges if they are greater than the charges imposed. [Soc. Sec. Act § 1813(a)(1).] In connection with the lifetime reserve days provision, however, when the actual charge is equal to or less than the coinsurance amount, the beneficiary is deemed to have elected not to use one of the lifetime reserve days. Thus, the day is treated as a noncovered day and no coinsurance amount is chargeable to the patient (see ¶ 224). [42 C.F.R. § 409.83(c).]

[¶ 223] Whole Blood and Packed Red Blood Cells

In addition to the inpatient hospital deductible, there is another deductible, equal to the cost of the first three pints of whole blood (or packed red blood cells) received by a beneficiary in a calendar year. This deductible can be satisfied under either Part A or Part B (see ¶ 335), or a combination of the two. [Soc. Sec. Act § 1813(a)(2).]

"Whole blood" is human blood from which none of the liquid or cellular components have been removed. Components of whole blood such as plasma and gamma globulin are not subject to the blood deductible because they are covered as biologicals (see ¶ 212). [*Medicare General Information, Eligibility and Entitlement Manual*, Pub. 100-01, Ch.3, § 20.5.3.]

The patient may not be charged for the first three pints of whole blood or equivalent quantities of packed red blood cells if the patient arranges for their replacement on a pint-for-pint basis. [Soc. Sec. Act § 1866(a)(2)(C); Pub. 100-01, Ch. 3, § 20.5.]

The difference, if any, between the cost of the whole blood (or equivalent quantities of packed red blood cells) to the provider and the charge to the beneficiary will be deducted from the payments that otherwise would be made to the provider under Part A. Thus, a hospital cannot make a profit on the blood or packed red blood cells for which it charges a beneficiary. No charge may be imposed on the patient for the cost of administering, storing, and processing the blood. [Soc. Sec. Act § 1866(a)(2)(C); Pub. 100-01, Ch. 3, § 20.5.]

When a beneficiary elects to replace deductible pints or units, it is considered replaced if the beneficiary, another individual, or a group or organization acting on the beneficiary's behalf (*e.g.*, a blood assurance plan) offers replacement pints or units, whether or not the provider actually accepts the offer. Thus a provider may not charge a beneficiary merely because its policy is not to accept blood from a particular organization that has offered to replace blood on behalf of the beneficiary. A provider would not be barred from charging a beneficiary for deductible blood, however, if there is a reasonable basis for believing replacement blood offered by or on behalf of the beneficiary would endanger the health of either the donor or a recipient. [Pub. 100-01, Ch. 3, §§ 20.5.4, 20.5.4.1.]

When a provider accepts blood donated in advance for or by a beneficiary in anticipation of need, such donations are considered as replacement for any deductible pints or units subsequently furnished the beneficiary. [Pub. 100-01, Ch. 3, § 20.5.4.1.]

A provider must not participate or permit its blood suppliers to participate in any practice that denies Medicare patients the same opportunity available to non-Medicare patients for replacing blood. Thus, when non-Medicare patients are permitted to replace the full amount of blood they have used, Medicare beneficiaries also must be permitted to do so. [Pub. 100-01, Ch. 3, § 20.5.4.1.]

[¶ 224] Duration of Covered Inpatient Hospital Services

Beneficiaries who are covered under Part A are entitled to have payment made on their behalf for up to 150 days of inpatient hospital services during a single "spell of illness" (see ¶ 210). These 150 days of entitlement are calculated as follows: the first 60 days of coverage are fully paid, subject only to the initial deductible amount (see ¶ 221); the next 30 days of coverage are subject to a coinsurance amount (see ¶ 222); and the last 60 days of coverage are subject to a coinsurance amount double the coinsurance amount for days 61 through 90 (see the chart at ¶ 220 for the current amount of deductible and coinsurance). The last 60 days are "lifetime reserve" days, which may be used only once in an individual's lifetime. Thus, if a beneficiary is hospitalized for 150 days during the first covered spell of illness, all lifetime reserve days will be expended. If a beneficiary is hospitalized for only 100 days during the first spell of illness, 50 lifetime reserve days would be left for use during a subsequent spell of illness that requires hospitalization for more than 90 days. Medicare will pay for lifetime reserve days used on the basis of the beneficiary's request for payment unless the individual elects in writing not to have the program pay for the additional days, thereby saving reserve days for a later time. [Soc. Sec. Act §§ 1812(a)(1), 1812(b)(1); *Medicare Benefit Policy Manual*, Pub. 100-02, Ch. 5, § 20.]

The rules for lifetime reserve day described above may not apply in certain situations when a hospital is paid under the prospective payment system (see the discussion under "Period Covered by Election" below).

There is an additional lifetime limitation of 190 days on inpatient psychiatric hospital services (see ¶ 225). [Soc. Sec. Act § 1812(b)(3).]

For coverage under Part B of inpatient "ancillary" services furnished after a beneficiary's days of entitlement under Part A are exhausted, see ¶ 361.

Election by Beneficiary Not to Use Reserve Days

An election not to use lifetime reserve days may be made by the beneficiary (or by someone acting on the beneficiary's behalf) at the time of admission to a hospital or at any time thereafter, subject to the limitations on retroactive elections described below.

Election made prospectively. Ordinarily, an election *not* to use reserve days will apply prospectively. If the election is filed at the time of admission to a hospital, it may be made effective beginning with the first day of hospitalization or with any day thereafter. If the election is filed later, it may be made effective beginning with any day after the day it is filed. [42 C.F.R. § 409.65; Pub. 100-02, Ch. 5, § 30.2.]

Retroactive election. A beneficiary, while still in the hospital or within 90 days following discharge, may elect retroactively not to use reserve days provided: (1) the beneficiary (or some other source) offers to pay the hospital for any of the services not payable under Part B, or (2) the hospital agrees to accept the retroactive election. [42 C.F.R. § 409.65; Pub. 100-02, Ch. 5, § 30.3.]

A beneficiary may file an election not to use the lifetime reserve days later than 90 days following discharge only if benefits are available from a third-party payer and the hospital agrees to the retroactive election. [Pub. 100-02, Ch. 5, § 30.1.]

Example • • • _____

Prior to July 1, Henry Wong had used 90 days of inpatient hospital services in a spell of illness. Beginning July 1, he was hospitalized for ten more days during the same spell of illness. Henry was informed of his election right on July 1 at the time of his admission and indicated that he wanted to use his reserve days for that stay. One month after being discharged from the hospital, Henry informed the hospital that he now wished to save his reserve days for a future stay. Henry agreed to pay the hospital for the services he received during the ten days of hospitalization and was permitted to file a retroactive election not to use his reserve days for those ten days.

On July 1, Walter Brown was discharged from a hospital after being hospitalized for 105 days. The hospital billed Medicare for 90 regular days plus 15 lifetime reserve days. On October 20 (more than 90 days following discharge), Walter learned that a private insurer could pay for the last 15 days of the stay. Walter informed the hospital that he wished to file a retroactive election not to use lifetime reserve days for the last 15 days of the stay. The hospital agreed to the request, and Walter filed an election form. The hospital refunded the Medicare payment and billed the private carrier instead.

¶224

Medicare Part A

Period Covered by Election

General rule. A beneficiary election *not* to use reserve days for a particular hospital stay may apply to the entire stay or to a single period of consecutive days in the stay but cannot apply to selected days in a stay. If an election (whether made prospectively or retroactively) not to use reserve days is made effective with the first day for which reserve days are available, it may be terminated at any time. After termination of the election, all hospital days would be covered to the extent that reserve days are available. (Thus, an individual who has private insurance that covers hospitalization beginning with the first day after 90 days of benefits have been exhausted may terminate the election as of the first day not covered by the insurance plan.) If an election not to use reserve days is made effective beginning with any day after the first day for which reserve days are available, it must remain in effect until the end of that stay unless the entire election is revoked. [42 C.F.R. § 409.65; Pub. 100-02, Ch. 5, § 30.4.1.]

A beneficiary is deemed to have elected not to use lifetime reserve days if the charges for those days are less than the beneficiary's coinsurance obligation. [42 C.F.R. § 409.65; Pub. 100-02, Ch. 5, § 30.1.]

Exception for hospitals reimbursed under the prospective payment system. For hospital reimbursed under the prospective payment system (PPS), the rules stated above apply with the following exceptions.

The beneficiary has one or more regular benefit days available at time of admission. If the beneficiary has one or more regular benefit (non-lifetime reserve) days remaining in the benefit period upon entering the hospital, Medicare will pay the entire prospective payment amount for non-outlier days (see ¶ 810 for an explanation of the term "outlier days"). Thus, there will be no advantage to a beneficiary in using any lifetime reserve days for non-outlier days if at least one day of the regular 90 days of coverage remains when the beneficiary enters the hospital. In this situation, the beneficiary will be deemed to have elected *not* to use any lifetime reserve days for the non-outlier part of the stay. The beneficiary also may elect not to use lifetime reserve days for outlier days but such an election must apply to all outlier days. [Pub. 100-02, Ch. 5, § 30.4.2.1.]

Example • • •

Olivia Gonzalez was admitted to a hospital on April 1 and discharged on June 29, utilizing 89 regular days of inpatient care. On August 1, Olivia entered the hospital again. For this diagnosis-related group (DRG), outlier days would have begun August 26, but Olivia was discharged on August 23, prior to the commencement of outlier days. Because the first two days of the second stay were regular coverage days, Medicare will reimburse the hospital the prospective payment amount for the entire stay. Because no outlier days are involved, there is no advantage to the beneficiary in using lifetime reserve days. Therefore, Olivia will be deemed to have elected *not* to use any lifetime reserve days for that stay.

Although lifetime reserve days are not used for non-outlier days when the beneficiary has at least one regular day available at the time of admission, payment will be made for outlier days occurring after regular coverage days have been exhausted unless (a) the beneficiary elects not to use lifetime reserve days for the outlier days or (b) the beneficiary is deemed to have elected not to use lifetime reserve days for the outlier days. A beneficiary is deemed to have elected not to use lifetime reserve days for outlier days if the average daily charge for the outlier days for which lifetime reserve days otherwise would be available is equal to or less than the daily coinsurance amount for the lifetime reserve days. In that situation, the beneficiary would be required to pay for all of the hospital's charges for such outlier days regardless of election and, therefore, would not benefit from the use of lifetime reserve days. If the beneficiary elects *not* to use lifetime reserve days for outlier days, such an election must apply to all outlier days. If the beneficiary elects not to use lifetime reserve days for outlier days, Medicare will pay for the non-outlier portion of the stay and will make no payment for the outlier days. [42 C.F.R. § 409.65; Pub. 100-02, Ch. 5, § 30.1.]

Example • • • _____

Stuart Desmond, who had never used any of his lifetime reserve days, was admitted to the hospital on April 1, 2006, and discharged on June 29, utilizing 89 regular days of covered inpatient care. On August 1, Stuart entered the hospital again; he was discharged on September 5. For this DRG, outlier days began on August 26. Medicare will reimburse the hospital the prospective payment amount for the non-outlier portion of the stay. The average daily charges were $800 for the outlier portion of the stay. The lifetime reserve day coinsurance amount is $476 in 2006. Because the average daily charge for the outlier days is more than the daily coinsurance amount for lifetime reserve days, there is no deemed election not to use lifetime reserve days for the outlier portion of the stay. For outlier days Stuart has the option: (1) to make no election and, therefore, use his lifetime reserve days, in which case Medicare will pay for the non-outlier portion of the stay and for the ten outlier days, August 26 through September 4, and Stuart will have utilized ten lifetime reserve days; or (2) to elect *not* to use his lifetime reserve days for the ten outlier days, in which case Medicare will pay only for the non-outlier portion of the stay, and Stuart will not have used any lifetime reserve days.

_____

The beneficiary has exhausted regular benefit days. An election by a beneficiary not to use lifetime reserve days must apply to the entire hospital stay when no regular benefit days are available. If the beneficiary elects not to use lifetime reserve days, Medicare will not pay for any portion of the stay. [42 C.F.R. § 409.65 (e)(2).] A beneficiary whose 90 days of benefits are exhausted before cost outlier status is reached must elect to use lifetime reserve days for the hospital to be paid cost outlier payments. Cost outlier status is reached the day that charges reach the cost outlier status for the applicable DRG under the inpatient prospective payment system (PPS) (see ¶ 810). Use of reserve days must begin on the day following that day, to permit payment for outlier charges. If the beneficiary elects not to use lifetime reserve days when benefits are exhausted the hospital may charge the beneficiary for the charges that would have been paid as cost outlier. [42 C.F.R. § 409.65(e)(2); Pub. 100-02, Ch. 5, § 30.4.2.]

Example • • •

Frances McDonald was admitted to a hospital on March 10, 2005, and discharged on June 8, utilizing 90 regular days of coverage. On August 1, Frances entered the hospital again; she was discharged on September 10. For this DRG, outlier days began on August 26. At the time of the second admission, Frances still has 60 lifetime reserve days available. The hospital charges for this stay were $28,000. The sum of the coinsurance amounts for the lifetime reserve days needed to pay for this stay is $17,520 ($438 per day × 40 days). Because the charges for the stay are greater than the sum of lifetime reserve days coinsurance amounts, there is no deemed election not to use lifetime reserve days. Frances has the option: (1) of making no lifetime reserve election, in which case Medicare will pay for the entire stay, including the outlier days, and Frances will use 40 lifetime reserve days; or (2) of electing *not* to use lifetime reserve days, in which case Medicare will not pay for any portion of the stay.

"Inpatient Day of Care" Defined

The number of days of care charged to a beneficiary for inpatient hospital services is always in units of full days. A day begins at midnight and ends 24 hours later. A part of a day, including the day of admission, counts as a full day, but *the day of discharge or death, or a day on which a patient begins a leave of absence, is not counted as a day.* If admission and discharge occur on the same day, the day is considered a day of admission and counts as one day. As noted, the day on which a patient begins a leave of absence is treated as a day of discharge and not counted (unless the patient returns to the hospital by midnight of the same day), each day during the leave is not counted as an inpatient day, and the day the patient returns to the hospital from the leave is treated as a day of admission and counted if the patient is present at midnight of that day. [Pub. 100-02, Ch. 3, § 20.1.]

Late Discharge

When a patient chooses to continue to occupy hospital accommodations beyond the checkout time for personal reasons, the hospital may charge the beneficiary for the continued stay. Such a stay beyond the checkout time, for the comfort or convenience of the patient, is not covered under the program and the hospital's agreement to participate in the program does not preclude it from charging the patient. Medicare expects that hospitals will not impose late charges on a beneficiary unless the beneficiary has been given reasonable notice (for example, 24 hours) of impending discharge. When the patient's medical condition is the cause of the stay past the checkout time (for example, the patient needs further services, is bedridden and awaiting transportation to his home or to a skilled nursing facility, or dies in the hospital), the stay beyond the discharge hour is covered under the program and the hospital may not charge the patient. [Pub. 100-02, Ch. 3, § 20.1.1.]

[¶ 225] Psychiatric Hospital Restrictions

If an individual is an inpatient of a participating psychiatric hospital on the first day for which the individual is entitled to hospital insurance benefits (see ¶ 200–¶ 206), the days (not necessarily consecutive) on which the individual was an inpatient of a psychiatric hospital in the 150-day period immediately before this first day are deducted from the 150 days of inpatient hospital services for which the individual otherwise is entitled to have payment made *during the first spell of illness,* if these services were furnished in a psychiatric hospital or in a hospital in which the individual was an inpatient primarily for the diagnosis or treatment of mental illness. [Soc. Sec. Act § 1812(c); 42 C.F.R. § 409.63; *Medicare Benefit Policy Manual,* Pub. 100-02, Ch. 4, § 10.]

The term "mental illness" means the specific psychiatric conditions described in the American Psychiatric Association's "Diagnostic and Statistical Manual—Mental Disorders." [Pub. 100-02, Ch. 4, § 30.]

In determining the number of days to be deducted, the days of admission and the days on which the patient returned from leave of absence are included. Days of discharge, days on which the patient began a leave of absence, and the days of leave during all of which the individual is absent from the hospital are not counted. [Pub. 100-02, Ch. 3, § 20.1.]

Payment may not be made for more than a total of 190 days of inpatient psychiatric hospital services during the patient's lifetime. The period spent in a psychiatric hospital prior to entitlement does not count against the patient's 190-day lifetime limitation, however, even though pre-entitlement days may have been counted against the 150 days in the first spell of illness. [Pub. 100-02, Ch. 4, § 50.]

Example • • •

Mark DeSoto was an inpatient of a participating psychiatric hospital on his first day of entitlement on February 1. He had been in such a hospital in the pre-entitlement period for 20 days. Therefore, Medicare payment can be made for 130 days during the patient's first spell of illness. Payment would be made in the following order: 60 full benefit days, 30 coinsurance days, 40 coinsurance (lifetime reserve) days.

Partial hospitalization services are covered under Part B when these services would prevent the need for inpatient psychiatric care (see ¶ 387).

[¶ 226] Physicians' Professional Services

The medical and surgical services provided to inpatients by physicians and other healthcare professionals (*e.g.*, physician's assistants, nurse practitioners, psychologists, clinical social workers) normally are covered under Part B and are, therefore, excluded from coverage under Part A. [Soc. Sec. Act § 1861(b)(4).]

The exclusion of physicians' professional services under Part A also applies to the services rendered to individual patients by such hospital-based physicians as radiologists, anesthesiologists, pathologists, and psychiatrists. The services of nonphysician technicians (*e.g.*, an X-ray technician) aiding hospital-based physicians in these services generally are covered under Part A, however.

The services of hospital-based physicians that are not related to the care of an individual patient—*e.g.*, research, administration, supervision of professional or technical personnel, service on hospital committees, etc.—are covered under Part A and no charge can be made to the patient for these services. [Soc. Sec. Act § 1861(b).]

As discussed at ¶ 215, the services of interns and residents in an approved teaching program also are covered under Part A.

Coverage and payment for the services of hospital-based physicians are further discussed at ¶ 340 and ¶ 820, respectively.

For general coverage of physicians' services under Part B, see ¶ 340.

[¶ 227] Emergency Services

There are emergency situations in which an individual who is eligible for Medicare goes or is taken to a hospital that does not participate in the program. For example, an accident victim might have to be taken immediately to the nearest hospital, either for outpatient diagnosis and treatment or for admission as an inpatient. The law permits the payment of benefits for emergency outpatient services or inpatient care in the United States in such cases until it is no longer necessary from a medical standpoint to care for the patient in the nonparticipating institution. Payment will be made only when, taking into account the availability of any nearby participating hospitals, the nonparticipating facility was the most accessible hospital able to furnish necessary emergency care. [Soc. Sec. Act § 1814(d)(1).]

The following discussion applies *only* to emergency services in a hospital *not participating* in Medicare. Emergency services in a participating hospital are covered under Medicare in the same manner as nonemergency services. The special requirements applicable to participating hospitals with respect to the treatment of emergency room cases are discussed at ¶ 730.

Payment for Emergency Services in Nonparticipating Hospitals

There are two possible methods of payment to a nonparticipating hospital for emergency services. If the hospital so elects and meets the conditions described below, payment can be made to it. Otherwise, payment is made to the individual on the basis of an itemized bill. For payment to be made to the hospital:

1. the services *must* be emergency services;

2. the services must be covered inpatient hospital services under Part A or covered outpatient services;

3. the hospital must meet the definition of "emergency services hospital" (see below);

4. the hospital must agree not to charge for covered items or services (except to the extent that a participating hospital would be permitted to charge for these services (see ¶ 730)), and must agree to return any money incorrectly collected; and

5. the hospital must have signed a statement of election to claim payment for all inpatient and outpatient services furnished during the year. [Soc. Sec. Act §§ 1814(d)(1), 1835(b)(1); 42 C.F.R. §§ 424.104, 424.108; *Medicare General Information, Eligibility, and Entitlement Manual*, Pub. 100-01, Ch. 5, § 20.1.]

If the hospital does not elect to claim payment as discussed above, payment may be made to the beneficiary on the basis of an itemized bill, subject to applicable deductibles and coinsurance amounts. [Soc. Sec. Act §§ 1814(d)(2), 1835(b).]

Definition of "Emergency Services Hospital"

A facility qualifies as an "emergency services hospital" if it is licensed as a hospital under applicable state or local laws; has a full-time nursing service; is engaged primarily in furnishing medical care under the supervision of a physician; and is not engaged primarily in providing skilled nursing care and related services for inpatients who require medical or nursing care. Psychiatric hospitals that meet these requirements also can qualify as emergency services hospitals. [Soc. Sec. Act § 1861(e).] A federal hospital need not be licensed under state or local licensing laws to meet the definition of an emergency services hospital.

Definition of "Emergency Services"

"Emergency services" are inpatient or outpatient hospital services that are necessary to prevent the death or serious impairment of the health of an individual, and which, because of the threat to the life or health of the individual, necessitate the use of the most accessible hospital available and equipped to furnish the services. [42 C.F.R. § 424.101.]

The medical necessity of emergency services is not established by the death of the patient during hospitalization, by a lack of adequate care at home, or by a lack of transportation to a participating hospital, unless there also is an immediate threat to the life and health of the patient. [42 C.F.R. § 424.102.]

The finding of accessibility is intended to limit emergency services to situations in which transport of the patient to a participating hospital is medically inadvisable. [42 C.F.R. § 424.106.]

Termination of Emergency Services

Payment to a nonparticipating hospital for emergency services under Part A ceases when the emergency has ended. Payment under Part B may be made, however, for certain ancillary services furnished during nonemergency inpatient stays (see ¶ 361). An emergency no longer exists when it becomes safe from a medical standpoint to move the patient to a participating institution or to discharge the patient, whichever occurs first. The determination that an emergency has ended ordinarily will be based on the physician's supporting statement (see below). [42 C.F.R. § 424.103(b)(3).]

Physician's Supporting Statements

Claims filed by a nonparticipating hospital for payment for emergency services must be accompanied by a physician's statement that describes the nature of the emergency, includes relevant clinical information about the patient's condition, and states that the emergency services rendered were necessary to prevent death or serious impairment of the individual's health. A bare statement that an emergency existed is not sufficient. It must be comprehensive enough to support a finding that an emergency existed. In addition, when inpatient services are involved, this statement must include the date on which, in the physician's judgment, the emergency ceased. [*Medicare Claims Processing Manual*, Pub. 100-04, Ch. 3, §§ 110.2; 110.12.2.]

Most emergencies will be of relatively short duration so that only one bill will be submitted in a case. Thus, generally only one physician's statement will be necessary. However, in the rare situation where the emergency exists over an extended period, requests for payment following the initial one are to be accompanied by a physician's statement containing sufficient information to indicate clearly that the emergency situation still existed. A bare statement that the emergency continued to exist is not sufficient. [Pub. 100-04, Ch. 3, § 110.2.]

Emergency Services Outside the United States

Medicare will pay for emergency inpatient hospital services furnished to a beneficiary outside the United States by a foreign hospital if, at the time of the emergency, the beneficiary was (1) in the United States, or (2) in Canada, traveling between Alaska and another state without unreasonable delay and by the most direct route. (An emergency occurring within the Canadian inland waterway between the states of Washington and Canada is considered to have occurred in Canada.) [42 C.F.R. § 424.122(a); Pub. 100-04, Ch. 3, § 110.5.].

The hospital must be appropriately licensed in the country in which it is located and must be closer to, or substantially more accessible from, the place where the emergency arose than the nearest adequately equipped hospital within the United States. While typically the foreign exclusion exception involves hospital services that are furnished in Canada or Mexico, under Social Security Act § 1841(f), the United States includes the 50 states, the District of Columbia, Puerto Rico, the Virgin Islands, Guam, American Somoa, the Northern Mariana Islands, and, for purposes of services rendered on board a ship, the territorial waters adjoining the land areas of the United States. [42 C.F.R. § 424.122(b).]

¶227

At the time the emergency services are furnished, the foreign hospital also must meet accreditation requirements equal to standards adopted by the Joint Commission on Accreditation of Healthcare Organizations (JCAHO). [*Medicare Benefit Policy Manual*, Pub. 100-02, Ch. 16, § 60.] Payment to foreign hospitals is based on the hospital's customary charges. [42 C.F.R. § 413.74.]

In addition to inpatient hospital services, necessary physicians' and ambulance services that are furnished in connection with a period of covered foreign hospitalization are covered under Part B. Regular deductible and coinsurance requirements apply to physicians' and ambulance services rendered outside the United States. [Pub. 100-02, Ch. 16, § 60.]

Physicians' services in connection with foreign hospitalization. Physicians' services furnished to a Medicare beneficiary outside a hospital on the day of the beneficiary's admission as an inpatient are covered, provided the services were for the same condition for which the beneficiary was hospitalized. The physician must be legally licensed to practice in the country in which the services were furnished. This provision would include the services of a Canadian ship's physician who furnishes emergency treatment in Canadian waters on the day a beneficiary is admitted to a Canadian hospital for a covered emergency stay. [42 C.F.R. § 424.124(a), (b); Pub. 100-02, Ch. 16, § 60.]

Ambulance service in connection with foreign hospitalization. Payment may be made for necessary ambulance service to a hospital in conjunction with a beneficiary's admission as an inpatient. Return trips from a foreign hospital are not covered, however. [42 C.F.R. § 424.124(a), (c); Pub. 100-02, Ch. 16, § 60.]

Note that the coverage of foreign inpatient hospital services, emergency or otherwise, does not apply to those voluntarily enrolling in the hospital insurance program (see ¶ 203). [Soc. Sec. Act § 1814(d).]

[¶ 228] Religious Nonmedical Health Care Institutions

Prior to enactment of the Balanced Budget Act of 1997 (BBA) (PubLNo 105-33), Medicare provided special coverage rules for services performed in Christian Science sanatoria operated or listed and certified by the First Church of Christ, Scientist, Boston, Mass. The law allowed Christian Science sanatoria to qualify both as "hospitals" and as "skilled nursing facilities" for purposes of Medicare coverage, even though these sanatoria did not meet the regulatory requirements applicable to other Medicare providers.

Congress originally enacted the Christian Science exception to accommodate elderly individuals who had contributed to the Medicare and Medicaid programs through their payroll taxes but who otherwise would have been ineligible for reimbursement for needed nonmedical care without violating their religious beliefs. In *Children's Healthcare Is A Legal Duty v. Vladeck*, 938 F. Supp. 1466, 1485 (D.Minn.1996), invalidated the provisions exempting Christian Science sanatoria from Medicare's normal rules, finding that the provisions violated the Establishment Clause of the U.S. Constitution, favoring one religious sect over all others.

Responding to this ruling in the BBA, Congress changed the Christian Science provisions of the law to include all "religious nonmedical health care institutions." As was the case with Christian Science sanatoria, providers qualifying as religious nonmedical health care institutions will be included as hospitals and skilled nursing facilities for Medicare purposes. [Soc. Sec. Act §§ 1861(e), 1861(y)]. To qualify, an institution must:

(1) be a tax-exempt organization under § 501(c)(3) of the Internal Revenue Code;

(2) be lawfully operated under all applicable federal, state, and local laws and regulations;

(3) provide only nonmedical nursing items and services exclusively to individuals who choose to rely solely upon a religious method of healing, through experienced nonmedical personnel, and on a 24-hour basis;

(4) not provide medical items or services (including screening, examination, diagnosis, or administration of drugs) to its patients, or be affiliated by common ownership or otherwise with an institution that provides such services; and

(5) have in effect a specialized utilization review plan and must provide the Secretary with information required to monitor quality of care and to provide for coverage determinations. [Soc. Sec. Act § 1861(ss); 42 C.F.R. § 403.720.]

Patients being treated in a religious nonmedical health care institution must make an election to receive such benefits. [Soc. Sec. Act §§ 1821(a)(1), 1821(b).] Additionally, Medicare reimbursement in these institutions is available only to individuals having a condition such that they would be inpatients in a hospital or skilled nursing facility were it not for their religious beliefs. [Soc. Sec. Act § 1821(a)(2).] Payment is on a reasonable cost basis and may be made only for items and services normally furnished in such institutions (*i.e.*, nonmedical nursing services and related items). [Soc. Sec. Act §§ 1861(e), 1861(y); 42 C.F.R. § 403.752.]

Medicare will cover specified durable medical equipment and intermittent religious nonmedical health care institution nursing visits provided in the home to beneficiaries. The remainder of the services covered under the Medicare home health benefit are medical in nature and must be provided under the order of a physician. The specified DME items include canes, crutches, walkers, commodes, a standard wheelchair, hospital beds, bedpans, and urinals. [*Medicare Claims Processing Manual*, Pub. 100-04, Ch. 3.]

[¶ 229] "Hospital" Defined—Qualified Hospitals

As a general rule, a beneficiary's stay in a hospital will not be covered by Medicare unless the hospital is "participating" in the Medicare program; that is, the hospital has been approved for Medicare participation by the government and has signed a participation agreement (see ¶ 730). Services provided in a nonparticipating hospital, however, may be covered by Medicare in emergency situations (see ¶ 227).

To participate as a hospital in the Medicare program, an institution must be a "hospital" within the meaning of § 1861(e) of the Social Security Act. The section lists several requirements hospitals must meet, the most important of which is that the hospital is primarily engaged in providing, by or under the supervision of physicians, to inpatients (1) diagnostic services and therapeutic services for medical diagnosis, treatment, and care of injured, disabled, or sick persons, or (2) rehabilitation services for the rehabilitation of injured, disabled, or sick persons. [Soc. Sec. Act § 1861(e)(1).] In addition, § 1861(e) requires hospitals to provide 24-hour nursing care, have in effect a utilization review plan, and meet certain health and safety requirements.

Psychiatric hospitals also must participate in Medicare for the services they furnish to be covered. The requirements for these hospitals are similar to the requirements for other hospitals, although they differ in some respects due to their different purpose. Section 1861(f) of the Social Security Act lists the requirements psychiatric hospitals must meet, the most important of which is that the hospital be primarily engaged in providing, by or under the supervision of a physician, psychiatric services for the diagnosis and treatment of mentally ill persons. [Soc. Sec. Act § 1861(f)(1).]

Medicare Part A

Hospital Providers of Extended Care Services ("Swing-Bed" Facilities)

Because of the shortage of rural skilled nursing facility (SNF) beds for Medicare patients, rural hospitals with fewer than 100 beds may be paid under Part A for furnishing covered nursing home services to Medicare beneficiaries. Such a hospital, known as a swing-bed facility, can "swing" its beds between hospital and SNF levels of care on an as-needed basis if it has obtained a swing-bed approval from CMS. [Soc. Sec. Act § 1883.]

A hospital providing extended care services will be treated as a SNF for purposes of applying coverage rules. This means that those services are subject to all of the Part A coverage, physician certification, deductible, and coinsurance provisions that are applicable to SNF extended care services. For example:

(1) SNF level of care days in a swing-bed facility are counted against total SNF benefit days available to Medicare beneficiaries,

(2) Medicare beneficiaries receiving a SNF level of care in a swing-bed facility must first meet the three-day prior hospital stay requirement, and

(3) services needed and provided must be of the type and at the level to constitute extended care or SNF level services. [Soc. Sec. Act § 1883(d).]

Regulations Governing Conditions of Participation

Medicare regulations describing the conditions of participation for hospitals are found at 42 C.F.R. Ch. IV, Subch. E, Part 482.

¶229

Nursing Home Services

[¶ 230] Extended Care Services

Extended care services furnished to inpatients of a skilled nursing facility (SNF) are covered under Part A. A SNF is an institution or a distinct part of an institution, such as a skilled nursing home or rehabilitation center, which has a transfer agreement in effect with one or more participating hospitals and which is primarily engaged in providing skilled nursing care and related services for residents who require medical or nursing care; or rehabilitation services for the rehabilitation of injured, disabled, or sick persons. (Conditions of participation for SNFs are discussed at ¶ 231.) [Soc. Sec. Act § 1819(a);*Medicare General Information, Eligibility, and Entitlement Manual*, Pub. 100-01, Ch. 5, § 30.]

Extended care services, which involve skilled nursing or rehabilitation services, are similar to the kinds of services provided to hospital inpatients, but at a lower level of care. [Soc. Sec. Act §§ 1811, 1814(a)(2)(B).]

Patients using this Part A coverage are entitled to have payment made on their behalf for covered extended care services furnished by the facility or by a hospital with which the facility has a transfer agreement, or by other providers under arrangements with the facility. Generally, only the kinds of services that would be covered if furnished to a hospital inpatient are covered during a stay in a skilled nursing facility. [Soc. Sec. Act § 1814(a)(2)(B).]

Extended care services include the following:

- nursing care provided by or under the supervision of a registered professional nurse;
- bed and board in connection with furnishing of such nursing care;
- physical or occupational therapy and/or speech-language pathology services furnished by the skilled nursing facility or by others under arrangements with them made by the facility;
- medical social services;
- drugs, biologicals, supplies, appliances, and equipment, furnished for use in the skilled nursing facility, as are ordinarily furnished by such facility for the care and treatment of inpatients;
- medical services provided by an intern or resident-in-training of a hospital with which the facility has in effect a transfer agreement under an approved teaching program of the hospital, and other diagnostic or therapeutic services provided by a hospital with which the facility has such an agreement in effect, and
- other services necessary to the health of the patients as are generally provided by skilled nursing facilities, or by others under arrangements. [Soc. Sec. Act § 1861(h).]

For Medicare purposes, SNFs do not include any institution that is primarily for the care and treatment of mental diseases, or swing bed hospitals authorized to provide and be paid for extended care services. [Soc. Sec. Act § 1819(a), Pub. 100-01, Ch. 5, § 30.]

Services furnished to an inpatient of a skilled nursing facility for which payment cannot be made under Part A (usually because the beneficiary has exhausted his entitlement to benefits) are reimbursable under Part B if they constitute "medical and other health services" and the beneficiary is otherwise entitled to Part B benefits.

CMS will cover SNF care for beneficiaries involuntarily disenrolled from Medicare Advantage (MA) plans as a result of a MA plan termination when they do not have a three-day hospital stay before SNF admission. [*Medicare Benefit Policy Manual,* Pub. 100-02, Ch. 8, § 10; Soc. Sec. Act § 1861(h).]

Prior Hospitalization Requirement

An individual must be an inpatient of a hospital for at least three consecutive calendar days and then transfer to a participating skilled nursing facility usually within 30 days after discharge from the hospital to qualify for Medicare reimbursement of post-hospital extended care services. [Soc. Sec. Act § 1861(i).]

Three-day prior hospitalization. In determining whether the individual's prior hospital stay meets the required minimum of three consecutive calendar days, the day of admission is counted as a hospital inpatient day, but the day of discharge is not. The hospital discharge must have occurred on or after the first day of the month in which an individual attains age 65 or becomes entitled to Medicare benefits under the disability or end-stage renal disease provisions.

An inpatient hospital stay satisfies the prior hospitalization requirement if the hospital is either a participating hospital or a hospital that meets the requirements for an emergency hospital. The hospital need not be one with which the skilled nursing facility has a transfer agreement.

A three-day stay in a psychiatric hospital satisfies the prior hospital stay requirement but stays in religious nonmedical health care institutions do not. A three-day stay in a foreign hospital satisfies the prior hospital stay requirement if the foreign hospital meets the requirements of an emergency hospital.

To be covered, the post-hospital extended care services must have been necessitated by the condition which occasioned the patient's qualifying hospital stay, or by a condition which arose while in the facility for treatment of a condition for which the patient was previously hospitalized. In addition, the qualifying hospital stay must have been medically necessary.

In short, the qualifying hospital may or may not be a participating provider of services and it may or may not have a transfer agreement with the SNF. But if it meets the definition of an emergency hospital and if the patient's stay was medically necessary and lasted at least three days, then the services furnished the patient in the SNF satisfy the three-day prior hospitalization requirement. [Pub. 100-02, Ch. 8, § 20.1.]

Beneficiaries affected by hurricanes. In 2005, many beneficiaries and providers in the Gulf Coast regions were affected by hurricanes. CMS issued a statement recognizing that it may often be difficult to determine whether the three-day stay requirement has been met. This policy applies to any Medicare beneficiary: evacuated from a nursing home in the emergency area; discharged from a hospital (in the emergency or receiving locations) in order to provide care to more seriously ill patients; and who needs SNF care as a result of the emergency, regardless of whether that individual was in a hospital or nursing home prior to the hurricane.

Providers must document both the medical need for the SNF admission and how the admission was related to the crisis created by a hurricane and its aftermath. [*CMS Frequently Asked Questions,* http://questions.cms.hhs.gov.]

Thirty-day transfer requirements. Post-hospital extended care services represent an extension of care for a condition for which the individual received inpatient hospital services. Extended care services are "post-hospital" if initiated within 30 days after the date of discharge from a hospital following a stay which included at least three consecutive days of medically necessary inpatient hospital services.

In determining the 30-day transfer period, the day of discharge from the hospital is not counted. For example, a patient discharged from a hospital on August 1 and admitted to an SNF on August 31 was admitted within 30 days. Thus, the 30-day period begins to run on the day following actual discharge from the hospital and continues until such time as the individual is admitted to a participating SNF, and requires and receives a covered level of care. Thus, an individual who is admitted to an SNF within 30 days after discharge from a hospital, but does not require a covered level of care until more than 30 days after such discharge, does not meet the 30-day requirement.

If an individual whose SNF stay was covered upon admission is later determined not to require a covered level of care for a period that continues for more than 30 days, payment could not be resumed for any extended care services he may subsequently require even though he has remained in the facility, since the services could not be deemed to be "post-hospital" extended care services. [Pub. 100-02, Ch. 8, § 20.2.1.]

If the individual leaves the SNF and is readmitted to the same or any other participating SNF within 30 days, the 30-day transfer requirement is satisfied. Thus, the period of extended care services may be interrupted briefly and then resumed, if necessary, without hospitalization preceding the readmission to the facility. [Pub. 100-02, Ch. 8, § 20.2.3.]

Exceptions. The law provides an exception to the 30-day transfer requirement—if a patient is not admitted to an SNF within 30 days after his discharge from a hospital because to admit him within that time would not be medically appropriate, his admission to the SNF will be covered if he is admitted within such time as would be medically appropriate to begin an active course of treatment. [Soc. Sec. Act § 1861(i).]

[¶ 231] "Skilled Nursing Facility"—Conditions of Participation

As a general rule, a beneficiary's stay in a skilled nursing facility (SNF) will not be covered by Medicare unless the SNF is "participating" in the Medicare program; that is, the SNF has been approved for Medicare participation by the government and has signed a participation agreement (see ¶ 730).

To participate as a skilled nursing facility in the Medicare program, an institution must fit the statutory definition at Soc Sec. Act § 1819(a). The law defines "skilled nursing facility" as an institution or a distinct part of an institution that has in effect a transfer agreement with one or more participating hospitals. "Distinct part" and "transfer agreement" are further explained below.

A SNF also must:

(1) be primarily engaged in providing skilled nursing care and related services for residents who require medical or nursing care, or rehabilitation services for the rehabilitation of injured, disabled, or sick residents; and

(2) meet detailed requirements relating to services provided, residents' rights, professional standards, health and safety standards, and notification to the state of changes in ownership or control.

The term "skilled nursing facility" includes institutions operated or listed as a religious nonmedical health care institutions. A Medicare beneficiary may choose to have services in these facilities covered as post-hospital extended care services. [Soc. Sec. Act § 1861(y).]

A single set of requirements is applicable to SNFs under both Medicare and Medicaid. Thus, a SNF eligible to participate under one program is eligible to participate under the other, provided it agrees to contract terms. The identical definition also permits a single consolidated survey to determine a facility's qualifications to participate in either program.

A state may require higher health and safety standards of SNFs than those mandated by federal statute and regulation, which then become standards applicable under both programs in that state. [42 C.F.R. § 488.3.]

A SNF of the Indian Health Service (IHS), whether operated by the IHS or a tribal organization, is eligible for Medicare payments if it meets all of the Medicare requirements for skilled nursing facilities [Soc. Sec. Act § 1880.] Facilities that primarily treat mental illness are specifically excluded from the SNF definition. This definition also applies to nursing facility participation in the Medicaid program. A single survey determines a facility's qualifications to participate in either program. [Soc. Sec. Act § 1919(a).]

Skilled Nursing Beds in Hospitals

It is possible to treat part of an institution as a SNF. This may be done either by having a "distinct part" of the institution certified as a SNF or by having an agreement with the Secretary under which inpatient hospital beds may be used for skilled nursing care on a "swing" basis (see ¶ 229). When a beneficiary who no longer meets the Medicare skilled level of care (required for a covered Part A stay) is moved from the Medicare certified "distinct part" to a Medicare non-certified area of the institution, the beneficiary has technically ceased to reside in the SNF and, thus, is appropriately billed as a "nonresident" of the SNF. [*Medicare Claims Processing Manual*, Pub. 100-04, Ch. 6, § 100.]

To qualify for participation in the program as a "distinct part" SNF, the "distinct part" must be physically separated from the rest of the institution, that is, it must represent an entire, physically identifiable unit consisting of all the beds within that unit, such as a separate building, floor, wing, or ward. Although it is required that the distinct part be identifiable as a separate unit within the institution, it need not necessarily be confined to a single location within the institution's physical plant. The distinct part may, for example, consist of several floors or wards scattered throughout several different buildings within the institutional complex. In each case, however, the patients of the distinct part would have to be located in units that are physically separate from those units housing all other patients of the institution. Various beds scattered throughout the institution would not comprise a distinct part for purposes of being certified as a SNF. [*Medicare General Information, Eligibility, and Entitlement Manual*, Pub. 100-01, Ch. 5, § 30.3.]

Transfer Agreements

To participate in Medicare, a SNF must have a written transfer agreement with one or more participating hospitals, providing for the transfer of patients between the hospital and the facility, and for the interchange of medical and other information. If an otherwise qualified SNF has attempted in good faith, but without success, to enter into a transfer agreement, this requirement may be waived. [Pub. 100-01, Ch. 5, § 30.2.]

Although a SNF must have a transfer agreement in effect with one or more hospitals, the entitlement of a patient otherwise entitled to post-hospital extended care services will not be affected if the patient is transferred from a hospital to a SNF that does not have an agreement in effect with the particular hospital from which the patient is transferred. [Pub. 100-01, Ch. 1, § 10.1.]

[¶ 232] Accommodations

The coverage of ward, semiprivate, private, and deluxe accommodations in a skilled nursing facility is treated in the same way as hospital accommodations (see ¶ 211). [42 C.F.R. § 409.22.]

Unlike the Medicaid program, Medicare does not make payments to a nursing facility to hold a bed for a patient who takes a temporary leave of absence from the facility. [42 C.F.R. § 489.22(d)(1).]

Patients in inappropriate beds When patients requiring inpatient hospital services occupy beds in an SNF or in the hospital's distinct part SNF, they are considered inpatients of the SNF. In such cases, the services furnished in the SNF may not be considered inpatient hospital services, and payment may not be made under the program for those services. Such a situation may arise where the SNF is a distinct part of an institution the remainder of which is a hospital, and either there is no bed available in the hospital, or for any other reason the institution fails to place the patient in the appropriate bed. The same rule applies where the SNF is a separate institution.

For the same reason, where patients who require extended care services occupy beds in a hospital, payment cannot be made on their behalf for the services furnished to them in the hospital, unless the services are extended care services furnished pursuant to a swing bed approval.

When patients who require SNF services are placed in a noncertified part of an institution that contains a participating distinct part SNF, the services may be paid under certain conditions, based on the limitation of liability provisions. [*Medicare Benefit Policy Manual*, Pub 100-02, Ch. 8, § 50.]

Exceptions. Patients who are denied coverage because they have been placed in the wrong bed may nevertheless be entitled to Medicare coverage under the "waiver of liability" provision. The law recognizes that the patient is not in a position to make a choice or influence an incorrect action taken by hospital or SNF.

In the special case of patients who require extended care services but occupy beds in a hospital, the general rule is that no payment will be made on their behalf for the hospital services furnished them. However, when such patients occupy hospital beds because there are no SNF beds available to them, the general rule may not apply. A physician or a utilization review committee may certify to the need for continued hospitalization in these situations. [42 C.F.R. § 424.13(b).] Similarly, under Soc. Sec. Act § 1861(v)(1)(G), a peer review organization or the Secretary may also require continued coverage for the extended care services at a special nursing home rate of payment. Finally, rural hospitals entering into "swing-bed" agreements, as well as other hospitals without such agreements, are eligible for special rates of reimbursement for patients inappropriately occupying hospital beds because there are no SNF beds available. [Pub. 100-02, § 10.3]

[¶ 233] Physical, Occupational, and Speech Therapy

Physical and occupational therapy, and speech-language pathology furnished by a skilled nursing facility (SNF) or by others under arrangements made by the facility are covered when provided in accordance with a physician's orders and are furnished by or under the supervision of a qualified therapist. [Soc. Sec. Act § 1861(h)(3); 42 C.F.R. § 409.23.]

Coverage of outpatient physical therapy, occupational therapy, and outpatient speech language pathology services under Part B includes such services furnished directly by the provider and also services furnished under arrangements made by a provider, a physician, a non-physician practitioner, a therapist or a supplier qualified to provide the service. This includes individual practitioners and approved clinics, rehabilitation agencies, and public health agencies as well as participating hospitals, SNFs, home health agencies, comprehensive occupational rehabilitation facilities, and other rehabilitation facilities. Reimbursement for therapy provided to Part A inpatients of hospitals or SNFs is included in the respective PPS rate. [*Medicare Benefit Policy Manual*, Pub. 100-02, Ch. 15, § 220; *Final rule*, 70 FR 45026, Aug. 4, 2005.]

Coverage limits on therapy services provided on an patient basis under Part B are scheduled to be implemented on January 1, 2006. Medicare will cover $1740 of charges for physical therapy and speech-language pathology services combined for dates of service from January 1, 2006, through December 31, 2006. The separate limitation for occupational therapy services is also $1740 for these same dates of service (see ¶ 100.) [*Medicare Claims Processing Manual,* Pub. 100-04, Transmittal No. 759, Nov. 18, 2005.]

[¶ 235] Drugs and Biologicals

Drugs and biologicals for use in the skilled nursing facility (SNF) that are ordinarily furnished by the facility for the care and treatment of inpatients are covered. Such drugs and biologicals are not limited to those routinely stocked by the SNF but include those obtained for the patient from an outside source, such as a pharmacy in the community. Drugs and biologicals are included in the SNF prospective payment system except for those Part B drugs specifically excluded. Because the provision of drugs and biologicals is considered an essential part of skilled nursing care, a facility must assure their availability to inpatients to be found capable of furnishing the level of care required for participation in the program. When a facility secures drugs and biologicals from an outside source, their availability is assured only if the facility assumes financial responsibility for the necessary drugs and biologicals, that is, the supplier looks to the facility, not the patient, for payment. [*Medicare Benefit Policy Manual,* Pub. 100-02, Ch. 8, § 50.5.]

Payment may not be made for particular uses of drugs that the Food and Drug Administration has expressly disapproved or that are designated as not covered in the *Medicare National Coverage Determinations Manual,* Pub. 100-03, Chapter 2. If the intermediary has reason to question whether the FDA has approved a drug or biological for marketing, it will obtain satisfactory evidence of FDA's approval.

A drug that is not included in the drug compendia is nevertheless covered in a SNF if the drug: (1) was furnished the patient during his or her prior hospitalization; (2) was approved for use in the hospital by the hospital's pharmacy and drug therapeutics committee; (3) is required for the continuing treatment of the patient in the SNF; and (4) is reasonable and necessary. Under these limited circumstances, a combination drug approved by a hospital pharmacy and drug therapeutics committee also may be covered as an extended care service. Rules for drugs and biologicals applicable to hospital inpatients are found in the *Medicare Benefit Policy Manual,* Pub. 100-02, Ch. 1, § § 30, 30.3, and 30.5, also apply to inpatients of SNFs. Theses rules include general information concerning drugs and biologicals furnished to inpatients; combination drugs; and drugs for use outside the SNF. [Pub. 100-02, Ch. 8, § 50.5.]

With respect to drugs or biologicals furnished to an *inpatient* for use *outside* a SNF, see the comparable provisions pertaining to hospital inpatients at ¶ 212. Special limitations on payment for certain "less than effective" drugs applicable under the Part B program are described at ¶ 644.

Prescription drug plans. Medicaid will no longer cover prescription drugs covered by Medicare prescription drug coverage as of January 1, 2006. Beneficiaries who don't join a Medicare drug plan by December 31, 2005, will be automatically enrolled in a Medicare drug plan. Medicare drug coverage started January 1, 2006; however, beneficiaries can choose and join a different plan. [42 C.F.R. § 423.34.]

[¶ 236] Supplies, Appliances, and Equipment

Supplies, appliances, and equipment are covered as extended care services only if they are ordinarily furnished by the skilled nursing facility (SNF) for the care and treatment of inpatients and if furnished to an inpatient for use in the SNF. [42 C.F.R. § 409.25.]Examples of covered SNF supplies include oxygen, surgical dressings, splints, casts, and personal hygiene items and services. [*Medicare Benefit Policy Manual,* Pub. 100-02, Ch. 1, § 40.]

Covered extended services for which payment may be made under Part A include the amount of unreplaced whole blood or packed red blood cells and the administration of blood to inpatients of participating SNFs.

Under certain circumstances, supplies, appliances, and equipment used during the beneficiary's stay are covered even though they leave the facility with the patient when discharged. These are circumstances in which it would be unreasonable or impossible from a medical standpoint to limit the patient's use of the item to the periods during which the individual is an inpatient. An example of a covered item which may leave the facility with the patient is a leg brace temporarily attached to the patient's body while he is receiving treatment as an inpatient and which is also necessary to permit or facilitate the patient's release from the facility. [Pub. 100-02, Ch. 1, § 40.]

Supplies, appliances, and equipment furnished to a patient for use only outside the facility would not, in general, be covered as extended care services. However, a temporary or disposable item, such as a sterile dressing, provided to a patient that is medically necessary to permit or facilitate his or her departure from the facility and is required until such time as the patient can obtain a continuing supply would be covered as an extended care service. [Pub. 100-02, Ch. 1, § 40.]

Other Diagnostic and Therapeutic Items or Services

Other services that are necessary to the health of the patients are covered if the services are generally provided by, or under arrangements made by, skilled nursing facilities (SNFs). Items or services that would not be included as inpatient hospital services if furnished to an inpatient of a hospital also are excluded from coverage as extended care services. For instance, the provision of personal laundry services by SNFs is not a covered service under Medicare because it would not be covered if provided to an inpatient of an acute care hospital. The use of an operating room and any special equipment, supplies, or services would not constitute covered extended care services except when furnished to the facility by a hospital with which the facility has a transfer agreement because operating rooms are not generally maintained by SNFs. However, supplies and nursing services connected with minor surgery performed in a SNF that does not require the use of an operating room or any special equipment or supplies associated with such a room would be covered extended care services and paid as part of inpatient SNF prospective payment system. [Pub. 100-02, Ch. 8, § 50.8.1.]

[¶ 237] Interns and Residents-in-Training

Medicare pays for medical services that are furnished by an intern or a resident-in-training under a hospital teaching program as posthospital skilled nursing facility (SNF) care, if the intern or resident is in (1) a participating hospital with which the SNF has in effect a transfer agreement; or (2) a hospital that has swing-bed approval, and is furnishing services to a SNF-level inpatient of that hospital. [42 C.F.R. § 409.26(a).]

The medical and surgical services furnished to the facility's patients by interns and residents-in-training of a hospital with which the facility has a transfer agreement (see ¶ 248) are covered under Part B if the services are not covered under Part A. [*Medicare Benefit Policy Manual*, Pub. 100-02, Ch. 8, § 50.7.]

[¶ 238] Whole Blood and Packed Red Blood Cells

Medicare coverage includes the cost of unreplaced blood (after satisfaction of the three-pint blood deductible discussed at ¶ 223) and the cost of administering the blood to inpatients of participating skilled nursing facilities (SNF). Blood transfusions, however, ordinarily are performed by hospitals and not by SNFs. Thus, in the usual case, when a SNF facility patient needs blood, a participating hospital will provide the blood and the laboratory services and perform the transfusion under arrangements with the facility. In such a case, the SNF pays the hospital's charge for these services, and this amount becomes the facility's cost. [*Medicare General Information, Eligibility, and Entitlement Manual*, Pub. 100-01, Ch. 3, § 20.5.]

[¶ 239] Other Services

The medical and other health services listed below are covered under Part B when furnished by a participating SNF either directly or under arrangements to inpatients who are not entitled to have payment made under Part A or outpatients:

- diagnostic x-ray tests, diagnostic laboratory tests, and other diagnostic tests;

- X-ray, radium, and radioactive isotope therapy, including materials and services of technicians;

- surgical dressings, and splints, casts, and other devices used for reduction of fractures and dislocations;

- prosthetic devices (other than dental) which replace all or part of an internal body organ (including contiguous tissue), or all or part of the function of a permanently inoperative or malfunctioning internal body organ, including replacement or repairs of such devices;

- leg, arm, back, and neck braces, trusses, and artificial legs, arms, and eyes including adjustments, repairs, and replacements required because of breakage, wear, loss, or a change in the patient's physical condition;

- outpatient physical therapy, outpatient speech pathology services, and outpatient occupational therapy screening mammography services;

- screening mammography services;

- screening pap smears and pelvic exams;

- influenza, pneumococcal pneumonia, and hepatitis B vaccines;

- some colorectal screening;

- diabetes self-management;

- prostate screening;

- ambulance services;

- hemophilia clotting factors; and

- Epoetin Alfa (EPO) for ESRD beneficiaries when given in conjunction with dialysis.

[42 C.F.R. § 409.27; *Medicare Benefit Policy Manual*, Pub. 100-02, Ch. 8, § 70.]

Routine personal hygiene items and services required to meet the needs of residents also are covered items and services. These include, but are not limited to, hair hygiene supplies, comb, brush, bath soap, disinfecting soaps or specialized cleansing agents when indicated to treat special skin problems or to fight infection, razor, shaving cream, toothbrush, toothpaste, denture adhesive, denture cleaner, dental floss, moisturizing lotion, tissues, cotton balls, cotton swabs, deodorant, incontinence care and supplies, sanitary napkins and related supplies, towels, washcloths, hospital gowns, over the counter drugs, hair and nail hygience services, bathing, and basic personal laundry. [42 C.F.R. § 483.10.]

[¶ 242] Skilled Nursing Facility Coinsurance

The beneficiary is required to pay a coinsurance amount equal to one-eighth of the inpatient hospital deductible for each day after the 20th and before the 101st day of skilled nursing facility (SNF) services furnished during a spell of illness. A "spell of illness" is defined as a period of consecutive days that begins with the first day on which a beneficiary is furnished inpatient hospital or SNF services by a qualified provider (see ¶ 210.) This coinsurance amount, like the inpatient hospital deductible on which it is dependent, is subject to annual change. The coinsurance charge in calendar year 2006 is $119 per day. [*Medicare General Information, Eligibility and Entitlement Manual*, Pub. 100-01, Ch. 3, § 10.2.1; *Notice*, 70 FR 55885, Sept. 23, 2005.]

[¶ 243] Duration of Covered SNF Services

A patient having hospital insurance coverage is entitled to have payment made on his or her behalf for up to 100 days of covered inpatient extended care services in each spell of illness subject to the coinsurance requirement discussed at ¶ 242. [Soc. Sec. Act § 1812(a)(2), (b)(2).]

The number of days of care charged to a beneficiary for inpatient skilled nursing facility services is counted in units of full days. A day begins at midnight and ends 24 hours later. The midnight-to-midnight method is to be used in reporting days of care for beneficiaries, even if the facility uses a different definition of day for statistical or other purposes.

A part of a day, including the day of admission, counts as a full day. The day of discharge, death, or a day on which a patient begins a leave of absence, however, is not counted as a day. (Charges for ancillary services on the day of discharge or death or the day on which a patient begins a leave of absence are covered.) If admission and discharge or death occur on the same day, the day is considered a day of admission and counts as one inpatient day. [*Medicare Benefit Policy Manual*, Pub. 100-02, Ch. 3, § 20.1.]

When a patient chooses to occupy accommodations in a facility beyond the normal check-out time for personal reasons, the facility may charge the patient for a continued stay. Such a stay beyond the check-out time, for the comfort or convenience of the patient, is not covered under the program and the facility's agreement to participate in the program does not preclude it from charging the patient. The hospital, however, must provide the beneficiary with an Advance Beneficiary Notice (ABN) before the noncovered services are provided.

When the patient's medical condition is the cause of the stay past the checkout time (e.g., the patient needs further services, is bedridden and awaiting transportation to their home or in the case of a hospital, transfer to a skilled nursing facility (SNF), or dies in the SNF or hospital), the stay beyond the discharge hour is covered under the program and the hospital or SNF may not charge the patient.

The imposition of a late checkout charge by a hospital or SNF does not affect the counting of days for: (1) ending a benefit period; (2) the number of days of inpatient care available to the individual in a hospital or SNF; and (3) the 3-day prior hospitalization requirement for coverage of post hospital extended care services and Part A home health services. A late charge by a hospital does not affect counting of days for meeting the prior inpatient stay requirement for coverage of extended care services. The quality improvement organization is responsible for reviewing the appropriateness of early discharges. [Pub. 100-02, Ch. 3, § 20.1.1.]

Leaves of absence. The day on which the patient begins a leave of absence is treated as a day of discharge and is not counted as an inpatient day unless the patient returns to the facility by midnight of the same day. The day the patient returns to the facility from a leave of absence is treated as a day of admission and is counted as an inpatient day if he or she is present at midnight of that day. [Pub. 100-02, Ch. 3, § 20.1.2.]

Days counting toward maximum. Post-hospital extended care services count toward the maximum number of benefit days payable per benefit period only if: (1) payment for the services is made, or (2) payment for the services would be made if a request for payment were properly filed, the physician certified that the services were medically necessary, and the provider submitted all necessary evidence. When payment cannot be made because of the extended care coinsurance requirement, the day(s) used nevertheless count toward the beneficiary's maximum days of extended care. [Pub. 100-02, Ch. 3, § 30.]

[¶ 244] Noncovered Levels of Care

Payment cannot be made for posthospital extended care unless a physician certifies—and recertifies when required—that "such services are or were required to be given because the individual needs or needed on a daily basis skilled nursing care (provided directly by or requiring the supervision of skilled nursing personnel) or other skilled rehabilitation services, which as a practical matter can be provided only in a skilled nursing facility (SNF) on an inpatient basis, for any of the conditions with respect to which he was receiving inpatient hospital services." [Soc. Sec. Act § 1814(a)(2)(B).]

Thus, for a patient to be eligible for posthospital extended care as an inpatient of a SNF, the patient must require the type and level of care that is defined in the regulations as "posthospital extended care," a level of care often distinguished from "custodial care" (see ¶ 625), which is excluded.

In determining whether the services a patient requires constitute the level of care covered under the extended care benefit, three criteria must be met: (1) skilled nursing services or skilled rehabilitation services must be required on a daily basis; (2) the services must be furnished for a condition for which the beneficiary received inpatient hospital or inpatient critical access hospital (CAH) care or a condition that arose while the beneficiary was receiving care in a SNF for a condition for which the beneficiary had received inpatient hospital or inpatient CAH services; and (3) as a practical matter, the service can be provided only in a SNF on an inpatient basis. [42 C.F.R. § 409.31(b).]

See ¶ 908 for a discussion of waiver of liability when a beneficiary is improperly transferred to a lower level of care.

"Skilled Nursing/Rehabilitation Services" Defined

Skilled nursing and skilled rehabilitation services are services that are (1) ordered by a physician; (2) require the skills of technical or professional personnel, for example, a registered nurse, licensed practical (vocational) nurse, physical therapist, occupational therapist, speech pathologist, or audiologist; and (3) are provided either directly by or under the supervision of such personnel. [42 C.F.R. § 409.31(a).] In determining whether a service is skilled, the following criteria apply:

(1) If the inherent complexity of a service prescribed for a patient is such that it can be performed safely and effectively only by or under the supervision of technical or professional personnel, the service would constitute a skilled service;

(2) A service that is usually nonskilled may be considered skilled when, because of special medical complications, its performance or supervision, or the observation of the patient, requires the use of skilled nursing or skilled rehabilitation personnel. For example, having a plaster cast on an extremity generally does not indicate a need for skilled care, but a patient with a preexisting acute skin problem or a need for special traction of the injured extremity might need to have technical or professional personnel properly adjust traction or

observe the patient for complications. In such cases, the complications and special services involved must be documented by physicians' orders and nursing or therapy notes; and

(3) The restoration potential of a patient is not the deciding factor in determining whether skilled services are needed. Even when full recovery or medical improvement is not possible, skilled care may be needed to prevent, to the extent possible, deterioration of the patient's condition or to sustain current capacities. For example, even though no potential for rehabilitation exists, a terminal cancer patient may require skilled services. [42 C.F.R. § 409.32.]

Examples of Levels of Care

The following are examples of skilled nursing, skilled rehabilitation services, and nonskilled services that are specified in the Medicare regulations:

Services That Could Qualify as Either Skilled Nursing or Skilled Rehabilitation Services:

(1) overall management and evaluation of care plan;

(2) observation and assessment of the patient's changing condition; and

(3) patient education services. [42 C.F.R. § 409.33(a).]

Services That Qualify as Skilled Nursing Services:

(1) intravenous or intramuscular injections and intravenous feeding;

(2) enteral feeding that comprises at least 26 percent of daily calorie requirements and provides at least 501 milliliters of fluid per day;

(3) nasopharyngeal and tracheotomy aspiration;

(4) insertion and sterile irrigation and replacement of suprapubic catheters;

(5) application of dressings involving prescription medications and aseptic techniques;

(6) treatment of extensive decubitus ulcers or other widespread skin disorder;

(7) heat treatments that specifically have been ordered by a physician as part of active treatment and that require observation by nurses to evaluate adequately the patient's progress;

(8) initial phases of a regimen involving administration of medical gases;

(9) rehabilitation nursing procedures, including the related teaching and adaptive aspects of nursing, that are part of active treatment; for example, the institution and supervision of bowel and bladder training programs. [42 C.F.R. § 409.33(b).]

Services That Would Qualify as Skilled Rehabilitation Services:

(1) ongoing assessment of rehabilitation needs and potential: services concurrent with the management of a patient care plan, including tests and measurements of range of motion, strength, balance, coordination, endurance, functional ability, activities of daily living, perceptual deficits, speech and language or hearing disorders;

(2) therapeutic exercises or activities: therapeutic exercises or activities which, because of the type of exercises employed or the condition of the patient, must be performed by or under the supervision of a qualified physical therapist or occupational therapist to ensure the safety of the patient and the effectiveness of the treatment;

(3) gait evaluation and training: gait evaluation and training furnished to restore function in a patient whose ability to walk has been impaired by neurological, muscular, or skeletal abnormality;

¶244

(4) range-of-motion exercises: range-of-motion exercises that are part of the active treatment of a specific disease state that has resulted in a loss of, or restriction of, mobility (as evidenced by a therapist's notes showing the degree of motion lost and the degree to be restored);

(5) maintenance therapy: maintenance therapy, when the specialized knowledge and judgment of a qualified therapist is required to design and establish a maintenance program based on an initial evaluation and periodic reassessment of the patient's needs, and consistent with the patient's capacity and tolerance. For example, a patient with Parkinson's disease who has not been under a rehabilitation regimen may require the services of a qualified therapist to determine what type of exercises will contribute the most to the maintenance of his present level of functioning;

(6) ultrasound, short-wave, and microwave therapy treatments by a qualified physical therapist;

(7) hot pack, hydrocollator, infrared treatments, paraffin baths, and whirlpool; hot pack, hydrocollator, infrared treatments, paraffin baths, and whirlpool in particular cases in which the patient's condition is complicated by circulatory deficiency, areas of desensitization, open wounds, fractures, or other complications, and the skills, knowledge, and judgment of a qualified physical therapist are required; and

(8) services of a speech pathologist or audiologist when necessary for the restoration of function in speech or hearing. [42 C.F.R. § 409.33(c).]

Specific Examples of Personal Care Services:

Personal care services that do not require the skills of qualified technical or professional personnel are not skilled services, except under the circumstances specified in 42 C.F.R. § 409.32(b) (that is, when "special medical complications" are involved—see "Skilled Nursing/Rehabilitation Services Defined" above). Personal care services include, but are not limited to, the following:

(1) administration of routine oral medications, eye drops, and ointments;

(2) general maintenance care of colostomy and ileostomy;

(3) routine services to maintain satisfactory functioning of indwelling bladder catheters;

(4) changes of dressings for noninfected postoperative or chronic conditions;

(5) prophylactic and palliative skin care, including bathing and application of creams, or treatment of minor skin problems;

(6) routine care of the incontinent patient, including use of diapers and protective sheets;

(7) general maintenance care in connection with a plaster cast;

(8) routine care in connection with braces and similar devices;

(9) use of heat as a palliative and comfort measure, such as whirlpool and hydrocollator;

(10) routine administration of medical gases after a regimen of therapy has been established;

(11) assistance in dressing, eating, and going to the toilet;

(12) periodic turning and positioning in bed; and

(13) general supervision of exercises that have been taught to the patient, including the actual carrying out of maintenance programs. Helping a patient repeat exercises required to maintain bodily function do not require the skills of a therapist and would not constitute

¶244

skilled rehabilitation services. Similarly, repetitive exercises to improve gait, maintain strength, or endurance; passive exercises to maintain range of motion in paralyzed extremities, which are not related to a specific loss of function; and assistive walking do not constitute skilled rehabilitation services. [42 C.F.R. § 409.33(d).]

"Daily Basis" Requirement

Skilled nursing services or skilled rehabilitation services must be required and provided on a "daily basis" (essentially a seven-day-a-week basis). If skilled rehabilitation services are not available on a seven-day-a-week basis, however, a patient whose inpatient stay is based solely on the need for skilled rehabilitation services would meet the "daily basis" requirement if the patient needs and receives such services at least five days a week. If a facility provides physical therapy only five days a week, and the patient requires and receives physical therapy on each of the days on which it is available, the "daily basis" requirement would be met. This requirement is not applied so strictly that it would not be met merely because there is a break of a day or two during which no skilled rehabilitation services are furnished and discharge from the facility would not be practical. For example, a patient who normally requires skilled rehabilitation services on a daily basis exhibits extreme fatigue that results in his physician's suspending therapy sessions for a day or two. Payment would be made for these days because discharge in such a case would not be practical. [42 C.F.R. § 409.34.]

Need for Institutionalization

In determining whether the care needed by a beneficiary can, as a practical matter, only be provided in a skilled nursing facility (SNF) on an inpatient basis (see 42 C.F.R. § 409.31(b)(3)), consideration is given to the patient's condition and to the availability and feasibility of using more economical alternative facilities and services. If the needed service is not available in the area in which the individual resides, and transporting him to the closest facility furnishing such services would be an excessive physical hardship, it is appropriate to conclude that the needed care can, as a practical matter, only be provided in a SNF. This is also true, even though the patient's condition might not be adversely affected, if it would be more economical or more efficient to provide the covered services in the institutional setting. For example, if the patient's condition is such that daily transportation by ambulance is necessary, it might be more economical to provide the needed care in an institutional setting. [42 C.F.R. § 409.35.]

In determining the availability of alternative facilities and services, availability of Medicare payment for the services furnished by the alternative facilities is not a factor to be considered. For instance, an individual in need of daily physical therapy might be able to receive the needed services from an independent physical therapy practitioner. The existence of an annual limit on Medicare payment for services furnished by such a practitioner (see ¶ 381) should not be the basis for determining that the needed care can be provided only in a SNF. [Soc. Sec. Act § 1833(g); 42 C.F.R. § 409.35(a).]

Discharge planning. Medicare-participating hospitals, as part of the discharge planning process, must include a discharge planning evaluation of a patient's likely need for posthospital extended care services and the availability of these services through facilities that participate in the Medicare program and that serve the geographic area in which the patient resides. The hospital must inform the patient or the patient's family of their freedom to choose among participating Medicare providers of posthospital services and must, when possible, respect patient and family preferences when they are expressed. In addition, the hospital may not use the discharge plan to specify or otherwise limit the patient's choice of qualified providers that may provide home health care or posthospital extended care services. [42 C.F.R. § 482.43.]

[¶ 248] Rights of SNF Residents

A skilled nursing facility (SNF) must promote and protect the rights of each resident, including: (1) free choice with respect to medical care and treatment; (2) freedom from restraints; (3) privacy; (4) confidentiality; (5) accommodation of needs; (6) grievance procedures; (7) participation in resident and family groups; (8) participation in social, religious, and community activities; (9) examination of state certification survey results; and (10) refusal of a transfer to a nonskilled nursing part of the facility. [Soc. Sec. Act § 1819(c).]

The facility is required to (1) give notice, orally and in writing at the time of admission to the facility, of the resident's legal rights during the stay at the facility; (2) make available to each resident, upon reasonable request, a written statement of such rights; (3) inform each resident, in writing before or at the time of admission and periodically during the resident's stay, of services available in the facility and of related charges for such services, including any charges for services not covered under Medicare or by the facility's basic per diem charge; and (4) provide written information including a policy statement related to the resident's rights to make decisions concerning medical care (see the discussion on advance directives at ¶ 730). [Soc. Sec. Act § 1819(c)(1)(B).]

The written description of legal rights must include a description of the protection of personal funds and a statement that a resident may file a complaint with a state survey and certification agency respecting resident abuse and neglect or misappropriation of resident property in the facility. [Soc. Sec. Act § 1819(c).]

Payment Issues

If a beneficiary requests a noncovered service or a service that is more expensive than the amount of Medicare payment, the provider must inform the beneficiary that there will be a specific charge for that service. [42 C.F.R. § 489.32.] On the other hand, providers, including a SNF, may not impose any of the following prepayment requirements:

(1) require an individual entitled to hospital insurance benefits to prepay in part or in whole for inpatient services as a condition of admittance as an inpatient, or require a promissory note except where it is clear upon admission that payment under Medicare Part A cannot be made;

(2) deny covered inpatient services to an individual entitled to have payment made for those services on the ground of inability or failure to a pay a requested amount at or before admission;

(3) evict, or threaten to evict, an individual for inability to pay a deductible or a coinsurance amount required under Medicare;

(4) charge an individual for an agreement to admit or readmit the individual on some specified future date for covered inpatient services; or

(5) charge a resident for failure to remain an inpatient for any agreed-upon length of time or for failure to give advance notice of departure from the provider's facilities. [42 C.F.R. § 489.22(d).]

Payment adjustment for AIDS residents in SNFs. The temporary 128 percent increase in the PPS per diem payment for any SNF resident with Acquired Immune Deficiency Syndrome (AIDS), which went into effect October 1, 2004, has been continued for FY 2006. [Soc. Sec. Act § 1888(e); *Final rule,* 70 FR 45026, Aug. 4, 2005.]

Privacy Issues

Healthcare facilities must be compliant with regulations that protect the privacy of individually identifiable information. HHS regulations protect the privacy of individually identifiable information in accordance with the Health Insurance Portability and Accountability Act (HIPAA) (PubLNo 104-191). Under these regulations, facilities must provide notice to patients on the first service visit regarding the facilities' use of the beneficiary's medical data and the beneficiary's right to access that data. [45 C.F.R. §§ 164.520, 164.534.] Other than very specific uses, such as a patient directory or emergency care, the identity of patients and information about their health status must be protected unless an authorization describing to whom and for what purpose the information is being released is obtained from the beneficiary. [45 C.F.R. § 164.508.] These regulations apply to all communications including written, verbal, and electronic communications.

Patients have the right to see their medical records, to request copies or amendment of their records, and to be given a list of others who have accessed their records during the previous six years. [45 C.F.R. §§ 164.522, 164.524, 164.526, 164.528.] (See ¶ 715 for a full description of medical record protections.)

Home Health Services

[¶ 250] Home Health Services: Qualifying Conditions for Coverage

home health services are covered only if furnished by a home health agency (HHA) participating in the Medicare program and acting on a physician's certification that the individual (1) is confined to the home; (2) needs skilled nursing care on an intermittent basis or is in need of physical or occupational therapy, or speech-language pathology services; (3) is under a physician's care who has established the plan; and (4) the plan is reviewed at least every 60 days by a physician. [42 C.F.R. § 409.42; *Medicare Benefit Manual*, Pub. 100-02, Ch. 7, § 30.] If the patient does not need therapy, skilled nursing care must be needed at least once every 60 days for the patient to qualify for home health benefits. [Pub. 100-02, Ch. 7, § 40.1.3.]

Parts A and B Coverage

Home health services are covered under Part A hospital insurance and Part B supplementary medical insurance. Part C Medicare Advantage health plans also provide home health benefits, but must do so only through Medicare-approved HHAs. (see ¶ 400 for a discussion of the Medicare Advantage program). Prior to the enactment of the Balanced Budget Act of 1997 (BBA) (PubLNo 105-33), home health services were covered under Part A when the patient was eligible under both Part A and Part B. [Soc. Sec. Act § 1833(d).] Effective January 1, 1998, for beneficiaries enrolled in Parts A and B, home health visits that are not a part of the first 100 visits following a beneficiary's stay in a hospital or skilled nursing facility are considered Part B home health services. If the beneficiary is enrolled only in Part A and qualifies for the home health benefit, all of the home health services are financed under Part A. [Soc. Sec. Act §§ 1812(a)(3), 1832(a); Pub. 100-02, Ch. 7, § 60.1.]

For beneficiaries enrolled in Parts A and B, Part A will pay only for "post-institutional home health services" furnished during a home health spell of illness for up to 100 visits during such spell of illness for all beneficiaries. [Soc. Sec. Act §§ 1812(a)(3), 1812(b).] Covered home health services that do not meet the definition of post-institutional are covered under Part B. There is no prior hospitalization requirement for a beneficiary to receive home health services. [42 C.F.R. § 409.42.]

The monthly Part B premium increased to compensate for the extra costs due to the transfer of payment responsibility from Part A to Part B. Between 1998 and 2003, premiums were increased by one-seventh of the extra costs each year. [BBA § 4611(e)(3).]

Home health services are covered without a deductible or coinsurance charge, except for (1) durable medical equipment (DME) and (2) osteoporosis drugs. [Soc. Sec. Act § 1833(a)(2)(A), (b)(2); *Medicare General Information, Eligibility, and Entitlement Manual*, Pub. 100-01 Ch. 3, § 20.4.] A 20 percent coinsurance charge applies to DME furnished as a home health benefit. [Soc. Sec. Act §§ 1814(k), 1834(a)(1); Pub. 100-02, Ch. 7, § 50.4.2.] Both the Part B coinsurance and deductible apply to osteoporosis drugs furnished by an HHA as well as to services not covered under the HHA plan of care (see ¶ 262). [Pub. 100-2, Ch. 7, § 60.4.]

See ¶ 351 for coverage of home health services provided to homebound patients in medically underserved areas where HHAs are not available. Certain home health services also may be covered when provided by a rural health clinic (see ¶ 382) or a hospice (see ¶ 270).

The BBA required the Secretary to base home health service payments on a prospective payment system (HH PPS) by October 1, 1999. The Omnibus Consolidated and Emergency

Supplemental Appropriations Act for Fiscal Year 1999 (OCESAA) (PubLNo 105-277), delayed the date for implementation of HH PPS until October 1, 2000 (see ¶ 835).

Definitions

"Post-institutional home health services" are defined as the services furnished to a beneficiary after discharge from a hospital in which the individual was an inpatient for not less than three consecutive days before discharge and the services are initiated within 14 days of discharge, or after discharge from a skilled nursing facility in which the beneficiary was provided post-hospital extended care services and services are initiated within 14 days after discharge. [Soc. Sec. Act § 1861(tt)(1).] If the first home health visit is not initiated within 14 days of discharge or if the three-consecutive-day stay requirement is not met, then home health services are furnished under Part B. [Pub. 100-02, Ch. 7, § 60.1.]

"Home health spell of illness" refers to a period of consecutive days beginning with the first day that an individual is furnished post-institutional home health services during a month in which the individual is entitled to benefits under Part A. It ends when the beneficiary has not received hospital, critical access hospital, skilled nursing facility, or home health services for 60 days. [Soc. Sec. Act § 1861(tt)(2).]

An "episode of care" is a 60-day period starting on the day that the first billable services are provided to a beneficiary under a plan of care and ending 60 days later. On the 61st day that services are being provided, a new episode of care commences. A beneficiary can have an unlimited number of episodes of care, and an episode can be shorter than 60 days. A beneficiary may have only one episode of care at a time. The 60-day episode of care is used to determine the amount of payment made on behalf of a beneficiary (see payment rates at ¶ 835). [*Medicare Claims Processing Manual*, Pub. 100-04, Ch. 10, § 10.1.5.]

"Home health services" are defined as the following items and services, provided on a visiting basis in a place of residence used as the individual's home, except as noted in item (7), below:

(1) part-time or intermittent nursing care provided by or under the supervision of a registered professional nurse;

(2) physical or occupational therapy, or speech-language pathology services;

(3) medical social services under the direction of a physician;

(4) part-time or intermittent services of a home health aide who has completed an approved training program successfully;

(5) medical supplies (other than drugs and biologicals) and durable medical equipment;

(6) medical services of interns and residents-in-training under an approved teaching program of a hospital with which the HHA is affiliated; and

(7) any of the foregoing items and services that (a) are provided on an outpatient basis under arrangements made by the HHA at a hospital or skilled nursing facility, or at a rehabilitation center meeting standards prescribed in regulations, and (b) involve the use of equipment of such a nature that the items and services cannot be made readily available to the individual in the place of residence, or that are furnished at the facility while the individual is there to receive any item or service involving the use of such equipment. Transportation of the individual is not covered (see ¶ 257). [Soc. Sec. Act § 1861(m); 42 C.F.R. §§ 409.44, 409.45.]

¶250

[¶ 251] Skilled Nursing Care

If a patient qualifies for home health services, Medicare covers either part-time or intermittent skilled nursing services. For purposes of receiving home health care, the term "part-time or intermittent care" means skilled nursing and home health aide services furnished up to 28 hours per week combined over any number of days per week so long as they are furnished fewer than eight hours per day. Additional time up to 35 hours per week but fewer than eight hours per day may be approved by Medicare on a case-by-case basis. For purposes of an individual qualifying for home health benefits when the individual needs intermittent skilled nursing care and for payment of provider claims, the term intermittent means skilled nursing care that is either provided or needed on fewer than seven days each week, or fewer than eight hours of each day for periods of 21 days or less with extensions in exceptional circumstances. [Soc. Sec. Act § 1861(m); *Medicare Benefit Manual*, Pub. 100-02, Ch. 7, § 50.7.]

Skilled nursing care in excess of the amounts of care that meet the definitions of "part-time" or "intermittent" may be provided to a home care patient or purchased by other payers without bearing on whether the care is covered to the extent allowed by Medicare. An HHA may bill the home care patient or other payor for care that exceeds the hours of care that Medicare allows, as reasonable and necessary. [Pub. 100-02, Ch. 7, § 50.7.]

Skilled nursing services are services that:

(1) require the skills of a registered nurse or a licensed practical nurse (or licensed vocational nurse) under the supervision of a registered nurse;

(2) are reasonable and necessary to the treatment of the patient's illness or injury; and

(3) are needed on an intermittent basis. [Pub. 100-02, Ch. 7, § 40.1.]

In general, the last requirement is met if a patient needs skilled nursing care at least once every 60 days. A one-time nursing service, such as giving a gamma globulin injection following exposure to hepatitis, for example, would not be considered a need for intermittent skilled nursing care because a recurrence of the problem every 60 days is not medically predictable. If the need for a skilled nursing visit at least once every 60 days is medically predictable but a situation arises after the first visit making additional visits unnecessary—for example, the patient is institutionalized or dies—the one visit made would be covered. [Pub. 100-02, Ch. 7, § 40.1.3.]

[¶ 252] Physical and Occupational Therapy and Speech-Language Pathology Services

Physical and occupational skilled therapy and speech-language pathology services furnished by a home health agency (HHA) or by others under arrangements made by the HHA are covered when provided in accordance with a physician's orders and by, or under the supervision of, a qualified therapist. For occupational therapy services to qualify initially for home health coverage, they must be part of a plan of care that also includes intermittent skilled nursing care, physical therapy, or speech-language pathology services. The skilled services must be reasonable and necessary for the treatment of the beneficiary's illness or injury or for the restoration or maintenance of the function affected by the illness or injury. [42 C.F.R. § 409.44(c).] Payment for therapy services is included in the home health prospective payment amount received by an HHA for the episode of care. See ¶ 267 and ¶ 835 for a discussion on consolidated billing and the home health prospective payment system. These therapy services also are discussed at ¶ 381.

The service of a physical or occupational therapist, or speech-language pathologist, is a skilled therapy service if the inherent complexity of the service is such that it can be performed safely and/or effectively only by or under the general supervision of a skilled therapist. Services involving activities for the general welfare of any patient, *e.g.*, general exercises to promote overall fitness or flexibility and activities to provide diversion or general motivation, do not constitute skilled therapy. Those services can be performed by nonskilled individuals without the supervision of a therapist. On the other hand, services of skilled therapists for the purpose of teaching the patient or the patient's family or caregivers necessary techniques, exercises, or precautions are covered to the extent that they are reasonable and necessary to treat illness or injury. [42 C.F.R. § 409.44; Pub. 100-02, Ch. 7, § 40.2.]

Coverage limits on therapy services are scheduled to be implemented on January 1, 2006. Medicare will cover $1,740 of charges for physical therapy and speech-language pathology services combined for dates of service from January 1, 2006, through December 31, 2006. The separate limitation for occupational therapy services is also $1,740 for these same dates of service (see ¶ 100.) [*Medicare Claims Processing Manual*, Pub. 100-04, Transmittal No. 759, Nov. 18, 2005.]

From December 8, 2004, through December 31, 2005, there was no upper limit on the amount of physical and occupation therapy benefit and the speech-language pathology services provided by Medicare. [§ 624 of the Medicare Prescription Drug, Improvement, and Modernization Act of 2003 (PubLNo 108-173); Soc. Sec. Act § 1833(g).]

For physical and occupational skilled therapy and speech-language pathology service claims received between September 1, 2003, until December 7, 2003, Medicare covered only $1,590 of charges for physical therapy and speech-language pathology services combined. [*Medicare Benefit Policy Manual*, Pub. 100-02, Ch. 7, § 10.12.]

[¶ 253] Medical Social Services

Medical social services are covered as home health services if ordered by a physician and included in the plan of care. The frequency and nature of the services must be reasonable and necessary for the treatment of the Medicare beneficiary's condition. Medical social services are "dependent" services that are covered only if the beneficiary needs skilled nursing care on an intermittent basis, physical therapy or speech-language pathology services, or occupational therapy services on a continuing basis. [42 C.F.R. § 409.45(c).]

Treatment for a patient's social problems will be covered under the program only if (1) the services are necessary to resolve social or emotional problems that are, or are expected to become, an impediment to the effective treatment of the patient's medical condition or rate of recovery, and (2) the plan of care indicates how, to be performed safely and effectively, the required services necessitate the skills of a qualified social worker or social worker assistant under the supervision of a qualified medical social worker. [42 C.F.R. § 409.45(c); *Medicare Benefit Policy Manual*, Pub. 100-02, Ch. 7, § 50.3.]

Covered services include, but are not limited to, the following: (1) assessment of the social and emotional factors related to the patient's illness, need for care, response to treatment, and adjustment to care; (2) appropriate action to obtain community services to assist in resolving problems in these areas; (3) assessment of the relationship of the patient's medical and nursing requirements to the home situation, financial resources, and availability of community resources; and (4) counseling services required by the patient. Counseling services furnished to the patient's family are covered only when the HHA can demonstrate that a brief intervention (that is, two or three visits) by a medical social worker is necessary to remove a clear and direct impediment to the effective treatment of the patient's medical condition or to his or her rate of recovery. To be considered clear and direct, the behavior or actions of the family member or caregiver must plainly obstruct, contravene, or prevent the patient's medical treatment or rate of recovery. Medical social services to address general problems that do not clearly and directly impede treatment or recovery as well as long-term social services furnished to family members, such as ongoing alcohol counseling, are not covered. [42 C.F.R. § 409.45(c); Pub. 100-02, Ch. 7, § 50.3.]

[¶ 254] Home Health Aides

Medicare covers part-time or intermittent services of a home health aide who has successfully completed a training program approved by the Secretary, when ordered by a physician for a beneficiary who qualifies for home health services. The reason for the visits by the home health aide must be to provide hands-on personal care to the beneficiary or services that are needed to maintain the beneficiary's health or to facilitate treatment of the beneficiary's illness or injury. Services provided by the home health aide must be reasonable and necessary. The physician's order should indicate the frequency of the home health aide services required. [Soc. Sec. Act § § 1861(m)(4), 1891(a)(3); 42 C.F.R. § 409.45(b).]

Covered home health aide services include the following: (1) personal care of a patient; (2) simple dressing changes that do not require the skills of a licensed nurse; (3) assistance with medications that ordinarily are self-administered and do not require the skills of a licensed nurse; (4) assistance with activities that are directly supportive of skilled therapy, such as routine exercises and the practice of functional communication skills; and (5) routine care of prosthetic and orthotic devices. [42 C.F.R. § 409.45(b); *Medicare Benefit Policy Manual*, Pub. 100-02, Ch. 7, § 50.2.]

The discussion on intermittent services at ¶ 251 is applicable also to home health aides.

[¶ 255] Medical Supplies and Durable Medical Equipment

Covered medical supplies are items that, due to their therapeutic or diagnostic characteristics, are essential to enable the home health agency (HHA) to carry out effectively the plan of care that the physician has ordered for the treatment or diagnosis of the patient's illness or injury. They include such items as catheters and catheter supplies; ostomy bags and ostomy care supplies; dressings and wound care supplies, such as sterile gloves, gauze, and applicators; and intravenous supplies. [Soc. Sec. Act § 1861(m)(5); 42 C.F.R. § 409.45(f); *Medicare Benefit Policy Manual*, Pub. 100-02, Ch. 7, § 50.4.]

Durable medical equipment (DME) furnished by an HHA is reimbursed under Medicare Part B based on a fee schedule with the beneficiary responsible for a 20 percent coinsurance (see ¶ 356). [Soc. Sec. Act § § 1814(k), 1834(a)(1), 1861(m)(5); Pub. 100-02, Ch. 7, § 50.4.2.] DME is not included in the home health prospective payment rate and has been eliminated from the consolidated billing requirement. [42 C.F.R. § 484.205(b).]

Exclusion of Drugs and Biologicals

Drugs and biologicals generally are excluded from coverage as a home health benefit. [Soc. Sec. Act § 1861(m)(5); 42 C.F.R. § 409.49(a).] In certain cases they may be covered under Part B; however, if administered by a physician as a part of his professional services, the drugs cannot be self-administered (see ¶ 351). In addition, the administration of medication may be covered if the services of a licensed nurse are required to administer the medications safely and effectively for the reasonable and necessary treatment of the illness or injury. [Pub. 100-02, Ch.7, § 40.1.2.4.]

Injections of osteoporosis drugs are covered as non-routine medical supplies for female beneficiaries in certain circumstances (the nursing visit to perform the injection may be the individual's qualifying service for home health coverage) if:

(1) the individual sustained a bone fracture that a physician certifies was related to postmenopausal osteoporosis; and

(2) the individual's physician certifies that she is unable to learn the skills needed to self-administer the drug, or is otherwise physically or mentally incapable of administering the drug, and that her family or caregivers are unable or unwilling to administer the drug. [Soc. Sec. Act § 1861(kk); *Medicare Claims Processing Manual*, Pub. 100-04, Ch. 10, § 90.1.]

[¶ 256] Interns and Residents-in-Training

Home health services include the medical services of interns and residents-in-training under an approved hospital teaching program if the services are ordered by the physician who is responsible for the plan of care and the home health agency is affiliated with, or is under common control of, a hospital providing the medical services. Approved means:

(1) approved by the Accreditation Council for Graduate Medical Education;

(2) in the case of an osteopathic hospital, approved by the Committee on Hospitals of the Bureau of Professional Education of the American Osteopathic Association;

(3) in the case of an intern or resident-in-training in the field of dentistry, approved by the Council on Dental Education of the American Dental Association; or

(4) in the case of an intern or resident-in-training in the field of podiatry, approved by the Council on Podiatric Education of the American Podiatric Association. [42 C.F.R. § 409.45(g); *Medicare Benefit Policy Manual*, Pub 100-02, Ch. 7, § 50.5.]

[¶ 257] Outpatient Services

In certain instances, the services described in ¶ 251–¶ 256, provided on an outpatient basis, can be included as home health services (see ¶ 250, item (7)). While the individual ordinarily must be homebound to be eligible for home health services, such services are covered if furnished under arrangements at a hospital, skilled nursing facility, or rehabilitation center that (1) require the use of equipment (for example, hydrotherapy) that cannot be made available at the beneficiary's home or (2) are furnished while the beneficiary is at the facility to receive services requiring the use of the equipment in (1) above. The hospital or skilled nursing facility must be a qualified provider of services. [42 C.F.R. § 409.47(b); *Medicare Benefit Policy Manual*, Pub. 100-02, Ch. 7, § 50.6.]

In some cases, special transportation arrangements may have to be made to bring the homebound patient to the institution providing these special services. The cost of transporting an individual to a facility cannot be reimbursed as a home health service. [42 C.F.R. § 409.49(b); Pub. 100-02, Ch. 7, § 50.6.]

[¶ 260] Care of a Physician

The patient must be under the care of a physician who established the plan of care (POC). The physician must be qualified to sign the physician certification and the POC (see ¶ 262). Such a physician may be a doctor of medicine, osteopathy, or podiatric medicine. A podiatrist may establish a POC only if consistent with the functions authorized for that specialty by state law. It is expected, but not required for coverage, that the physician who signs the POC will see the patient, but there is no specified interval of time within which the patient must be seen. [42 C.F.R. § 409.42(b); *Medicare Benefit Policy Manual*, Pub. 100-02, Ch. 7, § 30.3.]

[¶ 262] Establishment of a Plan of Care

Items and services must be furnished under a plan established and periodically reviewed by a physician. [Soc. Sec. Act § 1861(m); 42 C.F.R. § 409.42(d).] The same physician must certify the medical necessity of the home health services, signing the certification at the time the plan of treatment is established. [42 C.F.R. § 424.22.]

Home health services may not be certified or recertified, and a plan of care may not be established and reviewed, by a physician who has a financial relationship with the home health agency (HHA) furnishing the service. [42 C.F.R. § 424.22(d).] See ¶ 720 on fraud and abuse.

Recertification is required at least every 60 days when a new episode of care commences (see ¶ 250). Recertification also is required if a beneficiary elects to transfer to another home health agency (HHA), or is discharged and returns to the same HHA during an episode of care. The recertification must be signed by the physician who reviews the plan of care. [42 C.F.R. § 424.22(b).]

Content of the Plan of Care

The plan of care must contain all pertinent diagnoses, including the beneficiary's mental status; types of services, supplies, and equipment required; frequency of visits; prognosis; rehabilitation potential; functional limitations; activities permitted; nutritional requirements; all medications and treatments; safety measures to protect against injury; instructions for timely discharge or referral; and any additional items the HHA or physician chooses to include. [42 C.F.R. § 484.18(a); *Medicare Benefit Policy Manual*, Pub. 100-02, Ch. 7, § 30.2.]

The term "plan of care" is used to refer to the medical treatment plan established by the treating physician with the assistance of the home health care nurse. It is anticipated that a discipline-oriented plan of care will be established, when appropriate, by an HHA nurse regarding nursing and home health aide services and by skilled therapists regarding specific therapy treatment. These plans of care may be incorporated within the physician's plan of care or separately prepared. [Pub. 100-02, Ch. 7, § 30.2.]

The physician's orders in the plan of care must indicate the type of services to be provided to the beneficiary, both with respect to the professional who will provide them and with respect to the nature and frequency of the individual services. [42 C.F.R. § 409.43(b); Pub. 100-02, Ch. 7, § 30.2.]

Since July 1, 2000, physician orders are no longer required for pneumococcal pneumonia, influenza virus and Hepatitis B vaccinations. Beneficiaries may receive these vaccinations upon request. [*Medicare Claims Processing Manual*, Pub. 100-04, Ch. 18, § 10.]

Services that are provided from the beginning of the certification period and before the physician signs the plan of care are considered to be provided under a plan of care established and approved by the physician if (1) there is a documented verbal order for the care prior to rendering the services, and (2) the services are included in a signed plan of care. [42 C.F.R. § 409.43(d); Pub. 100-02, Ch. 7, § 30.2.]

Review of Plan of Care

The plan of care must be reviewed and signed by a physician in consultation with an HHA professional personnel no less frequently than every 60 days. Note that, in the case of physical, occupational, and speech therapy plans, the plan of care may be designed by the qualified therapist providing the services (see ¶ 381). In such cases, the physician still must review the plan. [42 C.F.R. § 409.43(e); Pub. 100-02, Ch. 7, § 30.2.]

The plan of care must be signed by the physician before a claim for payment is submitted. Services may be provided prior to the plan of care being signed because a claim is not submitted until the end of a 60-day episode of care. [Pub. 100-02, Ch. 7, § 30.2.]

Effective January 1, 2001, physicians are eligible for payment from Medicare for signing plans of care and for recertification. [*Final rule*, 65 FR 65376, Nov. 1, 2000.]

¶262

[¶ 264] Patient Confined to Home

For a beneficiary to be eligible to receive covered home health services, the items and services must be furnished to an individual who is confined to home, except as discussed at ¶ 257. The law requires a physician to certify this confinement in all cases. [Soc. Sec. Act § 1814(a)(2)(C); 42 C.F.R. §§ 409.42(a), 424.22(a).]

An individual is considered "confined to home" if, due to an illness or injury, a condition exists that restricts the individual's ability to leave home except with the assistance of another person or with the aid of a supportive device, such as crutches, a cane, a wheelchair, or a walker, or if a condition exists that medically contraindicates leaving the home. While an individual does not have to be bedridden to be considered confined to home, the condition should be such that there exists a normal inability to leave home, that leaving home requires a considerable and taxing effort, and that absences from the home are infrequent or of relatively short duration, or are attributable to the need to receive medical treatment. [*Medicare Benefit Policy Manual*, Pub. 100-02, Ch. 7, § 30.1.1.]

Beneficiaries are considered homebound even if they take an occasional absences from the home for nonmedical purposes such as: a trip to the barber; a walk around the block; a drive; or attend a family reunion, funeral, graduation, or other infrequent or unique event. The absences must be infrequent, relatively short in duration and does not indicate that the patient has the ability to obtain healthcare outside of the home. These examples are not an all—inclusive list, but are meant to be illustrative of the kinds of infrequent or unique events a beneficiary may attend. In determining whether a beneficiary has the general inability to leave home and leaves the home only frequently or for periods of short duration, it is necessary to look at the patient's condition over a period of time, rather than for short periods. [Pub. 100-02, Ch. 7, § 30.1.1.]

Attendance at a religious service was defined as an absence of infrequent or short duration by the Benefits Improvement and Protection Act of 2000 (BIPA) (PubLNo 106-544). BIPA also allows beneficiaries to receive therapeutic, psychosocial or medical treatment in a state-licensed adult day-care program on a regular basis and still be considered homebound. [Soc. Sec. Act §§ 1814(a), 1835(a).]

Patient's Place of Residence

Home health services must be furnished on a visiting basis in a place used as the patient's residence. This may be his or her own dwelling, an apartment, a relative's home, a home for the aged, or some other type of institution. However, an institution may not be considered a patient's place of residence if the institution meets at least the most important requirement in the definition of "hospital" (see ¶ 229), or in the definition of "skilled nursing facility" (see ¶ 231). [Pub. 100-02, Ch. 7, § 30.1.2.]

[¶ 266] Visits

A visit is a personal contact in the patient's residence made for the purpose of providing a covered service by a health worker on the staff of the home health agency (HHA) or by others under contract or arrangement with the HHA; or a visit by a patient on an outpatient basis to a hospital, skilled nursing facility, or rehabilitation center, or outpatient department affiliated with a medical school when arrangements have been made by the HHA for one or more of the covered services. [42 C.F.R. § 409.48(c); *Medicare Benefit Policy Manual*, Pub. 100-2, Ch. 7, § 70.2.]

An HHA may furnish services via a telecommunication system if such services do not substitute for in-person home health services ordered as part of a plan of care certified by a physician. Telecommunication services are not considered a home health visit for purposes of eligibility or payment. As with all services provided under the Medicare home health benefit, physician certification is required for payment of home health services furnished via telecommunication systems. Telemedicine does not constitute a visit under the home health prospective payment. [Soc. Sec. Act § 1895(e); BIPA § 223(b); Pub. 100-02, Ch.7 § 110; *Final rule*, 65 FR 41128, July 3, 2000.]

Evaluation Visits

When personnel of the HHA make an initial evaluation visit, the cost of this visit is considered an administrative expense of the HHA because at this point the patient has not been accepted for care. If, however, during the course of this initial evaluation visit, the patient is determined suitable for home health care by the HHA, and is furnished the first skilled service as ordered under the physician's plan of treatment, the visit would become the first billable visit. [Pub. 100-02, Ch. 7, § 70.2.]

An observation and evaluation, or reevaluation visit made by a nurse or other appropriate personnel, ordered by the physician for the purpose of evaluating the patient's condition and his or her continuing need for skilled services, is covered as a skilled visit. [Pub. 100-2, Ch. 7, § 70.2.]

A supervisory visit made by a nurse or other personnel to evaluate the specific personal care needs of the patient or to review the manner in which the personal care needs of the patient are being met by the aide is considered an administrative function and is not chargeable to the patient as a skilled visit. [Pub. 100-02, Ch. 7, § 70.2.]

OASIS

Since July 19, 1999, HHAs participating in the Medicare program have been required to conduct patient-specific comprehensive assessments on certain patients using a standard core assessment data set, the "Outcomes and Assessment Information Set (OASIS)." OASIS is a fundamental component of CMS' efforts to achieve broad-based and measurable improvements in the quality of health care and patient satisfaction in the Medicare and Medicaid home health benefit. [42 C.F.R. § 484.55.]

With the enactment of the Medicare Prescription Drug, Improvement, and Modernization Act of 2003 (MMA) (PubLNo 108-173), effective December 8, 2003, home health agencies will no longer have to collect OASIS data on patients who are not Medicare beneficiaries or Medicaid enrollees. [§ 704 of MMA.]

HHAs are required to incorporate OASIS data items into the HHA's own assessment instrument using the language and groupings of the OASIS items. The items include information regarding demographics and patient history, living arrangements, supportive assistance, sensory status, integumentary status, elimination status, neuro/emotional/behavioral status, activities of daily living, medications, equipment management, emergent care, and discharge.

HHAs should use assessments to identify the patient's need for home care and the patient's medical, nursing, rehabilitative, social and discharge planning needs. For Medicare patients, identifying the need for home care will include assessment of the beneficiary's eligibility for Medicare's home health benefit, including the patient's homebound status. [42 C.F.R. § 484.55(e).]

OASIS data must be submitted electronically. HHAs have seven calendar days from the completion of the patient-specific assessment to enter and submit the OASIS data to the designated state agency or CMS OASIS contractor. Accurate, complete, encoded, and locked data must be submitted for each patient at least monthly. [42 C.F.R. § 484.20.]

¶266

Except for a patient whose physician orders only physical, occupational or speech therapy, the assessment must be completed by a registered nurse. A speech pathologist or physical therapist may conduct the assessment if the physician ordered only these types of therapy. [42 C.F.R. § 484.55(b).]

Initial assessment. An initial assessment must be completed by a registered nurse or an appropriate therapist, if that therapy is the only component of a plan of care, within 48 hours of the patient's referral, within 48 hours of the patient's return home, or on the start-of-care date ordered by the physician. Eligibility for the Medicare home health benefit must be evaluated during the initial assessment and when the comprehensive assessment is completed. [42 C.F.R. § 484.55(a).]

Comprehensive assessments. The comprehensive assessment should reflect the patient's current health status accurately and include information that may be used to demonstrate the patient's progress toward achievement of desired outcomes. Comprehensive assessments must be completed within five calendar days after the start of care and updated when there is a:

(1) significant change in condition resulting in a new case-mix assignment (see ¶ 853);

(2) transfer to another HHA elected by the beneficiary;

(3) discharge and then a return to the same HHA during a 60-day episode; or

(4) discharge.

Comprehensive assessments also must be updated within 48 hours of a beneficiary's return home from a hospital stay longer than 24 hours for any reason other than diagnostic testing, and during the last five days of an episode of care. [42 C.F.R. § 484.55(d).]

Drug regimen review. Drug regimen review is part of the comprehensive assessment of the patient and includes all medications the patient is using at the time of the assessment. The purpose of the review is to identify any potential adverse effects and drug reactions including ineffective drug therapy, duplicate drug therapy, significant side effects, significant drug interactions, and noncompliance with drug therapy. [42 C.F.R. § 484.55(c).]

Discharge or transfer. A discharge occurs when the patient dies, is released from home care by the HHA, or is admitted to another facility such as a nursing home or hospital. Patient transfer occurs, when the physician orders care to be provided by another facility such as a nursing home. [42 C.F.R. § 484.55.]

Confidentiality. The HHA must ensure the confidentiality of all patient identifiable information contained in the clinical record, including OASIS data, and may not release patient-identifiable OASIS information to the public. [42 C.F.R. § 484.11.] Under the conditions of participation for HHAs, patients whose data will be collected and used by the federal government must receive a notice of their privacy rights, including the right to refuse to answer questions. Two standard statements notifying patients of their privacy rights have been prepared by CMS. The statements, one for Medicare/Medicaid patients and one for non-Medicare/non-Medicaid patients, must be incorporated into HHAs' admission processes. [*Notice*, 64 FR 32983, June 18, 1999.]

Under rules required by the Health Insurance Portability and Accountability Act of 1996 (HIPAA) (PubLNo 104-191), an HHA must provide each beneficiary at the first service visit with a notice regarding the use of protected identifiable health information and make a good faith effort to obtain a written acknowledgement by the beneficiary of receipt of the notice. Beneficiaries also will have a right to review, obtain a copy and amend the medical records maintained by the HHA. HHAs were to be compliant with these HIPAA privacy provisions no later than April 14, 2003. [45 C.F.R. §§ 164.520, 164.524, 164.526, 164.534.] See ¶ 715 for more discussion on the privacy of beneficiaries' medical data and the requirements of providers, including the need to obtain authorizations from beneficiaries prior to the release of individually identifiable health information in certain circumstances.

Prospective payment system. The weighted answers to several OASIS items, including the need for therapy, provide a key element of Medicare reimbursement under the home health prospective payment system (HH PPS) (see ¶ 835). The sum of the weighted answers creates a profile of the beneficiary that fits into a specific category that has been developed for the case-mix adjustment. The case-mix adjustment is used to raise or lower the rate of reimbursement from the standard national rate of payment under HH PPS based on the medical needs of the beneficiary. HH PPS became effective October 1, 2000. [42 C.F.R. § 484.210(e).]

Advance Directives

Beneficiaries must be informed about advance directives and their choices must be documented in their medical record. HHAs must provide the information to the beneficiary during the initial visit before care is provided. [42 C.F.R. § 489.102.]

Advance medical directives are legal documents that enable individuals to express their wishes regarding their own healthcare prior to the time when such care may be necessary and while they are still capable of making rational decisions. [Soc. Sec. Act § 1866(f)(3).]

Beneficiaries are not *required* to make advance directives, and the amount and type of care cannot be conditioned upon the completion or noncompletion of an advance directive. HHAs must provide written information to beneficiaries about their rights under state law to make decisions concerning their medical care, including the right to accept or refuse medical care and the right to formulate medical directives before care is started. [Soc. Sec. Act § 1866(f); 42 C.F.R. § 489.102.]

[¶ 267] Specific Exclusions from Coverage

Any service that would not be covered if furnished to an inpatient of a hospital is excluded from coverage as a home health service, such as private-duty nurse services (see ¶ 217). [Soc. Sec. Act §§ 1861(b), 1861(m); 42 C.F.R. § 409.49(c).]

In addition to the general exclusions applicable to both parts of the Medicare program, which are discussed at ¶ 600 *et seq.*, the following are excluded from home health services: (1) meals-on-wheels, or similar food service arrangements; (2) domestic or housekeeping services unrelated to patient care; (3) transportation services from place of residence to a facility to receive home health services on an outpatient basis (see ¶ 257); (4) drugs and biologicals, except for osteoporosis drugs (see ¶ 255); (5) end-stage renal disease services covered under the ESRD program; (6) prosthetic devices covered under Part B (but catheters, ostomy bags, etc. are not considered prosthetic devices if furnished under a home health plan of care and are not subject to this exclusion); (7) medical social services provided to members of the beneficiary's family that are not incidental to covered social services being provided to the beneficiary; (8) respiratory care furnished by a respiratory therapist in a beneficiary's home; (9) in-home visits by dietitians or nutritionists, and (10) services that would not be covered as inpatient services. [42 C.F.R. § 409.49; *Medicare Benefit Policy Manual*, Pub. 100-02, Ch. 7, § 80.]

Consolidated Billing

Medicare will not reimburse providers other than the home health agency (HHA) that has established a 60-day home health episode of care (see ¶ 250) for claims that contain: (1) routine medical supplies, (2) certain listed non-routine medical supplies, (3) part-time or intermittent or nursing home health aides services; (4) physical therapy, occupational therapy and speech therapy services; (5) medical social services; (6) Medicare services of an intern or resident in training in a hospital under an approved teaching program in the case of a home health agency that is affiliated with a teaching hospital; (7) services furnished at hospitals, rehabilitation centers or skilled nursing facilities when they involve equipment too cumbersome to be provided in the home; and (8) covered osteoporosis drugs. [Soc. Sec. Act § 1861(m).] All Medicare covered home health services listed in § 1861(m) of the Social Security Act and ordered by the physician in a plan of care must be billed to Medicare by the home health agency.

The payment made to an HHA for a 60-day home health episode of care includes payment for these items. If these services are provided to a beneficiary from a provider other than the HHA during the 60-day home health episode of care, the HHA is to pay the provider not Medicare. HHAs and hospitals, as part of their discharge planning, are required by the Medicare conditions of participation to inform beneficiaries of these payment policies. [Soc. Sec. Act § 1842(b)(6)(F); *Medicare Claims Processing Manual,* Pub. 100-4, Ch. 10, §§ 20, 20.1 and 20.2.]

Venipuncture

Since February 5, 1998, venipuncture has been excluded as a basis for qualifying for Medicare home health services if it is the sole skilled service required by a beneficiary. Medicare will pay for a blood draw, however, if the beneficiary needs another qualified skilled service and meets all home health eligibility criteria. [Soc. Sec. Act § 1814(a)(2)(C).]

Home Health Advance Beneficiary Notices and Demand Billing

Whenever a home health agency (HHA) believes that home health services ordered by a physician would not be covered by Medicare, the HHA must inform the patient, orally and with written notice of: (1) the extent to which payment may be expected from Medicare, Medicaid, or any other federally funded or aided program known to the HHA; (2) the charges for services that will not be covered by Medicare; and (3) the charges that the individual may have to pay. [42 C.F.R. § 484.10(e); *Medicare Claims Processing Manual*, Pub. 100-04, Ch. 30, § 60.2.3.1.]

Beneficiaries must be given the opportunity to submit a "demand bill" after being notified that an HHA believes services will not be covered by Medicare. Demand billing requires an HHA to submit a bill to CMS for coverage determination even though the HHA believes the services will not be covered. [Pub. 100-4, Ch. 10, § 50.]

Effective March 1, 2001, HHAs must use Home Health Advance Beneficiary Notices (HHABN) CMS Form R-296 to provide notice to a beneficiary on the first occasion that a triggering event occurs after the Form's effective date of March 1, 2001. Triggering events include those in which the HHA (1) advises a beneficiary that the HHA will not initiate services for him as a Medicare patient, (2) proposes to reduce services, or (3) proposes to terminate services because the HHA believes Medicare is not likely to pay for otherwise-covered home health services. HHAs may produce a version of CMS Form R-296 electronically as long as they meet all of the format requirements of the approved Form CMS-R-296. HHA created HHABNs that are found to be defective will result in the HHA being liable for services provided after the HHABN was delivered. [Pub. 100-04, Ch. 30, §§ 60.2.3.1, 60.4.1.2.]

Effective July 1, 2005, expedited determination and reconsideration procedures are available to beneficiaries when an HHA informs them of a decision that Medicare coverage of their provider services is about to end. There will be a two-step notification process: a simple, generic notice to each beneficiary before a discharge or service termination, and, for

¶267

a beneficiary who objects to the service termination, a detailed notice of the reason for this decision.

Quality improvement organizations, which currently conduct similar expedited review for inpatient hospital discharges, will carry out the expedited determination process, and quality independent contractors will conduct expedited reconsiderations. A provider is financially liable for continued services until two days after valid delivery of the termination notice or until the service termination date specified on the notice, whichever is later. [*Final rule*, 69 FR 69253, Nov. 26, 2004.]

[¶ 268] "Home Health Agency" Defined—Qualified Home Health Agencies

As a general rule, services furnished by a home health agency (HHA) will not be covered by Medicare unless the HHA is participating in the Medicare program; that is, the HHA has been approved for Medicare participation by the government and has signed a participation agreement (see ¶ 730). [42 C.F.R. § 409.41.]

To participate in Medicare as a "home health agency," an organization must be a public agency or private organization, or a subdivision of such an agency or organization. It also must be primarily engaged in providing skilled nursing services and other therapeutic services, have policies established by a group of professional personnel (including at least one physician and one registered nurse) associated with the agency, provide for supervision of services by a physician or nurse, and meet certain health and safety and financial stability requirements. [Soc. Sec. Act § 1861(o); *Medicare General Information, Eligibility and Entitlement Manual*, Pub. 100-01, Ch. 5, § 50.]

For Part A, but not for Part B, the definition of a home health agency does not include any agency or organization that is primarily for the care and treatment of mental diseases. [Soc. Sec. Act § 1861(o).]

Arrangements may be made by an HHA with other HHAs to furnish items or services under certain circumstances. Whether the services and items are furnished by the HHA itself or by another HHA under arrangements made by the HHA, both must agree not to charge the patient for covered services and items and must also agree to return money incorrectly collected (see ¶ 835). [Pub. 100-01, Ch. 5, § 50.2.]

Conditions of Participation

The statutory requirements to be met by participating HHAs and the additional health and safety requirements prescribed by the Secretary have been incorporated into conditions of participation for HHAs. These conditions are included in the regulations governing the Medicare program. [42 C.F.R. Part 484.]

Home Health Quality Initiative

CMS makes available to the public 11 measures of care provided at every Medicare certified home health agency. The measures include: (1) four measures related to improvement in mobility; (2) four measures related to meeting basic daily needs; (3) two measures related to medical emergencies, and (4) one measure related to improvement in mental health. These measures are calculated based upon responses to 41 questions in the Outcome and Assessment Information Set (OASIS) (see ¶ 266) evaluations completed for each beneficiary. From time to time, CMS plans to print these quality of care measures in newspapers throughout the country. These measures are also available at www.medicare.gov. Medicare quality improvement organizations will work with home health agencies to improve the quality of care administered. [*HHS Release*, Nov. 3, 2003.]

Surety Bonds

CMS issued, and subsequently suspended, additional regulations establishing a surety bond requirement for HHAs participating in the Medicare and Medicaid programs, as mandated by the Balanced Budget Act of 1997 (BBA) (PubLNo 105-33). The purpose of the regulations is to protect the Medicare program from sham businesses set up to collect Medicare reimbursement fraudulently. [*Final rule*, 63 FR 292, Jan. 5, 1998; *Final rule*, 63 FR 41170, July 31, 1998.]

The Balanced Budget Refinement Act of 1999 (BBRA) (PubLNo 106-113), which became effective November 29, 1999, modified the BBA surety bond requirements. Under the BBRA, an HHA must obtain a surety bond that is the lesser of $50,000 or 10 percent of the aggregate amount of payments made to the HHA by Medicare. [Soc. Sec. Act § 1861(o)(7).] The surety bond obtained by an HHA to satisfy the Medicare requirement also will satisfy the Medicaid surety bond requirement so long as the bond applies to guaranteed return of overpayments under both programs. [Soc. Sec. Act § 1128F.] The regulations enforcing these provisions have been suspended by CMS and have not been replaced. [*Final rule*, 63 FR 41170, July 31, 1998.]

Since January 1, 1998, an HHA entering the Medicare or Medicaid program must demonstrate that it has available sufficient capital to start and operate the HHA for the first three months. [42 C.F.R. § 489.28.]

Hospice Care

[¶ 270] Hospice Care

Hospice care is an interdisciplinary approach to caring for the terminally ill that provides comfort rather than seeking a cure. The patient and family or household are considered a unit receiving care. Pain control, counseling, including bereavement counseling for the patient's family, and social services are required aspects of hospice care. A hospice program must be a public agency or private organization that meets Medicare conditions of participation in order to qualify as a Medicare provider. [Soc. Sec. Act § 1861(dd)(2).]

A Medicare beneficiary becomes eligible for hospice care upon a physician's certification that he or she has a terminal illness, *i.e.*, is expected to live six months or less if the illness proceeds at its normal course. The prognosis is based on the physician's clinical judgment regarding the normal course of the individual's illness. [Soc. Sec. Act §§ 1814(a)(7)(A), 1861(dd)(3)(A).]

Hospice Care Defined

Hospice care includes the following services and supplies:

(1) nursing care provided by or under the supervision of a registered professional nurse;

(2) physical or occupational therapy or speech-language pathology services;

(3) medical social services under the direction of a physician;

(4) homemaker services and the services of a home health aide who has successfully completed an approved training program;

(5) medical supplies (including drugs and biologicals, but only those that are reasonable and necessary for palliation and management of terminal illness) and the use of medical appliances;

(6) physicians' and nurse practitioners' services; nurse practitioners may serve many of the functions of the physician, but they cannot serve as medical director, certify or recertify terminal illness, or direct the plan of care in place of the physician;

(7) short-term inpatient care, including both procedures necessary for pain control and symptom management and respite care to relieve family members caring for the beneficiary;

(8) counseling (including dietary counseling) with respect to care of the terminally ill beneficiary and the immediate family's adjustment to the beneficiary's death; and

(9) any other item or service that is specified in the plan of care and which is otherwise covered by Medicare.

Nursing care and homemaker services may be provided on a 24 hour, continuous basis during periods of crisis as necessary to maintain the terminally ill individual at home. Respite care will be covered if provided only occasionally and may not exceed five consecutive days. Bereavement counseling is a required service but is not reimbursable. [Soc. Sec. Act § 1861(dd)(1); 42 C.F.R. § 418.202; 42 C.F.R. § 418.204(b), (c); *Medicare Benefit Policy Manual*, Pub. 100-02, Ch. 9, § 40.1.]

Hospice services that are not reasonable and necessary for the palliation or management of terminal illness are excluded from Medicare coverage. [Soc. Sec. Act § 1862(a)(1)(C).] A beneficiary who is denied coverage for hospice care because services received were determined not to have been reasonable or necessary may nevertheless be entitled to Medicare coverage under the waiver-of-liability rules discussed at ¶ 908. The exclusions of custodial care and personal comfort items applicable to other Medicare services do not apply to hospice services (see ¶ 616 and ¶ 625). [42 C.F.R. § 411.15(g), (j).]

Hospice Program Requirements

To qualify as a Medicare provider, a hospice program must be a public agency or a private organization that is primarily engaged in providing the care and services described above and that makes these services available as needed, on a 24-hour basis. The hospice program must provide care and services in individuals' homes, on an outpatient basis, and on a short-term inpatient basis and must meet the requirements described in the following paragraphs. [Soc. Sec. Act § 1861(dd)(2).]

Hospices must have an interdisciplinary group of staff which includes at least a physician medical director, a registered nurse, a social worker, and a pastoral or other counselor. All must be hospice employees except the physician and the pastoral counselor. The functions of the group are:

- to establish and review the plan of care for each patient;
- to maintain central records on each patient;
- to provide or supervise the provision of hospice care and services;
- to govern and set policy for the hospice;
- to assure the Secretary that it will continue providing service even if the patient is no longer able to pay;
- to use volunteers in accordance with standards set by the Secretary,
- to maintain records on the use of volunteers and the costs savings and expanded services achieved; and
- to assure that the hospice complies with state licensing laws and state and federal regulations.

[Soc. Sec. Act § 1861(dd)(2)(B)-(G).]

In addition, a hospice program is required to provide bereavement counseling for the immediate families of the terminally ill individual, although Medicare does not reimburse for this counseling. [Pub. 100-02, Ch. 9, § 40.2.3.]

Generally, hospice services must be provided directly, *i.e.*, by hospice employees and volunteer staff. The nursing, counseling, and medical social service obligations are considered "core services" which must be provided directly by hospice employees. Hospices may contract with third parties to provide other hospice services, however. The Medicare Modernization Act of 2003 (MMA) (PubLNo 108-173) allows hospices to contract with other hospices to provide nursing or medical social services only services in exigent circumstances, such as unusually high patient load, and to provide highly specialized services that are not frequently required. Hospices in non-urbanized areas may apply for waivers to contract for nursing services if: (1) they were operating before January 1, 1983, and (2) they demonstrate that they have made a good faith effort to employ nurses but cannot do so because of the nursing shortage. Finally, a hospice but may contract with independent physician or physician groups for their services. [Soc. Sec. Act §§ 1861(dd)(2)(B)(i)(I), 1861(dd)(5).]

A hospice that contracts for services remains responsible for provision and supervision of those services professionally, administratively and financially. All authorizations and all services provided by the contractor must be documented. A contract provider may not charge the beneficiary for services rendered under arrangement with the hospice. [Soc. Sec. Act § 1861(dd)(2)(A)(i)-(ii); 42 C.F.R. § 418.80.]

A provider that is certified for Medicare participation as a hospital, skilled nursing facility, or home health agency may also be certified as a hospice. If so, the provider must have separate provider agreements and must file separate cost reports. [Soc. Sec. Act § 1861(dd)(4).]

Prior to enactment of the Balance budget Act of 1997 (BBA) (PubLNo 105-33), a hospice was required to employ one physician as part of the interdisciplinary group. Since August 5, 1997, however, a hospice may contract with independent physician or physician groups. [Soc. Sec. Act § 1861(dd)(2)(B)(i)(I).]

Benefit Periods

A Medicare beneficiary may elect to receive hospice care for up to two periods of 90 days each and an unlimited number of subsequent periods up to 60 days each. [Soc. Sec. Act § 1812(a)(4); 42 CFR § 418.21(a).] A beneficiary electing to receive hospice care must choose to receive it through a particular hospice program. [Soc. Sec. Act § 1812(d)(1).] By making the election, the beneficiary agrees to accept treatment for pain and palliative care and gives up the right to be treated for the terminal illness. [Soc. Sec. Act § 1812(d)(2)(A).]

Beneficiary Rights During A Hospice Benefit Period

When choosing a particular hospice program, , the beneficiary gives up the right during the benefit period, to receive (1) hospice care provided by other hospice programs and (2) other services related to the treatment of the terminal illness or equivalent to or duplicative of hospice care. This waiver does not apply to (1) physicians' services furnished by the patient's attending physician or (2) services provided by or under arrangements made by the hospice program. [Soc. Sec. Act § 1812(d)(2)(A).]

A beneficiary may revoke a hospice care election before the period has expired; revocation reinstates eligibility for other Medicare benefits. At any time after a revocation, a beneficiary who is otherwise entitled to hospice care may make a new hospice care election. [Soc. Sec. Act § 1812(d)(2)(B); Pub. 100-02, Ch. 9, § 20.2.]

A beneficiary also is entitled to change from one hospice program to another hospice program once per period. Such a change is not considered to be a revocation of an election if the individual is otherwise entitled to hospice care benefits within that period. [Soc. Sec. Act § 1812(d)(2)(C).]

Example • • •

Sam Green has elected to receive hospice care for a 90-day period at Hospice A. He now wants to move to Hospice B. During the 90 day period, he may elect to change programs to Hospice B, or Hospice A can make arrangements for services to be provided by Hospice B. Within that 90 day period, he cannot change to Hospice C, but Hospice B can make arrangements for the Hospice C to provide services for the remainder of the period. At the end of the period, Sam may change to Hospice C for the next period.

Beginning January 23, 2006, a beneficiary's election of hospice care need not be renewed at each benefit period, but will continue in effect until election of a different hospice, revocation or discharge. [*Final rule*, 70 FR 70532, Nov. 22, 2005; 42 CFR § 418.24(c).]

Admission Requirements

New regulations, effective January 23, 2006, govern the admission of new patients to a hospice and the certification of terminal illness. In addition to certifying the patient's terminal illness, the hospice medical director must recommend the patient for admission to the hospice in consultation with, or with input from, the patient's attending physician, if any. The recommendation must be signed by the physician and included in the patient's medical records. [*Final rule*, 70 FR 70532, Nov. 22, 2005; 42 CFR § 418.25.]

Certification and Recertification of Terminal Illness

At the beginning of the first hospice benefit period, a 90-day period, both the individual's attending physician, if any, and the medical director or physician member of the hospice interdisciplinary group must certify in writing that the individual is terminally ill. At the beginning of each subsequent period, only the hospice physician must recertify that the individual is terminally ill. Although nurse practitioners may serve as the attending physician, they may not certify or recertify the beneficiary's terminal illness or prognosis. [Soc. Sec. Act § 1814(a)(7)(A).]

Additional requirements for the certification and recertification of terminal illness become effective January 23, 2006. In reaching a decision to certify that the patient is terminally ill, the hospice medical director must consider at least the following information: (1) diagnosis of the terminal condition of the patient; (2) other health conditions, whether related or unrelated to the terminal condition; and (3) current clinically relevant information supporting all diagnoses. Documentation must support the certification or recertification.

The initial certification of terminal illness must be made within two days of admission to the hospice. If the hospice cannot obtain a written certification within two days, an oral certification must be obtained, and the written certification must be obtained before submission of a claim for payment. Subsequent certifications may be made orally, but the written certification must be made before submission of the claim for payment, and documentation must support the certification. [*Final rule*, 70 FR 70532, Nov. 22, 2005; 42 CFR § 418.22.]

Written Plan of Care

All hospice care must be provided according to a written plan of care, established by the hospice medical director in conjunction with the hospice's interdisciplinary staff before hospice care begins. The written plan of care must be established by the hospice medical director in conjunction with the hospice's interdisciplinary staff. The plan of care must be reviewed periodically both by the beneficiary's attending physician and by the hospice medical director and interdisciplinary staff. Care must be provided according to the established plan of care. [Soc. Sec. Act § 1814(a)(7); 42 C.F.R. § 418.58.] Nurse practitioners may act as attending physicians and review the plan of care as part of the interdisciplinary group, but they may not act as the physician designee of the group to establish or update the plan of care. [Pub. 100-02, Ch. 9, § 40.]

Discharge from Hospice Care

New regulations govern the discharge of a living patient from hospice care. A patient may be discharged in three situations:

    1. medical stabilization, so that the patient is no longer terminally ill;

    2. departure from the hospice service area; or

    3. for cause, because of the behavior of the patient or another individual in the patient's home. [*Final rule*, 70 FR 70532, Nov. 22, 2005; 42 CFR § 418.26.]

To qualify for discharge for cause, the hospice must determine that the behavior of the patient or household member must be disruptive, abusive, or uncooperative to the extent that delivery of care to the patient or the ability of the hospice to operate effectively is seriously impaired. Before discharging a patient, the hospice must:

    1. advise the patient that discharge is being considered;

¶270

2. ascertain that the patient's proposed discharge is not due to the patient's use of necessary hospice services;

3. make a serious effort, to resolve the problem(s) presented by the patient or family;

4. document in the patient's records both the problems and the efforts made to resolve them; and

5. obtain a written discharge order from the hospice medical director. It an attending physician is involved in the patietn's care, that physician must be consulted, and the consultation, review and decision must be documented. [*Final rule*, 70 FR 70532, Nov. 22, 2005; 42 CFR § 418.25.]

Beginning January 23, 2006, hospices must have a process for discharge planning and must begin planning when staff begins to consider discharge. The discharge planning process must include planning for any necessary family counseling, patient education, or other services before the patient is discharged because he or she is no longer terminally ill. [*Final rule*, 70 FR 70532, Nov. 22, 2005; 42 CFR § 418.22.]

Effect of Discharge

A living patient who has been discharged from hospice care no longer has an election of hospice care in effect. A patient whose condition remains terminal or becomes terminal again may make a new election of hospice care. Until a new election is made, the patient is not eligible for hospice care, but is eligible for all of the care is covered by Medicare. [*Final rule*, 70 FR 70532, Nov. 22, 2005.]

Deductibles and Coinsurance

A beneficiary's responsibility for deductibles and coinsurance extends for a "hospice coinsurance period", which begins with the date of the election and extends through the fourteenth consecutive day that the beneficiary has no hospice election is in effect. Thus, a beneficiary who renews or continues hospice care elections without a 14-day break will be responsible for only one maximum inpatient deductible. [Soc. Sec. Act § 1813(a)(4)(B).]

An individual who has elected hospice care is liable for coinsurance payments for the following services or supplies:

Drugs and biologicals. An individual is liable for a coinsurance payment for each palliative drug and biological prescription furnished by the hospice except when the individual is an inpatient. The amount of coinsurance for each prescription must approximate 5 percent of the cost of the drug or biological to the hospice, up to $5, in accordance with the hospice's established drug copayment schedule approved by the Medicare intermediary. The cost of the drug or biological may not exceed what a prudent buyer would pay in similar circumstances. [Soc. Sec. Act § 1813(a)(4)(A); 42 C.F.R. § 418.400.]

Respite care. The amount of coinsurance for each respite care day is to 5 percent of the Medicare payment for a respite care day. The amount of the individual's coinsurance liability for respite care during a hospice coinsurance period may not exceed the inpatient hospital deductible applicable for the year that the hospice coinsurance period began (see ¶ 221).

During the hospice coinsurance period, when an election of hospice care is effective, no other deductible or copayment may be charged for services that constitute hospice care, regardless of the location where the services are provided. [Soc. Sec. Act § 1813(a)(4)(B).]

¶270

Hospice Reimbursement

Hospice providers are reimbursed on the basis of a cost-related prospective payment method, subject to an annual cap that is determined and applied at the end of each hospice cap period. The cap amount is calculated by the intermediary at the end of the hospice cap period. The cap period runs from November 1 of each year through October 31 of the next year. Any payments in excess of the cap must be refunded by the hospice once the cap is determined. The hospice cap for the year ending October 31, 2005 is $19,777.51 per beneficiary, up from $19,635.67 from the previous year. The next adjustment to the hospice cap will occur in the fall of 2006. [Soc. Sec. Act § 1814(i)(2); *Medicare Claims Processing Manual*, Pub. No. 100-04, Ch. 11, § 30.2, Transmittal No. 663, Aug. 26, 2005..]

CMS establishes daily payment amounts for hospices that are adjusted annually for inflation and adjusted to reflect local differences in wages. Hospice per diem payment rates for the period from October 1, 2005, through September 30, 2006, for the four separate categories of care are as follows: routine home care—$126.49, continuous home care—$738.26 (or $30.76 per hour), inpatient respite care—$1130.85, and general inpatient care—$562.69. [Soc. Sec. Act § 1814(i)(1)-(2); 42 C.F.R. § 418.306; Pub. No. 100-04, Transmittal No. 663, Aug. 26, 2005.]

Hospice programs must submit cost data to the Secretary for each fiscal year. [Soc. Sec. Act § 1814(i)(1)(C)(ii)(VI); 42 C.F.R. § 413.24, § 418.310.] Hospice will have to file cost reports electronically for cost reporting periods ending on or after December 31, 2004. Until May 31, 2007 hospices will have to file paper copies of their cost reports as well. The paper copies will serve as the official copy of the cost report. [42 C.F.R. § 413.24(f)(4).]

Physician Reimbursement

Physicians' services furnished to hospice patients are reimbursed as "physicians' services" under Part B if the physician is the patient's attending physician and is not employed by the hospice. [Social Security Act § 1861(d)(2)(A); 42 C.F.R. § 414.39.] Effective January 1, 2001, physicians are eligible for payment from Medicare for signing hospice plans of care and recertification. [42 C.F.R. § 414.39.] Beginning with services provided on or after January 1, 2005, a physician on staff of a hospice may be paid to evaluate a patient who has not yet elected hospice care, to determine the patient's need for pain and symptom management and for hospice care and to help with advance care planning. [Medicare Modernization Act, § 512]. Other physician services performed by a physician on the staff of the hospice are "hospice services" and are reimbursed under Part A, whether or not the hospice staff physician is the patient's attending physician. [42 C.F.R. § 418.304(c).]

Chapter 3—MEDICARE PART B—SUPPLEMENTAL INSURANCE

Eligibility and Enrollment

[¶ 300] Eligibility for Part B Benefits

Unlike the hospital insurance benefits program (Part A), which is provided automatically to eligible individuals and is largely financed by payroll FICA taxes, the supplementary medical insurance benefits program (Part B) is provided only to eligible individuals who elect to enroll in the program and pay its monthly premiums.

For most individuals who become entitled to Part A benefits, enrollment in Part B occurs automatically unless they elect to decline enrollment (see ¶ 310).

Enrollment in Part B is open to all persons who are entitled to Part A benefits (see ¶ 200). It is also permissible for a person to enroll in Part B even if he or she is not entitled to Part A benefits if certain conditions are met. Those conditions are that the person be (1) age 65 or over, (2) a resident of the United States, and (3) either (a) a citizen of the United States or (b) an alien lawfully admitted to the United States for permanent residence who has resided in the United States continuously during the five years immediately preceding the month in which application for enrollment was made. [Soc. Sec. Act § 1836; 42 C.F.R. § 407.10(a).]

The term "United States" includes the Commonwealth of Puerto Rico, the Virgin Islands, Guam, American Samoa and the Northern Mariana Islands. [Soc. Sec. Act §§ 210(i), 1861(x).] An individual becomes a resident the first day of arrival in the U.S. and establishes a home with intent to remain indefinitely.

For the disabled under age 65 (see ¶ 204), neither Part A nor Part B coverage can begin before the 25th month of the individual's entitlement to disability benefits, except for ALS patients (see ¶ 204). [Soc. Sec. Act § 226(b).] See ¶ 847 for the beginning of coverage for persons diagnosed with end-stage renal disease (ESRD).

Turning 65

The great majority of persons affected will, upon reaching age 65 (see ¶ 200), satisfy the conditions stated above. Accordingly, their first eligibility for enrollment usually will be governed by the attainment of age 65. Although the full retirement age for purposes of qualifying for Social Security retirement benefits is rising, age 65 remains the starting date for Medicare eligibility.

Suspended Benefits of Aliens

Part B benefits are suspended in the same manner they are suspended under Part A in the case of certain aliens who are or were outside the United States (see ¶ 200). [Soc. Sec. Amendments of 1965 (PubLNo 89-97) § 104(b)(1).]

Conviction of Subversive Activities

An individual convicted of any of the offenses stipulated in § 202(u) of the Social Security Act, relating to subversive activities, cannot enroll in the Part B plan. [Soc. Sec. Amendments of 1965 (PubLNo 89-97) § 104(b)(2); 42 C.F.R. § 407.10(b).]

¶300

How the Part B Program Is Financed

In general, the Part B program is financed from premium payments by enrollees, contributions from funds designated by the federal government, and the patient deductible and cost-sharing (coinsurance) provisions of the Part B program.

[¶ 310] Enrollment in Part B

Persons entitled to Medicare benefits under Part A are enrolled automatically and covered for Medicare benefits under Part B, unless they indicate they do not want to be enrolled in the Part B plan (see ¶ 312).

In order to enroll, in the case of the few individuals who are not enrolled automatically, the eligible individual must file a written request for enrollment, signed by or on behalf of the individual, during an enrollment period (see ¶ 311). [42 C.F.R. § 407.22.]

The written request for enrollment may be made by (1) completing a special Part B enrollment form (which may be obtained from the local Social Security office), (2) answering the Part B enrollment questions on an application for monthly Social Security benefits, or (3) signing a simple statement of request. [42 C.F.R. § 407.11.]

Note that the coverage period—the period during which premiums are due and during which an individual is entitled to benefits under Part B—is not the same as the enrollment period (see ¶ 313).

Health Insurance Card

As evidence of eligibility, each beneficiary entitled to Part A or Part B benefits is issued a Health Insurance Card, Form CMS-40 (G-43, in the case of railroad beneficiaries). This card gives the beneficiary's name, claim number, sex, extent of entitlement, and effective date(s) of entitlement—the beginning dates of the beneficiary's Part A and Part B coverage.

[¶ 311] Enrollment Periods

An individual ordinarily may enroll in the Part B program, either by a positive act or through automatic enrollment (see ¶ 312) only during an "enrollment period." There are two kinds of enrollment periods: (1) the "initial enrollment period," which is based on the date when an individual first meets the eligibility requirements for enrollment (see ¶ 300) and (2) the "general enrollment period," during which individuals may enroll if they have missed their initial enrollment period. [Soc. Sec. Act § 1837; 42 C.F.R. § 407.12.]

The "initial enrollment period" is seven months long. It begins with the third month before the month in which an individual first meets the eligibility requirements (see ¶ 300), and ends seven months later. For example, an individual first meeting the eligibility requirements in July 2006 would have a seven-month enrollment period beginning April 1, 2006, and ending October 31, 2006. An individual age 65 qualifying solely on the basis of hospital insurance entitlement (see ¶ 300) is deemed to meet the eligibility requirements on the first day on which he or she becomes entitled to hospital insurance benefits. [Soc. Sec. Act §§ 1837(c), 1837(d).]

The law also provides a "general enrollment period" for those who failed to enroll in their initial enrollment period, or for those who terminated their enrollment but want to re-enroll. The "general enrollment period" is from January 1 through March 31 of each year. [Soc. Sec. Act § 1837(e).] Coverage is effective the following July 1. An individual who fails to enroll during the initial enrollment period, or whose enrollment has been terminated, may enroll thereafter only during a general enrollment period. [42 C.F.R. § 407.12(a)(2).]

In most cases, individuals who do not enroll in the supplementary medical insurance program within a year of the close of their initial enrollment period will be required to pay a permanently increased premium. Individuals who drop out of the program and reenroll later also will have to pay an increased premium in most cases. Increased premiums are discussed at ¶ 320.

Example • • •

Roger Green became a Social Security beneficiary when he reached age 65 in May 2005. His initial enrollment period was February 1, 2005–August 31, 2005. Because he failed to enroll during this period, his next chance to enroll was during the next general enrollment period, January 1, 2006–March 31, 2006. He also did not enroll during this period. He may now enroll during any subsequent general enrollment period (January 1 to March 31 of each year), but he will be required to pay an increased premium due to his late enrollment (see ¶ 320).

Individuals Covered by Employer Health Plans

Elderly or disabled employees and their spouses who receive primary health coverage under an employer group health plan, as discussed at ¶ 639, are not required to enroll in the same enrollment period applicable to other individuals. (They may wish to delay enrollment because Part B benefits may duplicate the employer plan's benefits.) A special enrollment period applicable to these individuals is available for eight full months after they terminate participation in the employer plan (or six months in the case of disabled individuals whose group plan is involuntarily terminated). [Soc. Sec. Act § 1837(i).]

The coverage period for an individual enrolling during this type of special enrollment period begins on the first day of the month in which the individual enrolls, if the individual enrolls in the first month of the special enrollment period, or the first day of the month following the month in which the individual enrolls, if the enrollment occurs in a month after the first month of the special enrollment period. [Soc. Sec. Act § 1838(e).]

[¶ 312] Automatic Enrollment

As the aged and disabled become entitled to Medicare Part A, they also become entitled to Part B. They are automatically enrolled in Part B by the Social Security Administration, unless they elect to decline coverage. [42 C.F.R. § 407.17.]

The enrollee must reside in the United States, excluding Puerto Rico (see ¶ 300). [Soc. Sec. Act § 1837(f).] Persons eligible for automatic enrollment are, to the extent possible, fully informed of the automatic enrollment provisions and given an opportunity to decline coverage. [42 C.F.R. § 407.17(b).] Those who do not decline coverage before it is scheduled to begin are deemed to have enrolled automatically.

An individual who is receiving Social Security retirement or disability benefits or otherwise is entitled to Medicare benefits on the first day of the initial enrollment period (see ¶ 311) or who becomes entitled to Social Security retirement benefits during any one of the first three months of the initial enrollment period, is *deemed* to have enrolled in the third month of the initial enrollment period, thus permitting coverage to begin with the first day of the following month. [Soc. Sec. Act §§ 1837(f), 1837(g).]

An individual who first becomes entitled to Social Security retirement or survivors benefits during the last four months of the seven-month initial enrollment period will be deemed to have enrolled automatically in the month in which the individual files the application establishing entitlement to Medicare. A person who defers establishing entitlement to Medicare until after the end of the initial enrollment period will be deemed to have enrolled in Part B on the first day of the general enrollment period in effect at the time, or immediately following the time, at which the individual establishes entitlement to Part A. [Soc. Sec. Act § § 1837(g)(2)(B), 1837(g)(3).]

In the case of disability beneficiaries, the initial enrollment period cannot be determined on the basis of attainment of age 65. The law provides that the initial enrollment period for an individual eligible for Part B by reason of entitlement to disability benefits for a period of 24 months will begin on the first day of the third month before the 25th month of entitlement to disability benefits. Enrollment periods will recur with each continuous period of eligibility and upon attainment of age 65. [Soc. Sec. Act § 1837(g)(1).]

Examples • • •

(1) Bill Miller, a Social Security retirement beneficiary who elected to receive Social Security benefits at age 62, reached age 65 and became automatically entitled to Medicare Part A in May 2005. His initial enrollment period under Part B (see ¶ 311) began February 1, 2005, and extended through August 31, 2005. Bill automatically was deemed to have enrolled in the Part B program in the third month (April) of his enrollment period, and coverage became effective May 1, 2005.

(2) Jennifer Green became age 65 and potentially entitled to Social Security benefits in August 2005. She did not file an application for Social Security benefits, however, until January 2006. Because her application for Medicare benefits, which was made automatically when she filed for Social Security benefits (see ¶ 200), did not occur until after the end of her first enrollment period (November 30, 2005—see ¶ 311), her enrollment in Part B was deemed to have occurred on January 1, 2006, the first day of the then current general enrollment period. As to when her coverage period began, see ¶ 313.

[¶ 313] Coverage Period

The "coverage period" of an individual enrolled in the Part B program is the period during which the individual is entitled to Part B benefits. Except in the case of an individual who is enrolled automatically (see ¶ 312), the earliest possible coverage can be obtained if an individual enrolls during the three months of the initial enrollment period that are *before* the month in which the individual reaches age 65.

An individual's coverage period begins on whichever of the following dates is the *latest*:

(1) For an individual who enrolls in the initial enrollment period, (a) if the individual enrolls during the first three months, coverage begins with the first month of eligibility; (b) if the individual enrolls during the fourth month, coverage begins with the following month; (c) if the individual enrolls during the fifth month, coverage begins with the second month after the month of enrollment; and (d) if the individual enrolls in either the sixth or seventh month, coverage begins with the third month after the month of enrollment;

(2) For an individual who enrolls in a general enrollment period, coverage becomes effective the July 1 following the month of enrollment;

(3) For an individual deemed to have enrolled automatically in the first three months of the enrollment period (see ¶ 312), Part B coverage begins on the first day of the month he meets the eligibility requirements (see ¶ 300). If an individual automatically enrolled is deemed to have enrolled after the first three months of his enrollment period (see ¶ 312), then his coverage period will begin as described in (1) and (2), above. [Soc. Sec. Act § 1838(a); 42 C.F.R. § 407.25.]

Example • • •

An individual first meets the eligibility requirements for enrollment in April of 2006. Therefore, the initial enrollment period runs from January through July 2006. Depending upon the month of enrollment, the coverage period will begin as follows [42 C.F.R. § 407.25(a)(5).]:

Enrolls in—	Coverage period begins on—
Initial enrollment period:	
January	April 1 (month eligibility requirements first met).
February	April 1 (month eligibility requirements first met).
March	April 1 (month eligibility requirements first met).
April	May 1 (month following month of enrollment).
May	July 1 (second month after month of enrollment).
June	September 1 (third month after month of enrollment).
July	October 1 (third month after month of enrollment).

The beginning of coverage for ESRD beneficiaries is described at ¶ 205. For details on the coverage period for elderly and disabled employees and their spouses who receive primary health coverage under an employer group health plan, see ¶ 311.

Termination or Cancellation of Coverage

An individual's coverage period continues until enrollment is terminated or upon death. An individual's enrollment may be terminated: (1) by the filing of notice that the individual no longer wishes to participate in the program, or (2) for nonpayment of premiums. If an enrollment is terminated by the filing of a notice, the termination will take effect at the close of the month following the month in which the notice is filed. A termination for nonpayment of premiums will take effect with the end of the grace period (see ¶ 320) during which overdue premiums may be paid and coverage continued. [Soc. Sec. Act § 1838(b).]

A termination request filed by an individual deemed to have enrolled automatically (see ¶ 312) before the month in which Part B coverage becomes effective will cancel the coverage. A termination request filed by an automatically enrolled individual on or after the first day coverage is effective will cancel the coverage as of the close of the month following the month in which the notice is filed. [Soc. Sec. Act § 1838(b).]

In the case of an individual entitled to Medicare on the basis of 24 or more months of disability, rather than on the basis of having reached age 65, coverage and enrollment under Part B ends with the close of the last month for which the individual is entitled to hospital insurance benefits. [Soc. Sec. Act § 1838(c).]

An individual whose enrollment has terminated may reenroll only during a general enrollment period or a special enrollment period, if the requirements are met (see ¶ 311).

[¶ 320] Premiums

The following table shows the standard monthly premium rates in effect under the Part B program during the past several years:

Year	Premium	Year	Premium
1996	42.50	2001	50.00
1997	43.80	2002	54.00
1998	43.80	2003	58.70
1999	45.50	2004	66.60
2000	45.50	2005	78.20
		2006	88.50

Part B premiums are set by actuaries to cover 25 percent of the costs of the Part B program. [Soc. Sec. Act § 1839(a)(3); 42 C.F.R. § 408.20.] The federal government is required by statute to supplement the remainder of Part B costs out of general revenues. [Soc. Sec. Act § 1844(a).] Currently, all Medicare beneficiaries who elect Part B during their initial enrollment period pay the same Part B premium, regardless of their income. Under the Medicare Prescription Drug, Improvement, and Modernization Act of 2003 (PubLNo 108-173), beginning in 2007, Medicare beneficiaries with incomes over $80,000 for an individual (or $160,000 for a married couple) will pay a higher premium on a sliding scale. [Soc. Sec. Act § 1839(i).]

The law provides that, in the case of beneficiaries who have premiums deducted from their Social Security checks, if there is a Social Security cost-of-living adjustment that is less than the amount of the increased premium, the premium increase otherwise applicable will be reduced to avoid a reduction in the beneficiaries' Social Security checks. [Soc. Sec. Act § 1839(f).]

Increased Premium for Late Enrollment

In the case of an individual who enrolls after the "initial enrollment period" (see ¶ 311) or who reenrolls after terminating enrollment, the monthly premium otherwise applicable will be increased by 10 percent for each full 12 months (in the same "continuous period of eligibility") in which the individual could have been, but was not, enrolled. For these purposes, the length of the period of delay is computed by totalling (1) the months that elapsed between the close of the initial enrollment period and the close of the enrollment period in which enrollment occurred, plus (2) in the case of an individual who reenrolls, the months that elapsed between the date of the termination of the previous coverage period and the close of the enrollment period in which reenrollment occurred. Any premium that is not a multiple of 10 cents will be rounded to the nearest multiple of 10 cents. [Soc. Sec. Act §§ 1839(b), 1839(c).]

The beginning of a disabled individual's "continuous period of eligibility" serves as the beginning of an initial enrollment period for purposes of determining whether the premium increase applicable to late enrollees should apply. In general, a "continuous period of eligibility" is (1) the period beginning with the first day a person is eligible to enroll in Part B (see ¶ 300) and ending with the person's death, or (2) a period during all of which an individual is entitled to disability benefits and which ended in or before the month preceding the month in which the individual became 65 years of age. [Soc. Sec. Act § 1839(d).]

Examples • • •

(1) Paul Jones was eligible to enroll in an initial enrollment period that ended May 31, 2004. He actually enrolled in the general enrollment period January 1, 2006–March 31, 2006. There were 22 months between the close of his initial enrollment period (May 31, 2004) and the close of the period in which he actually enrolled (March 31, 2006). Because there was only one full 12-month period during which he could have been, but was not, enrolled, his premium was (permanently) increased 10%.

(2) Marlene Blum became age 65 in July 2000 and first enrolled in March 2002. She paid premiums increased by 10% above the regular rate because there was one 12-month period (17 total months) between the end of her initial enrollment period, October 2000 (see ¶ 311), and the end of the general enrollment period, March 2002, in which she actually enrolled. A few years later, she failed to pay the premiums and her coverage was terminated (after the end of her grace period) on June 30, 2004. She enrolled for a second time in January 2006. Added to her previous 17 months of delinquency is the period of 9 months between July 2005 through March 2006 (the end of the general enrollment period in which she reenrolled), for a grand total of 26 months. Since this totals two full 12-month periods, her monthly premium is (permanently) increased 20 percent.

(3) John Foley was late in enrolling by 38 months and, accordingly, his Part B premium was permanently increased by 30% every year. Thus, in 2006 when the standard premium is $88.50 per month, he is required to pay $115.10 per month ($88.50× 30% = $26.55. $88.50 + $26.55= $115.05. Monthly premiums are rounded to the nearest multiple of 10 cents, which in this case is $115.10.)

Elderly and disabled employees and their spouses who delay enrollment in the Part B program because they elect primary health coverage under an employer group plan, as discussed at ¶ 639, have been accorded a special enrollment period (see ¶ 311). Therefore, the months in which they are enrolled in such a plan are not counted in determining the penalty for delinquent enrollment. [Soc. Sec. Act § 1839(b).]

Military retirees. The Medicare Prescription Drug, Improvement, and Modernization Act of 2003 (MMA)(PubLNo 108-173) waives the Part B late enrollment penalty for military retirees who enrolled in Part B from 2001 to 2004. The penalty is waived for Part B monthly premiums beginning in January 2004. The waiver applies to military retirees who are enrolled in the TRICARE for Life military health insurance program. [Soc. Sec. Act § 1839(b).]

Collection of Premiums

Social Security and railroad retirement beneficiaries, and civil service annuitants—except those enrolled by a state as public assistance recipients—have their premiums deducted, when possible, from their monthly benefit, annuity, or pension checks paid in the preceding month. [Soc. Sec. Act § 1840(a)-(d).] The premiums of public assistance recipients enrolled under a state "buy-in" agreement (see ¶ 707) are paid by the state that enrolled them. [Soc. Sec. Act § § 1840(h), 1843.]

Premiums are paid by direct remittance in certain circumstances. Direct payment must be made by individuals who are (1) not entitled to a monthly cash Social Security benefit, a railroad retirement annuity or pension, or a federal civil service annuity, or (2) entitled to one of these benefits, but for some reason the benefit cannot be paid during the period in question. These individuals are sent premium notices, together with a card and envelope for use in sending payment to the proper servicing center. [42 C.F.R. § 408.60 *et seq.*]

¶320

Premiums are payable for the period commencing with the first month of the individual's coverage period and ending with the month in which the individual dies or, if earlier, in which the individual's coverage period ends. [Soc. Sec. Act § 1840(g).]

Refund of Excess Premiums

Premiums received for any month after the month in which a Part B enrollee dies are refunded. Refunds are paid to (1) the person or persons who paid the premiums, (2) the legal representative of the estate, if the enrollee paid the premiums prior to death, or (3) the person or persons in the priorities specified in the law, if there is no person meeting the requirements in (1) or (2). [Soc. Sec. Act § 1870(g); 42 C.F.R. § 408.112.]

Failure to Pay Premiums

Enrollment (see ¶ 311) is terminated for nonpayment of premiums. A grace period is provided for payment of premiums by beneficiaries who are billed directly. The grace period extends from the date payment is due through the last day of the third month following the month in which such payment is due. For example, if an enrollee's premium payment became due on March 1 of any given year, the grace period would extend to June 30 of that year. [42 C.F.R. § 408.8(a).] If payment is not made on or before the end of the grace period, coverage and enrollment terminate. [42 C.F.R. § 408.8(c).]

The initial grace period may be extended for up to an additional three months if there is a finding that the enrollee had good cause for not paying the overdue premiums during the initial grace period. [Soc. Sec. Act § 1838(b); 42 C.F.R. § 408.8(d).] Good cause will be found if the enrollee establishes that the failure to pay within the initial grace period was due to conditions (1) over which the enrollee had no control or (2) which the enrollee reasonably could not have been expected to foresee. [42 C.F.R. § 408.8(d)(2).] Good cause, for example, may be found if the enrollee was mentally or physically incapable of paying premiums on a timely basis, or had some reasonable basis to believe that payment had been made, or the failure to pay was due to administrative error. [*Medicare General Information, Eligibility, and Entitlement Manual,* Pub. 100-01, Ch. 2, § 40.7.4.]

Benefits

[¶ 330] Part B Benefits: In General

The supplementary medical insurance benefits plan (Part B) provides benefits that supplement the coverage provided by the hospital insurance benefits plan (Part A). Part A covers inpatient institutional services: hospitals, skilled nursing facilities, hospices, and home health services after hospitalization. Part B covers the services of physicians and other health practitioners as well as a variety of "medical and other health services" not covered under Part A. The kinds of "medical and other health services" included in Part B are described beginning at ¶ 350, Physicians' services are discussed separately at ¶ 340. Physical, occupational, and speech therapy services are discussed at ¶ 381, rural and community health clinic services at ¶ 382, home health services at ¶ 383, comprehensive outpatient rehabilitation facility services at ¶ 385, ambulatory surgical services at ¶ 386, and mental health services at ¶ 387.

Method of Payment

In general, there are two methods of payment for items or services covered by the Medicare program:

(1) In the case of all services furnished by an institutional provider of services (*for example,* a hospital, skilled nursing facility, home health agency, hospice, or end-stage renal disease facility) or by others under arrangements made by a provider of services; rural and community health clinic services; comprehensive outpatient rehabilitation services; and ambulatory surgical center services, Medicare pays the provider or facility that provided the services *on the patient's behalf.* [Soc. Sec. Act § 1832(a)(2).] The provider or facility files the claim for payment, and the patient's obligation is fully satisfied once he or she has paid any required deductible or coinsurance amounts (¶ 335). The Medicare payment amount is determined by the payment methodology in effect for the services provided (see ¶ 800 *et seq.*).

(2) In the case of all other Part B services—the services of physicians and other healthcare practitioners (see ¶ 340, ¶ 351, ¶ 366, and ¶ 381), and the "medical and other health services" furnished by suppliers or practitioners (see ¶ 350–¶ 370 and ¶ 387)—Medicare pays either the one who provided the service or the patient, depending on whether the one who provided the service accepts the "assignment" payment method (see ¶ 831, ¶ 903). [Soc. Sec. Act § 1832(a)(1); 42 C.F.R. § 410.150.] If assignment is accepted, Medicare pays the supplier or practitioner, and the patient's obligation is fully satisfied once he or she has paid any required deductible or coinsurance amounts (¶ 335). If the supplier or practitioner does not accept assignment, Medicare pays the patient, and the patient is responsible for paying the supplier or practitioner.

Medicare payment rules in general are discussed at ¶ 800 *et seq.* Payment for end-stage renal disease facilities is discussed at ¶ 205. "Assignment" agreements are discussed at ¶ 831 and ¶ 903.

Limitations

There are limitations on the benefits provided under the Part B program. Financial limitations include an annual $124 deductible in 2006 and a 20 percent coinsurance, which are applicable to most services covered under Part B (see ¶ 335). There is also a blood deductible (see ¶ 335) and a cap on how much Medicare will pay for mental health services (see ¶ 387).

There are benefit limitations in that only named items and services listed as covered benefits by the Medicare program are covered, and coverage is often limited to certain kinds of services or frequencies. In addition, a number of items and services are listed as excluded from Medicare coverage. Exclusions are discussed beginning at ¶ 600

Finally, payment may not be made under Part B for services furnished an individual if that individual is entitled to have payment made for those services under Part A. [Soc. Sec. Act § 1833(d).] In general, all services provided to an inpatient of a hospital (except for (1) the services of physicians and most other healthcare practitioners and (2) pneumococcal and hepatitis B vaccine) will be paid for by Part A if they are covered Medicare services (see ¶ 635).

[¶ 335] Deductible and Coinsurance

In addition to the monthly premium charged individuals enrolled in Part B (see ¶ 320), an annual deductible and a 20 percent "coinsurance" or "copayment" are normally required (see "Exceptions" to this rule, below). For 2006, the Part B deductible is $124. This is a $14 increase from 2005, when the deductible was $110. The law requires the deductible to be indexed to the growth in Part B expenditures. [Soc. Sec. Act § 1833(b).]

Application of the Deductible and Coinsurance

The deductible. The annual deductible applies only to services covered by Medicare. If the deductible is not applied because the service is not covered or because the service is included in the list under "Exceptions" below, the deductible for that year remains unsatisfied. [42 C.F.R. § 410.160.]

The deductible is satisfied by the initial expenses incurred in each calendar year. Even in cases in which an individual is not eligible for the entire calendar year (for example, when coverage begins after the first month of the year), the individual still is subject to the full deductible. The date of service generally determines when expenses were incurred, but expenses are allocated to the deductible in the order in which the bills are received by the carrier administering the Part B program. [*Medicare General Information, Eligibility, and Entitlement Manual*, Pub. 100-01, Ch. 3, § 20.2.]

Coinsurance. Medicare patients normally are required to pay 20 percent of the cost of each Medicare covered service. Medicare pays the other 80 percent. For Medicare purposes, the cost of a Medicare service is the "Medicare-approved charge" for that service. It is to the "Medicare-approved charge" that the coinsurance percentage applies. [Soc. Sec. Act §§ 1833(a), 1833(b).]

Example • • • _____

(1) Robert White visited his doctor in January 2006 for his annual routine checkup. This checkup, which indicated that Mr. White was in good condition, cost $150. Later in the year, however, it was discovered that he had high blood pressure. Successive visits to the doctor during the remainder of the year in connection with the treatment for this condition resulted in a total of $600 in Medicare-approved charges for the doctor's services. The $150 for the routine checkup cannot be counted toward the $124 deductible because it is not a covered expense (see ¶ 619). Accordingly, of the remaining $600 in covered expenses, $124 satisfies the deductible for the year and 80% of the remaining $476 ($380.80) is paid by Medicare. Mr. White's charges total $369.20. $150 (noncovered routine checkup) + $124 deductible + $95.20 coinsurance = $369.20.

Note the special rule for the "Welcome to Medicare" exam described below.

(2) Sarah visits her doctor and has various clinical diagnostic laboratory tests performed in the doctor's office lab. Because the doctor accepts assignment for these tests and is paid under the fee schedule applicable to these services, no deductible (or coinsurance) is

required (see "Exceptions" below) for the lab tests. Later, Sarah visits the doctor on another matter, incurring $250 in Medicare-approved charges for the doctor's services. She then has to pay the $124 deductible and an additional $25.20 as coinsurance ($250 − $124 × 20% = $25.20). Medicare pays $100.80.

(3) Mary needs emergency surgery in 2006. She is taken to a participating hospital in an ambulance. She has no previous medical expenses of any kind for the year, and she has no previous "spell of illness" (see ¶ 210). Her hospital stay lasts 16 days. Her expenses are as follows:

Hospital costs (including room and board, nursing services, drugs, and use of the operating room)	$9,000
Fees for services to her of personal physician, surgeon, and anesthesiologist	$2,500
Emergency ambulance services	$300
Follow-up visits to personal physician following hospital discharge	300
	$12,100

After payment of the $952 inpatient hospital deductible (¶ 220), the remainder of Mary's hospital costs are paid for under Part A (see ¶ 210 *et seq.*). The non-hospital portion of her expenses ($3,100) is covered under Part B, except that Mary is required to pay the $124 deductible, plus 20 percent of the remaining $2,976 in expenses, or $595.20. Mary pays a total of $1,671.20 ($952 + $124 + $595.20). The rest is paid for by Medicare.

Note that if Mary has Medicare supplement (or "Medigap") insurance (see ¶ 740), some or all of what she is required to pay in the above example will be paid by her Medigap insurance.

Exceptions

Noncovered services. When coverage is denied for services because the services were not medically necessary or because the care provided was custodial, no deductible or coinsurance is required if the beneficiary is not liable (see ¶ 908 concerning waiver of beneficiary liability). [Pub. 100-01, Ch. 3, § 20.4.1.]

Clinical diagnostic laboratory tests. Medicare payment for clinical diagnostic laboratory tests (other than tests performed by a hospital or other provider for its inpatients) is made according to fee schedules established by the Secretary (see ¶ 827 for details). The laboratory or physician providing these tests must accept assignment (defined at ¶ 831). Medicare pays for such services at 100 percent of the fee schedule rate, and the deductible and coinsurance are waived. [Soc. Sec. Act §§ 1833(a)(1)(D), 1833(a)(2)(D), 1833(b)(3), 1833(h)(1).]

In the case of a diagnostic laboratory test that is paid on the basis of a negotiated rate instead of a fee schedule, the amount paid under the negotiated rate is considered the full charge for the test, and the deductible and coinsurance do not apply. [Soc. Sec. Act §§ 1833(a)(1)(D), 1833(a)(2)(D), 1833(b)(3), 1833(h)(6).]

Home health services. No deductible or coinsurance generally is applied to home health services. [Soc. Sec. Act §§ 1833(a)(2)(A), 1833(b)(2).] However, when a home health agency furnishes services that are not included in the definition of "home health services," the deductible and coinsurance do apply. Also, the coinsurance applies to supplies, drugs, durable medical equipment and prosthetics/orthotics furnished by home health agencies. [Soc. Sec. Act §§ 1833(a)(1), 1833(a)(2)(A), 1833(b)(2).]

Donation of kidney for transplant surgery. There are no deductible or coinsurance requirements with respect to services furnished to an individual in connection with the donation of a kidney for transplant surgery. [42 C.F.R. § 410.163.]

Pneumococcal and influenza vaccines. Pneumococcal and influenza vaccines and their administration are covered without imposition of deductible or coinsurance requirements (see ¶ 362). [Soc. Sec. Act §§ 1833(a)(1)(B), 1833(b)(1).]

Community health center services. No deductible is required for federally qualified health center services (see ¶ 382). [Soc. Sec. Act § 1833(b)(4).]

Prevention services. No deductible is required for screening mammography services, screening pap smears, or screening pelvic exams (see ¶ 369). [Soc. Sec. Act §§ 1833(b)(5), 1833(b)(6).]

Blood Deductibles

Part B requires a deductible for the expenses incurred during any calendar year for the first three pints of whole blood (or equivalent quantities of packed red blood cells) furnished to outpatients. As in the case of the similar deductible for inpatients under Part A (see ¶ 223), this deductible is reduced to the extent that the blood (or equivalent quantities of packed red blood cells) has been appropriately replaced. [42 C.F.R. § 410.161.] Satisfaction of the deductible through replacement is discussed in greater detail at ¶ 223.

The blood deductible under Part B is not required to the extent it has been satisfied under Part A. [Soc. Sec. Act § 1833(b).]

Welcome to Medicare Exam

Effective January 1, 2005, Medicare covers an initial preventive physical exam (IPPE), which is called the "Welcome to Medicare" exam (see ¶ 340). Payment for this service would be applied to the required deductible if the deductible has not been met, with the exception of federally qualified health centers (FQHCs), and the usual coinsurance provisions would apply to all providers. The FQHC encounter is exempt from the Medicare deductible. The contractors apply coinsurance and deductible to payments for the IPPE except for payments by the fiscal intermediaries to FQHCs where only co-insurance applies. [*Medicare Claims Processing Manual,* Ch. 18, § 80.]

[¶ 340] Physicians' Services

Part B covers reasonable and medically necessary physicians' services. "Physicians' services" means professional services performed by physicians *for a patient,* including diagnosis, therapy, surgery, consultation, and care plan oversight. "Physicians' services" under Part B does not include services provided by interns or residents or administrative services performed by physicians for a provider—these are covered under Part A (see ¶ 215). [Soc. Sec. Act § 1861(q); *Medicare Benefit Policy Manual,* Pub. 100-02, Ch. 15, § 30.]

A service may be considered to be a physician's service if the physician either examines the patient in person or is able to visualize some aspect of the patient's condition without the interposition of a third person's judgment. Direct visualization would be possible by means of X-rays, electrocardiogram and electroencephalogram tapes, tissue samples, etc. Thus, for example, the interpretation by a physician of an actual electrocardiogram or electroencephalogram reading that had been transmitted via telephone (for example, electronically rather than by means of a verbal description) is a covered service. Physicians' professional services are covered if provided within the United States, and may be performed in a home, office, institution, or at the scene of an accident. A patient's home, for this purpose, is anywhere the patient makes his or her residence, such as a home for the aged, a nursing home, or a relative's home. [Pub. 100-02, Ch. 15, § 30.]

Consultations. Services by means of a telephone call between a physician and a beneficiary (or between a physician and a member of a beneficiary's family) are covered under Part B, but the Medicare program does not make separate payment for these services. The physician work resulting from telephone calls is considered to be an integral part of the pre-work and post-work of other physician services. [Pub. 100-02, Ch. 15, § 30B.] However, Medicare covers consultations and certain other services furnished via interactive telecommunications systems for Medicare patients located in rural health professional shortage areas and in counties that are not in a metropolitan statistical area (see ¶ 388). [42 C.F.R. § 410.78.]

A consultation is reimbursable when it is a professional service furnished to a patient by a second physician at the request of the attending physician. A consultation includes the history and examination of the patient as well as the written report, which is furnished to the attending physician for inclusion in the patient's permanent medical record. Regarding laboratory consultations, the consultation must involve a medical judgment that ordinarily requires a physician—if a nonphysician laboratory specialist could furnish the information, the service of the physician is not a consultation payable under Part B. [Pub. 100-02, Ch. 15, § 30C.]

Second Opinions. Patient-initiated "second opinions" relating to the medical need for surgery or for major nonsurgical diagnostic and therapeutic procedures are covered by Medicare. In the event that the recommendations of the first and second physician differ regarding the need for surgery (or other major procedure), a third opinion is also covered. Second and third opinions are covered even though the surgery or other procedure, if performed, is determined not to be covered. Payment may be made for the history and examination of the patient, and for other covered diagnostic services required to properly evaluate the patient's need for a procedure and to render a professional opinion. [Pub. 100-02, Ch. 15, § 30D.]

Physician Defined

The term "physician" means a doctor of medicine or osteopathy legally authorized to practice in the state in which the services are performed. [Soc. Sec. Act § 1861(r).] "Legally authorized" means the physician is licensed by the state in which the physician practices. If state licensing law limits the scope of practice of a particular type of medical practitioner—for example, in some states osteopaths are limited in their practice to the manipulation of bones and muscles—only the services within these limitations will be covered. Physicians performing services in hospitals operated by the federal government may be considered as meeting the definition of physician with respect to services performed within the scope of their federal employment, even though they may not be licensed to practice in the state in which they are employed. [*Medicare General Information, Eligibility, and Entitlement Manual*, Pub. 100-01, Ch. 5, §§ 70, 70.1, 70.4.]

For certain purposes, dentists, optometrists, podiatrists, and chiropractors are defined as physicians. The term physician does not include a Christian Science practitioner, naturopath, or other such practitioners. [Pub. 100-01, Ch. 5, § 70.]

Dentists

A doctor of dental surgery or dental medicine having state authorization to practice and acting within the scope of his or her license is defined as a "physician" for Medicare purposes. Services covered when performed by a dentist include any service that would be covered if performed by a doctor of medicine—for example, dental examinations to detect

¶340

infections prior to certain surgical procedures, treatment of oral infections, and interpretations of diagnostic x-ray examinations in connection with covered services. [Pub. 100-01, Ch. 5, §70.2.] The dentist also may provide the physician's certification required for inpatient hospital services connected with a dental procedure when the patient requires hospitalization (see ¶ 634). [42 C.F.R. §424.13(c)(2).]

Because of the general exclusion of payment for dental services (see ¶ 634), medical procedures involving the teeth or structures directly supporting the teeth generally are not covered unless, for example, this type of medical procedure is a necessary part of a larger covered surgical procedure. Note that the coverage or exclusion of any given dental service is not affected by whether the person rendering the service is classified as a physician. Rather, it depends on whether the service itself is classified as covered or excluded. [Soc. Sec. Act §1861(r)(2); Pub. 100-01, Ch.5, §70.2.]

A description of inpatient hospital services connected with dental procedures is at ¶ 218.

Optometrists

A doctor of optometry is considered a physician with respect to all services the optometrist is authorized to perform under state law. The scope of coverage is based on the covered vision care services the optometrist is legally authorized to perform in the state in which the services are performed. [Soc. Sec. Act §1861(r)(4); Pub. 100-01, Ch. 5, §70.5.] Note, however, that many vision care services are excluded from Medicare coverage—see ¶ 619.

Podiatrists and Chiropractors

The term physician also includes a doctor of podiatric medicine, but only with respect to functions the podiatrist is legally authorized to perform by the state in which the services are performed. Certain types of foot treatment or foot care, however, are excluded (see ¶ 622), whether performed by a doctor of medicine or a doctor of podiatric medicine. Also, a doctor of podiatric medicine is considered a physician with respect to certification or recertification of the medical necessity for services, home health services, and serving as a member of a utilization review committee. [Soc. Sec. Act §§1861(p)(1), 1861(r)(3); Pub. 100-01, Ch. 5, §70.3.]

A chiropractor licensed or legally authorized by the state in which the chiropractic services are furnished is included in the definition of physician. Chiropractors must meet certain minimum standards pertaining to their age and education for their services to be covered by Medicare. In addition, a chiropractor's services are covered only with respect to manual manipulation of the spine to correct a subluxation. Chiropractic maintenance therapy—that is, services that seek to prevent disease, promote health, and prolong and enhance the quality of life, or maintain or prevent the deterioration of a chronic condition—is not covered by Medicare. [Soc. Sec. Act §1861(r)(5); Pub. 100-01, Ch. 5, §70.6; Pub. 100-02, Ch.15, §§30.5, 240.]

Hospital- and Other Provider-Based Physicians

The services of hospital- or other provider-based physicians (for example, radiologists, anesthesiologists, and pathologists) include two distinct elements: the professional (patient care) component and the provider component. [Pub. 100-02, Ch.15, §30.1.]

The *professional component* of provider-based physicians' services includes those services directly related to the medical care of the individual patient. Payment for those services is made according to the Medicare physician fee schedule (see ¶ 820) by the Part B carrier. The *provider component* of their services includes those services not directly related to the medical care of individual patients, *e.g.*, teaching, administrative, and autopsy services, and other services that benefit the provider's patients as a group. Those services are reimbursed to the provider as provider services under Part A. [Pub. 100-02, Ch. 15, § 30.1.]

Teaching Physician Services. Part B covers services that attending physicians (other than interns and residents) furnish in the teaching setting to individual patients. The medical record must contain signed or countersigned notes by the physician that show the physician personally reviewed the patient's diagnoses, visited the patient at more critical times of the illness, and discharged the patient. For other services, such as surgical procedures, notes in the record by interns, residents, or nurses, indicating that the physician was physically present when the service was rendered, are sufficient. To pay a teaching physician under Part B, the teaching physician must at least be present during the key portion of a service rendered by a resident or intern. When a resident performs a visit without a teaching physician's presence, the teaching physician must repeat the key portions of the visit and have his own documentation to receive payment. [Pub. 100-02, Ch. 15, § 30.2.]

Payment for the services of provider-based physicians is discussed in greater detail at ¶ 820.

Residents and Interns

The services of interns and residents provided in the hospital setting as part of their training program normally are paid under Part A as hospital services and not under Part B as physicians' services. Medical and surgical services furnished by interns and residents that are not related to their training program and are performed outside the hospital are covered if (1) the services are identifiable physician services that require performance by a physician in person and contribute to the diagnosis and treatment of the patient's condition, and (2) the intern or resident if fully licensed to practice medicine, osteopathy, dentistry, or podiatry by the state in which the services are performed. Services performed by interns and residents that are not related to their training program and are performed in the outpatient department or emergency room of the hospital where they have their training program are covered if the above two criteria are met and if, in addition, the services can be separately identified from those services required as part of the training program. [42 C.F.R. §§ 415.200–415.208.]

Psychiatrists and Psychologists

Psychiatrists are medical doctors, and their services are covered by Medicare to the same extent as other physicians' services. Note, however, that there are special limits on Medicare coverage of psychiatric services—see ¶ 225 and ¶ 387. Psychiatric services also may be covered as incident to physicians' services as an outpatient hospital benefit (see ¶ 352).

Psychologists generally are not considered physicians. Their services can be covered as "incident to" physicians' services (see ¶ 351), and their diagnostic services can be covered as "other diagnostic tests" (see ¶ 353). In addition, the services of clinical psychologists in rural health clinics and risk-basis HMOs are covered even when provided without physician supervision, and the services of a "qualified psychologist" are covered as a separate Part B benefit (see ¶ 366). [Soc. Sec. Act §§ 1861(s)(2)(M), 1833(a)(1)(L); *Medicare Benefit Policy Manual*, Pub. 100-02, Ch. 15, § 160.]

Payment Considerations

Payment for physicians' services is discussed at ¶ 820 and ¶ 821. With respect to the coverage of services and supplies furnished as an incident to a physician's professional services, see ¶ 351. Services excluded from coverage are discussed beginning at ¶ 600. The "assignment" method of billing for physicians' services and the "participating physician" program are discussed at ¶ 831 and ¶ 833, respectively.

¶340

Physicians' services furnished to an outpatient of a rural health clinic or comprehensive outpatient rehabilitation facility are considered furnished by the facility and payment is made to the facility (see ¶ 382 and ¶ 385). Physicians' services furnished to hospice patients are reimbursed as "physicians' services" under Part B if the physician is the patient's attending physician and is not employed by the hospice. If the physician is on the staff of the hospice, the services are considered "hospice services" and payment is made to the hospice under Part A (see ¶ 270). [*Medicare Claims Processing Manual*, Pub. 100-04, Ch. 23, § 30.]

[¶ 350] Medical and Other Health Services

The law divides the kinds of services covered under Part B into various categories: home health services (see ¶ 383), comprehensive outpatient rehabilitation facility services (¶ 385), outpatient ambulatory surgical services (¶ 386), and "medical and other health services." [Soc. Sec. Act § 1861(s).]

"Medical and other health services" includes the following items or services:

- *physicians' services* (see ¶ 340);

- *services and supplies furnished incident to a physician's professional services*, of kinds that commonly are furnished in physicians' offices and that commonly either are rendered without charge or are included in the physician's bills (see ¶ 351);

- *outpatient hospital services furnished incident to physicians' services* (see ¶ 352) and *partial hospitalization (mental health) services incident to such services* (see ¶ 387);

- *outpatient diagnostic services furnished by a hospital* (see ¶ 352);

- *outpatient physical, occupational, and speech therapy services* (see ¶ 381);

- *services of nonphysician healthcare practitioners, including physician assistants, nurse practitioners and clinical nurse specialists, certified registered nurse anesthetists (CRNAs) and anesthesia assistants, nurse-midwives, qualified psychologists, and clinical social workers* (see ¶ 351 and ¶ 366);

- *diagnostic X-ray tests, laboratory tests, and other diagnostic tests* (see ¶ 353);

- *X-ray, radium, and radioactive isotope therapy,* including materials and services of technicians (see ¶ 354);

- *surgical dressings, splints, casts, and other devices* used for reduction of fractures and dislocations (see ¶ 359);

- *rental or purchase of durable medical equipment for use in the patient's home* (see ¶ 356);

- *prosthetic devices* (other than dental) that replace all or part of an internal body organ (including *colostomy bags and supplies directly related to colostomy care*), and replacement of such devices (see ¶ 357);

- *leg, arm, back, and neck braces, and artificial legs, arms, and eyes* (including required adjustments, repairs, and replacements) (see ¶ 358);

- *certain drugs and biologicals,* including pneumococcal pneumonia, influenza, and hepatitis B vaccines, antigens, blood clotting factors for hemophilia patients, immunosuppressant therapy drugs furnished to an individual who receives an organ transplant, erythropoietin (EPO) for dialysis patients, oral anti-cancer drugs, and anti-emetic drugs used in conjunction with chemotherapy treatments (see ¶ 362)

- *ambulance service,* if the use of other methods of transportation is contraindicated by the individual's condition (see ¶ 355);

- *ambulatory surgical center services* (see ¶ 386)

- *rural health clinic and federally qualified health center services* (see ¶ 382);

- *certain preventive and screening services* (if specifically exempted from the exclusion for routine checkups), including screening tests and services for colorectal cancer, prostate cancer, glaucoma, pap smears, pelvic exams, mammograms, and bone mass measurement tests (see ¶ 369);

- *diabetes outpatient self-management training services* (see ¶ 369);

- *home dialysis supplies and equipment, self-care home dialysis support services, and institutional dialysis services and supplies* (see ¶ 205); and

- *therapeutic shoes* for individuals with severe diabetic conditions (see ¶ 370 and ¶ 622).

In general, all "medical and other health services" provided to an inpatient of a qualified hospital (except for the services of physicians and other practitioners and pneumococcal and hepatitis B vaccine) will be paid for by Part A if Part A coverage is available. Payment may not be made under Part B for services furnished to an inpatient if the inpatient is entitled to have payment made for services under Part A. [*Medicare Benefit Policy Manual*, Pub. 100-02, Ch. 15, § 10.]

Some medical services may be considered for coverage under more than one of the above categories. For example, electrocardiograms can be covered as physician's services, services incident to a physician's service, or as other diagnostic tests. Medicare payment is permitted so long as the requirements for coverage under one category are met.

None of the medical and other health services listed above (except physicians' services and services incident to physicians' services) furnished to a patient in a nonqualified hospital are covered unless the facility meets the definition of "hospital" for emergency services (see ¶ 227) and unless it meets such health and safety requirements as are appropriate for the item or service furnished, as determined by the Secretary. [Soc. Sec. Act § 1861(s).]

[¶ 351] Services and Supplies Furnished Incident to Physicians' Services

To be covered incident to the services of a physician, services and supplies (including drugs and biologicals not usually self-administered by the patient) must be: (1) furnished in a setting other than a hospital or skilled nursing facility; (2) an integral, although incidental, part of the physician's professional services in the course of diagnosis or treatment of an injury or illness; (2) commonly rendered without charge or included in the physician's bill; (3) of a type commonly furnished in physician's offices or clinics; and (4) furnished by the physician or by auxiliary personnel under the physician's direct supervision. A "physician," for this purpose, means a physician or other practitioner (physician assistant, nurse practitioner, clinical nurse specialist, nurse midwife, or clinical psychologist) legally authorized to receive Medicare payment for services incident to his or her own services. "Incident to" services must be furnished in a noninstitutional setting to noninstitutionalized patients but they may be covered as outpatient hospital therapeutic services—see ¶ 352. [42 C.F.R. § 410.26.]

The incident to requirements should not be applied to services that have their own Medicare benefit category. Rather, such services should meet the requirements of their own benefit category. For example, diagnostic tests are covered under a separate provision of the Social Security Act and are subject to their own coverage requirements. Depending on the particular tests, the supervision requirement for diagnostic tests or other services may be more or less stringent than supervision requirements for incident to services. Diagnostic tests also need not meet the incident to requirement. Likewise, pneumococcal, influenza, and hepatitis B vaccines are covered under a separate statutory provision and need not also meet incident to requirements. [*Medicare Benefit Policy Manual*, Pub. 100-02, Ch. 15, § 60.]

Physician assistants, nurse practitioners, clinical nurse specialists, certified nurse midwives, clinical psychologists, clinical social workers, physical therapists, and occupational therapists all have their own benefit categories and may provide services without direct physician supervision and bill directly for those services. When their services are provided as auxiliary personnel (that is, under a physician's direct supervision), they may be covered as incident to services. [42 C.F.R. § 410.26(b)(5); Pub. 100-02, Ch. 15, § 60.]

Services and supplies commonly furnished in physicians' offices are covered under the incident to provision. This requirement is not met when supplies are clearly of a type a physician would not be expected to have on hand in the office or the services are of a type not considered medically appropriate to provide in the office setting. [Pub. 100-02, Ch. 15, § 60.1.]

Services furnished in a prospective payment system (PPS) hospital to hospital inpatients that are incident to a physician's services (except for some anesthetist services) are included within the hospital's prospective payment rate and are paid under Part A. See ¶ 635 and ¶ 810.

Direct Supervision Requirement

Services and supplies provided in a private practice setting are considered "incident to" services only if there is direct personal supervision by the physician. This rule applies to services of auxiliary personnel working under the physician's supervision, such as nurses, anesthetists, psychologists, technicians, therapists, and other aides. For example, if a physician employs a nurse, and the charges for the nurse's services are included in the physician's bills, the services of the nurse are considered to be incident to the physician's services if (1) there was a physician's service rendered to which the services of the nurse were an incidental part, and (2) there was direct personal supervision by the physician. [Pub. 100-02, Ch. 15, § 60.1.]

Auxiliary personnel may be employees, leased employees, or independent contractors of the supervising physician, or of the legal entity that employs or contracts with the physician. Likewise, the supervising physician may be an employee, leased employee, or independent contractor of the legal entity billing and receiving payment for the services or supplies. The supervising physician must have a relationship with the legal entity billing and receiving payment for the services or supplies that satisfies the requirements for reassignment (see ¶ 831). [42 C.F.R. § 410.26; Pub. 100-02, Ch. 15, § 60.1.]

This does not mean, however, that for each occasion of service by auxiliary personnel, the physician must also render a personal professional service. A service or supply can be considered incident to when furnished during a course of treatment where the physician performs the initial service and subsequent services at a frequency that reflects the physician's active participation in and management of the course of treatment. However, the direct supervision requirement must still be met. [Pub. 100-02, Ch. 15, § 60.1.]

"Direct supervision" in the office setting does not mean that the physician must be present in the same room with an aide. However, the physician must be present in the office suite and immediately available to provide assistance and direction throughout the time the aide is performing services. [Pub. 100-02, Ch. 15, § 60.1.]

If auxiliary personnel perform services outside the office setting, such as in a patient's home or an institution (other than a hospital or skilled nursing facility), their services likewise are covered as incident to the physician's services only if there is direct supervision by the physician. For example, if a nurse accompanies a physician on house calls and administers an injection, the nurse's services are covered. If the same nurse makes the calls alone and administers the injection, the services are not covered (even when billed by the physician) because the physician is not providing direct supervision. Note, however, that this requirement has been modified somewhat with respect to patients who are considered "homebound"—see "Homebound Patients," below.

Services provided by auxiliary personnel in an institution (*e.g.*, hospital, skilled nursing facility, nursing or convalescent home) present a special problem in determining whether direct physician supervision exists. The availability of the physician by telephone, and the presence of the physician somewhere in the institution, would not constitute direct supervision. For patients in a hospital or skilled nursing facility (SNF) who are in a Medicare-covered stay, Part B does not cover services of physician-employed auxiliary personnel as incident to services. Such services can only be covered under the Medicare hospital or SNF benefit and payment for such services can be made only to the hospital or SNF by a Medicare intermediary. [Pub. 100-02, Ch. 15, § 60.1.]

Nonphysician Practitioners

Nonphysician practitioners may be licensed under state law to assist or act in the place of the physician. Such practitioners include, for example, certified nurse midwives, certified registered nurse anesthetists, physician assistants, nurse practitioners, and clinical nurse specialists. Services performed by nonphysician practitioners incident to a physician's professional services include not only services ordinarily rendered by a physician's office staff (for example, taking blood pressure and temperatures, giving injections, and changing dressings), but also services ordinarily performed by the physician himself or herself (for example, performing minor surgery, setting casts and simple fractures, and reading X-rays. [Pub. 100-02, Ch. 15, § 60.2.]

The services of nonphysician practitioners, such as physician assistants and nurse practitioners, may be covered as "incident to" a physician's services, or they may be separately payable as "medical and other health services." For services of a nonphysician practitioner to be covered as incident to a physician's services, the services must meet all the requirements for incident to coverage discussed above. For example, the services, must be an integral, although incidental, part of the physician's personal professional services and must be performed under the physician's direct supervision. If the nonphysician practitioner meets the requirements for separate payment (see ¶ 366) and bills Medicare independently for his or her services, then the services are "medical and other health services." [Soc. Sec. Act § 1862(s) (2) (K); Pub. 100-02, Ch. 15, § 60.2.]

In some circumstances, nurse practitioners giving hospice care may serve as attending physicians. The services provided by a nurse practitioner that are medical in nature must be reasonable and necessary, be included in the plan of care and must be services that, in the absence of a nurse practitioner, would be performed by a physician. If the services performed by a nurse practitioner are such that a registered nurse could perform them in the absence of a physician, they are not considered attending physician services and are not separately billable. Services that are duplicative of what the hospice nurse would provide are also not separately billable. [*Medicare Benefit Policy Manual*, Pub. 100-02, Transmittal No. 22, Sept. 24, 2004.]

The amount of separate Medicare payment for the services of nonphysician practitioners is discussed at ¶ 826.

¶351

Supplies

Supplies usually furnished by the physician in the course of diagnosis and treatment, such as gauze, ointments, bandages (including ace bandages), oxygen, etc., also are covered. Charges for the supplies must be included in the physician's bill. To be covered, supplies, including drugs and biologicals (see below), must represent an expense to the physician. For example, if a patient purchases a drug and the physician administers it, the cost of the drug would not be covered. [Pub. 100-02, Ch. 15, § 60.1.]

Clinic Setting

Except in the case of rural health clinics, to which special rules apply (see ¶ 382), the guidelines for coverage of services and supplies incident to a physician's service in a "physician-directed clinic" or group association are generally the same as those described above. However, in highly organized clinics, particularly those that are departmentalized, "direct physician supervision" may be the responsibility of several physicians, as opposed to an individual attending physician. In this situation, medical management of all services provided in the clinic is assured. The physician ordering a particular service need not be the physician who is supervising the service. Therefore, services performed by auxiliary personnel and other aides are covered even though they are performed in another department of the clinic. [Pub. 100-02, Ch. 15, § 60.3.]

Supplies provided by the clinic during the course of treatment also are covered. When auxiliary personnel perform services outside the clinic premises, the services are covered as incident to the professional services of a physician only if performed under the direct supervision of a clinic physician. If the clinic refers a patient for auxiliary services performed by personnel who are not supervised by the clinic physicians, these services would not be incident to a physician's service. [Pub. 100-02, Ch. 15, § 60.3.]

A "physician-directed clinic" is one in which (1) a physician (or a number of physicians) is present to perform medical (rather than administrative) services at all times the clinic is open; (2) each patient is under the care of a clinic physician; and (3) the nonphysician services are under medical supervision. [Pub. 100-02, Ch. 15, § 60.3.]

Hospital Outpatient Department

Therapeutic services provided by the hospital in connection with the physician's treatment of outpatients are covered under Part B as incident to physicians' services (unless otherwise specifically excluded). This includes the use of the hospital's facilities and the services of nurses, nonphysician anesthetists, psychologists, technicians, therapists (other than physical, occupational, and speech therapists), and other aides. Therapeutic services also include clinic services and emergency room services. [Pub. 100-02, Ch. 6, § 20.4.1.]

Outpatient therapeutic services must meet the "incident to" requirements for Medicare coverage—that is, the services and supplies must be furnished as an integral, although incidental, part of the physician's professional service, and must be furnished on a physician's order and under physician supervision. The physician supervision requirement is generally assumed to be met where the services are performed on hospital premises; the hospital medical staff that supervises the services need not be in the same department as the ordering physician. However, if the services are furnished outside the hospital, they must be rendered under the direct personal supervision of a physician who is treating the patient. [Pub. 100-02, Ch. 6, § § 20.4.1, 40.]

Medical supplies provided by the hospital that are necessary and incident to physicians' services rendered to hospital outpatients are covered under Part B, for example, gauze, oxygen, ointments, and other supplies. [Pub. 100-02, Ch. 6, § 40.]

¶ 351

Outpatient hospital services are discussed at ¶ 352. The special rules concerning ambulatory surgical centers are discussed at ¶ 386.

Drugs and Biologicals

Drugs and biologicals furnished as incident to physicians' services are covered under Part B only if they are of the type that *are not usually self-administered by the patient (i.e., are not usually taken by the patient without professional assistance)* and generally are limited to those that are administered by injection. Thus, most prescription drugs that are in pill form and are swallowed are not covered by Medicare Part B because they do not meet the criteria that they are not usually self-administered. See ¶ 362 for more details and for a list of exceptions to this rule. [Pub. 100-02, Ch. 15, § 50.]

Drugs and biologicals also must meet all the general requirements for coverage of items as incident to a physician's services. Thus, a drug or biological must be furnished by a physician and must be administered by the physician or by auxiliary personnel under the physician's personal supervision. The charge for the drug or biological must be included in the physician's bill and the cost must represent an expense to the physician. Drugs and biologicals furnished by other healthcare practitioners may also meet these requirements. [Pub. 100-02, Ch. 15, § 50.3.]

Whole blood is a biological that is not usually self-administered and is covered when furnished incident to a physician's services. It is, however, subject to the blood deductible (see ¶ 335). [Pub. 100-02, Ch. 15, § 50.3.]

Drugs that the Secretary determines to be "less than effective" are not covered under the Part B program (see ¶ 644). [Pub. 100-02, Ch. 15, § 50.4.6.] The payment rates for drugs and biologicals covered under Part B are described at ¶ 362.

Beginning on January 1, 2006, prescription medications will be covered under Medicare Part D. This benefit was provided in the Medicare Modernization Act of 2003 (MMA) (PubLNo 108-173). The description of Medicare's prescription drug benefit under Part D begins at ¶ 500.

Homebound Patients

In some medically underserved areas there are only a few physicians available to provide services over broad geographic areas or to a large patient population. The lack of medical personnel (and, in many instances, absence of a home health agency to serve the area) reduces significantly the availability of certain medical services to homebound patients. Some physicians and physician-directed clinics, therefore, call upon nurses and other paramedical personnel to provide these services under general (rather than direct) supervision. [Pub. 100-02, Ch. 15, § 60.4.]

General supervision means that the physician need not be physically present at the patient's place of residence when the service is performed. However, the service must be performed under the physician's overall supervision and control. Homebound means the patient is generally unable to leave home and leaves the home only infrequently or for periods of short duration (see more on this at ¶ 264). [Pub. 100-02, Ch. 15, § 60.4.1.]

Direct supervision is not required for many services to homebound patients that can be performed safely by licensed nonphysicians when the services are (1) an integral part of the physician's service to the patient, (2) performed under general physician supervision by employees of the physician or clinic; and (3) included in the physician's/clinic's bill and the physician or clinic incurred an expense for them. If the services can be furnished by a local home health agency, they normally cannot be covered when furnished by a physician/clinic. [Pub. 100-02, Ch. 15, § 60.4.]

[¶ 352] Outpatient Hospital Services

Hospitals provide two distinct types of services to outpatients: (1) *therapeutic* services—services that aid the physician in the treatment of the patient and (2) *diagnostic* services—for example, diagnostic X-rays or diagnostic laboratory services. Both kinds of services furnished by hospitals to outpatients are covered under Part B. [*Medicare Benefit Policy Manual*, Pub. 100-02, Ch. 6, § 20.]

A "hospital outpatient" is a person who has not been admitted by the hospital as an inpatient, is registered on the hospital records as an outpatient, and receives services (rather than supplies alone) from hospital personnel. If a hospital uses the category "day patient," that is, an individual who receives hospital services during the day and is not expected to be lodged in the hospital at midnight, the individual is classified as an outpatient. An inpatient of a participating hospital may not be considered an outpatient of that or any other hospital. However, an inpatient of a SNF may be considered an outpatient of a participating hospital. [Pub. 100-02, Ch. 6, § 20.1.]

When a tissue sample, blood sample, or specimen is taken by personnel that are neither employed nor arranged for by the hospital and is sent to the hospital for the performance of tests, the tests are not outpatient hospital services since the patient does not receive services directly from the hospital. Similarly, supplies provided by a hospital supply room for use by physicians in the treatment of private patients are not covered as an outpatient service since the patients receiving the supplies are not outpatients of the hospital. [Pub. 100-02, Ch. 6, § 20.1.]

Diagnostic services are covered when provided by the hospital, whether furnished in the hospital or at other locations. Outpatient therapeutic services, which must be incident to physicians' services, are covered when furnished outside the hospital only if there is direct personal supervision by a physician. Thus, it may be necessary to distinguish between diagnostic and therapeutic services when services are provided outside the hospital. [Pub. 100-02, Ch. 6, § 20.2.]

Outpatient observations services. Outpatient observations services are those services furnished by a hospital on the hospital's premises, including use of a bed and at least periodic monitoring by a hospital's nursing or other staff which are reasonable and necessary to evaluate an outpatient's condition or determine the need for a possible admission to the hospital as an inpatient. These services must be ordered by a physician in order to qualify for Medicare part B coverage. [*Medicare Benefit Policy Manual*, Pub. 100-02, Transmittal No. 19, Sept. 10, 2004.]

Outpatient Hospital Therapeutic Services

Therapeutic services that hospitals provide on an outpatient basis are those services and supplies (including the use of hospital facilities) that are incident to the services of physicians in the treatment of patients. Therapeutic services also include clinic services and emergency room services. Drugs and biologicals are covered as therapeutic services if they are of the type that are usually not self-administered by the patient, as described at ¶ 362. [Pub. 100-02, Ch. 6, § 20.4.1.]

To be covered as incident to physicians' services, the services and supplies must be furnished as an integral, although incidental, part of the physician's professional service in the course of diagnosis or treatment of an illness or injury. The services and supplies must be furnished on a physician's order by hospital personnel under a physician's supervision.

This does not mean that each occasion of service by a nonphysician need also be the occasion of the actual rendition of a personal professional service by the physician. However, during any course of treatment rendered by auxiliary personnel, the physician must personally see the patient periodically and sufficiently often to assess the course of treatment and the patient's progress and, where necessary, to change the treatment regimen. A hospital service or supply would not be considered incident to a physician's service if the attending physician merely wrote an order for the services or supplies and referred the patient to the hospital without being involved in the management of that course of treatment. [Pub. 100-02, Ch. 6, § 20.4.1.]

The physician supervision requirement generally is assumed to be met if the services are performed on hospital premises; the hospital medical staff that supervises the services need not be in the same department as the ordering physician. However, if the services are furnished outside the hospital, they must be rendered under the direct personal supervision of a physician who is treating the patient. For example, if a hospital therapist (other than a physical, occupational, or speech language pathologist) goes to a patient's home to give treatment unaccompanied by a physician, the therapist's services would not be covered. [Pub. 100-02, Ch. 6, § 20.4.1.]

Outpatient physical, occupational, and speech-language services (¶ 381) are not subject to the direct physician supervision requirement. [Pub. 100-02, Ch. 6, § 20.2.]

Outpatient Hospital Diagnostic Services

A service is "diagnostic" if it is an examination or procedure to which the patient is subjected, or which is performed on materials derived from the patient, to obtain information to aid in the assessment of a medical condition or the identification of a disease. Among these examinations and tests are diagnostic laboratory services such as hematology and chemistry, diagnostic X-rays, isotope studies, EKGs, pulmonary function studies, thyroid function tests, psychological tests, and other tests given to determine the nature and severity of an ailment or injury. [Pub. 100-02, Ch. 6, § 20.3.1.]

Covered diagnostic services to outpatients include the services of nurses, psychologists, and technicians; drugs and biologicals necessary for diagnostic study; and the use of supplies and equipment. When a hospital sends hospital personnel and hospital equipment to a patient's home to furnish a diagnostic service, the service is covered as if the patient had received the service in the hospital outpatient department. [Pub. 100-02, Ch. 6, § 20.3.2.]

Hospital personnel may provide diagnostic services outside the hospital premises without the direct personal supervision of a physician. For example, if a hospital laboratory technician is sent by the hospital to a patient's home to obtain a blood sample for testing in the hospital's laboratory, the technician's services are a covered hospital service even though a physician was not with the technician. [Pub. 100-02, Ch. 6, § 20.3.2.]

Payment may not be made for outpatient diagnostic services unless the same service would be covered as an inpatient hospital service if furnished to a hospital inpatient. [Pub. 100-02, Ch. 6, § 20.3.2.]

When the hospital makes arrangements with another facility for diagnostic services furnished on an outpatient basis, the services can be covered whether furnished in the hospital or in other facilities. Independent laboratory services furnished to an outpatient under an arrangement with the hospital are covered only under the diagnostic laboratory tests provision of Part B, but are to be billed along with other services to outpatients. [Pub. 100-02, Ch. 6, § 20.3.3.]

¶352

Outpatient Surgery

There are special rules concerning outpatient surgery in hospital outpatient departments, freestanding ambulatory surgical centers, and hospital-affiliated ambulatory surgical centers. See ¶ 386.

Psychiatric Services

There is a wide range of services and programs that a hospital may provide to its outpatients who need psychiatric care, ranging from a few individual services to comprehensive, full-day programs, and from intensive treatment programs to those that provide primarily supportive, protective or social activities. To be covered by Medicare, such services must be incident to a physician's services and be reasonable and necessary for the diagnosis or treatment of the patient's condition. The services must be for the purpose of diagnostic study or must reasonably be expected to improve the patient's condition. [Pub. 100-02, Ch. 6, § 70.1.]

Payment Rules

For a discussion of payment methods for outpatient hospital items and services, see ¶ 837.

[¶ 353] Diagnostic X-Ray, Laboratory, and Other Diagnostic Tests

Diagnostic X-ray, laboratory, and other diagnostic tests, including materials and the services of technicians, are covered under Part B. [Soc. Sec. Act § 1861(s)(3); 42 C.F.R. § 410.10(e).] In most cases, the services must be furnished by a physician or be incident to a physician's services. As a general rule, diagnostic tests must be ordered by the physician who is treating the beneficiary—that is, the physician furnishes a consultation or treats the beneficiary for a specific medical problem and uses the test results in the management of the beneficiary's medical problem. Nonphysician practitioners entitled to provide physician services under state law are also subject to the physician ordering requirement. [42 C.F.R. § 410.32(a).]

There are two exceptions to the treating physician requirement: (1) a physician may order an x-ray for a chiropractic patient in order to demonstrate spinal subluxation, even though the physician does not treat the patient; and (2) a physician who meets the qualification requirements for an interpreting physician under § 354 of the Public Health Service Act may order a diagnostic mammogram based on the findings of a screening mammogram, even though the physician does not treat the patient. These rules also apply to nonphysician practitioners (that is, clinical nurse specialists, clinical psychologists, clinical social workers, nurse-midwives, nurse practitioners, and physician assistants) who furnish services that would be physician services if furnished by a physician and are operating within the scope of their authority under state and Medicare law. [42 C.F.R. § 410.32(a).]

Payment under the physician fee schedule is made for diagnostic tests performed by a physician, a group practice of physicians, an approved supplier of portable X-ray services, a nurse practitioner, or a clinical nurse specialist when he or she performs a test authorized under state law, or an independent diagnostic testing facility (IDTF). [42 C.F.R. § 410.33(a).]

Physician supervision. Some degree of physician supervision is required for most diagnostic tests payable under the physician fee schedule. The degree of physician supervision (general supervision, direct supervision, or personal supervision) required at the time the test is conducted will depend on the difficulty and risk of the test. [42 C.F.R. § 410.32(b).] Nurse practitioners, clinical nurse specialists, and physician assistants cannot function as supervisory physicians under the diagnostic tests benefit. [*Medicare Benefit Policy Manual,* Pub. 100-02, Ch. 15, § 80.]

Some diagnostic tests are covered when performed by a technician without direct personal physician supervision if the technician's general supervision and training, as well as the maintenance of the necessary equipment and supplies, are the continuing responsibility of a physician. [Pub. 100-02, Ch. 15, § 80.]

Portable X-ray Suppliers

Diagnostic X-ray services furnished by a portable X-ray supplier are covered when furnished in the patient's home and in nonparticipating institutions. Such services are also covered under Part B when provided in participating SNFs and hospitals, under circumstances in which they cannot be covered under Part A, that is, the services are not furnished by the participating institution either directly or under arrangements that provide for the institution to bill for the services. Portable X-ray services must be performed under the general supervision of a physician, the supplier must meet Food and Drug Administration certification requirements, and Medicare-prescribed health and safety conditions must be met. Coverage for portable X-ray services is limited to skeletal films involving the extremities, pelvis, vertebral column, and skull; chest and abdominal films that do not involve the use of contrast media; and diagnostic mammograms if the supplier is approved for this service. [42 C.F.R. § 410.32(c); Pub. 100-02, Ch. 15, § § 80.4–80.4.5]

Diagnostic Laboratory Tests

Part B pays for covered diagnostic laboratory tests when furnished by a qualified hospital, physician's office laboratory, rural health clinic, clinical laboratory, federally qualified health center, or skilled nursing facility. [42 C.F.R. § 410.32(d).]

National coverage and administrative policies. CMS established national coverage and administrative policies for clinical diagnostic laboratory services payable under Part B, in order to promote program integrity and national uniformity, and to simplify administrative requirements for clinical diagnostic laboratory services. [*Final rule*, 66 FR 58788, Nov. 23, 2001.] National coverage decisions (NCDs) are published in the CMS Internet-only *Medicare National Coverage Determinations Manual,* CMS Pub. 100-03. The NCDs describe CMS policy concerning the circumstances under which diagnostic tests are considered reasonable and necessary for Medicare purposes.

Prohibited referrals. The law prohibits Medicare payment to a laboratory that has a financial relationship with the referring physician. Violators are subject to civil money penalties and exclusion from the program. Laboratories are required to include information on referring physicians when submitting claims for payment (see ¶ 720). [Soc. Sec. Act § § 1833(q), 1877.]

Licensing requirements. Diagnostic laboratory services furnished by laboratories in physician offices or independent laboratories are covered under Part B only if the laboratories are licensed pursuant to state or local law or are approved as meeting the requirements for licensing by the state or local agency responsible for licensing laboratories. These laboratories also must meet the standards prescribed in the Medicare regulations (42 C.F.R. Part 493) pursuant to the Clinical Laboratory Improvement Amendments of 1988 (CLIA) (PubLNo 100-578).

Payment for clinical diagnostic laboratory tests is discussed at ¶ 827.

Other Diagnostic Tests

"Other diagnostic tests" are covered under Part B if the services are furnished by a physician or incident to a physician's services, except for psychological tests, otologic evaluations, and electrocardiograms. Some examples of "other diagnostic tests" are basal

¶353

metabolism readings, electroencephalograms, electrocardiograms, respiratory function tests, cardiac evaluations, allergy tests, psychological tests, and otologic evaluations.

Psychological tests. In addition to covering psychological tests when furnished by a physician or as an incident to a physician's services, Part B covers diagnostic testing services when performed by a qualified psychologist (who is not a clinical psychologist) practicing independently of an institution, agency, or physician's office, if a physician orders such testing. Examples of psychologists whose services are covered under this provision include educational psychologists and counseling psychologists. Expenses for such testing are not subject to the payment limitation on treatment for mental disorders. Independent psychologists are not required by law to accept assignment when performing psychological tests. [Pub. 100-02, Ch. 15, § 80.2.]

Hearing evaluations. Diagnostic testing performed by a qualified audiologist is covered when a physician orders such testing to evaluate the need for, or appropriate type of, treatment of a hearing deficit or related medical problem. Diagnostic services performed only to determine the need for, or the appropriate type of, a hearing aid are not covered. However, if a physician refers a beneficiary to an audiologist for evaluation of signs or symptoms associated with hearing loss or ear injury, the audiologist's diagnostic services are covered, even if the only outcome is the prescription of a hearing aid. [Pub. 100-02, Ch. 15, § 80.3.]

Payment for diagnostic audiology tests is determined by the reason the tests were performed, rather than the diagnosis or the patient's condition. Payment is based on the physician fee schedule amount, except that audiological services furnished in a hospital outpatient department are paid under the outpatient prospective payment system. (see ¶ 837). [Pub. 100-02, Ch. 15, § 80.3.]

Independent Diagnostic Testing Facilities

Diagnostic tests provided by an independent diagnostic testing facility (IDTF) are covered and paid under the physician fee schedule. IDTFs replaced the provider category known as independent physiological laboratories. An IDTF may be a fixed location, a mobile entity, or an individual nonphysician practitioner. An ITDF is independent of a physician's office or hospital, but it may furnish diagnostic procedures in a physician's office. In most cases, an IDTF must have one or more supervising physicians who are responsible for direct and ongoing oversight of the quality of the testing performed, proper operation and calibration of testing equipment, and the qualification of nonphysician personnel who use the equipment. All procedures performed by the IDTF must be ordered in writing by the physician who is treating the beneficiary, although nonphysician practitioners may order tests in accordance with the scope of their licenses. The supervising physician for the IDTF may not order tests to be performed by the IDTF, unless the IDTF's supervising physician is in fact the beneficiary's treating physician. [42 C.F.R. § 410.33.]

[¶ 354] X-Ray, Radium, and Radioactive Isotope Therapy

X-ray, radium, and radioactive isotope therapy are covered under the Part B program. These services also include materials and the services of technicians. The services must be performed by a physician or furnished under a physician's supervision. [Soc. Sec. Act § 1861(s)(4); *Medicare Benefit Policy Manual,* Pub. 100-02, Ch. 15, § 90.]

[¶ 355] Ambulance Services

Medicare Part B covers ambulance services if the supplier meets the applicable vehicle, staff, and billing and reporting requirements and the service meets the medical necessity and origin and destination requirements.

Levels of ambulance service. Ambulance services are divided into different levels of ground (including water) and air ambulance services based on the medically necessary treatment provided during transport. Medicare covers the following levels of ambulance service:

- Basic life support (BLS) (emergency and nonemergency)
- Advanced life support, level 1 (ALS1) (emergency and nonemergency)
- Advanced life support, level 2 (ALS2)
- Paramedic ALS intercept (PI)
- Specialty care transport (SCT)
- Fixed wing air ambulance (FW)
- Rotary wing air ambulance (RW) [42 C.F.R. § 410.40(a).]

These levels of service are defined in the Medicare regulations. [42 C.F.R. § 414.605.]

Air ambulance services. Air ambulance services are covered only when (1) the applicable vehicle and crew requirements are met; (2) the beneficiary's medical condition requires immediate and rapid ambulance transportation that could not have been provided by ground ambulance; and (3) either (a) the point of pickup is inaccessible by ground vehicle, or (b) great distances or other obstacles are involved in getting the patient to the nearest hospital with appropriate facilities. Air ambulance services are not covered for transport to a facility that is not an acute care hospital, such as a nursing facility, physician's office, or a beneficiary's home. Medical appropriateness is only established when the time needed to transport the beneficiary by ground, or the instability of transportation by ground, poses a threat to the beneficiary's survival or seriously endangers the beneficiary's health. [*Medicare Benefit Policy*, Pub. 100-02, Ch. 10, § § 10.4.1-10.4.5.]

Vehicle and crew standards. The Medicare regulations prescribe standards that vehicles must meet to be used as an ambulance, and standards concerning the qualifications of ambulance crews. [42 C.F.R. § 410.41(a), (b).] Ambulances must have customary patient care equipment and first aid supplies, including reusable devices and equipment such as backboards, neckboards and inflatable leg and arm splints. Ambulance equipment and supplies are considered part of the general ambulance service and payment for them is included in the payment for the transport. [Pub. 100-02, Ch. 10, § 10.1.5.]

Effect of beneficiary death. In general, if the beneficiary dies before being transported in an ambulance, no Medicare payment may be made. Therefore, in situations where the beneficiary dies, whether any Medicare payment can be made under the ambulance benefit depends on the time at which the beneficiary is pronounced dead by an individual authorized by the state to make such pronouncements. [Pub. 100-02, Ch. 10, § 10.2.6.]

The services of ambulance paramedics outside the ambulance, *e.g.,* in the patient's home, are not covered unless they are provided under the supervision of a physician as "incident to" a physician's services (see ¶ 351).

With respect to ambulance services furnished in conjunction with inpatient hospital services in a foreign country, see ¶ 227 and ¶ 610.

Medical Necessity Requirements

Medicare covers ambulance services only if they are furnished to a beneficiary whose medical condition is such that other means of transportation are contraindicated. To satisfy the medical necessity requirement, the beneficiary's condition must require both the ambulance transportation itself and the level of service provided. In addition, the reason for the

¶355

transport must be medically necessary—that is, the transport must be to obtain a Medicare-covered service or return from such a service. The presence (or absence) of a physician's order for an ambulance transport does not necessarily prove (or disprove) whether the transport was medically necessary; the ambulance service must meet all Medicare coverage criteria for payment to be made. [42 C.F.R. § 410.40(d); Pub. 100-02, Ch. 10, § 10.2.1.]

For nonemergency ambulance transportation, medical necessity is satisfied if either (1) the beneficiary is bed-confined, and it is documented that other methods of transportation are contraindicated, or (2) the beneficiary's medical condition, regardless of bed confinement, is such that ambulance transportation is medically required. Bed confinement is not the sole criterion in determining the medical necessity of ambulance transportation—rather, it is one factor considered in medical necessity determinations. For a beneficiary to be considered bed-confined, the beneficiary must be unable to (1) get up from bed without assistance, (2) ambulate, or (3) sit in a chair or wheelchair. [42 C.F.R. § 410.40(d); Pub. 100-02. Ch. 10, § 10.2.3.]

Scheduled nonemergency services. Medicare covers nonemergency, scheduled, repetitive ambulance services if the ambulance provider or supplier, before furnishing the service, obtains a written order from the beneficiary's attending physician certifying that the medical necessity requirements discussed above are met. The physician's order must be dated no earlier than 60 days before the date the service is furnished. [42 C.F.R. § 410.40(d) (2).]

Unscheduled nonemergency services. If a beneficiary resides in a facility and is under the care of a physician, Medicare will cover unscheduled nonemergency ambulance transportation (or nonemergency ambulance services scheduled on a nonrepetitive basis) if the beneficiary's attending physician certifies within 48 hours after the transport that the medical necessity requirements discussed above were met. For a beneficiary residing at home, or a beneficiary residing in a facility who is not under the direct care of a physician, Medicare will cover nonemergency ambulance services without requiring physician certification. [42 C.F.R. § 410.40(d) (3).]

Rural air ambulance services. The Medicare Prescription Drug, Improvement, and Modernization Act of 2003 (MMA)(PubLNo 108-173) specifies medical necessity requirements pertaining to rural air ambulance services. [Soc. Sec. Act § 1834(l) (14).] These requirements are discussed below in the Ambulance Fee Schedule section.

Origin and Destination Requirements

Medicare coverage of the ambulance trip is provided for a beneficiary who is transported by ambulance (1) from any point of origin to the nearest hospital, critical access hospital (CAH), or skilled nursing facility (SNF) that is capable of furnishing the required level and type of care for the beneficiary's illness or injury; (2) from a hospital, CAH, or SNF to the beneficiary's home; (3) from a SNF to the nearest supplier of medically necessary services not available at the SNF where the beneficiary is a resident, including the return trip; and (4) from an ESRD beneficiary's home to the nearest renal dialysis facility, including the return trip. [42 C.F.R. § 410.40(e).]

As a general rule, only local transportation by ambulance is covered and only to the nearest appropriate facility equipped to treat the beneficiary's condition. If two or more facilities that meet the destination requirements can treat the beneficiary appropriately and the place where the ambulance transportation began is within each facility's locality, than the full mileage from any one of the facilities is covered. In exceptional situations, full Medicare payment may be made where the ambulance trip originates beyond the locality of the institution to which the beneficiary was transported, if the institution is the nearest one with appropriate facilities.

¶355

"Locality" means the service area surrounding the institution to which individuals normally travel or are expected to travel to receive hospital or skilled nursing services. "Appropriate facilities" means that the institution is generally equipped to provide the needed hospital or skilled nursing care for the illness or injury involved. In the case of a hospital, it also means that a physician or a physician specialist is available to provide the necessary care required to treat the patient's condition. The fact that a particular physician does or does not have staff privileges in a hospital is not a consideration in determining whether the hospital has appropriate facilities. Thus, ambulance service to a more distant hospital solely to avail a patient of the service of a specific physician or physician specialist does not make the hospital in which the physician has staff privileges the nearest hospital with appropriate facilities. [Pub. 100-02, Ch. 10, §§ 10.3, 10.3.5, 10.3.6.]

Ambulance Fee Schedule

Effective April 1, 2002, a fee schedule payment system was established for ambulance services, including volunteer, municipal, private, independent, and institutional providers. Under the fee schedule, Medicare-covered ambulance services are paid based on the lower of the actual billed amount or the ambulance fee schedule amount. Except for services furnished by certain critical access hospitals (CAHs), all ambulance services are paid under the fee schedule. Payment for ambulance items and services furnished by a CAH, or by an entity owned and operated by a CAH, is based on reasonable cost if the CAH is the only provider or supplier of ambulance services that is located within a 35-mile drive of that CAH. [Soc. Sec. Act § 1834(l); 42 C.F.R. §§ 414.610(a), 414.615.]

The ambulance fee schedule was phased in over a five-year period ending in 2006 and replacing the former reasonable cost reimbursement system for providers and the reasonable charge system for suppliers. During the five-year transition period, the Medicare allowed amount for ambulance services, mileage, and separately billable supplies comprised a blended rate. The blended rate included a portion based on the fee schedule and a portion based on the provider's reasonable cost or the supplier's reasonable charge. The fee schedule amount comprised an increasing percentage of the blended amount over the five-year period. For services furnished in calendar year 2006 and thereafter, the payment is based solely on the ambulance fee schedule amount. [Soc. Sec. Act § 1834(l)(10); 42 C.F.R. § 414.615.]

The MMA also increased the Medicare payment rate for certain long ambulance trips. For ground ambulance services furnished on or after July 1, 2004, and before January 1, 2009, if the trip is longer than 50 miles, the payment rate per mile will be increased by 25 percent for each mile over 50 miles. This payment increase applies regardless of where the transportation originates. [Soc. Sec. Act § 1834(l)(11).]

The base rate of the fee schedule for ground ambulance trips that originate in a qualified rural area also were increased by the MMA. The payment increase applies to ground ambulance services furnished on or after July 1, 2004, and before January 1, 2010. CMS will identify qualified rural areas for purposes of this payment adjustment. [Soc. Sec. Act § 1834(l)(12).]

In addition, payments for ground ambulance services was temporarily increased for services furnished on or after July 1, 2004, and before January 1, 2007. For trips originating in a rural area or a rural census tract, the Medicare payment rate will increase by two percent. For trips originating in urban areas, the payment rate will increase by 3.3 percent. This payment increase is calculated after applying the increases for long trips and rural areas discussed above. [Soc. Sec. Act § 1834(l)(13).]

¶355

Rural air ambulance services furnished on or after January 1, 2005, will be reimbursed at the air ambulance rate if the air ambulance service (1) is reasonable and necessary based on the health condition of the patient being transported at or immediately prior to the time of transport, and (2) the service complies with the Medicare program's equipment and crew requirements for ambulances. The medical necessity requirement is deemed to be met for a rural air ambulance service if (1) the service is requested by a physician or other qualified medical personnel who reasonably determines or certifies that the patient's condition is such that the time needed to transport the patient by land, or the instability of transportation by land, poses a threat to the patient's survival or seriously endangers the patient's health, or (2) the service is furnished pursuant to a protocol established by a state or regional emergency medical service (EMS) agency and recognized or approved by CMS, under which the use of an air ambulance is recommended.

The EMS agency cannot have an ownership interest in the entity furnishing the service. Restrictions are also specified concerning employment and financial relationships between medical personnel requesting rural air ambulance services and the entity that provides the service. [Soc. Sec. Act § 1834(l) (14).]

Billing and reporting requirements. An ambulance supplier must use Medicare-designated billing forms and billing codes and must be able to document (1) the origin and destination of transports, (2) physician certifications, and (3) compliance with emergency vehicle and staff licensure and state and local certification requirements. [42 C.F.R. § 410.41(c).] Effective with implementation of the ambulance fee schedule (that is, for services furnished on or after April 1, 2002), ambulance suppliers must accept Medicare assignment (see ¶ 831). Thus, suppliers must accept the Medicare allowed charge as payment in full and may not bill or collect from a beneficiary any amount other than unmet Part B deductible and coinsurance amounts. [42 C.F.R. § 414.610(b).] Medicare does not require that the beneficiary's signature to authorize claim submission be obtained at the time of transport for the purpose of accepting assignment of Medicare payment. If the provider or supplier cannot obtain the beneficiary's signature at the time of transport, it may obtain the signature any time prior to submitting the claim to Medicare for payment. [Pub. 100-02, Ch. 10, § 20.1.2.]

[¶ 356] Durable Medical Equipment

Durable medical equipment (DME) furnished to a beneficiary for use in the patient's home is covered under the Part B program, whether furnished on a rental basis or purchased. The equipment must meet the definition of DME, it must be reasonable and necessary for the treatment of an illness or injury or to improve the functioning of a malformed body member, and it must be used in the patient's home. The decision whether to rent or purchase an item of DME generally rests with the beneficiary, while the decision on how to pay rests with the Medicare program. [*Medicare Benefit Policy Manual*, Pub. 100-02, Ch. 15, § 110.]

"Durable Medical Equipment" Defined

"Durable medical equipment" is equipment that (1) can withstand repeated use, (2) is primarily and customarily used to serve a medical purpose, (3) generally is not useful to a person in the absence of illness or injury, and (4) is appropriate for use in the home. All of these requirements must be satisfied before an item can be considered to be DME. [Pub. 100-02, Ch. 15, § 110.1.]

Durability. An item is considered durable if it can withstand repeated use, *i.e.,* the type of equipment that normally could be rented. Medical supplies of an expendable nature, such as incontinent pads, catheters, bandages, and elastic stockings are not considered durable

Medical equipment. Medical equipment is equipment that is primarily and customarily used for medical purposes and is not generally useful in the absence of illness or injury. Items such as hospital beds, wheelchairs, hemodialysis equipment, iron lungs, respirators, intermittent positive pressure breathing machines, medical regulators, oxygen tents, crutches, canes, trapeze bars, walkers, inhalators, nebulizers, commodes, suction machines, and traction equipment presumptively constitute medical equipment. [Pub. 100-02, Ch. 15, § 110.1B.]

Equipment that is used primarily and customarily for a nonmedical purpose is not considered medical equipment for Medicare purposes, even though the item has some remote medically related use. For example, in the case of a cardiac patient, an air conditioner possibly might be used to lower room temperature to reduce fluid loss in the patient and to restore an environment conducive to maintenance of the proper fluid balance. Nevertheless, because the primary and customary use of an air conditioner is a nonmedical one, the air conditioner *cannot* be considered DME for which payment can be made. [Pub. 100-02, Ch. 15, § 110.1B.]

Other devices and equipment used for environmental control or to enhance the environmental setting in which the beneficiary resides are not considered covered DME. These include, for example, room heaters, humidifiers, dehumidifiers, and other equipment that basically serve comfort or convenience functions. Equipment that primarily serves the convenience of a person caring for the patient, such as elevators or posture chairs, does not constitute medical equipment. Similarly, physical fitness equipment, such as an exercycle, first-aid or precautionary-type equipment, self-help devices, and training equipment are considered nonmedical in nature. [Pub. 100-02, Ch. 15, § 110.1B.]

Special exception items. Specified items of equipment may be covered under certain conditions even though they do not meet the definition of DME. These items are covered if it is clearly established that they serve a therapeutic purpose in an individual case, and would include heat lamps for a medical rather than a soothing or cosmetic purpose, and gel pads and pressure and water mattresses when prescribed for a patient who has bed sores or if there is medical evidence indicating the patient is highly susceptible to ulceration. [Pub. 100-02, Ch. 15, § 110.1B.]

Items limited or excluded by law. The law excludes the following items from coverage as DME *when furnished by a home health agency*: (1) intraocular lenses, and (2) medical supplies (including catheters, catheter supplies, ostomy bags, and supplies relating to ostomy care). [Soc. Sec. Act § 1834(a)(13).]

Seat lift chairs are covered only for the seat-lift mechanism, not for the chair itself. [Soc. Sec. Act § 1861(n).]

Use in Patient's Home

An item of DME must be used in the patient's home in order to be covered. For purposes of rental or purchase of DME, a patient's home may be the patient's own dwelling, an apartment, a relative's home, a home for the aged, or some other type of institution. However, neither a hospital nor a skilled nursing facility may be considered a patient's home. [Pub. 100-02, Ch. 15, § 110.1D.]

¶356

Coverage Criteria

Although an item may be classified as DME, it may not be covered in every instance. Coverage in a particular case is subject to the requirement that the equipment be necessary and reasonable for treatment of an illness or injury, or to improve the functioning of a malformed body member. [Pub. 100-02, Ch. 15, § 110.1C.]

Medicare requires a physician's prescription for DME, prosthetics, orthotics, and other supplies (DMEPOS). A supplier must have an order signed and dated by the beneficiary's treating physician before dispensing any DMEPOS item to a beneficiary. A nurse practitioner, clinical nurse specialist, or physician assistant may give the dispensing order and sign the written order for an item of DMEPOS under certain conditions. Suppliers may dispense most items of DMEPOS based on a verbal order that includes a description of the item, the beneficiary's name, the physician's name, and the start date of the order. However, a written order prior to delivery is required for pressure reducing pads, mattress overlays, mattresses, beds, seat lift mechanisms, TENS units, and power-operated vehicles. For items that are dispensed based on a verbal order, the supplier must also obtain a written order. For some items of DME, a certificate of medical necessity (CMN) is required (see "Certificate of Medical Necessity" below). In addition, for any DME item to be covered by Medicare, there must be clinical information in the beneficiary's medical record that supports the necessity for the type and quantity of items ordered and for the frequency of use or replacement. [*Program Integrity Manual*, Pub. 100-08, Ch. 5, §§ 5.1-2.]

Effective December 8, 2003, Medicare will no longer pay for motorized or power wheelchairs unless a physician, physician assistant, nurse practitioner, or clinical nurse specialist has conducted a face-to-face examination of the beneficiary and has written a prescription for the wheelchair. [Soc. Sec. Act § 1834(a)(1)(E)(iv).]

Certificate of Medical Necessity

For certain DME items or services billed to Medicare, the supplier must receive a signed Certificate of Medical Necessity (CMN) from the treating physician. The CMN can serve as the physician's order if the narrative description is sufficiently detailed. There are rules concerning who should and should not fill out various parts of the CMN between the physician and supplier. For example, the information in section B (estimated length of need, diagnosis codes, and clinical information used to determine medical necessity), may only completed by health care professionals, and not by suppliers. However, the information in section C of the CMN (fee schedule amount, narrative description of the items furnished, and the supplier's charge for the equipment or supplies) must be completed by the supplier prior to furnishing the CMN to the beneficiary's physician. A supplier that knowingly and willfully completes section B of the CMN, or that knowingly and willfully fails to include the required information in section C of the CMN, may be subject to a civil money penalty of up to $1,000 for each form or document distributed. Suppliers and physicians may use an electronic CMN (e-CMN). E-CMNs must adhere to all privacy, security, and electronic signature rules and regulations. [Soc. Sec. Act § 1834(j)(2)(A); Pub 100-08, Ch. 5, § 5.3.3.]

The use of the CMNs for motorized wheelchairs, manual wheelchairs and power operated vehicles has been phased out for claims with dates of service on or after May 5, 2005. [Pub. 100-08, Transmittal No. 121, Sept. 14, 2005.]

Repairs, Maintenance, Replacement, and Delivery

Under the circumstances discussed below, payment may be made for repair, maintenance, and replacement of medically required DME that the beneficiary owns or is purchasing, including equipment which had been in use before the user enrolled in Medicare Part B. [42 C.F.R. § 414.210(e)(2); Pub. 100-02, Ch. 15, § 110.2.]

Repairs. Repairs to equipment a beneficiary is purchasing or already owns are covered when necessary to make the equipment serviceable. If the expense for repairs exceeds the estimated expense of purchasing or renting another item of equipment for the remaining period of medical need, no payment can be made for the amount of the excess. [Pub. 100-02, Ch. 15, § 110.2A.]

Maintenance. Medicare pays for maintenance and servicing of DME in the following classes: inexpensive or frequently purchased items, customized items, other prosthetic and orthotic devices, and capped rental items. Maintenance and servicing for items that require frequent and substantial servicing, and for oxygen equipment, is not reimbursed. Payment is not made for maintenance and servicing of rented equipment except for PEN pumps, which Medicare covers every three months after the 15th paid rental month, and the maintenance and servicing fee established for capped rental items. [*Medicare Claims Processing Manual*, Pub. 100-04, Ch. 20, § 40.1.]

Routine periodic servicing, such as testing, cleaning, regulating, and checking of the beneficiary's equipment is *not* covered. Such routine maintenance generally is expected to be done by the owner rather than by a retailer or some other person who would charge the beneficiary. Normally, purchasers of DME are given operating manuals that describe the type of servicing an owner may perform to maintain the equipment properly. Thus, hiring a third party to do this work would be for the convenience of the beneficiary and would not be covered. However, more extensive maintenance, which, based on the manufacturers' recommendations, is to be performed by authorized technicians, would be covered as repairs. This might include, for example, breaking down sealed components and performing tests that require specialized testing equipment not available to the beneficiary. [Pub. 100-02, Ch. 15, § 110.2B.]

Capped rental items. For capped rental items that have reached the 15-month rental cap, Medicare pays for maintenance and servicing fees after six months have passed from the end of the final paid rental month or from the end of the period the item is no longer covered under the supplier's or manufacturer's warranty, whichever is later. The maintenance and servicing fee for capped rental items may be paid only once every six months. [42 C.F.R. § 414.229(e); Pub. 100-04, Ch. 20, § 40.2.]

Replacement. Replacement of equipment is covered in cases of loss, irreparable damage, wear, or when required because of a change in the patient's condition. Expenses for replacement due to loss or irreparable damage may be reimbursed without a physician's order when, in the judgment of the DME Regional Carrier, the equipment as originally ordered still fills the patient's medical needs. Claims involving replacement due to wear or a change in the patient's condition must be supported by a current physician's order. If a capped rental item of equipment has been in continuous use by the patient for the equipment's useful lifetime, or if the item is lost or irreparably damaged, the patient may choose to obtain a replacement. Carriers determine the reasonable useful lifetime of capped rental equipment, but in no case can it be less than five years. Payment will not be made for items covered under a manufacturer's or supplier's warranty. [42 C.F.R. §§ 414.210(f), 414.229(g); Pub. 100-02, Ch. 15, § 110.2C.]

Delivery. Delivery and service charges are covered but the related payment is included in the fee schedule for the item. Under special circumstances, such as if a beneficiary lives in a remote area, or equipment could not be obtained from a local dealer, the Medicare contractor may allow a separate charge at its discretion. [Pub. 100-02, Ch. 15, § 110.2D; Pub. 100-04, Ch. 20, § 60.]

¶356

Supplies and Accessories

Reimbursement may be made for supplies, for example, oxygen, that are necessary for the effective use of DME. Such supplies include those drugs and biologicals that must be put directly into the equipment in order to achieve the therapeutic benefit of the DME or to assure the proper functioning of the equipment, for example, tumor chemotherapy agents used with an infusion pump or heparin used with a home dialysis system. However, the coverage of such drugs or biologicals does not preclude the need for a determination that the drug or biological itself is reasonable and necessary for treatment of the illness or injury or to improve the functioning of a malformed body member. [Pub. 100-02, Ch. 15, § 110.3.]

A supplier that furnishes a drug (other than oxygen) used in conjunction with DMEPOS must be licensed by the state to dispense drugs, regardless of whether the drug requires a prescription. Medicare will deny claims for drugs, and related equipment, supplies, and accessories when billed on the same claim, if the supplier does not have a license to dispense drugs. A supplier of drugs must bill and receive payment for the drug in its own name. A physician enrolled as a DMEPOS supplier may dispense and bill for drugs only if authorized under state law as part of the physician's license. The entity that dispenses the drug must furnish it directly to the patient for whom the prescription is written. A supplier that does not dispense the drugs cannot purchase the drugs used in conjunction with DME for resale to the beneficiary. [42 C.F.R. § 424.57(b)(4); Pub. 100-02, Ch. 15, § 110.3.]

Reimbursement may be made for replacement of essential accessories such as hoses, tubes, mouthpieces, etc., for necessary DME, only if the beneficiary owns or is purchasing the equipment. [Pub. 100-02, Ch. 15, § 110.3.]

Oxygen Services in the Home

Oxygen and oxygen equipment provided in the home are covered by Medicare under the DME benefit. Initial claims for oxygen services provided in the beneficiary's home must include a completed CMN to establish whether coverage criteria are met and to ensure that oxygen services are provided consistent with the physician's prescription or other medical documentation. The treating physician's prescription or other medical documentation must indicate that other forms of treatment have been tried, have not been sufficiently successful, and that oxygen therapy is still required. The documentation must specify a diagnosis of the disease requiring home use of oxygen, the oxygen flow rate, and an estimate of the frequency, duration of use (for example, 2 liters per minute, 10 minutes per hour, 12 hours per day), and duration of need (for example, six months or lifetime). The initial claim also must include the results of a blood gas study, but a measurement of arterial oxygen saturation obtained by ear or pulse oximetry is acceptable. [*Medicare National Coverage Determinations Manual*, Pub. 100-03 Ch. 1, § 240.2.]

A portable oxygen system is covered either as a necessary complement to a stationary system or by itself to provide an intermittent supply of oxygen for use during exercise by a patient who has a medical diagnosis of exercise-induced hypoxemia. Respiratory therapists' services are not covered under the DME benefit, but they may be covered as incident to a physician's services. [Pub. 100-03, Ch. 1, § 240.2.]

A new physician certification is required every 90 days for certain patients receiving home oxygen therapy. The recertification must be made if, at the time the home oxygen therapy is initiated, the patient has an initial arterial blood gas value at or above a partial pressure of 56 or an arterial oxygen saturation at or above 89 percent. The recertification must be based on a follow-up test of these indications within the final 30 days of the 90-day period. [Soc. Sec. Act § 1834(a)(5)(E); Pub. 100-03, Ch. 1 § 240.2; Pub. 100-04, Ch. 20 § 100.2.3.]

¶356

Supplier Rules

Suppliers (including physicians) that sell or rent Medicare covered durable medical equipment, prosthetics, orthotics, and other supplies (called DMEPOS) are required to obtain a Medicare billing number. [42 C.F.R. § 424.57.] Four regional carriers have been specially designated to process all DMEPOS claims.

To obtain and keep a Medicare billing number, a supplier must meet, and certify that it meets, several conditions, including delivering supplies and equipment to beneficiaries, honoring all warranties, answering questions and complaints, maintaining and repairing the equipment, accepting returns of substandard and unsuitable items, and complying with disclosure of ownership provisions. [42 C.F.R. § 424.57(c).]

The MMA requires CMS to establish quality standards for suppliers of DME; prosthetic devices; orthotics and prosthetics; medical supplies; home dialysis supplies and equipment; therapeutic shoes; parenteral and enteral nutrients, equipment, and supplies; electromyogram devices; salivation devices; blood products; and transfusion machines. CMS must designate one or more independent accreditation organizations no later than one year after the quality standards are implemented. [Soc. Sec. Act § 1834(a).]

Payment Rules

Durable medical equipment, prosthetics, orthotics, and other supplies (DMEPOS) are paid for by Medicare under a set of regional fee schedules. Payment for those items equals 80 percent of the lower of the actual charge for the equipment or the fee schedule amount. [Soc. Sec. Act §§ 1834(a)(1), 1834(h)(1).] As a result of the 2003 amendments to the Medicare Act, however, Medicare will shift from paying for DMEPOS based on fee schedules to paying amounts determined through competitive bidding. See the discussion below regarding the competitive acquisition program.

Fee schedule classes. DMEPOS are categorized into classes for purposes of fee schedule payment. The classes include [42 C.F.R. § 414.210]:

- Inexpensive or routinely purchased items,
- Items requiring frequent and substantial servicing,
- Certain customized items,
- Oxygen and oxygen equipment,
- Prosthetic and orthotic devices,
- Other DME—Capped rental items, and
- Transcutaneous electrical nerve stimulators (TENS).

The DMEPOS fee schedules are generally updated annually using the consumer price index (the "covered item update"). Under the MMA, the update to the DMEPOS fee schedules will be zero percentage points from 2004 through 2008. After 2008, for those items not included in the competitive acquisition program, the update will be the percentage increase in the consumer price index for all urban consumers (CPI-U). For class III medical devices, the update from 2004 through 2006 is the percentage increase in the CPI-U. Class III medical devices are devices that require premarket approval because neither general nor special controls provide a reasonable assurance of safety and effectiveness. In 2007, CMS will determine the update for class III devices after taking into account recommendations made by the General Accounting Office. [Soc. Sec. Act § 1834(a)(14).]

The DMEPOS fee schedules include application of national payment floors and ceilings. For inexpensive or routinely purchased DME, items that require frequent and substantial servicing, capped rental items, and oxygen and oxygen equipment, the floor is equal to 85 percent of the weighted median (mid-point) of all local payment amounts, and the ceiling is equal to 100 percent of the weighted median of all local payment amounts. For prosthetics and orthotics, the floor and ceiling are equal to 90 percent and 120 percent of the nationwide average purchase price, respectively. [Soc. Sec. Act §§ 1834(a)(2), 1834(a)(3), 1834(a)(8), 1834(a)(9); 42 C.F.R. §§ 414.220-414.228.]

PEN fee schedule. Effective for items and services furnished on or after January 1, 2002, Medicare pays for parenteral and enteral nutrition (PEN) nutrients, equipment, and supplies on the basis of 80 percent of the lesser of: (1) the actual charge for the item or service, or (2) the fee schedule amount. For each year after 2002, the fee schedule amounts are updated by the percentage increase in the consumer price index. [Soc. Sec. Act § 1842(s); 42 C.F.R. §§ 414.102, 414.104.]

Inexpensive or routinely purchased items. Payment for inexpensive or routinely purchased items is made on a rental basis or in a lump-sum purchase amount, based on the applicable fee schedule amount. Equipment is "inexpensive" if the purchase price does not exceed $150. Equipment is "routinely purchased" if it is acquired at least 75 percent of the time by purchase. If rental rather than lump-sum purchase is chosen, the total amount of rental payments may not exceed the fee schedule amount recognized for purchase of that item. Payment for ostomy supplies, tracheostomy supplies, urologicals, and surgical dressings, not furnished as incident to a physician's professional service or furnished by a home health agency, is made using the methodology for the inexpensive and routinely purchased class of equipment. [42 C.F.R. § 414.220; Pub. 100-04, Ch. 20, § 30.1.]

For payment purposes, used equipment is considered routinely purchased equipment and is any equipment that has been purchased or rented by someone before the current purchase transaction. Used equipment also includes equipment that has been used under circumstances where there has been no commercial transaction (such as equipment used for trial periods or as a demonstrator). If a beneficiary rents a piece of new equipment and subsequently purchases it, the payment amount for the purchase should be high enough that the total combined rental and purchase amounts at least equal the fee schedule amount for purchase of comparable new equipment. [Pub. 100-04, Ch. 20, § 30.1.1.]

Equipment requiring frequent and substantial servicing. Equipment requiring frequent and substantial servicing in order to avoid risk to the patient's health (for example, ventilators, continuous and intermittent positive pressure breathing machines, and continuous passive motion machines) is paid for only on a monthly rental basis. [42 C.F.R. § 414.222.]

Customized items. To be considered a customized item, a covered item (including a wheelchair) must be uniquely constructed or substantially modified for a specific beneficiary according to the description and orders of a physician, and must be so different from another item used for the same purpose that the two items cannot be grouped together for pricing purposes. Customized items are paid on a lump-sum purchase basis, based on the carrier's consideration of a reasonable payment amount. [42 C.F.R. § 414.224.]

Oxygen and oxygen equipment. Payment for rental of oxygen equipment and purchase of oxygen contents is based on a monthly fee schedule amount. Monthly fee schedule amounts are separately calculated for the following items: (1) stationary oxygen equipment and oxygen contents (stationary and portable oxygen contents); (2) portable oxygen equipment only; (3) stationary and portable oxygen contents only; and (4) portable oxygen contents only. [42 C.F.R. § 414.226.]

Prosthetic and orthotic devices. Payment for prosthetic and orthotic devices is made only on a lump-sum purchase basis. This class of DMEPOS consists of all prosthetic and orthotic

¶356

devices except: equipment in the "items requiring frequent and substantial servicing" and "customized items" classes of DME, parenteral and enteral nutritional supplies and equipment, and intraocular lenses. [42 C.F.R. § 414.228; Pub. 100-04, Ch. 20, § 30.4.]

Other DME—Capped rental items. Payment is made on a rental or purchase option basis for other DME not included in the categories listed above. Payment for rented equipment during the first three months of use is limited to 10 percent of the purchase price; thereafter, payment is limited to 7.5 percent of the purchase price. [42 C.F.R. § 414.229.]

Transcutaneous electrical nerve stimulators (TENS). Payment for TENS equipment is made on a purchase basis. However, to permit an attending physician time to determine whether the purchase of TENS equipment is medically appropriate for a particular patient, two months of rental payments may be made in addition to the purchase price. The rental payments are equal to 10 percent of the purchase price. [42 C.F.R. § 414.232.]

Parenteral and enteral nutrition items and services. Payment for parenteral and enteral nutrition (PEN) items and services is made in a lump sum for nutrients and supplies that are purchased and on a monthly basis for equipment that is rented. [42 C.F.R. § 414.104.] Claims for rental of parenteral and enteral pumps are limited to payments for a total of 15 months during a period of medical need. Payment policies for these pumps generally follow the rules for capped rental items. [Pub. 100-04, Ch. 20, § 30.7.1.]

Blood-testing strips and glucose monitors. Payment for blood-testing strips and glucose monitors is discussed at ¶ 369 under "Diabetes Self-Management Services."

Competitive Acquisition Program

As a result of the MMA, Medicare will shift from paying for DMEPOS on the basis of fee schedules to paying amounts determined through competitive bidding. Competitive acquisition programs will replace fee schedule payments for DME (including items used in infusion and drugs); medical supplies; home dialysis supplies; therapeutic shoes; enteral nutrients, equipment, and supplies; electromyogram devices; salivation devices; blood products; transfusion medicine; and off-the-self orthotics (requiring minimal self-adjustment). The competitive acquisition program does not include inhalation drugs; parenteral nutrients, supplies, and equipment; and class III devices under the Federal Food, Drug, and Cosmetic Act. [Soc. Sec. Act § 1847.]

CMS will establish competitive acquisition areas throughout the United States in order to award contracts for furnishing of competitively priced items and services. In carrying out the competitive acquisition program, CMS may exempt rural areas and areas of low population density within urban areas that are not competitive, unless a significant national market exists through mail order for a particular item or service. CMS also may exempt items and services for which competitive acquisition is not likely to result in significant savings. The program will be phased in so that competition occurs in 10 of the largest metropolitan statistical areas in 2007, 80 of the largest metropolitan statistical areas in 2009, and remaining areas after 2009. Existing rental agreements for DME and supply arrangements for oxygen, entered into before implementation of the competitive acquisition program, will not be affected. [Soc. Sec. Act § 1847.]

Payment for items and services will be based on competitive bids, and CMS will determine a single payment amount for each item or service in each competitive acquisition area. Medicare will pay 80 percent of the payment amount determined through competitive bidding, with beneficiaries paying the remaining 20 percent (after meeting the Part B deductible). [Soc. Sec. Act § 1847.]

¶356

Purchase Option for Capped Rental Items

For DME in the capped rental items category, suppliers must offer a purchase option to beneficiaries during the 10th continuous rental month. Beneficiaries have one month from the date the supplier makes the offer to accept the purchase option. For power-driven wheelchairs, the supplier must also offer a purchase option to beneficiaries when the equipment is initially furnished. If the beneficiary does not accept the purchase option, payment continues on a rental basis for up to 15 months. After 15 months of rental payments, the supplier must provide the item without charge, other than a charge for maintenance and servicing fees, until medical necessity ends or Medicare coverage ceases. If the beneficiary accepts the purchase option, payment continues on a rental basis not to exceed a period of continuous use of 13 months. After 13 continuous rental months, the supplier must transfer title to the equipment to the beneficiary. [42 C.F.R. §§ 414.229(d), 414.230.]

Suppliers must offer beneficiaries the option of purchasing power-driven wheelchairs when the supplier first furnishes the item. If the beneficiary chooses the purchase option, payment is on a lump-sum fee schedule purchase basis. If the beneficiary declines to purchase the electric wheelchair initially, contractors make rental payments in the same manner as for any other capped rental item. [42 C.F.R. § 414.229(d).]

Upgraded DMEPOS and the Advance Beneficiary Notice

A beneficiary may purchase or rent an upgraded item of DME other than the standard allowable item, but the beneficiary is responsible for the difference between the supplier's charge for the upgrade and the Medicare payment amount for the standard item. [Soc. Sec. Act § 1834(a)(17).] Suppliers may bill for upgraded DME using the Advance Beneficiary Notice (ABN). An ABN is a written notice that a physician or supplier gives to a Medicare beneficiary before items or services are furnished, when the physician or supplier believes that Medicare probably or certainly will not pay for some or all of the items or services based on certain exclusions in the Medicare statute. Under the ABN process, the supplier is permitted to bill on an assigned or unassigned basis for Medicare-covered DME, and the supplier can bill the beneficiary for the difference between Medicare's allowed amount and the cost of the upgraded feature. [Pub. 100-04, Ch. 30, § 50.7.5.]

A DMEPOS upgrade consists of an item that includes an "excess component." An excess component is an item, feature, or the extent of, number of, duration of, or expense for an item or feature, that is in addition to, or is more extensive or more expensive than, the item that is medically necessary under Medicare coverage requirements. When upgraded DMEPOS is furnished and the supplier expects a Medicare reduction in payment for the additional expenses attributable to the upgrade, an ABN should first be delivered to the beneficiary, and the signature of the beneficiary, agreeing to be personally and fully responsible for payment of those additional expenses, should be obtained. For items and services furnished on or after January 1, 2003, the ABN-G (Form CMS-R-131) should be used. [Pub. 100-04, Ch. 30, § 50.7.5.]

For DMEPOS upgrades, the ABN should specify, in the "Items or Services" box, the excess components for which denial is expected, and in the "Because" box, the reason that Medicare is expected to deny payment for the excess components related to the upgrade. In other words, the subject of the ABN is the upgraded features that are expected to be denied, not the standard items or services for which payment is expected. Any cost estimate provided on the ABN must relate to the extra expense for the upgrade features, not the total cost of the item or service. [Pub. 100-04, Ch. 30, § 50.7.5.]

¶356

Change in the Patient's Condition

When equipment is sold by a patient and later reacquired. A beneficiary may sell or otherwise dispose of equipment purchased under the program and for which there is no further use, for example, because of recovery from the illness or injury that gave rise to the need for the equipment. (There is no authority for the program to repossess the equipment.) If, after disposal, there is again medical need for similar equipment, payment can be made for the rental or purchase of that equipment. [Pub. 100-02, Ch. 15, § 110.4.]

When equipment is purchased and patient's condition changes. When payments stop because the beneficiary's condition has changed and the equipment is no longer medically necessary, the beneficiary is responsible for the remaining noncovered charges. Similarly, when payments stop because the beneficiary dies, the patient's estate is responsible for the remaining noncovered charges. [Pub. 100-02, Ch. 15, § 110.4.]

[¶ 357] Prosthetic Devices

Prosthetic devices (other than dental) that replace all or part of an internal body organ (including contiguous tissue) or that replace all or part of the function of a permanently inoperative or malfunctioning internal body organ, and replacements or repairs for those devices, are covered when furnished incident to physicians' services or on a physician's order. This does not require a determination that there is no possibility that the patient's condition may improve sometime in the future. If the medical record, including the judgment of the attending physician, indicates the condition will be of long and indefinite duration, the test of permanence will be considered met. [*Medicare Benefit Policy Manual*, Pub. 100-02, Ch. 15, § 120A.]

Medicare does not cover a prosthetic device dispensed to a beneficiary prior to the time at which the beneficiary undergoes the procedure that necessitates the use of the device. For example, Medicare will not make a separate Part B payment for an intraocular lens or pacemaker that a physician, during an office visit prior to the actual surgery, dispenses to the beneficiary for the beneficiary's use. [Pub. 100-02, Ch. 15, § 120A.]

Examples of prosthetic devices include artificial limbs, parenteral and enteral nutrition, cardiac pacemakers, prosthetic lenses, breast prostheses, maxillofacial devices, and devices that replace all or part of the ear or nose. A urinary collection and retention system with or without a tube is a prosthetic device replacing bladder function in case of permanent urinary incontinence. The foley catheter is also considered a prosthetic device when ordered for a patient with permanent urinary incontinence. However, chucks, diapers, rubber sheets, etc., are supplies that are not covered under this provision. Colostomy (and other ostomy) bags and other items and supplies directly related to ostomy care also are covered as prosthetic devices. Payment also can be made for *supplies* that are necessary for the effective use of a prosthetic device (for example, the batteries needed to operate an artificial larynx). [Pub. 100-02, Ch. 15, § § 120A, 120D.]

Although hemodialysis equipment is a prosthetic device, payment for rental or purchase of such equipment in the home is made only for use under the payment provisions applicable to durable medical equipment. However, if payment cannot be made on an inpatient's behalf under Part A, hemodialysis equipment, supplies, and services required by the patient can be covered under Part B as a prosthetic device that replaces the function of a kidney. [Pub. 100-02, Ch. 15, § 120A.]

Repairs, adjustments, and replacement. Adjustment of prosthetic devices required by wear or by a change in the patient's condition is covered when ordered by a physician. Necessary supplies, adjustments, repairs and replacements are covered even for devices in use before the user enrolled in Medicare Part B, so long as the device continues to be medically required. The Benefits Improvement and Protection Act of 2000 (BIPA) (PubLNo 106-554) requires Medicare to pay for replacement of prosthetic devices that are artificial limbs, or the replacement of any part of such devices, without regard to continuous use or useful lifetime restrictions, if an ordering physician determines that the replacement device or part is necessary because of (1) a change in the patient's physiological condition; (2) an irreparable change in the condition of the device; (3) or the condition of the device requires repairs that would cost more than 60 percent of the cost of a replacement device. [Pub. 100-02, Ch. 15, §§ 120A, 120D.]

No payment may be made for prosthetics and certain custom-fabricated orthotics unless they are furnished by a qualified practitioner and fabricated by a qualified practitioner or a qualified supplier at an approved facility. Affected custom-fabricated orthotics are those items that require education, training, and experience to custom fabricate and that are included on a list to be published by the Secretary. [Soc. Sec. Act § 1834(h)(1)(F).]

Prosthetic Lenses

The term "internal body organ" includes the lens of an eye. Prostheses replacing the lens of an eye include postsurgical lenses customarily used during convalescence from eye surgery in which the lens of the eye was removed. In addition, permanent lenses also are covered when required by an individual lacking the organic lens of the eye because of surgical removal or congenital absence. Prosthetic lenses obtained on or after the beneficiary's date of entitlement to Part B benefits may be covered even though the surgical removal of the crystalline lens occurred before the beneficiary's date of entitlement. [Pub. 100-02, Ch. 15, § 120B.]

Payment may be made for one of the following combinations of prosthetic lenses when determined to be medically necessary to restore the vision provided by the crystalline lens of the eye: (1) prosthetic bifocal lenses in frames, (2) prosthetic lenses in frames for far vision, and prosthetic lenses in frames for near vision, or (3) when a prosthetic contact lens for far vision is prescribed (including cases of binocular and monocular aphakia). The law provides coverage for one pair of conventional eyeglasses or contact lenses furnished subsequent to each cataract surgery with insertion of an intraocular lens. Lenses that have ultraviolet absorbing or reflecting properties may be covered, in lieu of payment for regular untinted lenses, if such lenses are medically reasonable and necessary for the patient.

Payment may not be made for cataract sunglasses obtained in addition to the regular (untinted) prosthetic lenses, because the sunglasses duplicate the restoration of vision function performed by the regular prosthetic lenses. Payment for intraocular lenses inserted during, or subsequent to, cataract surgery in a Medicare-certified ambulatory surgical center (ASC) is included with the payment for ASC facility services (see ¶ 386). [Soc. Sec. Act § 1861(s)(8); Pub. 100-02, Ch. 15, § 120B.]

Claims for cataract eyeglasses or cataract contact lenses and the professional services associated with them may not be billed to Medicare under one comprehensive service code. The items and the services must be billed separately. In addition, payment for an intraocular lens implanted during cataract surgery in a physician's office may not exceed the actual acquisition cost for the lens plus up to a 5 percent handling fee. [Soc. Sec. Act § 1842(b)(11).]

With respect to the coverage of an optometrist's services, see ¶ 340. Limitations on the use of surgery assistants in cataract operations are discussed at ¶ 654 and ¶ 820.

Enteral and Parenteral Nutrition Therapy

Accessories and/or supplies that are used directly with an enteral or parenteral device in order to achieve the therapeutic benefit of the prosthesis or to assure the proper functioning of the device are covered under the prosthetic device benefit. The following supplies and equipment are included: catheters, filters, extension tubing, infusion bottles, pumps (either food or infusion), I.V. poles, needles, syringes, dressings, tape, heparin sodium (parenteral only), volumetric monitors (parenteral only), and parenteral and enteral nutrient solutions. Baby food and regular grocery products that can be blenderized and used with an enteral system are not covered. [Pub. 100-02, Ch. 15, § 120A.]

Note that some of these items, for example, a food pump and an I.V. pole, qualify as durable medical equipment (see ¶ 356). Effective for items and services furnished on or after January 1, 2002, Medicare pays for parenteral and enteral nutrients, equipment, and supplies on the basis of 80 percent of the lesser of the actual charge for the item or service, or the applicable fee schedule amount (see ¶ 356). [42 C.F.R. § 414.102; Pub. 100-02, Ch. 15, § 120A.] CMS is required to implement competitive bidding to replace the fee schedule method of payment for durable medical equipment, prosthetics, orthotics or supplies and certain other equipment and supplies. Enteral nutrients, equipment, and supplies will be included in the competitive acquisition program, but parenteral nutrients, equipment, and supplies are exempt from competitive bidding. [Soc. Sec. Act § 1847.] See the discussion of the competitive acquisition program at ¶ 356.

Dentures

Dentures are not covered unless a denture or a portion thereof is an integral part of a covered prosthesis (for example, an obturator to fill an opening in the palate). [Pub. 100-02, Ch. 15, § 120C.]

Payment Rules

Payment for prosthetic and orthotic devices is made on a lump-sum purchase basis. See ¶ 356 under "Payment Rules."

[¶ 358] Braces, Artificial Limbs, Etc.

Leg, arm, back, and neck braces; trusses; and artificial legs, arms, and eyes are covered when furnished incident to physicians' services or on a physician's order. [*Medicare Benefit Policy Manual*, Pub. 100-02, Ch. 15, § 130.]

A "brace" includes rigid and semi-rigid devices used for the purpose of supporting a weak or deformed body member or for restricting or eliminating motion in a diseased or injured part of the body. Elastic stockings, garter belts, and similar devices do not come within the scope of the definition of a brace. Back braces include, but are not limited to, special corsets (sacroiliac, sacrolumbar, and dorsolumbar corsets) and belts. [Pub. 100-02, Ch. 15, § 130.]

A terminal device (for example, a hand or hook) is covered regardless of whether an artificial arm is required by the patient. Stump stockings and harnesses (including replacements) also are covered when these appliances are essential to the effective use of the artificial limb. [Pub. 100-02, Ch. 15, § 130.]

Adjustments to an artificial limb or other appliance required by wear or by a change in the patient's condition are covered when ordered by a physician. Adjustments, repairs, and replacements are covered even when the item had been in use before the user enrolled in Part B of the program, so long as the device continues to be medically required. [Pub. 100-02, Ch. 15, § 130.]

[¶ 359] Surgical Dressings, Splints, Casts, Etc.

Surgical dressings, splints, casts, and other devices used for the reduction of fractures and dislocations are covered under the Part B program. Surgical dressings are limited to primary and secondary dressings required for the treatment of a wound caused by, or treated by, a surgical procedure that has been performed by a physician or other healthcare professional. In addition, surgical dressings required after debridement of a wound are also covered, irrespective of the type of debridement. "Primary dressings" are therapeutic or protective coverings applied directly to wounds or lesions either on the skin or caused by an opening to the skin. Secondary dressing materials that serve a therapeutic or protective function and are needed to secure a primary dressing are also covered. Secondary dressings include adhesive tape, roll gauze, bandages, and disposable compression material.

Examples of items *not* ordinarily covered as surgical dressings include elastic stockings, support hose, foot coverings, leotards, knee supports, surgical leggings, gauntlets, and pressure garments for the arms and hands. Some items, such as transparent film, may be used as a primary or secondary dressing. [*Medicare Benefit Policy Manual*, Pub. 100-02, Ch. 15, § 100.]

If a physician or other qualified practitioner applies surgical dressings as part of a professional service that is billed to Medicare, the surgical dressings are considered incident to the practitioner's professional services. When surgical dressings are not covered incident to the services of a healthcare practitioner, and are obtained by a patient from a supplier pursuant to an order from a physician or other healthcare professional, the dressings are covered separately under Part B. [Pub. 100-02, Ch. 15, § 100.]

The coverage of splints and casts includes dental splints. [Pub. 100-02, Ch. 15, § 100.]

[¶ 361] Inpatient Ancillary Services

No payment may be made under Part B with respect to any services furnished to an individual to the extent that the individual is entitled (or would be entitled, except for the deductible and coinsurances) to have payment made for these services under Part A. [Soc. Sec. Act § 1833(d).] This precludes payment under Part B and Part A for the same services. Part B payment can be made for certain medical and other health services, even though they are furnished to an inpatient of a hospital or skilled nursing facility (SNF) if payment for those services cannot be made under Part A. These services are called "Part B ancillary services."

For hospitals paid under the prospective payment system (PPS) (see ¶ 810), Part B payment can be made for ancillary services if:

• no Part A prospective payment is made for the hospital stay because the patient exhausted his or her benefit days before admission;

• the admission was disapproved as not reasonable and necessary (and waiver of liability payment was not made);

• the days of the otherwise covered stay during which the services were provided were not reasonable and necessary (and no payment was made under waiver of liability);

• the patient was not otherwise eligible for or entitled to coverage under Part A; or

• no Part A day outlier payment is made (for discharges before October 1997) for one or more outlier days due to patient exhaustion of benefit days after admission but before the case's arrival at outlier status, or because outlier days are otherwise not covered and waiver of liability payment is not made. [*Medicare Benefit Policy Manual*, Pub. 100-02, Ch. 6, § 10.]

However, if only day outlier payment is denied under Part A (for discharges before October 1997), Part B payment may be made for only the services covered under Part B and furnished on the denied outlier days. [Pub. 100-02, Ch. 6, § 10.]

In non-PPS hospitals, Part B may pay for services on any day for which Part A payment is denied (that is, benefit days are exhausted, services are not at the hospital level of care, or the patient is not otherwise eligible or entitled to Part A payment). [Pub. 100-02, Ch. 6, § 10.]

Payment can be made for the following Part B ancillary services furnished by a participating hospital (either directly or under arrangements) to an inpatient if payment for these services cannot be made under Part A:

- diagnostic X-ray tests, diagnostic laboratory tests, and other diagnostic tests;
- x-ray, radium, and radioactive isotope therapy, including materials and services of technicians;
- surgical dressings and splints, casts, and other devices used for reduction of fractures and dislocations;
- prosthetic devices (other than dental) that replace all or part of an internal body organ (including contiguous tissue) or all or part of the function of a permanently inoperative or malfunctioning internal body organ, including replacement or repair of such devices;
- leg, arm, back, and neck braces; trusses; and artificial legs, arms, and eyes, including adjustments, repairs, and replacements required because of breakage, wear, loss, or a change in the patient's physical condition;
- outpatient physical and occupational therapy services and outpatient speech pathology services;
- screening mammography services, screening pap smears, colorectal screening, and prostate screening;
- influenza, pneumococcal pneumonia, and hepatitis B vaccines;
- bone mass measurements;
- diabetes self-management;
- ambulance services;
- blood clotting factors for hemophilia patients competent to use these factors without supervision;
- immunosuppressive drugs;
- oral anti-cancer drugs, and oral anti-emetic drugs used as part of an anti-cancer chemotherapeutic regimen; and
- Epoetin Alfa (EPO). [Pub. 100-02, Ch. 6, § 10.]

With the exception of the last two items above, the same services are payable under Part B when furnished by a participating SNF either directly or under arrangements to inpatients who are not entitled to have payment made under Part A (for example, benefits exhausted or three-day prior-stay requirement not met) or to outpatients. Drugs, biologicals, and blood are not covered under Part B when furnished by a SNF. [Pub. 100-02, Ch. 8, § 70.]

The services listed below, when provided to a hospital inpatient, may be covered under Part B *even if* the patient has Part A coverage for the hospital stay, because these services are covered under Part B and not covered under Part A:

- physicians' services (including the services of residents and interns in unapproved teaching programs);
- influenza, pneumococcal pneumonia, and hepatitis B vaccines;
- screening mammography services, screening pap smears and pelvic exams, colorectal screening, and prostate screening;

¶361

- bone mass measurements; and
- diabetes self-management training services. [Pub. 100-02, Ch. 6, § 10.]

However, in order to have any Medicare coverage at all (Part A or Part B), any nonphysician service rendered to a hospital inpatient must be provided directly or arranged for by the hospital. [Pub. 100-02, Ch. 6, § 10.]

[¶ 362] Listed Drugs and Biologicals

Drugs and biologicals must meet the same Medicare criteria for coverage under Part B as under Part A. These requirements are discussed at ¶ 212.

There are, however, significant limitations on Part B coverage of drugs and biologicals that do not apply under Part A. Drugs and biologicals generally are covered under Part B only if they are (1) of the type that are not usually self-administered by the patient; (2) reasonable and necessary to diagnose or treat an existing illness or condition; (3) administered by a physician or other health professional as an "incident to" service (see ¶ 351); (4) not excluded as immunizations (see ¶ 619); and (5) not found by the Food and Drug Administration (FDA) to be "less than effective" (see ¶ 644). [Soc. Sec. Act § 1861(s)(2); *Medicare Benefit Policy Manual*, Pub. 100-02, Ch. 15, § 50.]

The key limitation here is that drugs and biologicals that patients usually can take without assistance, such as most prescription drugs and drugs used to immunize patients against potential diseases, are not covered under Part B. Nevertheless, the law has been amended from time to time to specify that a particular drug or biological will be covered regardless of whether it meets these general criteria. The drugs and biologicals specifically mentioned by law as covered, and the specific criteria that must be met, are discussed in the paragraphs under "Statutory Exceptions to Above Rules," below.

Prescription drugs will be covered under Part D of Medicare, which will become effective on January 1, 2006. Medicare coverage of prescription drugs begins at ¶ 500.

Determining Self-Administration

Each Medicare contractor must make its own individual determination for each drug as to whether the drug is usually self-administered. Contractors must describe on their websites the process they use to determine whether a drug is usually self-administered. In addition, contractors must publish on their websites a list of the injectable drugs that are subject to the self-administered exclusion, including the supporting data and rationale. Contractors must provide notice 45 days prior to the date that such drugs will not be covered. [Pub. 100-02, Ch. 15, § 50.2.]

The term "administered" refers to the physical process by which the drug enters the patient's body, not whether the process is supervised by a medical professional. Only injectable (including intravenous) drugs are eligible for inclusion under the "incident to" benefit. Other methods of administration, including oral drugs, suppositories, and topical medications, are considered to be usually self-administered by the patient. The term "by the patient" means Medicare beneficiaries as a collective whole, but does not include instances when drugs are administered on an inpatient basis. The carrier determines whether beneficiaries as a collective whole self-administer on a drug-by-drug basis, not a beneficiary-by-beneficiary basis. [Pub. 100-02, Ch. 15, § 50.2.]

In determining whether a drug is usually self-administered, the term "usually" means more than 50 percent of the time for all Medicare beneficiaries who use the drug. Thus, if a drug is self-administered by more than 50 percent of Medicare beneficiaries, the drug is excluded from Medicare coverage. In arriving at a single determination as to whether a drug is usually self-administered, Medicare contractors are to make a separate determination for each indication for that drug. Contractors should determine the relative contribution of each indication to total use of the drug (that is, a weighted average) to make an overall determination as to whether the drug is usually self-administered. [Pub. 100-02, Ch. 15, § 50.2.]

For certain injectable drugs, it will be apparent due to the nature of the conditions for which they are administered or the usual course of treatment for those conditions, whether the drugs are usually self-administered. For example, an injectable drug used to treat migraine headaches is usually self-administered. An injectable drug, administered at the same time as chemotherapy, used to treat anemia secondary to chemotherapy is not usually self-administered. The fact that a drug's FDA label includes instructions for self-administration is not, by itself, a determining factor that a drug is subject to the self-administered exclusion. [Pub. 100-02, Ch. 15, § 50.2.]

Reliable statistical information on the extent of self-administration by patients may not always be available. In the absence of such data, contractors are to consider the following presumptions:

- Drugs delivered intravenously are not usually self-administered.
- Drugs delivered by intramuscular injection are not usually self-administered. The contractor may consider the depth and nature of the particular intramuscular injection in applying this presumption. However, contractors should examine use of the particular drug and consider (1) whether the drug is used for an acute condition (if so, it is less likely that a patient would self-administer the drug), and (2) how often the injection is given (for example, if the drug is administered once or more per week, it is likely to be self-administered by the patient).
- Drugs delivered by subcutaneous injection are self-administered. However, contractors should examine use of the particular drug and consider whether it is used for an acute condition and the frequency of administration, as described above. [Pub. 100-02, Ch. 15, § 50.2.]

Exclusion of Immunizations

Vaccinations and inoculations are excluded as "immunizations" (see ¶ 619) unless they are directly related to the treatment of an injury or direct exposure to a disease or condition, such as antirabies treatment, tetanus antitoxin or booster vaccine, botulin antitoxin, antivenin sera, or immune globulin. In the absence of injury or direct exposure, preventive immunizations (vaccinations or inoculations) against such diseases as smallpox, polio, diphtheria, etc., are not covered. However, pneumococcal pneumonia, hepatitis B, and influenza virus vaccines are exceptions to this rule and are covered (see below). [Pub. 100-02, Ch. 15, § 50.4.4.2.]

Statutory Exceptions to Above Rules

There are a number of exceptions to the rule against self-administered drugs and preventive immunizations:

Antigens. Payment may be made for a reasonable supply of antigens that have been prepared for a particular patient if: (1) the antigens are prepared by a physician who is a doctor of medicine or osteopathy, and (2) the physician who prepared the antigens has examined the patient and has determined a plan of treatment and a dosage regimen. Antigens must be administered in accordance with the plan of treatment and by a physician or by a properly instructed person (who could be the patient) under the supervision of the physician. A reasonable supply of antigens is considered to be not more than a 12-week supply of antigens that has been prepared for a particular patient at any one time. The

¶362

purpose of the reasonable supply limitation is to assure that the antigens retain their potency and effectiveness over the period in which they are to be administered to the patient. [Soc. Sec. Act § 1861(s)(2)(G); Pub. 100-02, Ch. 15, § 50.4.4.1.]

Pneumococcal pneumonia vaccine. In order to protect the elderly from pneumococcal pneumonia, a disease to which they are particularly susceptible, pneumococcal pneumonia vaccine and its administration is covered without deductible or coinsurance. Coverage includes revaccination of patients at highest risk of pneumococcal infection. The vaccine may be requested by the patient; neither a physician's order nor physician supervision is required. [Soc. Sec. Act § 1861(s)(10)(A); Pub. 100-02, Ch. 15, § 50.4.4.2.]

Hepatitis B vaccine. Hepatitis B vaccine and its administration is covered when furnished to an individual who is at high or intermediate risk of contracting Hepatitis B. [Soc. Sec. Act §§ 1861(s)(10)(B).] High-risk groups include: end-stage renal disease (ESRD) patients; hemophiliacs who receive Factor VIII or IX concentrates; clients of institutions for the mentally retarded; persons who live in the same household as a Hepatitis B Virus carrier; homosexual men; and illicit injectable drug abusers. Intermediate risk groups include staff in institutions for the mentally retarded, healthcare workers who have frequent contact with blood or blood-derived body fluids during their routine work, and heterosexually active persons with multiple sexual partners (*i.e.*, those Medicare beneficiaries who have had at least two documented episodes of sexually transmitted diseases within the past five years). However, persons in these groups are not considered at high or intermediate risk of contracting Hepatitis B if they have tested positive for Hepatitis B antibodies. [42 C.F.R. § 410.63; Pub. 100-02, Ch. 15, § 50.4.4.2.]

A special Hepatitis B vaccine, Engerix-B, has been approved for adults undergoing hemodialysis. Payment for Hepatitis B vaccine is made on a reasonable-charge basis and is not included in the prospective payment amount paid to ESRD facilities or in the comprehensive fee amount paid to physicians for treating ESRD patients. [Soc. Sec. Act § 1881(b)(11).]

Influenza virus vaccine. Influenza virus vaccine and its administration is covered without deductible or coinsurance when furnished in compliance with any applicable state law by any provider of services or any entity or individual with a supplier number. Typically, these vaccines are administered once a year in the fall or winter. Medicare does not require for coverage purposes that the vaccine be ordered by physician. Therefore, the beneficiary may receive the vaccine upon request without a physician's order and without physician supervision. [Soc. Sec. Act § 1861(s)(10)(A); Pub. 100-02, Ch. 15, § 50.4.4.2.]

Blood clotting factors. Medicare covers blood clotting factors for hemophilia patients competent to use such factors to control bleeding without medical or other supervision. Items related to the administration of the factors also are covered. This coverage is subject to utilization controls deemed necessary by the Medicare program for the efficient use of the factors. [Soc. Sec. Act § 1861(s)(2)(I); Pub. 100-02, Ch. 15, § 50.5.5.] Medicare will make a separate payment for administration of clotting factors furnished on or after January 1, 2005. The separate payment may take into account the mixing and delivery of clotting factors to a beneficiary, including special inventory management and storage requirements, as well as ancillary supplies and patient training necessary for self-administration. [Soc. Sec. Act § 1842(o)(5).]

Immunosuppressive drugs. Medicare covers prescription drugs used in immunosuppressive therapy when furnished to an individual who receives a covered organ transplant. [Soc. Sec. Act § 1861(s)(2)(J).] Prior to December 21, 2000, Medicare imposed time limits on coverage of immunosuppressive drugs. The Benefits Improvement and Protection Act of 2000 (BIPA) (PubLNo 106-554) eliminated the time limit on Medicare coverage for immunosuppressive drugs furnished on or after December 21, 2000. [Pub. 100-02, Ch. 15, § 50.5.1.]

¶362

Coverage is limited to those immunosuppressive drugs that specifically are labeled as such and approved for marketing by the Food and Drug Administration. Also included are prescription drugs, such as prednisone, that are used in conjunction with immunosuppressive drugs as part of a therapeutic regimen reflected in FDA-approved labeling for immunosuppressive drugs. Antibiotics, hypertensives, and other drugs not directly related to preventing organ rejection are not covered. [Pub. 100-02, Ch. 15, § 50.5.1.]

Erythropoietin (EPO). EPO is covered, even when self-administered, for the treatment of anemia for patients with chronic renal failure who are on dialysis. It is covered for self-administration by a home dialysis patient if the patient (or an appropriate caregiver) is trained to inject EPO. The patient's doctor or the renal dialysis facility also must develop a protocol for follow-up review and reevaluation of the patient's condition and the patient's ability to use the drug safely and effectively. [Soc. Sec. Act § 1861(s)(2)(O); Pub. 100-02, Ch. 15, § 50.5.2.]

Osteoporosis drugs. Medicare covers injectable drugs approved for the treatment of a bone fracture related to post-menopausal osteoporosis if (1) the drugs are administered by a home health agency, (2) the patient's attending physician certifies that the patient has suffered a bone fracture related to post-menopausal osteoporosis and the patient is incapable of self-administering the drugs, and (3) the patient is confined to her home. [Soc. Sec. Act §§ 1861(m)(5), 1861(kk).]

Oral anti-cancer and anti-emetic drugs. Oral anti-cancer chemotherapeutic drugs are covered, even when self-administered, if they contain the same active ingredients as intravenously administered anti-cancer drugs. [Soc. Sec. Act §§ 1861(s)(2)(Q), 1861(t)(2); Pub. 100-02, Ch. 15, § 50.5.3.]

Coverage is provided also for self-administered anti-emetic drugs when prescribed by a physician for use with a covered anti-cancer drug when necessary for the administration and absorption of the oral anti-cancer drug (*e.g.*, when a high likelihood of vomiting exists). The anti-emetic must be used during the period that begins immediately before and ends within 48 hours after the time of the administration of the anti-cancer drug and it must be used as a full replacement for the anti-emetic therapy that otherwise would be administered intravenously. [Soc. Sec. Act § 1861(s)(2)(T); Pub. 100-02, Ch. 15, § 50.5.4.]

Payment Rates

Prior to 2004, outpatient drugs covered under Part B were generally paid based on 95 percent of the average wholesale price (AWP). The MMA made significant changes to Medicare reimbursement for Part B drugs and biologicals. These changes were driven by concern that the AWPs for certain Medicare-covered drugs were much higher than the prices generally paid by healthcare providers to drug companies, resulting in significant Medicare overpayments to providers, as well as inflated beneficiary copayments. Under the MMA, certain categories of drugs and biologicals will continue to be paid at 95 percent of the AWP—these include:

- drugs and biologicals furnished before January 1, 2004;

- blood clotting factors furnished during 2004;

- a drug or biological furnished during 2004 that was not available for Part B payment as of April 1, 2003;

- pneumococcal, influenza, and hepatitis B vaccines furnished on or after January 1, 2004;

- a drug or biological (other than erythropoietin) furnished in connection with renal dialysis services that is separately billed by renal dialysis facilities;

¶362

- radiopharmaceuticals; and
- blood products.

Payments for other drugs furnished in 2004 will equal 85 percent of the AWP (determined as of April 1, 2003). CMS may substitute a different percentage of the April 1, 2003 AWP, but not less than 80 percent. [Soc. Sec. Act § 1842(o)(4)(A).]

Beginning in 2005, drugs and biologicals, except for pneumococcal, influenza, and hepatitis B vaccines and drugs associated with certain renal dialysis services, are paid using either (1) the average sales price methodology or (2) through a competitive acquisition program. Under the average sales price method, Medicare pays 106 percent of the applicable price for a drug, subject to the beneficiary deductible and copayment requirements. The applicable price for multiple source drugs is the volume-weighted average of sales prices. The applicable price for single source drugs is the lesser of (1) the average sales price for all National Drug Codes assigned to that drug or (2) the wholesale acquisition cost. A manufacturer's average sales price for a particular drug will be calculated for each calendar quarter by dividing the manufacturer's total sales in the United States for the drug by the total number of units of that drug sold in that quarter. The average sales price takes into account various discounts, chargebacks, and rebates. Medicare payment amounts for Part B drugs and biologicals are updated on a quarterly basis. [Soc. Sec. Act § 1847A.]

As an alternative to reimbursement under the average sales price methodology, physicians will be able to choose to participate in a competitive acquisition program under which payment amounts for Part B drugs and biologicals are determined through competitive bidding. The competitive acquisition program will be phased in starting in 2006. Competitive acquisition areas will be established throughout the United States. Each year, a physician will be able to select a contractor to supply Part B drugs and biologicals directly to the physician. Payments will be based upon the bids submitted by competing contractors, and CMS will determine a single payment amount for each drug in each competitive acquisition area. [Soc. Sec. Act § 1847B.]

Discarded drugs and biologicals. If a physician must discard the remainder of a vial or other package after administering a drug to a beneficiary, Medicare pays for the amount of drug discarded along with the amount administered. Payment for discarded drugs applies only to single-use vials. Multi-use vials are not subject to payment for discarded amounts of drug. [*Medicare Claims Processing Manual*, Pub. 100-04, Ch. 17, § 40.]

Assignment. All billing for drugs and biologicals covered under Part B must be on an assignment-related basis. Therefore, no charge or bill may be rendered to anyone for drugs and biologicals for any amount, except for any applicable Part B deductible and coinsurance amounts. This means that the physician, nonphysician practitioner, pharmacy, or supplier cannot charge the patient more than Medicare allows (*i.e.*, balance billing is prohibited). Sanctions can be imposed against violators. Mandatory assignment does not apply to the dispensing fee for nebulizer drugs. [Soc. Sec. Act § 1842(o); Pub. 100-04, Ch. 17, § 50.]

If an approved pharmacy dispenses the drug or biological, the pharmacy may collect an appropriate dispensing fee. As a result of the MMA, Medicare will pay pharmacies a supplying fee for covered immunosuppressive drugs, oral anti-cancer drugs, and oral anti-nausea drugs used as part of a chemotherapy regimen. [Soc. Sec. Act § 1842(o).]

[¶ 366] Other Healthcare Practitioners

Medicare increasingly has expanded coverage for the services of nonphysician healthcare practitioners. Included in this group are physician assistants, nurse practitioners and clinical nurse specialists, certified registered nurse anesthetists and anesthesia assistants, nurse midwives, qualified psychologists, and clinical social workers. See ¶ 826 for the details of payment rules for these practitioners.

Physician Assistants and Nurse Practitioners

The services of physician assistants and nurse practitioners are covered as "medical and other health services" under Part B if certain conditions are met. [Soc. Sec. Act § 1861(s) (2) (K); 42 C.F.R. §§ 410.74-410.76.]

The services of a physician assistant (PA) are covered only if they are performed under the general supervision of a physician and they are of the type that would be covered if provided by a physician. The PA must be legally authorized to perform the services in the state where the services are rendered. If the PA's services are covered, services and supplies furnished as incident to those services also are covered. The PA's physician supervisor is primarily responsible for overall direction and management of the PA's professional activities and for assuring that the services provided are medically appropriate for the patient. The supervising physician need not be physically present when the PA is performing services (unless required by state law), but the supervising physician must be immediately available to the PA for consultation. [Soc. Sec. Act § 1861(s) (2) (K) (i); 42 C.F.R. § 410.74.]

Payment for a PA's services may be made only to the PA's actual qualified employer, and the employer must be eligible to enroll in the Medicare program under existing provider/supplier categories. If the employer of a PA is a professional corporation or other qualified legal entity (*e.g.*, a limited liability company or a limited liability partnership) that permits PA ownership as a stockholder or member, that corporation or entity may bill for PA services, even if a PA is a stockholder or officer of the entity, as long as the employer is entitled to enroll as a Medicare provider or supplier. PAs may not otherwise organize or incorporate and bill Medicare directly for their services, including as sole proprietorships or general partnerships. A group of PAs that incorporate to bill for their services is *not* a qualified employer. Leasing agencies and staffing companies do not qualify under Medicare as providers or suppliers of services. [*Medicare Benefit Policy Manual*, Pub. 100-02, Ch. 15, § 190D.]

The services of a nurse practitioner, as well as a clinical nurse specialist, are covered only if they are performed in collaboration with a physician and they are of the type that would be covered if provided by a physician. They must also be authorized to provide those services in the state where the services are rendered. If the nurse practitioner's or clinical nurse specialist's services are covered, services and supplies furnished as incident to those services also are covered. [Soc. Sec. Act § 1861(s) (2) (K) (ii); 42 C.F.R. §§ 410.75, 410.76.]

Collaboration is a process in which a nurse practitioner or clinical nurse specialist works with one or more physicians to deliver healthcare services, with medical direction and appropriate supervision as required by the law of the state in which the services are furnished. In the absence of state law governing collaboration, nurse practitioners and clinical nurse specialists should demonstrate collaboration by documenting their scope of practice and indicating the relationships they have with physicians to deal with issues outside their scope of practice. The collaborating physician does not have to be present when the nurse practitioner or clinical nurse specialist furnishes services, nor does the collaborating physician have to make an independent evaluation of each patient who is seen by a nurse practitioner or clinical nurse specialist. [42 C.F.R. §§ 410.75(c), 410.76(c); Pub. 100-02, Ch. 15, §§ 200D, 210D.]

Physician assistant, nurse practitioner, and clinical nurse specialist services commonly include taking blood pressure and temperatures, giving injections, changing dressings, performing routine physical examinations, performing minor surgery, setting casts for

¶366

simple fractures, and interpreting X-rays. If authorized under the scope of their state license, physician assistants, nurse practitioners, and clinical nurse specialists may furnish services billed under all levels of CPT evaluation and management codes. In addition, if authorized under state law, physician assistants may perform diagnostic tests under the general supervision of a physician, and nurse practitioners and clinical nurse specialists may perform diagnostic tests in collaboration with a physician. [Pub. 100-02, Ch. 15, §§ 60.2, 190, 200, 210.]

CRNAs and Anesthesia Assistants

Medicare covers the services of qualified nurse anesthetists (certified registered nurse anesthetists (CRNAs) and anesthesia assistants (AAs) when they provide reasonable and necessary anesthesia and related care services. Payment for an anesthesia service furnished by a CRNA may be made to the CRNA or to any individual or entity (for example, a hospital, critical access hospital, physician, group practice, or ambulatory surgical center) with which the CRNA has an employment or contractual relationship that provides for payment to be made to the individual or entity. [42 C.F.R. § 414.60; *Medicare Claims Processing Manual*, Pub. 100-04, Ch. 12, §§ 140, 140.2.]

Nurse-Midwife Services

Medicare covers nurse-midwife services (as well as services and supplies furnished incident to a nurse-midwife's services) to the same extent the services would be covered if furnished by a physician, including obstetrical and gynecological services. The services must be authorized under state law. [Pub. 100-02, Ch. 15, § 130.]

Clinical Psychologists

Medicare covers diagnostic and therapeutic services furnished by a clinical psychologist, if the services would be covered if furnished by a physician or as incident to a physician's services. Services and supplies furnished incident to a clinical psychologist's services are covered if the requirements that apply to services incident to a physician's services are met. Other kinds of psychologists are paid as incident to physician services (see ¶ 340). [42 C.F.R. § 410.71; Pub. 100-02, Ch. 15, § 160.]

Contingent upon the patient's consent, a clinical psychologist must attempt to consult with the patient's primary care or attending physician to obtain information on any conditions contributing to the patient's symptoms. However, if the patient's primary care or attending physician referred the patient to the clinical psychologist, this consultation requirement does not apply. Neither a clinical psychologist nor a primary care or attending physician may bill Medicare or the patient for this required consultation. [42 C.F.R. § 410.71; Pub. 100-02, Ch. 15, § 160.]

All covered therapeutic services furnished by qualified clinical psychologists are subject to the Part B outpatient mental health services limitation (see ¶ 387). The limitation does not apply to diagnostic services. [Pub. 100-02, Ch. 15, § 160.]

Clinical Social Workers

Coverage for clinical social worker services includes the diagnosis and treatment of mental illnesses that the clinical social worker is legally authorized to perform under state law and that otherwise would be covered if performed by a physician or as incident to a physician's services. Not included in this coverage are services furnished to an inpatient of a hospital or skilled nursing facility (SNF), if the services furnished in the SNF are those that the SNF must furnish as a condition of participation in Medicare. [42 C.F.R. § 410.73; Pub. 100-02, Ch. 15, § 170.]

¶ 366

All covered therapeutic services furnished by clinical social workers are subject to the Part B outpatient mental health services limitation (see ¶ 387). This limitation does not apply to diagnostic services. [Pub. 100-02, Ch. 15, § 170.]

[¶ 369] Prevention Services

Medicare covers several kinds of preventive health services that have been specially exempted from the routine checkups exclusion (discussed at ¶ 619). Medicare coverage for initial preventive physical examinations, cardiovascular screening blood tests, and diabetes screening tests began in 2005. [Soc. Sec. Act § 1861(s)(2).]

Welcome to Medicare Exams

Medicare will pay for one "Welcome to Medicare Physical" within the first six months after the effective date of the beneficiary's first Part B coverage period, but only if the coverage begins on or after January 1, 2005. [*Final rule*, 69 FR 66235, Nov. 15, 2004.]

The initial exam includes: (1) a physical examination, including measurement of weight, height, blood pressure, and an electrocardiogram (but excluding clinical laboratory tests), with the goal of health promotion and disease detection; and (2) education, counseling, and referral for screening and other covered preventive benefits separately authorized under Part B. The education, counseling, and referral are for the following statutory screening and other preventive services authorized under Part B:

- pneumococcal, influenza, and hepatitis B vaccine and their administration;
- screening mammography;
- screening pap smear and screening pelvic exam services;
- prostate cancer screening services;
- diabetes outpatient self-management training services;
- bone mass measurements;
- screening for glaucoma;
- medical nutrition therapy services for individuals with diabetes or renal disease;
- cardiovascular screening tests; and
- diabetes screening tests.

The usual coinsurance and deductible provisions apply to the "Welcome to Medicare Physical." [*Final rule*, 69 FR 66235, Nov. 15, 2004.]

Mammograms

Medicare covers both screening and diagnostic mammography. Diagnostic mammography is a radiological procedure furnished to a man or woman who has signs or symptoms of breast disease, or a personal history of breast cancer, or a personal history of biopsy-proven benign breast disease. Screening mammography is a radiological procedure furnished to a woman without signs or symptoms of breast disease, for the purpose of the early detection of breast cancer. Medicare coverage includes the radiological procedure itself as well as a physician's interpretation of the results of the procedure. Diagnostic mammographies are covered when furnished on a physician's order. A doctor's prescription or referral is not necessary for a screening mammography to be covered. Payment may be made for a screening mammography furnished to a woman at her direct request, if she meets the age and frequency criteria discussed below. [42 C.F.R. § 410.34; *Medicare Benefit Policy Manual*, Pub. 100-02, Ch. 15, § 280.3.]

Medicare will not pay for screening mammography performed on a woman under age 35. Women between the ages of 35-39 are entitled to coverage for one screening mammogram during that age period. Asymptomatic women age 40 and over are entitled to one screening mammogram per 12-month period. [Soc. Sec. Act § 1834(c)(2)(A); 42 C.F.R. § 410.34(d).]

The usual Part B deductible is waived for screening mammography services. Physicians and suppliers are paid for screening mammography under the physician fee schedule. Diagnostic mammography is also reimbursed under the physician fee schedule. [Soc. Sec. Act §§ 1833(b), 1834(c)(2)(A), 1848(j)(3); 42 C.F.R. § 414.2; *Medicare Claims Processing Manual*, Pub. 100-04, Ch. 18, § 20.3.2.] A film and digital screening mammography, or film and digital diagnostic mammography, should not be billed together, as Medicare will not pay for both procedures when performed on the same patient. Diagnostic mammography and screening mammography can both be paid when performed on the same beneficiary on the same day if the diagnostic test is medically necessary and if the applicable periodicity requirement for the screening mammography is met. [Pub. 100-04, Ch. 18, § 20.3.2.2.]

Part B payment may not be made for screening or diagnostic mammography services unless they are conducted by a facility that holds a certificate of compliance or a provisional certificate issued by the Food and Drug Administration. The certification requirements for suppliers of diagnostic and screening mammography are set forth in § 354 of the Public Health Service Act and 21 C.F.R. Part 900, Subpart B. [42 C.F.R. § 410.34(c).]

Pap Smears and Pelvic Exams

Effective July 1, 2001, Medicare covers biennial screening pap smears and biennial screening pelvic examinations. More frequent pap smears or pelvic exams may be covered if the beneficiary meets certain criteria. The Part B deductible is waived for these exams. [42 C.F.R. § 410.56; Pub. 100-02, Ch. 15, § 280.4; Pub. 100-04, Ch. 18, § 40.]

Colorectal Cancer Screening Tests

Covered colorectal screening tests for prevention purposes include (1) an annual fecal-occult blood test for individuals age 50 and older; (2) flexible sigmoidoscopy every four years for individuals age 50 and older; (3) colonoscopy for high-risk individuals every two years and for other individuals every ten years; (4) screening barium enemas every four years for individuals age 50 and older who are not at high risk of developing colorectal cancer or every two years for individuals who are at high risk. [Soc. Sec. Act § 1834(d); 42 C.F.R. § 410.37; Pub. 100-02, Ch. 15, § 280.2.2.] Effective July 1, 2004, Medicare covers fecal-occult blood tests, flexible sigmoidoscopies, and colonoscopies furnished in skilled nursing facilities when used for colorectal cancer screenings. [Pub. 100-04, Transmittal No. 80, Feb. 6, 2004.]

Payment is made according to the applicable payment system for the test provider (for example, the physician fee schedule, the fee schedule for laboratories, the payment rate for ambulatory surgical center services, etc.). [Soc. Sec. Act § 1834(d).] In the case of flexible sigmoidoscopies and colonoscopies, the usual 20 percent Part B coinsurance is increased to 25 percent. [Soc. Sec. Act §§ 1834(d)(2)(C)(ii), 1834(d)(3)(C)(ii).]

Diabetes Self-Management Services

Medicare covers diabetes outpatient self-management educational and training services furnished by a certified provider who meets certain quality standards. This program is intended to educate beneficiaries in the successful self-management of diabetes. [Soc. Sec. Act § 1861(qq).] The program includes instructions in self-monitoring of blood glucose, education about diet and exercise, an insulin treatment plan developed specifically for the patient who is insulin-dependent, and motivation for patients to use these skills for self-management. [42 C.F.R. § 410.141(c); Pub. 100-02, Ch. 15, § 300.1.]

The doctor or qualified nonphysician practitioner who is managing the beneficiary's diabetic condition must certify that these services are needed. The services must be provided under a comprehensive plan of care to ensure therapy compliance or to provide the patient with the necessary skills and knowledge (including the skill to self-administer injectable drugs) to participate in the management of his or her own condition. Up to 10 hours of initial training and two hours of additional training are authorized. [Pub. 100-02, Ch. 15, §§ 300.1, 300.3.]

CMS has designated all providers and suppliers that bill Medicare for other individual services as "certified providers" for purposes of providing diabetes outpatient self-management training. This includes hospital outpatient departments, renal dialysis facilities, physicians, and durable medical equipment suppliers. Medicare will not reimburse diabetes self-management training services provided to an inpatient of a hospital or skilled nursing facility, an individual in hospice care, a resident in a nursing home, or an outpatient in a rural health clinic (RHC) or federally qualified health center (FQHC). Although separate payment is not made to RHCs and FQHCs for this service, the service is covered but is considered as included in the encounter rate. All certified providers must be accredited as meeting quality standards. Payment to providers is based on rates established under the physician fee schedule. [Pub. 100-02, Ch. 15, §§ 300.2, 300.4.]

Blood glucose monitors and blood-testing strips. Blood glucose monitors and blood-testing strips are covered for both Type I and Type II diabetes without regard to whether the patient uses insulin; however, prescription coverage for supplies, which must be renewed every six months, may or may not be dependent on whether the patient is using insulin. [*Program Memorandum*, No. B-99-32, Aug. 1, 1999.] Blood-testing strips and blood glucose monitors are covered as durable medical equipment (see ¶ 356). [Soc. Sec. Act §§ 1834(a)(2)(B), 1861(n).]

Only home glucose monitors are covered. Medicare does not pay for certain monitors, such as reflectance colorimeters, that are used in clinical settings. However, Medicare does pay for specialized glucose monitors, such as those adapted for home use by the visually impaired. [*Medicare National Coverage Determinations Manual*, Pub. 100-03, Ch. 1, § 40.2.]

Insulin. Generally, injectable and oral insulin are excluded from Part B coverage because they are customarily self-administered or administered by the patient's family. [Pub. 100-02, Ch. 7, § 40.1.2.4, and Ch. 12, § 40.10.] However, under the MMA, insulin and supplies associated with the administration of insulin will be covered under Part D.

Bone Mass Measurement Tests

Medicare covers bone mass measurement tests to identify bone mass, detect bone loss, or determine bone quality. Also included is the doctor's interpretation of the results of the tests. [42 C.F.R. § 410.31.]

Individuals to whom the coverage applies include (1) estrogen-deficient women at clinical risk for osteoporosis, (2) individuals with vertebral abnormalities, (3) individuals receiving long-term glucocorticoid steroid therapy, (4) individuals with primary hyperparathyroidism, and (5) individuals being monitored to assess the response to or efficacy of an approved osteoporosis drug therapy. [42 C.F.R. § 410.31.]

Bone mass measurement tests may be performed with either a bone densitometer (other than dual-photon absorptiometry) or a bone sonometer system. The test must be ordered by a physician (or a qualified nonphysician practitioner) after a need for the test has

¶369

been determined, and the test must include a physician's interpretation of the results. Tests normally may be performed no more often than biannually, although more frequent testing is allowed for patients who have special needs or conditions. [42 C.F.R. § 410.31.]

Prostate Cancer Screening Tests

Medicare covers annual prostate cancer screening tests for men over age 50. Tests covered include a digital rectal exam and a prostate-specific antigen (PSA) blood test. The tests may be performed (or in the case of the PSA blood test, ordered) by the patient's physician, physician assistant, nurse practitioner, clinical nurse specialist, or certified nurse-midwife. [42 C.F.R. § 410.39.]

The screening PSA test is not subject to the Part B deductible and coinsurance requirements. The deductible and coinsurance requirements apply to screening rectal examinations. [Pub. 100-04, Ch. 18, § 50.2.]

Screening Glaucoma Tests

Effective January 1, 2002, Medicare coverage is provided for annual screening glaucoma tests for individuals determined to be at high risk for glaucoma. High risk individuals include (1) individuals with diabetes mellitus; (2) individuals with a family history of glaucoma; and (3) African-Americans age 50 and over. [Soc. Sec. Act §§ 1861(s)(2)(U), 1861(uu); 42 C.F.R. §§ 410.23(a)(2), 410.23(c).]

Covered screening tests include (1) a dilated eye exam with an intraocular pressure measurement and (2) a direct ophthalmoscopy exam, or a slit-lamp biomicroscopic exam. Glaucoma screening examinations must be furnished by, or under the direct supervision of, an optometrist or opthalmologist. "Direct supervision" means the optometrist or opthalmologist must be present in the office suite and be immediately available to furnish assistance and direction throughout the performance of the procedure. [42 C.F.R. § 410.23.]

Medical Nutrition Therapy Services

Effective January 1, 2002, Medicare coverage is provided for medical nutrition therapy (MNT) services for beneficiaries with diabetes or a renal disease who (1) have not received diabetes outpatient maintenance self-management training services within a specified time period and (2) are not receiving maintenance dialysis benefits. Services covered include nutritional diagnostic, therapy, and counseling services for the purpose of disease management. The services must be provided by a registered dietitian or nutritional professional pursuant to a referral by the beneficiary's treating physician. Non-physician practitioners cannot make referrals for this service. [42 C.F.R. §§ 410.130-410.134.]

Effective October 1, 2002, basic coverage of MNT for the first year a beneficiary receives MNT is three hours, and basic coverage for subsequent years is two hours. Also effective October 1, 2002, if the beneficiary's treating physician determines that both MNT and diabetes self-management training are medically necessary in the same episode of care, Medicare will cover both services, without decreasing either benefit, *as long as* MNT and diabetes self-management training are not provided on the same date of service. Additional hours are covered if the treating physician determines that there is a change in medical condition, diagnosis, or treatment regimen that requires a change in MNT, and orders additional hours during that episode of care. [*Medicare National Coverage Determinations Manual*, Pub. 100-03, Ch. 1, § 180.1.]

Payment is based on the lower of actual charges or 85 percent of the physician fee schedule on an assignment-related basis. [42 C.F.R. § 414.64.]

¶369

[¶ 370] Therapeutic Shoes

Therapeutic shoes and inserts are covered for beneficiaries with severe diabetic foot disease. Diabetic shoes are not considered durable medical equipment nor orthotics; instead, they are a separate category of coverage under Medicare Part B. [Soc. Sec. Act § 1861(s)(12); *Medicare Benefit Policy Manual*, Pub. 100-02, Ch. 15, § 140.]

The need for diabetic shoes must be certified by a physician who is responsible for treating the beneficiary's diabetes. The footwear must be fitted and furnished by a podiatrist or other qualified individual such as a pedorthist, orthotist, or prosthetist. The certifying physician may not furnish the therapeutic shoes unless the physician is the only qualified individual in the area. [Pub. 100-02, Ch. 15, §§ 140C, 140D.]

Coverage is limited to one of the following within a calendar year: (1) one pair of custom-molded shoes (including inserts provided with such shoes) and two additional pairs of inserts, or (2) one pair of depth shoes (not including the noncustomized inserts provided with such shoes) and three pairs of inserts. Inserts may be covered and dispensed independently of diabetic shoes if the supplier of the shoes verifies in writing that the patient has appropriate footwear into which the insert can be placed. An individual may substitute modifications of custom-molded or depth shoes instead of obtaining a pair of inserts. Payment for the modification may not exceed the limit set for the inserts to which the beneficiary is entitled. [Pub. 100-02, Ch. 15, § 140B.]

Orthopedic shoes generally are not covered. However, this exclusion does not apply to orthopedic shoes that are an integral part of a leg brace. When an individual qualifies for both diabetic shoes and a leg brace, those items are covered separately. The brace may be covered when furnished incident to physicians' services or on a physician's order. A brace includes rigid and semi-rigid devices. Elastic stockings, garter belts, and similar devices do not come within the scope of the definition of a brace. [Pub. 100-02, Ch. 15, § 140B.]

Payment is made on a reasonable charge basis, subject to upper limits established by the Medicare program. The payment limits are updated annually by the same percentage increase that applies to payments for durable medical equipment. [Soc. Sec. Act § 1833(o).]

Under the Medicare Modernization Act of 2003 (PubLNo 108-173), beginning in 2005, payments for diabetic shoes and inserts will be limited to the amount that would be paid if they were considered a prosthetic or orthotic device. In addition, the Secretary must establish a payment amount for individuals substituting modifications to covered shoes that would assure there is no net increase in Medicare expenditures. [Soc. Sec. Act § 1833(o).]

[¶ 381] Physical, Occupational, and Speech Therapy Services

The Part B program covers physical, occupational, and speech therapy services. The coverage and payment rules for outpatient physical, occupational, and speech therapy are essentially the same. The only significant difference is that speech therapy may not be performed by a therapist in independent practice. The following discussion refers to physical, occupational, and speech therapy services collectively as "therapy" services. Part B includes the following types of therapy services [42 C.F.R. §§ 410.59, 410.60, 410.62]:

(1) *outpatient* therapy services furnished by (or under arrangements with) a participating provider of services, clinic, rehabilitation agency, or public health agency;

(2) therapy *in the therapist's office or the patient's home*, in the case of a qualified physical or occupational therapist in independent practice; and

(3) *inpatient* therapy services furnished by (or under arrangements with) a participating provider of services, clinic, rehabilitation agency, or public health agency to an inpatient of a hospital or skilled nursing facility.

In order for therapy services to be covered, the patient must be under the care of a physician, a plan of treatment must be developed by either the physician or the therapist, and the plan must be reviewed periodically by the physician. Any item or service that would be excluded as an inpatient hospital benefit also would be excluded as a therapy benefit. [42 C.F.R. §§ 410.59, 410.60, 410.61.]

Physical, occupational, and speech therapy services also can be covered under Part B as incident to physician services (¶ 351) or as comprehensive outpatient rehabilitation facility services (see ¶ 385).

Services furnished under arrangements. A provider or clinic may have others furnish outpatient therapy services under arrangements. However, it is not intended that the provider or clinic merely serve as a billing mechanism for the other party. For such services to be covered, the provider or clinic must assume professional responsibility for the services. The provider's or clinic's professional supervision over the services requires applying many of the same controls that are applied to services furnished by salaried employees. [*Medicare Benefit Policy Manual*, Pub. 100-02, Ch. 15, § 220.1.]

"Therapy Services" Defined

To be covered by Medicare, physical therapy, occupational therapy, or speech-language pathology services must relate directly and specifically to an active written treatment regimen established by the beneficiary's physician or nonphysician practitioner after any needed consultation with the qualified therapist, and the services must be reasonable and necessary to treat the individual's illness or injury. The physician, nonphysician practitioner, or the qualified physical therapist providing such services may establish a treatment plan for outpatient therapy services. Services related to activities for the general good and welfare of patients, such as general exercises to promote overall fitness and flexibility, do not constitute therapy services for Medicare purposes. For physical therapy, occupational therapy, or speech-language pathology services to be considered reasonable and necessary, the following conditions must be met [Pub. 100-02, Ch. 15, § 230]:

(1) the services must be considered, under accepted standards of medical practice, to be a specific and effective treatment for the patient's condition;

(2) the services must be of such a level of complexity and sophistication, or the condition of the patient must be such, that the services required can be performed safely and effectively only by a qualified therapist or under a therapist's supervision;

Speech-language pathology services must meet the following additional conditions to be considered reasonable and necessary [Pub. 100-02, Ch. 15, § 230.3]:

(1) the services must be provided with the expectation that the patient's condition will improve significantly in a reasonable, and generally predictable, period of time, or the services must be necessary to the establishment of a safe and effective maintenance program required in connection with a specific disease state;

(2) the amount, frequency, and duration of services must be reasonable.

Restorative therapy. If the patient's expected restoration potential would be insignificant in relation to the extent and duration of speech language pathology services required to achieve this potential, the therapy will not be considered reasonable and necessary. In addition, there must be an expectation that the patient's condition will improve significantly in a reasonable (and generally predictable) period of time. However, if at any point in the treatment of an illness or injury it is determined that the expectations will not materialize, the services will no longer be considered reasonable and necessary. [Pub. 100-02, Ch. 15, §§ 230.3C, 230.4B.]

¶381

If a valid expectation of improvement exists at the time the occupational therapy program is instituted, the services would be covered even though the expectation may not be realized. However, in such situations the services would be covered only up to the time at which it would have been reasonable to conclude that the patient is not going to improve. Once a patient has reached the point where no further significant practical improvement can be expected, the skills of an occupational therapist will not be required in the carrying out of any activity and/or exercise program required to maintain function at the level to which it has been restored. Consequently, while the services of an occupational therapist in designing a maintenance program and making infrequent but periodic evaluation of its effectiveness would be covered, carrying out the program is not considered reasonable and necessary for the treatment of illness or injury and such services are not covered. [Pub. 100-02, Ch. 15, § 230.4B.]

Maintenance therapy. The repetitive services required to maintain function generally do not involve the use of complex and sophisticated therapy procedures and, consequently, the judgment and skill of a qualified therapist are not usually required for safety and effectiveness.

However, in certain instances, the specialized knowledge and judgment of a qualified speech language pathologist or occupational therapist may be required to establish a maintenance program if the treatment aims of the physician are to be achieved. For example, a multiple sclerosis patient may require the services of a speech-language pathologist to establish a maintenance program designed to fit the patient's level of function. In such a situation, the initial evaluation of the patient's needs, the designing by the qualified speech-language pathologist of a maintenance program that is appropriate to the capacity and tolerance of the patient and the treatment objectives of the physician, the instruction of the patient or family members in carrying out the program, and such infrequent reevaluations as may be required, would constitute covered speech therapy. After the maintenance program has been established and instructions have been given for carrying out the program, the services of the speech-language pathologist would no longer be covered, as they would no longer be considered reasonable and necessary for the treatment of the patient's condition. [Pub. 100-02, Ch. 15, § § 230.3C, 230.4B.]

Therapy provided by physicians and physician employees. For outpatient therapy services provided by physicians, qualified nonphysician practitioners, and employees providing services incident to practitioner services, the services must be provided by, or under the direct supervision of, a physician and the services must be of a level of complexity that requires physician performance or direct physician supervision. [Pub. 100-02, Ch. 15, § 220.2.]

Independently Practicing Therapists

Physical and occupational therapy (but not speech pathology) also are covered when provided by a therapist in private practice, when furnished by the therapist, or under the therapist's direct supervision, in the office or in the patient's home. Services furnished by a therapist in the therapist's office under arrangements with hospitals in rural communities and public health agencies, or furnished in the beneficiary's home under arrangements with a provider of outpatient therapy services, are not covered under this provision. [42 C.F.R. § § 410.59(c), 410.60(c); Pub. 100-02, Ch. 15, § 230.1.]

A qualified physical or occupational therapist is considered to be in private practice if the therapist (1) is legally authorized to engage in the private practice of occupational or physical therapy by the state in which he or she practices; (2) engages in the private practice of occupational or physical therapy on a regular basis as an individual; (3) bills Medicare only for services furnished in his or her private practice office space, which is owned, leased, or rented by the practice and used for the exclusive purpose of operating the practice, or in the patient's home; (3) treats his or her own patients, for whom the practice collects fees for the services furnished. [42 C.F.R. §§ 410.59(c), 410.60(c); Pub. 100-02, Ch. 15, § 230.1.]

While the therapist need not be in full-time private practice, the therapist must be engaged in private practice on a regular basis, *i.e.*, recognized as a private practitioner who has access to the necessary equipment to provide an adequate program of therapy. [Pub. 100-02, Ch. 15, § 230.1C.]

The services must be furnished either by, or under the direct supervision of, the therapist, and the services of support personnel must be included in the therapist's bill. The supporting personnel, including other therapists, must be employees of the independently practicing therapist. [Pub. 100-02, Ch. 15, § 230.1F.]

Clinic or Rehabilitation Agency Standards

A physical therapy clinic or agency must (1) provide an adequate program of physical therapy services for outpatients and have the facilities and personnel required for the supervision of such a program and (2) have policies established by a group of professional personnel, including one or more physicians (associated with the clinic or rehabilitation agency) and one or more qualified physical therapists, to govern the physical therapy services. A public health agency need only satisfy the Secretary that it has adequate health and safety standards in order to qualify for outpatient physical therapy payments. The Secretary has the authority to demand a surety bond of up to at least $50,000 from an outpatient therapy provider. [Soc. Sec. Act § 1861(p)(4).]

Outpatient rehabilitation services must be provided pursuant to a written plan of treatment established by a physician, a therapist, or other qualified health practitioner. The plan must prescribe the type, amount, frequency, and duration of the services provided and indicate the diagnosis and anticipated goals. [42 C.F.R. § 410.61.]

The conditions of participation for rehabilitation agencies, clinics, and public health agencies are contained in Subpart H of Part 485 of the Medicare regulations (42 C.F.R. Part 485).

Payment Methodology and the Annual Payment Limit

Reimbursement for therapy provided to Part A inpatients of hospitals or skilled nursing facilities (SNFs) is included in the prospective payment system (PPS) rate. Reimbursement for therapy provided by home health agencies under a home health plan of care is included in the home health PPS rate. The Medicare physician fee schedule is the method of payment for outpatient therapy services furnished by comprehensive outpatient rehabilitation facilities (CORFs), outpatient physical therapy providers (OPTs), other rehabilitation facilities, physical and occupational therapists in private practice, physicians, and certain nonphysician practitioners. Outpatient therapy services also are paid under the physician fee schedule when rendered by hospitals to outpatients and to inpatients not in a covered Part A stay, by SNFs to residents not in a covered Part A stay and to nonresidents who receive outpatient therapy services from the SNF, and by home health agencies for individuals who are not homebound or otherwise are not receiving services under a home health plan of care. Outpatient therapy services furnished by critical access hospitals are paid on a reasonable cost basis. [Pub. 100-02, Ch. 15, § 220; *Medicare Claims Processing Manual*, Pub. 100-04, Ch. 5, § 10.]

Annual payment limit. Therapy caps have been reinstated on outpatient physical therapy, speech language pathology services, and occupational therapy services under Medicare Part B beginning January 1, 2006. The dollar amount for the therapy caps in calendar year

2006 is $1,740. Physical therapy services that are performed by chiropractors under the two-year demonstration project provided for in the MMA, are included under the therapy cap because chiropractors are subject to the same rules as medical doctors for therapy services under the demonstration. [*Final rule*, 70 FR 70266, Nov. 21, 2005.]

Previously, the Balanced Budget Act of 1997 (BBA) (PubLNo 105-33) imposed annual payment limits on outpatient therapy services provided on or after January 1, 1999. The limit was an annual per beneficiary cap of $1,500 on all outpatient physical therapy services (including speech-language pathology services). A separate $1,500 limit was applied to occupational therapy services. The limits are adjusted annually for inflation. The limits do not apply to services furnished directly or under arrangement by a hospital to an outpatient or to an inpatient who is not in a covered Part A stay. [Soc. Sec. Act § 1833(g); 42 C.F.R. § § 410.59(e), 410.60(c).]

The payment limits on therapy services were suspended by Congress for a three-year period, from January 1, 2000 through December 31, 2002. There was no moratorium on therapy payment limits during 2003, but due to a delay in implementation, the payment limits only went into effect beginning on September 1, 2003. Section 624 of the Medicare Modernization Act of 2003 (PubLNo 108-173) imposes another moratorium on implementation of the caps, from December 8, 2003 through December 31, 2005. The payment limits did not apply to claims received from December 8, 2003 through December 31, 2005. For claims received when the limits were in effect (from September 1 through December 7, 2003), the inflation-adjusted limit for outpatient physical therapy and speech-language pathology was $1,590, and the limit for occupational therapy was $1,590. [Soc. Sec. Act § 1833(g); Pub. 100-04, Ch. 5, § 10.2.]

[¶ 382] Rural Health Clinics and Federally Qualified Health Centers

Part B covers rural health clinic (RHC) and federally qualified health center (FQHC) services in medically underserved localities. [Soc. Sec. Act § § 1832(a)(2)(D), 1861(aa).]

RHC and FQHC services reimbursable under Part B include [42 C.F.R. § § 405.2411, 405.2446, 410.45; *Medicare Benefit Policy Manual*, Pub. 100-2, Ch. 13, § 30.1.]:

(1) physicians' services, and services and supplies incident to a physician's services;

(2) similar services furnished by a physician assistant, nurse practitioner, clinical nurse specialist, clinical psychologist, or clinical social worker, and services and supplies incident to their services;

(3) visiting nurse services furnished to homebound patients in areas where there is a shortage of home health agencies;

(4) services of registered dietitians or nutritional professionals for diabetes training services and medical nutrition therapy; and

(5) otherwise covered drugs furnished by, and incident to, services of physicians and nonphysician practitioners.

In addition to the services listed above, Medicare covers certain preventive primary services furnished by FQHCs, including physical examinations, visual acuity screening, hearing screening, cholesterol screening, and blood pressure measurement. Preventive primary services furnished by FQHCs do *not* include group or mass information programs, health education classes, group education activities, eyeglasses, hearing aids, or preventive dental services. Screening mammography is not considered an FQHC service, but may be provided at an FQHC if the center meets the applicable regulatory requirements. [42 C.F.R. § 405.2448.]

RHC and FQHC services are reimbursable when furnished to a patient at the clinic or center, at a hospital or other medical facility, the patient's place of residence, or elsewhere such as the scene of an accident. [42 C.F.R. §§ 405.2411(b), 405.2446(c); Pub. 100-2, Ch. 13, §§ 30.1, 30.2.]

A clinic certified as an RHC or FQHC may furnish services beyond the scope of the services covered under the RHC or FQHC benefit. If covered under another separate Medicare benefit category, the services must be separately billed to the Medicare carrier or intermediary (as appropriate) under the proper benefit category. Items and services that are *not* RHC/FQHC services include certain laboratory services that RHCs are required to furnish; durable medical equipment; prosthetic devices; leg, arm, back, and neck braces and artificial legs, arms, and eyes; ambulance services; technical components of diagnostic tests; and the technical component of various preventive services such as screening pap smears and pelvic exams, prostate cancer screening, colorectal cancer screening, and screening mammography. [Pub. 100-2, Ch. 13, § 30.3.]

RHCs and FQHCs are paid by means of an "all-inclusive rate" per beneficiary visit (except for pneumococcal and influenza vaccines and their administration, which are paid at 100 percent of reasonable cost). The payment rate includes covered services provided by an RHC/FQHC physician or non-physician practitioner and related services and supplies. The rate is paid, subject to the Part B deductible and coinsurance requirements, for each covered visit with a Medicare beneficiary. No deductible, however, applies to FQHC services. [42 C.F.R. §§ 405.2462, 405.2410; *Medicare Claims Processing Manual*, Pub. 100-4, Ch. 9, §§ 20-20.4.]

The RHC/FQHC payment rate is subject to a per-visit upper limit that is adjusted annually for inflation. RHCs based in hospitals with less than 50 beds are eligible for an exception to the payment limit. This exception to the payment limit does not apply to provider-based FQHCs. Similarly, there is no exception for independent RHCs or FQHCs. [42 C.F.R. §§ 405.2462; Pub. 100-4, Ch. 9, § 20.6.3.]

As discussed at ¶ 607, services paid for directly or indirectly by a governmental entity usually are excluded from coverage under the Medicare program. The law, however, makes a specific exception to this exclusion in the case of RHC and FQHC services. [Soc. Sec. Act § 1862(a)(3).]

[¶ 383] Home Health Services

The scope of the home health services benefit changed, effective January 1, 1998. Formerly, home health services were provided primarily under Part A, and coverage was for an unlimited number of visits, without a deductible or coinsurance (except in the case of durable medical equipment furnished by a home health agency). Part B coverage was available only in those rare instances when Part A coverage was not available.

Congress transferred most home health services from Part A to Part B for those beneficiaries who are enrolled in both programs (beneficiaries enrolled in Part A only or Part B only experienced no change in benefits). The transfer involved the following services for beneficiaries enrolled in both Part A and Part B [Soc. Sec. Act § 1812(a)(3); *Medicare Benefit Policy Manual*, Pub. 100-02, Ch. 7, §§ 60.1, 60.2]:

(1) If the beneficiary uses more than 100 home health visits during a "post-institutional spell of illness" that began with a hospital or skilled nursing facility stay, the additional visits used are paid for under Part B instead of Part A.

(2) If the beneficiary uses any home health visits during a period that is not a "post-institutional spell of illness," all the visits are paid for under Part B instead of Part A.

Home health services are considered "post-institutional" if they were furnished to a beneficiary (1) after discharge from a hospital in which the individual was an inpatient for not less than three consecutive days before discharge and the services are initiated within 14 days of discharge, or (2) after discharge from a skilled nursing facility in which the beneficiary was provided post-hospital extended care services and services are initiated within 14 days after discharge. [Pub. 100-02, Ch. 7, § 60.1.]

A "spell of illness" in the case of home health services furnished under Part B means a period of consecutive days beginning with the first day that the individual is furnished post-institutional home health services and that occurs in a month for which the individual is entitled to benefits under Part A. The home health spell of illness ends when the individual has not received inpatient hospital, skilled nursing facility, or home health services for 60 consecutive days. [Pub. 100-02, Ch. 7, § 60.1.]

The effect of this partial transfer of responsibilities from Part A to Part B is that Part B premiums, which are statutorily set at 25 percent of program expenses (see ¶ 320), have been raised to reflect the additional coverage responsibilities. The required premium increases were phased in over a six-year period beginning in 1998. [§ 4611(e) of the Balanced Budget Act (PubLNo 105-33).]

To qualify for home health benefits, a beneficiary must meet the following requirements: be confined to the home; under a physician's care; receiving services under a plan of care established and periodically reviewed by a physician; be in need of skilled nursing care on an intermittent basis, or physical therapy or speech pathology services; or have a continued need for occupational therapy. [Pub. 100-02, Ch. 7, § 30.]

Part A home health benefits are discussed beginning at ¶ 250. Concerning the coverage of services rendered to certain homebound patients when provided by employees of a physician or clinic, or when performed by a rural health clinic, see ¶ 351 and ¶ 382, respectively.

[¶ 385] Comprehensive Outpatient Rehabilitation Facility Services

A "comprehensive outpatient rehabilitation facility" (CORF) is a public or private institution that is capable of providing a broad array of rehabilitation services on an outpatient basis at a central location in a coordinated fashion. The CORF must provide a comprehensive, coordinated, skilled rehabilitation program for its patients that includes, at a minimum, physicians' services, physical therapy services, and social psychological services. Covered items and services include: (1) physicians' services; (2) physical, occupational, and respiratory therapy and speech-language pathology services; (3) prosthetic and orthotic devices, including testing, fitting, or training in the use of such devices; (4) social and psychological services; (5) nursing care provided by or under the supervision of a registered professional nurse; (6) drugs and biologicals that are administered by or under the supervision of a physician or registered nurse, and are not usually self-administered by the patient; (7) supplies and durable medical equipment; and (8) other items and services that are medically necessary for the rehabilitation of the patient and ordinarily are furnished by CORFs (for example, home environment evaluation visits). Any service that would not be covered if furnished to a hospital inpatient also is excluded from coverage as a CORF service. [42 C.F.R. §§ 410.100, 410.102; *Medicare Benefit Policy Manual*, Pub. 100-2, Ch. 12, §§ 10, 20.1, 20.2, 40.]

As a general rule, services must be furnished on the premises of the CORF. Physical therapy, occupational therapy, speech pathology services, and a home environment evaluation may be furnished away from the premises of the CORF. [42 C.F.R. § 410.105(b).]

Certain administrative services provided by physicians associated with a CORF are considered CORF services and are paid to the CORF. These services include administrative services provided by the physician associated with the CORF, consultation with and medical supervision of nonphysician staff, team conferences, case reviews, and other facility medical and administration activities relating to the comprehensive coordinated skilled rehabilitation service. [Pub. 100-2, Ch. 12, § 40.1.]

Physicians' diagnostic and therapeutic services furnished to an individual patient are not CORF physicians' services. The physician must bill the Part B carrier for these services, and payment is based on the Medicare physician fee schedule. [Pub. 100-2, Ch. 12, § 40.1.]

CORF services are subject to the same annual payment limitation rules applicable to other therapy and rehabilitation services (see ¶ 381).

Note that Part B also covers rehabilitation services in a variety of other settings under various other coverage provisions (see ¶ 350). In addition, rehabilitation services are included among the services that may be covered as "incident to" the services of a physician (¶ 351). Coverage of rehabilitation services under Part A is described at ¶ 214.

CORF services are paid under a special prospective payment system. The Medicare physician fee schedule constitutes the prospective payment system for these services, effective January 1, 1999. [Soc. Sec. Act § 1834(k); *Medicare Claims Processing Manual*, Pub. 100-4, Ch. 5, § 10.]

The conditions of participation applicable to CORFs are contained in 42 C.F.R. Chapter IV (Subchapter E, Part 485, Subpart B) of the regulations.

[¶ 386] Ambulatory Surgical Services

There are a number of surgical procedures that Medicare has identified that are sometimes performed on an inpatient basis but may, consistent with sound medical practice, be performed on an outpatient basis for far less cost. These surgical procedures are covered by Medicare when performed in an ambulatory surgical center (ASC) or in a hospital outpatient department. When performed in a hospital outpatient department, ambulatory surgical services are reimbursed under the outpatient prospective payment system or other applicable outpatient payment rules.

An ASC is a distinct entity that operates exclusively for the purpose of furnishing outpatient surgical services, has entered into an agreement with CMS to participate in Medicare as an ASC, and meets the conditions of participation set forth in 42 C.F.R. §§ 416.40-416.49. [42 C.F.R. § 416.2.] An ASC is either independent (that is, not part of a provider of services or any other facility), or operated by a hospital under the common ownership, licensure or control of a hospital). If a hospital-based outpatient surgery center is certified as an ASC, it is subject to the Medicare rules for ASCs. If a hospital-based outpatient surgery center is not certified as an ASC, it continues to operate under the Medicare program as part of the hospital, and the applicable outpatient payment rules apply (the outpatient prospective payment system (OPPS) for most hospitals, or other provisions for hospitals excluded from OPPS). To be covered as an ASC operated by a hospital, a facility must: (1) elect to be covered as an ASC; (2) constitute a separately identifiable entity that is physically, administratively, and financially independent and distinct from the hospital's other operations, with costs for the ASC treated as a non-reimbursable cost center on the hospital's cost report; (3) meet all health and safety requirements, and agree to the assignment, coverage, and payment rules that apply to independent ASCs; and (4) be surveyed and approved as complying with the ASC conditions of coverage at 42 C.F.R. §§ 416.40–416.49. [*Medicare Benefit Policy Manual*, Pub. 100-02, Ch. 15, § 260.1; *Medicare Claims Processing Manual*, Pub. 100-04, Ch. 14, § 10.1.]

Covered ASC Services

Generally, there are two elements in the total charge for a covered surgical procedure—a charge for the facility services (such as use of an operating room) and a charge for the physician's professional services for performing the procedure.

ASC "facility" services are those services furnished in an ASC in connection with a covered surgical procedure that otherwise would be covered under Medicare if furnished on an inpatient or outpatient basis in a hospital in connection with that procedure. ASC facility services include, but are not limited to:

(1) nursing, technician, and related services;

(2) use by the patient of the ASC's facilities;

(3) drugs, biologicals, surgical dressings, supplies, splints, casts, and appliances and equipment directly related to the provision of surgical procedures;

(4) diagnostic or therapeutic services or items directly related to the provision of a surgical procedure;

(5) administrative, recordkeeping, and housekeeping items and services;

(6) materials for anesthesia;

(7) intra-ocular lenses (IOLs); and

(8) blood or blood products, except those to which the blood deductible applies.

[42 C.F.R. § 416.61(b); Pub. 100-02, Ch. 15, §§ 260.3, 260.4.]

Excluded from facility services are items and services for which payment can be made under other Medicare provisions. Items and services excluded from ASC facility reimbursement include: physicians' services; laboratory, X-ray, or diagnostic procedures (other than certain simple tests that are included in the ASC's facility charges); prosthetic devices (except IOLs); ambulance services; leg, arm, back, and neck braces; artificial limbs; durable medical equipment for use in the patient's home; and anesthetist services. [42 C.F.R. § 416.61(b).]

The list of ASC-covered procedures is published periodically in the *Federal Register* and on the CMS website. CMS issues a public use file for ASCs each year to update the list of procedures for which an ASC may be paid. This file can be obtained at http://www.cms.hhs.gov/ASCPayment. The list of Medicare-covered ASC procedures was updated, effective for services furnished on or after July 5, 2005, and corrected on June 24, 2005. [*Final rule*, 70 FR 23690, May 4, 2005, and *Final rule, correction* 70 FR 36533, June 24, 2005.] Additions and deletions to the list, effective January 1, 2006, were published in a CMS manual transmittal in October 2005. [*Medicare Claims Processing Manual*, Pub. 100-04, Transmittal No. 720, Oct. 21, 2005.]

Payment for Facility Services

To receive the ASC facility fee for a surgical procedure, that procedure must be on the list of Medicare-covered ASC procedures. Each covered service is assigned to a payment group. Each group has a specified payment rate that applies to all services assigned to that group. These payment rates are normally updated annually to account for inflation. Under § 626 of the Medicare Modernization Act of 2003 (PubLNo 108-173) (MMA), for fiscal year (FY) 2004 (starting April 1, 2004), the inflation update for ASC payment rates was the consumer price index for all urban consumers (CPI-U) minus 3 percentage points. In FY 2005, the last quarter of calendar year 2005, and calendar years 2006 through 2009, the inflation update is zero percent. [Soc. Sec. Act § 1833(i)(2).] The ASC payment rate must be set so as to insure that the amount paid to an ASC will be substantially less than would have been paid if the procedure had been performed on an inpatient basis. [42 C.F.R. § 416.125.]

Current ASC payment rates and wage index values remain in effect for FY 2006. The MMA mandated a zero percent increase for inflation in each calendar year from 2006 through 2009, until CMS determines the impact of changes in the FY 2006 inpatient hospital wage index on payment amounts for individual ASC's. For services furnished on or after October 1, 2005, carriers should continue using the FY 2004 hospital inpatient wage index to calculate payments to ASC's and the payment rates that were effective for services furnished after April 1, 2004. , The ASC payment rates for FY 2006 will remain as follows [*Medicare Claims Processing Manual*, Pub. 100-04, Transmittal No. 690, Sept. 30, 2005].

Group 1—$333	Group 5—$717
Group 2—$446	Group 6—$826
Group 3—$510	Group 7—$995
Group 4—$630	Group 8—$973
	Group 9—$1,339

To make these payment rates applicable to the area in which an ASC is located, individual ASC payment amounts must be calculated using the appropriate wage index values. [Pub. 100-04, Ch. 14, § 40.2.]

Payment groups 6 and 8 include a $150 allowance for intra-ocular lenses. IOLs classified as "new technology IOLs" are normally accorded a $200 allowance. [42 C.F.R. § 416.185(f).]

Ambulatory surgical services performed in hospital outpatient departments are reimbursed under the outpatient prospective payment system or other applicable outpatient payment rules for hospitals excluded from OPPS. [Pub. 100-02, Ch. 15, § 260.1.]

Under the MMA, the General Accounting Office (GAO) must conduct a study on the applicability of the hospital outpatient prospective payment system to payment for services furnished in ASCs. CMS is required to implement a revised payment system for ASC surgical services, taking into account GAO's recommendations. The revised payment system is to take effect on or after January 1, 2006 and no later than January 1, 2008. [Soc. Sec. Act § 1833(i)(2)(D).]

[¶ 387] Mental Health Services

Part B pays 62½ percent of covered expenses incurred in a calendar year in connection with the treatment of mental, psychoneurotic, and personality disorders of a person who is not a hospital inpatient. This limitation is called the outpatient mental health treatment limitation. Because the Part B deductible also applies, Medicare pays for about half of the allowed amount recognized for mental health therapy services. Expenses for diagnostic services (such as psychiatric testing and evaluation to diagnose the patient's illness) are not subject to this limitation. The limitation applies only to therapeutic services and to services performed to evaluate the progress of a course of treatment for a diagnosed condition. If treatment services are rendered for both a psychiatric condition and other nonpsychiatric conditions, the charges are separated to apply the limitation only to the mental health charge. [*Medicare General Information, Eligibility, and Entitlement Manual*, Pub. 100-01, Ch. 3, § 30.]

This 62½ percent payment limitation applies to mental health services furnished to an individual who is not a hospital inpatient. Thus, the limitation applies to mental health services furnished in a physician's office, in the patient's home, in a skilled nursing facility, etc. [Pub. 100-1, Chapter 3 § 30.1.] It also applies to services furnished by a comprehensive outpatient rehabilitation facility (CORF) (see ¶ 385). [42 C.F.R. § 410.155(b)(1).]

The limitation does not apply to (1) services furnished to hospital inpatients, (2) brief office visits used to monitor or change drug prescriptions for mentally ill patients, (3) partial hospitalization services not directly provided by a physician, (4) psychological testing and other diagnostic testing performed to establish a diagnosis, and (5) medical management services provided to a patient diagnosed with Alzheimer's disease or a related disorder. [Soc. Sec. Act § 1833(c); 42 C.F.R. § 410.155(b)(2).]

The 62½ percent limitation is subject to Part B deductible and coinsurance requirements (see ¶ 335). For example, if a beneficiary submits a bill of $1,000 to Medicare for Part B mental illness treatments, Medicare will treat only $625 of that amount as "incurred expenses." Medicare then will pay 80 percent of this amount, that is, $500, assuming the Part B deductible already has been paid. [42 C.F.R. § 410.155.]

Partial Hospitalization Coverage

Medicare also covers partial hospitalization services connected with the treatment of mental illness. Partial hospitalization services are covered only if the individual otherwise would require inpatient psychiatric care. The treatment program of partial hospitalization programs closely resembles that of a highly structured, short-term hospital inpatient program. [Soc. Sec. Act §§ 1833(c), 1835(a)(2)(F), 1861(s)(2)(B); *Medicare Benefit Policy Manual*, Pub. 100-02, Ch. 6, § 70.3.]

Under this benefit, Medicare covers: (1) individual and group therapy with physicians or psychologists (or other authorized mental health professionals); (2) occupational therapy; (3) services of social workers, trained psychiatric nurses, and other staff trained to work with psychiatric patients; (4) drugs and biologicals furnished for therapeutic purposes that cannot be self-administered; (5) individualized activity therapies that are not primarily recreational or diversionary; (6) family counseling (for treatment of the patient's condition), (7) patient training and education; and (8) diagnostic services. Meals and transportation are excluded specifically from coverage. Programs involving primarily social, recreational, or diversionary activities are not considered partial hospitalization. [Soc. Sec. Act § 1861(ff)(2); 42 C.F.R. § 410.43; Pub. 100-02, Ch. 6, § 70.3.]

The services must be reasonable and necessary for the diagnosis or active treatment of the individual's condition. They also must be reasonably expected to improve or maintain the individual's condition and functional level and to prevent relapse or hospitalization. The course of treatment must be prescribed, supervised, and reviewed by a physician. The program must be hospital-based or hospital-affiliated and must be a distinct and organized intensive ambulatory treatment service offering less than 24-hour-daily care. The program is also covered when provided in a community health center (see ¶ 382). [Soc. Sec. Act § 1861(ff); 42 C.F.R. § 410.43; Pub. 100-02, Ch. 6, § 70.3.]

[¶ 388] Telehealth Services

Effective October 1, 2001, Medicare covers professional consultations, office and other outpatient visits, individual psychotherapy, and pharmacologic management delivered via a telecommunications system. Effective March 1, 2003, the psychiatric diagnostic interview examination was added to the list of Medicare telehealth services. [Soc. Sec. Act § 1834(m)(1); *Medicare Benefit Policy Manual*, Pub. 100-02, Ch. 15, §§ 270, 270.2.] End stage renal disease-related services with two or more visits a month also was added to the list of Medicare telehealth services. [*Final rule*, 69 FR 66235, Nov. 15, 2004.]

An interactive telecommunications system is required as a condition of payment. An interactive telecommunications system must include, at a minimum, audio and video equipment permitting two-way, real-time interactive communication between the patient and the distant site physician or practitioner. Telephones, facsimile machines, and electronic mail systems do not meet the definition of an interactive telecommunications system. However, asynchronous "store and forward" technology can be used to deliver telehealth services when the originating site is a federal telemedicine demonstration program in Alaska or Hawaii. [Soc. Sec. Act § 1834(m)(1); 42 C.F.R. § 410.78; Pub. 100-02, Ch. 15, § § 270, 270.3.]

The originating site (for example, the location of the beneficiary at the time the telehealth service is furnished) can be a physician or practitioner's office, a critical access hospital, a rural health clinic, a federally qualified health center, or a hospital. The originating site must be located in either a rural health professional shortage area or in a county that is not included in a metropolitan statistical area. Federal telemedicine demonstration projects in operation as of December 31, 2000, may serve as the originating site regardless of geographic location. A "telepresenter" (a physician or practitioner who presents the patient at the originating site) is not required unless the distant site physician or practitioner determines that a telepresenter is medically necessary. BIPA expanded Medicare payment to include a $20 facility fee for the originating site. The facility fee is adjusted annually for inflation. [Soc. Sec. Act § 1834(m)(4)(C)(ii); 42 C.F.R. § 410.78; *Medicare Benefit Policy Manual*, Pub. 100-02, Ch. 15, § § 270, 270.1, 270.5.]

The physician or practitioner at the distant site must be licensed to provide the service under state law. Medicare covers telehealth services furnished by physicians, physician assistants, nurse practitioners, clinical nurse specialists, nurse-midwives, clinical psychologists, and clinical social workers. BIPA specified that payment for the professional service performed by the distant site physician or practitioner is equal to what would have been paid without the use of telemedicine. Medicare will not pay for medical evaluation and management services furnished by clinical psychologists and clinical social workers via a telecommunications system. [Soc. Sec. Act § 1834(m)(1); 42 C.F.R. § 410.78; Pub. 100-02, Ch. 15, § 270.4.]

[¶ 390] National and Local Coverage Decisions

The Medicare program expands the services available as new treatments and services become accepted. To the extent a specific item or service is not mentioned in the law, the Secretary of HHS has authority to make coverage decisions within a broad range of categories. Items and services that are not specifically excluded from coverage must be determined by the Secretary to be reasonable and necessary for the diagnosis and treatment of illnesses and injuries, or to improve the functioning of a malformed body member. HHS decisions whether Medicare will cover new services are issued as national coverage determinations (NCDs) [Soc. Sec. Act § 1862(l).]

In an effort to make the process of NCD development more efficient and to ensure improved public access to all relevant information, effective October 27, 2003, CMS revised its NCD process. The changes include: (1) a tracking system that provides public notice of acceptance of a complete, formal request and subsequent actions in a web-based format; (2) a process to allow notice and opportunity to comment before implementation of an NCD; (3) standardization of the information required to complete a formal request; (4) a process for asking CMS to reconsider an existing NCD based on new information, including new medical or scientific evidence; and (5) the publication of a decision memorandum explaining the purpose and basis of the decision. CMS considers coverage of additional services with the help of the Medical Care Advisory Committee, which is composed of members of the healthcare industry and consumer groups, or other consultants. [*Notice*, 68 FR 55634, Sept. 26, 2003.]

There two tracks for making a request for a new or reconsidered NCD. One track is available only to aggrieved parties, as defined in § 522 of BIPA. The other track is open to anyone, including beneficiaries, manufacturers and other members of the public, and offers a more collaborative process with more flexible deadlines.

CMS ordinarily will respond in writing to the requestor within 90 calendar days of receiving the complete request. If the requestor submits additional medical and scientific information during this 90-day period, a new 90-day response period is triggered. When CMS is unable to complete a review within the 90-day timeframe, it must issue a notice that identifies the remaining steps in the review process and a deadline for the completed review. [Soc. Sec. Act § 1862(l); 42 C.F.R. § 426.547.]

After CMS posts the acceptance of a complete and formal request on its web site, a 30-day comment period is initiated. The public and requestor of the NCD may submit additional information or evidence regarding the NCD issue under review during this time. CMS provides responses to public comments in its decision memoranda. [Soc. Sec. Act § 1862(l).]

Information about the coverage process can be accessed at http://www.cms.hhs.gov/DeterminationProcess/. The web site contains information on NCD analyses, determinations, lab NCDs, technology assessments, national clinical trials, and Medicare Coverage Advisory Committee information on recent and upcoming meetings. The NCD analyses link also provides a vehicle for interested individuals to make comments, which helps to insure public participation and review of the entire process.

Recent Announcements of Coverage Decisions. During the past year, CMS has announced new or expanded coverage of the following services as a result of the NCD process:

- Smoking and anti-tobacco use counseling; [*Medicare National Coverage Determinations Manual,* Pub. Transmittal No. 36, May 20, 2005.]

- Mobility-assistive equipment, including powered equipment; [Pub. 100-03, Transmittal No. 37, June 3, 2005.]

- non-invasive ultrasound stimulation for the treatment of nonunion bone fractures prior to surgical intervention; Pub. 100-03, Transmittal No. 42, June 24, 2005.]

- Aberlix ® for the treatment of prostate cancer; [Pub. 100-03, Transmittal No. 34, April 25, 2005.]

- oral anti-emetic three-drug combination of aprepitant (Emend®), a 5-HT3 antagonist, and examethasone for individuals undergoing certain chemotherapy regimens [Pub. 100-03, Transmittal No. 40, June 24, 2005.]

- Percutaneous Transluminal Angioplasty (PTA) of the carotid artery concurrent with the placement of a Food and Drug Administration (FDA) -approved carotid stent with embolic protection. [Pub. 100-03, Transmittal No. 33, April 22, 2005.]

- High-dose melphalan together with autologous stem cell transplantation (AuSCT) for treatment of primary amyloid light chain amyloidosis, under certain conditions. [Pub. 100-03, Transmittal No. 32, April 15, 2005.]

- implantable automatic defibrillators (approved for additional conditions) [Pub. 100-03, Transmittal No. 29, March 4, 2005.]

- blood glucose and lipid testing procedures are covered as diabetic and cardiovascular screening benefits, respectively [Pub. 100-03, Transmittal No. 28, Feb. 11, 2005.]

- 2-[F-18] Fluoro-D-Glucose Positron Emission Tomography (FDG PET) scans for certain cancer indications, when providers are participating in, and patients are enrolled in, an approved FDG PET clinical study or an FDG PET clinical trial meeting Federal Drug Administration category B Investigational Device requirements; [Pub. 100-03, Transmittal No. 31, April 1, 2005.]

¶390

- off-label use of certain drugs for the treatment of colorectal cancer, in clinical trials sponsored jointly with the National Cancer Institute. [Pub. 100-03, Transmittal No. 38, June 17, 2005.]

- expanded coverage of cochlear implantation; [Pub. 100-03, Transmittal No. 39, July 1, 2005.]

- fasting beta cell autoantibody test as an adequate diagnostic criterion for insulopenia as an alternative to the updated C-peptide level; [Pub. 100-03, Transmittal No. 35, May 6, 2005.]

Local Coverage Determinations. The Medicare contractors that process claims also make local decisions about coverage of services not addressed in any National Coverage Decision. BIPA introduced the new process of local coverage decisions (LCDs), which is replacing the previous local medical review policies. LCDs are made only on the reasonableness and necessity of a service, unlike the LMRPs, which also addressed statutory and other exclusions. In November 2003, the contractors began converting all of the former LMRPs that contained language about reasonableness or necessity to LCDs. Providers may ask the contractor to review a decision or consider a new service. [*Medicare Program Integrity Manual*, Pub. 100-08, § 13.1.]

Chapter 4—MEDICARE PART C—MEDICARE ADVANTAGE

[¶ 400] Overview

Starting with the 2006 plan year, Medicare beneficiaries have more options to receive basic healthcare as well as prescription drug coverage through the Medicare Advantage (MA) program, which replaces the Medicare+Choice managed care program.

The Medicare Advantage program is administered according to federal regulations found at 42 C.F.R. Part 422. CMS also published a *Final rule* specific to Medicare Advantage in 2005 that outlined the implementation plans for the MA program. [*Final rule,* 70 FR 4587, Jan. 28, 2005, corrected at *Final rule,* 70 FR 52023, Sept. 1, 2005.] CMS also publishes updates to information regarding the administration of the Medicare Advantage program in the *Medicare Managed Care Manual,* CMS Pub. 100-16.

Types of Plans

Medicare Advantage organizations can offer three types of plans to beneficiaries: a coordinated care plan (which include special needs plans); a combination of a medical savings account (MSA) plan and a contribution into a MSA; a private fee-for-service plan. [42 C.F.R. § 422.4.]

A coordinated care plan. These plans include a network of providers that are under contract or arrangement with the Medicare Advantage organization to deliver a benefit package approved by CMS. These plans may include health maintenance organizations (HMOs), provider-sponsored organizations (PSOs), regional or local preferred provider organizations (PPOs), and other network plans (other than private fee-for-service plans). As of October 1, 2005, 5.077 million beneficiaries were enrolled in one of 302 coordinated care plans. [CMS website, http://cms.hhs.gov/healthplans/statistics/monthly.]

Special needs MA plans are an option for MA eligible individuals who are institutionalized, eligible for Medicaid, or have a severe or disabling chronic condition that would benefit from enrollment in a specialized MA plan. Special needs MA plans are paid the same as other MA plans; there are no special payment features to these plans. [Soc. Sec. Act § 1852(a)(2)(A)(ii).]

A private fee-for-service plan. This type of plan reimburses providers at a rate determined by the plan on a fee-for-service (FFS) basis, without putting the provider at risk. These plans do not vary reimbursement based on utilization; and they do not limit the selection of providers. As of October 1, 2005, 165,471 beneficiaries were enrolled in one of 17 private fee-for-service plans. [42 C.F.R. § 422.4(a)(3).]

A combination plan. These plans have two parts: (1) a Medicare Advantage medical savings account (MSA) health insurance plan that pays for a basic set of health benefits as approved by CMS, and includes a uniform premium and a uniform level of cost sharing for beneficiaries in the plan's service area, and (2) a MSA, which is a trust or custodial account into which CMS will make deposits. No MA organization currently offers this type of plan. [42 CFR § 422.4(a)(2).]

Part D coverage. An organization that offers a MA coordinated plan in a specific area must offer qualified Part D prescription drug coverage in that plan or in another MA plan in the same area. MA organizations offering MSA plans generally are not permitted to offer prescription drug coverage. MA organizations offering private fee-for-service plans can choose whether or not to offer Part D coverage. [42 CFR § 422.4(c).]

[¶ 401] Eligibility, Election, and Enrollment

Eligibility. In general, an individual is eligible to elect a Medicare Advantage (MA) plan if he or she is entitled to Medicare Part A and enrolled under Part B; and either resides in the service area of the Medicare Advantage plan or resides outside this service area but is enrolled in a health plan offered by the MA organization during the month immediately preceding the month in which the individual is entitled to both Medicare Part A and Part B. An individual who has end-stage renal disease (ESRD) is not eligible to elect an MA plan unless he or she develops ESRD while enrolled in an MA plan or in a health plan offered by an MA organization. An individual with ESRD may elect coverage by an MA special needs plan, if that plan has opened enrollment to individuals with ESRD. [42 C.F.R. § 422.50.]

Continuation of enrollment. A Medicare Advantage organization may offer a continuation of enrollment option to enrollees when they no longer reside in the service area of a plan and permanently move into the area designated as the MA organization's "continuation area". The beneficiary may choose whether to continue enrollment in the plan after the move, or to disenroll. [42 C.F.R. § 422.54.]

Election

Election process. Aside from some exceptions spelled out in the regulations, each MA organization must accept without restriction individuals who are eligible to elect a MA plan that the MA organization offers and who elect the plan during initial coverage election periods and annual election periods. MA organizations may submit information on enrollment capacity of plans they offer by July 1 of each year. If CMS determines that a plan has a capacity limit, the MA organization may limit enrollment in the plan under certain circumstances. [42 C.F.R. § 422.60.]

Election of coverage. Beneficiaries may make elections during four different election periods:

- the annual election period (AEP);
- the initial coverage election period (IEP);
- a special election period (SEP); or
- the open enrollment period (OEP).

Annual election period. The annual election period (AEP) occurs November 15 through December 31 of every year. For the 2006 plan year, the AEP extended from November 15, 2005, through May 15, 2006. For the 2007 plan year, the AEP will be from November 15, 2006, until December 31, 2006.

During the annual coordinated election period, an individual may change his or her election from an MA plan to original Medicare or to a different MA plan, or from original Medicare to an MA plan. If an individual changes his or her election to original Medicare, he or she may also elect a prescription drug plan. [42 CFR § 422.60(a)(2); *Medicare Managed Care Manual*, Pub. 100-16, Ch. 2, § 30.1.]

Initial coverage election period. The initial election period begins three months prior to the month an individual is first entitled to Medicare Part A and Part B and ends the last day of the month preceding the month of entitlement, or, if after May 15, 2006, the last day of the individual's Pat initial enrollment period. [42 C.F.R. § 422.62(a)(1).]

Open enrollment period. An individual who is not enrolled in an MA plan, but who is eligible to elect an MA plan in 2006, may elect an MA plan only once during the first six months of 2006. An individual who is enrolled in a Medicare Advantage Prescription Drig (MA-PD) plan may elect another MA-PD plan or original Medicare and coverage under a prescription drug plan (PDP). Such an individual may not elect an MA plan that does not provide qualified prescription drug coverage. An individual who is enrolled in an MA plan that does not provide qualified prescription drug coverage may elect another MA plan that does not provide that coverage or original Medicare. Such an individual may not elect an MA-PD plan or coverage under a PDP.

An individual who becomes MA-eligible during 2006 may elect an MA plan or change his or her election once during the period that begins the month the individual is entitled to both Part A and Part B and ends on the last day of the 6th month of the entitlement, or on December 31, whichever is earlier. [42 CFR § 422.62(a)(3); Pub. 100-16, Ch. 2, § 30.3.1.]

Special election period. SEPs include situations where:

    1. An individual has made a change in residence outside of the service area or continuation area or has experienced another change in circumstances as determined by CMS (other than termination for non-payment of premiums or disruptive behavior) that causes the individual to no longer be eligible to elect the MA plan;

    2. CMS or the MA organization has terminated the MA organization's contract for the MA plan in the area in which the individual resides, or the organization has notified the individual of the impending termination of the plan or the impending discontinuation of the plan in the area in which the individual reside;

    3. the individual demonstrates that the MA organization offering the plan substantially violated a material provision of its contract under MA in relation to the individual, or the MA organization materially misrepresented the plan when marketing the plan; or

    4. the individual meets other exceptional conditions as CMS may provide. [Pub. 100-16, Ch. 2, § 30.4.]

Coordination of enrollment and disenrollment through MA organizations. An individual who wishes to elect a MA plan may make or change his or her election during the election periods specified above by filing the appropriate election forms with the MA organization, or through other mechanisms approved by CMS. An individual who wishes to disenroll from a MA plan may change his or her election during the election periods by either filing a new election form or by filing the appropriate disenrollment form with the MA organization or through other mechanisms determined by CMS. [42 C.F.R. § 422.66(a), (b).]

Alternate employer group election mechanism. MA organizations that offer MA plans to employer groups may choose to accept voluntary elections directly from an employer group without obtaining an MA election form from each individual. The elections reported to the MA organization will reflect the choice of retiree coverage individual enrollees made using their employer's process for selecting a health plan. This election mechanism is optional for MA organizations, and may not be required. Therefore, MA organizations may specify the employer groups, if any, from which they will accept this election format and may choose to accept enrollment and/or voluntary disenrollment elections. [Pub. 100-16, Ch. 2, § 20.4.1.]

Passive elections. CMS allows for enrollment in an MA plan under a passive election process in limited circumstances generally associated with the MA plan renewal process. A passive election is a process by which a beneficiary is informed that he or she may make an election of a new MA plan by taking no action.

When a passive election is used in connection with a service area reduction (SAR) or plan termination, the MA organization must send a modified Annual Notice Of Change (ANOC) to the enrollees setting forth the available options, including Medigap rights. Although the ANOC information ordinarily may not be due until a later date, the MA organization must provide the ANOC information for the new MA plan by October 2 of the

¶401

current calendar year for the following year's plan(s). When a passive election is used in an MA plan renewal that does not include a termination or SAR, there are no Medigap rights. The MA organization should use the regular ANOC and include passive enrollment language to inform enrollees about their respective plans and other choices for the upcoming year. [Pub. 100-16, Ch. 2, § 20.4.2.]

Election by default. An individual who fails to make an election during the initial coverage election period is deemed to have elected original fee-for-service Medicare. [42 C.F.R. § 422.66(c).]

Conversion of enrollment. A MA plan must accept any individual (even if the individual has end-stage renal disease) who is enrolled in a health plan offered by the MA organization during the month immediately preceding the month in which he or she is eligible for Medicare. [42 C.F.R. § 422.66(d).]

Closed plans and capacity limits. An MA organization may specify a capacity limit for one or all of the MA plans it offers and reserve spaces for individual and employer group commercial members who are converting from a commercial product to an MA product at the time the member becomes eligible (i.e., conversion enrollments). When an MA plan is closed due to a capacity limit, the MA plan must remain closed to all prospective enrollees (with the exception of reserved vacancies) until space becomes available. Unlike the mandatory election periods (AEP, ICEP and SEP), an MA organization has the option to be open for elections made during the OEP.

The decision to be open or closed for OEPs rests with the MA organization and does not require CMS approval. However, if an MA organization has a plan that is open during an OEP, and decides to change this process, it must notify CMS and the general public 30 calendar days in advance of the new limitations on the open enrollment process. Further, each MA plan may be open for all or only part of the OEP.

If an MA organization has a plan that is approved by CMS for a capacity limit, it should estimate when a capacity limit will be reached and notify CMS and the general public 30 calendar days in advance of the closing of the open enrollment process. If CMS approves the capacity limit for immediate closing of enrollment, the MA organization must notify the general public within 15 calendar days of CMS approval that it has closed for enrollment. [Pub. 100-16, Ch. 2, § 30.8.1.]

Effective dates of elections.

    1. An election made during an initial coverage election period is effective as of the first day of the month of entitlement to both Part A and Part B.

    2. Elections or changes of election made during the annual coordinated election period are effective the first day of the following calendar year; however, elections made after December 31, 2005, through May 15, 2006, are effective the first day of the first calendar month following the month in which the election is made.

    3. Elections made during an open enrollment period are effective the first day of the first month following the month in which the election is made

    4. The effective date of elections made during special election periods depend on the circumstances. [42 C.F.R. § 422.68.]

Enrollment

Disenrollment by the MA organization. With certain exceptions, a MA organization may not disenroll an individual from any MA plan it offers. The exceptions include the following: (1) if the enrollee does not pay any monthly basic or supplementary premium in a timely manner; (2) if he or she engages in disruptive behavior; or (3) if he or she provides fraudulent information on an election form or permits the fraudulent use of an enrollment card.

The MA organization must disenroll an individual if he or she moves out of the MA's service area, loses entitlement to Part A or Part B benefits, or dies. In addition, an MA organization must disenroll individuals enrolled in a specialized MA plan for special needs individuals who no longer meet the special needs status of that plan.

The MA organization also must disenroll enrollees if the organization has its contract with CMS terminated; if it terminates the MA plan; or if it discontinues the plan in an area where it had previously been available. [42 C.F.R. § 422.74(a),(b).]

Consequences of disenrollment. An individual who is disenrolled for nonpayment of premiums, disruptive behavior, or fraud and abuse is deemed to have elected original Medicare. If the individual is disenrolled because the plan was terminated, the area covered by the plan was reduced, or because the individual moved, he or she will have a special election period to make a new choice. [42 C.F.R. § 422.74(e).]

Members who change residence. MA organizations may offer extended "visitor" or "traveler" programs to members who have been out of the service area for up to 12 months. MA organizations that offer such programs do not have to disenroll members in these extended programs who remain out of the service area for more than six months but less than 12 months. MA organizations must make this option available to all enrollees who are absent for an extended period from the MA plan's service area. However, MA organizations may limit this option to enrollees who travel to certain areas, as defined by the MA organization and who receive serves from qualified providers. MA organizations without these programs must continue to disenroll members who have been out of the area for more than six months. [Pub. 100-16, Ch. 2, § 50.2.1.]

Medigap rights. MA organizations are required to notify members of their Medigap guaranteed issue rights when members disenroll to original Medicare during a special election period. [Pub. 100-16, Ch. 2, § 50.1.7.]

ESRD beneficiaries. Except as provided below, an individual is not eligible to elect an MA plan if he/she has been medically determined to have end stage renal disease. ESRD means that stage of kidney impairment that appears irreversible and permanent and requires a regular course of dialysis or kidney transplantation to maintain life.

An individual who receives a kidney transplant and who no longer requires a regular course of dialysis to maintain life is not considered to have ESRD for purposes of MA eligibility. Such an individual may elect to enroll in a MA plan, if he/she meets other applicable eligibility requirements. In addition, an individual who initiated dialysis treatments for ESRD, but subsequently recovered native kidney function and no longer requires a regular course of dialysis to maintain life is not considered to have ESRD for purposes of MA eligibility. Such an individual may also elect to enroll in a MA plan, if he/she meets other applicable eligibility requirements. [Pub. 100-16, Ch. 2, § 20.2]

[¶ 402] Benefits and Beneficiary Protections

A Medicare Advantage organization offering an MA plan must provide enrollees, at a minimum, with all basic Medicare-covered services by furnishing the benefits directly or through arrangements, or by paying for the benefits. MA organizations also may provide mandatory and optional supplemental benefits through their plans. [42 C.F.R. § 422.100.]

Requirements relating to basic benefits. Generally, each MA organization must provide coverage for all Medicare Part A and Part B benefits that are available to beneficiaries residing in the plan's service area. In addition, each MA organization must comply with

CMS's national coverage decisions, general coverage guidelines included in original Medicare manuals and instructions (unless superseded by regulations), and written coverage decisions of local Medicare contractors. If an MA organization covers geographic areas encompassing more than one local coverage policy area, the MA organization may elect to uniformly apply to plan enrollees in all areas the coverage policy that is the most beneficial to MA enrollees. [42 C.F.R. § 422.101.]

Supplemental benefits. An MA organization may require enrollees of an MA plan (other than an MA MSA) to accept and pay for services in addition to the basic benefits. An MA organization also may offer optional supplemental benefits that may be purchased at the discretion of enrollees. Beginning with the 2006 plan year, an MA plan also may reduce cost sharing below the plan's actuarial value only as a mandatory supplemental benefit. [42 C.F.R. § 422.102.]

Benefits under an MA MSA plan. An MA organization offering an MSA plan must provide at least the basic services available under Medicare Part A and Part B, after the enrollee incurs expenses equal to the plan's annual deductible. [42 C.F.R. § 422.103.] An MA organization offering an MSA plan may not provide supplemental benefits that cover expenses that count toward the deductible. [42 C.F.R. § 422.104(a).]

Point-of-service option. A point-of-service (POS) benefit is an option that an MA organization may offer as part of a coordinated care plan or MSA plan to provide enrollees with additional choice in obtaining healthcare services. An MA organization may not offer a POS option until CMS approves it. A coordinated care plan may offer the POS option as either a mandatory or optional supplemental benefit. [42 C.F.R. § 422.105(a),(b).]

Coordination of benefits with employer or union group health plans and Medicaid. If an MA organization contracts with an employer group health plan (EGHP) or labor union that covers enrollees in an MA plan, or with a state Medicaid agency to provide Medicaid benefits to enrollees who are eligible for both Medicare and Medicaid and who are enrolled in an MA plan, the enrollees must be provided the same benefits as all other enrollees in the MA plan, with the EGHP, labor union, or Medicaid benefits supplementing the MA plan benefits. [42 C.F.R. § 422.106(a).]

Permissible employer, labor organization, or Medicaid plan benefits include (1) payment of a portion or all of the MA basic and supplemental premiums; (2) payment of a portion or all of other cost-sharing amounts approved for the MA plan; or (3) other employer-sponsored benefits that may require additional premium and cost-sharing, or other benefits provided by the organization under a contract with the state Medicaid agency. [42 C.F.R. § 422.106(b).]

CMS has authority to waive or modify requirements that hinder the design of, the offering of, or the enrollment in, Part D arrangements sponsored by employers or unions for their retirees. This waiver authority can assist employer and union plan sponsors direct-contract with Medicare to become Medicare Prescription Drug Plans (PDPs) and Medicare Advantage plans that include prescription drugs (MA-PDs), as well as to contract with existing PDPs and MA-PDs to provide enhanced Medicare prescription drug coverage to their retirees. [42 C.F.R. § 422.106(c), (d).]

Medicare as secondary payer. A state cannot take away an MA organization's right under federal law and the Medicare Secondary Payer (MSP) regulations to bill, or to authorize providers and suppliers to bill, for services for which Medicare is not the primary payer. The MA organization will exercise the same rights to recover from a primary plan, entity, or individual that the Secretary exercises under the MSP regulations. [42 C.F.R. § 422.108(f).]

¶402

Effect of national coverage determinations (NCDs) and legislative changes in benefits. If CMS determines that an individual NCD or legislative change in benefits meets the criteria for "significant cost," an MA organization is not required to assume risk for the costs of that service or benefit until the contract year for which payments are appropriately adjusted to take into account the cost of the NCD service or legislative change in benefits. If CMS determines that an NCD or legislative change in benefits does not meet the "significant cost" threshold, the MA organization is required to provide coverage for the NCD or legislative change in benefits and assume risk for the costs of that service or benefit as of the effective date stated in the NCD or specified in the legislation.

"Significant cost" is defined as either (1) the average cost of furnishing a single service that exceeds a cost threshold of the preceding year's dollar threshold adjusted to reflect the national per capita growth percentage; or (2) the estimated cost of all Medicare services furnished as a result of a particular NCD or legislative change in benefits representing at least 0.1 percent of the national average per capita costs. [42 C.F.R. § 422.109.]

Discrimination against beneficiaries prohibited. An MA organization may not discriminate against beneficiaries on the basis of health status, including medical condition, claims experience, receipt of health care, medical history, genetic information, evidence of insurability (including conditions arising out of acts of domestic violence), or disability. An MA organization may not enroll an individual who has been medically determined to have end-stage renal disease (ESRD). However, if an individual is diagnosed with ESRD while enrolled in an MA plan, he or she may not be disenrolled for that reason. [42 C.F.R. § 422.110.]

Disclosure requirements. An MA organization must disclose to each beneficiary enrolling in an MA plan offered by the organization a detailed content of plan description, including the plan's service area, benefits, access (including out-of-area coverage), emergency coverage, supplemental benefits, prior authorization and review rules, grievance and appeals procedures, quality improvement program, disenrollment rights and responsibilities, and catastrophic caps and single deductible. This information must be offered at the time of enrollment and at least annually after that, in a clear, accurate, and standardized form. [42 C.F.R. § 422.111.]

Access to services. An MA organization that offers an MA coordinated care plan or an MSA plan may specify the networks of providers that enrollees can use, as long as the organization ensures that all covered services, including additional or supplemental services contracted for the Medicare enrollee, are available and accessible under the plan.

To accomplish this, the MA organization must do the following: (1) maintain and monitor a network of appropriate providers that is sufficient to provide sufficient access to meet the needs of enrollees; (2) establish a panel of primary care providers (PCPs) from which an enrollee may choose a PCP; (3) provide or arrange for necessary specialty care; in particular, give women enrollees the option of direct access to a women's health specialist; (4) ensure that each of its MA plans has CMS-approved procedures in place to identify individuals with serious medical conditions and to establish and implement a treatment plan for those individuals; (5) demonstrate, if seeking to expand the service area of an MA plan, that the number and type of providers available to the plan are sufficient to meet the needs of the population; (6) demonstrate to CMS that its providers in a plan are credentialed; (7) establish written standards for timely access to care, medical necessity determinations, and provider consideration of enrollee input for treatment plans; (8) establish convenient hours of operation; (9) ensure that services are provided in a culturally competent manner to all enrollees; and (10) provide coverage for ambulance services. [42 C.F.R. § 422.112(a).]

MA organizations also must ensure continuity of care and integration of services through arrangements with contracted providers. [42 C.F.R. § 422.112(b).]

¶402

An MA regional plan may seek, upon application to CMS, to designate a noncontracting hospital as an essential hospital. [42 C.F.R. § 422.112(c).]

Special rules for ambulance services, emergency and urgently needed services, and maintenance and post-stabilization care services. The MA organization is financially responsible for ambulance services, including ambulance services dispatched through 911 or its local equivalent, where other means of transportation would endanger the beneficiary's health. The MA organization is financially responsible for emergency and urgently needed services regardless of whether the services are obtained within or outside the MA organization, and regardless of whether there is prior authorization for the services.

The MA organization also is financially responsible for post-stabilization care services obtained within or outside the MA organization that (1) are pre-approved by a plan provider or other MA organization representative; (2) are NOT pre-approved by a plan provider or other MA organization representative, but administered to maintain the enrollee's stabilized condition within one hour of a request to the MA organization for pre-approval of further post-stabilization care services; and (3) are NOT pre-approved by a plan provider or other MA organization representative, but administered to maintain, improve, or resolve the enrollee's stabilized condition under certain conditions.

The MA organization's financial responsibility for post-stabilization care services it has not pre-approved ends when (1) a plan physician with privileges at the treating hospital assumes responsibility for the enrollee's care; (2) a plan physician assumes responsibility for the enrollee's care through transfer; (3) an MA organization representative and the treating physician reach an agreement concerning the enrollee's care; or (4) the enrollee is discharged. [42 C.F.R. § 422.113.]

The MA organization is not responsible for the care provided for an unrelated nonemergency problem during treatment for an emergency situation. For example, the MA organization is not responsible for any costs, such as a biopsy, associated with treatment of skin lesions performed by the attending physician who is treating a fracture. [*Managed Care Manual*, Pub. 100-16, Ch. 4, § 130.2.]

Access to services under private fee-for-service plans. An MA organization that offers a private fee-for-service plan must demonstrate to CMS that it has a sufficient number and range of providers willing to furnish services under the plan. [42 C.F.R. § 422.114(a)(1).]

Skilled nursing facility services. MA plans must provide coverage of posthospital extended care services to Medicare enrollees through a home skilled nursing facility (SNF) if the enrollee elects to receive the coverage through the home SNF, and if the home SNF either has a contract with the MA organization or agrees to accept substantially similar payment under the same terms and conditions that apply to similar SNFs that contract with the MA organization. A home skilled nursing facility is (1) the SNF in which the enrollee resided at the time of admission to the hospital preceding the receipt of posthospital extended care services; (2) a SNF that is providing posthospital extended care services through a continuing care retirement community in which the MA plan enrollee was a resident at the time of admission to the hospital; or (3) the SNF in which the spouse of the enrollee is residing at the time of discharge from the hospital. [42 C.F.R. § 422.133.]

Confidentiality of enrollee records. For any medical records or enrollment information it maintains, an MA organization must abide by all federal and state laws regarding confidentiality and disclosure of medical records; ensure that medical information is released only in accordance with federal or state laws, or under court orders or subpoenas; maintain the records in an accurate manner; and ensure timely access by enrollees to their own records. [42 C.F.R. § 422.118.]

¶402

[¶ 403] Beneficiary Grievances, Appeals, and Notifications

Medicare Advantage plans must provide meaningful procedures for hearing and resolving grievances between the plan and enrolled beneficiaries. [42 C.F.R. § 422.560.]

Grievance Procedures and Benefit Determination Reviews

A Medicare Advantage organization must have a procedure for determining whether an enrolled beneficiary is entitled to receive a health service and how much the enrollee may be required to pay for the service. The organization also must have a procedure for reconsidering its determinations. [42 C.F.R. § 422.562.] In the case of a care denial based on lack of medical necessity, an appeal request must be decided by a physician with appropriate expertise in the specialty at issue. This may not be the same physician who made the original claim denial. [42 C.F.R. § 422.590(g).]

Grievance procedures. Each MA organization must provide meaningful procedures for timely hearing and resolving grievances between enrollees and the organization or any other entity or individual through which the organization provides health care services under any MA plan it offers. Grievance procedures are separate and distinct from appeal procedures, which address organization determinations. Upon receiving a complaint, an MA organization must promptly determine and inform the enrollee whether the complaint is subject to its grievance procedures or its appeal procedures.

The grievance procedure also is distinguished from the quality improvement organization (QIO) complaint process. While the QIO must review beneficiaries' written complaints about the quality of services they have received under the Medicare program. For quality of care issues, an enrollee may file a grievance with the MA organization; file a written complaint with the QIO, or both. For any complaint submitted to a QIO, the MA organization must cooperate with the QIO in resolving the complaint.

An MA organization must respond to an enrollee's grievance within 24 hours if: (1) the complaint involves an MA organization's decision to invoke an extension relating to an organization determination or reconsideration; or (2) the complaint involves an MA organization's refusal to grant an enrollee's request for an expedited organization determination or reconsideration. [42 C.F.R. § 422.564.]

Organization determinations. Each MA organization must have a procedure for making timely organization determinations regarding the benefits an enrollee is entitled to receive under an MA plan, including basic benefits and mandatory and optional supplemental benefits; and the amount, if any, that the enrollee is required to pay for a health service. The MA organization must have a standard procedure for making determinations, and an expedited procedure for situations in which applying the standard procedure could seriously jeopardize the enrollee's life, health, or ability to regain maximum function.

An organization determination is any determination made by an MA organization regarding any of the following:

(1) payment for temporarily out of the area renal dialysis services, emergency services, post-stabilization care, or urgently needed services;

(2) payment for any other health services furnished by a provider other than the MA organization that the enrollee believes are covered under Medicare; or if not covered under Medicare, should have been furnished, arranged for, or reimbursed by the MA organization;

(3) the MA organization's refusal to provide or pay for services, in whole or in part, including the type or level of services, that the enrollee believes should be furnished or arranged for by the MA organization;

(4) discontinuation or reduction of a service if the enrollee believes that continuation of the services is medically necessary; and

(5) failure of the MA organization to approve, furnish, arrange for, or provide payment for health care services in a timely manner, or to provide the enrollee with timely notice of an adverse determination, such that a delay would adversely affect the health of the enrollee.

Individuals or entities who can request an organization determination include the enrollee; any provider that furnishes, or intends to furnish, services to the enrollee; or the legal representative of a deceased enrollee's estate. Those who can request an expedited determination include an enrollee; or a physician (regardless of whether the physician is affiliated with the MA organization). [42 C.F.R. § 422.566.]

Expedited determinations and reconsiderations. Generally, Medicare Advantage plans must maintain procedures for expediting determinations and reconsiderations when, on the request of an enrollee or a physician, the organization determines that the normal timeframe for a determination or reconsideration could seriously jeopardize the affected enrollee's life or health. When it has received such a request, the MA organization must notify the enrollee or the physician, as appropriate, of its determination or the results of its reconsideration within time limits established by the Secretary of HHS. Although the Secretary may allow a longer time limit in specified cases, generally, the plan's determination or reconsideration must be relayed to the enrollee or physician within 72 hours of the plan's receipt of the request. [42 C.F.R. § 422.570 *et seq.*]

Expedited reviews in certain provider settings. As of January 1, 2004, enrollees have the right to an expedited review by a QIO when they disagree with their MA organization's decision that Medicare coverage of their services from a skilled nursing facility (SNF), home health agency (HHA), or comprehensive outpatient rehabilitation facility (CORF) should end.

When an MA organization has approved coverage of an enrollee's admission to a SNF, or coverage of HHA or CORF services, the enrollee must receive a Notice of Medicare Non-Coverage (NOMNC) at least two calendar days in advance of the services ending. It is similar to the long-standing right of a Medicare beneficiary to request a QIO review of a discharge from an inpatient hospital. If the enrollee does not agree that covered services should end, the enrollee may request an expedited review of the case by the QIO in the state where the services are being provided. The enrollee's MA organization must furnish a detailed notice explaining why services are no longer necessary or covered. The review process generally will be completed within less than 48 hours of the enrollee's request for a review. [Pub. 100-16, Ch. 13, § 90.2.]

Administrative Determinations, Reconsiderations, and Appeals

Historically, administrative law judges (ALJs) within the Social Security Administration (SSA) have been responsible for holding hearings on most types of Medicare appeals, including those related to the Medicare managed care program as it has evolved over the years. Section 931 of the Medicare Modernization Act of 2003 (MMA) (PubLNo 108-173) required that the functions of ALJs responsible for hearing cases for the Medicare program would be transferred from the SSA to HHS. Accordingly, the Office of Medicare Hearings and Appeals has been created. [*Notice,* 70 FR 36386, June 23, 2005.] The transition plan provided for CMS contractors to send to HHS all Medicare appeals that would otherwise have been sent to SSA, beginning July 1, 2005.

¶403

Medicare Part C

Hearing and Judicial Review

Plan enrollees who are dissatisfied, either because they have not received health care to which they believe they are entitled, or because they contest the cost of a service they have received, are entitled to a hearing before the Secretary of HHS when the amount in controversy is $100 or more. If the amount in controversy is $1,000 or more (prior to 2005), either the enrollee or the health plan, upon notifying the other party, is entitled to judicial review. [42 C.F.R. § 422.612.]

In 2005, the minimum amount in controversy for judicial review of Medicare claims was increased to $1,050 and is increased each year by a dollar amount equal to the percentage increase in the medical care component of the consumer price index for July 2003 to the July preceding the year involved, rounded to the nearest multiple of $10. [MMA § 940; *Medicare Claims Processing Manual*, Pub. 100-04, Ch. 29, § 30.8.]

Reconsidered Determinations or Decisions

Standard requests. If, on reconsideration of a *request for service*, the MA organization completely reverses its organization determination, the organization must authorize or provide the service under dispute as expeditiously as the enrollee's health condition requires, but no later than 30 calendar days after the date the MA organization receives the request for reconsideration.

If, on reconsideration of a *request for payment*, the MA organization completely reverses its organization determination, the organization must pay for the service no later than 60 calendar days after the date the MA organization receives the request for reconsideration.

If, on reconsideration of a *request for service*, the MA organization's determination is reversed in whole or in part by the independent outside entity, the MA organization must authorize the service under dispute within 72 hours from the date it receives notice reversing the determination, or provide the service under dispute as expeditiously as the enrollee's health condition requires, but no later than 14 calendar days from that date.

If, on reconsideration of a *request for payment*, the MA organization's determination is reversed in whole or in part by the independent outside entity, the MA organization must pay for the service no later than 30 calendar days from the date it receives notice reversing the organization determination.

If the independent outside entity's determination is reversed in whole or in part by the administrative law judge (ALJ), or at a higher level of appeal, the MA organization must pay for, authorize, or provide the service under dispute as expeditiously as the enrollee's health condition requires, but no later than 60 calendar days from the date it receives notice reversing the determination. [42 C.F.R. § 422.618.]

Expedited requests. If on reconsideration of an expedited request for service, the MA organization completely reverses its organization determination, the MA organization must authorize or provide the service under dispute as expeditiously as the enrollee's health condition requires, but no later than 72 hours after the date the MA organization receives the request for reconsideration.

If the MA organization's determination is reversed in whole or in part by the independent outside entity, the MA organization must authorize or provide the service under dispute as expeditiously as the enrollee's health condition requires but no later than 72 hours from the date it receives notice reversing the determination.

If the independent outside entity's expedited determination is reversed in whole or in part by the ALJ, or at a higher level of appeal, the MA organization must authorize or provide the service under dispute as expeditiously as the enrollee's health condition requires, but no later than 60 days from the date it receives notice reversing the determination. The MA organization must inform the independent outside entity that the organization has effectuated the decision.

If the MA organization requests Departmental Appeals Board (the Board) review consistent with 42 C.F.R. § 422.608, the MA organization may await the outcome of the review before it authorizes or provides the service under dispute. A MA organization that files an appeal with the Board must concurrently send a copy of its appeal request and any accompanying documents to the enrollee and must notify the independent outside entity that it has requested an appeal. [42 C.F.R. § 422.619.]

Notification of Noncoverage of Inpatient Hospital Care

Enrollee's entitlement. Where an MA organization has authorized coverage of the inpatient admission of an enrollee, either directly or by delegation (or the admission constitutes emergency or urgently needed care), the MA organization (or hospital that has been delegated the authority to make the discharge decision) must provide a written notice of noncoverage when (1) the beneficiary disagrees with the discharge decision; or (2) the MA organization (or the hospital that has been delegated the authority to make the discharge decision) is not discharging the individual but no longer intends to continue coverage of the inpatient stay. An enrollee is entitled to coverage until at least noon of the day after such notice is provided.

Before discharging an individual or changing the level of care in an inpatient hospital setting, the MA organization must obtain the concurrence of the physician who is responsible for the enrollee's inpatient care The written notice of noncoverage must be issued no later than the day before hospital coverage ends. The written notice must include the following elements: (1) the reason why inpatient hospital care is no longer needed; (2) the effective date and time of the enrollee's liability for continued inpatient care; (3) the enrollee's appeal rights; (4) additional information specified by CMS. [42 C.F.R. § 422.620.]

An enrollee who wishes to appeal a determination by an MA organization or hospital that inpatient care is no longer necessary must request immediate QIO review of the determination: An enrollee who requests immediate QIO review may remain in the hospital with no additional financial liability. [42 C.F.R. § 422.622.]

Termination of Provider Services

A termination of service is the discharge of an enrollee from covered provider services, or discontinuation of covered provider services, when the enrollee has been authorized by the MA organization, either directly or by delegation, to receive an ongoing course of treatment from that provider (including home health agencies, skilled nursing facilities, and comprehensive outpatient rehabilitation facilities). Termination includes cessation of coverage at the end of a course of treatment preauthorized in a discrete increment, regardless of whether the enrollee agrees that such services should end.

Advance written notification of termination. Prior to any termination of service, the provider of the service must deliver valid written notice to the enrollee of the MA organization's decision to terminate services. The provider must use a standardized notice, required by the Secretary, and follow specific procedures regarding timing and content of the notice. The standardized termination notice must include the date that coverage of services ends; the date that the enrollee's financial liability for continued services begins; and a description of the enrollee's right to a fast-track appeal. [42 C.F.R. § 422.624.]

¶403

[¶ 404] MA Regional Plans

CMS established 26 regions for Medicare Advantage (MA) preferred provider organizations (PPOs) and 34 regions for prescription drug plans (PDPs). CMS considered four key principles in establishing the regions:

- *Appropriate Size of Eligible Population.* At least 200,000 eligible beneficiaries must live in a region to make the formation of networks viable. If the size of the region is too large (i.e. greater than 3 million eligibles), plans may have difficulty enrolling and providing services to beneficiaries, especially in the start-up year.

- *Multiple Potential Plan Entrants.* A sufficient number of existing plans (commercial preferred provider organizations (PPOs), Federal Employees Health Benefits (FEHB) plans and local Medicare Advantage plans) are necessary to assume that potential plan entrants will participate.

- *Limited Variation in Health Plan Costs.* Adequate payments are necessary to encourage plan participation, and providing adequate payments for quality services in all areas within a region may be more difficult if there is high variation in health care costs within a region. Therefore, to avoid the potential effects of cross subsidization, CMS generally did not join states that have large differences in average payments or that would substantially add to the variability of payments within the region.

- *Preserve Medicare Patient Flows.* CMS attempted to limit disruption to natural Medicare "patient flows," where patients who live in one state seek care in another. Patient flow is determined using Medicare expenditures data. In areas in which beneficiaries are more likely to seek care in another state, CMS has generally kept those states together. [*Principles for Establishing Prescription Drug Plan Regions to Maximize Access to High-Quality Plans,* Dec. 6, 2004.]

CMS may periodically review and revise service areas if it determines the revision to be appropriate, using the following criteria:

- There will be no fewer than 10 regions, and no more than 50 regions.

- The main purpose of the regions is to maximize the availability of MA regional plans to all MA eligible individuals without regard to health status, or geographic location, especially those residing in rural areas. [42 C.F.R. § 422.455.]

Moratorium. CMS will not approve the offering of a local preferred provider organization plan during 2006 or 2007 in a service area unless the MA organization seeking to offer the plan was offering a local preferred provider organization plan in the service area before December 31, 2005. [42 C.F.R. § 422.451.]

Risk Sharing in 2006 and 2007

Application of risk corridors. For the 2006 and 2007 plan years, an MA organization that offers an MA regional plan in an MA region must notify CMS of the following:

- the total amount of costs that the organization incurred in providing benefits covered under the original Medicare fee-for-service program option for all enrollees under the plan;

- the total amount of costs that the organization incurred in providing rebatable integrated benefits for all enrollees under the plan, as well as the portion of those costs attributable to administrative expenses beyond the administrative expense incurred in providing benefits under the original Medicare fee-for-service program option. [42 C.F.R. § 458(b).]

Adjustment of payment. If the allowable costs for the plan for the year are at least 97 percent, but do not exceed 103 percent, of the target amount for the plan and year, there will be no payment adjustment under this section for the plan and year.

If the allowable costs for the plan for the year are greater than 103 percent, but not greater than 108 percent, of the target amount for the plan and year, CMS will increase the total of the monthly payments made to the organization offering the plan for the year by an amount equal to 50 percent of the difference between those allowable costs and 103 percent of that target amount.

If the allowable costs for the plan for the year are greater than 108 percent of the target amount for the plan and year, CMS will increase the total of the monthly payments made to the organization offering the plan for the year by an amount equal to the sum of: 2.5 percent of that target amount; and 80 percent of the difference between those allowable costs and 108 percent of that target amount. [42 C.F.R. § 458(c).]

Reduction in payment. If the allowable costs for the plan for the year are less than 97 percent, but greater than or equal to 92 percent, of the target amount for the plan and year, CMS will reduce the total of the monthly payments made to the organization offering the plan by an amount equal to 50 percent of the difference between 97 percent of the target amount and those allowable costs.

If the allowable costs for the plan for the year are less than 92 percent of the target amount for the plan and year, CMS will reduce the total of the monthly payments made to the organization offering the plan by an amount (or otherwise recover from the plan an amount) equal to the sum of: 2.5 percent of that target amount; and 80 percent of the difference between 92 percent of that target amount and those allowable costs. [42 C.F.R. § 458(c)(3).]

Organizational and Financial Requirements

Regional MA plans offered by MA organizations must be licensed under state law as a risk-bearing entity eligible to offer health insurance or health benefits coverage in each state in which it offers one or more plans. MA organizations offering MA regional plans, however, may obtain a temporary waiver of state licensure.

In the case of an MA organization that is offering a regional plan, and is not licensed in each state in which it offers such a plan, the following rules apply:

- the MA organization must be licensed to bear risk in at least one state of the region.

- for the other states in a region in which the organization is not licensed to bear risk, if it demonstrates to CMS that it has filed the necessary application to meet those requirements, CMS may temporarily waive the licensing requirement with respect to each state for a period of time as CMS determines appropriate for the timely processing of the application by the state or states.

In the case of an MA organization to which CMS grants a waiver and that is licensed in more than one state in a region, the MA organization will select one of the states, the rules of which shall apply in states where the organization is not licensed for the period of the waiver. [42 C.F.R. § 458(e).]

Regional Stabilization Fund

The MA Regional Plan Stabilization Fund is available beginning in 2007 to provide incentives to have MA regional plans offered in each MA region and to retain MA regional plans in certain MA regions with below-national-average MA market penetration. [42 C.F.R. § 422.458(f).]

Cost Sharing Under Regional Plans

MA regional plans must provide for the following:

- MA regional plans, to the extent they apply a deductible, are permitted to have only a single deductible related to combined Medicare Part A and Part B services.

- MA regional plans are required to provide for a catastrophic limit on beneficiary out-of-pocket expenditures for in-network benefits under the original Medicare fee-for-service program (Part A and Part B benefits);

- MA regional plans are required to provide an additional catastrophic limit on beneficiary out-of-pocket expenditures for in-network and out-of-network benefits under the original Medicare fee-for-service program.

- MA regional plans are required: to track the deductible and catastrophic limits of incurred out-of-pocket beneficiary costs for original Medicare-covered services; and to notify members and health care providers when the deductible or a limit has been reached.

- MA regional plans are required to provide reimbursement for all covered benefits, regardless of whether those benefits are provided within the network of contracted providers. [*Medicare Managed Care Manual* Pub. 100-16, Ch. 4, § 30.2.]

[¶ 405] Contracts with Medicare Advantage Organizations

To qualify as a Medicare Advantage (MA) organization, enroll Medicare beneficiaries, or be paid on behalf of enrolled beneficiaries, an organization must be under contract with CMS. Any entity seeking to contract as an MA organization must:

- complete an application;

- be licensed by the State as a risk bearing entity in each State in which it seeks to offer an MA plan;

- meet minimum enrollment requirements; and

- have administrative and management arrangements satisfactory to CMS. [42 C.F.R. § 422.503.]

In order to obtain a determination on whether it meets the requirements to become a MA organization and is qualified to provide a particular type of MA plan, an entity must complete a certified application, in the form and manner required by CMS. The application must include documentation that the entity has (1) the appropriate state license or certification to offer health insurance or health benefits coverage, and (2) is authorized by the state to accept prepaid capitation for providing, arranging, or paying for the comprehensive healthcare services to be offered under the MA contract. In the case of MA regional plans, the entity must provide documentation of application for state licensure in any state in the region that the organization is not already licensed. [42 C.F.R. § 422.501.]

Basis for evaluation. CMS evaluates an application for an MA contract on the basis of information contained in the application itself and any additional information that CMS obtains through other means such as on-site visits, public hearings, and any other appropriate procedures. After evaluating all relevant information, CMS determines whether the application meets the applicable requirements.

CMS will make one of three determinations: approval, intent to deny, or denial. If CMS approves the application, it gives written notice to the applicant, indicating that it qualifies to contract as an MA organization.

If CMS finds that the applicant does not appear to be able to meet the requirements for an MA organization or has not provided enough information, CMS gives the contract applicant notice of intent to deny the application and a summary of the basis for this preliminary finding. The applicant has 10 days to revise its application.

If CMS denies the application, it gives written notice to the contract applicant indicating that the applicant is not qualified to contract as an MA organization; the reasons why the applicant is not qualified; and the applicant's right to request reconsideration. [42 C.F.R. § 422.502.]

Contract period and effectiveness. Contracts with MA plans are for a term of one year. Contracts are renewed annually if CMS authorizes renewal and so informs the MA organization, and the organization has not notified CMS of its intention not to renew. [42 C.F.R. § 422.505.]

Nonrenewal of contract. An MA organization may elect not to renew its contract with CMS as of the end of the term of the contract for any reason, provided it meets specific timeframes for doing so. If an MA organization does not intend to renew its contract, it must notify:

- CMS, in writing, by the first Monday in June of the year in which the contract would end.

- Each Medicare enrollee, at least 90 days before the date on which the nonrenewal is effective. This notice must include a written description of alternatives available for obtaining Medicare services within the service area, including alternative MA plans, Medigap options, and original Medicare and must receive CMS approval prior to issuance.

- The general public, at least 90 days before the end of the current calendar year, by publishing a notice in one or more newspapers of general circulation in each community located in the MA organization's service area.

CMS may accept a nonrenewal notice submitted after July 1 if the MA organization notifies its Medicare enrollees and the public as noted above; and acceptance is not inconsistent with the effective and efficient administration of the Medicare program. If an MA organization does not renew a contract, CMS will not enter into a contract with the organization for two years unless there are special circumstances that warrant special consideration, as determined by CMS. [42 C.F.R. § 422.506.]

The Secretary may cancel a contract at any time, however, if a plan substantially fails to carry out the contract; carries it out in a manner that is inconsistent with the efficient, effective administration of the MA program; no longer meets specified requirements of the MA program; or there is credible evidence that the MA organization committed or participated in false, fraudulent, or abusive activities affecting the Medicare program, including submission of false or fraudulent data. [42 C.F.R. § 422.510.]

Termination of contract. The MA organization may terminate the contract if CMS fails to substantially carry out the terms of the contract. The MA organization must give advance notice to CMS at least 90 days before the intended date of termination, and advance notice to its Medicare enrollees at least 60 days before the termination effective date. The notice to beneficiaries must include a written description of alternatives available for obtaining Medicare services within the services area, including alternative MA plans, Medigap options,

¶405

original Medicare and must receive CMS approval. The MA organization also must provide notice to the general public at least 60 days before the termination effective date by publishing a CMS-approved notice in one or more newspapers of general circulation in each community or county located in the organization's geographic area.

CMS's liability for payment to the MA organization ends as of the first day of the month after the last month for which the contract is in effect. CMS does not enter into an agreement with an organization that has terminated its contract within the preceding two years unless there are circumstances that warrant special consideration, as determined by CMS. [42 C.F.R. § 422.512.]

Periodic audits of contractors. CMS is required to conduct an annual audit of the financial records, including data on Medicare utilization, costs and computation of the adjusted community rate, of at least one-third of the Medicare Advantage organizations. The agency may inspect or evaluate the quality, propriety and timeliness of services performed under the contract, as well as the facilities of the organization if there is reasonable evidence of the need for such inspection. CMS may audit and inspect any books or records of an MA organization. [42 C.F.R. § 422.504.]

Minimum enrollment requirements. CMS will not enter into a contract with a managed care organization unless the organization enrolls at least 5,000 individuals (or 1,500 individuals if the organization is a provider-sponsored organization (PSO)) in urban areas or at least 1,500 individuals (or 500 individuals if the organization is a PSO) in rural areas. CMS may waive the minimum enrollment requirement at the time of application or during the first three years of the contract if the organization demonstrates to CMS's satisfaction that it is capable of administering and managing a Medicare Advantage contract and is able to manage the level of risk required under the contract. [42 C.F.R. § 422.514(d).]

Sanctions

The following intermediate sanctions and civil money penalties may be imposed on Medicare Advantage organizations: (1) civil money penalties ranging from $10,000 to $100,000 depending upon the violation; (2) suspension of enrollment of Medicare beneficiaries; (3) suspension of payment to the MA organization for Medicare beneficiaries who enroll; and (4) requirement that the MA organization suspend all marketing activities to Medicare beneficiaries for the MA plan subject to the intermediate sanctions. The enrollment, payment, and marketing sanctions continue in effect until CMS is satisfied that the deficiency on which the determination was based has been corrected and is not likely to recur. [42 C.F.R. § 422.750.]

Intermediate sanctions. CMS may impose a civil money penalty of not more than $25,000 for each determination of a violation, or suspension of enrollment or payments, if an MA plan:

- fails to provide a beneficiary with medically necessary services;

- imposes premiums that exceed the MA monthly basic and supplemental beneficiary premiums;

- expels or refuses to re-enroll a beneficiary in violation of MA requirements;

- engages in any practice that would have the effect of denying or discouraging the enrollment of eligible individuals;

- misrepresents or falsifies information;

- interferes with practitioners' advice to enrollees;

- fails to limit on balance billing under a private fee-for service plan; or

¶405

- employs or contracts with providers who are excluded from Medicare participation. [42 C.F.R. § 422.752.]

Procedures for imposing sanctions. Before imposing intermediate sanctions CMS must sends a written notice to the MA organization stating the nature and basis of the proposed sanction; and send the HHS office of Inspector General a copy of the notice. CMS allows the MA organization 15 days from receipt of the notice to provide evidence that it has not committed an act or failed to comply. If the MA organization submits a timely response to CMS' notice of sanction, CMS will conducts an informal reconsideration that: (1) consists of a review of the evidence by a CMS official who did not participate in the initial decision to impose a sanction; and (2) gives the MA organization a concise written decision setting forth the factual and legal basis for the decision that affirms or rescinds the original determination.

If CMS affirms the initial determination, it may (1) require the MA organization to suspend accepting new enrollment applications from Medicare beneficiaries during the sanction period; (2) suspend payments to the MA organization for Medicare beneficiaries enrolled in the sanctioned MA plan during the sanction period; and (3) require the MA organization to suspend all marketing activities for the sanctioned MA plan to Medicare enrollees.

A sanction is effective 15 days after the date that the organization is notified of the decision to impose the sanction or, if the MA organization timely seeks reconsideration, on the date specified in the notice of CMS's reconsidered determination. If CMS determines, however, that the MA organization's conduct poses a serious threat to an enrollee's health and safety, CMS may make the sanction effective on a date before issuance of CMS's reconsidered determination. The sanction remains in effect until CMS notifies the MA organization that CMS is satisfied that the basis for imposing the sanction has been corrected and is not likely to recur.

CMS also may decline to authorize the renewal of an organization's contract, or terminate the contract. [42 C.F.R. § 422.756.]

Civil money penalties. If CMS determines that an MA organization has committed an act or failed to comply with a requirement described in § 422.752, CMS notifies the HHS office of Inspector General (OIG) of this determination, and also notifies OIG when CMS reverses or terminates a sanction. The OIG may impose civil money penalties on the MA organization in addition to, or in place of, the sanctions that CMS may impose. [42 C.F.R. § 422.756.]

[¶ 406] Medicare Contract Determinations and Appeals

Contract determinations. CMS can make three types of contract determinations:

(1) a determination that an entity is not qualified to enter into a contract with CMS,

(2) a determination to terminate a contract with a Medicare Advantage organization, and

(3) a determination not to authorize a renewal of a contract with an MA organization. [42 C.F.R. § 422.641.]

Notice of contract determination. When CMS makes a contract determination, it gives the Medicare Advantage organization written notice. The notice specifies the reasons for the determination and the MA organization's right to request reconsideration. For CMS-initiated terminations, CMS mails a notice 90 days before the anticipated effective date of the termination. For terminations based on initial determinations described at 42 C.F.R. § 422.510(a)(5), CMS immediately notifies the MA organization of its decision to terminate the organization's MA contract. When CMS determines that it will not authorize a contract renewal, CMS mails the notice to the MA organization by May 1 of the current contract year. [42 C.F.R. § 422.644.]

Medicare Part C

The MA organization is provided an opportunity to request reconsideration of a determination which CMS may then act upon. [42 C.F.R. §§ 422.650, 422.654]. Depending on the outcome of that reconsideration, the MA organization may request a hearing concerning the determination and then, if applicable, a review of the hearing decision by the CMS Administrator [42 C.F.R. §§ 422.660, 422.692.]

[¶ 407] Bids, Negotiations and Premiums

This section discusses the requirements for Medicare Advantage (MA) bidding payment methodology, including the calculation of benchmarks by CMS, submission of plan bids by MA organizations, establishment of beneficiary premiums and rebates, and negotiation and approval of bids by CMS.

Submission of Bids

Not later than the first Monday in June, each MA organization must submit to CMS an aggregate monthly bid amount for each MA plan (other than a medical savings account plan) the organization intends to offer in the upcoming year in a given service area. The monthly aggregate bid amount submitted by an MA organization for each plan is the organization's estimate of the revenue required for the following categories for providing coverage to an MA eligible beneficiary with a national average risk profile:

- the unadjusted MA statutory non-drug monthly bid amount, which is the MA plan's estimated average monthly required revenue for providing benefits under the original Medicare fee-for-service program option;
- the amount to provide basic prescription drug coverage, if any; and
- the amount to provide supplemental health care benefits, if any.

Each bid is for a uniform benefit package for the service area. Each bid submission must contain all estimated revenue required by the plan, including administrative costs and return on investment. [42 C.F.R. § 422.254(a), (b).]

Required information. MA organizations' submission of bids for coordinated care plans, including regional MA plans and specialized MA plans for special needs beneficiaries, and for MA private fee-for-service plans must include the following information:

- The plan type for each plan.
- The monthly aggregate bid amount for the provision of all items and services under the plan.
- The proportions of the bid amount attributable to (1) the provision of benefits under original Medicare fee-for-service; (2) the provision of basic prescription drug coverage; and (3) the provision of supplemental health care benefits.
- The projected number of enrollees in each MA local area used in calculation of the bid amount, and the enrollment capacity, if any, for the plan.
- The actuarial basis for determining the bid amount and the projected number of enrollees.
- A description of deductibles, coinsurance, and copayments applicable under the plan and the actuarial value of the deductibles, coinsurance, and copayments.
- For qualified prescription drug coverage, information related to coverage, actuarial value, bid, service area, and level of risk assumed.
- For the purposes of calculation of risk corridors, MA organizations offering regional MA plans in 2006 or 2007 must submit the following information developed using the appropriate actuarial bases:

(1) projected allowable costs;

(2) the portion of projected allowable costs attributable to administrative expenses incurred in providing these benefits; and

(3) the total projected costs for providing rebatable integrated benefits and the portion of costs that is attributable to administrative expenses.

- For regional plans, the relative cost factors for the counties in a plan's service area, for the purposes of adjusting payment for intra-area variations in an MA organization's local payment rates. [42 C.F.R. 422.254(c).]

Beneficiary rebate information. In the case of a plan required to provide a monthly rebate for a year, the MA organization offering the plan must inform CMS how the plan will distribute the rebate. [42 C.F.R. 422.254(d).]

MSA plans. MA organizations intending to offer MA MSA plans must submit: (1) the enrollment capacity (if any) for the plan; (2) the amount of the MSA monthly premium for basic benefits under the original Medicare fee-for-service program option; (3) the amount of the plan deductible; and (4) the amount of the beneficiary supplemental premium, if any. [42 C.F.R. 422.254(e).]

Separate bids must be submitted for Part A and Part B enrollees and Part B-only enrollees for each MA plan offered. [42 C.F.R. 422.254(f).]

Review and Negotiation of Bids

CMS has the authority to review the aggregate bid amounts submitted by MA organizations and conduct negotiations with these organizations regarding these bids (including the supplemental benefits) and the proportions of the aggregate bid attributable to basic benefits, supplemental benefits, and prescription drug benefits. [42 C.F.R. 422.256(a).]

Standards of bid review. CMS can only accept bid amounts or proportions if it determines that the bid amount and proportions are supported by the actuarial bases provided by MA organizations, and that the bid amount and proportions reasonably and equitably reflect the plan's estimated revenue requirements for providing the benefits under that plan. For coordinated care plans (including regional MA plans and specialized MA plans) and private fee-for-service plans (other than MSA plans), the actuarial value of plan basic cost sharing, reduced by any supplemental benefits, may not exceed the actuarial value of deductibles, coinsurance, and copayments that would be applicable for the benefits to individuals entitled to benefits under Part A and enrolled under Part B in the plan's service area if they were not members of an MA organization for the year. [42 C.F.R. 422.256(b).]

Negotiation process. The negotiation process may include the resubmission of information to allow MA organizations to modify their initial bid submissions to account for the outcome of CMS' regional benchmark calculations and the outcome of CMS' calculation of the national average monthly bid amount. [42 C.F.R. 422.256(c).]

Exceptions. For private fee-for-service plans, CMS will not review, negotiate, or approve the bid amount, proportions of the bid, or the amounts of the basic beneficiary premium and supplemental premium. CMS also does not review, negotiate, or approve amounts submitted with respect to MA MSA plans, except to determine that the deductible does not exceed the statutory maximum. [42 C.F.R. 422.256(d), (e).]

Calculation of Benchmarks

Area plans. The term "MA area-specific non-drug monthly benchmark amount" means, for a month in a year:

¶407

- for MA local plans with service areas entirely within a single MA local area, 1/12th of the annual MA capitation rate for the area, adjusted as appropriate for the purpose of risk adjustment.

- for MA local plans with service areas including more than one MA local area, an amount equal to the weighted average of annual capitation rates for each local area (county) in the plan's service area, using as weights the projected number of enrollees in each MA local area that the plan used to calculate the bid amount, and adjusted as appropriate for the purpose of risk adjustment.

For MA local plans with service areas including more than one MA local area, an amount equal to the weighted average of annual capitation rates for each local area (county) in the plan's service area, using as weights the projected number of enrollees in each MA local area that the plan used to calculate the bid amount, and adjusted as appropriate for the purpose of risk adjustment. [42 C.F.R. 422.258(a).]

Regional plans. For MA regional plans, the term "MA region-specific non-drug monthly benchmark amount" is:

- the sum of two components: the statutory component (based on a weighted average of local benchmarks in the region), and the plan bid component (based on a weighted average of regional plan bids in the region); and

- announced before November 15 of each year, but after CMS has received the plan bids. [42 C.F.R. 422.258(b).]

Calculation of MA regional non-drug benchmark amount. CMS calculates the monthly regional non-drug benchmark amount for each MA region as follows:

(1) CMS will determine the number of MA eligible individuals in each local area, in each region, and nationally as of the *reference month*, which is a month in the previous calendar year CMS identifies.

(2) CMS will determine the *statutory national market share* percentage as the proportion of the MA eligible individuals nationally who were not enrolled in an MA plan.

(3) CMS calculates the unadjusted region-specific non-drug amount by multiplying the county capitation rate by the county's share of the MA eligible individuals residing in the region (the number of MA eligible individuals in the county divided by the number of MA eligible individuals in the region), and then adding all the enrollment-weighted county rates to a sum for the region. CMS then multiplies the unadjusted region-specific non-drug amount by the statutory market share to determine the statutory component of the regional benchmark.

(4) For each regional plan offered in a region, CMS will multiply the plan's unadjusted region-specific non-drug bid amount by the plan's share of enrollment and then sum these products across all plans offered in the region. CMS then multiples this by 1 minus the statutory market share to determine the plan-bid component of the regional benchmark.

(5) CMS will calculate the plan's *share of MA enrollment* in the region as follows:

- In the first year that any MA regional plan is being offered in a region, and more than one MA regional plan is being offered, CMS will determine each regional plan's share of enrollment based on one of two possible approaches. CMS may base this factor on equal division among plans, so that each plan's share will be 1 divided by the number of plans offered. Alternatively, CMS may base this factor on each regional plan's estimate of projected enrollment.

- If two or more regional plans are offered in a region and were offered in the reference month, the plan's share of enrollment will be the number of MA eligible individuals enrolled in the plan divided by the number of MA eligible individuals enrolled in all of the plans in the region, as of the reference month.

- If a single regional plan is being offered in the region, the plan's share of enrollment is equal to 1. [42 C.F.R. 422.258(c).]

Beneficiary Premiums and Co-Payments

The amount a beneficiary pays out of pocket each year depends on several factors, including:

- whether the MA plan charges a monthly premium in addition to a monthly Part B premium. MA plans will charge one premium that includes coverage for Part A and B benefits, prescription drug coverage (if offered) and extra benefits (if offered);

- whether the plan reduces the monthly premium using a rebate;

- how much the beneficiary pays for each visit or service; and

- the type of healthcare needed, and how frequently it is needed. [42 C.F.R § 422.262.]

Determination of monthly premium. If an MA plan has an unadjusted statutory non-drug bid amount that is less than the relevant unadjusted non-drug benchmark amount, the monthly basic beneficiary premium is zero. If the plan's bid amount that is equal to or greater than the relevant unadjusted non-drug benchmark amount, the basic beneficiary premium is the amount by which the bid amount exceeds the benchmark amount. [42 C.F.R § 422.262.]

Consolidated monthly premium. MA organizations must charge enrollees a consolidated monthly MA premium, which is equal to the sum of the MA monthly basic beneficiary premium (if any), the MA monthly supplementary beneficiary premium (if any), and the MA monthly prescription drug beneficiary premium (if any). For an individual enrolled in an MSA plan offered by an MA organization, the monthly beneficiary premium is the supplemental premium (if any). [42 C.F.R § 422.262.]

Monetary inducement prohibited. An MA organization may not provide for cash or other monetary rebates as an inducement for enrollment or for any other reason or purpose. [42 C.F.R § 422.262.]

Calculation of Savings

The *risk-adjusted MA statutory non-drug monthly bid amount* is the unadjusted plan bid amount for coverage of original Medicare benefits adjusted using the factors for local and regional plans.

The risk-adjusted MA *area-specific* and *region-specific* non-drug monthly benchmark amounts are the unadjusted benchmark amount for coverage of original Medicare benefits by a local MA plan, adjusted as follows:

CMS will publish the first Monday in April before the upcoming calendar year the risk adjustment factors used in calculating savings amounts for MA local and regional plans. For area plans, CMS has the authority to apply risk adjustment factors that are plan-specific average risk adjustment factors, statewide average risk adjustment factors, or use other factors. If CMS applies statewide average risk adjustment factors, the statewide factor for each state is the average of the risk factors based on all enrollees in MA local plans in that state in the previous year.

¶407

For regional plans, CMS has the authority to apply risk adjustment factors that are plan-specific average risk adjustment factors, region-wide average risk adjustment factors, or factors determined on a basis other than MA regions. In the event that CMS applies region-wide average risk adjustment factors, the region-wide factor for each MA region is the average of all risk factors, based on all enrollees in MA regional plans in that region in the previous year. [42 C.F.R. § 422.264.]

Beneficiary Rebates

An MA organization must provide to an enrollee a monthly rebate equal to 75 percent of the average per capita savings (if any) for both MA local plans and MA regional plans.

The rebate can take the form of one or more of the following:

- supplemental health care benefits;
- payment of premium for prescription drug coverage; or
- payment toward Part B premium. [42 C.F.R. § 422.266.]

[¶ 408] Payments to Medicare Advantage Organizations

CMS makes advance monthly payments to Medicare Advantage (MA) plans for coverage of original fee-for-service benefits for an individual in an MA payment area for a month. For MA plans that have average per capita monthly savings, i.e., bids below the benchmark, CMS pays:

- the unadjusted MA statutory non-drug monthly bid amount risk-adjusted and adjusted (if applicable) for variations in rates within the plan's service area and for the effects of risk adjustment on beneficiary premiums; and
- the amount (if any) of any rebate.

For MA plans that do not have average per capita monthly savings, i.e., plans with bids at or above benchmark, CMS pays the unadjusted MA area-specific non-drug monthly benchmark amount, risk-adjusted and adjusted (if applicable) for variations in rates within the plan's service area and for the effects of risk adjustment on beneficiary premiums. [42 C.F.R. § 422.304.]

Federal drug subsidies. In the case of an enrollee in an Medicare Advantage Prescription Drug (MA-PD) plan, the MA organization offering such a plan also receives: (1) direct and reinsurance subsidy payments for qualified prescription drug coverage, and (2) reimbursement for premium and cost sharing reductions for low-income individuals. [42 C.F.R. § 422.304(b).]

Enrollees with ESRD. For enrollees with end-stage renal disease (ESRD), CMS establishes special rates that are actuarially equivalent to rates in effect before the enactment of the Medicare Modernization Act of 2003 (MMA) (PubLNo 108-173). CMS publishes annual changes in these capitation rates no later than the first Monday in April each year. [42 C.F.R. § 422.304(c)(1).]

MSA enrollees. In the case of an Medicare Savings Account (MSA) plan, CMS pays the unadjusted MA area-specific non-drug monthly benchmark amount for the service area, subject to risk adjustment, less 1/12 of the annual lump sum amount (if any) CMS deposits to the enrollee's MA MSA. [42 C.F.R. § 422.304(c)(2).]

RFB plan enrollees. For enrollees in religious fraternal benefit plans (RFB), CMS adjusts the capitation payments otherwise determined under this subpart to ensure that the payment level is appropriate for the actuarial characteristics and experience of these enrollees. This adjustment can be made on an individual or organization basis. [42 C.F.R. § 422.304.]

Annual MA Capitation Rates

The annual capitation rate for each MA local area is equal to the minimum percentage increase rate, which is the greater of (1) 102 percent of the annual capitation rate for the preceding year; or (2) the annual capitation rate for the area for the preceding year increased by the national per capita MA growth percentage for the year. [42 C.F.R. § 422.306.]

The annual capitation rate for each MA local area is the greater of (1) the minimum percentage increase rate; or (2) the amount determined, no less frequently than every three years, to be the adjusted average per capita cost for the MA local area, based on 100 percent of fee-for-service costs for individuals who are not enrolled in an MA plan for the year, adjusted as appropriate for the purpose of risk adjustment; to exclude costs attributable to payments for the costs of direct graduate medical education; and to include CMS' estimate of the amount of additional per capita payments that would have been made in the MA local area if individuals entitled to benefits under this title had not received services from facilities of the Department of Defense or the Department of Veterans Affairs. [42 C.F.R.§ 422.306.]

All payment rates are annual rates, determined and promulgated by HHS. For 2006 and subsequent years, the Secretary will determine and announce, not later than the 1st Monday in April before the calendar year concerned, the annual capitation rate, payment area, and risk adjustment factors. Proposed changes to the payment methodology must be published no later than 45 days before annual announcement of rates. [42 C.F.R. § 422.312.]

Changes to the 2006 MA Capitation Rates

The base beneficiary premium is equal to the product of the beneficiary premium percentage and the national average monthly bid amount. *The Part D base beneficiary premium for 2006 is $32.20.* [*CMS Letter,* August 9, 2005.]

The national average monthly bid amount is the weighted average of the standardized bid amounts for each prescription drug plan (not including fallbacks) and for each Medicare Advantage Prescription drug (MA-PD) plan described in Soc. Sec. Act § 1851(a)(2)(A)(i). The calculation does not include bids submitted by medical savings account (MSA) plans, MA private fee-for-service plans, specialized MA plans for special needs individuals, PACE programs under Soc. Sec. Act § 1894, and contracts under reasonable cost reimbursement contracts under Soc. Sec. Act § 1876(h). The national average monthly bid amount for 2006 is $92.30.

The standardized benchmark for each MA region is a blend of two components: a statutory component consisting of the weighted average of the county capitation rates across the region; and a competitive, or plan-bid, component consisting of the weighted average of all of the standardized bids for providing Part A and Part B services for regional plans in the region. The two components are then blended, with the statutory components reflecting the market share of traditional Medicare and the plan-bid component reflecting the market share of all MA organizations in the Medicare population nationally. For 2006, the weights applied to the statutory and plan-bid components are 87.4 and 12.6 percent, respectively. [*CMS Letter to Medicare Advantage Organizations, Prescription Drug Plan Sponsors, and Other Interested Parties,* August 9, 2005.]

Special Rules

Special rules for beneficiaries enrolled in MA MSA plans. A beneficiary who elects coverage under a Medicare Advantage MSA plan must establish a MA MSA with a trustee. If he or she has more than one MA MSA, the beneficiary must designate the particular account to which payments under the plan are to be made.

The payment is calculated as follows: (1) The monthly MA MSA premium is compared with 1/12 of the annual capitation rate for the area determined under 42 C.F.R. § 422.252, and (2) if the monthly MA MSA premium is less than 1/12 of the annual capitation rate, the difference is the amount to be deposited in the MA MSA for each month for which the beneficiary is enrolled in the MSA plan.

CMS deposits the full amount to which a beneficiary is entitled for the calendar year, beginning with the month in which MA MSA coverage begins. If the beneficiary's coverage under the MA MSA plan ends before the end of the calendar year, CMS recovers the amount that corresponds to the remaining months of that year. [42 C.F.R. § 422.314.]

Special rules for payments to federally qualified health centers. If an enrollee in an MA plan receives a service from a federally qualified health center (FQHC) that has a written agreement with the MA organization offering services to the plan, CMS will pay the FQHC directly for the services, less the amount the FQHC would receive for the MA enrollee from the MA organization and taking into account the cost sharing amount paid by the enrollee [42 C.F.R. § 422.316.]

Special rules for coverage that begins or ends during an inpatient hospital stay. If coverage under an MA plan begins while the beneficiary is an inpatient, payment for inpatient services until the date of the beneficiary's discharge is made by the previous MA organization or original Medicare, as appropriate. The MA organization offering the newly-elected MA plan is not responsible for the inpatient services until the date after the beneficiary's discharge. The MA organization is paid the full amount otherwise payable. [42 C.F.R. § 422.318.]

If coverage under an MA plan ends while the beneficiary is an inpatient, the MA organization is responsible for the inpatient services until the date of the beneficiary's discharge. Payment for those services during the remainder of the stay is not made by original Medicare or by any succeeding MA organization offering a newly-elected MA plan. The MA organization that no longer provides coverage receives no payment for the beneficiary for the period after coverage ends. [42 C.F.R. § 422.318.]

Special rules for hospice care. A MA organization must inform each Medicare enrollee eligible to elect hospice care about the availability of hospice care if a Medicare hospice program is located within the plan's service area or if it is common practice to refer patients to hospice programs outside that area. [42 C.F.R. § 422.320.]

Unless the enrollee disenrolls from the MA plan, a beneficiary electing hospice continues his or her enrollment in the MA plan and is entitled to receive, through the MA plan, any benefits other than those that are the responsibility of the Medicare hospice. [42 C.F.R. § 422.320(b).]

Payment. No payment is made to an MA organization on behalf of a Medicare enrollee who has elected hospice care, except for the portion of the payment attributable to the beneficiary rebate for the MA plan plus the amount of the monthly prescription drug payment (if any). This no-payment rule is effective from the first day of the month following the month of election to receive hospice care, until the first day of the month following the month in which the election is terminated. [42 C.F.R. § 422.320(c).]

Special rules for payments to VA facilities. An MA enrollee who is enrolled in the VA Medical Benefits Plan has dual entitlement to separate government-funded health care systems. This means that the individual may elect to receive his or her health care either through the VA system or through his or her MA plan. If the individual elects to receive routine or non-emergency services through the VA system, the VA would be obligated by law to pay for those services and the MA organization would not be permitted to reimburse

¶408

for such services under the same law. [*Medicare Managed Care Manual*, Pub. 100-16, Ch. 7, § 165.]

[¶ 409] Marketing

Marketing materials, in general, are informational materials targeted to Medicare beneficiaries that promote the Medicare health plan or any plan offered by the Medicare health plan, or communicate or explain a Medicare health plan.

Medicare Advantage organizations can use the term "Medicare" or the term "Advantage" in their plan names. Furthermore, all plans in existence as of January 1, 2004, who had the name "Medicare Advantage" may continue to use that name indefinitely. However, new plans are not allowed to do business under the name "Medicare Advantage." If an organization chooses to retain the Medicare Advantage plan name it must insert the company name before "Medicare Advantage" beginning with all 2005 plan year materials. This will help prevent any confusion with the national Medicare Advantage program. [*Medicare Managed Care Manual*, Pub. 100-16, Ch. 3, § 10.]

Approval of marketing materials and enrollment forms. An MA organization may not distribute any marketing materials or election forms unless it has submitted the materials or forms to CMS for approval at least 45 days before the date of distribution and CMS has not disapproved the materials or forms. If the MA organization uses for its materials and forms proposed model language specified by CMS, the approval period may be reduced to 10 days. [42 C.F.R. § 422.80.]

Standards for MA organization marketing. In conducting marketing activities, MA organizations may not (1) offer cash inducements for enrollment, (2) engage in discriminatory activity such as targeted marketing to beneficiaries from high-income areas without making comparable attempts to enroll beneficiaries from low-income areas, (3) solicit door-to-door for beneficiaries, (4) engage in activities that could mislead or confuse beneficiaries or misrepresent the MA organization, (5) distribute marketing materials that CMS has disapproved, (6) use providers to distribute printed information comparing the benefits of different health plans unless the materials have the concurrence of all MA organizations involved and CMS' approval, (7) accept applications in provider offices, or (8) employ MA plan names that suggest that a plan is not available to some beneficiaries. [42 C.F.R. § 422.80.]

HIPAA compliance. Health plans/MA organizations may use or disclose their members' protected health information as permitted by the "Standards for Privacy of Individually Identifiable Health Information" (45 C.F.R. Part 164). Specifically, they may use or disclose this information without beneficiary authorization for treatment, payment or health operations (as those terms are defined by the rule) and for a number of public policy purposes, such as public health and research, recognized in the rule. Health plans/MA organizations are not required to obtain authorization from beneficiaries prior to marketing their plan benefit packages. [Pub. 100-16, Ch. 3, § 10.1.]

Streamlined marketing campaign. CMS offers a streamlined marketing review process to MA organizations for certain marketing materials to ensure that the materials can be available to Medicare beneficiaries in time to make decisions about their health insurance coverage. In particular, the streamlined marketing review process only applies to marketing materials developed for the fall campaign (i.e., the annual notice of change, the summary of benefits, and materials necessary to develop an annual enrollment period marketing package in the fall to encourage members to join the plan) and marketing materials developed to notify members of any mid-year benefit enhancements. [Pub. 100-16, Ch. 3, § 20.3.]

File and Use program. The File and Use program is designed to streamline the marketing review process. Under this process, organizations that can demonstrate to CMS that they can continually meet a particular standard of performance will be able to publish and distribute certain marketing materials without prior CMS approval. [Pub. 100-16, Ch. 3, § 20.5.]

Health plan web sites. CMS considers a health plan's web site as simply another vehicle for the distribution of marketing information. Therefore, all marketing regulatory rules and requirements are applicable to Medicare health plan marketing activity on the Internet. The specific requirements that apply depend on the type of material. For example, the advertising guidelines would apply to postings on the Internet that fall within the definition of advertising.

Independent insurance agents. A regional PPO or MA/PD plan can pay agent/broker fees for selling and servicing membership in the plan. CMS recognizes that independent insurance agents can provide a necessary service to Medicare beneficiaries and potential enrollees. CMS is aware that sales by independent insurance agents are typically tied to compensation, and that agents are often given incentives to steer enrollees towards the carrier offering the most compensation. Marketing by an independent insurance agent shall be deemed to be marketing by the Medicare health plan. Therefore, Medicare health plans should stipulate in their contracts with independent insurance agents that any coordinated marketing to be carried out by the agent must be done in accordance with all applicable CMS markering guidelines. [Pub. 100-16, Ch. 3, § 50.3.]

[¶ 410] Quality Improvement Programs

Quality assessment. Each MA organization that offers one or more MA plans must have an ongoing quality improvement program for services it provides to enrollees. An MA plan must (1) include a chronic care improvement program, (2) conduct quality improvement projects that can be expected to have a favorable effect on health outcomes and enrollee satisfaction, and (3) encourage its providers to participate in CMS and HHS quality improvement initiatives. [42 C.F.R. § 422.152.]

Requirements for MA coordinated care plans. An MA coordinated care plan's (except for regional PPO plans and local PPO plans) quality improvement program must (1) in processing requests for initial or continued authorization of services, follow written policies and procedures that reflect current standards of medical practice; (2) have in effect mechanisms to detect both underutilization and overutilization of services; and (3) measure and report performance. [42 C.F.R. 422.152(b).]

Requirements for MA regional plans and MA local plans. MA organizations offering an MA regional plan or local PPO plan must: (1) measure performance under the plan using standard measures required by CMS and report its performance to CMS, and (2) evaluate the continuity and coordination of care furnished to enrollees. If the organization uses written protocols for utilization review, the organization must: (1) base those protocols on current standards of medical practice, and (2) have mechanisms to evaluate utilization of services and to inform enrollees and providers of services of the results of the evaluation. [42 C.F.R. 422.152(e).]

Requirements for all plans. For all types of plans that it offers, an organization must (1) maintain a *health information system* that collects, analyzes, and integrates the data necessary to implement its quality improvement program; (2) ensure that the information it receives from providers of services is reliable and complete; and (3) make all collected information available to CMS. For each plan, there must be in effect a *process for formal evaluation*, at least annually, of the impact and effectiveness of its quality improvement program. For each plan, the organization must *correct all problems* that come to its attention through internal surveillance, complaints, or other mechanisms. [42 C.F.R. 422.152(f).]

Compliance deemed on the basis of accreditation. Congress gave CMS the authority to deem MA organizations compliant with Medicare requirements in the following six areas: (1) quality assurance; (2) antidiscrimination; (3) access to services; (4) confidentiality and accuracy of enrollee records; (5) information on advance directives; and (6) provider participation rules.

An MA organization is deemed to meet any of these requirements if it is fully accredited for the standards related to one of the areas listed above by a private, national accreditation organization, and the accreditation organization uses standards approved by CMS for assessing the MA organization's compliance with Medicare requirements. [42 C.F.R. § 422.156.] Currently, CMS contracts with the National Committee for Quality Assurance (NCQA), the Joint Commission on Accreditation of Healthcare Organizations (JCAHO) and the Accreditation Association for Ambulatory Health Care, Inc. (AAAHC) to be deeming accrediting organizations. [*Managed Care Manual,* Pub. 100-16, Ch. 5, § 35.1.]

[¶ 411] Relationships with Providers

A Medicare Advantage organization that operates a coordinated care plan or network MSA plan must provide for the participation of individual physicians through reasonable procedures that include written notice of the following: (1) rules of participation, including terms of payment, credentialing, and other rules relating to participation decisions; (2) changes in participation rules before the changes are put into effect; (3) participation decisions that are adverse to physicians; and (4) a process for appealing adverse participation procedures, including the right of physicians to present information and their views on the decision. [42 C.F.R. § 422.202(a).]

The MA organization must establish a formal mechanism to consult with the physicians who have agreed to provide services under the MA plan offered by the organization, regarding the organization's medical policy, quality improvement programs, and medical management procedures. The MA organization must ensure that practice guidelines and utilization management guidelines are communicated to providers and, as appropriate, to enrollees. [42 C.F.R. § 422.202(b).]

Suspension or termination of contract. An MA organization that suspends or terminates a provider agreement must give the individual provider written notice of the reasons for the action and of the provider's right to appeal the action. The organization also must give written notice of the suspension or termination to licensing or disciplinary authorities. [42 C.F.R. § 422.202(d).]

Provider selection and credentialing. An MA organization must have written policies and procedures for the selection and evaluation of providers, physicians, and other healthcare professionals. Providers must be licensed to operate in the state and must be reviewed and approved by an accrediting body, or must meet the standards of the MA organization itself. Physicians and other healthcare professionals must undergo an initial credentialing process and be recredentialed at least every three years thereafter. [42 C.F.R. § 422.204.]

Provider antidiscrimination rules. An MA organization may not discriminate, in terms of participation, reimbursement, or indemnification, against any healthcare professional who is acting within the scope of his or her license or certification, based on that license or certification. If an MA organization declines to include a given provider or group of providers in its network, it must furnish written notice to the affected providers of the reason for the decision. [42 C.F.R. § 422.205.]

Prohibition of interference with professional advice to enrollees. An MA organization may not prohibit or restrict a healthcare professional from advising an enrollee about his or her health status, medical care, or treatment options; the risks, benefits, or consequences of treatment; or the opportunity for the enrollee to refuse treatment. This rule, however, (the so-called "gag clause" rule) does not require an MA plan to cover a counseling or referral service if the plan objects to the service on religious or moral grounds. [42 C.F.R. § 422.206.]

Physician incentive plans. A physician incentive plan is any compensation arrangement to pay a physician or physician group that directly or indirectly may have the effect of reducing or limiting the services provided to any plan enrollee. An MA organization may not make a specific payment, directly or indirectly, to a physician or physician group as an inducement to reduce or limit medically necessary services to enrollees. If the MA organization has a physician incentive plan that puts a physician or physician group at substantial financial risk, the organization must assure that the providers at risk have either aggregate or per-patient stop-loss protection. [42 C.F.R. § 422.208(a), (c).]

Each MA organization must provide to CMS information concerning its physician incentive plans as requested. Each MA organization must provide the following information to any Medicare beneficiary who requests it: (1) whether the MA organization uses a physician incentive plan that affects the use of referral services; (2) the type of incentive arrangement; (3) whether stop-loss protection is provided; and (4) if the MA organization was required to conduct a survey, a summary of the survey results. [42 C.F.R. § 422.210.]

Special rules for services furnished by noncontract providers. Healthcare providers (other than hospitals, critical access hospitals, skilled nursing facilities, comprehensive outpatient rehabilitation facilities, home health agencies, or hospice programs) that do not have a contract with an MA plan must accept, as payment in full, the amounts that the provider could collect if the beneficiary were enrolled in original Medicare. [42 C.F.R. § 422.214.]

Special rules for MA private fee-for-service plans. An MA organization must establish uniform payment rates for all items and services that apply to all contracting providers and make those payment rates available to all providers that furnish services under an MA private fee-for-service contract. [42 C.F.R. § 422.216(a).]

Contract providers may charge enrollees no more than the cost-sharing and balance billing amounts that are permitted under the plan. The organization may permit balance billing no greater than 15 percent of the set uniform payment rate, and it must specify the amount of cost sharing and balance billing allowed in its contracts with providers. A noncontract provider may not collect from an enrollee more than the cost sharing established by the MA organization, unless the provider has opted out of Medicare. [42 C.F.R. § 422.216(b).]

[¶ 412] Provider-Sponsored Organizations

A *provider-sponsored organization (PSO)* is a public or private entity that (1) is established or organized, and operated, by a provider or group of affiliated providers; (2) provides a substantial proportion of the healthcare services under the Medicare Advantage contract directly through the provider or affiliated group of providers; and (3) when it is a group, is composed of affiliated providers who share, directly or indirectly, substantial financial risk for the provision of services that are the obligation of the PSO under the Medicare Advantage contract and have at least a majority financial interest in the PSO. [42 C.F.R. § 422.350.]

For purposes of this definition, CMS has determined that a "substantial proportion" means at least 70 percent of the Medicare items and services covered under a PSO contract.

[42 C.F.R. § 422.352(b)(1).] The substantial proportion threshold has been reduced to 60 percent, however, for rural PSOs. [42 C.F.R. § 422.352(b)(2).]

The PSO must demonstrate to CMS's satisfaction that it apportions a significant part of the financial risk of the PSO enterprise under the Medicare Advantage contract to each affiliated provider. The PSO must demonstrate that the financial arrangements among its affiliated providers constitute "substantial" risk in the PSO for each affiliated provider. The following may constitute risk-sharing arrangements: (1) agreement by a healthcare provider to accept capitation payment for each Medicare enrollee; (2) agreement by a healthcare provider to accept as payment a predetermined percentage of the PSO premium or the PSO's revenue; (3) the PSO's use of significant financial incentives for its affiliated providers, with the aim of achieving utilization management and cost containment goals; and (4) other mechanisms that demonstrate significant shared financial risk.[42 C.F.R. § 422.356(a).] Maintaining effective control of a PSO will be accepted by CMS as evidence of a "majority financial interest" for purposes of this definition. [42 C.F.R. § 422.356(b).]

Other basic requirements. In addition to satisfying the definition, to be a PSO for purposes of a Medicare Advantage contract, an organization must be licensed by all states in which it plans to operate, or obtain a waiver. The PSO also must be controlled effectively by the provider or affiliated providers that established and operate it. Finally, a PSO must demonstrate that it can deliver Medicare enrollees the full range of services required under the MA contract. [42 C.F.R. § 422.352.]

PSO waiver. The Secretary may approve a PSO waiver if:

• a state has failed to complete action on a PSO's licensing application within 90 days of the state's receipt of a substantially complete application;

• a PSO experiences discrimination in a state's denial of its application;

• a state imposes financial solvency standards that differ from those established by CMS; or

• a state has notified an organization in writing that it will not accept a license application from a PSO. [42 C.F.R. § 422.372(b).]

PSO solvency requirements. A Medicare Advantage PSO that is not licensed by a state, and for which CMS has approved a waiver, must meet these financial solvency standards:

• a minimum start-up net worth, generally $1.5 million [42 C.F.R. § 422.382(a)(1)];

• a minimum continuing operations net worth based on a regulatory formula [42 C.F.R. § 422.382(b),(c)];

• an approved financial plan [42 C.F.R. § 422.384];

• sufficient cash flow to meet financial obligations [42 C.F.R. § 422.386]; and

• an insolvency deposit of $100,000. [42 C.F.R. § 422.388.]

[¶ 415] Map of 2006 MA Regions

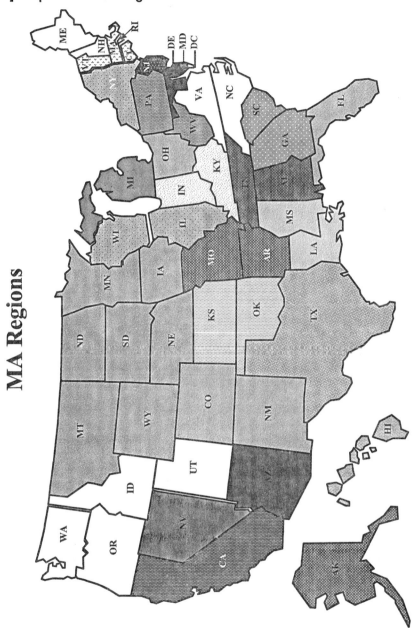

Chapter 5—MEDICARE PART D—PRESCRIPTION DRUG BENEFIT

[¶ 500] Overview

Beneficiaries entitled to Part A and enrolled in Part B, enrollees in Medicare Advantage private fee-for-service plans, and enrollees in Medicare Savings Account plans are eligible individuals for the prescription drug benefit (see ¶ 505). The prescription drug benefit is available to eligible individuals beginning January 1, 2006. Eligible individuals have access to at least two prescription drug plans (PDPs) in their region. [Soc. Sec. Act §§ 1860D-1(a), 1860D-3(a).] In regions where eligible individuals do not have access to at least two PDPs, limited risk or fallback prescription drug plans must be offered (see ¶ 525). As a practical matter, fallback plans have not been necessary as at least two qualified PDPs have been offered in each region.

Under the PDP program, eligible individuals have the choice of either a standard coverage plan or an alternative coverage plan with actuarially equivalent benefits. In addition to the standard coverage plan, participating plans may offer a supplemental benefit. For 2006, standard coverage will have a $250 deductible and a 25 percent coinsurance for costs between $251 and $2250. Beneficiaries will pay 100 percent for the cost of prescription drugs for amounts spent between $2251 and $5100 each year. At this point, beneficiaries will have spent $3600 out of their own pockets on the cost of prescription drugs. From this point forward, beneficiaries will pay $2 for generic drugs and $5 for nonpreferred drugs or 5 percent of the cost of the prescription medication, whichever is greater (see ¶ 510). Subsidies are established for deductibles, premiums, and cost-sharing for low-income individuals with incomes below 150 percent of the federal poverty line (see ¶ 535). Low-income determinations will be made by state Medicaid plans. [Soc. Sec. Act § 1860D-2(b).]

CMS established a state pharmaceutical assistance transition commission to deal with transitional issues facing state programs and participants due to the implementation of Part D. [Soc. Sec. Act § 1860D-31.]

[¶ 505] Prescription Drug Benefit

The voluntary prescription drug benefit, created under a new Part D of the Medicare program by § 101(a) of the Medicare Prescription Drug, Improvement, and Modernization Act of 2003 (MMA) (PubLNo 108-173), is available to eligible individuals beginning January 1, 2006. [*Final rule*, 70 FR 4193, Jan. 28, 2005.]

Under the benefit, beneficiaries will choose drugs from formularies, i.e. lists of discounted drugs. The transitional drug card formularies had 209 therapeutic categories of drugs and were required to provide beneficiaries with a choice of at least one drug in each category, but the prescription drug benefit formularies that go into effect on January 1, 2006, will have fewer categories. The formularies will have to provide beneficiaries with at least two choices in each category, whenever possible. The United States Pharmacopeial Convention, Inc., which was charged by the MMA with creating a model formulary for all prescription drug plans, proposed a formulary with only 146 therapeutic categories and pharmacologic classes of drugs. CMS considered public comments on the makeup of a model formulary. [*Medicare Prescription Drug Benefit Draft Model Guidelines*, United States Pharmacopeial Convention, Inc., CMS Cooperative Agreement No. 18-C-92305/3-01, August 19, 2004.]

[¶ 506] Eligibility and Enrollment

To be eligible for prescription drug benefits under Part D, an individual must be entitled to Medicare benefits under Part A or enrolled in Medicare Part B and live in the service area of a Part D plan. Except for those enrolled in a Medicare Advantage prescription drug plan (MA-PD), a Program of All-inclusive Care for the Elderly plan (PACE), or a cost-based health maintenance organization (HMO) or competitive medical plan (CMP), individuals may enroll in prescription drug plans (PDPs) if they are eligible for Part D, live in the PDP service area, and are not enrolled in another Part D plan. [42 C.F.R. § 423.30(a).]

Medicare Advantage (MA) plan enrollees. A Part D eligible individual enrolled in a MA-PD plan must obtain qualified prescription drug coverage from that plan. MA enrollees may not enroll in a PDP unless they are enrolled in a MA private fee-for-services plan that does not provide qualified prescription drug coverage or they are enrolled in a Medicare savings account plan. [42 C.F.R. § 423.30(b).]

Program of All-inclusive Care for the Elderly (PACE) plan enrollees. A Part D eligible individual enrolled in a PACE plan offering qualified prescription drug coverage must obtain coverage through that PACE plan. [42 C.F.R. § 423.30(c).]

Cost-based HMO or competitive medical plan (CMP) enrollees. A Part D eligible individual enrolled in a cost-based HMO or CMP that provides qualified prescription drug coverage is eligible to enroll in a PDP only if the individual does not elect prescription drug coverage under the cost-based HMO or CMP and otherwise meets general PDP eligibility requirements. [42 C.F.R. § 423.30(d).]

Incarcerated individuals. Individuals incarcerated in correctional facilities are not eligible to enroll in PDPs. Despite the fact that incarcerated individuals may be located within a PDP service area, CMS believes it is unlikely that they will have access to Part D services through network pharmacies. As a result, CMS has determined that it is inappropriate for PDP service areas to include correctional facilities. [*Final rule*, 70 FR 4202, Jan. 28, 2005.]

State mental institution patients. Unlike incarcerated individuals, CMS does not consider individuals who are residing in state mental institutions to be out of service areas. Medicare beneficiaries residing in such institutions have access to Medicare benefits under Parts A and B and are entitled to enroll in Part D plans. CMS, however, recognizes that individuals in state mental institutions may be limited to enrolling in the pharmacy network that contracts with their institution. As a result, CMS will provide a special enrollment period to enable them to join the appropriate Part D plan based upon their situation. [*Final rule*, 70 FR 4203, Jan. 28, 2005.]

The Enrollment Process

An individual eligible for a Part D benefit may enroll in a private prescription drug plan (PDP) during the specified regulatory enrollment periods by filing the appropriate enrollment form with the PDP or through other CMS-approved enrollment mechanisms. [42 C.F.R. § 423.32(a).]

Enrollment forms. The enrollment must be completed by the beneficiary and must include an acknowledgement of the disclosure and exchange of necessary information between CMS and the PDP sponsor. Individuals who assist in the completion of an enrollment, including authorized representatives of the beneficiary, must indicate that they provided assistance and disclose their relationship to the beneficiary. Part D eligible individuals must provide information regarding reimbursement through other insurance, group health plans, other third-party payment arrangements, or other sources, and consent to the release of such information. [42 C.F.R. § 423.32(b).]

Timely processing and prompt notice. A PDP sponsor must timely process an enrollment request in accordance with CMS enrollment guidelines and enroll a Part D eligible who elects to enroll or is enrolled in the plan during the specified enrollment periods. A sponsor also must provide an individual with prompt notice of acceptance or denial of an enrollment request. [42 C.F.R. § 423.32(c) and (d).]

Maintenance of enrollment. An enrolled individual remains enrolled in a PDP until: (1) the individual successfully enrolls in another PDP or MA-PD; (2) the individual voluntarily disenrolls from the PDP; (3) the individual is involuntarily disenrolled from the PDP; (4) the PDP is discontinued within the individual's area of residence; or (5) the individual is enrolled after the initial enrollment. [42 C.F.R. § 423.32(e).]

Cost-based HMOs, CMPs, and PACE plans. Individuals enrolled in cost-based health maintenance organizations (HMOs), competitive medical plans (CMPs) or Program for All-inclusive Care for the Elderly (PACE) plans that offer prescription drug coverage as of December 31, 2005, will remain enrolled in those plans as of January 1, 2006, and receive Part D benefits offered by the plans until one of the five conditions for disenrollment are met (see above). [42 C.F.R. § 423.32(f).]

Appeals process. A formal appeals process will not be available for beneficiaries who are denied enrollment into PDPs. Beneficiary complaints regarding PDP enrollment will be addressed in a manner similar to the Medicare Advantage (MA) program. Under the MA program, individuals are advised through their notices of denial of enrollment that if they disagree with a decision, they may contact the MA organization. [*Final rule*, 70 FR 4204, Jan. 28, 2005.]

Enrollment of Individuals Eligible for Medicare and Medicaid

Those individuals eligible for both Medicare and Medicaid (referred to as full-benefit dual eligible individuals) who fail to enroll in prescription drug plans (PDPs) will be automatically enrolled by the Center for Medicare Services (CMS). [42 C.F.R. § 423.34(a).]

Automatic enrollment. CMS will automatically enroll full-benefit dual eligible individuals who fail to enroll in Part D plans into PDPs offering basic prescription drug coverage in the areas where the individuals reside. These basic plans must have monthly beneficiary premiums that do not exceed the low-income premium subsidy amount. If there is more than one eligible PDP in a service area, individuals will be auto-enrolled in such PDPs on a random basis. Full-benefit dual eligible individuals enrolled in a Medicare Advantage private fee for service plan, a cost-based health maintenance organization, a competitive medical plan that does not offer qualified prescription drug coverage, or a Medicare savings account plan, and who fail to enroll in a Part D plan, also will be enrolled automatically. [42 C.F.R. § 423.34(d).]

Declining enrollment or disenrollment by dual eligible individuals. A full-benefit dual eligible individual may decline enrollment in Part D or disenroll from a Part D plan and elect to enroll in another Part D plan during the special enrollment period. Late enrollment penalties are waived for these individuals. [42 C.F.R. § 423.34(e).]

Dual eligibles' effective date of enrollment. Enrollment for full-benefit dual eligible individuals must be effective: (1) January 1, 2006, for individuals who are full-benefit dual eligible individuals as of December 31, 2005, (2) the first day of the month the individual is eligible for Part D under the rule of general eligibility for individuals who are Medicaid-eligible and subsequently become newly eligible for Part D under the general eligibility rule on or after January 1, 2006; and (3) for individuals who are eligible for Part D under the rule of general eligibility and subsequently become newly eligible for Medicaid on or after January 1, 2006, as soon as practicable after being identified as a newly full-benefit dual eligible individual. [42 C.F.R. § 423.34(f).]

Voluntary Disenrollment

An individual may disenroll from a prescription drug plan (PDP) during the specified enrollment periods by enrolling in a different PDP, by submitting a disenrollment request to a PDP, or by filing an appropriate disenrollment request through other mechanisms approved by CMS. The PDP sponsor must submit a disenrollment notice to CMS within the timeframes CMS specifies, provide the enrollee with a notice of disenrollment as CMS determines and approves, and file and retain disenrollment requests for the period specified in CMS instructions. CMS may grant retroactive disenrollment if there never was a legally valid enrollment or if a valid request for disenrollment was properly made but not processed or acted upon. [42 C.F.R. § 423.36.]

Enrollment Periods

The Medicare Modernization Act of 2003 mandates an initial enrollment period (IEP), an annual coordinated election period (AEP), and special enrollment periods (SEPs) for prescription drug plans (PDPs).

Initial enrollment period. The initial enrollment period (IEP) is the period during which an individual is first eligible to enroll in a Part D plan. Generally, the IEP for Part D is the same as the IEP established for Part B. [42 C.F.R. § 423.38(a).]

Prior to January 31, 2006. An individual who is first eligible to enroll on or prior to January 31, 2006, has an IEP from November 15, 2005 through May 15, 2006. [42 C.F.R. § 423.38(a)(1).]

February 2006. An individual who is first eligible to enroll in February 2006, has an IEP from November 15, 2005 through May 31, 2006. [42 C.F.R. § 423.38(a)(2).]

On or after March 2006. The IEP for an individual who is first eligible to enroll on or after March 2006, is the same as the IEP for Medicare Part B, generally a six month period. Exceptions: For individuals not eligible to enroll in Part D at any time during their IEP for Part B, their IEP runs from three months before becoming eligible for Part D to three months following eligibility. In addition, for individuals who become entitled to Medicare Part A or enrolled in Part B for a retroactive effective date, their IEP under Part D starts with the month in which notification of Medicare determination is received and ends on the last day of the third month in which the notification was received. [42 C.F.R. § 423.38(a)(3).]

Annual coordinated election period. The annual coordinated election period (AEP) for Part D is concurrent with the annual coordinated election period for Medicare Advantage prescription drug plans (MA-PDs). For coverage beginning in 2006, the AEP begins on November 15, 2005, and ends on May 15, 2006. For 2007 and subsequent years, the AEP will run from November 15 through December 31 for coverage beginning on January 1 of the following year. [42 C.F.R. § 423.38(b).]

Special enrollment periods. Special enrollment periods (SEPs) allow an individual to disenroll from one PDP and enroll in another PDP. SEPs required by the MMA are provided below. Those SEPs that are established for exceptional circumstances for PDPs and MA-PDs will be provided in CMS manual instructions. [42 C.F.R. § 423.38(c).]

A Part D eligible individual may enroll in a PDP or disenroll from a PDP and enroll in another PDP or MA-PD plan at any time if:

¶506

(1) creditable prescription drug coverage is lost or involuntarily reduced so that it is no longer creditable coverage, but loss of coverage due to failure to pay premiums is not considered involuntary;

(2) the individual is not adequately informed that he or she has lost creditable prescription drug coverage, that he or she never had credible prescription drug coverage, or the coverage is involuntarily reduced so that the coverage is no longer creditable;

(3) the individual's enrollment or non-enrollment in a Part D plan is unintentional, inadvertent, or erroneous because of error, misrepresentation, or inaction of a federal employee, or any person authorized to act on behalf of the federal government;

(4) the individual is a full-benefit dual eligible;

(5) the individual elects to disenroll from a MA-PD plan and elects coverage under Medicare Part A and Part;

(6) the PDP's contract is terminated by the PDP or CMS or the PDP plan no longer is offered in the area where the individual resides;

(7) the individual no longer is eligible for the PDP because of a change of residence;

(8) the individual demonstrates in accordance with CMS guidelines that the PDP sponsor substantially violated a material provision of its contract, including: (a) failure to provide benefits on a timely basis; (b) failure to provide benefits in accordance with applicable quality standards; or (c) material misrepresentation of the plan's provisions during marketing; or

(9) the individual meets other exceptional circumstances as determined by CMS. [42 C.F.R. § 423.38(c).]

Additional special enrollment periods (SEPs). CMS plans to issue guidance regarding additional SEPs that it chooses to establish in the future. In this future guidance, CMS plans to establish SEPs for:

(1) individuals eligible for the low-income subsidy whose enrollment into a Part D plan will be facilitated;

(2) individuals in long-term care facilities;

(3) individuals enrolled in, or desiring to enroll in the Program for All-inclusive Care for the Elderly (PACE);

(4) individuals enrolled in employer group health plans; and

(5) individuals who will receive the low-income subsidy but who are not full-benefit dual eligible individuals to change to a plan of their choosing. CMS also reserves the right to establish SEPs on a case-by-case basis, when warranted by an immediate exceptional circumstance, such as when an individual has a life-threatening condition or illness. [*Final rule*, 70 FR 4212, Jan. 28, 2005.]

Effective Dates of Coverage and Change of Coverage

The Medicare Modernization Act of 2003 directs CMS to apply the effective date requirements provided under the Medicare Advantage (MA) program to Part D enrollments. The three enrollment periods for Part D are the initial enrollment period (IEP), the annual coordinated enrollment period (AEP), and the special enrollment period (SEP). The effective dates for these enrollment periods are described below:

(1) *Initial enrollment period.* An enrollment made prior to the month of entitlement to Medicare Part A or enrollment in Part B is effective the first day of the month

the individual is entitled to or enrolled in Part A or enrolled in Part B. Except as indicated for full-benefit dual eligible individuals, an enrollment made during or after the month of entitlement to Part A or enrollment in Part B is effective the first day of the calendar month following the month in which the enrollment in Part D is made. If the individual, however, is not eligible to enroll in Part D on the first day of the calendar month following the month in which the election to enroll is made, the enrollment is effective the first day of the month the individual is eligible for Part D. Because the Part D regulations are not effective until January 1, 2006, in no case is an enrollment in Part D effective prior to this date or before entitlement to Part A or enrollment in Part B. [42 C.F.R. § 423.40(a).]

(2) *Annual coordinated election period.* Except for enrollment elections between January 1, 2006 and May 15, 2006, for an enrollment or change of enrollment in Part D made during an AEP, the coverage or change in coverage is effective as of the first day of the following calendar year. Enrollment elections made during the AEP between January 1, 2006 and May 15, 2006, are effective the first day of the calendar month following the month in which the enrollment in Part D is made. [42 C.F.R. § 423.40(b).]

(3) *Special enrollment periods.* For an enrollment or change of enrollment in Part D made during a SEP, the effective date is determined by CMS in a manner consistent with protecting the continuity of health benefits coverage. [42 C.F.R. § 423.40(c).]

Involuntary Disenrollment

Generally, a prescription drug plan (PDP) sponsor is prohibited from involuntarily disenrolling an individual from a PDP it offers or requesting or encouraging an individual to disenroll, either through verbal or written communication, or through action or inaction. Mandatory disenrollment, however, is required by the PDP sponsor under various conditions and an option to disenroll an individual may be exercised by the PDP sponsor for monthly premiums that are not timely paid or for disruptive behavior by the enrollee. [42 C.F.R. § 423.44(a).]

As with the Medicare Advantage (MA) program, PDP sponsors will be required to provide proper notice to the beneficiary prior to disenrollment, including due process procedures outlined in CMS operational instructions. PDP policies for optional disenrollment for nonpayment of premiums and disruptive behavior must be applied consistently among enrollees and unless CMS permits otherwise, in accordance with applicable discrimination and disability laws.

Mandatory disenrollment. A PDP sponsor must disenroll an individual from a PDP it offers if:

(1) the individual no longer resides in the PDP's service area;

(2) the individual loses eligibility for Part D;

(3) the individual dies;

(4) the PDP's contract is terminated by CMS or by the PDP or through mutual consent; and

(5) the individual materially misrepresents information to the PDP sponsor as to whether or not the individual's costs are expected to be reimbursed through insurance or other third-party means. CMS does not intend to apply this provision to disenroll individuals who simply make an error, but rather, to those who "knowingly" provide false information. [42 C.F.R. § 423.44(b)(2).]

Disenrollment when temporarily outside the service area. CMS feels that disenrolling an individual for being temporarily out of the service area for a certain period of time may be inappropriate. CMS recognizes that the nature of the prescription drug benefit and the ability to access the benefit through mail order or chain drug stores provides flexibility for enrollees while temporarily out of a service area. CMS, however, will require that enrollees maintain their permanent residence within their service areas. [*Final rule,* 70 FR 4214, Jan. 28, 2005.]

Optional involuntary disenrollment for unpaid premiums. A PDP sponsor may disenroll an individual from a PDP it offers for failure to pay any monthly premium if the sponsor demonstrates to CMS that it made reasonable efforts to collect the unpaid premium and the PDP gives the enrollee proper notice of disenrollment. When disenrollment occurs for failure to pay monthly premiums, the PDP may refuse reenrollment of the individual until all past premiums have been paid. [42 C.F.R. § 423.44(b).]

Optional involuntary disenrollment for disruptive behavior. A PDP may disenroll an individual whose behavior is disruptive only after (1) the PDP sponsor makes an effort to resolve the problem, (2) the PDP sponsor documents the enrollee's behavior, and (3) CMS has reviewed and approved the proposed disenrollment. A PDP enrollee is considered disruptive if his or her behavior substantially impairs the PDP's ability to arrange or provide for services to the individual or other plan members. An individual cannot be considered disruptive if the behavior is related to the use of medical services or compliance (or noncompliance) with medical advice or treatment. As a result, an individual cannot be considered disruptive if his or her behavior is triggered by the prescribed use of a non-formulary drug instead of the drug originally prescribed. [42 C.F.R. § 423.44(d)(2).]

Reasonable accommodation for disruptive behavior. Arranging or providing care for individuals with mental illness, cognitive impairments such as Alzheimer's disease or other dementias, and medical conditions and treatments that may cause disruptive behavior warrant special consideration. As a result, PDP sponsors are required to provide a reasonable accommodation to individuals in such exceptional circumstances that CMS deems necessary. Reasonable accommodation will be determined by CMS on a case-by-case basis as part of CMS' review of the sponsor's request for disenrollment. Expert opinion from CMS staff with appropriate clinical or medical background will be utilized. [42 C.F.R. § 423.44(d)(2).]

Fallback prescription drug plan exception to disruptive behavior. CMS recognized that circumstances may arise when an individual is only able to obtain qualified prescription drug coverage from a fallback prescription drug plan operating in his or her service area. In such a case, allowing a fallback entity to disenroll an individual may create substantial barriers to accessing prescription medications under the Medicare program. The MMA grants CMS the authority to establish additional requirements specifically for fallback prescription plans. Under this authority, CMS reserves the right to deny a request from a fallback prescription drug plan to disenroll an individual for disruptive behavior. [42 C.F.R. § 423.44(d)(2)(vi).]

Effective date of disenrollment for disruptive behavior. If CMS permits a PDP to disenroll an individual for disruptive behavior, the termination is effective the first day of the calendar month after the month in which the PDP gives the individual the required written notice of the disenrollment. [42 C.F.R. § 423.44(d)(2)(vii).]

Loss of Part D eligibility. If an individual is no longer eligible for Part D, CMS notifies the PDP that the disenrollment is effective the first day of the calendar month following the last month of Part D eligibility. [42 C.F.R. § 423.44(d)(3).]

Death of the individual. If the individual dies, disenrollment is effective the first day of the calendar month following the month of death. [42 C.F.R. § 423.44(d)(4).]

¶506

Basis for disenrollment if the individual no longer resides in the PDP service area. The PDP must disenroll an individual if the individual notifies the PDP that he or she has permanently moved out of the PDP service area. [42 C.F.R. § 423.44(d)(5).]

Plan termination. When a PDP contract terminates, the PDP sponsor must give each affected PDP enrollee notice of the effective date of the plan termination and a description of alternatives for obtaining prescription drug coverage under Part D. The notice must be sent before the effective date of the plan termination or area reduction. [42 C.F.R. § 423.44(d)(6).]

Misrepresentation of third-party reimbursement. If CMS determines an individual has materially misrepresented information to the PDP sponsor, the termination is effective the first day of the calendar month after the month in which the sponsor gives the required individual written notice of the disenrollment. CMS does not intend this provision to disenroll individuals who simply make an error, but to disenroll those who "knowingly" provide false information. CMS will review and issue the final decision in these cases. [42 C.F.R. § 423.44(d)(7).]

Late Enrollment Penalty

A Part D eligible individual must pay a late enrollment penalty if there is a continuous period of 63 days or longer at any time after the end of the individual's initial enrollment period (IEP) during which the individual was eligible to enroll in a prescription drug plan (PDP), was not covered under any creditable prescription drug coverage, and was not enrolled in a Part D plan. [42 C.F.R. § 423.46.]

Calculation of the late enrollment penalty. The late enrollment penalty for 2006 and 2007 will equal one percent of the base beneficiary premium or another amount specified by CMS based on available analysis or other information. As the base beneficiary premium changes, the late enrollment penalty also changes. This ensures that the late enrollment penalty is calculated in a manner consistent with the Part B penalty, where the penalty is always a percentage of the current year's premium. However, to the extent that historical data will support an actuarially determined amount providing a greater disincentive to late enrollment, CMS plans to move to that methodology given the fact that use of the larger penalty is mandated by statute and regulation. [*Final rule*, 70 FR 13397, March 21, 2005; 42 C.F.R. § 423.286(d).]

Determining the 63 day period. The count of the 63-day period will commence the day following the end of the individual's initial enrollment period (IEP) or, once the IEP has passed, the day following the last day of creditable coverage or Part D enrollment (in a PDP or Medicare Advantage plan). The application of the 63-day period will be consistently applied to all individuals, regardless of when an individual may or may not apply for the low-income subsidy. [*Final rule*, 70 FR 4217, Jan. 28, 2005.]

Clarifying notice of creditable coverage. An individual who is not adequately informed that his or her prescription drug coverage was not creditable may apply for CMS review. If CMS determines that the individual did not receive adequate notice or received incorrect information, CMS may deem the individual to have had creditable coverage, regardless of whether it was actually creditable, so that the late enrollment penalty will not be imposed. [*Final rule*, 70 FR 4217, Jan. 28, 2005.]

Waiver, delay, and reconsideration of the enrollment penalty. There is nothing in the Medicare Modernization Act that gives CMS the authority to waive or delay the late enrollment penalty unless an individual was not adequately informed that his or her prescription drug coverage was not creditable. Further, the penalty applies to full-benefit dual eligible individuals because the application of the penalty is specifically referenced in

¶506

the definition of the full premium subsidy in the MMA. [*Final rule*, 70 FR 4217, Jan. 28, 2005.]

Providing Information About Part D Plans to Beneficiaries

CMS will conduct activities designed to disseminate information about Part D coverage broadly to individuals who are either eligible or prospectively eligible for benefits. CMS will make this information available to beneficiaries at least 30 days prior to their initial enrollment periods. Each organization offering a prescription drug plan (PDP) or Medicare Advantage (MA-PD) plan must provide CMS annually with the information to disseminate to individuals who are currently or prospectively eligible for Part D benefits

Comparative information. CMS plans to include comparative information for qualified prescription drug coverage provided by PDPs and MA-PD plans as part of its efforts to promote informed beneficiary decisions, including information on:

(1) benefits and prescription drug formularies;

(2) monthly beneficiary premium;

(3) quality and performance;

(4) beneficiary cost-sharing; and

(5) results of consumer satisfaction surveys.

Late enrollment penalty methodology. CMS will provide information to beneficiaries regarding the methodology it will use for determining late enrollment penalties

Public information campaign. In carrying out the annual dissemination of Part D information, CMS will conduct a significant public information campaign to educate beneficiaries about the new Medicare drug benefit and to ensure the broad dissemination of accurate and timely information. [42 C.F.R. § 423.48; *Final rule*, 70 FR 4217-21, Jan. 28, 2005.]

Determining Creditable Status of Prescription Drug Coverage

Upon becoming eligible for Part D, beneficiaries must decide whether to enroll in Part D or forego that opportunity and face a possible late enrollment penalty should they later decide to enroll. Beneficiaries who decide not to enroll in Part D because they have creditable prescription drug coverage will not face such a penalty if they later decide to enroll.

The Medicare Modernization Act lists seven specific forms of potential creditable prescription drug coverage that CMS has incorporated into its Part D regulations, including:

(1) coverage under a prescription drug plan (PDP) or under a Medicare Advantage plan (MA-PD);

(2) Medicaid;

(3) a group health plan (including coverage provided by a federal or a nonfederal government plan and by a church plan for its employees);

(4) a State Pharmaceutical Assistance Program (SPAP);

(5) veterans' coverage of prescription drugs;

(6) prescription drug coverage under a Medigap policy; and

(7) military coverage (including Tricare). [42 C.F.R. § 423.56(b).]

In addition to the seven types of creditable prescription drug coverage specifically listed in the MMA, the Act also provided CMS with the flexibility to identify "other coverage" that could be considered creditable. As a consequence, in its regulations CMS expanded the list of coverage that could be considered creditable to include six more categories:

¶506

(1) individual health insurance coverage that includes coverage for outpatient prescription drugs and that does not meet the definition of an excepted benefit;

(2) coverage provided by the medical care program of the Indian Health Service, tribe or tribal organization, or Urban Indian Organization;

(3) coverage provided by a Program of All-inclusive Care for the Elderly (PACE) organization;

(4) coverage provided by a cost-based health maintenance organization (HMO) or competitive medical plan (CMP);

(5) coverage provided through a State High-Risk Pool; and

(6) and other coverage as CMS may determine appropriate. [42 C.F.R. § 423.56(b).]

Definition of creditable prescription drug coverage. A Part D enrollee who otherwise would be subject to a late enrollment penalty may avoid the penalty if his or her previous coverage meets the standards of "creditable prescription drug coverage." Previous coverage only will meet those standards if the coverage is determined (in a manner specified by CMS) to provide coverage of the cost of prescription drugs the actuarial value of which (as defined by CMS) to the individual equals or exceeds the actuarial value of standard prescription drug coverage. [42 C.F.R. § 423.56(a).]

Calculation of actuarial equivalence standard. The basic actuarial equivalence value test for the determination of creditable coverage or alternative coverage is determined by calculating whether the expected plan payout on average will be at least equal to the expected plan payout under defined prescription drug coverage. [*Final rule*, 70 FR 4226, Jan. 28, 2005.]

Retiree plans with multiple benefit options. CMS has addressed the application of the actuarial equivalence standard to retiree group health plans with multiple benefit options. CMS believes that sponsors have the flexibility to choose whether to apply the net prong of the actuarial equivalence test for each benefit option, or to apply the net prong of the actuarial equivalence test on an aggregate basis to 2 or more benefit options within a group health plan that satisfy the gross test and for which the sponsor is claiming the retiree subsidy. CMS believes the statutory language in question is ambiguous and can be reasonably interpreted to mean the actuarial value of a single benefit option or multiple benefit options within the group health plan in the aggregate. CMS has elected not to choose between these interpretations and has instead provided sponsors with flexibility to accommodate their offering a wide variety of benefit options for their retirees. [Soc. Sec. Act 1860D-22(a)(2)(A); *Final rule*, 70 FR 13397, March 21, 2005; 42 C.F.R. § 423.884(d)(5)(iv).]

Disclosure of creditable or non-creditable coverage status. With the exception of PDPs and MA-PD plans and PACE or cost-based HMO or CMP plans that provide qualified prescription drug coverage under Part D, CMS requires that any entity seeking to offer creditable coverage must attest to the actuarial equivalence (or non-equivalence) of its prescription drug coverage in its notice to Medicare beneficiaries and in a submission to CMS. The entity also must disclose to eligible individuals that there are limitations on the periods in a year in which the individual may enroll in Part D plans and that the individual may be subject to a late enrollment penalty. [42 C.F.R. § 423.56 (c)(d).]

[¶ 508] Payment of Premiums

Generally, the monthly beneficiary premium for a prescription drug plan (PDP) must be the same for all Part D eligible individuals enrolled in a plan. It is the base beneficiary premium adjusted to reflect: differences between the plan bid and a national average bid, supplemental benefits, and late enrollment penalties. [42 C.F.R. § 423.286(a).]

Calculation of the beneficiary premium. The beneficiary premium percentage for any year is a fraction, the numerator of which is 25.5 percent. The denominator is 100 percent minus a percentage equal to (a) the total estimated reinsurance payments for the coverage year divided by (b) the total estimated reinsurance payments plus total estimated payments to Part D plans attributable to the standardized bid amount during the coverage year. [42 C.F.R. § 423.286(b).]

Base beneficiary premium. The base beneficiary premium for a month is equal to the product of the beneficiary premium percentage and the national average monthly bid amount. If a sponsor's bid amount exceeds the adjusted national average monthly bid amount, then the base premium is increased by the excess; if the bid amount is less than the national average monthly bid amount, then the base premium is decreased by the excess. The base beneficiary premium also is increased for supplemental prescription drug benefits and late enrollment penalties, but it is decreased or eliminated for low-income subsidy-eligible individuals. [42 C.F.R. § 423.286(c).]

Premium collection. Plan enrollees have the option to make premium payments to PDP sponsors using any of the methods available to enrollees in Medicare Advantage Plans listed in 42 C.F.R. § 422.262(f), including withholding from Social Security payments, electronic funds transfers, or through employers or third parties specified by CMS. The agency will pay a plan sponsor only the portion of a late enrollment penalty attributable to increased PDP actuarial costs not taken into account through risk adjustment. [42 C.F.R. § 423.293. *Final Rule,* 70 FR 4303-4306, Jan. 28, 2005.]

Fallback plan premiums are not calculated under this rule (see ¶ 525 for fallback plan calculations). [42 C.F.R. § 423.293(d).]

[¶ 510] Benefits and Beneficiary Protections

CMS may approve as Part D sponsors only those entities proposing to offer qualified prescription drug coverage. Qualified prescription drug coverage may consist of either standard prescription drug coverage or alternative prescription drug coverage. Both standard and alternative prescription drug coverage provide access to Part D drugs at negotiated prices. A sponsor offering a prescription drug plan (PDP) must offer that plan to all Part D eligible beneficiaries residing in the plan's service area. [42 C.F.R. § 423.104(b).]

Standard prescription drug coverage. "Standard prescription drug coverage" consists of coverage of covered Part D drugs subject to an annual deductible, 25 percent coinsurance (or an actuarially equivalent structure) up to an initial coverage limit, and catastrophic coverage after an individual incurs out-of-pocket expenses above a certain annual out-of-pocket threshold. For 2006, the annual deductible will be $250, the initial coverage limit will be $2,250, and the annual out-of-pocket threshold will be $3,600. In 2006, once a prescription drug plan (PDP) enrollee reaches the annual out-of-pocket threshold, his or her nominal cost-sharing will be equal to the greater of five percent coinsurance or a co-payment of $2 for a generic drug or a preferred multiple source drug and $5 for any other drug, or an actuarially equivalent structure. [42 C.F.R. § 423.104(d).]

Beginning in 2007, the annual deductible, initial coverage limit, annual out-of-pocket threshold, and beneficiary cost-sharing after the annual out-of-pocket threshold is met will be adjusted annually. The amounts will be increased over the previous year's amounts by the annual percentage increase in average per capita aggregate expenditures for Part D drugs for the 12-month period ending in July of the previous year. [42 C.F.R. § 423.104(b).]

Alternative prescription drug coverage. Alternative prescription drug coverage provides coverage for Part D drugs and includes access to negotiated prices. Alternative prescription drug coverage also must:

(1) have an annual deductible that does not exceed the annual deductible for standard prescription drug coverage;

(2) impose cost-sharing no greater than that specified for standard prescription drug coverage once the annual out-of-pocket threshold is met;

(3) have a total or gross value that is at least equal to the total or gross value of defined standard coverage;

(4) have an unsubsidized value that is at least equal to the unsubsidized value of standard prescription drug coverage; and (*Note:* The unsubsidized value of coverage is the amount by which the actuarial value of the coverage exceeds the actuarial value of the subsidy payments for the coverage).

(5) provide coverage that is designed, based upon an actuarially representative pattern of utilization, to provide for the payment of costs that are equal to the initial coverage limit, in an amount at least equal to the product of: (i) the amount by which the initial coverage limit for the year exceeds the deductible and (ii) 100 percent minus the coinsurance percentage specified for standard prescription drug coverage. [42 C.F.R. § 423.104(e).]

Joint Enterprise Plans

Several health plans, each licensed by a State as a risk-bearing entity, have asked CMS whether they could jointly enter into a contract to offer a single PDP in a multi-state region. The participating health plans proposed contracting with each other to create a single "joint enterprise." They have asked CMS whether such a joint enterprise could be considered an "entity" under section 1860D-12(a)(1) of the Social Security Act, for purposes of offering a PDP. The Act generally requires that the "entity" be licensed by the State as a risk bearing entity where it offers benefits. CMS has determined that such a joint enterprise could be treated as a single "entity" for purposes of offering a PDP, as long as the enterprise as a whole meets all applicable Medicare requirements, and there is no substantive difference between this arrangement and a traditional entity from a Medicare enrollee's perspective. This means that the joint enterprise must, at a minimum:

(1) enter into a single contract under which it was accountable, through its participants individually or in the aggregate, for meeting all applicable Medicare requirements, including, since a regional entity cannot continue to operate in a service area that is less than the entire region, providing CMS with a description of the contracting entity's plan in the event that one or more parties in the joint enterprise terminates its participation (or is terminated by another party) in the enterprise in a contract year;

(2) submit a single bid covering the entire PDP Region, which includes a uniform benefit, uniform cost-sharing, as well as a uniform premium, including how the joint enterprise will allocate risk among the multiple parties in the region;

(3) offer a region-wide network of providers that is accessible to all enrollees in the plan, regardless of where in the region they live;

(4) market the plan under a single name throughout the region; and

(5) provide uniform enrollee customer service and appeal and grievance rights throughout the region.

In addition, where the regulations specifically govern the activities of the entity, such as the requirement for fidelity bonds for officers, or certifications associated with receipt of payment, each State-licensed plan comprising the joint enterprise will be required to meet such requirements individually. [*Final rule*, 70 FR 13397, March 21, 2005.]

Establishment of Prescription Drug Service Area

Before establishing service areas for prescription drug plans (PDPs), CMS conducted a market survey and analysis, including an examination of current insurance markets. The survey and analysis examined payment rates, eligible population size per region, preferred provider organization (PPO) market penetration, current existence of PPOs, Medicare Advantage (MA) plans, or other commercial plans, and the presence of PPO providers and primary care providers. CMS also considered solvency and licensing requirements, as well as capacity issues. [*Final rule*, 70 FR 4247, Jan. 28, 2005.]

On December 6, 2004, CMS announced the establishment of 26 MA regions and 34 PDP regions. PDP regions, were established in a manner that was consistent, to the extent practicable, with MA regions, usually on a state-by-state basis. Under the MMA, CMS was entitled to establish PDP regions that vary from MA regions if access to Part D benefits would be improved by establishing different regions. CMS was also entitled to designate a separate PDP region or regions for U.S. territories. CMS has the authority to revise the PDP regions. [*Final rule*, 70 FR 4246, Jan. 28, 2005.]

Convenient Access to Covered Part D Drugs

Prescription drug plans (PDPs) must secure the participation of a pharmacy network consisting of retail pharmacies sufficient to ensure that all beneficiaries residing in each state in a PDP's service area, each state in a regional (Medicare Advantage) MA-PD plan's service area, a local MA-PD plan's service area, or a cost plan's geographic area, have convenient access to covered drugs. As a result, PDPs must establish pharmacy networks in which:

(1) in urban areas, at least 90 percent of Medicare beneficiaries in the PDP service area live, on average, within two miles of the retail pharmacy participating in the plan's network;

(2) in suburban areas, at least 90 percent of Medicare beneficiaries in the PDP service area, on average, live within five miles of a retail pharmacy participating in the PDP's or MA-PD plan's network; and

(3) in rural areas, at least 70 percent of Medicare beneficiaries in the PDP service area, on average, live within 15 miles of a retail pharmacy participating in the plan's network. [42 C.F.R. § 423.120(a)(1).]

Part D plans may count Indian tribes and tribal organizations, and urban Indian organizations (I/T/U) pharmacies, and pharmacies operated by Federally Qualified Health Centers and Rural Health Centers toward the required percentages for urban, suburban, and rural areas. [42 C.F.R. § 423.120(a)(2).]

A PDP's contracted pharmacy network must provide adequate access to home infusion pharmacies and convenient access and standard contracting terms and conditions to all long-term care and I/T/U pharmacies in its service area. [42 C.F.R. § 423.120(a)(4)(5)(6).]

Part D sponsors will be required to permit the participation in their pharmacy networks of any pharmacy willing to accept the plan's terms and conditions. [42 C.F.R. § 423.120(a)(8).]

A PDP sponsor offering a plan that provides coverage other than defined standard coverage may reduce co-payments or coinsurance for covered drugs obtained through a

¶510

preferred pharmacy relative to the co-payments or coinsurance applicable for such drugs when obtained through a non-preferred pharmacy. [42 C.F.R. § 423.120(a)(9).]

A PDP sponsor must permit its enrollees to receive benefits, which may include an extended (90-day) supply of covered drugs, at any of its network pharmacies that are retail pharmacies. A Part D plan, however, may require an enrollee obtaining a covered drug at a retail network pharmacy to pay any higher cost-sharing applicable to that extended supply at a network retail pharmacy. [42 C.F.R. § 423.120(a)(10).]

Sponsor Transition Requirements

To address the needs of individuals who are stabilized on certain drug regimens, Medicare Part D prescription drug plans (PDPs) are required to establish a transition process to enroll new beneficiaries in Part D from other prescription drug coverage programs. This transition process must address the plan sponsor's method of educating both beneficiaries and providers to ensure a safe accommodation of an individual's medical needs with the plan's formulary. Features of this transition process include involvement of the pharmacy and therapeutics committee, temporarily filling one-time supplies of non-formulary drugs, and documenting transition timeframes.

Plan sponsors must also ensure that long term care (LTC) pharmacies in the plan's coordinate with LTC facilities to ensure a seamless transition of the facility's residents. Additionally, emergency drug supplies should be maintained for current enrollees with immediate needs for non-formulary drugs to protect beneficiaries from coverage gaps. CMS will review the plan's transition process as part of the formulary and plan benefit design review. [CMS Guidance, *Information for Part D Sponsors on Requirements for a Transition Process*, March 16, 2005.]

Long Term Care Pharmacy Requirements

Part D plans must offer a contract to any pharmacy willing to participate in its long term care (LTC) pharmacy network so long as the pharmacy is capable of meeting certain minimum performance and service criteria and any other standard terms and conditions established by the plan for its network pharmacies. The Part D plans must demonstrate that they have a network of participating LTC pharmacies that provide convenient access for LTC residents who are Part D enrollees.

Minimum performance and service criteria for pharmacies providing LTC service include: (1) comprehensive inventory and inventory capacity; (2) pharmacy operations and prescription orders; (3) special packaging required by LTCs; (4) IV medications; (5) compounding and alternative drugs; (6) on-call pharmacist service; (7) delivery service; (8) emergency boxes of medications; (9) emergency log books; and (10) various miscellaneous reports and forms.

Part D plans must accommodate the needs of LTC residents by providing coverage for all medically necessary medications at all levels of care within a single formulary structure. [CMS Guidance, *Long Term Care Guidance*, March 16, 2005.]

Out-of-Network Access to Covered Part D Drugs

Prescription drug plans (PDPs) are required to ensure that their enrollees have adequate access to drugs dispensed at out-of-network pharmacies when enrollees cannot reasonably be expected to obtain covered drugs at a network pharmacy. Provided the enrollees do not routinely access out-of-network pharmacies, CMS expects that PDPs guarantee out-of-network access if an enrollee:

¶510

(1) is traveling outside the plan's service area, runs out of or loses covered drugs or becomes ill and needs a covered drug, and cannot access a network pharmacy;

(2) cannot obtain a covered drug in a timely manner within a service area because, for example, there is no network pharmacy within a reasonable driving distance that provides 24 hour/7 day per week service;

(3) must fill a prescription for a covered drug, and that particular drug is not regularly stocked at accessible network retail or mail-order pharmacies; and

(4) is provided covered drugs dispensed by an out-of-network institution-based pharmacy while a patient in an emergency department, provider-based clinic, outpatient surgery, or other outpatient setting.

In addition, plans must provide coverage for vaccines or other covered Part D drugs that are appropriately dispensed and administered in a physician's office. CMS plans to closely monitor out-of-network access to ensure that Part D plans are adequately meeting beneficiaries' out-of-network access needs. [*Final rule*, 70 FR 4268, Jan. 28, 2005.]

Limits on out-of-network access. CMS understands that routine access to out-of-network pharmacies could undermine a Part D plan's ability to achieve cost-savings for both beneficiaries and the Medicare program. For this reason, CMS requires PDPs to establish reasonable rules to ensure that enrollees use out-of-network pharmacies in an appropriate manner, provided that the plans also ensure adequate access to out-of-network pharmacies on a non-routine basis when enrollees cannot reasonably access network pharmacies. For example, PDPs may wish to limit the amount of covered drugs dispensed at an out-of-network pharmacy, require that a beneficiary purchase maintenance medications via mail-order for extended out-of-area travel, or require a plan notification or authorization process for individuals who fill their prescriptions at out-of-network pharmacies. [42 C.F.R. § 423.124(a) and (c).]

Financial responsibility for out-of-network access. Enrollees obtaining covered Part D drugs at out-of-network pharmacies will not have access to the data needed to calculate PDP payment rates. These enrollees will have to pay the pharmacy's usual and customary (U&C) price at the point-of-sale, submit a paper claim to their PDP, and wait for reimbursement from the plan. This will make out-of-network pharmacies whole, relative to their U&C price for a covered Part D drug, at the point of sale. [42 C.F.R. § 423.120(b); *Final rule*, 70 FR 4268, Jan. 28, 2005.]

Out-of-network institution-based pharmacy coverage. CMS recognizes that enrollees who are provided covered Part D drugs by hospital and other institution-based pharmacies cannot reasonably be expected to obtain needed covered drugs at a network pharmacy. As a result, CMS expects that PDPs guarantee out-of-network access to covered drugs when an enrollee is provided covered drugs dispensed by an out-of-network institution-based pharmacy while a patient in an emergency department, provider-based clinic, outpatient surgery, or other outpatient setting. [42 C.F.R. § 423.120(a); *Final rule*, 70 FR 4268, Jan. 28, 2005.]

Dissemination of Part D Plan Information

To ensure that eligible or enrolled individuals in prescription drug plans receive the information they need to make informed choices about their coverage options, sponsors must disclose a detailed description of each qualified PDP. The description must be provided in a clear, accurate, and standardized form at the time of enrollment and annually thereafter, at a minimum. The information required is similar to the information Medicare Advantage plans must disclose to their enrollees. [42 C.F.R. § 423.128(a).]

The description must include information regarding:

(1) service area;

(2) benefits, including applicable conditions and limitations, premiums, cost-sharing, cost-sharing for subsidy eligible individuals, and other benefit-associated conditions;

(3) how to obtain more information on cost-sharing requirements, including tiered or other co-payment levels applicable to each drug;

(4) the plan's formulary, including a list of included drugs, the manner in which the formulary functions, the process for obtaining an exception to the plan's formulary or tiered cost-sharing structure, and a description of how an eligible individual may obtain additional information on the formulary;

(5) the number, mix, and addresses of network pharmacies from which enrollees may reasonably be expected to obtain covered drugs and how the sponsor meets the access requirements;

(6) provisions for access to covered drugs at out-of-network pharmacies;

(7) grievance, reconsideration, exceptions, coverage determination, reconsideration, exceptions, and appeal rights and procedures;

(8) policies and procedures for quality assurance and the medication therapy management program;

(9) disenrollment rights and responsibilities; and

(10) the fact that a sponsor may terminate or refuse to renew its contract, or reduce the service area, and the effect that this may have on plan enrollees. [42 C.F.R. § 423.128(b).]

Information available on request of the eligible individual. Upon request of a Part D eligible individual, a Part D sponsor must provide general coverage information; the procedures the sponsor uses to control utilization of services and expenditures; the number of grievances, appeals, and exceptions, and their disposition in the aggregate; and the financial condition of the Part D sponsor. This financial information must include the most recently audited information regarding the sponsor offering the plan. General coverage disclosure includes information on: (1) how to exercise election options; (2) procedural rights; (3) benefits; (4) premiums; (5) the plan's formulary; (6) the plan's service area; and (7) quality and performance indicators for benefits under the plan. [42 C.F.R. § 423.128(a).]

Mechanisms for providing specific information to enrollees. Part D sponsors must have mechanisms in place to provide specific information requested by current and prospective enrollees. The mechanisms include a toll-free customer call center, an Internet website, and responses in writing upon beneficiary request. The plans' customer call centers must be open during usual business hours and provide telephone service to customers, including pharmacists, pursuant to standard business practices.

CMS strongly recommends that plans provide some sort of 24 hour-per-day/seven day-per-week access to their call centers to provide timely responses to time-sensitive questions. In addition, CMS is requiring that plans maintain websites as one method of disseminating information to current and prospective enrollees. The websites must include a detailed plan description information, a current formulary (update monthly), and at least a 60-day notice of removal or change in the preferred or tiered cost-sharing status of a drug on a plan's formulary. [42 C.F.R. § 423.128(d).]

Explanation of benefits. Part D sponsors must furnish an explanation of benefits (EOB) to enrollees who receive covered Part D drugs. EOBs are required to be written in a form easily understandable to beneficiaries. EOBs must be provided at least monthly for those enrollees utilizing their prescription drug benefits in a given month. EOBs for Part D plans also must include:

(1) a listing of the item or service for which payment was made, as well as the amount of such payment for each item or service;

(2) a notice of the individual's right to request an itemized statement;

(3) information regarding the cumulative, year-to-date amount of benefits provided relative to the deductible, the initial coverage limit, and the annual out-of-pocket threshold for that year, and a beneficiary's cumulative, year-to-date total of incurred costs; and

(4) information regarding any applicable formulary changes. [42 C.F.R. § 423.128(e).]

Public Disclosure of Pharmaceutical Prices for Equivalent Drugs

Part D sponsors must ensure that pharmacies inform enrollees of any differential between the price of a covered Part D drug and the price of the lowest priced generic version available under the plan at that pharmacy. CMS expects that Part D plans will work with their network pharmacies to put this requirement into practice in the most efficient way possible. This generic price differential information must be provided at the time the plan enrollee purchases the drug, or in the case of drugs purchased by mail order, at the time of delivery. Disclosure of this information, however, is not necessary if the particular covered drug purchased by an enrollee is the lowest-priced generic version of that drug available at a particular pharmacy. CMS is permitted to waive the generic differential notice requirement when covered drugs are purchased at:

(1) any pharmacy, when the individual is enrolled in a Medicare Advantage private fee-for-service plan that offers qualified prescription drug coverage and provides plan enrollees with access to covered Part D drugs dispensed at all pharmacies, without regard to whether they are contracted network pharmacies, and does not charge additional cost-sharing for access to covered drugs dispensed at all pharmacies;

(2) out-of-network pharmacies;

(3) Indian tribes and tribal organizations, and urban Indian organizations' network pharmacies;

(4) network pharmacies located in any of the U.S. territories (American Samoa, the Commonwealth of the Northern Mariana Islands, Guam, Puerto Rico, and the Virgin Islands); and

(5) anywhere else, when CMS deems compliance is impossible or impracticable.

CMS also may waive the generic differential notice requirement when a Part D plan enrollee obtains a covered drug in a long-term care pharmacy or under other circumstances when CMS deems compliance impossible or impracticable. Long-term care pharmacies are required to provide the generic price differential information for Part D plans in their written explanation of benefits. [42 C.F.R. § 423.132.]

Privacy, Confidentiality, and Accuracy of Enrollee Records

To the extent that a prescription drug plan (PDP) offered by a PDP sponsor maintains medical records or other health information regarding Part D enrollees, the PDP sponsor must meet the same requirements regarding confidentiality and accuracy of enrollee records as Medicare Advantage (MA) organizations offering MA plans. Program of All-inclusive Care for the Elderly (PACE) organizations and cost plans offering qualified prescription drug

¶510

coverage are not subject to these requirements because these plans are already subject to similar requirements. Specifically, PDP sponsors must:

(1) abide by all federal and state laws regarding confidentiality and disclosure of medical records or other health and enrollment information, including the Health Insurance Portability and Accountability Act of 1996 (HIPAA) and the privacy rule promulgated under HIPAA;

(2) ensure that medical information is released only in accordance with applicable federal or state law or under court orders or subpoenas;

(3) maintain the records and information in an accurate and timely manner; and

(4) ensure timely access by enrollees to records and information pertaining to them.

Prescription drug plans are covered entities under the HIPAA privacy rule because they meet the definition of "health plan." Any violations by a PDP sponsor of its obligations under the privacy rule are subject to enforcement by the HHS Office for Civil Rights. [42 C.F.R. § 423.136; *Final rule*, 70 FR 4277, Jan. 28, 2005.]

[¶ 515] Grievances, Coverage Determinations, and Appeals

The regulations concerning grievances, coverage determinations and appeals under Part D, the prescription drug benefit, establish a process that largely mirrors the procedures for addressing coverage and determinations and appeals under the Medicare Advantage (MA) program.

Appeal. An appeal under Part D is the process for reviewing an adverse coverage determination made by a Part D plan sponsor on the benefits under a Part D plan that the enrollee believes he or she is entitled to receive, including delay in providing or approving the drug coverage when a delay would adversely affect the health of the enrollee, or on any amounts the enrollee must pay for the drug coverage. The levels of appeals for Part D determinations include:

(1) redeterminations by the plan,

(2) reconsiderations by the independent review entity,

(3) administrative law judge hearings,

(4) reviews by the Medicare Appeals Council, and

(5) judicial reviews.

Grievance. A grievance is any complaint or dispute expressing dissatisfaction with a Part D plan sponsor's operations or behavior. Grievances do not include coverage determinations.

Reconsideration. A reconsideration is a review of an adverse coverage determination by an independent review entity (IRE) and includes the evidence upon which the determination was based and any evidence the enrollee submits or the IRE obtains

Redetermination. A redetermination is a review of an adverse coverage determination by a Part D plan sponsor and includes the evidence upon which the determination was based and any evidence the enrollee submits or the plan obtains. [42 C.F.R. § 423.560.]

Responsibilities of Part D Plan Sponsors and Rights of Enrollees

For each prescription drug plan (PDP or plan) that it offers, a Part D plan sponsor must establish and maintain procedures for (1) grievances addressing issues unrelated to coverage determinations, (2) timely coverage determinations including determinations on requests for exceptions to a tiered cost-sharing formulary structure or exceptions to a formulary, and (3) appeal for issues related to coverage determinations that meet the requirements of the Part D regulations. [42 C.F.R. § 423.562(a)(1).]

A PDP must ensure that enrollees receive written information related to grievance and appeal procedures available to them through the plan and the complaint process available to the enrollee under the quality improvement organization process. In addition, a PDP must arrange with its network pharmacies to post or distribute notices instructing enrollees to contact their plans to obtain a coverage determination or request an exception if they disagree with the information provided by the pharmacist. [42 C.F.R. § 423.562(a)(2)(3).]

Rights of enrollees. Enrollees have the right to: (1) have grievances between the enrollee and the Part D plan sponsor heard and resolved by the plan; (2) have the plan make a timely coverage determination, including a request for an exception to the plan's tiered cost-sharing structure or formulary; and (3) request an expedited coverage determination from the plan.

If an enrollee is dissatisfied with any part of a coverage determination, the enrollee has the right to:

(1) a redetermination of the adverse coverage determination by the PDP sponsor;

(2) request an expedited redetermination;

(3) a reconsideration or expedited reconsideration by an independent review entity (IRE) contracted by CMS, if, as a result of a redetermination, a plan affirms, in whole or in part, its adverse coverage determination;

(4) an administrative law judge (ALJ) hearing if the IRE affirms the plan's adverse coverage determination, in whole or in part and the amount in controversy requirement is met;

(5) request a Medicare Appeals Council (MAC) review of the ALJ hearing decision, if the ALJ affirms the IRE's adverse coverage determination, in whole or in part;

(6) a judicial review of the MAC hearing decision, if the MAC affirms the ALJ's adverse coverage determination, in whole or in part; and the amount in controversy requirement is met. [42 C.F.R. § 423.562(b).]

Grievance Procedure

Prescription drug plans must have meaningful procedures for timely hearing and resolution of grievances between enrollees and the PDP sponsor or any other entity or individual through whom the plan provides covered benefits under any Part D plan it offers. The grievance procedures must be separate and distinct from appeals procedures. When the plan receives a complaint, it must promptly determine and inform the enrollee whether the complaint is subject to its grievance procedures or its appeal procedures. [42 C.F.R. § 423.564(a)(b).]

Method for filing a grievance. An enrollee may file a grievance with a plan either orally or in writing no later than 60 days after the event or incident that precipitated the grievance. [42 C.F.R. § 423.564(d).]

Disposition and notification. The plan must notify the enrollee of its decision as expeditiously as the case requires based on the enrollee's health status, but no later than 30 days after the date the plan receives the oral or written grievance. The 30-day timeframe may be extended by up to 14 days if the enrollee requests the extension or if the plan justifies a need for additional information and documents how the delay is in the interest of the enrollee. [42 C.F.R. § 423.564(e).]

Expedited grievances. A PDP is required to respond to an enrollee's grievance within 24 hours if the complaint involves a refusal by the plan to grant an enrollee's request for an expedited coverage determination or an expedited redetermination and the enrollee has not yet purchased or received the drug that is in dispute. [42 C.F.R. § 423.564(f).]

Recordkeeping. The PDP must maintain records on grievances received orally and in writing. Records minimally must include the date of receipt, final disposition of the grievance, and the date that the plan notified the enrollee of the disposition. [42 C.F.R. § 423.564(g).]

When a plan makes a decision on a grievance, its resolution is final and is not subject to appeal.

Coverage Determinations

Each prescription drug plan must have a procedure for making timely coverage determinations regarding the prescription drug benefits an enrollee is entitled to receive under the plan.

Only adverse coverage determinations are subject to the appeals process. Plan actions that constitute coverage decisions include:

(1) a decision not to provide or pay for a Part D drug that the enrollee believes may be covered by the plan; including a decision not to pay because: (i) the drug is not on the plan's formulary, (ii) the drug is determined not to be medically necessary, (iii) the drug is furnished by an out-of-network pharmacy, or (iv) the PDP determines that the drug is excludable from coverage if applied to Medicare Part D;

(2) failure to provide a coverage determination in a timely manner, when a delay would adversely affect the health of the enrollee;

(3) a decision concerning an exceptions request to the plan's tiered cost sharing structure;

(4) a decision concerning an exceptions request involving a nonformulary Part D drug; or

(5) a decision on the amount of cost sharing for a drug.

Cost utilization tools employed by PDPs may result in coverage determinations. For example, a denial based on an enrollee's exceeding a plan's quantity limitation constitutes a coverage determination. Enrollees may appeal such determinations if they believe that the cost-utilization requirements have been satisfied or the requirements cannot be satisfied for reasons of medical necessity. Enrollees, however, may not challenge that a plan has cost-utilization tools. In addition, although an enrollee may request an exception involving a nonformulary drug, the enrollee may not challenge a plan's formulary. [42 C.F.R. § 423.566(a).]

Individuals who can request a coverage determination. The enrollee or the enrollee's appointed representative, on behalf of the enrollee, or the prescribing physician, on behalf of the enrollee, may request a standard or expedited coverage determination. [42 C.F.R. § 423.566(a).]

Timeframes for requests for drug benefits and payment. When a party makes a request for a drug benefit, the plan must notify the enrollee and the prescribing physician involved, if appropriate, of its determination as expeditiously as the enrollee's health condition requires, but no later than 72 hours after receipt of the request. If the party has made an exceptions request, the plan must notify the enrollee of its determination as expeditiously as the enrollee's health condition requires, but no later than 72 hours after receipt of the physician's supporting statement. When a party makes a request for payment, the plan must notify the enrollee of its determination no later than 72 hours after receipt of the request. [42 C.F.R. § 423.568(b).]

¶515

If the plan fails to notify the enrollee of its determination in the appropriate timeframe the failure constitutes an adverse coverage determination, and the plan must forward the enrollee's request to the independent review entity (IRE) within 24 hours of the expiration of the adjudication timeframe. [42 C.F.R. § 423.568(e).]

Denial notice requirements. If a PDP decides to deny a drug benefit in whole or in part, it must give the enrollee written notice of the determination. The notice must: (1) use approved notice language in a readable and understandable form, (2) state the specific reasons for the denial, and (3) inform the enrollee of his or her right to a redetermination. [42 C.F.R. § 423.568(d).]

Point-of-sale transactions are not coverage determinations and do not trigger the notice requirements associated with adverse determinations. Plans are required, however, to arrange for their network pharmacies to notify enrollees of their right to receive, upon request, a detailed written notice from the Part D plan sponsor regarding the enrollee's prescription drug coverage, including information about obtaining a coverage determination and the exceptions process when enrollees disagree with the information provided by the pharmacist.

Effect of a coverage determination. A coverage determination is binding on the Part D plan and the enrollee unless it is reviewed and revised by a redetermination or it is reopened and revised. [42 C.F.R. § 423.576.]

Requirements for an Expedited Coverage Determination

An enrollee or an enrollee's prescribing physician may request that a prescription drug plan (plan or PDP) expedite a coverage determination. An expedited review is not available for requests for payment of Part D drugs that have been furnished. An enrollee or an enrollee's prescribing physician on behalf of the enrollee must submit an oral or written request directly to the plan, or if applicable, to the entity responsible for making the determination, as directed by the plan. The prescribing physician may provide oral or written support for an enrollee's request for an expedited determination. [42 C.F.R. § 423.570(a)(b).]

Processing the request. When a request for an expedited review is received, the PDP must provide for an expedited determination in the following situations:

- when the request has been made by an enrollee, if the plan determines that applying the standard timeframe for making a determination may seriously jeopardize the life or health of the enrollee or the enrollee's ability to regain maximum function; and

- when the request has been made or is supported by an enrollee's prescribing physician, if the physician indicates that applying the standard timeframe for making a determination may seriously jeopardize the life or health of the enrollee or the enrollee's ability to regain maximum function. [42 C.F.R. § 423.570.]

Timeframe and notice for denied requests. If a plan denies a request for expedited determination, it must make the determination within the 72 hour timeframe established for a standard determination. The 72 hour period begins on the day the plan receives the request for expedited determination, or, for an exceptions request, the day the plan receives the physician's supporting statement.

The PDP must give the enrollee and prescribing physician prompt oral notice of the denial that explains that the plan must process the request using the 72 hour timeframe for standard determinations and informs the enrollee of the right to file an expedited grievance if he or she disagrees with the plan's decision not to expedite. In addition, the PDP must inform the enrollee of the right to resubmit a request for an expedited determination with

¶515

the prescribing physician's support and provide instructions about the plan's grievance process and its timeframes. Within three calendar days of the oral notice, the plan must deliver an equivalent written notice. [42 C.F.R. § 423.570(d).]

Timeframe and notice requirements for expedited determinations. A plan that approves a request for expedited determination must make its determination and notify the enrollee and the prescribing physician involved, when appropriate, of its decision, whether adverse or favorable, as expeditiously as the enrollee's health condition requires, but no later than 24 hours after receiving the request, or, for an exceptions request, the physician's supporting statement. If the plan fails to notify the enrollee of its determination within the 24 hour timeframe, the failure constitutes an adverse coverage determination, and the plan must forward the enrollee's request to the independent review entity (IRE) within 24 hours of the expiration of the adjudication timeframe. [42 C.F.R. § 423.572(a).]

If the Part D plan sponsor first notifies an enrollee of an adverse expedited determination orally, it must mail written confirmation to the enrollee within three calendar days of the oral notification. The notice of any expedited determination must state the specific reasons for the determination in understandable language. If the determination is not completely favorable to the enrollee, the notice must inform the enrollee of his or her right to a redetermination and describe the standard and expedited redetermination processes, including the enrollee's right to request, and conditions for obtaining, an expedited redetermination, and the remainder of the appeal process. [42 C.F.R. § 423.572(b) and (c).]

Formulary Exception Procedures General Rules

A decision by a prescription drug plan concerning an exceptions request constitutes a coverage determination. If the plan fails to make a decision on an exceptions request and provide notice of the decision within the timeframe required for a standard determination or an expedited determination, as applicable, the failure constitutes an adverse coverage determination, and the plan must forward the enrollee's request to the independent review entity (IRE) within 24 hours of the expiration of the adjudication timeframe.

An enrollee may not use the exceptions process to request or be granted coverage for a prescription drug that does not meet the definition of a Part D drug. In addition, a physician's supporting statement required for an exceptions request, will not result in an automatic favorable determination. [42 C.F.R. § 423.578.]

Exceptions Process for a Plan's Tiered Cost-Sharing Structure

Prescription drug plan sponsors that manage the Part D prescription drug benefit through the use of a tiered formulary must establish and maintain reasonable and complete exceptions procedures subject to CMS' approval.

Under a tiered cost-sharing structure, drugs are assigned to different co-payment tiers based on cost-sharing, clinical considerations, or both. An enrollee's level of cost-sharing is based on the tier into which the prescribed drug falls. Typically, drugs fall into one of three tiers—generic drugs, preferred brand-name drugs, or non-preferred brand-name drugs. All of a plan's cost-sharing tiers make up its formulary.

CMS explained that a PDP's exception procedures must encompass all types of tiering exception requests. The plan must grant an exception to its tiered cost-sharing structure whenever it determines that the non-preferred drug for treatment of the enrollee's condition is medically necessary, consistent with the physician's statement.

Criteria. The PDP's exceptions criteria must include, but are not limited to: (1) a description of the criteria the plan uses to evaluate a determination made by the enrollee's prescribing physician; (2) consideration of whether the requested Part D drug that is the

¶515

subject of the exceptions request is the therapeutic equivalent of any other drug on the plan's formulary; and (3) consideration of the number of drugs on the plan's formulary that are in the same class and category as the requested prescription drug that is the subject of the exceptions request. [42 C.F.R. § 423.578(a).]

Requirements for a request for exception. An enrollee or the enrollee's prescribing physician may file a request for an exception. The prescribing physician must provide an oral or written supporting statement that the preferred drug for the treatment of the enrollee's condition: (1) would not be as effective for the enrollee as the requested drug; (2) would have adverse effects for the enrollee; or (3) would not be as effective for the enrollee as the requested drug and the preferred drug would have adverse effects for the enrollee. If the physician provides an oral supporting statement, the plan subsequently may require the physician to provide a written supporting statement to demonstrate the medical necessity of the drug as well as provide additional supporting medical documentation. [42 C.F.R. § 423.578(c)(3).]

Exception Process Involving a Non-Formulary Part D Drug

Part D plan sponsors that offer prescription drug plans with formularies must establish and maintain exceptions procedures subject to CMS' approval for PDP enrollees who require non-formulary drugs. A non-formulary drug is a drug that is not on a plan's formulary. If a plan organizes its drug benefits by providing coverage only for formulary drugs and requires enrollees to pay for prescriptions out-of-pocket if they are not on the formulary, the plan has established a closed formulary. A drug that is not on a plan's formulary under this type of cost-sharing arrangement also is considered a non-formulary drug.

Formulary use includes the application of cost utilization tools, such as: (1) a dose restriction, including the dosage form, that causes a particular Part D drug not to be covered for the number of doses prescribed, or (2) a step therapy requirement that causes a particular Part D drug not to be covered until the requirements of the plan's coverage policy are met, or (3) a therapeutic substitution requirement. [42 C.F.R. § 423.578(b).]

Exceptions process. The PDP must grant an exception whenever it determines that the drug is medically necessary, consistent with the physician's statement and that the drug would be covered except that it is an off-formulary drug. The plan's formulary exceptions process must address: (1) situations in which a formulary changes during the year, and situations in which an enrollee is using a given drug; (2) continued coverage of a particular Part D prescription drug that the PDP is discontinuing coverage on the formulary for reasons other than safety or because the Part D prescription drug cannot be supplied by or was withdrawn from the market by the drug's manufacturer; and (3) an exception to a plan's coverage policy that causes a Part D prescription drug not to be covered because of cost utilization tools, such as a requirement for step therapy, dosage limitations, or therapeutic substitution.

An enrollee, the enrollee's appointed representative, or the prescribing physician, on behalf of the enrollee, may file a request for an exception. The prescribing physician must provide an oral or written supporting statement that the requested prescription drug is medically necessary to treat the enrollee's disease or medical condition. [42 C.F.R. § 423.578(b).]

Impact on annual out of pocket threshold. If the plan covers a non-formulary drug, the costs incurred by the enrollee for that drug are treated as being included for purposes of calculating and meeting the annual out-of-pocket threshold.

Approval of a non-formulary exceptions request. When a non-formulary exception request is approved, the plan may not require the enrollee to request approval for a refill, or a new

¶515

prescription to continue using the Part D prescription drug after the refills for the initial prescription are exhausted, as long as (1) the enrollee's prescribing physician continues to prescribe the drug; (2) the drug continues to be considered safe for treating the enrollee's disease or medical condition; and (3) the enrollment period has not expired. [42 C.F.R. § 423.578(c)(4).]

Rules for Redeterminations

The first level of the appeals process is a redetermination. An enrollee must file a written request for redetermination with the plan that made the coverage determination within 60 calendar days from the date of the notice of the coverage determination. The plan, however, may adopt a policy for accepting oral requests. The plan may extend the timeframe for filing the request, if the enrollee can show good cause for late filing. The person who files a request for redetermination may withdraw it by filing a written request with the plan. [42 C.F.R. § 423.582.]

Who must conduct the review of an adverse coverage determination. A person or persons who were not involved in making the coverage determination must conduct the redetermination. When the issue is the denial of coverage based on a lack of medical necessity, the redetermination must be made by a physician with expertise in the field of medicine that is appropriate for the services at issue. The physician making the redetermination need not, in all cases, be of the same specialty or subspecialty as the prescribing physician. [42 C.F.R. § 423.590(f).]

Timeframes for standard redetermination requests. If the PDP makes a redetermination that is completely favorable to the enrollee, or makes a redetermination that affirms, in whole or in part, its adverse coverage determination, the plan must notify the enrollee in writing of its redetermination and effectuate it as expeditiously as the enrollee's health condition requires, but no later than seven calendar days from the date the plan receives the request for a standard redetermination. [42 C.F.R. § 423.590(b).]

If the PDP fails to provide the enrollee with a redetermination within the timeframes specified above, the failure constitutes an adverse redetermination decision, and the plan must forward the enrollee's request to the independent review entity (IRE) within 24 hours of the expiration of the adjudication timeframe. [42 C.F.R. § 423.590(c) and (e).]

Notice of adverse redetermination. The notice of any adverse determination must use approved notice language in a readable and understandable form, state the specific reasons for the denial, and inform the enrollee of his or her right to a reconsideration. For adverse drug coverage redeterminations, the notice must describe the standard and expedited reconsideration processes, including the enrollee's right to, and conditions for, obtaining an expedited reconsideration and the remainder of the appeals process. For adverse payment redeterminations, the notice must describe the standard reconsideration process and the remainder of the appeals process. [42 C.F.R. § 423.590(g).]

Expedited Redeterminations

For an expedited redetermination, an enrollee or an enrollee's prescribing physician acting on behalf of an enrollee, may request a redetermination of a coverage determinations. Requests for redetermination on payment of drugs already received, however, may not be expedited because a medical emergency does not exist for an enrollee who has obtained the medication in dispute. [42 C.F.R. § 423.584(a).]

Requests for expedited redetermination. To ask for an expedited redetermination, an enrollee or a prescribing physician acting on behalf of an enrollee must submit an oral or written request directly to the prescription drug plan or, if applicable, to the entity responsi-

¶515

ble for making the redetermination, as directed by the plan. A prescribing physician may provide oral or written support for an enrollee's request for an expedited redetermination. [42 C.F.R. § 423.584(b).]

The PDP must maintain procedures for processing requests for expedited redetermination: The PDP must establish (1) an efficient and convenient means for individuals to submit oral or written requests, (2) document all oral requests in writing, and (3) maintain the documentation in the case file. In addition, the PDP must decide promptly whether to expedite the redetermination or follow the timeframe for standard redetermination based on the following requirements:

- For a request made by an enrollee, the plan must provide an expedited redetermination if it determines that applying the standard timeframe for making a redetermination may seriously jeopardize the life or health of the enrollee or the enrollee's ability to regain maximum function.

- For a request made or supported by a prescribing physician, the plan must provide an expedited redetermination if the physician indicates that applying the standard timeframe for conducting a redetermination may seriously jeopardize the life or health of the enrollee or the enrollee's ability to regain maximum function. [42 C.F.R. § 423.584(c).]

If a PDP denies a request for expedited redetermination, it must make the determination within the seven-day timeframe that begins the day the plan receives the request for expedited redetermination. The plan must give the enrollee prompt oral notice of the denial that:

(1) explains that the plan processes the enrollee's request using the seven-day timeframe for standard redetermination;

(2) informs the enrollee of the right to file an expedited grievance if he or she disagrees with the decision by the plan not to expedite;

(3) informs the enrollee of the right to resubmit a request for an expedited redetermination with the prescribing physician's support; and

(4) provides instructions about the expedited grievance process and its timeframes.

Within three calendar days of the oral notice to the enrollee, the PDP must deliver an equivalent written notice, which contains the required information. [42 C.F.R. § 423.584(d).]

Timeframe for expedited redeterminations. A Part D plan sponsor that approves a request for expedited redetermination must complete its redetermination and give the enrollee and the prescribing physician involved, when appropriate, notice of its decision as expeditiously as the enrollee's health condition requires but no later than 72 hours after receiving the request. [42 C.F.R. § 423.590(d).]

Failure to meet timeframe for expedited redetermination. If the PDP fails to provide the enrollee or the prescribing physician, when appropriate, with the results of its expedited redetermination within the 72 hour timeframe, the failure constitutes an adverse redetermination decision, and the plan must forward the enrollee's request to the independent review entity (IRE) within 24 hours of the expiration of the adjudication timeframe. [42 C.F.R. § 423.590(e).]

Reconsideration by an Independent Review Entity

An enrollee who is dissatisfied with the redetermination of a prescription drug plan has a right to a reconsideration by an independent review entity that contracts with CMS.

¶515

Requirements for a request for reconsideration. An enrollee must file a written request for reconsideration with the IRE within 60 days of the date of the redetermination by the plan. When an enrollee files an appeal, the IRE is required to solicit the views of the prescribing physician orally or in writing. Because the IRE solicits the views of the prescribing physician, it is not necessary for the request to include a supporting statement from the prescribing physician. [42 C.F.R. § 423.600(a)(b).]

IRE records. A written account of the prescribing physician's views, prepared by either the prescribing physician or IRE, must be contained in the IRE's record. This will enable the administrative law judge, Medicare Appeals Council, or a federal court to review all of the evidence considered or disregarded by the IRE. [42 C.F.R. § 423.600(b).]

Requirements for reconsideration for non-formulary drugs. For an enrollee to request an IRE reconsideration of a determination by a plan not to provide for a Part D drug that is not on the formulary, the prescribing physician must determine that all covered Part D drugs on any tier of the formulary for treatment of the same condition would not be as effective for the individual as the non-formulary drug, would have adverse effects for the individual, or both. [42 C.F.R. § 423.600(c).]

Timeframe for reconsideration. The IRE must conduct the reconsideration as expeditiously as the enrollee's health condition requires but no later than seven calendar days from the date of a request for a reconsideration. When a request for an expedited reconsideration is received and granted, the IRE must conduct the reconsideration as expeditiously as the enrollee's health condition requires, but no later than 72 hours after receiving the request. [42 C.F.R. § 423.600(d).]

Medical necessity issues. When the issue is the denial of coverage based on a lack of medical necessity (or any substantively equivalent term used to describe the concept of medical necessity), the reconsideration must be made by a physician with expertise in the field of medicine that is appropriate for the services at issue. The physician making the reconsideration need not, in all cases, be of the same specialty or subspecialty as the prescribing physician. The IRE is prohibited, however, from ruling on the validity of a plan's exceptions criteria or formulary. [42 C.F.R. § 423.600(e).]

Notice of reconsideration determination. The IRE is responsible for mailing a notice of its reconsideration determination to the enrollee and the PDP, and for sending a copy to CMS. The notice must state the specific reasons for the IRE's decision in understandable language. If the reconsideration determination is adverse, the notice must inform the enrollee of his or her right to an administrative law judge (ALJ) hearing if the amount in controversy meets the threshold requirement and describe the procedures that the enrollee must follow to obtain an ALJ hearing. [42 C.F.R. § 423.602.]

Effect of a reconsideration determination. A reconsideration determination is final and binding on the enrollee and the plan, unless the enrollee files a request for an ALJ hearing. [42 C.F.R. § 423.604.]

Administrative Law Judge, Medicare Appeals Council, and Judicial Reviews

CMS has adopted most of the procedural rules currently used under the Medicare Advantage (MA) program for administrative law judge (ALJ), Medicare Appeals Council (MAC) and judicial reviews for prescription drug plans.

An enrollee who is dissatisfied with the independent review entity (IRE) reconsideration determination has a right to a hearing before an ALJ if the amount remaining in controversy meets the threshold requirement established annually. If the basis for the appeal is the refusal by the Part D plan sponsor to provide drug benefits, CMS uses the projected value of

¶515

those benefits to compute the amount remaining in controversy. The projected value of a Part D drug or drugs includes any costs the enrollee could incur based on the number of refills prescribed for the drug(s) in dispute during the plan year. [42 C.F.R. § 423.610(a)(b).]

Calculating the amount in controversy. The ALJ amount in controversy is a statutorily established threshold. To calculate the amount remaining in controversy, subtract the following amounts:

(1) payments made by third parties;

(2) any allowed amount under Part D;

(3) deductible and coinsurance amounts applicable to the particular Part D drug at issue from either the projected value of the drug; or

(4) (when the enrollee is seeking reimbursement) the actual amount the enrollee paid.

Aggregating appeals. An enrollee may aggregate two or more appeals to meet the amount in controversy threshold for an ALJ hearing if: (1) the appeals have been reconsidered by an IRE; (2) the request for ALJ hearing lists all of the appeals to be aggregated and each aggregated appeal meets the filing requirements, and (3) the ALJ determines that the appeals the enrollee seeks to aggregate involve the delivery of prescription drugs to a single enrollee.

Multiple enrollees may aggregate two or more appeals to meet the amount in controversy threshold for an ALJ hearing if (1) the appeals have been reconsidered by an IRE; (2) the request for ALJ hearing lists all of the appeals to be aggregated and each aggregated appeal meets the filing requirement, and (3) the ALJ determines that the appeals the enrollees seek to aggregate involve the same prescription drug. [42 C.F.R. § 423.610(c).]

Requirements for a request for an ALJ hearing. The enrollee must file a written request for a hearing with the entity specified in the IRE's reconsideration notice. Except when an ALJ extends the timeframe, the enrollee must file a request for a hearing within 60 days of the date of the notice of an IRE reconsideration determination. [42 C.F.R. § 423.612(a)(b).]

Insufficient amount in controversy. If a request for a hearing clearly shows that the amount in controversy is less than the amount in controversy threshold for an ALJ hearing, the ALJ dismisses the request. If, after a hearing is initiated, the ALJ finds that the amount in controversy is less than the threshold amount, the ALJ will discontinue the hearing and will not rule on the substantive issues raised in the appeal. [42 C.F.R. § 423.612(c).]

Medicare Appeals Council (MAC) review of an ALJ decision. An enrollee who is dissatisfied with an ALJ hearing decision may request that the MAC review the ALJ's decision or dismissal. The Medicare Advantage program regulations governing MAC review apply to MAC reviews to the extent applicable. However, unlike Medicare Advantage plans, PDPs do not have the right to request an appeal of an ALJ decision with which the plan disagrees; only Part D enrollees are permitted to appeal ALJs' decisions. [42 C.F.R. § 423.620.]

Judicial review. An enrollee may request judicial review of an ALJ's decision if: (1) the MAC denied the enrollee's request for review or if the MAC approves the request for review, (2) the MAC decision is the final decision of CMS, and (3) the amount in controversy meets the threshold requirement established annually by the Secretary. To request judicial review, an enrollee must file a civil action in a district court of the United States. [42 C.F.R. § 423.630.]

¶515

Effectuation of Standard Determinations, Reconsiderations, or Decisions and Expedited Determinations and Reconsiderations

In addition to shortening the adjudication timeframes, CMS has reduced the timeframes for effectuation for requests involving payment issues for both determinations and redeterminations. The effectuation timeframes for requests for benefits are shorter than the effectuation timeframes for payment issues because plans normally process claims in 30-day cycles. The timeframes for effectuation for both benefits and payment issues are described below.

Reversals by the Part D plan sponsor. If a prescription drug plan (plan or PDP) reverses its coverage determination in a redetermination of a request for benefits, the plan must authorize or provide the benefit under dispute as expeditiously as the enrollee's health condition requires, but no later than seven calendar days from the date it receives the request for redetermination.

If the PDP reverses its coverage determination on a redetermination of a request for payment, the Part D plan sponsor must authorize payment for the benefit within seven calendar days from the date it receives the request for redetermination, and make payment no later than 30 calendar days after the date the plan sponsor receives the request for redetermination.

On an expedited redetermination of a request for benefits, if the plan reverses its coverage determination, the plan must authorize or provide the benefit under dispute as expeditiously as the enrollee's health condition requires, but no later than 72 hours after the date the Part D plan sponsor receives the request for redetermination. [42 C.F.R. § 423.636(a).]

Reversals other than by the Part D plan sponsor. On appeal of a request for benefit, if the plan's determination is reversed in whole or in part by the independent review entity (IRE), or at a higher level of appeal, the PDP must authorize or provide the benefit under dispute within 72 hours from the date it receives notice reversing the determination.

On appeal of a request for payment, if the plan's determination is reversed in whole or in part by the independent review entity, or at a higher level of appeal, the Part D plan sponsor must authorize payment for the benefit within 72 hours, but make payment no later than 30 calendar days from the date it receives notice reversing the coverage determination. [42 C.F.R. § 423.636(b).]

If the expedited determination or expedited redetermination for benefits by the plan is reversed in whole or in part by the IRE, or at a higher level of appeal, the plan must authorize or provide the benefit under dispute as expeditiously as the enrollee's health condition requires but no later than 24 hours from the date it receives notice reversing the determination.

In all cases, when a plan's determination is reversed in whole or in part by the IRE or at any higher level of appeal, the plan must inform the IRE that it has effectuated the decision. [42 C.F.R. § 423.638.]

[¶ 520] Premiums and Cost-Sharing Subsidies for Low Income Individuals

CMS subsidizes the monthly beneficiary premium and cost-sharing amounts incurred by Part D eligible individuals with lower income and resources.

Requirements for Eligibility

CMS has stated that the primary goal under the low-income subsidy program is to have nationally uniform standards and rules for determining eligibility for a subsidy because the low-income subsidy is a national program and should be operated under the same rules regardless of where in the country an applicant lives. CMS has not permitted states to use the more liberal methodologies that they use to determine eligibility for Medicare Savings programs under Medicaid to determine Medicare Part D low-income subsidy eligibility because CMS does not have the authority to extend more liberal methodologies to the SSA. [*Final rule*, 70 FR 4374, Jan. 28, 2005.]

CMS explained that determinations for the low-income subsidy can be made in advance of a person enrolling in a Part D plan. States are required to take subsidy applications starting July 1, 2005, well in advance of the open enrollment period for the Part D benefit. A subsidy eligible individual is not entitled to the subsidy, however, until such time as the person's enrollment in the plan is effective. [*Final rule*, 70 FR 4374, Jan. 28, 2005.]

Subsidy eligible individual. A subsidy eligible individual is a Part D eligible individual residing in a state who (1) is enrolled in, or seeking to enroll in a Part D plan, has an income below 150 percent of the federal poverty level (FPL) applicable to the individual's family size, and (3) has resources that are at or below the resource thresholds described below. [42 C.F.R. § 423.773(a).]

A full subsidy eligible individual is a subsidy eligible individual who (1) has income below 135 percent of the FPL applicable to the individual's family size and (2) has resources that do not exceed:

- for 2006, three times the amount of resources an individual may have and still be eligible for benefits under the Supplemental Security Income (SSI) program under title XVI of the Act (including the assets or resources of the individual's spouse); and

- for subsequent years, the amount of resources allowable for the previous year increased by the annual percentage increase in the consumer price index (all items, U.S. city average) as of September of that previous year, rounded to the nearest multiple of $10. [42 C.F.R. § 423.773(b).]

Individuals treated as full subsidy eligible. An individual must be treated as meeting the eligibility requirements for full subsidy eligible individuals described above if the individual is a: (1) full-benefit dual eligible individual; (2) recipient of Social Security Income (SSI) benefits under title XVI of the Social Security Act; or (3) eligible for Medicaid as a qualified Medicare beneficiary (QMB), specified low income Medicare beneficiary (SLMB), or a qualifying individual (QI) under a state's plan. [42 C.F.R. § 423.773(c)(1).]

CMS has elected to exercise the authority granted under the Social Security Act to treat qualified Medicare beneficiaries, specified low income Medicare beneficiaries, and qualifying individuals who are not full benefit dual eligible individuals as full subsidy eligible individuals. Qualified disabled and working individuals, however, are not included.

Notification and period of eligibility. CMS will notify all individuals treated as full subsidy eligible persons that they do not need to apply for the subsidies and they are deemed eligible for a full subsidy for a period up to one year. CMS plans to begin sending notices to individuals deemed to be subsidy eligible in the spring of 2005, prior to the start of taking applications for individuals who are not deemed eligible for the low-income subsidy. [42 C.F.R. § 423.773(c)(2).]

Once a subsidy individual enrolls in a Part D plan, CMS will notify Part D plans through a data match that the individual qualifies for a low-income subsidy.

CMS has clarified that individuals who have met their spenddown obligation are eligible for a full subsidy under Part D for up to one year without interruption. An individual who periodically goes off Medicaid because he or she is required to meet a new spenddown budget will maintain full subsidy eligible individual status for the remaining period of the subsidy eligibility. In addition an individual who loses Medicaid during a year will be eligible for subsidy during the remainder of the year, but will no longer be automatically deemed for full subsidy in the next calendar year.

Other low-income subsidy individuals are subsidy eligible individuals who (1) have income less than 150 percent of the FPL applicable to the individual's family size; and (2) have resources that do not exceed:

- $10,000 if single or $20,000 if married (including the assets or resources of the individual's spouse) in 2006; and

- for subsequent years, the resource amount allowable for the previous year, increased by the annual percentage increase in the consumer price index (all items, U.S. city average) as of September of the previous year, rounded to the nearest multiple of $10. [42 C.F.R. § 423.773(d).]

CMS clarified that low income Part D eligible individuals who reside in the territories are not eligible to receive premium and cost-sharing subsidies. [42 C.F.R. 423.773.]

Eligibility Determinations, Redeterminations, and Applications

An application for subsidy assistance may be filed with a state's Medicaid program office or with the Social Security Administration (SSA). Part D plans are to refer individual inquiries concerning application or eligibility for the low-income subsidy to state agencies or SSA.

CMS has stated that individuals need not apply at state offices or SSA field offices in person, they may apply over the phone via SSA's toll free (1-800) number and they may send applications in the mail or over the Internet. In addition, they may have individuals assist them in completing the application on their behalf.

Eligibility determinations. If an individual applies with the state Medicaid agency, the determination of eligibility for subsidies is made by the state under its state plan under title XIX of the Social Security Act. If an individual applies with the SSA, the Commissioner of Social Security will make the determination. [42 C.F.R. § 423.774(a).]

Effective date of initial eligibility determinations. Initial eligibility determinations are effective beginning with the first day of the month in which the individual applies, but no earlier than January 1, 2006, and remain in effect for a period not to exceed one year. [42 C.F.R. § 423.774(b).]

Redeterminations and appeals of low-income subsidy eligibility. Redeterminations and appeals of low income subsidy eligibility determinations by states must be made in the same manner and frequency as the redeterminations and appeals are made under the state's Medicaid plan, which must be conducted at least annually. Redeterminations and appeals of eligibility determinations made by the Commissioner will be made in the manner specified by the Commissioner of Social Security. [42 C.F.R. § 423.774(c).]

If the eligibility determination for an individual not deemed to be a full subsidy eligible individual was processed by SSA, then SSA "owns" the beneficiary for redeterminations and appeals. If a beneficiary no longer resides in the state and the state processed the subsidy determination under its own system, the state no longer can be expected to be held liable for the subsidy redetermination and appeal. In this case, the beneficiary would need to apply in the new state of residence or could apply with SSA.

Application requirements. For subsidy applications to be considered complete, applicants or personal representatives applying on the individual's behalf, must (1) complete all required elements of the application; (2) provide any statements from financial institutions,

¶520

as requested, to support information in the application; and (3) certify, under penalty of perjury or similar sanction for false statements, as to the accuracy of the information provided on the application form. [42 C.F.R. § 423.774(c).]

Timeframes for determination. CMS does not have the authority to direct SSA to determine subsidy eligibility within a given time period and has decided not to impose a specified time period on states through the regulations. As a general guidance, CMS expects that states will determine subsidy eligibility within time periods that are at least consistent with the processing of state Medicaid applications. [*Final rule,* 70 FR 4378, Jan. 28, 2005.]

Retroactive eligibility. Retroactive eligibility for the low-income subsidy is only an issue if a full-benefit dual eligible individual currently is enrolled in a Part D plan and later qualifies for Medicaid. By being entitled to full benefits under Medicaid, the individual automatically is eligible for the low-income subsidy. In this case, the subsidy eligibility will extend back to the start date of Medicaid eligibility, which could be up to three months earlier if the individual would have qualified for Medicaid during the three month retroactive period. The individual will be reimbursed by the plan for any extra cost sharing he or she would not have paid as a full subsidy eligible individual. [*Final rule,* 70 FR 4378, Jan. 28, 2005.]

Reporting changes in financial circumstances. Changes in financial circumstances that could impact an individual's eligibility for the low-income subsidy should be reported to the agency that processed the subsidy application in accordance with that agency's rules.

Determinations by other entities. State pharmacy assistance programs and other entities such as community organizations and other non-Medicaid state offices can provide assistance to individuals in completing the SSA application. The entity, however, cannot be the entity ultimately responsible for determining eligibility for low income subsidies because under the statute, eligibility determinations must be made by the state Medicaid agency or SSA. [*Final rule,* 70 FR 4378.]

Premium Subsidy

The Part D premium subsidy amount available to subsidy eligible individuals vary depending upon the individual's income and resources/asset levels.

Full subsidy eligible individuals are entitled to a premium subsidy equal to 100 percent of the premium subsidy amount. [42 C.F.R. § 423.780(a).] The premium subsidy amount is equal to an amount which is the lesser of:

- under the Part D plan selected by the beneficiary,

  (1) the monthly beneficiary premium for a Part D plan other than a Medicare Advantage prescription drug (MA-PD) plan that is basic prescription drug coverage,

  (2) the portion of the monthly beneficiary premium attributable to basic prescription drug coverage for a Part D plan other than a MA-PD plan that is enhanced alternative coverage, or

  (3) the MA monthly prescription drug beneficiary premium as defined under the Social Security Act, or

- the greater of the low-income benchmark premium amount for a PDP region (see "Calculation of the low-income benchmark premium amount." below) or the lowest monthly beneficiary premium for a prescription drug plan that offers basic prescription drug coverage in the PDP region. [42 C.F.R. § 423.780(b)(1).]

Calculation of the low-income benchmark premium amount. The low-income benchmark premium amount for a prescription drug plan region is a weighted average of the monthly beneficiary premium amounts (see below) for the Part D plans, with the weight for each PDP

¶520

and MA-PD plan equal to a percentage, the numerator equal to the number of Part D eligible individuals enrolled in the plan in the reference month and the denominator equal to the total number of Part D eligible individuals enrolled in all PDP and MA-PD plans (but not including Program for All-inclusive Care for the Elderly (PACE), private fee-for-service plans or 1876 cost plans) in a PDP region in the reference month. [42 C.F.R. § 423.780(b)(2).]

Special rule for 2006 to weight the low-income benchmark premium. For purposes of calculating the low-income benchmark premium amount for 2006, CMS assigns equal weighting to PDP sponsors (including fallback entities) and assigns MA-PD plans a weight based on prior enrollment. New MA-PD plans are assigned a zero weight. PACE, private fee-for-service plans and 1876 cost plans are not included. [42 C.F.R. § 423.780(c).]

Premium amounts. The premium amounts used to calculate the low income benchmark premium amount are as follows: (1) the monthly beneficiary premium for a PDP that is basic prescription drug coverage; (2) the portion of the monthly beneficiary premium attributable to basic prescription drug coverage for a PDP that is enhanced alternative coverage; or (3) the MA monthly prescription drug beneficiary premium for a MA-PD plan. [42 C.F.R. § 423.780(b)(2).]

If a full subsidy eligible individual chose to enroll in a PDP with a higher premium that the premium subsidy amount, he or she would be obligated to pay the difference between the plan premium and the premium subsidy amount each month. CMS does not have the authority under the statute to limit these individuals' choices. The Part D plan with the higher premium may provide a benefit package that better meets these individuals' prescription needs than other plans. [*Final rule*, 70 FR 4384-87, Jan. 28, 2005.]

CMS has explained that the low income benchmark premium amounts are determined without the addition of any amounts attributable to late enrollment penalties.

Other low-income subsidy eligible individuals–sliding scale premium. Other low-income subsidy eligible individuals are entitled to a premium subsidy based on a linear sliding scale ranging from 100 percent of the premium subsidy amount as follows:

(1) the full premium subsidy amount for individuals with income at or below 135 percent of the federal poverty line (FPL) applicable to their family size;

(2) a premium subsidy equal to 75 percent of the premium subsidy amount for individuals with income greater than 135 percent but at or below 140 percent of the FPL applicable to the family size;

(3) a premium subsidy equal to 50 percent of the premium subsidy amount for individuals with income greater than 140 percent but at or below 145 percent of the FPL applicable to the family size; or

(4) a premium subsidy equal to 25 percent of the premium subsidy amount for individuals with income greater than 145 percent but below 150 percent of FPL applicable to the family size. [42 C.F.R. § 423.780(d).]

Premium subsidy for late enrollment penalty. Full subsidy eligible individuals who are subject to late enrollment penalties are entitled to an additional premium subsidy equal to 80 percent of the late enrollment penalty for the first 60 months during which the penalty is imposed and 100 percent of their late enrollment penalty thereafter.

CMS noted that late enrollment penalties for full subsidy eligible individuals enrolled in state pharmacy assistance programs (SPAPs) are subsidized in the same manner as full subsidy eligible individuals enrolled in other plans.

¶520

In contrast to full subsidy eligible individuals, other low-income subsidy eligible individuals subject to late enrollment penalties will be responsible for 100 percent of the penalties. [42 C.F.R. § 423.780(e).]

Cost-Sharing Subsidy

This section relates to the elimination of the deductible, continuation of coverage above the initial coverage limit (no coverage gap), and reductions in cost-sharing.

Full subsidy eligible individuals. Full subsidy eligible individuals have no annual deductible and there is no coverage gap for full subsidy individuals. In addition, they are entitled to a reduction in cost-sharing for all covered Part D drugs covered under the prescription drug plan (PDP) or Medicare Advantage (MA-PD) plan below the out-of-pocket limit, including Part D drugs covered under the PDP or MA-PD plan obtained after the initial coverage limit. Cost-sharing subsidies paid by Medicare under this provision count toward the out-of-pocket threshold. Finally, all cost-sharing for covered Part D drugs covered under the PDP or MA-PD plan above the out-of-pocket limit are eliminated for full subsidy eligible individuals. In other words, Medicare pays the full benefit once the catastrophic level is reached. [42 C.F.R. § 423.782(a).]

Reductions co-payments are applied as follows:

(1) For full-benefit dual eligible individuals who are not institutionalized and who have income above 100 percent of the federal poverty line (FPL) applicable to the individual's family size and for individuals who have income under 135 percent of the FPL applicable to the individual's family size who meet the resources test for costs up to the out-of pocket threshold, co-payment amounts are not to exceed $2 for a generic drug or preferred drug that is a multiple source drug and $5 for any other drug in 2006. For subsequent years, the copayment amounts for the previous year increased by the annual percentage increase rounded to the nearest multiple of five. Full-benefit dual eligible individuals who are institutionalized have no cost-sharing for covered Part D drugs covered under their PDP or MA-PD plans.

(2) Full-benefit dual eligible individuals who are institutionalized have no cost-sharing for covered Part D drugs covered under their PDP or MA-PD plans.

(3) Full-benefit dual eligible individuals with incomes that do not exceed 100 percent of the FPL applicable to the individual's family size, will pay, for costs below the out-of pocket threshold, the lesser of: (i) $1 for a generic drug or preferred drugs that are multiple source or $3 for any other drug in 2006, or for years after 2006 the percentage increase in the Consumer Price Index, rounded to the nearest multiple of 5 cents or 10 cents, respectively; or (ii) the amount charged to other full subsidy eligible individuals discussed in (1) above. [42 C.F.R. § 423.782(a).]

Medicare Advantage plans. CMS has noted that specialized Medicare Advantage plans offering benefits only to dual eligible individuals could choose to reduce or eliminate co-payments for their members as a supplemental benefit. Otherwise, the Part D co-payments for low-income individuals cannot be reduced or eliminated. For all other plans, Part D co-payments cannot be reduced or eliminated for dual eligible individuals unless reduced or eliminated for all other plan enrollees. This is because any reduction of the co-payments must apply to all plan members under the uniformity of benefits provisions. Therefore, MA-PD plans other than special MA-PD plans for dual eligibles may not offer their members who are dual eligible lower co-payments or coinsurance than those paid by its other plan members. [*Final rule*, 70 FR 4384-89, Jan. 28, 2005.]

Other low-income subsidy eligible individuals. In addition to continuation of coverage (no coverage gap), other low-income subsidy eligible individuals are entitled to the following:

¶520

(1) In 2006, reduction in the annual deductible from $250 to $50; this amount is increased each year beginning in 2007 by the annual percentage increase in average per capita aggregate expenditures for Part D drugs, rounded to the nearest multiple of $1;

(2) fifteen percent coinsurance for all covered Part D drugs obtained after the annual deductible under the plan up to the out-of-pocket limit;

(3) for covered Part D drugs above the out-of-pocket limit, in 2006, co-payments do not to exceed $2 for a generic drug or preferred drugs that are multiple source drugs and $5 for any other drug. For years beginning in 2007, the amounts specified for the previous year increased by the annual percentage increase in average per capita aggregate expenditures for covered Part D drugs, rounded to the nearest multiple of five cents.

CMS has stated that the cost-sharing subsidies will count toward the application of the out-of pocket threshold.

Pharmacies may waive or reduce cost-sharing requirements on behalf of a subsidy eligible individual provided the waiver is not offered as part of any advertisement or solicitation. In the alternative, states may elect to pay copayments on behalf of these individuals and provide supplemental drug coverage although they will not receive a federal match under Medicaid if they choose to do so. [42 C.F.R. § 423.782(b).]

Administration of Subsidy Program

CMS will issue further operational guidance on the notification methodology Part D plans must use to notify CMS that the reductions in premiums and cost-sharing have been implemented in a timely fashion and on the amount of the subsidy reductions received by beneficiary. CMS will have a plan in place to pay plans directly for their incurred and paid expenses related to reimbursement of beneficiaries who have incurred and paid expenses while waiting for a low-income subsidy eligibility determination. CMS will provide further operational guidance on this issue as well.

Notification of eligibility for low income subsidy. CMS notifies the Part D sponsor offering the Part D plan in which a subsidy eligible individual is enrolled of the individual's eligibility for a subsidy and the amount of the subsidy. [42 C.F.R. § 423.800(a).]

Reduction of premium or cost-sharing by PDP sponsor or organization. The Part D sponsor offering the Part D plan in which a subsidy eligible individual is enrolled must reduce the individual's premiums and cost-sharing as applicable, and provide information to CMS on the amount of those reductions, in a manner determined by CMS. The Part D sponsor must track the application of the subsidies to be applied to the out-of-pocket threshold. [42 C.F.R. § 423.800(b).]

Reimbursement for cost-sharing paid before notification of eligibility for low-income subsidy. The Part D sponsor must reimburse subsidy eligible individuals and organizations such as state pharmacy assistance programs and Ryan White AIDS Drug Assistance program that may pay cost-sharing on behalf of such individuals, any excess premiums and cost-sharing paid by such individual or organization after the effective date of the individual's eligibility for a subsidy. [42 C.F.R. § 423.800(c).]

Retroactive eligibility. Retroactive eligibility is only an issue if an individual is enrolled in a Part D plan and subsequently applies for and is determined eligible as a full-benefit dual eligible individual. Because the individual is entitled to full benefits under Medicaid, he or she automatically will be eligible for the low-income subsidy. Subsidy eligibility will extend back to the start date of Medicaid eligibility, which could be three months earlier if the individual would have qualified for Medicaid during the three-month retroactive period. The individual will be reimbursed for the extra cost sharing he or she otherwise would not have paid as a full subsidy eligible individual.

This also applies to an individual under a Medicare Savings Program specified as a low-income Medicare beneficiary or qualifying individual but not as a qualified Medicare beneficiary (QMB) because QMBs cannot receive retroactive benefits under the Medicaid statute. For QMBs and other individuals who are enrolled in Part D plans and later apply and are determined eligible for low-income subsidy assistance, consistent with the statute, their eligibility would be effective on the first day of the month in which they applied for the low-income subsidy. In future guidance, CMS will specify how these reimbursements will be made. [*Final rule*, 70 FR 4389-91.]

[¶ 525] Fallback Plans

Fallback prescription drug plans may be offered in areas where eligible individuals would not otherwise have a choice of enrollment in at least two qualifying plans. To date, because there are at least two qualified plans offered in each region, no fallback plans have been offered. Fallback plans must offer only defined standard or actuarially equivalent standard prescription drug coverage, provide access to negotiated prices (including discounts from manufacturers), and meet all other requirements established for prescription drug plans (PDPs). There may be only one fallback plan per fallback service area, and there may not be any national fallback plan covering the whole country. [42 C.F.R. §§ 423.855, 423.859, 423.863(b)(6).]

If CMS determines that Part D eligible individuals in a prescription drug plan (PDP) region, or some portion of the region, do not have available a choice of enrollment in a minimum of two qualified plans, CMS will designate the region or portion of a region as a "fallback" service area.

CMS will monitor prescription drug plan (PDP) sponsors, Medicare Advantage (MA-PD) organizations and their subcontractors to ensure that the same legal entity is not operating both plans in a fallback area. CMS noted that there is no prohibition against a pharmacy benefit plan (PBM) operating as a subcontractor to an MA-PD plan as well as being a sponsor of a fallback PDP. CMS also noted that a PBM can operate as a subcontractor to all kinds of PDPs, including fallback PDPs, and to MA-PDs in any region. There also is no prohibition against an MA organization offering both an MA-PD plan and a fallback plan in the same region. [42 C.F.R. § 423.871.]

CMS has said that risk plans should not be concerned about competing against fallback plans. Risk plans will have the competitive advantages of corporate marketing, brand recognition, and the ability to offer more varied benefit designs (including supplemental benefits) and coverage to all enrollees in a region, not just to those in fallback service areas. CMS also anticipates that efficient risk plans may have the opportunity to earn higher levels of profit. Although there is a possibility that a fallback plan could enter a region if there is only one risk plan, it would be unlikely that a risk plan and a fallback plan would compete.

Submission of bids. CMS determines when fallback plans are necessary and then solicits bids at three-year cycles, or if need be, at mid-cycle to replace fallback contractors. If a mid-cycle contractor change is necessary, CMS will approve the change within 90 days of notice. Fallback plan sponsors need not be risk-bearing entities, and they may not submit risk bids at the same time that they submit fallback bids. [42 C.F.R. § 423.863.]

Premiums. The monthly beneficiary premium under a fallback PDP must be uniform for all fallback service areas in a PDP region. It must equal 25.5 percent of the CMS estimate of the average monthly per capita actuarial cost, including administrative expenses. There are no late enrollment penalties associated with fallback plans. [42 C.F.R. § 423.867; *Final rule*, 70 FR 4391–4400, Jan. 28, 2005.]

[¶ 530] Payments to Sponsors of Retiree Prescription Drug Plans

Subsidy payments will be paid to the sponsors of qualified retiree prescription drug plans. The sponsors of these subsidy plans can receive an annual subsidy equal to 28 percent of specified retiree drug costs. [Soc. Sec. Act § 1860D-22; 42 C.F.R. § 423.880.]

Requirements for Qualified Retiree Prescription Drug Plans

An employment-based retiree health coverage is considered to be a qualified retiree prescription drug plan if all of the following requirements are satisfied:

(1) an actuarial attestation is submitted;

(2) Part D eligible individuals covered under the plan are provided with creditable coverage notices; and

(3) records are maintained and made available for audit. [42 C.F.R. § 423.884(a).]

Disclosure of information. The sponsor must have a written agreement with its health insurance issuer, or group health plan regarding disclosure of information to CMS, and the issuer or plan must disclose to CMS, on behalf of the sponsor, the information necessary for the sponsor to comply with CMS requirements. [42 C.F.R. § 423.884(b).]

Submitting an Application for Subsidy

The sponsor must submit an application for the subsidy to CMS that is signed by an authorized representative of the sponsor. The sponsor must submit the following:

(1) employer tax ID number;

(2) sponsor name and address;

(3) contact name and e-mail address;

(4) actuarial attestation that satisfies the standards (specified below) and any other supporting documentation required by CMS for each qualified retiree prescription drug plan for which the sponsor seeks subsidy payments;

(5) a list of all individuals the sponsor believes are qualifying covered retirees enrolled in each prescription drug plan, including spouses and dependents, if Medicare eligible, along with the listed individual's: (a) full name, (b) Health Insurance Claim (HIC) number or Social Security number, (c) date of birth, (d) gender, and. (e) relationship to the retired employee.

(6) a sponsor may satisfy item (5) by entering into a voluntary data sharing agreement with CMS;

(7) a signed sponsor agreement; and

(8) any other information specified by CMS. [42 C.F.R. § 423.884(c)(1) and (2).]

An authorized representative of the requesting sponsor must sign the completed application and certify that the information contained in the application is true and accurate. [42 C.F.R. § 423.884(c)(4).]

Terms and conditions for subsidy payment. To receive a subsidy payment, the sponsor must specifically accept and agree to: (1) comply with the terms and conditions of eligibility for a subsidy payment; (2) acknowledge that the information in the application is being provided to obtain federal funds; and (3) require that all subcontractors, including plan administrators, acknowledge that information provided in connection with the subcontract is used for purposes of obtaining federal funds. [42 C.F.R. § 423.884(c)(3).]

Application timing and required updates. An application for a given plan year must be submitted by no later than 90 days prior to the beginning of the plan year. For plan year ending in 2006, an application was required by September 30, 2005. The sponsor must provide updates of the applications information to CMS on a monthly basis or at a frequency specified by CMS. [42 C.F.R. § 423.884(c)(5) and (6).]

CMS data match. Once the full application for the subsidy payment is submitted, CMS matches the names and identifying information of the individuals submitted as qualifying covered retirees with the Medicare Beneficiary Database (MBD) to determine which retirees are Part D eligible individuals who are not enrolled in a Part D plan and provides information concerning the results of the search to the sponsor. [42 C.F.R. § 423.884(c)(7).]

Actuarial Attestation Requirements

The sponsor of the plan must provide to CMS an attestation that the actuarial value of the retiree prescription drug coverage under the plan is at least equal to the actuarial value of the defined standard prescription drug coverage. The contents of the attestation must include the following assurances.

(1) The actuarial gross value of the retiree prescription drug coverage under the plan for the plan year is at least equal to the actuarial gross value of the defined standard prescription drug coverage under Part D for the plan year in question.

(2) The actuarial net value of the retiree prescription drug coverage under the plan for that plan year is at least equal to the actuarial net value of the defined standard prescription drug coverage under Part D for the plan year in question.

(3) The actuarial values must be determined using the methodology described below. [42 C.F.R. § 423.884(d)(1).]

Actuarial requirements. The attestation must be made and signed by a qualified actuary (member of the American Academy of Actuaries) and must state that the attestation is true and accurate. Applicants may use qualified outside actuaries, including actuaries employed by the plan administrator or an insurer providing benefits under the plan. If an applicant uses an outside actuary, the attestation can be submitted directly by the outside actuary or by the plan sponsor. The attestation must contain an acknowledgement that the information being provided in the attestation is being used to obtain federal funds. [42 C.F.R. § 423.884(d)(2)(3)(4).]

Methodology. The attestation must be based on generally accepted actuarial principles and any actuarial guidelines established by CMS. To the extent CMS has not provided guidance on a specific aspect of the actuarial equivalence standard, an actuary providing the attestation may rely on any reasonable interpretation of the CMS regulations and Soc. Sec. Act § 1860D-22(a) consistent with generally accepted actuarial principles in determining actuarial values. [42 C.F.R. § 423.884(d)(5).]

Specific rules for determining actuarial value of the sponsor's retiree prescription drug coverage. The gross value of coverage under the sponsor's retiree prescription drug plan must be determined using the actual claims experience and demographic data for Part D eligible individuals who are participants and beneficiaries in the sponsor's plan, provided that sponsors without creditable data due to their size or other factors, may use normative databases as specified by CMS. Sponsors may use other actuarial approaches specified by CMS as an alternative to the actuarial valuation specified under this paragraph.

The net value of coverage provided under the sponsor's retiree prescription drug plan must be determined by reducing the gross value of such coverage by the expected premiums paid by Part D eligible individuals who are plan participants or their spouses and

¶530

dependents. For sponsors of plans that charge a single, integrated premium or contribution to their retirees for both prescription drug coverage and other types of medical coverage, the attestation must allocate a portion of the premium/contribution to prescription drug coverage under the sponsor's plan, under any method determined by the sponsor or its actuary. [42 C.F.R. § 423.884(d)(5)(ii)(A) and (B).]

Specific rules for calculating the actuarial value of defined standard prescription drug coverage. The gross value of defined standard prescription drug coverage under Part D must be determined using the actual claims experience and demographic data for Part D eligible individuals in the sponsor's plan, provided that sponsors without credible data due to their size or other factors may use normative databases as specified by CMS. Sponsors may use other actuarial approaches specified by CMS as an alternative to the actuarial valuation.

To calculate the net value of defined standard prescription drug coverage under Part D, the gross value of defined standard prescription drug coverage under Part D is reduced by the following amounts:

(1) the monthly beneficiary premiums expected to be paid for standard prescription drug coverage; and

(2) an amount calculated to reflect the impact on the value of defined standard prescription drug coverage of supplemental coverage provided by the sponsor. [42 C.F.R. § 423.884(d)(5)(iii)(A) and (B).]

Valuation of standard prescription drug coverage. The valuation of defined standard prescription drug coverage for a given plan year is based on the initial coverage limit cost-sharing and out-of-pocket threshold for defined standard prescription drug coverage under Part D in effect at the start of such plan year.

The attestation must be submitted to CMS no later than 60 days after the publication of the Part D coverage limits for the upcoming calendar year, otherwise such valuation is based on the initial coverage limit, cost-sharing amounts, and out-of-pocket threshold for defined standard prescription drug coverage under Part D for the upcoming calendar year. For example, if a sponsor's retiree prescription drug plan operates under a plan year that ends March 30, the attestation for the year April 1, 2007, through March 30, 2008, is based on the coverage limit, cost-sharing and out-of-pocket threshold that apply to defined standard prescription drug coverage under Part D in 2007, provided the attestation is submitted within 60 days after the publication of the Part D coverage limits for 2008. If the attestation is submitted more than 60 days after the 2008 coverage limits have been published, the 2008 coverage limits would apply. [42 C.F.R. § 423.884(d)(5)(iii)(C) and (D).]

Employment-based retiree health coverage with two or more benefit options. For the assurance required for the actuarial gross value of the retiree prescription drug coverage under the plan for the plan year, the assurance must be provided separately for each benefit option for which the sponsor requests a subsidy under this subpart.

For the assurance required for the actuarial net value of the retiree prescription drug coverage under the plan for the year, the assurance may be provided either separately for each benefit option for which the sponsor provided assurances for the actuarial gross value of the retiree prescription drug coverage, or in the aggregate for all benefit options for which the sponsor provided assurances for the actuarial gross value of the retiree prescription drug coverage under the plan for the plan year. [42 C.F.R. § 423.884(d)(5)(iv).]

Submission of attestation following material change. The attestation must be provided no later than 90 days before the implementation of a material change to the drug coverage of the sponsor's plan that impacts the actuarial value of the coverage. [42 C.F.R. § 423.884(d)(6)(ii).]

¶530

Retiree Drug Subsidy Amounts

For each qualifying covered retiree enrolled with the sponsor of a qualified retiree prescription drug plan in a plan year, the sponsor receives a subsidy payment in the amount of 28 percent of the allowable retiree costs in the plan year that are attributable to gross retiree costs that exceed the cost threshold and do not exceed the cost limit (see below). The subsidy payment is calculated by first determining gross retiree costs between the cost threshold and cost limit, and then determining allowable retiree costs attributable to the gross retiree costs. [42 C.F.R. § 423.886(a).]

Cost threshold and cost limit. The following cost threshold and cost limits apply:

(1) the cost threshold is equal to $250 for plan years that end in 2006, subject to an annual adjustment described in item (3);

(2) the cost limit is equal to $5,000 for plan years that end in 2006; subject to an annual adjustment described in item (3);

(3) for subsequent years after 2006, the cost threshold and cost limit specified in (1) and (2) are adjusted in the same manner as the annual Part D deductible and the annual Part D out-of-pocket threshold are adjusted annually [42 C.F.R. § 423.886(b).]

Payment Methods and Providing Necessary Information

The provisions governing payment to Part D plan sponsors for qualified prescription drug coverage, including requirements to provide information necessary to ensure accurate subsidy payments, also govern the subsidy payment to sponsors of retiree prescription drug plans. Payment by CMS is conditioned on provision of accurate information. The information must be submitted, in a form and manner and at the times provided by CMS. CMS will make payment after the submission of the cost data by the sponsor and in a time and manner specified by CMS. [42 C.F.R. § 423.888(a) and (b)(3).]

Timing and submission of cost data. Payment can be made on a monthly, quarterly or annual basis, as elected by the plan sponsor, unless CMS determines that the options must be restricted because of operational limitations. If annual payments are elected, the sponsor must submit to CMS actual rebate and other price concession data within 15 months after the end of the plan year. If the plan sponsor elects to receive payment on a monthly or quarterly basis, it must submit to CMS the gross covered retiree plan related prescription drug costs incurred for its qualifying covered retirees during the payment period for which it is claiming a subsidy payment, and any other data CMS may require. The sponsor also must submit, using historical data and generally accepted actuarial principles, an estimate of the extent to which its expected allowable retiree costs differ from the gross covered retiree plan-related prescription drug costs, based on expected rebates and other price concessions for the upcoming plan year. The estimate must be used to reduce the periodic payments for the plan year. Final allocation of price concession data must occur after the end of the year under the reconciliation provisions (see below). [42 C.F.R. § 423.888(b)(1) and (2)(i).]

If the plan sponsor elects a one-time final annual payment, it must submit, within 15 months, or within any other longer time limit specified by CMS, after the end of the plan year, the total gross covered retiree plan-related prescription drug costs for the plan year for which it is claiming a subsidy payment, actual rebate and other price concession data, and any other data CMS may require. [42 C.F.R. § 423.888(b)(2)(ii).]

In the alternative, the sponsor can elect an interim annual payment, in which case it must submit to CMS:

¶530

- the gross covered retiree plan-related prescription drug costs incurred for all of its qualifying covered retirees during the payment period for which it is claiming a subsidy payment;

- an estimate using historical data and generally accepted actuarial principles of the difference between such gross costs and allowable costs based on expected rebates and other price concessions for the upcoming plan year; and

- any other data CMS may require. [42 C.F.R. § 423.888(b)(2)(ii).]

Reconciliation. Within 15 months or any other longer time limit specified by CMS, after the end of its plan year, sponsors who elect either monthly, quarterly or an interim annual payment must submit to CMS: (1) the total gross covered retiree plan-related prescription drug costs, (2) actual rebate and other price concession data for the plan year in question, and (3) any other data CMS may require. When this data is received, CMS will adjust the payments made for the plan year in question. [42 C.F.R. § 423.888(b)(4)(i) and (ii).]

Special rule for insured plans. Sponsors of group health plans that provide benefits through health insurance coverage and that choose either monthly payments, quarterly payments or an interim annual payment may elect to determine gross covered plan-related retiree prescription drug costs for purposes of the monthly, quarterly or interim annual payments based on a portion of the premium costs paid by the sponsor or by the qualifying covered retirees. Premium costs that are determined using generally accepted actuarial principles may be attributable to the gross prescription drug costs incurred by the health insurance issuer for the sponsor's qualifying covered retirees, except that administrative costs and risk charges must be subtracted from the premium. [42 C.F.R. § 423.888(b)(5)(i).]

At the end of the plan year, actual gross retiree plan related prescription drug costs incurred by the insurer (or the retiree), and the allowable costs attributable to the gross costs, are determined for each of the sponsor's qualifying covered retirees and submitted for reconciliation after the end of the plan year (see above). The insurer may submit the data for the reconciliation can be submitted directly to CMS. When it receives this data, CMS will adjust the payments made for the relevant plan year. [42 C.F.R. § 423.888(b)(5)(ii).]

Use of information provided. Officers, employees and contractors of the Department of Health and Human Services, including the Office of Inspector General (OIG), may use information collected only for the purposes of, and to the extent necessary in, carrying out payments to sponsors of retiree prescription drug plans, including, but not limited to, determination of payments and payment-related oversight and program integrity activities. This restriction does not limit OIG authority to conduct audits and evaluations necessary for carrying out these requirements. [42 C.F.R. § 423.888(c).]

Maintaining records. The sponsor of the qualified retiree prescription drug plan or a designee must maintain, and furnish to CMS or the OIG upon request, the records listed below. The records must be maintained for six years after the expiration of the plan year in which the costs were incurred for the purposes of audits and other oversight activities conducted by CMS to assure the accuracy of the actuarial attestation and the accuracy of payments. In addition, the sponsor of the qualified retiree prescription drug plan or a designee must maintain the records longer than six years if it knows or should know that the records are the subject of an ongoing investigation, litigation or negotiation involving civil, administrative or criminal liability. CMS or the OIG may extend the six-year retention requirement for the records in the event of an ongoing investigation, litigation, or negotiation involving civil, administrative or criminal liability. The records that must be retained include:

(1) reports and working documents of the actuaries who wrote the attestation;

¶530

(2) all documentation of costs incurred and other relevant information utilized for calculating the amount of the subsidy payment, including the underlying claims data;

(3) any other records specified by CMS. [42 C.F.R. § 423.888(d).]

Appeals

Informal written reconsideration. A sponsor is entitled to an informal written reconsideration of an adverse initial determination by CMS. An initial determination is a determination regarding the amount of the subsidy payment; the actuarial equivalence of the sponsor's retiree prescription drug plan; whether or not an enrollee in a retiree prescription drug plan is a qualifying covered retiree; or any other similar determination affecting eligibility for, or the amount of, a subsidy payment. An initial determination is final and binding unless reconsidered. [42 C.F.R. § 423.890(a)(1) and (2).]

A request for reconsideration must be made in writing and filed with CMS within 15 days of the date on the notice of adverse determination. The request for reconsideration must specify the findings or issues with which the sponsor disagrees and the reasons for the disagreements and may include additional documentary evidence the sponsor wishes CMS to consider. [42 C.F.R. § 423.890(a)(3) and (4).]

In conducting the reconsideration, CMS reviews the subsidy determination, the evidence and findings upon which it was based, and any other written evidence submitted by the sponsor or by CMS before notice of the reconsidered determination is made. CMS is required to inform the sponsor of the decision orally or through electronic mail, but will send a written decision to the sponsor upon the sponsor's request. A reconsideration decision, whether delivered orally or in writing, is final and binding unless a request for hearing is filed or it is revised. [42 C.F.R. § 423.890(a)(5), (6), and (7).]

Informal hearing request. A sponsor dissatisfied with the CMS reconsideration decision is entitled to an informal hearing. A request for a hearing must be made in writing and filed with CMS within 15 days of the date the sponsor receives the CMS reconsideration decision. The request for informal hearing must include a copy of the CMS reconsideration decision and must specify the findings or issues in the decision with which the sponsor disagrees and the reasons for the disagreements. [42 C.F.R. § 423.890(b)(1) and (2).]

CMS must provide written notice of the time and place of the informal hearing at least 10 days before the scheduled date. The hearing is conducted by a CMS hearing officer who neither receives testimony nor accepts any new evidence that was not presented with the reconsideration request. The CMS hearing officer is limited to the review of the record that was before CMS when CMS made both its initial and reconsideration determinations.

If CMS did not issue a written reconsideration decision, the hearing officer may request, but not require, a written statement from CMS or its contractors explaining CMS' determination, or CMS or its contractors may, on their own, submit the written statement to the hearing officer. Failure of CMS to submit a written statement does not result in any adverse findings against CMS and may not in any way be taken into account by the hearing officer in reaching a decision. [42 C.F.R. § 423.890(b)(3).]

The CMS hearing officer decides the case and sends a written decision to the sponsor, explaining the basis for the decision. The hearing officer decision is final and binding, unless the decision is reversed or modified by the Administrator. [42 C.F.R. § 423.890(b)(4) and (5).]

Review by the Administrator. A sponsor that has received a hearing officer decision upholding a CMS initial or reconsidered determination may request review by the Administrator within 15 days of receipt of the hearing officer's decision. The Administrator may

¶530

review the hearing officer's decision, any written documents submitted to CMS or to the hearing officer, as well as any other the hearing officer's decision and determine whether to uphold, reverse or modify the hearing officer's decision. The Administrator's determination is final and binding. [42 C.F.R. § 423.890(c).]

Reopening of initial or reconsidered determination. CMS may reopen and revise an initial or reconsidered determination upon its own motion or upon the request of a sponsor within one year of the date of the notice of determination for any reason, within four years for good cause, and at any time when the underlying decision was obtained through fraud or similar fault. [42 C.F.R. § 423.890(d)(1).]

A finding of good cause requires the existence of new and material evidence that was not readily available at the time the initial determination was made, a clerical error in the computation of payments, or the evidence that was considered in making the determination clearly shows on its face that an error was made. CMS does not find good cause if the only reason for reopening is a change of legal interpretation or administrative ruling upon which the initial determination was made. [42 C.F.R. § 423.890(d)(4) and (5).]

A decision by CMS not to reopen an initial or reconsidered determination is final and binding and cannot be appealed. [42 C.F.R. § 423.890(d)(6).]

Change of Ownership

Sponsors who apply for a retiree drug subsidy payment must comply with certain change of ownership requirements. A change of ownership includes:

- the removal, addition, or substitution of a partner, unless the partners expressly agree otherwise as permitted by applicable state law;

- transfer of all or substantially all of the assets of the sponsor to another party; or

- the merger of the sponsor's corporation into another corporation or the consolidation of the sponsor's organization with one or more other corporations, resulting in a new corporate body. [42 C.F.R. § 423.892(a).]

Exception. The transfer of corporate stock or the merger of another corporation into the sponsor's corporation, with the sponsor surviving, will not ordinarily constitute change of ownership. [42 C.F.R. § 423.892(b).]

Notice requirement. A sponsor that has a retiree prescription drug plan in effect and is considering or negotiating a change in ownership must notify CMS at least 60 days before the anticipated effective date of the change. [42 C.F.R. § 423.892(c).]

Automatic assignment. When there is a change of ownership that results in a transfer of the liability for prescription drug costs, the existing sponsor agreement is automatically assigned to the new owner. [42 C.F.R. § 423.892(d).]

[¶ 535] Prescription Drug Discount Card and Transitional Assistance Program

The Medicare Prescription Drug Discount Card and Transitional Assistance Program was established by section 101(a) of the Medicare Prescription Drug, Improvement, and Modernization Act of 2003 (MMA) (PubLNo 108-173) (see Soc. Sec. Act § 1860D-31).

The discount card program was a temporary measure that continued until 2006, when the Medicare Part D prescription drug benefit is implemented. After December 31, 2005, beneficiaries will be able to use their drug discount cards during a short transition period while enrollment is under way for the Medicare prescription drug benefit. [*Interim final rule*, 68 FR 69840, Dec. 15, 2003.]

Eligibility and Enrollment

Beginning in the spring of 2004, Medicare beneficiaries began enrolling in prescription drug discount card programs offered by Medicare-endorsed sponsors for annual fees of up to $30. All Medicare beneficiaries, except individuals with outpatient drug coverage through Medicaid, were eligible to enroll in a discount card program, with benefits beginning in June 2004. Beneficiaries who were enrolled in discount card programs had access to drug prices negotiated by card sponsors. Sponsors could be pharmaceutical benefit management companies, insurance companies, retail pharmacies, Medicare Advantage plans, or other private organizations. [*Interim final rule*, 68 FR 69840, Dec. 15, 2003.]

Medicare managed care organizations (Medicare Advantage organizations that offer coordinated care plans, and Medicare reasonable cost reimbursement plans) offered "exclusive card programs" that limited enrollment to their own managed care plan members. Members of Medicare managed care plans offered by exclusive card sponsors could only enroll in such exclusive card programs. [*Interim final rule*, 68 FR 69840, Dec. 15, 2003.]

Transitional Assistance

Low-income beneficiaries participating in the drug discount card program could qualify for up to $600 per year in financial assistance toward drug purchases. This was referred to as "transitional assistance." A beneficiary was eligible for transitional assistance if (1) the beneficiary resided in one of the 50 states or the District of Columbia; (2) the beneficiary's income was not more than 135 percent of the poverty line for his or her family's size; and (3) the beneficiary was not receiving outpatient prescription drug coverage from certain other programs, including Medicaid, TRICARE, certain group health insurance or health insurance coverage (such as retiree coverage), or the Federal Employees Health Benefit Program. [*Interim final rule*, 68 FR 69840, Dec. 15, 2003.]

Beneficiaries with outpatient drug coverage under a Medicare Advantage plan or a Medigap policy were eligible for transitional assistance even if their employers payed all or a portion of the premium for such plans. Beneficiaries residing in U.S. territories were not eligible for transitional assistance under the Medicare drug discount card program. Territories were allowed to establish their own transitional assistance plans to be implemented separately. [*Interim final rule*, 68 FR 69840, Dec. 15, 2003.]

When applying the $600 in transitional assistance toward prescription drug purchases, beneficiaries with incomes at or below 100 percent of the poverty line payed a 5 percent copayment, and beneficiaries with incomes above 100 percent of the poverty line (but no more than 135 percent of the poverty line) payed a 10 percent copayment. To improve coordination between the benefits offered under Medicare managed care plans and drug discount card programs, Medicare managed care plans offering exclusive card programs were permitted to apply transitional assistance toward any copayments and deductibles incurred by enrollees for drugs obtained under their managed care plan's outpatient drug benefit. [*Interim final rule*, 68 FR 69840, Dec. 15, 2003.]

Prescription Drug Card Offering

Most prescription drugs that can be purchased at retail pharmacies were eligible for discounts and transitional assistance. Endorsed sponsors obtained manufacturer rebates, discounts, or other price concessions to help lower the cost of drugs purchased by their enrollees. There was no minimum requirement as to the levels of rebates, discounts, or other price concessions that endorsed sponsors could obtain or the share of those price concessions that could be passed through to card enrollees. CMS anticipated that discount card sponsors would pass a substantial share of drug manufacturers' price concessions through to beneficiaries. [*Interim final rule*, 68 FR 69840, Dec. 15, 2003.]

The government policed drug card fraud. Effective June 18, 2004, the Office of Inspector General (OIG) had the authority to impose civil money penalties (CMPs) of up to $10,000 per violation against drug card sponsors who knowingly mislead the public, defrauded beneficiaries, or misused transitional assistance funds. The OIG was authorized to impose CMPs against sponsors who knowingly: misrepresented plan information in outreach materials, charged enrollees in violation of the terms of endorsed contracts, or misused transitional assistance funds. [*Interim Final rule*, 69 FR 28842, May 19, 2004.]

Beneficiary Information and Outreach

Each Medicare-endorsed discount card sponsor was required to provide to beneficiaries information and outreach materials describing its drug card program, including the enrollment fee, negotiated prices offered for prescription drugs, discounts on over-the-counter drugs (if offered), and any other products or services offered under the endorsement. CMS reviewed and approved a card sponsor's information and outreach materials before the sponsor could distribute the materials to beneficiaries. In addition, each discount card sponsor maintained a toll-free customer call center to respond to beneficiary questions. [*Interim final rule*, 68 FR 69840, Dec. 15, 2003.]

Beneficiaries were also able to obtain information from CMS on how drug discount card programs operated, who could qualify and how to enroll, as well as comparative information on card sponsors, by accessing the CMS website at www.medicare.gov or by calling 1-800-MEDICARE. CMS posted price comparison information on its website so that beneficiaries could compare negotiated prices, fees, and other card program features. [*Interim final rule*, 68 FR 69840, Dec. 15, 2003.]

Medicare Part D 225

[¶ 560] Map of 2006 PDP Regions

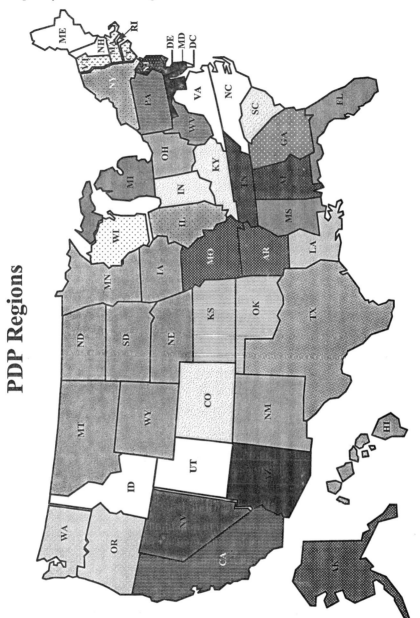

¶560

Chapter 6—EXCLUSIONS FROM COVERAGE

[¶ 600] Exclusions Under Both Plans

In addition to the limitations and exclusions discussed in the preceding chapters, other items or services are excluded under both Part A and Part B. The limitation on drugs discussed at ¶ 644, however, applies only to Part B drugs, which usually are administered in a physician's office. The coverage requirements for Part D prescription drugs are discussed at ¶ 500 through ¶ 535. These exclusions of particular procedures or services are discussed at ¶ 601, ¶ 602, and ¶ 654. Exclusions of services because of the existence of other responsible parties or available coverage are discussed at ¶ 607 through ¶ 644.

[¶ 601] Services Not Reasonable and Necessary

Items and services that are not reasonable and necessary for the diagnosis or treatment of illness or injury, or to improve the functioning of a malformed body part, are excluded. Many services are considered reasonable and necessary for some conditions but not for others, and coverage criteria relating to severity or trials of other treatments have been established for certain services. [Soc. Sec. Act § 1862(a)(1).]

The reasonable and necessary rule has been used to exclude procedures that are considered unsafe or ineffective and procedures that are experimental or investigational, that is, not yet established as safe and effective. See ¶ 602 for discussion of experimental and investigational procedures. It may also be used to exclude care that could be given as effectively in a less expensive setting. Procedures to assist a patient in committing suicide or to cause the patient's death are excluded, but this exclusion does not prevent the withholding or withdrawal of medical treatment, nutrition or hydration. [Soc. Sec. Act § 1862 (a)(16); 42 C.F.R. § 411.15(q).]

Medicare reviewers have been directed to form their own opinions about whether a procedure is reasonable and necessary. They have been directed to assign no presumptive weight to the treating physician's medical opinion in determining the medical necessity of the procedures performed. [*HCFA Ruling* No. 93-1.]

Note that a beneficiary can be "held harmless" (not required to pay) in certain situations in which claims are disallowed under this exclusion. This "waiver of liability" provision is discussed at ¶ 908.

[¶ 602] Experimental, Investigational and Other Excluded Procedures

Most exclusions are based on determinations of the safety or effectiveness of a service. These determinations, including decisions to cover new services, are compiled in the *National Coverage Determinations Manual*, CMS Pub. 100-03. Information about the review process, the services being reviewed, and final determinations is discussed at ¶ 390.

Excluded Procedures

National coverage decisions have been made ruling that the following treatments are not covered [*Medicare National Coverage Determinations Manual*, Pub. 100-03.]:

- colonic irrigation;
- heat treatment, including the use of diathermy and ultrasound, for pulmonary conditions;
- cellular therapy;
- thermogenic therapy;
- carotid body resection to relieve pulmonary symptoms;
- acupuncture;
- plastic surgery to correct "moon face";
- prolotherapy, joint sclerotherapy, and ligamentous injections with sclerosing agents;
- electrosleep therapy;
- intravenous histamine therapy;

- treatment of motor function disorders with electric nerve stimulation;
- electrical aversion therapy for treatment of alcoholism;
- biofeedback therapy for treatment of ordinary muscle tension states or for psychosomatic conditions;
- oxygen treatment of inner ear/carbon therapy;
- intestinal bypass surgery;
- fabric wrapping of abdominal aneurysms;
- extracranial-intracranial (EC-IC) arterial bypass surgery;
- cochleostomy with neurovascular transplant for Meniere's disease;
- hemodialysis for treatment of schizophrenia;
- refractive keratoplasty;
- transvenous (catheter) pulmonary embolectomy;
- electroencephalographic (EEG) monitoring during open-heart surgery;
- transsexual surgery;
- tinnitus masking;
- chelation therapy for treatment of atherosclerosis;
- gastric freezing;
- electrotherapy for treatment of facial nerve paralysis (Bell's palsy);
- stereotactic cingulotomy as a means of psychosurgery;
- gastric balloon for treatment of obesity;
- transcendental meditation training or use;
- partial ventriculectomy;
- vertebral axial decompression (VAX-D);
- bariatric surgery is being reconsidered by the Medical Care Adivsory Committee

The following drugs, diagnostic services and supplies are also excluded:

- vitamin B-12 injections to strengthen tendons, ligaments, etc., of the foot;
- Laetrile and related substances;
- transfer factor for treatment of multiple sclerosis;
- ethylenediamine-tetra-acetic (EDTA) chelation therapy for treatment of atherosclerosis;
- dimethyl sulfoxide (DMSO), except for treatment of interstitial cystitis;
- platelet-derived wound-healing formula, except for plasma-rich product in FDA-approved clinical trials;
- sublingual administration of antigens;
- thermography;
- hair analysis;
- human tumor stem cell drug sensitivity assays;
- transillumination light scanning, or diaphanography;
- cardiointegram (CIG) device tests;
- photokymography;
- cytotoxic leukocyte testing for food allergies;
- neutralization testing and therapy for food allergies (challenge ingestion testing is covered);
- peridex CAPD filter set;
- white cane for use by a blind person;
- intrapulmonary percussive ventilator (IPV);
- electrical continence aid;
- nutritional supplements between meals;
- bladder stimulators (pacemakers);
- abortions, except in the case of rape, incest or a life-endangering condition; and
- pocket Doppler ultrasound tests.
- unattended portable multi-channel sleep study testing for sleep apnea.

Until recently, CMS stated that obesity was not a disease, so that all treatment for obesity was excluded. In 2004, CMS acknowledged obesity as an illness without changing the policy of exclusion. Coverage for treatment of obesity is limited to situations where the obesity either is caused by another condition, such as hypothyroidism or Cushions disease, or aggravates another medical condition, such as diabetes or cardiovascular disease, where treatment of obesity is an integral part of the course of treatment for the other condition. Gastric bypass surgery may be approved under these limited conditions. [Pub. 100-03, No. 23, Oct. 1, 2004.]

Treatment of obesity which is not required to treat another medical condition is excluded from coverage as not reasonable and necessary. Supplemented fasting is not covered nationally, but local intermediaries have discretion to approve it under local coverage determinations. Gastric balloons are excluded from coverage because they are not established as safe and effective. [Pub. 100-03, Transmittal No. 23, Oct. 1, 2004.]

¶602

Recent national coverage decisions authorizing new covered services are discussed at ¶ 390.

Transplants. Previously, the "experimental or investigational" exclusion was interpreted to apply to heart and most other organ transplants. Medicare since has established a program to cover heart transplants "when performed in specialized facilities by trained personnel who have been carefully screened." Only specifically designated transplant centers with the necessary experience are qualified for Medicare coverage. [*Medicare National Coverage Determinations Manual*, Pub. 100-03, Ch. 1, § 260.9.] Liver and lung transplants are covered under a similarly structured program. [Pub. 100-03, Ch. 1, § 260.1.] Kidney transplants (see ¶ 847) have been covered since the beginning of the Medicare program.

Whole organ pancreas transplantation is covered by Medicare for diabetic patients only when it is performed simultaneously with or after a kidney transplant. Pancreas transplantation for diabetic patients who have not experienced end-stage renal failure secondary to diabetes continues to be excluded from Medicare coverage. Medicare covers of transplantation of pancreatic islet cells only in the context of a clinical trial. [Pub. 100-03, Ch. 1, § 310.1.]

Treatments in clinical trials are by definition experimental. Effective for items and services furnished on or after September 19, 2000, however, Medicare covers the routine costs of qualifying clinical trials as well as reasonable and necessary items and services used to diagnose and treat complications arising from participation in all clinical trials. All other Medicare rules apply. [Pub. 100-03, Ch. 1, § 310.1.] Coverage of participation in clinical trials is discussed more fully at ¶ 630.

[¶ 604] No Legal Obligation to Pay

Program payment may not be made for items or services for which neither the beneficiary nor any other person or organization has a legal obligation to pay or to provide. [Soc. Sec. Act § 1862(a)(2).] This exclusion applies when items and services are furnished free regardless of the beneficiary's ability to pay and without expectation of payment from any source. Examples are free X-rays or immunizations provided by health organizations. However, a physician, provider, or supplier may waive the right to charge a particular beneficiary without giving up the right to Medicare payment. Thus, if an individual is not charged because of indigency or lack of insurance, but the physician, provider, or supplier charges patients with insurance or those who are able to pay, Medicare will cover the services. The underlying reason the particular individual is not charged is the determinative factor in the application of this exclusion. [*Medicare Benefit Policy Manual*, Pub. 100-02, Ch. 16, § 40.]

Patient has other health coverage. Except as discussed at ¶ 636–¶ 639 (involving workers' compensation, automobile and liability insurance, and certain employer group health plans), payment is not precluded under Medicare even though the patient is covered by another health insurance plan or program that is obligated to provide or pay for the same services. The amount Medicare will pay is determined by rules discussed at ¶ 636.

Items covered under a warranty. When a defective medical device such as a cardiac pacemaker (see ¶ 358) is replaced under a warranty, hospital or other provider services rendered by parties other than the warrantor are covered despite the warrantor's liability. If, however, the device is replaced free of charge by the warrantor, no program payment may be made, because there was no charge involved. [Pub. 100-02, Ch. 16, § 40.4.]

Members of religious orders. A legal obligation to pay exists where a religious order either pays for or furnishes services to members of the order. Although medical services furnished in such a setting ordinarily would not be expressed in terms of a legal obligation, the order has an obligation to care for its members who have rendered life-long services, similar to that existing under an employer's prepayment plan. Thus, payment may be made for such services whether they are furnished by the order itself or by independent sources that customarily charge for their services. [Pub. 100-02, Ch. 16, § 40.5.]

Community health center services. The exclusion does not apply to services furnished in a federally qualified community health center (see ¶ 382). [Soc. Sec. Act § 1862(a)(2).]

State or local prisoners. Medicare payment may be made for services furnished to individuals who are in the custody of the police or other penal authorities if (1) state or local law requires the individuals to repay the cost of medical services they receive while in custody, and (2) the state or local government entity enforces the requirement to pay by billing all such individuals and by pursuing collection of the amounts they owe in the same way and with the same vigor that it pursues the collection of other debts. [42 C.F.R. § 411.4(b).]

[¶ 607] Services Paid for by Governmental Entity

Payment may not be made for expenses incurred for items or services that are paid for directly or indirectly by a governmental entity, including state and local governments, *except that payment may be made for:*

(1) services furnished under a health insurance plan established for employees of the governmental entity;

(2) services furnished under a program based on a title of the Social Security Act other than Medicare, such as Medicaid;

(3) services furnished in or by a participating hospital operated by a state or local governmental entity, if this hospital is a general or special hospital serving the general community;

(4) services paid for by a state or local governmental entity and furnished an individual as a means of controlling infectious diseases or because of the individual's medical indigency, regardless of whether these services are furnished in a hospital;

(5) services furnished by participating hospitals and skilled nursing facilities of the Indian Health Service;

(6) services furnished by a public or private health facility that receives United States government funds under a federal program that provides support to facilities furnishing healthcare services (other than a federal provider of services), provided the facility receiving federal support customarily seeks reimbursement for items and services not covered under Medicare from all resources available for the health care of its patients—for example, private insurance, patients' cash resources, etc.; and

(7) rural and community health clinic services (see ¶ 382). [Soc. Sec. Act § 1862(a)(3).]

In addition, payment cannot be made for expenses incurred for any items or services furnished by a federal provider of services, except that payment can be made (1) for emergency hospital services (see ¶ 227), (2) to a participating federal provider that the Secretary has determined to be furnishing services to the public generally as a community institution or agency, (3) for services furnished by a participating hospital or skilled nursing facility of the Indian Health Service, and (4) for services furnished under arrangements made by a participating hospital. [42 C.F.R. § 411.6.] Also, payment cannot be made for items or services that a provider of services (other than a hospital or skilled nursing facility of the Indian Health Service) or other person is obligated by a law of, or a contract with, the United States to furnish at public expense. [42 C.F.R. § 411.7.]

Exclusions from Coverage

Veterans Administration

Medicare payment may not be made for any item or service that a provider, physician, or supplier provided pursuant to an authorization issued by the Veterans Administration (VA) under which the VA agrees to pay for the services. An authorization issued by the VA binds the VA to pay in full for the items and services provided. However, when an authorization from the VA is not given to the party rendering the services, Medicare payment is not precluded even though the individual might have been entitled to have payment made by the VA if the individual had requested the authorization. [*Medicare Benefit Policy Manual,* Pub. 100-02, Ch. 16, § 50.1.]

It generally will be advantageous for Medicare beneficiaries who are veterans to have the VA pay for the services whenever possible, since in most cases the VA has no deductible or coinsurance requirements. The VA may charge veterans copayments for treatment of nonservice-connected conditions if a veteran's income exceeds a specified amount. If a beneficiary is charged a copayment by the VA for authorized services, a Medicare secondary benefit may be payable. [Pub. 100-02, Ch. 16, § 50.1.]

If a physician accepts a veteran as a patient and bills the VA, the physician must accept the VA's "usual and customary" charge determination as payment in full; *i.e.,* neither the patient nor any other party can be charged an additional amount. Therefore, Medicare cannot make payment if the physician's bill for authorized services exceeds the amount the VA paid the physician or reimbursed the beneficiary. Medicare can, however, pay secondary benefits to the beneficiary or physician to cover the VA copayment or deductible. Medicare also may pay for services not covered by the VA. For example, if a veteran is authorized "fee basis" care at VA expense for a service-connected back injury, and the veteran receives treatment for a different condition for which the VA does not pay, Medicare can pay for the services that are not reimbursable by the VA. [Pub. 100-02, Ch. 16, § 50.1.4.]

Under certain circumstances, Medicare reimbursement for care provided to a nonveteran Medicare beneficiary in a VA hospital is authorized if the care was provided on the mistaken (but good faith) assumption that the beneficiary was an eligible veteran. [Soc. Sec. Act § 1814(h).]

TRICARE and CHAMPVA

If a TRICARE (formerly CHAMPUS (Civilian Health and Medical Program of the Uniformed Services), and CHAMPVA (Civilian Health and Medical Program of the Veterans Administration) beneficiary also has Medicare coverage, Medicare is the primary payer. TRICARE or CHAMPVA will reduce its liability in all cases by the amount payable by Medicare. TRICARE or CHAMPVA covers the Medicare deductible and coinsurance amounts and portions of the bill not covered by Medicare. Thus, dually entitled individuals may be reimbursed up to 100 percent of expenses for items and services covered by both programs. [Pub. 100-02, Ch. 16, § 50.4.]

Medicare-participating hospitals are required to participate in the programs and to accept patients from those programs. [Soc. Sec. Act § 1866(a)(1)(J).]

[¶ 610] Services Outside the United States

Generally, items and services that are provided outside the United States are not covered. Exceptions exist for emergencies with certain requirements: (1) the emergency must have arisen while the beneficiary was in the United States or traveling directly between Alaska and the United States; and (2) the Canadian or Mexican hospital must have been the closest or most accessible with adequate facilities to care for the beneficiary's needs. U.S. residents for whom the closest hospital with adequate facilities is in Canada or Mexico will be covered for nonemergency services there. If the inpatient services are covered, Part B will cover physician and ambulance services.

Services provided on board a ship may be covered if furnished within six hours of before arrival at or after departure from a port in U.S. territory, which includes Puerto Rico, American Samoa, Guam, the Virgin Islands and the Northern Marianna islands. [*Medicare Benefit Policy Manual*, Pub. 100-02, Ch. 16, § 60.]

Qualified railroad retirement beneficiaries submit their claims for inpatient services received in Canada to the Railroad Retirement Board (RRB) for a determination of coverage. If the RRB finds the inpatient services are covered, Medicare will cover the accompanying Part B. RRB does not cover services furnished in Mexico; Medicare rules will apply to services received in Mexico. [Soc. Sec. Act §§ 1814(f), 1862(a)(4); 42 C.F.R. § 411.9.]

[¶ 613] War Claims

Items and services that are required as a result of war or an act of war occurring after the effective date of the patient's current coverage are not covered. [42 C.F.R. § 411.10.]

[¶ 616] Personal Comfort Items

Personal comfort items, items that do not contribute meaningfully to the treatment of an illness or injury or the functioning of a malformed body member, are not covered except when provided in the course of hospice care (see ¶ 270). [Soc. Sec. Act § 1862(a)(6); 42 C.F.R. § 411.15(j).] Charges for beauty and barber services and for special items requested by the patient, such as radios, televisions, telephones, or air conditioners, are examples of personal comfort items excluded from Medicare coverage. [*Medicare Benefit Policy Manual*, Pub. 100-02, Ch. 16, § 80.]

Basic personal services, such as simple barber and beautician services (for example, shaves, haircuts, shampoos and simple hair sets) that patients need and cannot perform for themselves, may be viewed as ordinary patient care when furnished by an institution, as they maintain least a minimum level of personal hygiene, decency, and presentability and are essential to patient well-being. Such services are covered costs when included in the flat rate charge and provided routinely without charge to the patient by a hospital or skilled nursing facility. However, under the personal comfort exclusion, more elaborate services, such as professional manicures and hair styling, are excluded, even when furnished routinely and without special charge. [Pub. 100-02, Ch. 16, § 80.]

Providers may charge patients for excluded personal comfort items that the patient requests only if the patient has knowledge that he will be charged for those items. To avoid misunderstandings and disputes, the provider should inform the beneficiary requesting a personal comfort item that it is not covered by Medicare and that the provider will charge the beneficiary a specified amount (which may not exceed the customary charge). Thereafter, the provider may not charge the patient more for the item or service than the amount specified. A provider may not require a beneficiary to request noncovered items or services as a condition of admission or of continued stay. [Pub. 100-02, Ch. 16, § 80.]

Providers also are allowed to charge patients when they request services that are more expensive than those covered by Medicare (see ¶ 730 under "Allowable Charges").

[¶ 619] Routine Checkups; Glasses; Eye Examinations; Immunizations

Historically, routine physical checkups, that is, examinations performed without relationship to diagnosis or treatment of any specific complaint, illness, symptom, or injury, were excluded from coverage. Originally, routine screening exams were also excluded. The following screening examinations are now covered, however, with limitations on frequency:

Exclusions from Coverage

- mammography;
- annual fecal occult blood test, flexible sigmoidoscopy every four years, colonoscopy, and other appropriate exams to detect colorectal cancer;
- pelvic exams and tests to detect cervical or vaginal cancer;
- prostate-specific antigen tests for prostate cancer;
- glaucoma tests;
- bone mass measurements for individuals at risk for osteoporosis, or who have certain other conditions; and
- fasting blood glucose and other appropriate tests for diabetes.
- blood lipid testing for cardiovascular screening.

[Soc. Sec. Act §§ 1861(s)(15); 1861(rr); and 1862(a)(1)(F),(G),(H),(L),(M); [Pub. 100-03, Transmittal No. 28, Feb. 11, 2005.]

Historically, preventive services also have been excluded from coverage. Coverage has been added for intermediate and intensive counseling for smoking cessation [*National Coverage Decisions Manual*, Pub. 100-03, Transmittal No. 36, May 20, 2005.]

Medicare beneficiaries whose coverage begins on or after January 1, 2005 are covered for one "Welcome to Medicare" comprehensive checkup, including an electrocardiogram and blood work to detect cardiovascular disease. [Soc. Sec. Act §§ 1862(a)(1)(K), 1862(a)(1)(L)] Examinations required by third parties, such as insurance companies, business establishments, or government agencies, are excluded from coverage. [Soc. Sec. Act § 1861(ww).]

Vision and hearing screening examinations, eyeglasses, and eye examinations for the purpose of prescribing, fitting, or changing eyeglasses; procedures performed (during the course of any eye examination) to determine the refractive state of the eyes; hearing aids (devices which produce as their output an electrical signal that directly stimulates the auditory nerve are not considered hearing aids of purposes of payment under Medicare) and examinations for hearing aids are not covered. [42 C.F.R. § 411.15; *Medicare Benefit Policy Manual*, Pub. 100-02, Ch. 16, §§ 90, 100.]

The exclusions apply to eyeglasses and contact lenses, as well as to eye examinations for the purpose of prescribing, fitting, or changing eyeglasses or contact lenses for refractive errors. The exclusions do not apply, except as indicated below, to services performed in conjunction with an eye disease, such as glaucoma or cataracts, or to postsurgical prosthetic lenses which are customarily used during convalescence from eye surgery in which the lens of the eye was removed, or to permanent prosthetic lenses (see ¶ 358) required by an individual lacking the organic lens of the eye, whether by surgical removal or congenital disease. [Pub. 100-02, Ch. 16, § 90.]

Coverage depends on the purpose of the eye examination rather than on the ultimate diagnosis of the patient's condition. If the beneficiary has a complaint or symptoms of an eye disease or injury, the examination is covered even though only eyeglasses were prescribed. However, if the beneficiary desires only an eye examination with no specific complaint, the expenses for the examination will not be covered, even though, as a result of the examination, the doctor discovers a pathological condition. [Pub. 100-02, Ch. 16, § 90.]

Note that the law specifically authorizes coverage for one pair of conventional eyeglasses or contact lenses furnished subsequent to each cataract surgery in which an intraocular lens is inserted. [Soc. Sec. Act §§ 1861(s)(8).]

¶619

Immunizations

Most vaccinations and inoculations are excluded as "immunizations" unless they are directly related to the treatment of an injury or direct exposure to a disease or condition, such as antirabies treatment, tetanus antitoxin or booster vaccine, botulin antitoxin, antivenin, or immune globulin. [Pub. 100-02, Ch. 16, §90.] Vaccinations to prevent hepatitis B, pneumococcal pneumonia, and influenza are covered, however. (See ¶ 362). [Soc. Sec. Act §1861(s)(10).] In addition, vaccinations and immunizations furnished in a federally qualified community health center (see ¶ 382) are covered if the patient receives other covered services during the visit. [*Medicare Claims Processing Manual*, Pub. 100-04, Ch. 9, §110.]

[¶ 622] Foot Care and Orthopedic Shoes

While most services of a doctor of podiatry or surgical chiropody are covered (see ¶ 340), payment generally will *not* be made for services, even when provided by a medical doctor or a doctor of podiatry, when they are:

(1) routine foot care (see below),

(2) the evaluation or treatment of subluxations (structural misalignments of the joints) of the feet, or

(3) the evaluation or treatment of flattened arches and the prescription of supportive devices. [42 C.F.R. §411.15(l)(1).]

These services may be covered, however, if they are (1) incident to, provided at the same time as, or a necessary integral part of a primary covered procedure performed on the foot; or (2) initial diagnostic services, regardless of the resulting diagnosis, in connection with a specific symptom or complaint that might arise from a condition for which treatment would be covered. [42 C.F.R. §411.15(l)(2)(iii).]

In addition, services may be covered (1) for the treatment of warts; (2) for the treatment of mycotic toenails if furnished no more often than every 60 days or the billing physician documents the need for more frequent treatment; and (3) when they are a necessary and integral part of otherwise covered treatment of systemic conditions, such as diabetic ulcers, arteriosclerosis, malnutrition, or alcoholism requiring scrupulous foot care by a professional to prevent severe circulatory embarrassment or diminished sensation in the individual's legs or feet. [42 C.F.R. §411.15(l)(2); *Medicare Benefit Policy Manual*, Pub. 100-02, Ch. 15, §290.]

Routine Foot Care

Routine foot care includes the cutting or removal of corns or calluses, the trimming of nails (including mycotic nails), and other hygienic and preventive maintenance care in the realm of self-care, such as cleaning and soaking the feet, the use of skin creams to maintain skin tone of both ambulatory and bedfast patients, and any services performed in the absence of localized illness, injury, or symptoms involving the foot. For example, foot care such as routine soaking and application of topical medication on a physician's order between required physician visits is not covered. [Pub. 100-02, Ch. 15, §290.]

Orthopedic Shoes

Expenses for orthopedic shoes or other supportive devices for the feet generally are not covered. This exclusion does not apply when the shoe is an integral part of a leg brace and its expense is included as part of the cost of the brace. [42 C.F.R. §411.15(f).] The exclusion also does not apply to therapeutic shoes and inserts for individuals with severe diabetic foot disease (see ¶ 370). [Soc. Sec. Act §1861(s)(12).]

[¶ 625] Custodial Care

Custodial care, except in the case of hospice care (see ¶ 270), is excluded. [Soc. Sec. Act § 1862(a)(9).] The custodial care exclusion precludes payment for that type of care, wherever furnished, that is designed essentially to assist the individual in meeting the activities of daily living—*i.e.*, services that constitute personal care, such as (1) help in walking and getting in or out of bed, (2) assistance in bathing, dressing, feeding, and using the toilet, (3) preparation of special diets, and (4) supervision over medication that usually can be self-administered—and does not entail or require the continuing attention of trained medical or paramedical personnel. [*Medicare Benefit Policy Manual*, Pub. 100-02, Ch. 16, § 110.] (For a discussion of noncovered levels of care in a skilled nursing facility, see ¶ 244.)

Note that a beneficiary can be "held harmless" (*i.e.*, not required to pay) in certain situations in which claims are disallowed under this exclusion. This provision is discussed at ¶ 908.

Custodial care is covered under the Medicaid program if the eligibility requirements of that poverty-related program are met. [Soc. Sec. Act § 1905(a)(24).]

[¶ 628] Cosmetic Surgery

Cosmetic surgery or expenses incurred in connection with such surgery are not covered. This exclusion applies to any surgical procedure directed at improving appearance, except when required for the prompt (*i.e.*, as soon as medically feasible) repair of accidental injury or for the improvement of the functioning of a malformed body member. Thus, this exclusion does not apply to surgery (1) in connection with treatment of severe burns or repair of the face following a serious automobile accident or (2) for therapeutic purposes that coincidentally also serves some cosmetic purpose. [*Medicare Benefit Policy Manual*, Pub. 100-02, Ch. 16, § 120.]

[¶ 630] Routine Costs in Clinical Trials

Medicare covers the routine costs of qualifying clinical trials, as well as reasonable and necessary items and services used to diagnose and treat complications arising from participation in all clinical trials. [*Medicare National Coverage Decisions Manual*, Pub. 100-03, Ch. 1, § 310.1.]

Routine costs. Routine costs of a clinical trial include all items and services that generally are available to Medicare beneficiaries that are provided in either the experimental or the control arms of a clinical trial, except (1) the investigational item, device or service, (2) items and services provided solely to satisfy data collection and analysis needs that are not used in the direct clinical management of the patient, and (3) items and services customarily provided by the research sponsors free of charge for any enrollee in the trial. [Pub. 100-03, Ch. 1, § 310.1.]

Examples of routine costs in clinical trials include items or services that (1) typically would be provided absent a clinical trial; (2) are required solely for the provision of the investigational item or service, the clinically appropriate monitoring of the effects of the item or service, or the prevention of complications; and (3) are needed for reasonable and necessary care arising from the provision of an investigational item or service—in particular, for the diagnosis or treatment of complications. [Pub. 100-03, Ch. 1, § 310.1.]

Local carriers are permitted to allow coverage of additional services they consider reasonable and necessary unless the services are not excluded by statute or a National Coverage Determination. These policies must be available on the carrier's web site. [Soc. Sec. Act § 1869(f)(2)(B); *Program Integrity Manual*, Pub. 100-08, Ch. 13, § 13.6.]

Any clinical trial receiving Medicare coverage of routine costs must meet the following three requirements: (1) the subject or purpose of the trial must be the evaluation of an item or service that falls within a Medicare benefit category (*e.g.,* physicians' service, durable medical equipment, diagnostic test) and is not statutorily excluded from coverage (*e.g.,* cosmetic surgery, hearing aids); (2) the trial must not be designed exclusively to test toxicity or disease pathophysiology, *i.e.,* it must have therapeutic intent; (3) trials of therapeutic interventions must enroll patients with diagnosed disease rather than healthy volunteers; however, trials of diagnostic interventions may enroll healthy patients to have a proper control group. [Pub. 100-03, Ch. 1, § 310.1.]

The three requirements above are insufficient by themselves to qualify a clinical trial for Medicare coverage of routine costs. Clinical trials also should have the following desirable characteristics: (1) the principal purpose of the trial is to test whether the intervention potentially improves the participants' health outcomes; (2) the trial is well-supported by available scientific and medical information, or it is intended to clarify or establish the health outcomes of interventions already in common clinical use; (3) the trial does not unjustifiably duplicate existing studies; (4) the trial design is appropriate to answer the research question being asked in the trial; (5) the trial is sponsored by a credible organization or individual capable of executing the proposed trial successfully; (6) the trial is in compliance with federal regulations relating to the protection of human subjects; and (7) all aspects of the trial are conducted according to the appropriate standards of scientific integrity. [Pub. 100-03, Ch. 1, § 310.1.]

[¶ 631] Charges by Relatives

Charges imposed by physicians or other persons who are immediate relatives of the patient or members of the patient's household are not covered. "Immediate relative" means spouse; natural or adoptive parent, child, and sibling; stepparent, stepchild, stepbrother, and stepsister; parent-in-law, child-in-law, brother-in-law, and sister-in-law; grandparent and grandchild; and spouse of grandparent and grandchild. "Members of the patient's household" means those persons sharing a common abode with the patient as part of a single family unit, including domestic employees and others who live together as part of a single family unit. A roommate or boarder is not included. [42 C.F.R. § 411.12(a), (b); *Medicare Benefit Policy Manual,* Pub. 100-02, Ch. 16, § 130.]

Note: A brother-in-law or sister-in-law relationship does not exist between a physician (or supplier) and the spouse of his wife's (her husband's) brother or sister. A father-in-law or mother-in-law relationship does not exist between a physician and the stepfather or stepmother of the physician's spouse. A step-relationship or an in-law relationship continues to exist even if the marriage upon which the relationship is based is terminated through divorce or through the death of one of the parties. Thus, for example, if a physician provides services to a stepparent after the death of (or divorce by) the natural parent, or if the physician provides services to an in-law after the death of the spouse of the physician, the services would be considered to have been furnished to an immediate relative and, therefore, excluded from coverage. [Pub. 100-02, Ch. 16, § 130.]

The exclusion extends also to charges for physicians' services rendered to immediate relatives of a provider's owner. This includes sole proprietorships, partnerships in which even one of the partners is related to the patient, and professional corporations. [Pub. 100-02, Ch. 16, § 130.]

In the case of nonphysician services, charges are excluded if they are provided by (1) an individually owned provider or supplier if the owner has an excluded relationship with the patient; or (2) a partnership if any of the partners has an excluded relationship with the patient. [42 C.F.R. § 411.12(c)(2).]

This exclusion does not apply to charges imposed by a corporation, other than a professional corporation, regardless of the patient's relationship to any of the stockholders, officers or directors of the corporation or to the person who furnished the service. [42 C.F.R. § 411.12(d); Pub. 100-02, Ch. 16, § 130.]

[¶ 634] Dental Services

Items and services in connection with the care, treatment, filling, removal, or replacement of teeth or structures directly supporting the teeth generally are not covered. However, payment may be made for inpatient hospital services furnished in connection with a dental procedure if the patient has impairments that are so severe that they require hospitalization or if the severity of the dental procedure requires hospitalization (see ¶ 218). [Soc. Sec. Act § 1862(a)(12).] "Structures directly supporting the teeth" means the periodontium, which includes the gingivae, dentogingival junction, periodontal membrane, cementum of the teeth, and alveolar process. [*Medicare Benefit Policy Manual*, Pub. 100-02, Ch. 16, § 140.]

When an excluded service is the primary procedure involved, it is not covered, regardless of the complexity or difficulty. If an otherwise noncovered procedure or service is performed by a dentist incident to, and as an integral part of, a covered procedure or service *performed by the dentist*, however, the total service performed by the dentist on such an occasion is covered. For example, the reconstruction of a ridge performed primarily to prepare the mouth for dentures is a noncovered procedure. When the reconstruction of a ridge is performed as a result of, and at the same time as, the surgical removal of a tumor (for other than dental purposes), the totality of surgical procedures would be a covered service. Medicare also would cover the wiring of teeth when it is done in connection with the reduction of a jaw fracture. [Pub. 100-02, Ch. 16, § 140.]

The extraction of teeth to prepare the jaw for radiation treatments of neoplastic disease also is covered. This is an exception to the requirement that to be covered, a noncovered procedure or service performed by a dentist must be incident to, and an integral part of, a covered procedure or service *performed by the dentist*. Ordinarily, the dentist extracts the patient's teeth, but another physician, for example, a radiologist, administers the radiation treatments. [Pub. 100-02, Ch. 16, § 140.]

[¶ 635] Services Not Provided In-House

The Medicare program requires hospitals and skilled nursing facilities caring for Medicare patients to provide in-house all the services that are furnished to those patients. This requirement is satisfied if the hospital or SNF has made arrangements to have the services provided by another entity, such as an independent laboratory or physical therapy group. Services not provided in-house that are supposed to be provided in-house are excluded from coverage and will not be paid for by Medicare. [Soc. Sec. Act §§ 1862(a)(14); 1862(a)(18).]

In addition, all services provided to an inpatient of a hospital (including all "medical and other health services" with the exception of (1) physician and health care practitioner services and (2) pneumococcal and hepatitis B vaccines and their administration) must be treated as "inpatient hospital services" and must be paid for under Part A if the patient is eligible for Part A benefits. [*Medicare Benefit Policy Manual*, Pub. 100-02, Ch. 6, § 10.]

The reason for this exclusion is that, under each prospective payment system (PPS), in-house services are included in the calculation of the hospital's and SNF's PPS DRG payment rate, and Medicare will not pay for these services twice (see ¶ 810 and ¶ 839).

The exclusion is applicable to all hospitals participating in Medicare, including those reimbursed under alternative arrangements such as state cost control systems, and to emergency hospital services furnished by nonparticipating hospitals. [Pub. 100-02, Ch. 6, § 10.]

This exclusion applies, but is not limited, to the following items and services: (1) clinical laboratory services; (2) pacemakers; (3) artificial limbs, knees, and hips; (4) intraocular lenses; (5) total parenteral nutrition; and (6) services and supplies furnished incident to physicians' services. [42 C.F.R. § 411.15(m).]

This exclusion does *not* apply to physicians' services, the services of anesthesiologists, or to the services of certain healthcare practitioners (for example, physician assistants, certified nurse-midwives, qualified psychologists, and CRNAs). [42 C.F.R. § 411.15(m).]

The exclusion also does not apply to SNF services furnished to patients whose stay is not covered by Medicare (except for outpatient therapy services, to which the exclusion applies even for noncovered stays). [Soc. Sec. Act § 1862(a)(18).]

Charges to Beneficiaries

Under the regulations governing provider agreements, hospitals are prohibited from charging beneficiaries for inpatient hospital services furnished by entities with which there is no arrangements agreement. Furthermore, because services furnished under arrangements are included in the hospital's DRG rate, if an entity other than the hospital charges the hospital inpatient for its services, that charge is treated as a charge by the hospital and is regarded as a violation of its provider agreement. [42 C.F.R. § 489.21(f).]

Outpatient Services

The in-house requirement also extends to hospital outpatient services. Only physician and certain healthcare practitioner services that are provided directly by the hospital or provided under arrangements with the hospital are covered. [Soc. Sec. Act § § 1862(a)(14); 1866(a)(1)(H).] Any person who bills or requests payment for hospital outpatient services inconsistent with this rule may be subject to up to $2,000 in civil money penalties. [Soc. Sec. Act § 1866(g).]

[¶ 636] Medicare as Secondary Payer

Medicare payment is excluded for services to the extent that payment has been made, or reasonably can be expected to be made, when the following alternate types of insurance are available:

(1) workers' compensation (see ¶ 637);

(2) automobile, no-fault, or liability insurance (see ¶ 638); and

(3) employer group health plans (see ¶ 639). [Soc. Sec. Act § 1862(b)(2)(A); 42 C.F.R. § 411.20.]

This exclusion is referred to as the Medicare Secondary Payer (MSP) rule.

To improve the Secretary's identification of MSP situations, questionnaires are mailed to individuals, before they become entitled to benefits under Part A or enroll in Part B, to determine possible coverage under a primary plan. Payment for otherwise covered services will not be denied, however, solely on the grounds that a beneficiary failed to complete the questionnaire properly. [Soc. Sec. Act § § 1862(b)(2)(C); 1862(b)(5)(D).]

Providers and suppliers also are required to furnish information concerning potential coverage under other plans. Payment may not be made for Part B claims if the provider or supplier fails to complete MSP questions on the claim form. Fines of up to $2,000 for each incident have been established for entities that knowingly, willfully, and repeatedly fail to complete a claim form or fail to provide accurate MSP information. [Soc. Sec. Act § 1862(b)(6)(B).]

Conditional Medicare Payments

In the case of workers' compensation and liability or no-fault insurance, Medicare conditional payments may be made if the alternate insurers are not expected to pay *promptly*. In general, a payment is considered to be made promptly if it is made within 120 days after receipt of the claim. In the case of liability insurance, however, a claim is considered paid promptly if it is paid within 120 days after the earlier of (1) the date a claim is filed or (2) the date the services were furnished. In the case of inpatient hospital services, services are considered to be furnished, for purposes of this provision, on the date of discharge. [Soc. Sec. Act § 1862(b)(2)(A); 42 C.F.R. §§ 411.21, 411.50(b).]

If Medicare payment is made only because the alternate insurer does not pay promptly or because the existence of the alternate insurer is not known, the Medicare payments are conditional and are subject to recovery if payment is made later by the alternate insurer or the alternate insurer's existence is discovered. [Soc. Sec. Act § 1862(b)(2)(B)(i).]

If conditional Medicare payments are made, Medicare can bring a subrogation action to recover the payments it made against (1) an alternate insurer that was supposed to pay for the services and (2) any entity, including a physician or provider, that has received payment from the alternate insurer and has not refunded such payment to Medicare. Medicare also is entitled to collect double damages against an alternate insurer that does not pay when it is required to do so. [Soc. Sec. Act §§ 1862(b)(2)(B); 1862(b)(3)(A).]

The beneficiary is required to cooperate in Medicare's attempt to recover conditional payments. If the beneficiary does not do so, Medicare is entitled to recover the payments from the beneficiary. If the beneficiary receives a payment from the alternate insurer, the beneficiary must reimburse Medicare within 60 days. [42 C.F.R. §§ 411.23, 411.24(g) and (h).]

Partial Payments by Alternate Insurer

If the alternate insurer pays less than the full amount of the charge for the services rendered, Medicare may make *secondary* payments to supplement the alternate insurer's payments. In no case, however, will the Medicare secondary payment exceed the amount that otherwise would have been payable if there were no alternate insurance. Also, the Medicare payment, when combined with the amount paid by the alternate insurer, cannot exceed the amount that otherwise would have been payable by Medicare. Medicare secondary payments also can be made to pay the alternate insurer's deductible and coinsurance requirements. [Soc. Sec. Act § 1862(b)(4); 42 C.F.R. §§ 411.32, 411.33.]

Some third-party payments obligate the provider, physician, or supplier to accept the payment as payment in full. No Medicare payment is payable in such a case. [42 C.F.R. § 411.32(b).]

For physicians and suppliers who are not obligated to accept the third-party payment as payment in full, the amount of the Medicare secondary benefit payable is the lowest of the following:

(1) the actual charge by the physician or supplier minus the amount paid by the third-party payer;

(2) the amount Medicare would pay if services were not covered by the third-party payer; or

(3) the higher of (a) the Medicare fee schedule or other amount payable under Medicare (without regard to any deductible and/or coinsurance amounts) or (b) the third-party payer's allowable charge (without regard to any deductible and/or coinsurance amounts imposed by the policy or plan), minus the amount actually paid by the third-party payer. [42 C.F.R. § 411.33(a).]

Example • • • _____

Lupe received treatment from a physician for which the physician charged $175. The third party payer allowed $150 of the charge and paid 80 percent of this amount, or $120. The Medicare fee schedule for this treatment is $125. Lupe's Part B deductible had been met. As secondary payer, Medicare pays the lowest of the following amounts:

(1) Excess of actual charge minus the third party payment: $175 − 120 = $55.

(2) Amount Medicare would pay if the services were not covered by a third party payer: .80 × $125 = $100.

(3) Third party payer's allowable charge without regard to its coinsurance (since that amount is higher than the Medicare fee schedule in this case) minus amount paid by the third party payer: $150 − 120 = $30.

The Medicare payment is $30. [42 C.F.R. § 411.33(b).]

___

The method of calculating the Medicare secondary amount is the same whether the claim is assigned or unassigned. However, a nonparticipating physician or supplier that does not accept assignment must reduce the actual charge to the Medicare limiting charge (see ¶ 821). [*Medicare Secondary Payer Manual*, Pub. 100-05, Ch. 5, § 40.7.3.]

For hospitals and other providers that are not obligated to accept third-party payments as payment in full, the Medicare secondary payment is the lowest of the following:

(1) the gross amount payable by Medicare minus the applicable deductible and/or coinsurance amount;

(2) the gross amount payable by Medicare minus the amount paid by the third-party payer for Medicare-covered services;

(3) the provider's charges (or the amount the provider is obligated to accept as payment in full) minus the amount paid by the third-party payer; or

(4) the provider's charges (or the amount the provider is obligated to accept as payment in full) minus the applicable Medicare deductible and/or coinsurance amount. [42 C.F.R. § 411.33(e).]

Effect of Medicare Agreements

The amount payable by Medicare does not affect the amount that a Medicare provider may bill or accept from a third party. If no other law or agreement limits the amount payable by the third party, receipt by a provider or supplier of third-party payments in excess of the amount Medicare would pay is not a violation of the conditions of assignment, or a violation of a Medicare provider agreement. [42 C.F.R. § 411.31.]

When a beneficiary has been paid by a third-party payer for services provided by a physician or supplier who accepts assignment, the physician or supplier may collect from the beneficiary the full amount paid by the third-party payer regardless of whether it exceeds the amount that would be payable by Medicare. If the third-party payment is less than the applicable Medicare deductible and coinsurance amounts, the physician or supplier may collect the difference between the fee schedule amount (or the amount the physician is obligated to accept as payment in full, if less) and the sum of the third-party payment and the Medicare secondary payment. [Pub. 100-05, Ch. 3, § 10.2.]

There are comparable rules for providers that receive direct payment from the Medicare program allowing them to retain third-party payments in full without violating their provider agreements. Providers may bill beneficiaries the amount by which Medicare deductible and coinsurance amounts exceed the third-party payment and the amount of any charges for the noncovered component of a partially covered service, such as the charge differential for a private room. [Pub. 100-05, Ch. 3, § 10.2.]

[¶ 637] Workers' Compensation

Payment is excluded for any items and services to the extent that payment has been made or reasonably can be expected to be made under a workers' compensation law or plan of the United States or a state. This exclusion is applicable to the workers' compensation plans of the 50 states, the District of Columbia, American Samoa, Guam, the Virgin Islands, and Puerto Rico, as well as federal workers' compensation laws. [42 C.F.R. § 411.40(a).]

The beneficiary is responsible for taking whatever action is necessary to obtain payment under workers' compensation when payment reasonably can be expected. Failure to take proper and timely action under such circumstances will preclude Medicare payment to the extent that payment reasonably could have been expected to be made under workers' compensation had the individual exhausted benefit rights under that system. [42 C.F.R. § 411.43.]

If a lump-sum workers' compensation award stipulates that the amount paid is intended to compensate the individual for all future medical expenses required because of the work-related injury or disease, Medicare payments for such services are excluded until medical expenses related to the injury or disease equal the amount of the lump-sum payment. [42 C.F.R. § 411.46(a).]

No Medicare payment will be made if workers' compensation pays an amount that (1) equals or exceeds the gross amount payable by Medicare without regard to deductible and coinsurance; (2) equals or exceeds the provider's, physician's, or supplier's charges for Medicare covered services; or (3) the provider accepts or is required under the worker's compensation law to accept as payment in full. If workers' compensation pays less than these amounts and the provider is not obligated to accept the amount as payment in full, secondary Medicare payments can be made. [42 C.F.R. § 411.32.]

Relationship with Other Insurers

When services are covered in part by workers' compensation and there also is coverage under automobile medical or no-fault insurance or under an employer group health plan (see ¶ 638 and ¶ 639), workers' compensation pays first, the automobile medical or no-fault insurance or employer plan pays second, and Medicare is the residual payer. [Pub. 100-05, Ch. 1, § 10.9.]

Liability claims. Most state laws provide that if an employee is injured at work due to the negligent act of a third party, the employee cannot receive payments from both workers' compensation and the third party for the same injury. Generally, the workers' compensation carrier pays benefits while the third-party claim is pending. However, once a settlement of the third-party claim is reached or an award has been made, the workers' compensation carrier may recover the benefits it paid from the third-party settlement and may deny any future claims for that injury up to the amount of the liability payment made to the individual. Regardless of the liabilities of any other parties to one another, Medicare is the residual payer. [Soc. Sec. Act § 1862(b)(2)(B)(ii).]

[¶ 638] Automobile and Liability Insurance Coverage

Medicare payment is excluded for any items and services to the extent that payment has been made or reasonably can be expected to be made promptly under an automobile or liability insurance policy or plan, including a self-insured plan, or under no-fault insurance. [Soc. Sec. Act § 1862(b)(2)(A); 42 C.F.R. §§ 411.20(a)(2), 411.50(c).]

In no-fault insurance cases, the beneficiary is responsible for taking whatever action is necessary to obtain any payments from the no-fault insurer that reasonably can be expected. Medicare normally will not make any payments until the beneficiary has exhausted all remedies to obtain payments from the no-fault insurer. Medicare may make conditional payments, however, if (1) a proper claim has been filed, but it appears that the no-fault insurer will not pay promptly; or (2) a claim has not been filed because of the beneficiary's physical or mental incapacity. [42 C.F.R. §§ 411.51, 411.53.]

In liability insurance cases, Medicare conditional payments can be made when the beneficiary has been treated for an injury or illness allegedly caused by another party but are subject to recovery if payments are made later by a liability insurer. [42 C.F.R. §§ 411.52, 411.54.]

It is common for insurance companies to settle claims without admitting liability. Therefore, any payment by a liability insurer constitutes a liability insurance payment regardless of whether there has been a determination of liability. Medicare is entitled to seek repayment of the amount it paid, less a proportionate share of procurement costs, from any payment a claimant receives from a liability insurer or self-insured party. [42 C.F.R. § 411.37(a).]

Generally, if settlement or other payment is greater than Medicare's claim, Medicare must be paid in full. If, however, a court or other adjudicator designates certain amounts as compensation for pain and suffering or other losses not related to medical services, Medicare will accept the designation and will not seek recovery from those portions of awards. [*Medicare Secondary Payer Manual*, Pub. 100-05, Ch. 7, § 50.4.4.]

[¶ 639] Employer Group Health Plans

Medicare payment is excluded for employees entitled to Medicare based on old age, disability, or (during a 30-month coordination-of-benefits period) end-stage renal disease to the extent that healthcare benefit payments have been made or reasonably can be expected to be made under an employer group health plan. [Soc. Sec. Act § 1862(b)(1)(B)(iii); 42 C.F.R. § 411.20.]

Working Aged

This exclusion applies to Medicare-eligible individuals age 65 or over whose employer group health coverage is based on the current employment of the individual or spouse by an employer that employ 20 or more employees. Health insurance plans for retirees or spouses of retirees are not affected because retirement does not constitute "current employment" condition and are not primary to Medicare. The exclusion does not apply to individuals who purchase Federal Employees Health Benefits available to certain family members under the Spousal Equity Act because their coverage is not based on either the current employment or the enrollment of the former spouse or relative. [Soc. Sec. Act § 1862(b)(1)(A); 42 C.F.R. § 411.170(a)(ii); *Medicare Secondary Payer Manual*, Pub. 100-05, Ch. 2, §§ 10, 10.3.]

Under this exclusion, employers are required to offer their employees age 65 or over the same group health plan coverage offered to younger workers. Similarly, employers are required to offer their workers with Medicare-eligible spouses age 65 or over the same spousal group health plan benefits they offer to workers with spouses that are not Medicare-eligible. [Soc. Sec. Act. § 1862(b)(1)(A)(i).] Employees and their spouses then have the option of choosing either the employer plan or Medicare as their primary health insurer. If the employee or spouse elects the employer plan, Medicare will assume back-up coverage. If the employee or spouse elects Medicare as the primary insurer, however, the employer plan may not offer back-up coverage. [42 C.F.R. § 411.172(c); Pub. 100-05, Ch. 2, §§ 10, 10.3.]

Example • • •

(1) Harold is age 68 and is currently employed (not retired). His wife Elizabeth is age 66 and is currently employed. Harold's employer must offer Harold the same health benefits package it offers younger employees, including coverage of Harold's wife if spousal coverage is part of the employer's plan. Likewise, Elizabeth's employer must offer her and her spouse the same coverage offered to younger employees.

(2) Bob is 69 and retired. His wife Heather is 58 and still working. Heather's employer must offer Bob the same spousal coverage it offers to younger spouses of its employees.

Medicare may assume primary responsibility in paying for a beneficiary's health care if the services furnished are not covered under the employer plan or the beneficiaries have exhausted their benefits under the plan. Conditional Medicare payments can be made if the employer plan denies the claim or the beneficiary failed to file a claim due to physical or mental incapacity. [42 C.F.R. § 411.175.]

The working aged employee provisions do not apply to disability beneficiaries or to end-stage renal disease beneficiaries. [Soc. Sec. Act § 1862(b)(1)(A), (B), (C).] Employer group health plan requirements pertaining to these beneficiaries are discussed below.

See ¶ 311 for the discussion of the special enrollment period applicable to older workers and their spouses.

Disabled Employees

Medicare is the secondary payer for individuals under age 65 entitled to Medicare based on disability (see ¶ 204) who are covered by a "large group health plan (LGHP)" and whose coverage is based on the current employment status of the individual or of a family member. When an employee (or a member of the employee's family) becomes disabled, the LGHP has primary coverage responsibility and Medicare has secondary coverage responsibility. [Soc. Sec. Act § 1862(b)(1)(B); 42 C.F.R. §§ 411.200-411.206.]

An LGHP is defined as a group health plan of either (1) a single employer or employee organization or (2) at least one of two or more employers or employee organizations that employed at least 100 full-time employees or part-time employees on 50 percent or more of its regular business days during the previous calendar year. [Soc. Sec. Act § 1862(b)(1)(B)(iii); Pub. 100-05, Ch. 2, § 30.3.]

As in the case of elderly employees, there is a special enrollment period for disabled employees who do not enroll in Part B because they have chosen disability coverage under the employer's plan. See ¶ 311.

End-Stage Renal Disease Beneficiaries

Medicare benefits also are secondary for a limited period of time, known as the coordination-of-benefits period (see below), for individuals who are eligible or entitled to Medicare benefits because of end-stage renal disease (ESRD) (see ¶ 847) and who are entitled to primary healthcare coverage under an employer group health plan regardless of the number of employees employed by the employer and regardless of the individual's current employment status. [42 C.F.R. § 411.162(a).]

¶639

The coordination-of-benefits period begins with the first month in which the individual becomes eligible for Medicare, or the first month in which the individual would have been eligible for Medicare if he or she had filed an application for Medicare ESRD benefits. The coordination-of-benefits period ends 30 months later. During the coordination-of-benefits period, Medicare has secondary payment responsibility. After the coordination-of-benefits period ends, Medicare has primary payment responsibility. After the 30 month period, the patient becomes entitled to Medicare. [Soc. Sec. Act § 1862(b)(1)(C); 42 C.F.R. § 411.162(a).]

Eligibility refers to the first month the individual would have become entitled to Medicare Part A on the basis of ESRD if the individual had filed an application for such benefits. No benefits are payable on behalf of an individual who is eligible for but not yet entitled to Medicare solely on the basis of ESRD. When an individual is eligible for Medicare based solely on ESRD, Medicare is effectively secondary payer because Medicare makes no payment during a period of eligibility. [42 C.F.R. § 411.162(a).]

During the coordination of benefits period, Medicare will pay primary benefits for Medicare covered services that are not covered by the employer plan, and it will make secondary payments to supplement the amount paid by the employer plan if that plan pays only a portion of the charge for the service. [42 C.F.R. § 411.162(a).]

Medicare benefits are primary without a coordination-of-benefits period for ESRD-eligible individuals if two conditions are met: (1) the beneficiary was already entitled to Medicare because of age or disability; and (2) either the group health insurance was not based on current employment status, or the employer had fewer than 20 employees (in the case of the aged) or fewer than 100 employees (in the case of the disabled.) The employer health plan may continue to pay benefits secondary to Medicare but may not differentiate in the services covered and the payments made between person who have ESRD and those who do not. [42 C.F.R. § 411.163.]

Conditional Payments

Medicare will pay conditional primary benefits if a proper claim has been submitted and (1) the employer's plan denies the claim, or (2) payment under the employer's plan can reasonably be expected but the insurer will not pay promptly. If the employer plan denied payment because of the Medicare coverage, however, Medicare will not make conditional payment. Medicare also will pay if the beneficiary failed to file a proper claim due to physical or mental incapacity. [Soc. Sec. § 1862(b)(2)(B); 42 C.F.R. § 411.165; Pub. 100-05, Ch. 1, § 10.7.]

If a beneficiary or employer appeals a denied claim, conditional payment may be made, but both the insurer and the beneficiary are responsible for reimbursing Medicare if, the claim is approved. The insurer is required to pay Medicare directly. [42 C.F.R. § 411.24; Pub. 100-05, Ch. 1, § 10.7.1.] (See also ¶ 636.)

Medicare has the authority to contact employers to verify the existence of employer responsibility. [Soc. Sec. Act § 1862(b)(5)(C)(i).] The employer must respond within 30 days of the date of the receipt of the inquiry. Employers who willfully or repeatedly fail to respond are subject to a penalty of not more than $1,000 for each individual for whom such an inquiry is made. [Soc. Sec. Act. § 1862(b)(5)(C)(ii).]

[¶ 644] Limitation on Payments for Certain Drugs

Prescription drugs that were approved prior to the 1962 amendments to the Federal Food, Drug and Cosmetic Act and that the Secretary subsequently determines to be "less than effective" in use are excluded under Part B. Also, no payment can be made for drug products that are identical, related, or similar to a drug that is excluded. To exclude a drug under this provision, the Secretary must publish a notice of an opportunity for hearing in accordance with §505(e) of the Federal Food, Drug and Cosmetic Act. [Soc. Sec. Act §1862(c).] This provision applies only under Part B. There is no comparable provision for excluding such drugs under Part A.

Drugs and biologicals also are excluded from coverage as items or services administered by home health agencies. [Soc. Sec. Act § 1861(m)(5).]

For a discussion of when drugs and biologicals are covered under Medicare, see ¶ 212 and ¶ 235, with respect to Part A, and ¶ 351 and ¶ 362, with respect to Part B. The new prescription drug benefit is discussed in Chapter 5 of this book.

[¶ 646] Individuals and Entities Guilty of Program Abuses

No Medicare payment may be made, except in an emergency, to an entity or individual, such as a provider, supplier, physician, or other healthcare practitioner, who has been excluded from the Medicare program due to program abuses (see ¶ 720). Similarly, Medicare payment will not be made for items or services furnished at the medical direction or on the prescription of a physician who is excluded from program participation if the person furnishing the items or services knew or had reason to know of the exclusion. [Soc. Sec. Act §1862(e)(1).]

If a beneficiary receives items or services from a physician or supplier who has been excluded from program participation, Medicare will pay for the items or services if the beneficiary did not know or did not have reason to know about the exclusion. [Soc. Sec. Act §1862(e)(2).]

[¶ 654] Surgery Assistants in Cataract Operations

Assistants at surgery in cataract operations, including subsequent insertions of intraocular lenses, may not be paid for by Medicare unless, before the surgery is performed, the appropriate quality improvement organization (see ¶ 710) or a carrier has approved the use of the assistant due to the existence of a complicating medical condition. [Soc. Sec. Act § 1862(a)(15)(A).]

No payment may be made for the assistant's services if the Secretary finds that assistants at surgery are used on a national basis less than five percent of the time for the particular surgical procedure involved. [Soc. Sec. Act § 1848(i)(2)(B).]

Chapter 7—ADMINISTRATIVE PROVISIONS

[¶ 700] Medicare Organizational Structure

Overall responsibility for administration of the Medicare program rests with the Secretary of Health and Human Services, but state and local agencies operating under agreements with the Secretary, and private insurance companies known as intermediaries and carriers operating under contracts with the Secretary, have a major administrative role. In addition to using such agencies or organizations under the conditions described below, the Secretary is authorized to purchase or contract separately for such services as auditing or cost analysis. [Soc. Sec. Act § 1874.]

HHS Programs

Specific responsibility within HHS for administration of the Medicare program rests with the Centers for Medicare and Medicaid Services (CMS), which changed its name from the Health Care Financing Administration (HCFA) in 2001. [*Final rule,* 66 FR 39450, July 31, 2001.] CMS also operates the state-federal Medicaid program, the Health Care Quality Improvement Program (¶ 710), and a variety of related programs designed to control program costs, assure appropriate utilization of health services by eligible beneficiaries and recipients, and eliminate provider fraud and abuse. Through these and related health quality and standards programs, CMS seeks to ensure that the best possible care is delivered in the most economical manner to eligible beneficiaries and recipients. CMS also provides national policy planning for health care financing and for delivery of health services within these operating programs. [*Notice,* 62 FR 24120, May 2, 1997.]

Medicare Integrity Program. Under the Medicare Integrity Program, the Secretary is authorized to contract with eligible private entities to perform specified review and audit functions. Those functions include: (1) medical utilization and fraud review; (2) cost report audits; (3) payment determinations and recovery; and (4) provider education. [Soc. Sec. Act § 1893.] Additional Medicare program integrity support, audits, and assessments are provided by the Office of the Inspector General (OIG) and the General Accounting Office (GAO), both of which work in collaboration with CMS Medicare fraud control and prevention initiatives. An entity is eligible to enter into a contract under this program if it meets certain requirements, one of which is to demonstrate to the Secretary that the entity's financial holdings, interests or relationships will not interfere with its ability to perform as required. Intermediaries and carriers are prohibited from entering into contracts under this provision. [Soc. Sec. Act § 1893.]

Standards for carrier and intermediary evaluation. Notice of performance standards for fiscal year 2006 that would be used to evaluate the performance of fiscal intermediaries, carriers, and Durable Medical Equipment, Prosthetics, Orthotics, and Supplies (DMEPOS) regional carriers in the administration of the Medicare program were open for public comment in September 2005. Performance standards are regularly considered by CMS in its determination to renew, enter into, or terminate an intermediary or carrier contract. The performance criteria and standards became effective on October 24, 2005. [*Notice,* 70 FR 55887, Sept. 23, 2005.]

Beneficiary incentive programs. The Secretary must issue all beneficiaries an "Explanation of Medicare Benefits" for all medical services or items furnished to each beneficiary, including a notice of the right to request itemized statements. Providers must furnish itemized statements of items or services within 30 days of a beneficiary's request or face a possible civil money penalty of not more than $100. Beneficiaries have 90 days after receiving the statement to submit written requests to the Secretary identifying billing irregularities.

The Secretary must take all appropriate measures to recover any amounts unnecessarily paid. [Soc. Sec. Act § 1806.]

The Secretary must provide an annual notice to beneficiaries including a statement of beneficiary rights to request itemized statements of items or services provided, as well as an instruction to check explanations of benefits and itemized statements carefully for accuracy. The notice also must contain a description of the Medicare fraud and abuse information collection program (see below) and a toll-free telephone number in order to report errors or questionable charges. [Soc. Sec. Act § 1804(c).]

Information collection program. The Secretary is required to establish a separate program to encourage individuals to report other individuals and entities who are engaging, or have engaged, in acts or omissions that qualify for the imposition of sanctions under the Office of Inspector General's civil penalty, exclusion, or law enforcement authorities (see below). A portion of the amount collected as the result of this information will be paid to the reporting individual when at least $100 is collected by the Secretary or the U.S. Attorney General. [§ 203 of the Health Insurance Portability and Accountability Act of 1996 (HIPAA) (PubLNo 104-191); 42 C.F.R. § 420.405.]

Information on program efficiency. The Secretary has established a program to encourage individuals to submit suggestions for improving the efficiency of the Medicare program. [42 C.F.R. § 420.410]. [42 C.F.R. § 420.400.] As with the fraud and abuse reporting program, this program also authorizes the Secretary to make an appropriate payment to individuals whose suggestions result in program savings. [HIPAA § 203(c), 42 C.F.R. § 420.410.]

CMS maintains ten regional offices, which are located in Atlanta, Boston, Chicago, Dallas, Denver, Kansas City (Mo.), New York, Philadelphia, San Francisco, and Seattle, as well as the central office in Baltimore. CMS regional offices are often the first point-of-contact for beneficiaries, health care providers, state and local governments, and the general public. About 35 percent of CMS employees work in the regional offices, performing essential day-to-day functions for Medicare, Medicaid, and the State Children's Health Insurance Program (SCHIP). The regional offices provide customer service, program management and education and outreach programs, as well as develop partnerships with state and local health and social service agencies. Additional information on the CMS regional offices can be found at www.cms.hhs.gov/about/agency/leader.asp.

The Social Security Administration also is involved in the administration of the Medicare program, primarily in the enrollment of beneficiaries in the program and the maintenance of beneficiary rolls.

Administrative improvements. Section 900 of the Medicare Prescription Drug, Improvement, and Modernization Act of 2003 (MMA)(PubLNo 108-173) provided improvements within the Centers for Medicare and Medicaid Services (CMS). A Center is to be established within CMS to: (1) administer Parts C and D of Medicare; and (2) provide notice and information to beneficiaries. The new Center is required to report to the Administrator of CMS. The Secretary is required to ensure that Center carries out these duties by no later than January 1, 2008. [Soc. Sec. Act §§ 1117(b), 1808.]

Office of Inspector General

The Office of Inspector General is an independent unit within HHS that is headed by an Inspector General and a Deputy Inspector General. OIG is charged with: (1) conducting audits and investigations relating to HHS programs and operations; (2) promoting economy and efficiency in the administration of HHS programs and operations, as well as preventing and detecting fraud and abuse; and (3) providing a means of keeping the Secretary and

Congress fully and currently informed about problems and deficiencies relating to the administration and operation of HHS programs and the necessity of corrective action. Reports on OIG activities must be submitted annually to Congress and quarterly to the Secretary and appropriate congressional committees. The OIG must report immediately on any serious problems or abuses. [Inspector General Act of 1978 (PubLNo 95-452).]

The OIG also has primary responsibility for detecting abuses and applying sanctions against providers, physicians, entities, and suppliers of health care items and services that commit federal health care program abuses. (See ¶ 720.)

Fraud and Abuse Control Program. The Health Insurance Portability and Accountability Act of 1996 (HIPAA) (PubLNo 104-191) established a national Health Care Fraud and Abuse Control Program (HCFAC) designed to coordinate federal, state and local law enforcement activities to combat fraud and abuse within federal health care programs. The program is administered under the joint direction of the U.S. Attorney General and the Secretary of the Department of Health and Human Services (HHS), acting through the OIG. HCFAC charges the Secretary with: (1) coordinating federal, state and local law enforcement programs to control fraud and abuse with respect to health care plans; (2) conducting investigations, audits, evaluations and inspections of health care delivery in the United States; (3) facilitating the enforcement of legal provisions that apply to exclusions from program participation, civil money penalties (CMPs), the anti-fraud and abuse amendments (including the anti-kickback provision), and other statutes related to health care fraud and abuse; (4) providing for the modification and establishment of safe harbors; (5) issuing advisory opinions and special fraud alerts pursuant to the provisions of Soc. Sec. Act § 1128D; and (6) reporting and disclosing adverse actions against health care providers, suppliers or practitioners under the data collection system established under the Health Care Fraud and Abuse Data Collection Program. [Soc. Sec. Act § 1128C(a)(1).] The scope of the agencies' coordinated efforts in investigations, audits, evaluations, and inspections is not limited to the Medicare and Medicaid programs, but encompasses issues common to *all* health plans. [Soc. Sec. Act § 1128C.]

Railroad Retirement Board

The Centers for Medicare and Medicaid Services (CMS) and the Railroad Retirement Board have agreed on a delegation of important responsibilities to the railroad agency in connection with Medicare Part B. Under this delegation, the Railroad Retirement Board has responsibility for enrolling railroad eligibles in Part B; for collecting their premiums; and for selecting "carriers" for railroad enrollees under Part B. (The Railroad Retirement Board has chosen one carrier, the Travelers Insurance Company, to act as the carrier for railroad beneficiaries, regardless of where the services are furnished.)

The Railroad Retirement Board applies the same policies and regulations as CMS in determining what expenses are covered and what payments are to be made. [Soc. Sec. Act §§ 226(a)(2)(B), 226(b)(2)(B).]

Use of Private Accrediting Organizations

The Secretary is authorized to contract with private accrediting organizations, such as the Joint Commission on Accreditation of Healthcare Organizations, the American Osteopathic Association, and other national accreditation bodies to determine whether hospitals, skilled nursing facilities, home health agencies, ambulatory surgical centers, hospices, rural health clinics, laboratories, clinics, rehabilitation agencies (including comprehensive outpatient rehabilitation agencies), psychiatric hospitals, and public health agencies meet Medicare requirements. [Soc. Sec. Act § 1865(a).]

¶700

The Secretary is prohibited from disclosing any accreditation survey made and released by any private national accreditation body. [Soc. Sec. Act § 1865(c).]

[¶ 703] Role of the State and Local Agencies

The law provides for state agencies, operating under an agreement with the Secretary, to determine whether a provider of items, services or and/or equipment meets the conditions of participation in federal health care programs. State agencies must later certify that a provider meets the conditions of participation with the Secretary. State agencies also make coverage certifications with respect to other health care entities, such as independent laboratories, suppliers of portable X-ray services, rural health clinics, rehabilitation agencies, and public health agencies providing outpatient physical and occupational therapy or speech pathology services under Part B. The Secretary is required to use the services of state health departments or other appropriate state or local agencies whenever the agencies are able and willing to perform such administrative functions. [Soc. Sec. Act § 1864(a).]

If a state enters into an agreement with Medicare to pay the Part B premium on behalf of its public assistance recipients, the agreement may provide for a designated state agency to serve as a carrier on behalf of its public assistance recipients. [Soc. Sec. Act § 1843(f).]

Disclosure of Information

Survey agency findings. The law requires the Secretary to make available to the public information from a state or local agency's survey of a health care facility, rural health clinic, laboratory, clinic, agency, or organization about the presence or absence of deficiencies relating to statutory and additional health and safety requirements. A statement of deficiencies or the survey report itself, including any pertinent written statements furnished by an institution or facility concerning this statement, will be disclosed within 90 days following the completion of the survey. Statements of deficiencies, reports, and pertinent written statements will be made available by the Secretary in a readily available form and place. [Soc. Sec. § 1864(a).]

Adverse fraud and abuse actions. Information concerning final adverse fraud and abuse actions against health care providers, suppliers, or practitioners must be made available to federal and state government agencies and private health plans. [Soc. Sec. Act § 1128E.] (See ¶ 720.) The Health Care Integrity and Protection Data Bank (HIPDB) is a national data bank that receives and discloses certain final adverse actions against health care providers, suppliers, or practitioners. OIG required reporting as of November 1999 on all reportable final adverse actions taken since the effective date of HIPAA's enactment (August 21, 1996). Reportable actions include civil judgments, criminal convictions, adverse licensing or certification decisions, and exclusions from any federal or state health care program. [45 C.F.R. Part 61; *Final rule,* 64 FR 57740, Oct. 26, 1999.] The definition of "any other negative action or finding" was corrected to exclude the reporting of administrative fines or citations, corrective action plans, and other personnel actions to the HIPDB unless they are (1) connected to the billing, provision, or delivery of health care services, and (2) taken in conjunction with other licensure or certification actions such as revocation, suspension, censure, reprimand, probation, or surrender. [*Final rule, corrective amendment,* 70 FR 53953, Sept. 13, 2005.] The information from the HIPDB is used in conjunction with the National Practitioner Data Bank. Settlement agreements in which a finding of liability has not been established are not be reported. [Soc. Sec. Act § 1128E.] (See ¶ 720.)

Federal and state government agencies, health plans, self-querying health care suppliers, and providers and practitioners have access to the data bank. [*Final rule,* 65 FR 34986, June 1, 2000.] Subjects of reports may obtain access to their own reports. Users of the

HIPDB wishing to perform a self-query can do so for a nominal fee (see ¶ 720). [*Final rule*, 64 FR 57740, Oct. 26, 1999.]

[¶ 705] Role of Fiscal Intermediaries, Carriers, and Medicare Administrative Contractors

The law provides a considerable role for the participation of private organizations in the administration of Medicare. The Part A program generally is administered by fiscal "intermediaries" and Part B is generally administered by "carriers." These organizations, which usually are insurance companies, contract with the federal government to process and pay Medicare claims and perform other administrative and operational tasks for the program, including the review of claims and the conduct of audits. [Soc. Sec. Act §§ 1816, 1842(a).]

Intermediaries Under Part A

Intermediaries are private organizations, usually insurance companies, that serve as CMS' agents in determining the amount of payment due providers and paying them for the Medicare services they have provided. An intermediary may be nominated by a group or association of providers (however, hospices may not nominate intermediaries) or may be designated by the Secretary to serve a class of providers on a national or regional basis. [42 C.F.R. §§ 421.104, 421.106, 421.114–421.117.] The Secretary is permitted to enter into an agreement with a nominated organization only pursuant to finding that (1) this will be consistent with effective and efficient administration, and (2) the organization is able and willing to assist in the application of safeguards against unnecessary utilization of covered services. The organization must agree to furnish the Secretary with such information, gathered by it in carrying out the agreement, as the Secretary finds necessary. [Soc. Sec. Act § 1816(b); 42 C.F.R. § 421.110.]

Besides paying Part A claims, intermediaries make initial coverage determinations and handle the early stages of beneficiary appeals.

Carriers Under Part B

Carriers are private organizations, usually insurance companies, that contract to serve as the government's fiscal agent for items and services provided under Part B. They are asked to make Part B program coverage and payment determinations for the items and services furnished by physicians and suppliers. They also handle beneficiary inquiries and initial appeals.

DME carriers. Durable Medical Equipment Regional Carriers (DMERCs) also serve as fiscal agents for durable medical equipment and services under Part B. While the service areas for DMERCs were previously listed in the regulations, a 2005 *Final rule* removed this information to allow for the selection of DMERCs, the alteration of their service areas, and increases or decreases in the total number of DMERCs without having to use the comment procedure required to amend the federal regulations. The criteria for selecting DMERCs remained unchanged, as did the selection process for new contractors to perform statistical analysis and maintain the National Supplier Clearing House. [*Final rule*, 70 FR 9232, Feb. 25, 2005.]

Medicare Administrative Contractors

Medicare administrative contractors (MACs) will replace intermediaries and carriers by September 30, 2011. The distinction between Part A contractors (fiscal intermediaries) and Part B contractors (carriers) will be eliminated. All functions of the current fiscal intermediaries and carriers will be assumed by the new MACs which include: (1) determining the amount of Medicare payments required to be made to providers and suppliers; (2)

making Medicare payments; (3) providing education and outreach to beneficiaries, providers and suppliers; (4) communicating with providers and suppliers; and (5) any additional functions as necessary. [Soc. Sec. Act § 1874A; *Medicare, Prescription Drug, Improvement, and Modernization Act of 2003*, § 911.]

The Secretary may begin the bidding process for MACs for annual contract periods that begin after October, 1 2005. The Secretary may competitively contract with any eligible entity to serve as a MAC. An entity is eligible to contract for the performance of a particular function of a MAC only if: (1) the entity has demonstrated capability to carry out such function; (2) the entity complies with conflict of interest standards as are generally applicable to federal acquisition and procurement; (3) the entity has sufficient assets to financially support the performance of the functions; and (4) the entity meets other requirements as the Secretary may impose. [Soc. Sec. Act § 1874A.]

The Secretary is permitted to renew the MAC contracts annually for up to five (5) years. All contracts must be re-competed at least every five (5) years using competitive processes. The Secretary is required to develop contract performance requirements to carry out the functions described in the provisions and to develop standards for measuring the extent to which a contractor has met the requirements. The Secretary is also required to consult with beneficiary and provider organizations and agencies performing other Medicare functions. The contractor performance requirements and measurement standards are made available to the public by the Secretary and must include provider and beneficiary satisfaction levels as one of the requirements. [Soc. Sec. Act § 1874A; *Medicare, Prescription Drug, Improvement, and Modernization Act of 2003*, § 911.]

[¶ 707] Role of Medicaid

Although the Medicaid program is administered separately from Medicare, a provision in the law requires Medicaid to pay Medicare premiums, deductibles, and coinsurance amounts for poverty-level Medicare beneficiaries (as defined under the Medicaid law). Medicare beneficiaries eligible for Medicaid cost-sharing assistance are called "Qualified Medicare Beneficiaries" (QMBs). [Soc. Sec. Act § 1905(p).]

States also may pay Medicare Part A and Part B premiums under "buy-in" agreements with Medicare for beneficiaries who do not qualify for QMB status. [Soc. Sec. Act §§ 1818(g), 1843.]

Prescription drug benefit. Section 103(a)(1) of the Medicare Prescription Drug, Improvement, and Modernization Act of 2003 (MMA) (PubLNo 108-173), requires states to provide the Secretary with eligibility information necessary to carry out transitional prescription drug assistance verification related to Medicare low-income subsidies under the new prescription drug benefit (see ¶ 520) and the prescription drug discount card program (see ¶ 535). States are required to provide this information as a condition of their state plans under the Medicaid Act to receive federal Medicaid assistance. The administrative costs expended by a state in providing eligibility information are reimbursable to the state. [Soc. Sec. Act § 1114.]

[¶ 710] Quality Improvement Organizations—QIOs

In 1982, the government established a utilization and quality control peer review program. The program established peer review organizations (PROs), which consisted of practicing local physicians and other professionally trained staff. These organizations must be sponsored by a significant number of physicians actively practicing in the service area, or must have available to it the services of a sufficient number of area physicians to assure adequate peer review. PROs were responsible for making determinations regarding the necessity and reasonableness of health care services provided under Medicare. PROs also were charged with evaluating the efficiency and economy of the health care services provided, as well as ensuring that such services met medically professional and accepted quality of care standards. [Soc. Sec. Act § 1154(a)(1).]

In May 24, 2002, CMS changed the name of peer review organizations to quality improvement organizations (QIOs) to reflect their instrumental role in supporting HHS' quality of care initiatives. These initiatives were launched in 2001 to provide Medicare and Medicaid beneficiaries and their families with user-friendly comparative information for selecting quality sources of healthcare. CMS revised all references in the regulations from "peer review organization" and "PRO" to "quality improvement organization" and "QIO" respectively. The definition and function of these organizations, however, remains the same. [*Final rule*, 67 FR 36539, May 24, 2002; *Medicare Quality Improvement Organization Manual*, Pub. 100-10.]

All hospitals, not just those under the prospective payment system (PPS), are required to have an agreement with a QIO as a condition of participation and to be eligible for Medicare program payments. [Soc. Sec. Act § 1866(a)(1)(F).] Each QIO reviews services and items provided to Medicare beneficiaries by hospital staff, physicians, and other healthcare practitioners in settings such as acute care hospitals, specialty hospitals, and ambulatory surgical centers. [Pub. 100-10, Ch. 1, § 1005 and Ch. 2, § 2020.]

QIOs also ensure that services (including both inpatient and outpatient) provided to beneficiaries in Medicare health maintenance organizations (HMOs) and competitive medical plans (CMPs) meet accepted quality standards of healthcare, including whether appropriate healthcare services have not been provided or have been provided in inappropriate settings. [42 C.F.R. § 476.72.] The determinations of QIOs on these matters are binding for purposes of determining whether Medicare benefits should be paid. [Soc. Sec. Act § 1154(a)(2).]

Pursuant to § 109(a) of the Medicare Prescription Drug, Improvement, and Modernization Act of 2003 (MMA) (PubLNo 108-173), the work of QIOs has been expanded to include review of the professional activities of Medicare Advantage organizations pursuant to contracts under Part C (see ¶ 400) and prescription drug sponsors pursuant to contracts under Part D (see ¶ 500). [Soc. Sec. Act § 1154(a)(1).]

Review of PPS Hospitals

QIOs review hospitals paid under the prospective payment system (PPS), under which hospitals are paid a fixed rate per discharge according to diagnosis-related groups of illnesses (see below and ¶ 810). QIOs ensure that hospitals do not make unnecessary or inappropriate admissions, inappropriate classification of discharge, unnecessary transfers of patients, or other inappropriate practices that would increase payments inappropriately. Based on a QIO's determination that a hospital has circumvented PPS, Medicare payment may be denied, or the hospital may be required to take corrective action. [Soc. Sec. Act § 1886(f)(2).]

Required Review Activities

The duties and review functions required of QIOs are specified in a document known as a Scope of Work (SOW). The first SOW covered the 1984-1986 contract period. Generally, duties and review functions include the implementation and operation of a system to assure the quality of services for which Medicare payment may be made, and to eliminate unreasonable, unnecessary, and inappropriate care provided to beneficiaries. [Pub. 100-10, Ch.1.]

Because CMS contracts with QIOs do not cover identical time periods, each contract reflects the SOW in effect when the contract is negotiated, and contract requirements may differ. QIOs have entered the seventh SOW on a staggered basis: one-third started on

August 1, 2002, one-third on November 1, 2002, and the final one-third will start on February 1, 2003. Under the seventh SOW, QIOs must improve the quality of care by completing specific tasks in the following areas: (1) clinical quality improvement; (2) information and communication; (3) beneficiary protection; and (4) developmental activities. The seventh SOW is described in further detail on the CMS website at www.cms.gov/qio.

In July 2004, new criteria for the evaluation of QIOs under their contracts with CMS was announced. The criteria are based on the tasks and related subtasks provided in the QIO Scope of Work (SOW). Section 1153 of the MMA requires the Secretary of HHS to publish general criteria and standards that will be used to evaluate the efficient and effective performance of contract obligations by QIOs. CMS has focused on the following four tasks to measure QIO performance: (1) improve beneficiary safety and health through clinical quality improvement; (2) improve beneficiary safety and health through information and communications; (3) improve beneficiary safety and health through Medicare beneficiary protection activities; and (4) improve beneficiary safety and health through developmental activities. [*Notice*, 69 FR 44031, July 23, 2004.]

Health Care Quality Improvement Program

The Health Care Quality Improvement Program (HCQIP) was initiated in 1992 to improve the health of beneficiaries. Under HCQIP, QIOs are required to analyze and change patterns of care to remedy widespread short-comings in the health care system. A HCQIP is defined as "an assessment, conducted by or for a QIO, of a patient care problem for the purpose of improving patient care through peer analysis, intervention, resolution of the problem, and follow-up." [42 C.F.R. § 480.101.] Quality improvement projects consist of : (1) the development of quality indicators based in science; (2) the identification of care improvement opportunities through measurement of health care patterns; (3) communication with professional and provider communities regarding patterns of care; (4) system improvements for quality improvement purposes; and (5) the evaluation of the effectiveness of quality improvement interventions. [www.cms.hhs.gov/qio/3.asp.]

Under HCQIP, QIOs participate in cooperative projects and data collection to address quality-of-care concerns. The requirement that QIOs review all ambulatory surgical procedures (or, at the Secretary's discretion, a sample of selected procedures) performed in ambulatory surgical centers and hospital outpatient departments are performed through cooperative project activities. [Soc. Sec. Act § 1154(a)(4)(A).]

Mandatory Case Review

Beneficiary complaints. QIOs must review all written beneficiary complaints about the quality of services they have received by screening patient care information to identify and verify problems. After the review is completed, the QIO must inform the beneficiary of the QIO's final disposition of the complaint. [Soc. Sec. Act § 1154(a).]

Denial notices issued by hospitals. Hospitals are permitted to issue noncoverage notices to Medicare beneficiaries denying coverage of their continued stay if the hospital determines (and the attending physician or QIO concurs) that inpatient care is no longer required. [Pub. 100-10, Chapter 7 § 7005.] QIOs are required to review noncoverage notices issued by a hospital on request of the beneficiary or his representative. [Soc. Sec. Act § 1154(e).]

Antidumping violations. QIOs are required to review allegations of hospital emergency rooms turning away or transferring patients without screening for, or stabilizing, emergency medical conditions. [Pub. 100-10, Chapter 9 § 9150.]

Review of assistants-at-surgery in cataract operations. QIOs review requests for surgical assistants based on medical necessity. [Pub. 100-10, Chapter 4 § 4020.] Medicare payment

¶710

for the services of an assistant at cataract surgery is prohibited unless a QIO approves the services prior to the surgery based on the existence of a complicated medical condition. [Soc. Sec. Act § 1862(a).]

Referrals. QIOs also must perform diagnosis related group (DRG) validation reviews of hospital requests for higher-weighted DRG adjustments. [42 C.F.R. § 476.71]. QIOs review all cases referred by CMS, the HHS Office of Inspector General, contractors (fiscal intermediaries and carriers), and clinical data abstraction centers. Cases referred by Medicare Advantage organization contractors or state Medicaid and survey and certification agencies also are reviewed by QIOs. [Pub. 100-10, Chapter 4 § 4070.] QIOs may review critical access hospital (CAH) patient records upon request.

CAH patient records. QIOs may review critical access hospital (CAH) patient records upon request. QIO review of CAH patient records only applies to Medicare inpatient admissions. [Pub. 100-10, Ch. 4, § 4080.]

Sanctions

If a QIO determines that a practitioner or provider has persisted in violating its obligations to furnish services that are economical, medically necessary, of proper quality, and properly documented, the organization is required to submit a report and recommendation to the Secretary on the action that should be taken, including possible exclusion from the Medicare and Medicaid programs or assessment of fines related to the costs of the improper services. A QIO recommendation to the Secretary for exclusion automatically becomes effective if the Secretary fails to act within a 120-day review period. [Soc. Sec. Act §§ 1156(a), 1156(b); Pub. 100-10, Chapter 9, § 9050.]

In addition, if a QIO finds that a PPS hospital has engaged in unnecessary admissions, early discharges and subsequent readmissions, or other improper practices in order to circumvent the prospective payment system, the Secretary may: (1) deny payment, in whole or in part, for the inappropriate practice; (2) require the hospital to take other corrective action necessary to prevent or correct the inappropriate practice; or (3) in the case of a pattern of inappropriate admissions and billing practices that have the effect of circumventing the prospective payment system, terminate the provider participation agreement. [Soc. Sec. Act § 1886(f)(2).]

If a practitioner or other person relocates to another QIO area prior to a finding of a violation or sanction recommendation, and the originating QIO is able to make a finding, the originating QIO must close the case or forward a sanction recommendation to the OIG. If the originating QIO cannot make a finding, it must forward all documentation regarding the case to the QIO with jurisdiction and notify the practitioner or other person of this action. [42 C.F.R. § 1004.30(e).]

Practitioners and providers are entitled to reasonable notice of a sanction determination and are provided the opportunity for a hearing, as well as judicial review. [Soc. Sec. Act § 1156(b)(4).]

Appeals from QIO Coverage Determinations

Any beneficiary, provider or practitioner who is dissatisfied with a QIO initial denial determination or change as a result of DRG validation is entitled to notice and reconsideration of the determination or change by the QIO. An initial denial determination consist of a finding that the health care services provider were unnecessary, unreasonable, and/or at an inappropriate level of care. QIOs are prohibited from publicizing payment denials without first offering the provider or practitioner notification and opportunity for a hearing. [Soc. Sec. Act § 1154(a)(3); 42 C.F.R. §§ 478.12, 478.15, 478.16.]

¶710

A dissatisfied party may obtain reconsideration by filing a written request within 60 days after the date of the initial denial determination, unless the time is extended for good cause. The date of receipt of the initial denial determination notice is presumed to be five (5) days after the date listed on the notice unless there is a showing to the contrary. [42 C.F.R. §§ 478.20, 478.22.]

If the QIO's reconsidered determination is adverse to the beneficiary, practitioner or provider, and the amount in controversy is at least $200, the affected party is entitled to a hearing by an Administrative Law Judge (ALJ). A request for a hearing must be filed within 60 days after the date of receipt of the notice of reconsidered determination. If the amount in controversy is $2,000 or greater, the affected party is entitled to judicial review of the ALJ's decision. [Soc. Sec. Act § 1155; 42 C.F.R. §§ 478.12, 478.20, 478.40, 478.46.]

Limitations on Beneficiary Liability

The law prohibits physicians, in the case of assigned claims, from billing beneficiaries for services for which payment has been denied by a QIO on the basis of substandard quality of care. [Soc. Sec. Act § 1842(b)(3)(B)(ii).] The beneficiary also is indemnified in the case of any deductible and coinsurance paid if a QIO has denied Medicare payment for services. [Soc. Sec. Act § 1879(b).]

[¶ 715] Privacy of Health Data

The Health Insurance Portability and Accountability Act of 1996 (HIPAA) (PubLNo 104-191) required the Department of Health and Human Services (HHS) to implement national standards to protect individually identifiable health information. The HIPAA privacy and security standards apply to all health care providers, employers, insurers, health care clearing-houses, and health plans, as well as government health programs (collectively called "covered entities"). Health care entities were required to be in full compliance with the provisions of the HIPAA regulations by April 14, 2003. [45 C.F.R. §§ 160.103, 164.534.]

Security rule. A final HIPAA security rule related to the transmission of electronic data was issued on February 20, 2003, which provided a series of administrative, technical, and physical security safeguards for hospitals and other covered entities to ensure the confidentiality of PHI. [*Final rule*, 68 FR 8334, Feb. 20, 2003.] Covered entities must have been compliant with the HIPAA electronic data security rules by April 20, 2005. [*OIG Supplemental Compliance Program Guidance for Hospitals*, Jan. 1, 2005.]

Definitions

Individually identifiable health information is defined as data that relates to any of the following: (1) the past, present or future physical or mental health condition of an individual; (2) the provision of health care to an individual; or (3) the past, present or future payment for the provision of health care that identifies the individual or that could reasonably be used to identify the individual. Protected health information is defined as individually identifiable health information that is transmitted or maintained in an electronic format or any other medium. The regulations cover all health data, including written records and oral communications, and not just electronically maintained or transmitted data. [45 C.F.R. § 164.501.] The disclosure of health information includes the release, transfer, provision of, access to, or divulging of patient health information, in any manner, to others outside of the entity holding the information. [45 C.F.R. § 160.103 (3).] More importantly, the term health care as it relates to HIPAA, includes any of the following services: (1) preventative, diagnostic, therapeutic, rehabilitative, counseling, service assessments, or any other procedure with respect to the physical, mental or functional condition of a patient; and (2) the sale or dispensing of prescription drugs, equipment, or devices in accordance with a prescription.

[45 C.F.R. § 106.103.] Thus, the disclosure of information for something as simple as an eyeglass prescription or the cost of services paid by a patient is a prohibited under HIPAA.

Patient Notice

Health care providers must issue a notice describing the provider's privacy policy to patients during the first delivery of service. Providers are required to conduct a good faith effort to obtain written acknowledgement from a patient of the receipt of the privacy notice. [45 C.F.R. § 164.520(c)(2)(ii).] The notice also must be available at any time and publicly displayed in a clear and prominent location in the provider's office. [45 C.F.R. § 164.520(c)(2).]

The notice must describe how the patient's medical information will be used and disclosed. The notice is required to inform patients that they have a right to inspect, copy, amend, and receive a list of people and organizations that have requested access to their protected health information. The notice must contain the name, title and telephone number of a contact person in the provider's office, as well as a description of the provider's legal duties with respect to the patient's protected health information. [45 C.F.R. §§ 164.520(b)(1)(iv), 164.520(a)(1).]

The notice might contain the following header statement: "THIS NOTICE DESCRIBES HOW MEDICAL INFORMATION ABOUT YOU MAY BE USED AND DISCLOSED AND HOW YOU CAN GET ACCESS TO THIS INFORMATION. PLEASE REVIEW IT CAREFULLY." Key to the compliance of the HIPAA notice provision is that the statement be placed as a header or otherwise prominently displayed. , [45 C.F.R. § 164.520(b)(1)(i).] In addition, providers must retain copies of the notices issued and, if applicable, any written acknowledgments of the patient's receipt of the notice, or any other documentation of the provider's good faith efforts to obtain a written acknowledgment of the patient's privacy rights. [45 C.F.R. § 164.520.]

Exception for inmates. Inmates do have a right to notice under the provisions of 45 C.F.R. § 164.520. The notice requirements of HIPAA do not apply to a correctional institution that is also a covered entity. [45 C.F.R. § 164.520(a)(3).]

Authorization

Health care providers may not release individually identifiable health information without an authorization unless the information is released: (1) for the provider's own treatment, payment or health care operations; (2) for treatment activities of another healthcare provider; (3) for payment activities of another covered entity; (4) to other providers of the patient's care; (5) to other providers in the provider's organized health care arrangement for the purposes of treating the patient; or (6) to the beneficiary. Patients may grant providers authorization to disclose individually identifiable health information for specific purposes. Disclosures of the information must be consistent with the authorization. Providers may not condition the provision of health care based on a patient's signing of such an authorization. [45 C.F.R. § 164.508.] In addition, patients have the right to request that providers restrict the use or disclosure of their personally identifiable health data. The provider, however, does not have to agree to a patient's requested restriction. [45 C.F.R. § 164.522.] A provider also may receive oral consent or authorization from a patient as long as the patient is informed about how their information will be used. [45 C.F.R. § 164.510.]

Providers must obtain an authorization from a patient before using the patient's individually identifiable health information for marketing purposes. Marketing includes communications between a provider, or another organization, and a patient that uses protected health information, which is made available by the patient's health care provider. [45 C.F.R. §§ 164.501, 164.514(e).]

¶715

Authorizations must contain: (1) a description of the information to be disclosed and a description of how the information will be used; (2) the name of the person or organization authorized to make the disclosure; (3) the name of the person or organization or a description of the class of organization to which the information will be disclosed; (4) an expiration date or event; (5) a statement of the individual's right to revoke the authorization at any time; (6) a statement that the individually identifiable health information is subject to unlimited further disclosure by the recipient of the information; and (7) the dated signature of the patient. [45 C.F.R. § 164.508(c) and (d).]

Exemptions

Health care facilities may provide a directory of patients that includes the patient's name, location in the facility, condition that does not communicate specific medical information, and the individual's religious affiliation. A patient must be given the opportunity to object to the hospital placing this information in its directory. [45 C.F.R. § 164.510(a)(2).]

Health care facilities may release individually identifiable health data to a business associate without authorization from the patient for the purpose of raising funds for the benefit of the health care facility or for marketing health care services provided at the facility. Health care facilities must remove personally identifiable data from fund raising and marketing lists upon request of the individual. [45 C.F.R. §§ 164.510(a), 164.514(e), (f).]

Protected health information may be released without authorization in the following instances: (1) in an emergency situation to a family member or friend; (2) to public health authorities for the purpose of preventing or controlling disease; (3) for research purposes when an authorization is independently approved by a privacy board or Institutional Review Board; (4) in judicial and administrative proceedings; (5) in limited law enforcement activities; in investigations of abuse or neglect; (6) for the identification of a deceased person or the cause of death; (7) and for activities related to national defense. [45 C.F.R. § 164.512.]

Business Associates

Providers are responsible for the use of protected information released to other organizations. A business associate is a person or organization who on behalf of a regulated entity or organized health care arrangement (such as a billing service or information processor), and who other than in the capacity of such an entity's workforce, uses protected health information to provide legal, actuarial, accounting, consulting, data aggregation, management, administrative, accreditation, or financial services. [45 C.F.R. § 160.103.] Health care providers and other covered entities must have a contract with each business associate detailing how the business associate will protect the individually identifiable information. [45 C.F.R. § 164.502(e)(2).] Business associates must provide the same protection to individually identifiable data as health care providers or other covered entities. If a provider suspects that an organization is using protected health information without the patient's consent or authorization, the provider is directed to terminate business relations and, if that is not possible, to contact HHS. Providers that do not obtain assurances from business associates that personally identifiable health data will be protected will be held in violation of these regulations. [45 C.F.R. §§ 164.504(e) and 164.534.]

Patients' Rights

Patients may: (1) view; (2) request a copy of; (3) amend; or (4) receive a list of individuals and organizations that have seen their medical information over the previous six years. A provider may deny access to a patient's records if the provider believes that release of that information will endanger the life or physical safety of the individual. In all other cases, providers have 60 days from the date of a request to make the information available.

Providers, with the consent of the patient, may provide a summary of the data instead of the actual data itself. Health care providers may charge a fee for providing access or copies of personally identifiable information. A provider does not have to include material submitted by a patient as an amendment if it was generated by another provider, is inaccurate or is not part of the requested records. Providers do not have to provide an accounting of the release of individually identifiable health information to patients when such a release conforms with an authorization. [45 C.F.R. §§ 164.524, 164.526, 164.528.]

Administrative Requirements

Health care providers must designate a privacy official who is responsible for the development and implementation of the privacy policies and procedures. Each health care provider must designate a contact person who is to receive complaints and requests. All staff members must have been trained on the privacy policies and procedures by the April 14, 2003 date described above. [45 C.F.R. § 164.530.]

The HIPAA privacy regulations are enforced by HHS's Office for Civil Rights. [*Final rule*, 65 FR 82462, Dec. 28, 2000.]

HIPAA Complaints

A new system of records (SOR) has been designed to assist the Office of E-Health Standards and Services (OESS) with the regulation and enforcement of the transaction and code sets, security, and unique identifier provisions of HIPAA. The SOR will: (1) store the results of OESS regional audits; (2) refer HIPAA violations to law enforcement agencies; (3) maintain and retrieve records of investigation results; and (4) generate reports concerning the status of current and closed complaints, reviews, and correspondence. The SOR, called the HIPPA Information Tracking System (HITS), is made up of a central, searchable electronic repository of all complaint documents supplemented by paper file. HITS will maintain a file of complaint allegations, information collected during the investigation, findings, the results of the investigation, and correspondence related to the investigation. Information collected is limited to the minimum personal data necessary to achieve the goals of HITS and includes the name, address, telephone number, health insurance claim number, geographic location, and background information of the complainant. OESS monitors the use of HITS and any disclosure of information from the SOR will be approved only if certain guidelines are met. Implementation of the SOR may be deferred pending the review of public comments. [*Notice*, 70 FR 38944, July 6, 2005.]

Complaint requirements. Complaints that a covered entity is not complying with HIPAA must be filed in writing (either on paper or electronically) and must describe the acts or omissions committed that are believed to be in violation of HIPAA rules. In addition, the complaint should contain the contact information of the complainant and must be filed within 180 days of when the complainant knew, or should have known, of the act or violation. CMS will make determinations of HIPAA violations and will advise covered entities that a complaint has been filed in an effort to promote voluntary compliance with HIPAA privacy and security rules. Finally, the covered entity must submit a written response demonstrating compliance with HIPAA, describing a plan of corrective action, or objecting to the allegations. [*Notice*, 70 FR 15329, March 25, 2005.]

Preemption of State Law

Federal regulations on administrative data standards and other requirements preempt conflicting state laws unless the state law provides more protection, or the Secretary determines that the state law may supersede any federal provisions. [45 C.F.R. § 160.203.]

[¶ 720] Fraud and Abuse Penalties

Criminal penalties. The Social Security Act contains criminal penalties for persons convicted of committing specified fraudulent acts including but not limited to: (1) filing false claims; (2) misrepresenting an institution's qualifications; (3) soliciting, receiving or offering kickbacks, bribes, or rebates; and (4) physician self-referrals to a "designated health facility" as defined under the Stark II law (see the paragraphs that follow for a detailed description of the changes in physician self-referral laws). [Soc. Sec. Act §§ 1126, 1128B(b), § 1877 and 42 C.F.R. § 411.354.]

Civil money penalties. Individuals determined by the Secretary to have filed fraudulent claims under the program, or to have charged beneficiaries for services in violation of the law or agreements with the Secretary, are subject to civil money penalties. Additionally, the regulations provide civil monetary penalties for any of the following acts: (1) failure to bill outpatient therapy services, rehabilitation services or ambulance service on an assignment-related basis; (2) failure to provide an itemized statement of Medicare items and services to program beneficiaries at their request; and (3) failure of physicians or non-physician practitioners to provide diagnostic codes for items or services furnished to beneficiaries. [*Final rule with comment period*, 66 FR 49544, Sept. 28, 2001.]

Exclusion and suspension from participation. The Social Security Act provides authority for the Secretary of the Department of Health and Human Services (HHS) to exclude providers, practitioners and entities from program participation who have previously been convicted of crimes involving federal health care programs. The Secretary may also suspend individuals and entities from participation in both the Medicare and Medicaid programs for fraud and abuse. The Secretary may, however, waive a provider's suspension if it is determined that, because of a shortage of providers or health care personnel in a particular area, program beneficiaries would suffer hardship resulting from the lack of access to care. [42 C.F.R. § 1003.105.]

Civil monetary penalty amount changes. The amount of civil monetary penalties (CMP) for violations of the anti-fraud and abuse provisions of the Social Security Act increased from $2,000 to $10,000 for each bill or request for payment in which a federal health care program beneficiary was billed in excess of the standard Medicare cost-sharing amounts. The increased CMP amounts reflect technical corrections to the regulations. [42 C.F.R. § 405.520(c).] The regulations further provided for the imposition of CMPs for: (1) failure to bill outpatient therapy services or comprehensive outpatient rehabilitation services on an assignment-related basis; (2) failure to bill ambulance services on an assignment-related basis; (3) failure to provide an itemized statement for Medicare items and services to a Medicare beneficiary upon his/her request; and (4) failure of physicians or non-physician practitioners to provide diagnostic codes for items or services they furnish or failure to provide this information to the entity furnishing the item or service ordered by the practitioner. [*Final rule*, 66 FR 49544, Sept. 28, 2001.]

CMS assessments of CMPs. The Social Security Act provisions allow for the additional imposition of civil monetary penalties and assessments by the Centers for Medicaid and Medicare. The *CMS Manuals* provide examples of instances for which CMS may impose penalties for false or fraudulent program related activities. Specific provisions are provided in the *Program Integrity Manual*, Ch. 4, Pub. 100-08, for: (1) provider and supplier billing; (2) payment collection; (3) telephone solicitation of and contact with beneficiaries; and (4) beneficiary refund payments. [*Program Integrity Manual*, Ch. 4, Pub. 100-08, § 4.20.2.1; *State Operations Manual*, Ch. 7, Pub. 100-07, § 7510.]

Criminal Penalties

Benefit and payment applications. The following acts constitute federal health care program fraud and abuse:

(1) knowingly and willfully making, or causing to be made, any false statement or representation of a material fact in an application for a Medicare benefit or payment;

(2) knowingly and willfully making, or causing to be made, any false statement or representation of a material fact for use in determining rights to such a benefit or payment;

(3) having knowledge of the occurrence of any event affecting the initial or continued right to such a benefit or payment, or the initial or continued right to the benefit or payment of any other individual in whose behalf a benefit or payment has been applied for or received, and concealing or failing to disclose the event with the intent to fraudulently secure the benefit or payment in a greater amount than is due, or when no benefit or payment is authorized;

(4) having made application to receive a benefit or payment for the use and benefit of another and, having received it, knowingly and willfully converting the benefit or payment to a use other than for the use and benefit of the other person;

(5) presenting, or causing to be presented, a claim for a physician's service for which payment may be made under Medicare, knowing that the individual who furnished the service was not a licensed physician; or

(6) for a fee, knowingly and willfully counseling or assisting an individual to dispose of assets (including transfers in trust) in order for the individual to become eligible for medical assistance under a state Medicaid plan if the disposing of the assets results in the imposition of a period of ineligibility under Medicaid law. (Government authorities have stated that this prohibition may not be enforced; *Letter* from Janet Reno, Attorney General, to Congress-Speaker of the House, (March 11, 1998).) [Soc. Sec. Act § 1128B(a).]

The commission of any of the above acts warrants the Secretary's imposition of administrative sanctions of CMPs and assessments against, any person, organization, agency, or public or private entity that causes the making of false or improper claims and requests for payment from Medicare, Medicaid, or any other federal health care program. Violators may be fined up to $10,000.00 as a penalty for each item or service fraudulently claimed and assessed up to three times the amount claimed for each item or service. [Soc. Sec. Act § 1128A(a).] In addition, the Secretary *must* exclude individuals and entities from program participation for convictions related to the delivery of health care items or services, patient abuse or controlled substance abuse. [Soc. Sec. Act § 1128(a); 42 C.F.R. § 1001.101.] Additionally, fraudulent acts committed in connection with the furnishing of items or services for which payments are, or may be made under a federal health care program constitute a felony that, upon conviction, may be punishable by a fine of up to $25,000, or imprisoned for not more than five (5) years, or both. In the case of a false statement, representation, concealment, or conversion made by any other person (*e.g.* a beneficiary), the crime is classified as a misdemeanor, and upon conviction, the guilty person can be fined not more than $10,000, or imprisoned for not more than one year, or both. [Soc. Sec. Act § 1128B.]

Health care fraud. Anyone who knowingly and willfully executes or attempts to execute a scheme or artifice to defraud *any* federal health care benefit program, or to obtain, by false or fraudulent pretenses, representations, or promises, any of the money or property owned or controlled by *any* federal health care program in connection with the delivery of or payment for health care items, benefits, or services, shall be fined, or imprisoned for not

¶720

more than 10 years, or both. Violations resulting in serious bodily harm are punishable by a fine, or imprisonment for no more than 20 years, or both. If the violation results in death, however, the penalty is a fine, or imprisonment for any term of years or for life, or both. [18 U.S.C. § 1347.]

Theft or embezzlement. Anyone who knowingly and willfully embezzles, steals, or otherwise, without authority, converts or intentionally misapplies any of the moneys, funds, securities, premiums, credits, property, or other assets of a health care benefit program will be fined, or imprisoned for no more than 10 years, or both. If the value of the property does not exceed $100, however, the penalty is a fine, or imprisonment for no more than one year, or both. [18 U.S.C. § 669.]

Other criminal activities. Criminal penalties also have been established for anyone who:

(1) knowingly and willfully falsifies or conceals a material fact or makes a materially false or fraudulent statement or uses any materially false document knowing that it is false, in connection with the delivery of, or payment for, health care benefits [18 U.S.C. § 1035];

(2) willfully prevents, obstructs, misleads, or delays the communication to a criminal investigator of information or records related to a federal health care offense, or attempts to do so [18 U.S.C. § 1518]; and

(3) engages in laundering of monetary instruments related to a federal health care offense [18 U.S.C. § 1956(c)(7)(F)].

Kickbacks, bribes and rebates. Anyone who knowingly and willfully solicits or receives any remuneration (including any kickback, bribe, or rebate) directly or indirectly, overtly or covertly, in cash or in kind: (1) in return for referring an individual to a person for the furnishing or arranging for the furnishing of any item or service for which payment may be made in whole or in part under a federal health care program, or (2) in return for purchasing, leasing, ordering, or arranging for or recommending purchasing, leasing or ordering any good, facility, service, or item for which payment may be made in whole or in part under a federal health care program, will be guilty of a felony and upon conviction fined not more than $25,000, or imprisoned for not more than five years, or both. [Soc. Sec. Act § 1128B(b)(1).]

Anyone who knowingly and willfully offers or pays any remuneration (including any kickback, bribe, or rebate) directly or indirectly, overtly or covertly, in cash or in kind, to any person to induce someone: (1) to refer an individual to a person for the furnishing or arranging for the furnishing of any item or service for which payment may be made in whole or in part under a federal health care program, or (2) to purchase, lease, order, or arrange for or recommend purchasing, leasing, or ordering any good, facility, service, or item for which payment may be made in whole or in part under a federal health care program, will be guilty of a felony and, upon conviction, fined not more than $25,000, or imprisoned for not more than five years, or both. [Soc. Sec. Act § 1128B(b)(2).]

Neither of the above penalties applies to activities or arrangements that fully fall within one or more "safe harbors" that have been established by CMS (see below). Congress also has authorized the Secretary of HHS to identify additional payment and business practice safe-harbors that will not be treated as a criminal offense (i.e. kickbacks, bribes, rebates, or other activities that would unlawfully induce payments under the Medicare or Medicaid programs) and that will not serve as a basis for an exclusion under the Act. [Soc. Sec. Act § 1128B(b.] The Secretary may, from time to time, solicit public comment on any additionally suggested safe-harbors.

¶720

The scope of the anti-kickback statute applies to *any* federal health care program, which is defined to include any plan or program that provides health benefits, whether directly, through insurance, or otherwise, and includes a health insurance policy, a contract of a service benefit organization, and or a membership agreement with a health maintenance organization or other prepaid health plan. [Soc. Sec. Act §§ 1128B, 1128C(c).]

False statements concerning qualification of providers. Any person who knowingly and willfully makes, or causes to be made, or induces or seeks to induce the making of, any false statement or representation of a material fact with respect to the conditions or operation of any institution or facility to enable it to qualify (either upon initial certification or upon recertification) as a hospital, critical access hospital, skilled nursing facility, nursing facility, intermediate care facility for the mentally retarded, home health agency, Medicare Advantage (MA) organization or other entity for Medicare purposes will be guilty of a felony and, when convicted, will be fined not more than $25,000, or imprisoned for not more than five years, or both. [Soc. Sec. Act §§ 1128B(c), 1876(b).]

Violation of assignment agreements. As discussed at ¶ 831, a physician or supplier who agrees to the assignment method of reimbursement must agree to accept Medicare's payment as payment in full for his services and may charge the beneficiary only for the coinsurance and any unmet deductible. Similarly, there are other situations—*e.g.,* ambulatory surgical services (see ¶ 386) or diagnostic clinical laboratory tests performed in the physician's office (see ¶ 827)—under which a physician must agree to accept assignment for Medicare payment to be made. A physician or supplier who knowingly, willfully, and repeatedly violates assignment terms by improperly charging beneficiaries will be guilty of a misdemeanor and, when convicted, will be fined not more than $2,000, or imprisoned for not more than six months, or both. [Soc. Sec. Act § 1128B(e).]

False representations about Medicare. Anyone who makes or causes to be made a false representation concerning the requirements of the Medicare Act, knowing such representations to be false and intending to defraud, will be guilty of a misdemeanor. Conviction is punishable by a fine not to exceed $1,000, or by imprisonment not exceeding one year, or both. [Soc. Sec. Act § 1107(a).]

Misrepresentation. Anyone who, with the intent to elicit information as to the Social Security account number, date of birth, employment, wages, or benefits of any individual, (1) falsely represents being such individual or the individual's relative to the Secretary, or (2) falsely represents being an employee or agent of the United States to any person, will be guilty of a felony punishable by a fine not exceeding $10,000, or by imprisonment not exceeding five years, or both. [Soc. Sec. Act § 1107(b).]

"Medigap" policy violations. See ¶ 740.

Civil Money Penalties

In lieu of (or in addition to) criminal proceedings against a person or entity that has committed a fraudulent act, the Secretary is authorized to administratively impose a civil money penalty (CMP). The penalty provisions include *all* federal health care programs. Civil money penalty liability extends to persons contracting with excluded individuals or violating the anti-kickback statutes. The amount of the fine is up to $10,000 for each item or service fraudulently claimed for reimbursement, and no more than $50,000 for each violating act against the anti-kickback statutes. In addition to the penalty, the Secretary also is authorized to impose a damage assessment that is three times the amount of the claim, and a damage assessment not more than three times the total amount of remuneration offered, paid, solicited, or received under the anti-kickback statutes. [Soc. Sec. Act §§ 1128A, 1128B(b).]

OIG imposition of CMPs for drug discount card fraud. As of June 2004, the Office of Inspector General (OIG) has the authority to impose CMPs of up to $10,000 per violation against drug card sponsors who knowingly mislead the public, defraud beneficiaries, or misuse transitional assistance funds. CMS will continue to have authority for drug card sponsor violations that concern operational requirements not directly related to beneficiary protections.

Prohibited submission of claims. Fines may be imposed on a person who knowingly presents, or causes to be presented, a claim :

(1) for an item or service that the person knows, or should know, was not provided as claimed including any person who engages in a pattern or practice of presenting or causing to be presented a claim for an item or service that is based on a code that the person knows, or should know, will result in a greater payment than the code the person knows, or should know, is applicable to the item or service actually provided [Soc. Sec. Act § 1128A(a)(1)(A)], or was falsely or fraudulently claimed [Soc. Sec. Act § 1128A(a)(1)(B)];

(2) for a physician's service (or an item or service incident to such a service) by someone who the person knows, or should know, was not a licensed physician; obtained a license through misrepresentation; or misrepresented qualification as a specialist [Soc. Sec. Act § 1128A(a)(1)(C)];

(3) for an item or service furnished while the person was excluded from the program under which the claim was made [Soc. Sec. Act § 1128A(a)(1)(D)]; or

(4) for a pattern of medical or other items or services that the person knows or should know are not medically necessary. [Soc. Sec. Act §§ 1128A(a)(1)(E) and 1842(k).]

Overcharging. The same penalties may be imposed on a physician who knowingly submits a Medicare payment claim in violation of: (1) a Medicare assignment agreement (see ¶ 831), (2) a Medicare participating physician or supplier agreement (see ¶ 833), (3) the Medicare "limiting charge" (see ¶ 821), or (4) other Medicare actual charge restrictions (see ¶ 821). [Soc. Sec. Act §§ 1128A(a)(2), 1842(j)(2), 1848(g)(1).]

Influencing level of patient care. The same penalties (except that the $10,000 penalty may be increased to $15,000) may be imposed on a physician who knowingly gives or causes to be given to any person information concerning inpatient hospital services under Medicare that the physician knows, or should know, is false or misleading and could reasonably be expected to influence a decision concerning when to discharge a patient. [Soc. Sec. Act § 1128A(a)(3).]

Ownership or controlling interest of excluded person. Individuals who retain an ownership or controlling interest, or who remain officers or managing agents in a participating entity after having been excluded from program participation in Medicare or Medicaid, also are subject to civil penalty liability. [Soc. Sec. Act § 1128A(a)(4).]

Payment of remunerations to patients. A prohibition against offering inducements to Medicare- or Medicaid-eligible individuals also may be imposed on persons who offer or pay such individuals remuneration that is likely to influence them to order or receive items or services from a specific provider or supplier. [Soc. Sec. Act § 1128A(a)(5).] Remuneration includes the waiver of coinsurance and deductible amounts and the transfer of items or services for free or for other than fair market value. [Soc. Sec. Act § 1128A(i)(6).]

Contracting with excluded individuals. Under the Balanced Budget Act of 1997 (BBA) (PubLNo 105-33), persons contracting with individuals or entities that they know or should know have been excluded from participation in any federal or state health care program (see the "Exclusion" section below) are subject to civil money penalties. The contract must be for

¶720

the provision of items or services resulting in payment under such federal or state program. [Soc. Sec. Act § 1128A(a)(6).]

Kickbacks, bribes and rebates. Anyone who violates the Medicare anti-kickback statutes is liable, in addition to criminal penalties, for civil money penalties of no more than $50,000 for each act and a damage assessment of not more than three times the total amount of remuneration offered, paid, solicited, or received. Thus, persons may not knowingly and willfully solicit or receive any remuneration (including kickbacks, bribes, or rebates) in return for referrals or for purchasing items or services, and may not knowingly or willfully offer or pay any remuneration (including kickbacks, bribes, or rebates) to induce any person to make a referral or to purchase items or services without liability. The Anti-kickback Statute requires the legal element of intent for violations. [Soc. Sec. Act § 1128A(a)(7), 1128B(b).]

Inducement to limit care. A penalty of up to $2,000 may be imposed on a physician who knowingly accepts payment from a hospital or a critical access center as an inducement to limit or reduce care to a patient entitled to benefits under a federal or state health care plan. [Soc. Sec. Act § 1128A(b)(2).]

False certification of home health services. The civil money penalty provisions also prohibit physicians from knowingly certifying an individual for Medicare-covered home health care when the individual does not meet Medicare requirements. The penalty for a false certification may not exceed the greater of $5,000 or three times the amount of payments made. [Soc. Sec. Act § 1128A(b)(3)(A).]

Patient "dumping." Civil money penalties may be imposed on participating hospitals that fail to provide proper treatment to emergency room patients (whether or not the patients are Medicare beneficiaries). (See ¶ 730 for details.) [Soc. Sec. Act § 1867(d).]

A penalty of up to $5,000 may be imposed for each violation resulting from the misuse of Departmental, CMS, Medicare, or Medicaid words, letters, symbols, or emblems related to printed media, and a penalty of not more than $25,000 may be imposed in the case of such misuse related to a broadcast or telecast. [42 C.F.R. § 1003.103(d)(1).]

In determining the amount of the penalty assessed, the Secretary is required to take into account the nature of the claims and the circumstances under which they were presented, as well as the degree of culpability, history of prior offenses, financial condition of the person presenting the claim, and other matters that justice may require. [Soc. Sec. Act § 1128A(d).] If more than one person is responsible for presenting or causing a false claim to be presented, each person may be held liable for the penalty and assessment, but the aggregate amount of the assessment collected may not exceed the amount that could be assessed if only one person were responsible. [42 C.F.R. § 1003.102(d)(1).]

The procedures set forth in the regulations (42 C.F.R. §§ 1003.109—1003.127) provide persons liable for civil money penalties and assessments an opportunity for a hearing on the record. Judicial review of the Secretary's final determination can be obtained in the U.S. Court of Appeals. [Soc. Sec. Act § 1128A(e).]

Fraud and abuse control account. A "Health Care Fraud and Abuse Control Account" was established within the Federal Hospital Insurance Trust Fund, funded with criminal fines recovered from federal health care offenses, civil money penalties, amounts resulting from the forfeiture of property due to federal health care offenses, and damages and penalties levied in the prosecution of false claims. Account funds will be appropriated to fund the fraud and abuse enforcement efforts of OIG and other federal agencies. [Soc. Sec. Act § 1817(k).]

¶720

Fraud and abuse data collection program. OIG regulations implement the Health Care Integrity and Protection Data Bank (HIPDB). [*Final rule*, 64 FR 57740, Oct. 26, 1999.] HIPDB collects information regarding actions that are inconsistent with sound fiscal, business or medical practice. Reportable actions include civil judgments, criminal convictions, adverse licensing or certification decisions, and exclusions from any federal or state health care program. [*Final rule*, 64 FR 57740, Oct. 26, 1999.] HIPDB became operational for reporting information on November 22, 1999. All reportable actions from August 21, 1996, the effective date of the authorizing statute, must be submitted to the HIPDB web site at www.npdb-hipdb.com. HHS has imposed a $10 fee for self-queries to the data bank by health care practitioners, providers or suppliers to offset the labor costs for manual data input, sorting and responding to calls for Help-line assistance. [*Notice*, 64 FR 58851, Nov. 1, 1999.] In addition, the fee charged to authorized entities for each query to access the HIPDB has been dropped from $5 to $4.25. [*Notice*, 68 FR 19838, April 22, 2003.] The information is available to federal and state government agencies and is used in conjunction with the National Practitioner Data Bank. Settlements in which no finding of liability has been made are not reported. Failure to report adverse actions may result in a civil money penalty up to $25,000 per occurrence. [Soc. Sec. Act § 1128E.]

Administrative actions, such as limited training permits, limited licenses for telemedicine, fines or citations that do not restrict a practitioner's practice, or personnel actions for tardiness would not be reportable to the HIPDB. Certain kinds of actions or findings were not intended to be included within the range of reportable actions. The definition of "any other negative action or finding" was revised to accommodate this situations. The revised definition, however, would not exclude administrative fines, citations, corrective action plans, or other personnel actions that are (1) connected to the billing, provision or delivery of health care services, and (2) taken in conjunction with other licensure or certification actions such as revocation, suspension, censure, reprimand, probation, or surrender. The correction became effective on September 13, 2005. [*Corrective amendment to final rule*, 70 FR 53953, Sept. 13, 2005.]

Exclusion from Program Participation

Mandatory exclusion. Under the mandatory exclusion provisions of the Social Security Act, an individual or entity that has been convicted of any felony under federal or state law for an offense must be excluded from participation in *any* federal health care program. [Soc. Sec. Act § 1128(a).]

Five-year exclusion for one conviction. In the case of a felony conviction related to:

(1) program-related crime,

(2) patient abuse,

(3) health care fraud, or

(4) a controlled substance,

the minimum period of exclusion is five years. [Soc. Sec. Act § 1128(a).] On the basis of a state's request, however, the Secretary may waive the exclusion in the case of an individual or entity that is the sole community physician or sole source of essential specialized services in a community. [Soc. Sec. Act § 1128(c)(3)(B).]

Ten-year exclusion for two convictions. For health care providers convicted a second time of a health care-related criminal offense on or after August 5, 1997, for which the provider is subject to mandatory exclusion, the penalty imposed will be a minimum ten-year exclusion from any federal health-care program. [Soc. Sec. Act § 1128(c)(3)(G)(i).]

¶720

Permanent exclusion for three convictions. The sanction is a permanent exclusion from any federal health care program for a health care provider convicted, on or after August 5, 1997, of a health care-related criminal offense for which the provider is subject to mandatory exclusion, and who has on two or more previous occasions been subject to exclusion for health care-related criminal convictions. [Soc. Sec. Act § 1128(c)(3)(G)(ii).]

Permissive exclusion. The Secretary *may* exclude individuals or entities that committed an offense resulting in a conviction under federal or state law, related to:

(1) misdemeanor fraud;

(2) obstruction of a criminal investigation; or

(3) misdemeanor manufacture, distribution, prescription, or dispensing of a controlled substance

for a minimum period of three years from any federal health care program, unless the Secretary designates a shorter period on the basis of mitigating circumstances, or a longer period based on the presence of aggravating factors. [Soc. Sec. Act § 1128(c)(3)(D).]

The Secretary also may exclude any individual or entity whose health care-related license has been revoked or suspended. The minimum period of exclusion is the same time period for which the license revocation or suspension is effective. [Soc. Sec. Act § 1128(c)(3)(E).]

Similarly, in the case of an exclusion or suspension under a federal or state health care program, the minimum period of exclusion is the period for which the individual or entity is excluded from the federal or state health program. [Soc. Sec. Act § 1128(c)(3)(E).]

The Secretary's permissive exclusionary authority against entities controlled by sanctioned individuals is considerable. Individuals are subject to exclusion for transferring ownership of a health care provider to a family member or member of the household in anticipation of, or following, a health care-related criminal conviction. Although the individual or entity that previously had at least a five percent ownership interest in the provider could no longer be described as having such interest, the provider may still be excluded by the Secretary. [Soc. Sec. Act § 1128(b)(8).] A member of the household is anyone sharing a common abode as part of a single family home, including domestic employees, but not roomers or boarders. [Soc. Sec. Act § 1128(j)(2).]

Other conduct subject to the Secretary's permissive exclusion authority includes:

(1) the submission of claims for excessive charges or unnecessary services, and failure to furnish medically necessary services;

(2) activities subject to civil money and criminal penalties;

(3) failure to disclose required information, requested information on subcontractors or suppliers, or payment information;

(4) failure to grant immediate access;

(5) failure to take corrective action;

(6) default on health education loan or scholarship obligations; and

(7) ownership or controlling interest in a sanctioned entity. This category of individuals subject to permissive exclusion affects any individual with a direct or indirect ownership or controlling interest in an entity that has been mandatorily excluded or permissively excluded for a conviction related to fraud, obstruction of an investigation, or a controlled substance. [Soc. Sec. Act § 1128(b).]

¶720

A minimum one-year exclusion period exists for providers sanctioned for failure to comply with statutory obligations related to quality of care. [Soc. Sec. Act § 1156(b)(1).]

The Secretary also has authority to refuse to enter into Medicare agreements with Part A or Part B health care providers who have been convicted of a felony, under federal or state law, that the Secretary determines to be detrimental to the Medicare program or its beneficiaries. The Secretary may also refuse to renew or may terminate an existing agreement for the same reasons. [Soc. Sec. Act § 1866(b)(2).] The Secretary's authority to refuse extends to all Medicare participating providers; some of the providers are specifically noted in the following statutes: physicians and suppliers [Soc. Sec. Act § 1842(h)(8)], and MA organizations. [Soc. Sec. Act §§ 1857(a), 1857(c)(2), 1857(c)(5), 1857(h).]

When a practitioner is excluded from Medicare participation, notice of the exclusion will be given to: the public; affected beneficiaries; other government agencies; quality improvement organizations; hospitals, nursing homes, managed care organizations and other providers; contractors; medical societies and other professional organizations; and state and local authorities responsible for licensing and the National Practitioner Data Bank. [Soc. Sec. Act § 1128(d)-(e); 42 C.F.R. § 1001.2006.]

If a patient submits claims for services furnished by an excluded practitioner, Medicare will pay the first claim submitted. It then will notify the patient that the practitioner is excluded and that, effective 15 days after the date of the notice or after the effective date of the exclusion, whichever is later, no more claims for services furnished by the practitioner will be paid. [42 C.F.R. § 1001.1901(c).]

Additionally, payment will be made for up to 30 days after the date of the exclusion for (1) inpatient hospital and skilled nursing facility services furnished to a patient who was admitted before the effective date of the exclusion, and (2) home health and hospice care furnished under a plan established before the effective date of the exclusion. [42 C.F.R. § 1001.1901(c).]

Safe Harbors

The prohibition against giving or receiving kickbacks, bribes, and rebates (see "Criminal Penalties" above) is worded broadly. It arguably prohibits some ostensibly non-problematic business activities in which some form of remuneration is received by the referring physician. The purpose of the prohibition is to prevent only truly abusive arrangements that could increase costs to the Medicare program and the patient.

The Office of Inspector General (OIG) has issued rules, called "safe harbors," that immunize various payment practices and business arrangements from criminal prosecution or civil sanctions under the anti-kickback provisions of the law.

The safe harbor list is not intended to be complete—activities not on the list are not necessarily prohibited—but the existence of the list does raise a red flag that non-listed activities might not be "safe." Because of the complicated nature of the safe harbor rules, it is recommended that practitioners consult an attorney when they have questions regarding any potentially problematic business arrangement.

Business activities that are included in the safe harbor list include:

(1) investment interests in (a) large publicly traded companies (worth at least $50 million) and (b) small companies (if certain criteria are satisfied);

(2) space rental;

(3) equipment rental;

(4) personal services and management contracts;

¶720

(5) sale of a practice;

(6) referral services by an organization whose primary business is to refer the public to practitioners;

(7) purchases made for a practitioner by a group purchasing organization;

(8) manufacturers' warranties;

(9) sellers' discounts;

(10) payments made by an employer to an employee;

(11) waiver of the Medicare deductible or coinsurance, under limited circumstances;

(12) increased coverage, reduced cost-sharing amounts, or reduced premium amounts offered by health plans;

(13) price reductions offered to health plans;

(14) payments to induce a practitioner to relocate to a designated Health Professional Shortage Area (HPSA);

(15) subsidies for obstetrical malpractice insurance premiums to practitioners in an HPSA;

(16) investments by providers into their solo or group practices;

(17) payments between a cooperative hospital service organization and its participating hospital;

(18) payments made as an investment in, or a dividend from, certain types of ambulatory surgical centers (ASC);

(19) limited agreements for referral of patients for specialty services;

(20) price reductions offered to eligible managed care organizations (MCOs); and

(21) price reductions offered to MCOs by contractors that assume substantial financial risk.

(22) ambulance restocking arrangements between hospitals or receiving facilities and ambulance providers. [42 C.F.R. § 1001.952]

A *Proposed rule*, published on September 25, 2002, would expand the existing safe harbor for certain waivers of beneficiary coinsurance and deductible amounts to policyholders of Medicare SELECT supplemental insurance. Waivers of coinsurance and deductible amounts under Part A and B owed by beneficiaries of the Medicare SELECT would be covered if the waiver was in accordance with the price reduction agreement covering such policyholders between the Medicare SELECT issuer and the provider or supplier offering the waiver and the waiver is otherwise permitted under the Medicare program. [*Proposed rule*, 67 FR 60202, Sept. 25, 2002.] A *Final rule* expanding this safe harbor has yet to be issued.

Electronic prescribing technology. A new safe harbor under the anti-kickback statute has been created for certain arrangements involving the provision of electronic prescribing technology and electronic health records. The safe harbor, which was required under the Medicare Modernization Act of 2003 (MMA)(PubLNo 108-73), would protect arrangements involving hospitals, group practices, prescription drug plan sponsors, and Medicare Advantage organizations. Additionally, the safe harbor would provide protections for certain non-monetary remunerations to recipients in the form of hardware, software, or other information technology (IT), as well IT training services for transmitting and receiving electronic drug prescription information. Donors would not be permitted to bundle software for general

¶720

office management, billing, scheduling, or other software with the electronic prescribing features if any purpose of the software package were to induce referrals. Items used only occasionally for electronic prescribing would not be protected. The proposed safe harbor also would apply as an exception under the physician self-referral prohibition (Stark laws). [*Proposed rule*, 70 FR 59182, Oct. 11, 2005.]

Federally Qualified Health Centers A safe harbor was also created for certain agreements involving health centers that receive section 330 funding under the Public Health Service Act and the Health Centers Consolidation Act of 1996 (PubLNo 104-299). Section 330 grant recipients are community based health organizations that provide cost effective care for communities with limited access to health care resources. The health centers traditionally serve low-income health care beneficiaries and medically underserved populations, including migratory and seasonal agricultural workers, the homeless, and residents of public housing. [42 U.S.C. 254b(a)(l).] Congress intended to permit some health centers to accept certain remuneration that might otherwise implicate the anti-kickback statute in instances where the remuneration furthers one of the core purposes of a federal health center's programs of ensuring available and quality health care services to otherwise under-served populations. The creation of the safe harbor is required under section 431(b) of the MMA. The new safe harbor, however, will not protect remuneration between a health center and an individual or entity that does not provide services, items, goods, donations, or loans to the health center. Any arrangements between a health center and an individual or entity will be evaluated on a case-by-case basis. [*Proposed rule*, 70 FR 38081, July 1, 2005.]

The Health Insurance Portability and Accountability Act of 1996 (HIPAA) (PubLNo 104-191) requires the Secretary to solicit, annually, public proposals and recommendations for new and existing safe harbors. [Soc. Sec. Act § 1128D(a)(1)(A).]

"Stark" Law: Physician Self-Referral Prohibitions

Under the physician self-referral prohibitions, known as the "Stark" laws (which are named for Rep. Fortney "Pete" Stark, D-Cal., the sponsor of the underlying laws), a physician or a physician's immediate family member may not refer a Medicare beneficiary for certain types of services or goods to an entity (such as a laboratory, clinic, or therapy center) in which the physician or a member of the physician's immediate family has a financial or compensation interest.

"Stark I" prohibits physicians from ordering clinical laboratory services for Medicare patients from an entity with which the physician has a financial relationship. In 1993 the "Stark II" law was passed by Congress. Stark II expanded on Stark I by extending the prohibition against self-referrals beyond clinical laboratory services to other designated health services (DHS). The list of designated health services includes the following:

- clinical laboratory services,
- physical and occupational therapy and speech-language pathology services,
- radiology and certain other imaging services,
- radiation therapy services and supplies,
- durable medical equipment,
- parenteral and enteral nutrients,
- prosthetics and orthotics,
- home health services,
- outpatient prescription drugs, and

¶720

- inpatient and outpatient hospital services. [Soc. Sec. Act § 1877 (h)(6); 42 C.F.R. § 411.351.]

Phase I of the Stark II regulations became effective January 4, 2002, except for the home health referral prohibition, which became effective April 6, 2001. Phase I provides key definitions and provisions directly addressing group practices under the self-referral prohibition. Phase I also includes general exceptions that protect physician ownership and compensation arrangements, including an in-office ancillary services exception. [*Final rule*, 66 FR 856, Jan. 4, 2001; *Final rule*, 66 FR 8771, Feb. 2, 2001.]

In July 2004, Phase II of the physician self-referral prohibitions (Stark II) was enacted. The regulations reflected that additional exceptions to the physician self-referral laws and serves to further broaden the scope of physician self-referral violations beyond the prohibition against physician (and immediate family member) financial ownership and compensation relationships in clinical laboratory service entities.

Definition of financial relationship. For purposes of the physician self-referral prohibition statute, a "financial relationship" includes a physician's or a physician's immediate family member's ownership, investment interest or compensation arrangements (i.e., contractual arrangements) in a DHS facility. Violations of the statute are punishable by the denial of payment for all DHS claims, refund of amounts collected for DHS claims, and CMPs for knowing violations of the prohibition. [42 C.F.R. § 411.] An ownership or investment interest also may be through equity, debt or other means and includes an interest in an entity that holds an ownership or investment interest in any entity providing the DHS. [42 C.F.R. § 411.354.]

New limited exceptions and other updated provisions. In addition to the broader language of Stark II (Phase II), the regulations provide for additional limited exceptions. Specifically, an exception for community-wide health information systems was established, as well as limited exceptions to allow physicians to refer business to immediate family members in rural areas, under certain circumstances, where no other physician is available. Additional exceptions were created to exempt hospital payments to retain physicians who would otherwise leave a health professional shortage area. Finally, exceptions were created for Medicaid managed care plans, professional courtesy arrangements, certain inadvertent and temporary lapses in compliance with an existing exception, and charitable contributions by physicians to entities that furnish designated health services. The hospital ownership exception has been revised to reflect the new 18-month moratorium on physician ownership of specialty hospitals, which was recently enacted by the Medicare Modernization Act of 2003 (MMA) (PubLNo 108-173). [*Interim final rule*, 69 FR 16053, March 26, 2003.]

Set-in-advance compensation arrangements. In June 2004, CMS released a final rule, which modified a March 26, 2004 final rule regarding the last sentence of 42 C.F.R. § 411.454(d)(1), which discusses "set in advance" compensation arrangements. Stark II (Phase II) would permit some physician hospital compensation arrangements to be "set in advance" if compensation calculations are established in advance and do not change over the course of the arrangement in any manner that reflects the volume or value of referrals or other business generated by the referring physician." [*Final rule*, 69 FR 35529, June 25, 2004.]

Gainsharing arrangements. Gainsharing programs refer to arrangements in which a hospital provides an incentive or a percentage share of savings in the hospital's costs for patient care that are attributable, in part, to the physician's efforts. While properly structured gainsharing arrangements can serve legitimate business and medical purposes, such as increasing efficiency, reducing waste, and, potentially increasing a hospital's profitability, the language of section 1128A(b)(1) of the Social Security Act prohibits tying a physician's compensation for services to reductions or limitations in items or services provided to patients under the physician's care. Hospitals that make (and physicians that receive) payments to directly or indirectly induce a physician to reduce or limit items or services furnished to Medicare or Medicaid beneficiaries are liable for CMPs of up to $2,000 per patient. Additionally, the anti-kickback statute may be implicated if (1) a gainsharing arrangement is intended to influence physicians to refer healthy patients to a particular hospital in exchange for gainsharing payments, or (2) in cases where the arrangement requires the physician to steer patients who have higher medical costs to hospitals that do not offer gainsharing payments. The statute also may be implicated if a hospital offers a cost-sharing program with the intent to foster physician loyalty and attract more referrals. [*OIG Supplemental Compliance Program Guidance for Hospitals*, Jan. 01, 2005.]

Speciality hospitals. As part of the updates to the prohibitions against physician self-referrals and effective on December 8, 2003 through June 8, 2005, a physician's ownership and investment interest in specialty hospitals will not qualify for the "whole hospital" exception under the physical self-referral laws. The change in exception policies also applies to specialty hospitals located in rural areas. Prior to the MMA the "whole hospital" exception of the physician self-referral law allowed physicians to refer Medicare patients to a hospital in which they had an ownership or investment interest as long as the physicians were authorized to perform services at the hospital, and their ownership or investment interest was in the hospital itself and not a subdivision of the hospital. Certain hospitals that offer specialized services are not "specialty hospitals" for purposes of section 507 of the MMA. Physician investment in and referrals to the following types of hospitals are permitted:

(1) psychiatric hospitals;

(2) rehabilitation hospitals;

(3) children's hospitals;

(4) long-term care hospitals;

(5) certain cancer hospitals; and

(6) existing specialty hospitals that satisfy the grandfather provision of section 507 of the MMA (entitled "grandfathered specialty hospitals"). [*One-Time Notification Manual*, Pub. No. 100-20, Transmittal No. 62, March 19, 2004.]

Stark law penalties. The penalties for making prohibited self-referrals includes any of the following:

(1) denial of payment for the DHS;

(2) refund of any money collected from the government for the DHS;

(3) imposition of a civil money penalty of up to $15,000 for each DHS for which a claim was submitted; and

(4) imposition of a civil money penalty of up to $100,000 and exclusion from participation in Medicare and other federal health care programs for circumvention schemes or arrangements that the physician or entity knows or should know violates the self-referral prohibitions. [42 C.F.R. § 411.353.]

OIG advisory opinions. To assist in this complex area, § 4314 of the BBA mandated that CMS provide advisory opinions, when requested, regarding the applicability of the Stark prohibitions to specific factual scenarios. This mandate expired in the fall of 2000, but in accordance with § 543 of the Benefits Improvement and Protection Act of 2000 (BIPA) (PubLNo 106-554), as of January 5, 2001, the OIG is again accepting advisory opinion requests.

¶720

Voluntary Compliance Guidelines

OIG has issued voluntary compliance guidelines to assist providers in designing and implementing programs to prevent and detect activities that do not comply with the requirements of federal and state health programs. OIG has released guidelines for hospitals, clinical laboratories, home health agencies, third-party medical billing companies, durable medical equipment suppliers, MA organizations, hospices, nursing facilities, and individual and small group physician practices.

OIG has released a voluntary provider self-disclosure protocol that is intended to encourage providers to make voluntary disclosures that will help resolve possible violations of federal criminal, civil, or administrative laws. [*Notice*, 63 FR 58399, Oct. 30, 1998.] Providers should conduct an initial assessment to substantiate that there is a problem with noncompliance with program requirements before making a disclosure to the OIG. When False Claims Act liability results from a disclosure, OIG may be more flexible in considering the terms of a Corporate Integrity Agreement (CIA). [*OIG Letter, Recommendations for Provider Self-Disclosure,* March 9, 2000.]

[¶ 730] Provider Participation Agreements

A "provider of services" for purposes of signing a participation agreement includes a hospital, a critical access hospital, a skilled nursing facility (SNF), a home health agency, hospice, a comprehensive outpatient rehabilitation facility, a fund for payments for physicians and other practitioners provided by hospitals, (but only with respect to outpatient physical and occupational therapy or speech pathology services) an eligible clinic, a rehabilitation agency, a public health agency, or a community health center with respect to partial hospitalization services. [Soc. Sec. Act §§ 1861(u), 1866(e).]

In addition, although they are not "providers of services" under the law, ambulatory surgical centers (see ¶ 386), rural health clinics (see ¶ 382), free-standing renal dialysis facilities, organ procurement organizations, and histocompatibility laboratories must sign an agreement in order to participate in the Medicare program. [Soc. Sec. Act §§ 1832(a)(2)(F)(i), 1861(aa)(2), 1881(b)(2)(A).]

Essentials of Provider Agreements

A provider of services is qualified to participate in the Medicare program if it files with the Secretary an agreement:

(1) to limit its charges to beneficiaries to the costs of noncovered services and to the deductible, coinsurance, and other charges allowed under federal law (see "Allowable Charges" below);

(2) to make adequate provision for the refund of amounts incorrectly collected from beneficiaries;

(3) to disclose the hiring of any individual who, at any time during the year preceding employment, was employed in a managerial, accounting, auditing, or similar capacity by the provider's Medicare intermediary or carrier;

(4) to release, upon request, patient data to a quality improvement organization (QIO, formerly PRO) (see ¶ 710) reviewing the provider;

(5) in the case of inpatient hospital services, to either furnish directly or make arrangements for all Medicare care and services (other than physician and certain healthcare practitioner services) (see ¶ 635);

(6) in the case of inpatient hospital services, to maintain an agreement with a QIO for the review of admissions, quality, and diagnostic information, and in the case of skilled

nursing facilities, home health agencies, and outpatient hospital services, to maintain an agreement with a QIO for review of services and beneficiary complaints regarding quality (see ¶ 710);

(7) to bill other primary payers before billing Medicare in accordance with statutory and regulatory requirements concerning alternate insurance coverage (see ¶ 636);

(8) in the case of hospitals with emergency departments, to meet the responsibilities imposed by the law with respect to treating emergency cases (see below under "Treatment of Emergency Cases");

(9) in the case of hospitals, to participate in the CHAMPUS and CHAMPVA programs (see ¶ 607), effective January 1, 1987;

(10) in the case of hospitals, to provide beneficiaries with a written notice, at the time of the beneficiaries' admission to the facility, explaining the beneficiary's right to Medicare benefits (see below);

(11) in the case of hospitals, to make available to beneficiaries directories of participating physicians in the area and to identify any qualified participating physicians in the area whenever a referral is made to a non-participating physician;

(12) in the case of hospitals and SNFs, to accept as payment in full any payments made by risk-basis HMOs (see ¶ 740) on behalf of their Medicare enrollees if the payments made are at Medicare levels; and

(13) in the case of home health agencies, to offer to furnish catheters, catheter supplies, ostomy bags, and supplies related to ostomy care to any individual who needs them as part of the provision of health services. [Soc. Sec. Act § 1866(a)(1); 42 C.F.R. § 489.20.]

Effective March 25, 2003, hospitals must also develop and maintain a quality assessment and performance improvement (QAPI) program. QAPI focuses provider efforts on the actual care delivered to patients, the performance of the hospital as an organization, and the impact of treatment furnished by the hospital on the health status of its patients. The QAPI program is not designed to measure a hospital's quality, but is rather a minimum requirement that the hospital systematically examine its quality and implement specific improvement projects on an ongoing basis. The QAPI program should include all activities required for measuring quality of care and maintaining it at acceptable levels. [*Final rule*, 68 FR 3435, Jan. 24, 2003.] CMS will not require Medicare Advantage (MA) organizations to implement a QAPI project in 2005, instead, MA organizations must undertake a project of their own choosing or participate in a local marketplace initiative. [*CMS Notice*, March 5, 2004.]

Treatment of Emergency Cases—Antidumping Rules

In its oversight of the national healthcare system, Congress received testimony that some hospitals have engaged in the practice of "patient dumping"—refusing to treat indigent individuals in their emergency rooms and sending them to other hospitals (usually public hospitals) that will treat them. To prevent these practices, Congress passed the Emergency Medical Treatments and Active Labor Act (EMTALA). Medicare statutes require that each provider agreement include a clause requiring the provider to comply with EMTALA. [Soc. Sec. Act § § 1866(a)(1)(I), 1867.]

Under this "antidumping" provision, a hospital must provide for an appropriate medical screening examination (within the capability of the hospital's emergency department) of any individual (*whether or not that individual is a Medicare beneficiary*) who comes to the emergency department and requests a medical examination or treatment. The hospital's emergency department is required to determine whether an emergency medical condition exists or whether the individual is in active labor. The hospital may not delay the examination or treatment in order to inquire as to the individual's method of payment or insurance status. [Soc. Sec. Act §§ 1867(a), 1867(h).]

If a hospital knowingly and willfully, or negligently, fails to handle emergency treatment cases, the hospital may have its provider agreement with Medicare terminated. In addition, the Secretary may impose civil money penalties of up to $50,000 (or not more than $25,000 in the case of a hospital with less than 100 beds) per violation on a participating hospital that knowingly violates the emergency treatment portion of its provider agreement. An identical civil money penalty may be imposed on the responsible physician in the hospital. Finally, the law provides for civil actions against a hospital (but not against physicians) by (1) any individual who suffers personal harm as a direct result of a participating hospital's violations, and (2) any medical facility that suffers a financial loss as a direct result of a participating hospital's violations. There is a two-year statute of limitations for civil actions under the provisions of this law. [Soc. Sec. Act § 1867(d).]

If an emergency medical condition exists (if the patient's health is in serious jeopardy or if there is a reasonable likelihood of serious impairment to bodily functions or of serious dysfunction of any bodily organ or part) or if a pregnant woman is in labor, the hospital must provide either (1) such further medical examination and treatment as may be required to stabilize the patient's medical condition or provide for treatment of the labor, or (2) transfer the individual to another medical facility if such a transfer is appropriate. [Soc. Sec. Act § 1867(b)(1).] If the patient refuses to be treated or does not consent to an appropriate transfer, the hospital will be deemed to have met its obligations under its provider agreement. State agencies may include medical record reviews, policy and procedure reviews, and staff interviews in investigations of antidumping violations. [Soc. Sec. Act §§ 1867(b)(2), 1867(b)(3).]

Emergency room services provided to screen and stabilize a Medicare beneficiary furnished after January 1, 2004, will be evaluated as reasonable and necessary on the basis of the information available to the treating physician or practitioner at the time the services were ordered. The evaluation as to whether the item or service was reasonable and necessary will include the patient's presenting symptoms or complaint and not the patient's principal diagnosis. The Secretary will not be able to consider the frequency with which the item or service was provided to the patient before or after the time of admission or visit. [Soc. Sec. Act § 1867.]

The transfer of an emergency room patient who has not been properly treated, as described above, is not appropriate unless the patient (or a person acting on the patient's behalf) requests a transfer in writing or a physician has certified that the medical benefits to be obtained from appropriate medical treatment outweigh the risks of transfer and the receiving facility has the space and qualified personnel for treating the patient. The receiving hospital must agree to accept the patient, and the hospital must be provided with all relevant medical records from the transferring hospital. Participating hospitals with specialized facilities cannot refuse to accept a patient who needs those facilities. The transfer must be effectuated by qualified personnel using appropriately equipped transportation. [Soc. Sec. Act § 1867(c).]

Hospitals are required to maintain records on transferred patients for five years. They also are required to maintain a list of physicians who are on call for duty after the initial examination to provide treatment necessary to stabilize an individual with an emergency medical condition. Each hospital must post a sign in its emergency department specifying patients' rights with respect to examination and treatment for emergency medical conditions and women in labor. The hospital must also maintain a central log of individual's who come to the dedicated emergency department seeking treatment and indicate the outcomes of that patients treatment. [Soc. Sec. Act §§ 1866(a)(1)(I), 1866(a)(1)(N)(iii); *CMS Letter to State Survey Agency Directors*, S&C-04-34, May, 13, 2004.]

The Office of Inspector General (OIG) and CMS have issued a special advisory bulletin stating that Medicare-participating hospitals must not delay required screening and stabilizing emergency treatment for managed care enrollees to obtain prior authorization from managed care plans. The bulletin recommends the following "best practices" to help hospitals ensure compliance with the law: (1) the hospital should not seek, or direct a patient to seek, authorization to provide screening or stabilizing services from the individual's health plan or insurance company until after the hospital has provided medical screening and necessary stabilization treatment; (2) a hospital should not delay a medical screening examination or necessary stabilizing treatment to prepare an Advanced Beneficiary Notice and obtain a beneficiary signature; (3) a hospital should ensure that either a physician or other qualified medical personnel provides an appropriate medical screening examination to all individuals seeking emergency care; (4) if a patient inquires about financial obligations for emergency services, the patient should be clearly informed that, regardless of the patient's ability to pay, the hospital will provide a medical screening and stabilizing treatment; and (5) if an individual intends to leave the hospital prior to the screening examination, a hospital should offer the individual further medical examination and treatment, inform the individual of the benefits of such examination and treatment, and take all reasonable steps to obtain the individual's written informed consent to refuse such examination and treatment. [*Notice*, 64 FR 61353, Nov. 10, 1999.]

QIO review. Except in the case where a delay would jeopardize the health and safety of individuals, the Secretary is required to request a quality improvement organization (QIO) review before making a compliance determination that would terminate a hospital's Medicare participation because of EMTALA violations. A period of five days is allowed for review, and the QIO must provide a copy of the report on its findings to the hospital or physician involved. [Soc. Sec. Act § 1867(d)(3).]

Notifying Beneficiaries of Medicare Rights

Hospitals are required to provide each Medicare beneficiary with a written statement (using language approved by the Secretary) explaining the beneficiary's Medicare rights. The rights explained must include: (1) rights to inpatient hospital services and post-hospital services; (2) the circumstances under which the beneficiary will and will not be liable for charges for a continued stay at the hospital; (3) the beneficiary's right to appeal a determination that a continued inpatient hospital stay is not covered (including practical steps to initiate such an appeal); and (4) the beneficiary's liability for payment for services if such a determination is upheld on appeal. This statement must be provided to the beneficiary at the time of his admission to the hospital. [Soc. Sec. Act § 1866(a)(1)(M).]

Advance Directives

Hospitals and other healthcare facilities must maintain written policies and procedures relating to advance directives (a written instruction, such as a living will or durable power of attorney for health care), which express a patient's wishes relating to the provision of care when the individual is incapacitated. Each facility must (1) inform Medicare and Medicaid patients of their rights under state law to make an advance directive, and (2) explain the written policies of the organization respecting the implementation of such rights. [Soc. Sec. Act §§ 1866(a)(1)(Q), 1866(f).]

¶730

Allowable Charges

As explained above, a provider agreement requires a provider of services to limit its charges to beneficiaries to the costs of noncovered services and to the deductible, coinsurance, and copayment charges allowed under federal law and regulations. Under these laws and regulations, the provider may charge a beneficiary the following:

(1) *Part A inpatient hospital deductible and coinsurance,* which consist of: (a) the amount of the inpatient hospital deductible or, if less, the actual charges for the services (see ¶ 221); (b) the amount of inpatient hospital coinsurance applicable for each day the individual is furnished inpatient hospital services after the 60th day during a benefit period (see ¶ 224); and (c) the post-hospital extended care services coinsurance amount (see ¶ 242). [42 C.F.R. §§ 489.30–489.32.]

(2) *Part B deductible and coinsurance,* which consist of an annual deductible, a coinsurance of 20 percent of the Medicare-approved Part B payment amount in excess of that deductible (see ¶ 335 for further details and exceptions), and a monthly premium. [Soc. Sec. Act § 1833(b).] For outpatient hospital services, allowable deductible charges depend on whether the hospital can determine the beneficiary's deductible status.

(3) *Blood deductible,* which consists of charges for the first three pints of blood or units of packed red blood cells furnished during a calendar year. Charges may not exceed the provider's customary charge. No charge may be made for any whole blood or packed red cells that are replaced by or on behalf of the beneficiary. If the charge exceeds the cost to the provider, that excess will be deducted from any Medicare payments due the provider (See ¶ 223.). [Soc. Sec. Act § 1833(b).]

(4) For costlier services *requested* by a beneficiary, the difference between the provider's customary charges for services covered under Medicare and the costlier services may be charged. Whenever a provider is permitted to charge for an item or service, it may not charge the individual or another person more than the amount customarily charged by the provider for such an item or service. [Soc. Sec. Act § 1866(a)(2)(B).] The provider is required to notify the intermediary of any amounts collected from or on behalf of a beneficiary. [42 C.F.R. § 489.35.]

Deposits and Prepayment Requests

A provider agreement contains specific requirements concerning prepayment. [42 C.F.R. § 489.22.] Under these provisions, the provider agrees not to:

(1) require an individual entitled to hospital insurance benefits to prepay in part or in whole for inpatient services as a condition of admittance, except where it is clear upon admission that payment under Part A cannot be made;

(2) deny covered inpatient services to an eligible individual on the ground of inability or failure to pay a requested amount at or before admission;

(3) evict, or threaten to evict, an individual for inability to pay a deductible or a coinsurance amount required under Medicare; and

(4) charge an individual for (a) an agreement to admit or readmit the individual on some specified future date for covered inpatient services, or (b) failure to remain an inpatient for any agreed-upon length of time, or (c) failure to give advance notice of departure from the provider's facilities.

Providers must not require advance payment of the inpatient deductible or coinsurance as a condition of admission. Additionally, providers may not require that the beneficiary prepay any Part B charges as a condition of admission, except where prepayment from non-

¶730

Medicare patients is required. In such cases, only the deductible and coinsurance may be collected. [*Medicare Claims Processing Manual*, CMS Pub. 100–04, Ch. 2, § 10.3.] A hospice is prohibited from discontinuing care to a patient because of the inability of the patient to pay. [Soc. Sec. Act § 1861(dd)(2)(D).]

Termination of Provider Agreements

A provider may terminate its participation in the Medicare program voluntarily or its participation may be terminated by the Secretary for cause. [Soc. Sec. Act § 1866(b).]

In general, no Medicare payment will be made to a provider after the effective date of the termination. However, in the case of inpatient hospital services (including inpatient psychiatric hospital services) and skilled nursing facility services, payments may be made for up to 30 days for services furnished to an individual who is admitted to the institution before the effective date of the termination. Similarly, home health services and hospice care furnished under a plan established before the termination date of the participation agreement will be covered for up to 30 days after termination. [Soc. Sec. Act §§ 1128(c)(2), 1866(b)(3); 42 C.F.R. § 489.55.]

[¶ 740] "Medigap" Insurance

The federal government has developed standardized packages for private health insurance policies sold as supplements to Medicare coverage. These "Medigap policies" are not needed, and would be unusable if Medicare benefits are obtained under Medicare Advantage organizations. Congress felt that these Medigap policies needed to be regulated because evidence indicated that the companies marketing these policies often were guilty of unethical sales practices and other abuses. Furthermore, it was found that the policies themselves often contained ineffective coverage or duplicated coverage already provided under Medicare.[Soc. Sec. Act §§ 1882(g)(1), 1882(o)(1).]

Preexisting conditions. Issuance of Medigap policies is guaranteed without a preexisting condition exclusion for the following Medicare beneficiaries:

(1) persons whose coverage under an employee welfare plan terminates;

(2) persons enrolled in a Medicare Advantage plan (see ¶ 400 *et seq.*) who disenroll for permissible reasons (plan termination or a move out of the plan area);

(3) persons enrolled in risk-or cost-based HMOs or other qualifying plan (see below) who disenroll for permissible reasons;

(4) persons whose enrollment in a Medigap policy ceases because of insurer bankruptcy or insolvency;

(5) persons previously enrolled under a Medigap policy who terminate to participate for the first time in a Medicare Advantage, HMO, or other qualifying plan and subsequently terminate within 12 months [Soc. Sec. Act § 1882(s)];

(6) persons previously enrolled in a Medigap policy who are enrolled in Medicare Advantage and are terminated involuntarily within the first 12 months from such an enrollment and who, without an intervening enrollment, enroll with a similar organization, provider, plan or program (for whom the subsequent enrollment is considered an initial enrollment, such as in (5) [Soc. Sec. Act § 1882(s)(3)(F)]; and

(7) persons who enroll in Medicare Advantage or in a PACE Program under § 1894 of the Social Security Act when first reaching Medicare eligibility but then disenroll within 12 months (see ¶ 400 *et seq.*). [Soc. Sec. Act § 1882(s).]

The preexisting condition exclusion may not be imposed during the six-month initial enrollment period of Medicare Advantage (see Chapter 4) when individuals have had six continuous months of creditable coverage on the date of application. Persons with fewer than six months of coverage are entitled to have the period of any preexisting condition exclusion reduced by the aggregate amount of periods of creditable coverage. [Soc. Sec. Act § 1882(s).]

An insurer may not impose an exclusion based on a pre-existing condition for individuals enrolling in Medicare Part D (see ¶ 500). Insurers are prohibited from discriminating in the pricing of such policies on the basis of the individual's health status, claims experience, receipt of health care or medical condition. [Soc. Sec. Act § 1882(s)(3)(A).]

A pamphlet containing Medigap insurance policy information for beneficiaries has been issued jointly by the Department of Health and Human Services (HHS) and the National Association of Insurance Commissioners (NAIC). It is entitled " Choosing a Medigap Policy: A Guide to Health Insurance for People with Medicare" and is available free from HHS at http://www.medicare.gov/ or ordered by calling 1-800-MEDICARE (1-800-633-4227).

Minimum Standards

Minimum standards for Medigap policies include:

Standardization. With limited exceptions, no more than the standard benefit packages may be offered in all states, by all issuers. Of the standard benefit packages, one must cover only a core group of basic benefits, and all others must include the core benefits;

Guaranteed renewability;

Suspension of Medigap premiums and benefits during Medicaid eligibility;

New and higher loss ratio requirements for individual policies and group policies and required refunds or credits if the policies do not meet the loss ratio requirements;

Pre-existing condition limitations. Such conditions may be imposed only in a replacement policy to the extent such conditions were not met under the original policy. There also is a six-month open enrollment period for new Part B enrollees who are age 65 or older; and

Prohibition of the sale of duplicative coverage. Virtually any sale of duplicative health insurance coverage to Medicare beneficiaries is prohibited. [*Notice,* 56 FR 47763, Sept. 20, 1991, corrected at 56 FR 65269, Dec. 16, 1991.]

The selling, issuance, or renewal of existing Medigap policies with prescription drug coverage for Part D enrollees is prohibited. [Soc. Sec. Act § 1882.]

Benefit packages. There are two Medigap benefit packages effective for 2006. The first provides, notwithstanding other provisions of law relating to core benefits: (1) coverage of 50 percent of the cost-sharing otherwise applicable (except coverage of 100 percent cost-sharing applicable for preventive benefits); (2) no coverage of the Part B deductible; (3) coverage of all hospital co-insurance for long stays and 365 extra lifetime days of coverage (as in the current core package); and (4) a limitation on annual out-of-pocket costs of $4,000 in 2006 (increased in future years by an appropriate inflation adjustment as specified by the Secretary). The second benefit package has the same benefit structure as the first new package except that: (1) coverage would be provided for 75 percent rather than 50 percent, of cost-sharing otherwise applicable; and (2) the limitation on out-of-pocket costs would be $2,000, rather than $4,000. Medigap issuers are not required to participate as a prescription drug plan sponsor under the new Part D and a state may not make such a requirement. [Soc. Sec. Act §§ 1882(s)(3)(C), 1882(w).]

¶740

The Secretary is authorized to approve states' Medigap regulatory programs and their enforcement efforts. State enforcement efforts, particularly with respect to assuring that policies comply with minimum loss ratios, are subject to periodic federal review.

Penalties

It is a criminal offense to engage in fraudulent activities connected with the sale of Medigap policies, including making false statements and misrepresentations, falsely claiming certification by the federal government, selling policies that duplicate Medicare benefits, including selling to Medicare Advantage beneficiaries (see ¶ 400), and mailing into a state Medigap policies that have been disapproved by that state. Violation of these provisions is a felony, entailing maximum penalties of $25,000, or five years' imprisonment, or both. [Soc. Sec. Act § 1882(d)(3)(A).]

Effective January 1, 2006, the Secretary is required to request the National Association of Insurance Commissioners (NAIC) to review and revise standards for benefit packages taking into account the changes in benefits for 2006. To the extent practicable, the revision will provide for implementation of revised standards. [Soc. Sec. Act § 1882.]

Medigap Policy Changes

As of January 1, 2006, the law prohibits the sale of new Medigap policies that include coverage for prescription drugs, and prohibit beneficiaries who enroll in Medicare Part D from purchasing a Medigap policy that provides drug coverage. Medigap prescription drug policies issued before January 1, 2006, may be renewed at the option of the policyholder, if the policyholder has not already enrolled in Medicare Part D. Beneficiaries who do not enroll during the initial enrollment period (IEP), but enroll later, will be charged higher Part D premiums unless they can show that they had "creditable prescription drug coverage" before enrolling in Medicare Part D. Individuals who enroll under Medicare Part D can keep their Medigap policy but the drug coverage will be eliminated and the premium for the policy must be adjusted. Individuals with a Medigap policy that provides prescription drug coverage who enroll under Medicare Part D during the IEP have the right, in most cases, to purchase another Medigap policy that does not include drug coverage, from the same issuer. Beneficiaries who enroll under Part D after the IEP lose the right to guaranteed issuance of a Medigap policy without outpatient drug coverage, but retain the right to keep their original Medigap policies without outpatient prescription drug coverage. [*Notice,* 70 FR 15394, March 25, 2005.]

Two new standardized benefit packages designated by the NAIC as Plan "K" and Plan "L" are effective in 2006. These two plans eliminate first dollar coverage for most Medicare cost-sharing and have a limit on annual out-of-pocket (OOP) expenditures incurred by a policyholder. When the OOP limit on annual expenditures is reached, the policy covers 100 percent of all cost-sharing under Medicare Parts A and B for the remainder of the year. For 2006, the OOP limit for Plan K will be $4,000 and the OOP limit for Plan L will be $2,000. These two plans do not cover the Medicare Part B deductible. [*Notice,* 70 FR 15394, March 25, 2005.]

Chapter 8—PAYMENT RULES

[¶ 800] Introduction

Medicare's method of paying for services provided to a beneficiary varies according to whether the services are furnished under Part A, Part B, Part C, or Part D.

Part A Payment

Payments made to most hospitals are made under the prospective payment system (PPS) for services covered by Medicare Part A, which covers institutional services (see ¶ 810). Prospective payment systems have been established for home health agencies (see ¶ 835), hospital outpatient services (combining elements of Part A and Part B; see ¶ 837), skilled nursing facilities (see ¶ 839), rehabilitation hospitals (see ¶ 841), long-term care facilities (see ¶ 843), and inpatient hospital services furnished in psychiatric hospitals and units (see ¶ 845). Other institutional providers and services not covered by a prospective payment system are paid on the basis of "reasonable costs." The Medicare payment is made directly to the provider that furnished the services.

Part B Payment

Part B services provided by physicians and other healthcare practitioners generally are paid on the basis of a physicians' fee schedule (see ¶ 820). Other suppliers of services and equipment paid under Part B are paid on the basis of different fee schedules (see, for example, the discussions about the durable medical equipment, prosthetic device, and clinical laboratory fee schedules at ¶ 356, ¶ 357, and ¶ 827, respectively), or on a "reasonable charge" basis (not covered in this book). The Medicare payment is made to the physician or supplier who furnished the services if assignment has been accepted (see ¶ 831). Otherwise, the payment is made to the beneficiary, who then has the obligation to pay the physician or supplier.

Part C Payment

Medicare managed care organizations (MCOs) are risk-bearing entities that can issue, within designated geographic areas, health plans offering a specific set of benefits offered at a uniform premium and uniform level of cost sharing to each Medicare beneficiary who chooses to enroll in a such a plan under Medicare Part C, which is called the Medicare Advantage (MA) program. The program was designed to give beneficiaries access to private health plan choices beyond traditional fee-for-service and the previous Medicare HMO program. The payment rules for MA organizations are at ¶ 407 and ¶ 408. Beginning in 2006, the MA program does the following:

- allows beneficiaries to choose among health maintenance organizations, preferred provider organization plans, fee-for-service plans, and medical savings account plans, for their health coverage;
- provides incentives to plans, and add specialized plans, to better serve those with complex and disabling diseases and conditions;
- provides a wider range of benefit choices available to enrollees, including prescription drug benefits;
- provides for regional plans that would make private plan options available to many more beneficiaries, especially in rural areas;
- bases payments for local and regional MA plans on competitive bids rather than administered pricing; and

- establishes uniform grievance and appeals procedures, as well as notice and timeliness procedures to ensure the beneficiary's rights are protected and understood. [Soc. Sec. Act § 1851.]

Part D Payments

Beginning January 1, 2006, Medicare covers the cost of prescription drugs. Section 101(a) of the Medicare Modernization Act of 2003 (MMA)(PubLNo 108-173) created a voluntary prescription drug benefit under a new Part D of the Social Security Act. The goal of the program is to provide beneficiaries with prescription drugs that cost less due to negotiated prices. Beneficiaries entitled to Part A and enrolled in Part B, enrollees in Medicare Advantage (formerly Medicare+Choice) private fee-for-service plans, and enrollees in Medicare Savings Account plans will be eligible for the prescription drug benefit.

The drug benefit permits eligible individuals to choose from at least two prescription drug plans (PDPs) in their region, either a standard coverage plan or an alternative coverage plan with actuarially equivalent benefits. In 2006, standard coverage has a $250 deductible and a 25 percent coinsurance for costs between $251 and $2250. Beneficiaries will pay 100 percent of prescription drugs costs between $2251 and $5100 for the year. At this point, beneficiaries will have spent $3600 out of their own pockets. Once the out-of-pocket threshold is met, beneficiaries will pay $2 for generic drugs and $5 for nonpreferred drugs or 5 percent of the cost of a drug, whichever is greater. Low-income individuals, those with incomes below 150 percent of the federal poverty line, will receive subsidies for deductibles, premiums, and cost-sharing amounts. Low-income eligibility determinations will be made by state Medicaid plans. [Soc. Sec. Act § 1860D-1.]

[¶ 810] Prospective Payment System for Inpatient Hospital Services

The reasonable cost method of reimbursing hospitals for the cost of furnishing inpatient services to Medicare beneficiaries was replaced by a prospective payment system (PPS) in 1983. Effective for cost reporting periods beginning after September 1983, with the exception of specified exempt hospitals, a hospital is paid a fixed amount for each Medicare discharge. Reimbursement for capital-related costs continued to be made on a reasonable cost basis until fiscal year 1988. [*Final rule*, 52 FR 33168, Sept. 1, 1987.] Other exceptions to prospective payments include direct medical education costs, a return on equity capital, and costs for administering blood clotting factors to individuals with hemophilia. [Soc. Sec. Act § 1886(a)(4), (d), (g), and (h).]

PPS has resulted in a substantial reduction in the average length of a hospital stay for Medicare beneficiaries. In addition, there has been a rapid increase in the number of one-day (or same-day) surgical procedures performed in hospital outpatient departments or ambulatory surgical centers.

DRG Classifications

Under PPS, all patient illnesses and injuries resulting in admission to a hospital are classified into different diagnosis-related groups (DRGs), that are clinically coherent and relatively homogeneous with respect to resources used by a hospital.

Using this classification system, Medicare has developed a system of payments to hospitals under which each DRG (each type of illness or injury) is paid at a set rate that is weighted geographically. The amount paid under PPS is based upon the DRG for each discharge, regardless of the number of services received or the length of the patient's stay in the hospital, and includes all inpatient operating costs. The DRG payment covers all items and services provided by the hospital to the patient. If the hospital's costs are less than that rate, the hospital keeps the difference; if the hospital's costs are more than the set rate, the hospital absorbs the loss. Not included in the DRG are services provided by the patient's physician, which are covered under Part B (see ¶ 820). This system was developed to hold down the rapidly escalating amounts that Medicare had been paying hospitals each year under the reasonable cost payment system. [Soc. Sec. Act § 1886(d); 42 C.F.R. §§ 412.2 et seq.]

A new number of DRGs and redesignated current diagnosis and procedure codes have been created by CMS. Specifically, new DRGs were created for spinal fusions that do not include the cervix with curvature of the spine or malignancy is composed of all noncervix-spinal fusions previously assigned to DRGs 497 and 498; and. for acute ischemic strokes that use thrombolytic agents. Addtionally, because Medicare coverage expanded to include the coverage of implantable defibrillators, CMS modified DRGs 515, 535, and 536 for patients that receive an electrophysiology test, but not a cardiac cathcrization. [*Final rule*, 70 FR 47278, Aug. 12, 2005.]

Payment Updates for FYs 2004–2007

Section 501(a) of the Medicare Modernization Act of 2003 (MMA) (PubLNo 108-173) provides that acute care hospitals will receive an update of the market basket percentage increase for fiscal years (FYs) 2004 through 2007. Receiving this update is contingent on the hospital submitting data before the start of the fiscal year on ten quality indicators established by the Secretary as of November 1, 2003. Although the Secretary provided a 30-day grace period for the submission of the required data for FY 2005, no such grace period exists for FY 2006 required data. Hospitals that participate in the quality reporting intiative will receive the full 3.7 percent increase. The update for a hospital that does not submit the required quality data to the Secretary will receive a 3.3 percent increase. [*Final rule*, 70 FR 47278, Aug. 12, 2005.].

The *Final rule* published on August 12, 2005, updating payment rates for 2006, announced that rural hospitals will receive an average 3.3 percent payment increase starting October 1, 2005. Large urban hospitals will receive an average 3.4 percent payment increase, while hospitals located in other urban areas will receive an average 3.6 percent payment increase under the inpatient prospective payment system (IPPS) update. [*Final rule*, 70 FR 47278, Aug. 12, 2005.]

This *Final rule* included other changes to the inpatient PPS mandated by the MMA in addition to the reduction of the amount of increase that a hospital will receive for failing to report quality data. These changes included in the final rule are: (1) expanding the number of DRGs that are subject to postacute care transfer policy; and (2) decreasing the outlier threshold from $25,800 for FY 2005, to $23,600 for FY 2006. [*Final rule*, 70 FR 47278, Aug. 12, 2005.]

Three-year transition. Beginning with FY 2005, CMS defined hospital labor market areas based on core based statical area (CBSAs). As a result, the Office of Management and Budget extensively revised the composition of many MSAs previously used to define labor markets. In the first year of this transition, FY 2005, hospitals whose wage indexes decreased due to this change were given a wage index based on 50 percent of the CBSA definitions and 50 percent of the wage index that the provider would have received under FY 2004 MSA boundaries. Beginning with FY 2006, hospitals will receive 100 percent of their wage index based on the new CBSA configurations. It is important to note, however, that CMS revised 42 C.F.R. § 412.64(k)(2), effective October 1, 2005, to specify that a change to a provider's wage index may be made retroactive to the beginning of the federal fiscal year under certain conditions. Although this provision may not be used to correct prior years' wage data, it can be used for the current federal fiscal year. [*Final rule*, 70 FR 47278, Aug. 12, 2005.]

¶810

Outlier Payments

For hospital stays that are extraordinarily long or costly, PPS provides for an additional payment to the hospital for treating a beneficiary's condition that is termed an "outlier". Prior to fiscal year (FY) 1998, PPS hospitals could receive either a "day outlier" payment, for cases in which a patient had an extraordinarily long length of stay compared to other patients in the DRG, or a "cost outlier" payment, if payment could not be made as a day outlier and the costs for treating a patient were extraordinarily high in relation to the costs for treating other patients in the same DRG. [42 C.F.R. §§ 412.82, 412.84.]

Payments for day outlier cases were phased out over a four-year period beginning in FY 1995. Day outlier payments completely ceased for discharges occurring during FY 1998. [Soc. Sec. Act § 1886(d)(5)(A)(i); 42 C.F.R. § 412.82.]

Cost outlier payments continue to be made, although it is more difficult for hospitals to qualify for them. For discharges in fiscal years prior to FY 1995, cases qualified for cost outlier payments if the hospital's charges exceeded a fixed multiple of the applicable DRG prospective payment rate, or a fixed dollar amount, whichever was greater. Beginning with discharges during FY 1995, a case qualifies for a cost outlier payment if the hospital's charges exceed the applicable DRG prospective payment rate *plus* any amounts payable as indirect medical education adjustments, disproportionate share hospital adjustments and a fixed dollar amount determined by the Secretary. [Soc. Sec. Act § 1886(d)(5)(A)(ii); 42 C.F.R. § 412.84.]

New Technology Payments

Beginning with FY 2003, new technologies are integrated more quickly into the inpatient hospital PPS, pursuant to § 533 of the Benefits Improvement and Protection Act of 2000 (BIPA) (PubLNo 106-554). CMS has implemented the BIPA mandate with a two-part strategy. First, it has shortened the timeframe for implementing new technology codes by adopting them in each year's inpatient PPS *Final rule* because they cannot be processed in time to be included in each year's *Proposed rule*. Second, CMS is working with the public to use categories 0 and 17 of the ICD-9-CM procedures, which will provide room for 200 additional procedure codes. [*Final rule*, 66 FR 46902, Sept. 7, 2001.] If the cost of a new technology requires a special add-on payment, the regulations authorize an add-on payment of up to the lesser of 50 percent of the amount by which the cost of the case exceeds the DRG payment for the case, or 50 percent of the cost of the new technology. Although, this rule still applies, for FY 2006, CMS is no longer required to ensure that any add-on payments for new technology under Soc. Sec. Act § 1886(d)(5)(K) are budget neutral. Because it is difficult to predict the actual new technology add-on payment for each case, however, CMS is estimating the increase in payment for FY 2006 as if every claim with these add-on payments will receive the maximum add-on payment. Reductions in this add-on payment may be made if the projected payment for the new technology exceeds the target amount for the year. [42 C.F.R. § 412.88.]

The high-cost threshold for new technologies applying for add-on payments for FY 2005 and subsequent years was lowered to 75 percent of one standard deviation beyond the geometric mean standardized charges for all cases in the diagnosis related group (DRG) to which the new medical service or technology is assigned. For FY 2006, CMS has approved two new technology applications: Restore®Rechargeable Implantable Neurostimulator; and GORE TAG. Addtionally, CMS is continuing to make add-on payments in FY 2006 for a FY 2005 new technology: Kinetra™implants. Overall, these approvals will increase FY 2006 payments by $6.01 million, $16.61 million and $12.82 million, respectively. [*Final rule*, 70 FR 47278, 47702, Aug. 12, 2005.]

¶810

Exemptions and Exceptions from Inpatient PPS

As noted above, there are certain hospitals that are exempt from inpatient PPS. These currently include psychiatric and rehabilitation hospitals, psychiatric and rehabilitation units of acute care hospitals, pediatric hospitals, and long-term care hospitals. Hospitals classified as cancer hospitals before December 31, 1990, also are exempt from PPS. Hospitals exempt from PPS are reimbursed on a reasonable cost basis but are subject to a ceiling on the rate of increase in inpatient costs of have their own prospective payment system. [Soc. Sec. Act § 1886(b)(1)(C), (j); 42 C.F.R. § 413.40.]

A prospective payment system for inpatient rehabilitation hospital services was phased in over the two-year period between October 1, 2000, and October 1, 2002, pursuant to § 4421 of the Balanced Budget Act of 1997 (BBA) (PubLNo 105-33) (see ¶ 841). [Soc. Sec. Act § 1886(j).] In addition, § 424 of BIPA provided that the planned implementation of PPS for ambulatory surgical centers would be delayed until at least January 1, 2002, and its planned phase-in period will be three years rather than two years. [§ 226 of the Balanced Budget Refinement Act of 1999 (BBRA) (PubLNo 106-113), as amended by BIPA § 424.]

A per discharge PPS for the inpatient hospital services of long-term care hospitals was implemented, effective October 1, 2002 (see ¶ 843) pursuant to § 123 of BBRA. [*Final rule*, 67 FR 55954, Aug. 30, 2002.] Section 124 of BBRA provides for implementation of a per diem PPS for the inpatient hospital services of psychiatric hospitals and units for cost reporting periods beginning on or after October 1, 2002. CMS issued a *Final rule*, 69 FR 66922, regarding PPS for psychiatric hospitals and units on December 7, 2004 (see ¶ 845).

Various types of hospitals are entitled to certain exceptions or adjustments to the amount paid under PPS. For instance, disproportionate share hospitals (DSH) (hospitals that serve a significantly disproportionate share of low-income patients) receive additional payments to cover the higher costs of treating such patients. As provided by § 211 of BIPA, for discharges occurring on or after April 1, 2001, all hospitals are eligible to receive DSH payments when their DSH percentage (threshold amount) exceeds 15 percent. [Soc. Sec. Act § 1886(d)(5)(F), 42 C.F.R. § 412.106(c).]

Sole community hospitals. Special rules apply to sole community hospitals (SCHs) (hospitals located in rural areas that are the sole source of care available to residents of the area) and to small rural hospitals that are not designated as sole community hospitals. [Soc. Sec. Act § 1886(d)(5)(D); 42 C.F.R. § 412.92.] Section 211 of BIPA required that the DSH payment formulas be modified, according to specified formulas, for SCHs, rural referral centers (RRCs), rural hospitals that are both SCHs and RRCs, small rural hospitals and urban hospitals with less than 100 beds. [Soc. Sec. Act § 1886(d)(5)(F).] BIPA also provided that (1) an otherwise qualifying small rural hospital will be able to be classified as a Medicare dependent hospital (MDH) if at least 60 percent of its days or discharges were attributable to Medicare Part A beneficiaries in at least two of the three most recent audited cost reporting periods for which the Secretary of HHS has a settled cost report [BIPA § 212], and (2) any sole community hospital will be able to elect payment based on hospital-specific, updated 1996 costs if this target amount results in higher Medicare payments. There will be a transition period with Medicare payment based completely on updated FY 1996 hospital-specific costs for discharges occurring after FY 2003. [BIPA § 213.]

Teaching hospitals. Large teaching hospitals receive an additional payment to account for the indirect costs of teaching interns and residents. There are limits on the total number of full-time equivalent interns and residents in allopathic and osteopathic medicine training programs established on or after January 1, 1995. [Soc. Sec. Act § 1886(d)(5)(B); 42 C.F.R. § 412.105.]

Graduate medical education costs. Soc. Sec. Act §1886(h) authorizes hospitals and hospital-based providers to receive additional payments to cover the costs of training and instructing residents in approved direct graduate medical education (GME) residency teaching programs. The GME payment is for costs associated with an approved residency teaching program in medicine, osteopathy, dentistry, and podiatry. Payment is based on a hospital's number of full-time equivalent (FTE) residents who are working in the hospital during a cost reporting period, multiplied by a hospital-specific, per-resident amount. If the hospital has a resident count less than its resident cap, however, a hospital's GME FTE resident cap will be reduced and the resident positions redistributed among other hospitals. The *Final rule* for FY 2006, however, has revised 42 C.F.R. §413.79(e)(1)(iv) so that new urban teaching hospitals that qualify for a GME adjustment under 42 C.F.R. §413.79(e)(1) may enter into a Medicare GME affiliation agreement under certain circumstances. Specifically, a new urban teaching hospital that qualifies for an adjustment to its FTE caps for a newly approved program may enter into an affiliation agreement if the resulting adjustments will increase the FTE cap. This policy change was made to allow new urban teaching hospitals flexibility to start new teaching programs without jeopardizing their ability to count additional FTE residents training at the hospital under an affiliation agreement. Rural hospitals with less than 250 acute care inpatient beds are exempt from this change. [*Final rule*, 70 FR 47278, 47452, Aug. 12, 2005.]

Managed care plans. Teaching hospitals may receive an additional payment for the indirect costs of GME associated with Medicare managed care discharges. Beginning in 2002, these payments are equal to the per discharge amount that would have been made for that discharge if the beneficiary were not enrolled in managed care, multiplied by 100 percent. [*Final rule*, 62 FR 45966, 45968, Aug. 29, 1997.]

Section 541 of the BBRA provides for an additional payment to hospitals that operate approved nursing and allied health education programs associated with services to Medicare Advantage enrollees and are reimbursed for these services on a reasonable cost basis under Soc. Sec. Act §1861(v)(1). The calculation that CMS uses to determine the amount of this additional payment can be found at 42 C.F.R. §413.87.

Three-Day Payment Window

Outpatient diagnostic services and most nonphysician services provided during the three calendar days immediately preceding the date of admission or during an inpatient stay are included in Medicare's fixed fee for inpatient services. [42 C.F.R. §412.2(c)(5).] The three-day payment rule (also known as the 72-hour payment rule) applies only if the services are diagnostic and furnished in connection with the principal diagnosis that requires the beneficiary to be admitted as an inpatient. Ambulance services and maintenance renal dialysis are specifically excluded from the three-day payment rule. [42 C.F.R. §412.2(c)(5).]

[¶ 820] Physicians' Fee Schedule

Physicians are paid by Medicare on the basis of a national physicians' fee schedule. The physicians' fee schedule applies to all "physicians' services" (see ¶ 340 for the meaning of "physician") and some services performed by other healthcare professionals. Specifically, the fee schedule applies to the following:

(1) physicians' professional services (see ¶ 340);

(2) supplies and services furnished "incident to" physicians' services (see ¶ 351), except for drugs;

(3) outpatient physical and occupational therapy (see ¶ 381);

(4) diagnostic X-ray tests and other diagnostic tests (see ¶ 353), except for clinical diagnostic laboratory tests, which have their own fee schedule (see ¶ 827);

(5) X-ray, radium, and radioactive isotope therapy, including materials and services of technicians (see ¶ 354);

(6) antigens (see ¶ 362);

(7) bone mass measurement (see ¶ 369); and

(8) screening mammography services (see ¶ 369). [Soc. Sec. Act § 1848(j)(3); 42 C.F.R. § 414.2.]

How the Fee Schedule Works

Under the fee schedule method, Medicare generally pays 80 percent of the lower of (1) the fee schedule amount or (2) the physician's actual charge (the other 20 percent is paid by the patient as a coinsurance—see ¶ 335). [Soc. Sec. Act §§ 1833(a), 1848(a)(1); 42 C.F.R. § 414.21.] The fee schedule amount is determined by multiplying the relative value for the procedure by a geographic adjustment factor and a conversion factor, which results in a specific dollar amount for that service in that area. [Soc. Sec. Act § 1848(b)(1); 42 C.F.R. § 414.20.]

The relative value of a procedure is a predetermined value established by the government that weighs the value of each procedure compared to every other procedure. The weight of a particular relative value is based on the resources needed to furnish a procedure. The value consists of three resources: (1) work required; (2) practice expense (non-facility or facility); and (3) malpractice insurance expense. The work component reflects the relative value of the physician's work for a particular procedure, in terms of time and intensity of effort, in comparison to the value of work required for other procedures. The practice expense component reflects the physician's overhead on a non-facility or facility basis. The malpractice insurance component attributes a portion of the physician's malpractice insurance premium to each procedure. [Soc. Sec. Act § 1848(c)(2)(C); 42 C.F.R. § 414.22.] Practice expenses were phased into the resource-based methodology over a four-year transition period from 1999 to 2002. Beginning in 2002, all three relative value unit (RVU) components are fully resource-based.

The "geographic adjustment factor" compares every locale to all other locales nationwide. [Soc. Sec. Act § 1848(e); 42 C.F.R. § 414.26.] The "conversion factor" (see the next paragraph) is used in the formula to convert the relative value and the geographic adjustment factor to dollars. It also is used to adjust the resulting payment amount for inflation. [Soc. Sec. Act § 1848(d); 42 C.F.R. §§ 414.28, 414.30.] Under the fee schedule method, each physician in a locale is paid the same amount for the same service as every other physician in that locale, without regard to physician specialization or reputation. [Soc. Sec. Act § 1848(c)(6).] Nonparticipating physicians (see ¶ 833) are paid 5 percent less than participating physicians. [42 C.F.R. § 414.20(b).]

Fee Schedule Updates

The physicians' fee schedule is updated annually by a formula that takes into consideration (1) changes in inflation as measured by the Medicare Economic Index (MEI) and (2) changes in the U.S. Gross Domestic Product as measured by a targeting standard called the Sustainable Growth Rate (SGR). The end result is the "conversion factor" discussed above, which converts RVUs and geographic adjustment factors to a Medicare payment amount under the fee schedule. The SGR's targeting standard may not result in an update that is more than three percentage points above or seven percentage points below the MEI. [Soc. Sec. Act § 1848(d).]

¶ 820

Changes in the conversion factor (called the "conversion factor update") have been the most important area to watch in terms of year-to-year fee schedule adjustments. In general, the conversion factor update is the figure resulting from adjusting the MEI upward or downward by the percentage by which the SGR target is missed. The conversion factor for 2006 is $36.1770, approximately a 4.5 percent decrease from the 2005 conversion factor (see the paragraph below). [*Final rule*, 70 FR 70116, Nov. 21, 2005.]

RVUs and geographic adjustment factors are usually changed annually. When this happens, the law requires that the overall effect of these changes be applied in a budget-neutral manner throughout the fee schedule. In general terms, this means that, if an RVU for a particular procedure is increased, other RVUs may have to be decreased to achieve budget neutrality. This result also reflects the "relative value" of comparing one procedure to other procedures. When wholesale changes are made to a group of RVUs, budget neutrality may require a change in the conversion factor. [Soc. Sec. Act § 1848(c)(2)(B)(ii).]

Provider-Based Physicians

As discussed at ¶ 340, hospital-based and other provider-based physicians are considered to provide two categories of services. Medicare payment for "provider component" services is made to the hospital or provider under Part A; Medicare payment for "professional component" services is made under Part B. In most cases, the professional component services of provider-based physicians are paid under the same fee schedule applicable to other physicians; however, anesthesiologists are paid according to a different fee schedule method that factors in time units as well as relative values.

Anesthesiologists. Reimbursement rates for anesthesiologists' services depend upon whether the physician personally performs the procedure or medically directs up to four concurrent procedures that are performed by qualified individuals. Payment for medical direction is based on a specific percentage of the payment allowance recognized for the anesthesia service personally performed by a physician alone. The Medicare payment allowance for the medical direction of a physician when a single procedure is involved is 50 percent of the payment allowance for personally performed services. The medical assistance team divides the other 50 percent. [42 C.F.R. § 414.46.]

Teaching anesthesiologists. To remedy the disproportionate payment policies for teaching anesthesiologists and teaching CRNAs, CMS has decided to allow teaching anesthetists to bill for their involvement in two concurrent cases, as teaching CRNAs are allowed to bill. [*Final rule*, 68 FR 63224, Nov. 7, 2003.]

Interns and residents. Medicare pays the hospital for the services of interns and residents furnished in connection with an accredited hospital teaching program. Services of interns and residents not connected with the teaching program are paid on a reasonable cost basis under Medicare Part B. No Medicare payment is made for the administrative costs related to the teaching activities of physicians or for other costs of unapproved programs. [42 C.F.R. § 415.202.]

Assistants-at-surgery. The law permits payment under Part B for a physician assistant-at-surgery in a teaching hospital under various conditions. Payment can be made for the services of an assistant-at-surgery only if the services:

(1) are required due to exceptional medical circumstances;

(2) are complex medical procedures performed by team physicians, each performing a discrete, unique function, integral to the performance of a complex medical procedure that requires the special skills of more than one physician;

¶ 820

(3) constitute concurrent medical care relating to a medical condition that requires the presence of, and active care by, a physician of another specialty during surgery;

(4) are medically required and are furnished by a physician who is primarily engaged in the field of surgery, and the primary surgeon does not utilize interns and residents in the surgical procedures the physician performs; or

(5) are not related to a surgical procedure for which CMS determines that assistants are used less than 5 percent of the time. [Soc. Sec. Act § 1842(b)(7)(D)(i); 42 C.F.R. § 415.190(c).]

Payment is *not* available for assistants-at-surgery in hospitals with (1) a training program relating to the medical specialty required for the surgical procedure, and (2) a qualified individual on the staff of the hospital available to serve as an assistant-at-surgery. [42 C.F.R. §§ 415.190(a)(1), 415.190(a)(2).]

When the conditions for payment for an assistant-at-surgery are met, the Medicare payment amount will be the lower of the actual charge or 16 percent of the physicians' fee schedule payment amount for the global surgical service. [Soc. Sec. Act § 1848(i)(2)(A).]

There are special rules concerning coverage of surgery assistants in cataract operations—see ¶ 654.

Payment for "Incident to" Services and Drugs

As discussed at ¶ 351, services and supplies furnished incident to a physician's services are covered if they are the types of services that commonly are rendered without charge or are included in the physician's bill.

Under the fee schedule system, these services and supplies sometimes are considered practice expenses of the physician and, therefore, are included in the fee schedule payment amount. In some cases, however, separate payment is made. The definitive criterion is whether the services and supplies are considered "routine." [42 C.F.R. § 414.34(a).]

Services provided by the physician's staff that are incident to the physician's services are paid under the schedule as if the physician had personally furnished the services. [42 C.F.R. § 414.34(b).] Services of certain healthcare practitioners (*e.g.*, nurse practitioners, physician assistants) can be billed and paid separately (see ¶ 366). When this occurs, no payment would be made to the physician.

Drugs and biologicals are paid separately under the fee schedule system. For covered drugs and biologicals furnished before January 1, 2004, the Medicare payment was the lowest of (1) the amount billed, (2) 95% of the median generic average wholesale price (AWP) of the drug (as published in the Red Book and similar price listings), or (3) 95% of the lowest brand-name AWP. For drugs and biologicals furnished during 2004, payment generally was based on 85% of the AWP. [42 C.F.R. § 405.517; 42 C.F.R. 707(a).]

This payment policy for drugs was applicable to all drugs furnished to Medicare beneficiaries that were not "paid for on a cost or prospective payment basis." Drugs furnished incident to a physician's services fall within this category. To be considered incident to a physician's services, a drug must be of a kind that is commonly furnished in a physician's office and is commonly either rendered without charge or included in the physician's bill. [Soc. Sec. Act § 1861(s)(2).] Also subject to the payment policy described above were drugs provided by independent end-stage renal disease facilities. [42 C.F.R. § 405.517.]

Sec. 303 of the Medicare Prescription Drug, Improvement, and Modernization Act of 2003 (MMA) (PubLNo 108-173), changed the basis for payment of drugs and biologicals not

¶820

paid on a cost or prospective payment basis. For January 1, 2004, through December 31, 2004, the payment limits for blood clotting factors were 95 percent of the AWP and the payment limits for new drugs or biologicals were 95 percent of the AWP. A new drug is defined as an unlisted drug (not currently covered by a HCPCS code) that was FDA approved subsequent to April 1, 2003. A drug would not be considered new if: the brand or manufacturer of the drug changed, a new formulation of the vial size is developed, or the drug received a new indication. The payment limits for pneumococcal and hepatitis B drugs and biologicals administered between January 1, 2004 through December 31, 2004, were 95 percent of the AWP and the payment limits for certain drugs studied by the OIG and GAO during that time period were based on the percentages of the April 1, 2003, AWPs specified in the *Medicare Claims Processing Manual*, Pub. 100-04, Ch. 17, § 20, as revised on March 15, 2004. Finally, the payment limits for infusion drugs furnished through an item of implanted durable medical equipment on or after January 1, 2004, will be 95 percent of the October 1, 2003 AWP. [42 C.F.R. 414.707.]

Drugs and biologicals not described above were paid at 85 percent of the April 1, 2003 AWP. [42 C.F.R. 414.707; *Medicare Claims Processing Manual*, Pub. 100-04, Ch. 17, § 20.]

Beginning in 2005, the law authorizes payments to physicians for drugs and biologicals under the Average Sales Price (ASP) method or a competitive bidding program. [Soc. Sec. Act § 1847A and Soc. Sec. Act. § 1847B.] A competitive acquisition program (CAP) for physicians who administer drugs in their offices will be available in 2006. CAP applies to physician-injectable drugs covered under Medicare's Part B program that are commonly provided incident to the physician's service. It does not apply to drugs included in the new Prescription Drug Benefit under Medicare Part D, which went into effect January 1, 2006, nor will it apply to drugs that are self-administered by the patient through a device such as a nebulizer, or to certain other drugs, such as intravenous immune globulin, immunosuppressive drugs and hemophilia blood clotting factor. [*Interim final rule*, 70 FR 39022, July 6, 2005.]

Physicians participating in CAP will obtain all of their drugs from one vendor. The vendor then bills Medicare directly and collects any deductible and coinsurance amounts from the beneficiary. Physicians bill Medicare only for their administrative services. While the vendor becomes their sole source for the drugs, physicians are allowed to obtain drugs from other sources in certain emergency situations. [*Interim final rule*, 70 FR 39022, July 6, 2005.]

Each year, physicians will have the option of participating in CAP or continuing to purchase drugs in the market, as they do currently, and being paid directly from Medicare. If a physician elected to purchase drugs, Medicare would pay the physician the ASP for the drug. Manufacturers would be required to furnish CMS with the ASP for each of their drugs quarterly. [42 C.F.R. 414.904.]

Global Surgery

Physicians' surgery services often are combined with related services to form one billable procedure under the fee schedule. The theory is that a global surgery package should reflect the total work required for the surgeon to complete the service once the decision for surgery is made. The global surgery package is considered to include preoperative visits, the operation itself, and postoperative hospital and office visits. The package does not include the initial evaluation or consultation with the surgeon. [42 C.F.R. § 414.40(b)(1).]

Professional and Technical Components

For some procedures, the physicians' fee schedule distinguishes between professional and technical components. The technical component typically involves a mechanical act, such as taking an X-ray or an EKG or performing a test on a specimen. The professional component involves the interpretation of the test. The physician may bill only for the component that he or she performed. If a technician performed the technical component, the technician can be paid under the fee schedule for that service. [42 C.F.R. § 414.40(b)(2); *Final rule*, 56 FR 59502, Nov. 25, 1991.]

Site-of-Service Differential

If physicians' services of the type routinely furnished in physicians' offices are furnished in facility settings, the physician fee schedule amount for those services reflects reduced practice expense RVUs for those services. Services furnished at least 50 percent of the time in physicians' offices are subject to this reduction. For services furnished after January 1, 1999, the site-of-service differential is reflected in the physician fee schedule columns showing nonfacility and facility practice expenses. The lower facility practice expense RVUs apply to services furnished to patients in a hospital, a skilled nursing facility, a community mental health center, or an ambulatory surgical center (ASC) (if the physician performs procedures on the ASC approved procedures list). The reduced practice expense RVUs do not apply to rural health clinics, anesthesiology services, radiology services, and outpatient therapy services. The higher non-facility practice expense RVUs apply to services performed in a physician's office, a patient's home, an ambulatory surgical center (if the procedure is not on the ASC approved procedures list), a nursing facility, and certain other facilities and institutions. [42 C.F.R. §§ 414.22(b)(5), 414.32(d).]

HPSA Bonus Payment

Medicare pays a bonus of 10 percent to physicians who furnish covered services to Medicare beneficiaries in areas designated as Health Professional Shortage Areas (HPSAs). The bonus is added to the reimbursement that otherwise would be paid under the fee schedule and applies to both urban and rural HPSAs. [Soc. Sec. Act § 1833(m).] Medicare also provides a five percent incentive payment to both primary care physicians and specialty physicians furnishing services in physician scarcity areas (PSAs). [Soc. Sec. Act § 1833(u).]

[¶ 821] Actual Charge Restrictions

In order to protect beneficiaries from excessive charges by Medicare physicians and suppliers, the Medicare program has several rules that limit how much beneficiaries can be charged (actual charge restrictions). These rules apply only to physicians and suppliers who do not accept assignment, which has its own rules (see ¶ 831). If these actual charge restrictions did not exist, a physician or supplier who does not accept assignment would be free to set any amount as the actual charge and could require the beneficiary to pay that amount. Medicare would, as usual, pay 80 percent of the amount it determines to be allowable, and the beneficiary would have to pay the difference between the Medicare payment amount and the physician's or supplier's actual charge.

The Limiting Charge

The most significant of the actual charge restrictions is the "limiting charge," which sets an upper limit on how much a physician (or other healthcare professional) or supplier may charge in excess of the Medicare payment amount. The limiting charge is 115 percent of the fee schedule amount for "non-participating" physicians and suppliers (see ¶ 833 for an explanation of the Participation Program). [Soc. Sec. Act § 1848(g)(2)(C); *Medicare Claims Processing Manual*, Pub. 100-4, Ch. 1, § 30.3.12.3.] The non-participating physician fee schedule amount is 95 percent of the listed fee schedule amount for each service. [Soc. Sec. Act § 1848(a)(3).]

Example • • •

Carla visits Dr. Kent for a series of medical tests and services for which Dr. Kent would charge private-pay patients $800. The physicians' fee schedule for those services, however, is $510. Carla already has paid the $124 Part B deductible for the year.

(1) If Dr. Kent is a participating physician, Medicare will pay Dr. Kent $408 and Carla will pay the $102 coinsurance (that is, 20 percent of $510).

(2) If Dr. Kent is a nonparticipating physician, the Medicare-approved amount is 5 percent less than the fee schedule ($485), and the Medicare payment amount is $388 (80 percent of the reduced approved amount).

(a) If Dr. Kent accepts assignment (see ¶ 831), and thus agrees to accept the reduced Medicare-approved amount as his full charge, Medicare will pay Dr. Kent $388 and Carla will pay the other $97.

(b) If Dr. Kent does not accept assignment and wants to charge Carla more than the reduced Medicare-approved amount, Dr. Kent may not charge Carla more than 15 percent over the reduced Medicare-approved amount (*i.e.*, 15 percent over $485, or $557.75). The Medicare-approved payment amount ($388) is sent to Carla, and Carla is responsible for paying the other $169.75.

A physician who charges a patient more than the limiting charge must refund the difference. [Soc. Sec. Act § 1848(g)(1)(A)(iv).] Medicare Summary Notices, which explain Medicare benefits to beneficiaries, indicate how much the limiting charge is for each bill submitted.

The Secretary is required to monitor each physician's actual charges, and if a physician knowingly and willfully bills above the limiting charge, the Secretary may apply sanctions, including (1) barring the physician from participating in the Medicare program for up to five years and/or (2) imposing a civil money penalty or assessment. [Soc. Sec. Act §§ 1842(j)(1)(A), 1842(j)(2).] The Secretary may use any penalties so collected to reimburse the beneficiary for the overcharge. [Soc. Sec. Act § 1842(j)(4).]

Billing Restrictions

Physicians, suppliers, and other healthcare practitioners are not allowed to bill or collect from Medicare beneficiaries amounts over the limiting charge. Should an incorrect billing be sent out, a corrected billing must follow. Any incorrect amounts collected must be refunded to the beneficiary within 30 days or offset against any outstanding balances. [Soc. Sec. Act § 1848(g)(1).]

Carriers are required to examine *each* claim for limiting charge violations before payment can be made. If a violation is detected, the beneficiary will be notified of the violation and of the right to a refund, and the physician, practitioner, or supplier will be sent a notice ordering the refund. [Soc. Sec. Act § 1842(h)(7)(D).]

The 30-day time limit for refunding overcharges begins to run when the carrier refund order is received. Sanctions in the form of fines or exclusion from program participation may result for knowing, willful, and repeated violations of these rules. [Soc. Sec. Act § 1848(g)(1)(B).]

Physician and Supplier Liability for Noncovered Services

When a physician furnishes otherwise covered services on an *unassigned* basis to a Medicare beneficiary, and a carrier or a quality improvement organization (QIO) determines that those services were not covered because they were not reasonable or necessary, the

¶821

physician is required to refund to the beneficiary any payments collected for those services. [Soc. Sec. Act § 1842(l)(1)(A); 42 C.F.R. § 411.408(a).]

A refund is not required if (1) the physician did not know, and reasonably could not have been expected to know, that the services were not covered, or (2) if, before the service was provided, the beneficiary was notified that Medicare payment would not be made and the beneficiary agreed to pay for the services (such a notification is called an Advance Beneficiary Notice (ABN)). [42 C.F.R. § 411.408(d).] If a refund is required and the physician knowingly and willfully fails to make the refund, the Secretary is authorized to impose civil money penalties and/or suspend the physician from participation in the program. [Soc. Sec. Act §§ 1842(l)(1)(C), 1842(l)(3); 42 C.F.R. § 411.408(g).]

When a refund is required, it must be made within 30 days after the date the physician receives the notice that Medicare payment will not be made. If the physician appeals the denial notice, the refund must be made within 15 days after the date the physician receives notice that the appeal was rejected, whether or not the physician further appeals the adverse determination. [Soc. Sec. Act § 1842(l)(1)(B); 42 C.F.R. § 411.408(b).]

Supplier rules. The refund requirement also applies to durable medical equipment, prosthetics, orthotics, and medical supplies. Suppliers are required to make refunds to beneficiaries when items are furnished on an *unassigned* basis if Medicare payment is denied for one of the following reasons: (1) lack of medical necessity [Soc. Sec. Act § 1862(a)(1)], (2) an item is furnished by a supplier who does not have a supplier number [Soc. Sec. Act § 1834(j)(1)], (3) the supplier violated the prohibition on unsolicited telephone contacts [Soc. Sec. Act § 1834(a)(17)(B)], or (4) payment is denied in advance [Soc. Sec. Act § 1834(a)(15)].

Suppliers are required to make refunds to beneficiaries when items are furnished on an *assigned* basis if: (1) the item is furnished by a supplier who does not have a supplier number, (2) the supplier violated the prohibition on unsolicited telephone contacts, or (3) payment is denied in advance.

For both unassigned and assigned claims, a refund is not required if (1) the supplier did not know, and reasonably could not have been expected to know, that Medicare would not pay for the medical equipment or supplies, or (2) if, before the medical equipment or supplies were furnished, the beneficiary was notified that Medicare payment would not be made and the beneficiary agreed to pay for the services (such a notification is called an Advance Beneficiary Notice). If the supplier is not required to make a refund, the beneficiary is liable for payment. However, for *assigned* claims which are denied because the item or service is not reasonable or necessary, the beneficiary will not be held liable for payment if the beneficiary did not know, and could not reasonably have been expected to know, that the items and services the beneficiary received were not covered. [*Program Memorandum*, No. B-03-003, Jan. 24, 2003.]

ABN requirements for physicians and suppliers

When an Advance Beneficiary Notice (ABN) is properly executed and given in a timely manner to a beneficiary, and, in fact, Medicare denies payment on the claim (whether unassigned or assigned), the physician or supplier may bill and collect from the beneficiary for that service. Medicare does not limit the amount that the physician or supplier (whether participating or nonparticipating in the Medicare program) may collect from the beneficiary in this situation. Medicare charge limits do not apply to unassigned and assigned claims when collection from the beneficiary is permitted on the basis of an ABN. [*Program Memorandum*, No. B-03-003, Jan. 24, 2003.]

To be acceptable, the ABN must: (1) be on the approved Form CMS-R-131, (2) clearly identify the particular item or service, (3) state that the physician or supplier believes

Medicare is likely (or certain) to deny payment for the item or service, and (4) give the physician's or supplier's reasons for believing that Medicare is likely (or certain) to deny payment. There are two versions of Form CMS-R-131. The ABN-G (Form CMS-R-131-G) may be used for all situations, including laboratory tests, by all physicians and suppliers. The ABN-L (Form CMS-R-131-L) may be used for laboratory tests by any person or entity furnishing laboratory tests. Effective January 1, 2003, the ABN-G and ABN-L are the only acceptable ABN forms for use with Part B items and services. In general, giving "routine" or "blanket" ABNs to beneficiaries for all claims or services, even when there is no specific identifiable reason to believe that Medicare will not pay, is not acceptable. Similarly, "generic" ABNs, which do no more than state that Medicare denial of payment is possible, or that the physician never knows whether Medicare will deny payment, are not acceptable. Routine, blanket, and generic ABNs are considered defective notices and will not protect the physician or supplier from liability. [*Program Memorandum*, No. AB-02-114, July 31, 2002.]

ABNs may be routinely given to beneficiaries only in the following circumstances [*Program Memorandum*, No. B-03-003, Jan. 24, 2003]:

Services which are always denied for medical necessity. When a national coverage decision provides that a particular service is never covered under any circumstances as reasonable and necessary (*e.g.*, currently all acupuncture services are denied as not reasonable and necessary) an ABN may routinely be given to beneficiaries. In the "Because" box, the ABN should state "Medicare never pays for this item/service."

Experimental items and services. When an item or service that Medicare considers to be experimental ("Research Use Only" and "Investigational Use Only" laboratory tests) is to be furnished, an ABN may routinely be given to beneficiaries, because all such services are denied as not reasonable and necessary. In the "Because" box, the ABN-G form should state "Medicare does not pay for services which it considers to be experimental or for research use." On an ABN-L with a test listed in the third column, the ABN should state "Medicare does not pay for experimental or research use tests." Alternatively, more specific language explaining Medicare coverage policy for clinical trials may be substituted as necessary.

Certain frequency limited items and services. When an item or service is furnished for which Medicare has established a frequency limitation on coverage, an ABN may routinely be given to beneficiaries, because virtually all beneficiaries may be at risk of having their claims denied. In the "Because" box, the ABN-G must state the frequency limitation.

Lack of a supplier number or prohibited telephone solicitation. Because Medicare denials of payment based on a supplier's lack of a supplier number, or based on the prohibition on unsolicited telephone contacts, apply to all varieties of equipment and supplies and to all beneficiaries, routine ABNs may be given under these circumstances.

Physicians and suppliers are prohibited from obtaining beneficiary signatures on blank ABNs and completing the ABNs later. To be effective, an ABN must be completed before delivery to the beneficiary. The ABN should be hand-delivered to the beneficiary or the beneficiary's authorized representative. As a general rule, the ABN should be delivered to the beneficiary before a procedure is initiated and before physical preparation of the patient (*e.g.*, disrobing, placement in or attachment of diagnostic or treatment equipment) begins. [*Program Memorandum*, No. B-03-003, Jan. 24, 2003.]

See ¶ 356 for a discussion of ABN requirements for upgraded durable medical equipment, prosthetics, orthotics, and supplies.

Payment Rules

Elective Surgery

When a physician performs an elective surgical procedure on an *unassigned* basis for a Medicare beneficiary, and the charge for that procedure is at least $500, the physician must refund to the patient any payment collected above the Medicare payment amount for the procedure, unless the physician discloses to the beneficiary in advance the difference between (1) the physician's estimated charge, (2) the estimated Medicare payment, and (3) the excess of the physician's actual charge over the estimated Medicare payment. [Soc. Sec. Act § 1842(m).]

This disclosure must be made in writing and in a form approved by the Secretary. A physician who knowingly and willfully fails to make a required refund for elective surgery procedures may be subject to civil money penalties or may be suspended from program participation. The Secretary is required to monitor elective surgery claims to assure that required refunds are being made. [Soc. Sec. Act § 1842(m).]

Diagnostic Tests

Carriers will pay for diagnostic procedures under the physician fee schedule only when performed by a physician, a group practice of physicians, an approved supplier of portable X-ray services, a nurse practitioner or clinical nurse specialist, or an independent diagnostic testing facility. [42 C.F.R. § 410.33(a).]

Physicians must accept assignment for clinical diagnostic laboratory tests provided in physician offices. See ¶ 827.

In the case of diagnostic tests other than clinical diagnostic laboratory tests (for example, diagnostic X-rays), the physician may not add a mark-up fee in billing Medicare or the beneficiary that adds to the charges of the supplier that performed the tests. If a physician submits a bill for a diagnostic test that does not show who performed the test and how much was charged for the test, no Medicare payment will be made and the beneficiary may not be billed. A physician who bills a beneficiary when not permitted to do so can be fined or excluded from the program. [Soc. Sec. Act § 1842(n); 42 C.F.R. § 414.50.]

[¶ 826] Nonphysician Practitioners

As discussed at ¶ 351, separate Medicare coverage is provided for several kinds of nonphysician healthcare practitioners. At one time, the services of healthcare practitioners such as physician assistants and nurse practitioners were covered only as "incident to" a physician's services (see ¶ 351), and payment for their services was included in Medicare's payment to the physician. Increasingly in recent years, healthcare practitioners have been permitted to bill separately when they perform specialized services or stand in the place of a physician. The Medicare payment amount for nonphysician practitioners is normally a certain percentage of the physicians' fee schedule for the same services (or less if their actual charges are less).

Nonphysician practitioners are required to accept assignment for all their Medicare claims. [42 C.F.R. §§ 410.74(d)(2), 410.75(e)(2), 410.76(e)(2), 410.77(d)(2), 414.60(c).]

Physician Assistants and Nurse Practitioners

Physician assistants. Physician assistants are paid at 85 percent of the physician fee schedule amount for the service. In the case of services performed as an assistant-at-surgery, payment is 85 percent of the amount that otherwise would be paid if performed by a physician serving as an assistant at surgery (see ¶ 820). [Soc. Sec. Act §§ 1848(a)(1), 1833(a)(1)(O); 42 C.F.R. § 414.52.]

Payment for the services of physician assistants may be made either to (1) the employer of the physician assistant or (2) directly to a physician assistant who was the owner of a rural health clinic. [Soc. Sec. Act § 1842(b)(6)(C).]

Nurse practitioners. Nurse practitioners (NPs) and clinical nurse specialists (CNSs) are paid at 85 percent of the physician fee schedule. In cases in which NPs and CNSs serve as assistants at surgery, payment is 85 percent of the physician fee schedule for assistants at surgery (see ¶ 820). [Soc. Sec. Act § 1833(a)(1)(O); 42 C.F.R. § 414.56.]

Payment for the services of an NP or CNS may normally be made only to the nurse's employer. However, when the services are provided in a rural area, payment can be made either directly to the NP or CNS or to the nurse's employer or contractor. [42 C.F.R. § 410.75(e).]

Nurse-midwives. Certified nurse-midwife services are paid at 65 percent of the physician fee schedule amount. [42 C.F.R. § 414.54.]

Certified Registered Nurse Anesthetists

Like anesthesiologists (see ¶ 820), the Medicare payment system for certified registered nurse anesthetists (CRNAs) is based on a modified version of the anesthesia payment system in effect before 1992. Anesthesia assistants (AAs) and anesthetists are paid in the same way as CRNAs. The allowance for an anesthesia service furnished by a medically directed CRNA is based on a fixed percentage of the allowance recognized for the anesthesia service personally performed by the physician alone. Payment may be made to a CRNA or to any individual or entity with whom the CRNA has an employment or contract relationship. [42 C.F.R. § 414.60.]

Clinical Psychologists and Social Workers

Clinical psychologists. Clinical psychologists (CPs) are paid under the physician fee schedule at the same rate as physicians for corresponding services. [Soc. Sec. Act § 1833(a)(1)(L); 42 C.F.R. § 414.62; *Medicare Claims Processing Manual*, Pub. 100-4, Ch. 12, § 170.]

Clinical social workers. Covered diagnostic tests furnished by clinical social workers (CSWs) are paid under the fee schedule, although psychological testing services are covered only if furnished by a physician or qualified psychologist. For therapeutic and other diagnostic services, CSWs are paid 75 percent of the fee schedule for comparable services furnished by CPs. [Soc. Sec. Act § 1842(b)(18)(A); Pub. 100-4, Ch. 12, § 150.]

Physical, Occupational, and Speech Therapists

Physical and occupational therapy services provided by a therapist in an independent practice are paid under the fee schedule. Payment is also made under the physician fee schedule for outpatient physical therapy (which includes speech-language pathology) and outpatient occupational therapy services furnished by rehabilitation agencies, hospitals when the beneficiary has exhausted their Part A benefits, skilled nursing facilities, and home health agencies for beneficiaries who are not homebound and are under not under a home health episode of care. [Soc. Sec. Act §§ 1833(a)(8), 1833(a)(9), 1834(k).]

Limits on the amount Medicare will pay for outpatient rehabilitation therapy services, generally called therapy caps, are being reinstated on outpatient physical therapy, speech language pathology services, and occupational therapy services under Medicare Part B beginning January 1, 2006. The dollar amount for the therapy caps in CY 2006 is $1,740. Physical therapy services that are performed by chiropractors under the two-year demonstration project provided for in the MMA, are included under the therapy cap because chiroprac-

¶826

tors are subject to the same rules as medical doctors for therapy services under the demonstration. [*Final rule*, 70 FR 70266, Nov. 21, 2005.]

Caps on therapy services were first effective January 1, 1999. Congress placed a moratorium on the application of the payment caps starting in January 2000. [*Final rule*, 67 FR 79966, Dec. 31, 2002.] From September 1, 2003, through December 7, 2003, therapy caps were reinstated, but were removed again by the Medicare Prescription Drug, Improvement, and Modernization Act of 2003 (MMA) (PubLNo 108–173). There was no limit on therapy services in effect from December 8, 2003, through December 31, 2005. [*Medicare Claims Processing Manual*, Pub. 100-04, No. 42, Dec. 8, 2003.]

[¶ 827] Clinical Diagnostic Laboratory Tests

Clinical diagnostic laboratory tests are paid according to special area-wide fee schedules established by the Secretary. These fee schedules apply to all services provided to Medicare beneficiaries by all clinical laboratories, including (1) laboratories in physicians' offices, (2) independent laboratories, and (3) hospital laboratories providing tests for the hospital's outpatients. Excluded from the fee schedules are provider-based laboratories performing clinical diagnostic laboratory tests for their own inpatients. [Soc. Sec. Act § 1833(h)(1).] Current exceptions to this rule are critical access hospital (CAH) laboratory services and services provided by hospitals in the State of Maryland. The areas may not include more than one state. [*Medicare Claims Processing Manual*, Pub. 100-04, Ch. 16, § 20.]

Each fee schedule is set at 60 percent of the prevailing charge levels that were in effect during the year beginning July 1, 1984. Laboratories in sole community hospitals are paid 62 percent of the prevailing charge level. The fee schedules are adjusted annually on a calendar year basis to reflect changes in the Consumer Price Index for All Urban Consumers (U.S. city average) and are subject to such other adjustments as the Secretary determines are justified by technological changes or the need to compensate adequately for emergency services or high utilization of sophisticated equipment and skilled personnel. [Soc. Sec. Act § 1833(h)(2).]

In accord with Medicare program rules, the fiscal intermediary pays the laboratory that provided the service for all separately billable ESRD clinical laboratory services furnished to patients of independent dialysis. Independent dialysis facilities with appropriate clinical laboratory certification may bill their intermediary for any separately billable clinical laboratory tests they perform. The intermediary pays both laboratories and independent dialysis facilities for separately billable clinical laboratory tests according to the Medicare clinical laboratory fee schedule. [Pub. 100-4, Ch. 16, § 40.6.2.2.]

The law imposes a ceiling on the amount that may be paid under a laboratory fee schedule. Since January 1, 1998, that ceiling has been 74 percent of the median of all the fee schedules established for a particular test in a particular laboratory setting. For new tests performed on or after January 1, 2001, for which no payment ceiling has previously been established, the ceiling is 100 percent of the median. [Soc. Sec. Act § 1833(h)(4)(B).] In addition, the annual inflation adjustment to the clinical diagnostic lab fee schedules for 2004 through 2008 will be zero percent. [Soc. Sec. Act § 1833(h)(2)(A)(ii)(IV).]

Fees for collection of samples. In addition to the amounts provided under the fee schedule, a nominal fee of up to $3 is allowed to cover services by physicians, independent laboratories, or hospital laboratories for drawing or collecting specimens, whether or not the specimens are referred to physicians or other laboratories for testing. This fee will not be paid to anyone who has not actually extracted the specimen from the patient. Only one collection fee will be allowed for each patient encounter, regardless of the number of specimens drawn. When a series of specimens is required to complete a single test (for

¶827

example, a glucose tolerance test), the series will be treated as a single encounter. A specimen collection fee is allowed in circumstances such as drawing a blood sample through venipuncture or collecting a urine sample by catheterization. A specimen collection fee is not allowed when the cost of collecting the specimen is minimal, such as a throat culture or a routine capillary puncture for clotting or bleeding time. [Pub. 100-4, Ch. 16, §§ 60.1-60.1.3.]

A specimen collection fee is allowed when it is medically necessary for a laboratory technician to draw the specimen from either a nursing home patient or homebound patient. A laboratory performing the specimen collection may receive payment both for the draw and for the associated travel to obtain the specimen. Payment may be made to the laboratory even if the nursing facility has on-duty personnel qualified to perform the specimen collection. [Soc. Sec. Act § 1833(h)(3)(B); Pub. 100-4, Ch. 16, § 60.1.2.]

Billing and Payment

In most cases, payment for clinical diagnostic laboratory tests may be made only to the person or entity that performed or supervised the performance of the test. Thus, no payment may be made to a physician for a test unless the physician (or another physician with whom a practice is shared) personally performed or supervised the performance of the test. Payment may be made, however, to a hospital when the tests are performed under arrangements made by the hospital and to a referring laboratory that meets certain conditions and that does not have a financial relationship with the referring physician. [Soc. Sec. Act §§ 1833(h)(5)(A), 1877.]

Mandatory assignment for independent and physician office labs. In most cases, payment for clinical diagnostic tests performed by clinical laboratories may be made only on an assignment-related basis (see ¶ 831). This rule also applies to services provided by (1) hospital laboratories to hospital outpatients, (2) hospital laboratories to non-hospital patients, and (3) laboratories in physician offices. This rule does not apply to rural health clinics, however, which have the option of choosing whether to accept assignment. [Soc. Sec. Act § 1833(h)(5)(C).]

Assignment acceptance. When assignment is accepted, payment is made at 100 percent of the fee schedule amount or the actual charges (whichever is less), and no deductible and coinsurance is required (see ¶ 335). When assignment is not accepted (for example, in the case of a rural health clinic), payment is made at 80 percent of the fee schedule or the actual charges (whichever is less), and deductible and coinsurance amounts are required. If assignment is not accepted by a laboratory that is not in a rural health clinic, no Medicare payment will be made. [Soc. Sec. Act §§ 1833(b)(3), 1833(h)(5)(C).]

Negotiated payment rate. In the case of diagnostic laboratory tests that are not paid on the basis of a fee schedule, the Secretary may negotiate a payment rate with the person or entity performing the test. This negotiated rate will be considered the full charge for the test, and no deductible or coinsurance will apply. [Soc. Sec. Act § 1833(h)(6).]

[¶ 831] Assignment

Medicare payments for services rendered by institutional providers under both Part A and Part B are made directly to the providers, and beneficiaries do not have the right to have the payments made to themselves first. However, in the case of Part B payments for the services of physicians and suppliers, the beneficiary does have this right. In these cases, Medicare's payment is sent to the beneficiary after the carrier has processed an itemized bill submitted to the carrier on the appropriate form (Form CMS-1500). The beneficiary is then responsible for paying the physician or supplier (see also ¶ 903). [42 C.F.R. §§ 424.51-424.55.]

Payment Rules

For convenience, the beneficiary may ask that the payment be made to the physician or supplier. Medicare will make direct payment to the physician or supplier only if the beneficiary assigns them this right by signing the assignment statement on the claims form and if the physician or supplier agrees to be paid under the rules governing assignment agreements (see below). Medicare then will pay the physician or supplier the Medicare-approved "fee schedule" amount (see ¶ 820), and the beneficiary is responsible for paying the coinsurance and any remaining deductible (see ¶ 335). [Soc. Sec. Act §§ 1842(b)(3)(B)(ii); 42 C.F.R. § 424.55; *Medicare Claims Processing Manual*, Pub. 100-4 Ch. 1, § 30.3.]

The law uses the terms "assignment" and "assignment-related basis" interchangeably. [Soc. Sec. Act § 1842(i)(1).]

Carriers are required to maintain toll-free telephone numbers at which beneficiaries can obtain the names, addresses, specialties, and telephone numbers of physicians and suppliers who are in the "participation program"—who have agreed to accept assignment for all services provided to all Medicare beneficiaries (this program is discussed at ¶ 833 and ¶ 903).

Assignment Agreements

By submitting the claims form with the beneficiary's assignment authorization, the physician or supplier agrees to accept the Medicare-approved charge as the full charge for the items or services provided. No additional charge may be collected from the beneficiary (except the coinsurance and deductible). If the physician or supplier is dissatisfied with the amount of the Medicare-approved charge, the physician's remedy is to request a review and hearing with the carrier (see ¶ 920). The physician may not ask the beneficiary for more money. [Soc. Sec. Act § 1842(b)(3)(B).]

If a beneficiary has private insurance in addition to Medicare (*e.g.*, a Medigap policy—see ¶ 740), the physician or supplier who has accepted assignment is in violation of the assignment agreement if that physician or supplier bills or collects from the beneficiary or the private insurer an amount which, when added to the Medicare benefit received, exceeds the limiting charge (see ¶ 821). [Pub. 100-4, Ch. 1, § 30.3.2.]

A physician or supplier who accepts assignment for some services (on a case-by-case basis) ordinarily is permitted to not accept assignment in other cases (unless, of course, the physician or supplier has joined the Participation Program—see ¶ 833). A physician or supplier may not fragment bills, however, by accepting assignment for some services or supplies and not others that are provided for the same beneficiary at the same place on the same occasion. *Exception:* When a physician is required to accept assignment for certain services as a condition of Medicare payment, (for example, for clinical diagnostic laboratory services (see ¶ 827) and the services of physician assistants (see ¶ 826), the physician may accept assignment for those services while billing on an unassigned basis for other services the physician furnishes at the same place and on the same occasion. [Pub. 100-4, Ch. 1, § 30.3.2.]

Breach of Assignment Agreement

A physician or supplier who charges a beneficiary more than the amount allowed under the assignment agreement is required to refund the overcharge to the beneficiary. A physician or supplier who refuses to refund the overcharge or who knowingly, willfully, and repeatedly violates the assignment agreement is subject to civil money penalties and/or exclusion from the Medicare program (see ¶ 720). [Soc. Sec. Act § 1128A.] Further, if a physician or supplier violates an assignment agreement or improperly reassigns Medicare

¶831

payments, the Medicare program may terminate the provider agreement or revoke the right to receive assigned benefits. [42 C.F.R. §§ 424.74, 424.82.]

Reassignment of Claims; "Factoring"

As a general rule, physicians and suppliers may not reassign the right to receive payments assigned to them. In effect, this prevents physicians, other practitioners, and suppliers from reassigning their rights to payment to an organization or group that submits claims and receives payments in its own name, a practice sometimes called "factoring." Such reassignments were found in the past to have been a source of incorrect or inflated claims or fraudulent operations. [Soc. Sec. Act § 1815(c); Pub. 100-4, Ch. 1, § 30.2.]

Exceptions. Payment may be made, however, to:

(1) the employer of the physician or other supplier providing the services, if the physician or other supplier is required as a condition of employment to turn over to the employer the fees for his or her services;

(2) to the entity if, under the contractual arrangement (where the service was provided under a contractual arrangement between such physician or other person and an entity), the entity submits the bill for the service and the contractual arrangement meets such program integrity and other safeguards as the Secretary may determine to be appropriate;

(3) an organized healthcare delivery system, if there is a contractual arrangement between the organization and the physician or other supplier under which the organization bills for the physician or other supplier's services;

(4) a physician (or a physician's medical group) for diagnostic laboratory tests (other than clinical diagnostic laboratory tests) that a physician (or group) purchases from an independent physician, medical group, or other supplier;

(5) a person or entity that provides diagnostic tests for interpretations, which that person or entity purchases from an independent physician or medical group;

(6) the patient's regular physician for services provided to his or her patients by another physician on an occasional reciprocal basis;

(7) the patient's regular physician for services of a substitute physician during the regular physician's absence, where the regular physician pays the substitute physician on a per diem or similar fee-for-time basis;

(8) a governmental agency or entity;

(9) an individual or entity designated pursuant to a court order by a court of competent jurisdiction;

(10) an agent who furnishes billing or collection services;

(11) a skilled nursing facility; and

(12) a home health agency. [Soc. Sec. Act § 1842(b)(6); Pub. 100-4, Ch. 1, § 30.2.]

A power of attorney may not be used to circumvent the prohibition against reassignment. [Soc. Sec. Act § 1842(b)(6); Pub. 100-4, Ch. 1, § 30.2.]

[¶ 833] Participation Program for Physicians and Suppliers

Under Medicare's "Participating Physicians and Suppliers Program," physicians and suppliers are encouraged to sign a "participation" agreement with Medicare binding them to accept assignment (see ¶ 831 for what this entails) for all services provided to all Medicare patients for the following calendar year. [Soc. Sec. Act § 1842(h)(1).]

Payment Rules

Participation agreements are effective for one year, but they are renewed automatically unless canceled. A physician or supplier who chooses not to participate in this program, known as "nonparticipating" physicians or suppliers, still may continue to accept assignment on a case-by-case basis. [*Medicare Claims Processing Manual*, Pub. 100-4 Ch. 1, § 30.3.12.]

Note that the "participation" program relates only to how physicians or suppliers are paid; it does not affect whether the services provided are covered. Thus, for coverage purposes, it makes no difference whether the physician or supplier providing the items or services is "participating" or "nonparticipating."

A participation agreement must be signed by the physician or supplier before the year in which it is to be effective. Once the year has begun, physicians and suppliers will not be permitted to enter or drop out of the program until the end of the year. However, a newly licensed physician, a physician who begins a practice in a new area, or a new supplier who begins a new business may enter into a participation agreement during the course of the year. [Soc. Sec. Act § 1842(h)(1).]

Incentives to Participate

The "participation program" provides incentives to encourage physicians and suppliers to participate. These include the following:

(1) the establishment and free distribution of participating physician and supplier directories (see below);

(2) carrier toll-free telephone lines through which beneficiaries may obtain the names, addresses, specialties, and telephone numbers of participating physicians and suppliers [Soc. Sec. Act § 1842(h)(2)];

(3) electronic transmission of claims to carriers [Soc. Sec. Act § 1842(h)(3)];

(4) certificates or emblems of participation are provided to all participating physicians and suppliers for display in their offices or places of business;

(5) higher payment rates (nonparticipating physicians are paid 95 percent of the payment rates applied to participating physicians);and

(6) limitations on the actual charges that can be billed by nonparticipating physicians, including important refund and disclosure rules (see ¶ 821).

Furthermore, as discussed at ¶ 821, the Secretary is required to monitor the actual charges of nonparticipating physicians to assure that these charges do not exceed the "limiting charge." The Secretary also is required to monitor whether the required refunds have been made. Failure by a physician to comply with the actual charge limitation rules can cause the physician to be fined or excluded from participation in the Medicare program. [Soc. Sec. Act § 1848(g)(2); *Medicare Claims Processing Manual*, Pub. 100-4, Ch. 1, § 30.3.12.3.]

Directory of Participating Physicians and Suppliers

At the beginning of each year, the Secretary is required to publish local directories containing the names, addresses, specialties, and telephone numbers of all local "participating" physicians and suppliers. [Soc. Sec. Act § 1842(h)(4).] These directories, called "Medicare Participating Physicians/Suppliers Directories" (abbreviated MEDPARD), are available at all Social Security offices and at some senior citizen organization centers. [*Medicare Contract Beneficiary and Provider Communications Manual*, Pub. 100-9, Ch. 1, § 30.1.12.] Carriers are required to mail directories to beneficiaries at no charge upon request. [Soc. Sec. Act § 1842(h)(2).]

¶833

[¶ 834] Private Non-Medicare Contracts with Healthcare Practitioners

Beginning in 1998, CMS allowed Medicare beneficiaries and their physicians (and certain nonphysician practitioners) to enter into private contracts that permit physicians to charge more than the Medicare program allows ("opt-out" contracts). A physician who enters into such a private contract, however, is not permitted to participate in the Medicare program for a two-year period. The "opt-out" provision is available to doctors of medicine, doctors of osteopathy, physician assistants, nurse practitioners, clinical nurse specialists, certified registered nurse anesthetists, certified nurse-midwives, clinical psychologists, and clinical social workers. CMS has added dentists, podiatrists, and optometrists to the definition/list of physicians who may opt out of Medicare as required by the enactment of the Medicare Modernization Act of 2003 (MMA) (PubLNo 108–173). Chiropractors, physical therapists in independent practice, and occupational therapists in independent practice *cannot* opt out of Medicare and provide services under private contract to Medicare beneficiaries.

Certain clauses must be included in the private contract to meet Medicare requirements. During the period the physician is not allowed to participate in Medicare, the physician is prohibited from receiving any Medicare payment (1) directly or (2) from any organization that receives Medicare payment. A physician or other practitioner who chooses to opt out of Medicare must opt out for all Medicare beneficiaries and for all covered items and services. Physicians and practitioners cannot have private contracts that apply to some covered services they furnish but not to others. [Soc. Sec. Act §§ 1802(b), 1862(a)(19); *Medicare Benefit Policy Manual*, Pub. 100-02, Ch. 15, §§ 40–40.40.]

The Medicare private contract rules provide that the contract must be in writing and signed by the patient before any item or service is provided. Furthermore, the contract may not be entered into at a time when the patient is facing an emergency or urgent healthcare situation. Finally, the physician must file an affidavit stating that for the following two-year period the physician will not submit any claims to Medicare or receive any payment from Medicare either directly or indirectly. If the physician knowingly and willfully submits a claim to Medicare or receives any payment from Medicare during the two-year period, the physician's right to enter into private contracts will be terminated for the remainder of the period and the physician will not be eligible to receive Medicare payments for the remainder of the period. [Soc. Sec. Act §§ 1128A, 1862(b); Pub. 100-02, Ch. 15, §§ 40.8, 40.9.]

Medicare will pay for services furnished by an "opt out" physician/practitioner who has not signed a private contract with a beneficiary, for emergency or urgent care items and services furnished to the beneficiary. The physician/practitioner may not charge the beneficiary more than the Medicare limiting charge for the service and must submit the claim to Medicare on the beneficiary's behalf. [Pub. 100-02, Ch. 15, §§ 40.6, 40.28.]

[¶ 835] Home Health Agencies

Section 4603 of the Balanced Budget Act of 1997 (BBA) (PubLNo 105-33) mandated the development of a prospective payment system (PPS) for all home health services for cost reporting periods beginning after September 1999. Section 5101 of the Omnibus Consolidated and Emergency Supplemental Appropriations Act for Fiscal Year 1999 (OCESAA) (PubLNo 105-277) postponed the implementation date of the home health PPS to October 1, 2000.

Prospective Payment System

Under the home health prospective payment system (HH PPS), a standardized payment, subject to several adjustments, is made for each 60-day episode of care a beneficiary receives from a home health agency (HHA). The payment covers the cost of skilled nursing and home health aide visits, covered therapy, medical social services, and supplies. [*Final rule*, 65 FR 41128, July 3, 2000.]

HHAs are paid 60 percent of their expected adjusted payment after submitting a request for anticipated payment (RAP). A RAP may be submitted at the start of care after the HHA receives verbal orders from a physician that are copied into the plan of care, including a description of the patient's condition and the services to be provided by the HHA. There must also be an attestation signed and dated by the registered nurse or qualified therapist responsible for furnishing or supervising the ordered service in the plan of care. The remainder of the adjusted payment will be made when care or the episode is completed. At that time, HHAs will be required to (1) have completed all Outcome and Assessment Information Set (OASIS) assessments, (2) have received a physician's certification, and (3) have a plan of care signed by a physician. Beneficiaries may have an unlimited number of episodes of care. [42 C.F.R. §§ 409.43(c), 484.205.]

The standard unadjusted national 60-day episode payment is calculated by computing the mean national cost-per-visit multiplied by the national mean utilization for each discipline. This amount then is added to the cost of the non-routine medical supplies and an adjustment for reporting costs associated with OASIS (see ¶ 266). The standard unadjusted national 60-day episode rate for calendar year (CY) 2006 is $2,327.68. For CY 2006 the CY 2005 rate of $2,264.28 was increased by the home health market basket update of 3.6 percent minus 0.8 percent in accordance with section 701 of the MMA which requires a full market basket update minus 0.8 percent for CY 2006. This 60-day episode rate will apply for care beginning on January 1, 2006 through December 31, 2006.[42 C.F.R. § 484.215(d); *Final rule*, 70 FR 68132, Nov. 9, 2005.]

The final CY 2005 updated national 60-day episode rate for the home health prospective payment system was $2,264.28. This amount represents the CY 2004 rate of 2,213.37 multiplied by the applicable home health market basket increase of 3.1 percent minus the 0.8 percentage point decrease mandated by the Medicare Modernization Act of 2003 (MMA). [*Final rule*, 69 FR 62123, Oct. 22, 2004.]

Since January 1, 2004, the annual adjustment to the standard unadjusted national 60-day episode payment rate is made on January 1 instead of October 1. [Soc. Sec. Act § 1895(b).]

Adjustments

The basic pay rate per 60-days of care is subject to adjustments based on (1) case mix, (2) outlier visits, (3) a significant change in a beneficiary's condition, (4) a partial period of care, (5) wage index, (6) budget neutrality, and (7) low utilization. [42 C.F.R. § 484.205.]

Case-mix adjustment. The case mix adjustment is determined based on responses to 22 questions in the OASIS evaluation. Based on these responses, a beneficiary is placed into one of 80 home health resource groups (HHRGs). An HHA adjusts the national prospective 60-day payment rate to account for HHA case mixing using an index to explain the resource utilization of different patients. The adjustment is also determined by the geographic differences in wage levels using an appropriate wage index based on the site of service of the beneficiary. [42 C.F.R. § 484.220.]

Outlier adjustment. The outlier adjustment provides additional payment to an HHA when the cost of providing care to a beneficiary exceeds a threshold amount. The total amount available for outlier payments is not to exceed five percent of the total amount paid for HHA services during the year. In 2005 and 2006, CMS adjusted the outlier formula so more episodes of care would qualify for this adjustment, however, this means that to meet the

¶835

requirement that outlier payments be limited to five percent of total expenditures the amount per episode is less. [42 C.F.R. § 484.240; *Final rule*, 70 FR 68132, Nov. 9, 2005.]

Significant change in condition (SCIC) adjustment. An HHA is provided additional funding when a significant change in a beneficiary's condition occurs. To realize this adjustment, an HHA must obtain the necessary change order from the physician; note the required changes in treatment in the beneficiary's plan of care; and complete a new OASIS evaluation, which will produce a new case-mix adjustment factor. The HHA will be reimbursed an amount proportionately between the HHRG prior to the change and HHRG after the significant change in condition. [42 C.F.R. §§ 484.237, 484.205(e).]

Partial episode payment adjustment. A partial period of care adjustment is made if a beneficiary transfers from one HHA to another HHA during a 60-day episode. The original 60-day episode payment is adjusted to reflect the length of time the beneficiary remained under the care of the original HHA based on the first billable visit date through and including the last billable visit date. The second HHA will conduct an assessment, and a new episode of care will begin. This is different from proration of care between HHAs when a beneficiary receives care from more than one HHA at the same time. [42 C.F.R. § 484.235.]

Low utilization adjustment. A low utilization adjustment applies to beneficiaries who receive four or fewer visits. HHAs will be paid the national average standardized per-visit amount by discipline for each visit type. These amounts will be updated annually by the applicable market basket for each type of visit in the episode. The savings from the "reduced" episode payment will be redistributed to all episodes. [42 C.F.R. § 484.230.]

The following amounts will be paid for service provided during a visit under the low utilization payment adjustment system in 2006; $46.01 will be paid for a home health aide visit, $162.89 will be paid for medical social services, $111.86 will be provided for occupational therapy services, $111.11 will be reimbursed for a physical therapy services, $101.62 will be reimbursed for skilled nursing services, $120.73 will be reimbursed for speech-language pathology services. [*Final rule*, 70 FR 68132, Nov. 9, 2005..]

Consolidated billing. Durable medical equipment (DME), a covered home health service when furnished to an eligible homebound beneficiary in his or her place of residence, was eliminated from the consolidated billing requirement. DME is paid under a fee schedule in an amount that is in addition to the prospective payment rate for home health services. Some non-routine medical supplies are included in the HH PPS, and some are billed separately. [*Final rule*, 65 FR 41128, July 3, 2000.]

Payment Basis and Updates

The Secretary will compute a standard payment amount initially based on the most current audited cost report data available. The total amounts payable under HH PPS will be equal to the total amount that would have been paid in the absence of such a system. [Soc. Sec. Act § 1895(b)(3)(A)(i)(I).] This amount will then be reduced by 15 percent for annual adjustments made after September 30, 2000. [Soc. Sec. Act § 1895(b)(3)(A)(ii).] For cost reporting periods beginning during each of fiscal years 2000, 2002 and 2003, the payment update were required to equal the market basket increase reduced by 1.1 percentage points. [OCESAA § 5101; Soc. Sec. Act § 1861(v)(1)(L).]

Payments were increased by five percent for home health service provided in rural areas from April 1, 2004 to March 31, 2005. [MMA § 421.]

Payment information requirements. Home health claims must include (1) the unique identifier of the physician prescribing or certifying the services and (2) in the case of skilled nursing care, physical and occupational therapy and speech language pathology services,

¶835

medical social services, and home health aide services, appropriately coded time information, as measured in 15-minute increments. [Soc. Sec. Act § 1895.] Payment for episodes of care that overlap fiscal years must be recorded in the fiscal year in which the episode was completed. [*Provider Reimbursement Manual*, Part 2, Chapter 32, line 3216.2; Form CMS 1728-94, Trans. No. 10, June 2001.]

[¶ 837] Hospital Outpatient Services

Outpatient services are paid under the outpatient prospective payment system (OPPS), and the annual Part B deductible ($124 in 2006) applies to payments. [42 C.F.R. § 419.21.]. Beneficiaries also have a copayment for each OPPS service, which in all cases is limited to the amount of the inpatient hospital deductible for the applicable year (2006 in $952). [*Final rule*, 70 FR 68515, Nov. 10, 2005.]

OPPS became effective on August 1, 2000, generally, and October 7, 2000, for provider-based facilities owned by hospitals. [Soc. Sec. Act § 1833(t).] Prior to OPPS, services provided to Medicare beneficiaries in hospital outpatient departments were reimbursed on the basis of the lower of charges or reasonable costs. [Soc. Sec. Act § 1814(b).] This cost-based reimbursement was reduced by 5.8 percent beginning in 1990 until OPPS became effective on August 1, 2000. The reimbursement reduction did not apply to sole community or rural primary care hospitals.

Background on Hospital Outpatient PPS

Historically, beneficiaries paid 20 percent of a hospital's *charges*, rather than 20 percent of what Medicare allowed, which is the opposite for most other Medicare-covered services. As a result, beneficiaries were required to pay substantially more than 20 percent of allowable costs. A combination of the beneficiary coinsurance rules and the blended payment systems for certain surgical, diagnostic and radiology services resulted in a rate of increase of Medicare payments for outpatient services that escalated faster than the increase for inpatient services. [*Proposed rule*, 63 FR 47552, 47572, Sept. 8, 1998.]

In addition, CMS determined that Medicare payments for the facility component of a procedure performed in an outpatient department, where it was reimbursed on a cost basis, were higher than payments for the technical component of the same procedure performed in a physician's office or freestanding clinic, where it was reimbursed on the basis of the physician's fee schedule (formerly, on the basis of the physician's reasonable charge). [*Final rule*, 65 FR 18434, 18437, April 7, 2000.] OPPS was designed to address the excessive payment liability experienced by beneficiaries and eliminated the formula-driven overpayments for outpatient services. The BBA amendments established an outpatient prospective payment system that was modified by BBRA and the Benefits Improvement and Protection Act of 2000 (BIPA) (PubLNo 106-554). [Soc. Sec. Act § 1833(t).]

Ambulatory Payment Classification Groups

To determine payment amounts for specific services under OPPS, CMS developed an outpatient department fee schedule and a classification system based on ambulatory payment classification groups (APCs), which bundle incidental costs associated with a procedure such as operating room time, lab tests and x-rays with the cost of the procedure itself. CMS chose to use the median cost to establish a payment amount for the grouped services. Each APC is assigned a relative weight that reflects the APC's use of resources as compared to other APCs. The APC payment rates are calculated on a national basis and then adjusted by geographic areas. The labor-related portion of the payment is wage adjusted using each hospital's wage index value. [*Proposed rule*, 63 FR 47552, Sept. 8, 1998.]

CMS bases the relative weights of APCs on the median cost for each APC group. Each APC represents the median hospital cost for services included in that APC relative to the median hospital cost of services included in APC 0601, mid-level clinic visits. APC weights are scaled to APC 0601 because it is one of the most frequently performed services in the outpatient setting. [*Final rule*, 69 FR 65682, Nov. 15, 2004.] Items and services within a group cannot be considered comparable with respect to the use of resources if the highest median cost for an item or service within the group is more than two times greater than the lowest median cost for an item or service within the group, referred to as the "two times rule". The Secretary may make an exception to the two-times limit in unusual cases such as low-volume items and services. [Soc. Sec. Act § 1833(t)(2)(G).]

The services within each group are related clinically and require comparable resources. [*Final rule*, 67 FR 66718, Nov. 1, 2002.] The items and services in an APC group are those that are recognized as contributing to the cost of the procedures or services. Provider concentration, when a procedure is offered only by a subset of hospitals, was taken into consideration in the creation of the APC groups, which CMS indicated it kept as broad and inclusive as possible to prevent upcoding and code fragmentation. The appropriate APC is assigned based on Healthcare Common Procedure Coding System (HCPCS) codes and International Classification of Disease (ICD-9-CM) codes on a patient's bill. [42 C.F.R. § 419.31; *Proposed rule*, 63 FR 47552, 47561, Sept. 18, 1998.]

The costs of drugs, pharmaceuticals and biologicals are packaged with the APC payment rate for the primary procedure or treatment with which they are used. Corneal tissue acquisition costs, however, are not packaged into the payment rate for corneal transplant procedures. A separate APC payment rate was created for the following items and services: blood and blood products; casting, splinting and strapping services; immunosuppressive drugs for patients following an organ transplant; hepatitis B vaccine; and certain other high cost drugs that are administered infrequently. Orphan drugs that meet certain criteria are paid separately. In 2006, CMS will continue to use the same criteria for establishing orphan drugs that was implemented in 2003. Payment for single indication orphan drugs has been set at the higher of 88 percent of the average wholesale price (AWP), or the average sales price (ASP) plus six percent, updated quarterly to reflect the most current AWP and ASP data. Influenza and pneumococcal pneumonia vaccines also are paid separately on a reasonable cost basis because CMS's payment methodology of using two year old claims data to recalibrate payment rates cannot take into account the yearly fluctuations. [42 C.F.R. § 419.2; *Final rule*, 69 FR 65682, Nov. 15, 2004.]

APC payment rates. The APC weights were converted to payment rates through the application of a conversion factor. [42 C.F.R. §§ 419.31(b), 419.32] The Secretary is authorized to adjust the conversion factor in later years to eliminate the effect of coding or classification changes if CMS determines that updates to the adjustment factor used to convert the relative utilization weights under OPPS into payment amounts have resulted or are likely to result in hospitals' changing their coding or classification of covered services. [Soc. Sec. Act § 1833(t)(3)(C); BIPA § 401(b).]

Payment for service under the OPPS is calculated based on grouping outpatient services into APC groups. The payment rate and coinsurance amount calculated for an APC apply to all of the services within the APC. APCs require no changes to the billing form; however, hospitals are required to include HCPCS codes for all services paid under OPPS. A hospital may receive a number of APC payments for the services furnished to a patient on a single day; however, multiple surgical procedures furnished on the same day are subject to discounting. [*Medicare Claims Processing Manual*, Pub. 100-04, Ch. 4, § 10.2.]

¶837

Bundling of Services

Hospitals participating in Medicare are required to furnish directly or under arrangements all covered nonphysician services required by their patients. [Soc. Sec. Act § 1866(a)(1)(H).] Separate payments for nonphysician services furnished to hospital inpatients or outpatients is prohibited, unless the services are furnished by the hospital either directly or under arrangements. [Soc. Sec. Act § 1862(a)(14).] All services furnished in a hospital encounter between an outpatient and physician or authorized nonphysician must be bundled. All diagnostic tests that are furnished by a hospital, directly or under arrangements to a registered hospital outpatient during an encounter at a hospital are also subject to the bundling requirements.

Hospitals are not required to bundle diagnostic services ordered during or as the result of an encounter in the hospital if the patient leaves the hospital and goes elsewhere to obtain the diagnostic test. In such cases, Medicare will pay the entity that furnishes the services if it is recognized by the program. Another exception to the bundling requirements has been provided for services furnished by hospitals to skilled nursing facility (SNF) residents when the services provided are subject to the consolidated billing requirement under SNF PPS. For those intensive hospital outpatient services that lie beyond the scope of care that a SNF would ordinarily furnish, such as cardiac catheterization, CAT scans, MRIs or radiation therapy, the patient would be considered a hospital outpatient. [42 C.F.R. § 410.42; *Final rule*, 70 FR 68749, Nov. 10, 2005].

To deter the unbundling of nonphysician services provided to hospital outpatients, civil money penalties have been established. [Soc. Sec. Act § 1866(g); 42 C.F.R. §§ 1003.102, 1003.103.]

Services and Costs Excluded From Coverage Under OPPS

In addition to services that are not covered, including services that are not reasonable or necessary, CMS excluded from coverage under OPPS those services furnished in an outpatient hospital setting that were already subject to an existing fee schedule or other prospectively determined payment rate. Services paid under fee schedules or other payment systems rather than under OPPS include ambulance services, screening and diagnostic mammographies (payment for both of these services will be based on the Medicare physician fee schedule (MPFS) for CY 2005 and 2006), services for patients with end-stage renal disease paid under the ESRD composite rate, professional services of physicians and nonphysician practitioners paid under the physician fee schedule, laboratory services paid under the clinical diagnostic laboratory fee schedule; and durable medical equipment, orthotics, prosthetics, and prosthetic devices, and supplies paid under the durable medical equipment, prosthetics and orthotics (DMEPOS) fee schedule when the hospital is acting as a supplier of these items. DMEPOS is billed to the DME regional carrier. [42 C.F.R. § 419.22; *Final rule*, 69 FR 65682, Nov. 15, 2004.]

Inpatient services. Generally, services that typically would be paid in an inpatient setting are not paid by Medicare under OPPS. These are services that require inpatient care because of the invasive nature of the procedure, the need for at least 24 hours of postoperative recovery time or monitoring before the patient can be safely discharged, or the underlying physical condition of the patient. CMS reviews the list of inpatient services so that procedures that can be appropriately performed in an outpatient setting are removed from the inpatient procedure list and moved to APCs. [42 C.F.R. § 419.22.] There are occasions, however, when a procedure on the inpatient list must be performed to resuscitate or stabilize a patient with a life-threatening condition whose status is that of an outpatient. Effective January 1, 2003, a hospital may submit a claim for inpatient-only procedures when four

¶ 837

conditions are met: (1) the patient's status is outpatient; (2) the patient has an emergent, life-threatening condition; (3) a procedure on the inpatient-only list has been performed to resuscitate or stabilize the patient; and (4) the patient dies while in surgery without being admitted as an inpatient. [*Final rule*, 67 FR 66718, Nov. 1, 2002.]

Outpatient services furnished to SNF patients. Hospital outpatient services furnished to skilled nursing facility (SNF) residents (as defined in 42 C.F.R. § 411.15(p)) as part of the patient's resident assessment or comprehensive care plan that are furnished by the hospital "under arrangements" are covered under SNF PPS and, therefore, are billable only by the SNF, regardless of whether or not the patient is in a Part A SNF stay (see ¶ 839). Outpatient services including emergency services that are not furnished pursuant to the SNF's comprehensive plan of care, however, are excluded from the SNF PPS consolidated billing requirement if those services lie well beyond the scope of care that any SNFs ordinarily would furnish. Those services may be covered under OPPS if they are within the scope of OPPS. [42 C.F.R. § 419.22.]

Costs outside the scope of OPPS. Hospitals subject to OPPS are paid for certain items and services that are outside the scope of OPPS on a reasonable cost or other basis. The following costs are outside the scope of OPPS:

- medical education;
- nursing and allied health programs;
- interns and residents not in approved teaching programs;
- teaching physicians' charges for Part B services in hospitals that elect cost-based payment for teaching physicians;
- anesthesia services furnished to hospital outpatients by qualified nonphysician anesthetists such as certified registered nurse anesthetists and anesthesiologists' assistants employed by the hospital or obtained under arrangements;
- bad debts for uncollectible deductible and coinsurance amount;
- organ acquisition costs paid under Part B; and
- corneal tissue acquisition costs. [42 C.F.R. § 419.2.]

Screening mammography. Section 614 of the Medicare Prescription Drug, Improvement, and Modernization Act of 2003 (MMA) (PubLNo 108-173) removed mammography services from coverage under OPPS. Screening mammography services have not been paid under OPPS since December 8, 2003. Unilateral and bilateral diagnostic mammograpy will not be paid under OPPS, effective January 1, 2005. [Soc. Sec. Act § 1833(t)(1)(B)(iv).]

Payment for Drugs, Biologicals, and Radiopharmaceuticals

Drugs, biological and radiopharmaceutical without pass-through status (see below) either are paid for separately (individual APCs established for the drug) or with the procedure performed (packaged). The threshold for establishing a separate APC for drugs, biologicals and radiopharmaceutical is set at $50 per administration for 2005 and 2006. CMS will pay separately for drugs, biologicals, and radiopharmaceuticals whose median cost per day exceeds $50 and will package the cost of drugs, biologicals, and radiopharmaceuticals whose median cost per day is less than $50 into the procedures with which they are an integral part. One exception to the packaging rule is anti-emetic treatments. There are seven drugs, biologicals and radiopharmaceuticals that also are excepted from the packaging rule. They will be paid according to their 2004 status as a package or separate APC drug. [Soc. Sec. Act § 1833(t)(16)(B); § 621(a)(2) of the MMA (PubLNo 108-173); *Final rule*, 69 FR 65682, Nov. 15, 2004.] During CY 2003, drugs costing $150 or less per patient encounter were folded into the associated APCs. [*Final rule*, 67 FR 66718, Nov. 1, 2002.]

¶837

Payment Rules

To ensure that Medicare beneficiaries will continue to have access to cutting-edge technology, CMS limited the impact of payment reductions for APCs that would have decreased by more than 15 percent in 2003. Most of the affected APCs include those drugs and devices that no longer are eligible for pass-through payments. To limit the impact of the reduction, CMS decreased the 2003 reduction in median cost by half of the difference between the value derived from the claims data and 15 percent. [*Final rule*, 67 FR 66718, Nov. 1, 2002.] For 2004, CMS limited the reduction in median costs to one-fourth of the difference between the value derived from claims data and a 15 percent reduction for separately payable drugs, biologicals and radiopharmaceuticals whose 2004 median costs decreased by more than 15 percent from the applicable 2003 median cost. CMS, however, has placed an upper limit on adjustments to the median costs used to calculate the 2004 payment rates. The upper limit will result in an adjusted median that is no greater than 95 percent of the AWP or the 2004 unadjusted median. In cases in which the 95 percent of AWP was higher than the adjusted median, CMS capped the adjustment at a value that was the higher of the 95 percent cap or the 2004 unadjusted median. [*Final rule*, 68 FR 63398, Nov. 7, 2003.]

Payment for Specified Covered Outpatient Drugs

Section 621 of the MMA has established a payment method for covered drugs that were paid on a pass-through basis on or before December 31, 2002. These drugs are referred to as "specified covered outpatient drugs." A specified covered outpatient drug is a covered outpatient drug for which a separate ambulatory payment classification group (APC) has been established and that is a radiopharmaceutical, a drug, or a biological. There are three categories of specified outpatient drugs: sole source drugs, innovator multiple source drugs and noninnovator multiple source drugs. A specified covered outpatient drug does not include a drug for which payment is first made on or after January 1, 2003, a drug for which a temporary Healthcare Common Procedure Coding System (HCPCS) code has not been assigned, or during 2004 and 2005, orphan drugs. [Soc. Sec. Act § 1833(t)(14)(B).]

Drugs, biologicals and radiopharmaceuticals with no assigned HCPCS. Although the MMA required CMS to make payment under OPPS in an amount equal to 95 percent of AWP for new drugs, biologicals and radiopharmaceuticals until HCPCS codes are assigned, effective January 1, 2004, CMS did not implement this provision, because it had not determined how hospitals would bill Medicare and receive payment without a HCPCS. For CY 2005, CMS will require hospitals to use HCPCS C9399 along with the National Drug Code (NDC) when billing these drugs. Once a HCPCS is assigned to the new drug, the hospital should bill using the new code. [*Final rule*, 69 FR 65682, Nov. 15, 2004.]

Payment method. For services furnished on or after January 1, 2004, a specified covered outpatient drug will be paid based on a percentage of the reference AWP for the drug. CMS has defined reference average wholesale price (AWP) to mean the AWP set under the single drug pricer (SDP) based on the Red Book (a recognized compendium listing the AWP of pharmaceuticals and other relevant information) for May 1, 2003. For services furnished on or after January 1, 2006, the payment rate is based on 106% of the manufacturer's average sales price (ASP), changed from between 83 percent and 95 percent of the reference AWP for 2005 dates of service. A "sole source drug" is a biological product approved under a biologics license application as defined by the Public Health Services Act or a single source drug produced or distributed under an original new drug application approved by the Food and Drug Administration (FDA). [*Final rule*, 70 FR 68749, Nov. 22, 2005.]

Innovator multiple source items payment rates are the lower of standard median cost or 68 percent of the reference AWP. An innovator multiple source drug is a multiple source drug that originally was marketed under an original new drug application approved by the

¶837

FDA. Noninnovator multiple source items are paid at the lower of the median cost or 46 percent of the reference AWP. A noninnovator multiple source drug is a multiple source drug that is not an innovator multiple source drug. Certain drugs are excepted from this rule and will be paid separately based on median cost based on CY 2003 claims data. [Soc. Sec. Act § 1833(t)(14); *Final rule*, 69 FR 65682, Nov. 15, 2004.]

In subsequent years, payment will be equal to the average acquisition cost for the drug for that year (which may vary by hospital group, taking into account hospital volume or other hospital characteristics) or if hospital acquisition cost data are not available, the average price for the drug in the year other than radiopharmaceuticals established under the Social Security Act as calculated and adjusted by the Secretary. [Soc. Sec. Act §§ 1833(t)(14)(A), (F), and (G).]

Transitional Pass-through Payments

Additional payments must be made to hospitals for a period of two to three years for current orphan drugs; current therapy drugs and biologicals and brachytherapy devices used for the treatment of cancer; current radiopharmaceutical drugs and biological products; and new or innovative medical devices, drugs and biologicals that were not being paid for as a hospital outpatient service as of December 31, 1996, and the cost of the item is "not insignificant" in relation to the hospital outpatient PPS payment amount. [Soc. Sec. Act § 1833(t)(6); 42 C.F.R. § 419.64.]

Criteria. To determine whether the costs of drugs and biologicals, and devices are "not insignificant" relative to the hospital outpatient department fee schedule amount, CMS uses the following criteria:

(1) For services furnished before January 1, 2003, the expected reasonable cost of a drug or biological must exceed 10 percent of the applicable APC payment amount for the service related to the drug or biological.

(2) For services furnished after December 31, 2002,

(a) The estimated average reasonable cost of the drug or biological in the category exceeds 10 percent of the applicable APC payment amount for the service related to the drug or biological.

(b) The estimated average reasonable cost of the drug or biological exceeds the cost of the drug or biological portion of the APC payment amount for the related service by at least 25 percent.

(c) The difference between the estimated reasonable cost of the drug or biological and the estimated portion of the APC payment amount for the drug or biological exceeds 10 percent of the APC payment amount for the related service. [42 C.F.R. § 419.64.]

Payment methodology. The MMA established the use of the average sales price (ASP) methodology for payment for drugs and biologicals described in the Act and furnished on or after January 1, 2005. For CY 2005, CMS is continuing pass-through status for eighteen drugs and biologicals Medicare will pay for these drugs and biologicals based on the average sales price (ASP) methodology at a rate that is equivalent to the payment these drugs and biologicals would receive in the physician office setting under the methodology set by the MPFS. The actual pass-through payment amount is the difference between the physician fee schedule payment less the ASP. For new drug and biologicals with status indicator G, CMS will make a separate payment at a rate equivalent to the physician office setting and has set the pass-through payment amount at zero. [42 C.F.R. § 419.64; *Final rule*, 69 FR 65682, Nov. 15, 2004.] The total amount of pass-through payments for a given year cannot be projected to exceed an "applicable percentage" of total outpatient payments. For 2004 and subsequent years, it cannot exceed 2.0 percent. [42 C.F.R. § 419.62; *Final rule,* 69 FR 65682, Nov. 15, 2004.] Additional payments may be reduced uniformly if the Secretary determines that total pass-through payments would exceed the caps. [Soc. Sec. Act § 1833(t)(6)(D)(ii).]

Pass-through for certain devices. Under the OPPS, a category of devices is eligible for transitional pass-through payments for at least two, but not more than three years. This period begins with the first date on which a transitional pass-through payment is made for any medical device that is described by the category. For CY 2005, CMS will continue to package the cost of a device that is no longer eligible for pass-through payment into the costs of the corresponding HCPCS code for that procedure. Six categories will expire on December 31, 2004, and three procedures will remain on the pass-through list for CY 2005. Prior to pass-through device categories, CMS paid for pass-through devices under the OPPS on a brand-specific basis. [Soc. Sec. Act § 1833(t)(6)(B)(ii); *Final rule,* 69 FR 65682, Nov. 15, 2004.]

Section 402 of the Benefits Improvement and Protection Act of 2000 (BIPA) (PubLNo 106-554) required CMS to establish categories of devices to be used in determining eligibility of a device for pass-through payments in two phases. In the first phase, all products that were determined to be pass-through devices were included in a single category. In the second phase, CMS was required to institute rulemaking by July 1, 2001, to establish criteria used to create additional categories, and the categories created cannot result in a device being described by more than one category. The criteria must include a test of whether the average cost of the devices that would be within the category is "not insignificant" as that phrase is used in determining whether a new drug, biological or device qualifies as a pass-through item. As new devices qualify for pass-through status, a new category must be created for devices that are not described by an existing category. [Soc. Sec. Act § 1833(t)(6)(B)(i)-(ii).]

Brachytherapy payment. As established by § 621(b) of the Medicare Modernization Act of 2003 (PubLNo 108-173) payment for brachytherapy devices furnished on or after January 1, 2004, and before January 1, 2007, will be equal to the hospital's charges for each device furnished, adjusted to the cost. Charges for such devices will not be included in determining any outlier payment. The Secretary is required to create additional groups of covered outpatient department services that classify brachytherapy devices separately from other services or groups of services, to reflect the number, isotope, and radioactive intensity of the devices furnished. Separate groups must be created for palladium-103 and iodine-125 devices. [Soc. Sec. Act § § 1833(t)(2)(H) and 1833(t)(16)(C); *Final rule,* 69 FR 65682, Nov. 15, 2004.]

New or innovative devices. CMS makes pass-through payments for new or innovative devices that meet specific criteria. Requests for a new category of devices are evaluated against the following criteria to determine if a device meets the substantial clinical improvement requirement: (1) the device offers a treatment option for a patient population unresponsive to, or ineligible for, currently available treatments; (2) the device can diagnose a medical condition, or provide earlier diagnosis of that condition, in a population in which that medical condition is currently undetectable; and (3) the device significantly improves clinical outcomes for a patient population as compared to currently available treatments. [*Interim final rule,* 66 FR 55850, Nov. 2, 2001.]

Incorporation of expiring transitional pass-through payments into APCs. Under Soc. Sec. Act § 1833(t)(6)(B)(iii), transitional pass-through drugs and devices are eligible for special payments for two to three years. Beginning January 1, 2003, 95 categories of devices and approximately 240 drugs, generally those that have received transitional pass-through payments since the first year of the OPPS, lost this eligibility. Although they continue to be paid under OPPS, they are paid under a different method. The final rule for calendar year (CY) 2003 included a method for incorporating expiring transitional pass-through devices and drugs into the regular payment system. For CY 2003, the costs for the expiring categories of devices are folded into the APCs with the procedures they were billed with in 2001. The MMA established the payment rules for expiring pas-through payment drugs for CY 2004 and subsequent years (see above). [*Final rule*, 67 FR 66718, Nov. 1, 2002.]

Copayment/Coinsurance

Under OPPS, coinsurance is defined as the percent of the Medicare-approved amount that beneficiaries pay for a service furnished in the hospital outpatient department (after they have met the Part B deductible, which is $124 for 2006). Copayment is defined as the set dollar amount that beneficiaries pay under OPPS. The coinsurance percentage is calculated as the difference between the program payment percentage and 100 percent. The coinsurance percentage in any year is defined for each APC group as the greater of the ratio of the APC group unadjusted copayment amount to the annual APC group payment rate, or 20 percent. [42 C.F.R. § 419.40.] As discussed above, historically, beneficiary's paid 20 percent of a hospital's *charges*, rather than 20 percent of what Medicare allowed. As a result, beneficiaries were required to pay substantially more than 20 percent of allowable costs. [*Proposed rule*, 63 FR 47552, 47572, Sept. 8, 1998.]

The Secretary must reduce the national unadjusted copayment amount each year so that the effective copayment rate for a covered service in the year does not exceed specified percentages. For all services paid under the OPPS in CY 20065, the specified percentage is 40 percent of the APC payment rate. For a covered service furnished in a year, the national unadjusted coinsurance amount cannot be less than 20 percent of the payment rate amount. [Soc. Sec. § 1833(t)(3)(B)(ii) and (8)(C); 42 C.F.R. § 419.41; *Final rule*, 70 FR 68749, Nov. 22, 2005.]

OPPS national unadjusted coinsurance amounts that exceed 20 percent of the APC payment rate are frozen until the payment rate increases to the point that the coinsurance amount is 20 percent of the payment rate. Section 111 of BIPA set limits on the national coinsurance amounts. Effective April 1, 2001, the national coinsurance amount cannot exceed 57 percent of the APC payment rate. The national coinsurance amount cannot exceed 55 percent in 2002 or 2003, 50 percent in 2004, 45 percent in 2005, and 40 percent thereafter. [Soc. Sec. Act 1833(t)(8); 42 C.F.R. § 419.41(c)(4).]

In addition, to a national unadjusted copayment amount, CMS established a minimum unadjusted copayment amount, which is an amount no less than 20 percent of the payment amount. A hospital may elect to bill beneficiaries at a wage-adjusted national copayment amount or the wage-adjusted reduced copayment amount (see below for details). [*Final rule*, 65 FR 18434, 18492-95, April 7, 2000.]

Coinsurance rates for certain pass-through drugs and biologicals. CMS made a one- time exception to the general methodology for certain drugs and biologicals eligible for transitional pass-throughs for which CMS could not obtain valid data to determine acquisition costs for OPPS implementation. One of the following ratios of acquisition cost to average wholesale price was applied to determine the applicable acquisition costs: .68 for drugs with one manufacturer, .61 for multi-source drugs, and .43 for multi-source drugs with generic competitors. In these situations, coinsurance amounts are set at 20 percent of this acquisition cost, not 20 percent of the APC rate. [*Final rule*, 65 FR 18434, 18481, April 7, 2000.]

Coinsurance limits. CMS implemented the statutory limit on coinsurance at the inpatient deductible ($952 for 2006) on an APC-by-APC basis, not based on all APCs in a hospital encounter. The coinsurance amount for the APC or APCs for a drug or biological furnished

¶837

on the same day has been aggregated with the coinsurance amount for the APC that reflects the administration of the drug or biological furnished on that day and treated as the coinsurance amount for one APC. [42 C.F.R. § 419.41(c)(4); *Final rule*, 70 FR 68749, Nov. 22, 2005.]

Coinsurance for new procedures. APCs for new procedures may be adopted when the new procedures do not fit well into another APC. When an APC is added that consists of HCPCS codes for which there was no 1996 charge data to calculate the unadjusted coinsurance amount, coinsurance is based on the minimum unadjusted coinsurance, which is 20 percent of the APC payment amount. Additional payments for outlier cases and for certain medical devices, drugs, and biologicals, and transitional corridor payments will not affect the coinsurance amounts. [*Final rule*, 65 FR 18434, 18487, April 7, 2000.]

Hospital election to reduce coinsurance. A hospital may elect to reduce coinsurance for any or all APC groups on a calendar year basis by selecting the minimum copayment amount, but may not reduce copayment for some, but not all, services within the same APC group. If a hospital reduces a coinsurance amount, it must notify the intermediary by December 1 of the preceding year by documenting the applicable APCs and the coinsurance amount that the hospital has selected. The coinsurance may not be less than 20 percent of the APC payment rate. The hospital may advertise that it has reduced the level of coinsurance identifying the specific outpatient services to which the reduction is applicable. Coinsurance reductions are not allowed in physicians' offices or other ambulatory settings. [Soc. Sec. Act § 1833(t)(8)(B); 42 C.F.R. § 419.42.]

Outlier Payments

The BBRA required that an additional payment be made for outpatient services for which a hospital's charges, adjusted to cost, exceed a fixed multiple of the OPPS payment as adjusted by pass-through payments. The final rule indicated specifically that, when billed charges, adjusted to cost, exceed 2.5 times the OPPS payments, the hospital will receive 75 percent of the costs beyond that threshold. [42 C.F.R. § 419.43(d).]

Prior to 2002, outlier payment was calculated based on the aggregate of OPPS services on the claim. Beginning with 2002, outlier payments are based on each individual OPPS service. Total outlier payments for 2003 cannot exceed 2 percent of total OPPS payments. For 2003, an OPPS service qualifies for outlier payment when costs of furnishing a service or procedure exceeds 2.75 times the APC payment amount. The outlier payment for 2003 equals 45 percent of the costs over and above 2.75 times the APC amount. [*Final rule*, 67 FR 66718, Nov. 1, 2002.]

For 2004, CMS set two separate outlier thresholds, one for hospitals and one for community mental health centers (CMHCs) because of the significant differences in costs between the two types of providers for providing partial hospitalization services. The hospital outlier threshold is met when costs of furnishing a service or procedure under APC 0033 exceed 2.6 times the APC payment amount and the outlier payment percentage is 50 percent of the amount of costs in excess of the threshold. For CMHCs, the threshold is met when costs of furnishing a service or procedure under APC 0033 exceed 3.65 times the APC payment amount. Because PHP is the only APC for which CMHCs may receive payment under the OPPS, CMS will not redirect outlier payments by imposing a second dollar threshold. The outlier payment percentage is 50 percent of the amount of costs in excess of the threshold. [*Final rule*, 68 FR 63398, Nov. 7, 2003.]

For CY 2005, to keep outlier payments within the budgeted amount of 2.0 percent of OPPS payments, to qualify for an outlier payment, the cost of a service must exceed 1.75 times the APC payment rate and the cost also must exceed the sum of the APC rate plus a fixed dollar amount of $1,175. Both of these thresholds must be met before a hospital is eligible for outlier payments. The threshold for a CMHC is 3.5 percent times the partial hospitalization program (PHP) APC. There is no separate fixed dollar threshold for a CMHC. The outlier payment percentage applicable to costs in excess of the threshold is 50 percent. [*Final rule*, 69 FR 65682, Nov. 15, 2004.]

For CY 2006, to keep outlier payments within the budgeted amount of 1.0 percent of OPPS payments, to qualify for an outlier payment, the cost of a service must exceed 1.75 times the APC payment rate and the cost also must exceed the sum of the APC rate plus a fixed dollar amount of $1,575. Both of these thresholds must be met before a hospital is eligible for outlier payments. As in 2005, the threshold for a CMHC is 3.5 percent times the partial hospitalization program (PHP) APC. There is no separate fixed dollar threshold for a CMHC. The outlier payment percentage applicable to costs in excess of the threshold is 50 percent. [*Final rule*, 70 FR 68749, Nov. 10, 2005.]

Transitional Corridor Payments

Section 411(a)(1) of the MMA extended transitional corridor payments until 2006 for hospitals located in rural areas that have no more than 100 beds and sole community hospitals located in a rural area. Transitional corridor payments have been discontinued for all other hospitals except cancer hospitals and children's hospitals, which are held harmless, effective January 1, 2004. [Soc. Sec. Act § 1833(t)(7)(D)(i); *Final rule*, 68 FR 63398, Nov. 7, 2003.]

Section 202 of the BBRA required payment adjustments, known as transitional corridor payments, to be made during a transition period to limit the decline in payments to hospitals under OPPS in addition to use of the wage index to adjust for local variation in labor costs through 2003. [Soc. Sec. Act § 1833(t)(7); 42 C.F.R. § 419.70.] The amount of payment adjustment for a hospital was dependent on the difference between the hospital's "PPS amount" and "pre-BBA amount." The "PPS amount" is the amount payable under OPPS for covered outpatient department (OPD) services, including coinsurance and deductibles, but excluding the effects of transitional corridor payments. The "pre-BBA amount" is the amount equal to the product of the hospital's reasonable cost for covered OPD services and the base OPD payment-to-cost ratio for the hospital. The base payment-to-cost ratio for the hospital is defined as a ratio of the hospital's Medicare payments for outpatient services during its cost reporting period ending in 1996, including beneficiary coinsurance and deductibles, to the hospital's reasonable cost for such services, without regard to the across-the-board percentage reductions for capital and operating costs. Final transitional corridor payments are based on the provider's settled cost report. [42 C.F.R. § 419.70; *Final rule*, 65 FR 18434, 18499-18501, April 7, 2000.]

[¶ 839] Skilled Nursing Facilities

Skilled nursing facilities (SNF) have been paid on a case-mix adjusted, *per diem* basis under a prospective payment system (PPS) since the cost reporting period that began July 1, 1998. The SNF PPS covers all routine, ancillary, and capital-related costs related to Part A SNF benefits (other than costs for approved educational activities), as well as many services for which payment may be made under Part B during a period in which the beneficiary is provided covered SNF care. Routine services costs are regular costs for which a separate charge is not made. Ancillary costs are costs for specialized services that are directly attributable to individual patients, such as therapy, drugs, and laboratory services. Capital-related costs include the costs of land, building, equipment, etc. [Soc. Sec. Act § 1888(e); *Interim final rule*, 63 FR 26251, May 12, 1998.]

The payment also covers any physical, occupational, or speech-language therapy, whether the services are furnished by, or under the supervision of, a physician or other healthcare professional and regardless of whether the resident who receives the services is in a covered Part A stay. Part A stays covers up to 100 days of SNF services in each spell of illness, while Part B covers medical and other health care services subject to specific coverage exclusions and conditions of coverage. Part B specifically excludes SNF services furnished to a SNF resident in a covered Part A stay and not furnished either directly by the SNF or under arrangement. [Soc. Sec. Act § 1888(e); 42 C.F.R. § 411.15(p); *Final rule*, 66 FR 39562, 38587, July 31, 2001.]

Payment for AIDS residents. Section 511 of the Medicare Modernization Act of 2003 (MMA) (PubLNo 108-173) provided for an increase in payment for services furnished to SNF residents with acquired immune deficiency syndrome (AIDS). Effective for services furnished on or after October 1, 2004, until there is an appropriate adjustment in the case-mix to compensate for increased costs associated with residents with AIDS, a temporary 128 percent increase in payment is made for SNF services for such residents. [Soc. Sec. Act § 1888(e)(12).]

Services and Items Excluded from SNF PPS

The *per diem* rate does not cover the following costs, for which separate Part B claims must be made:

(1) physician services furnished to individual SNF residents;

(2) certain nurse practitioner and physician assistant services;

(3) services of certified nurse-midwives, qualified psychologists, clinical social worker services, and certified registered nurse anesthetists;

(4) certain dialysis services (home dialysis supplies and equipment, self-care home dialysis support services, and institutional dialysis services and supplies) and drugs (specifically, erythropoietin for dialysis patients competent to use the drug without supervision); and

(5) only for services furnished in 1998, the transportation costs of electrocardiogram equipment.

(6) After January 1, 2005, services provided by a rural health clinic (RHC) and a federally qualified health center (FQHC), if such services would have been excluded if furnished by a physician or practitioner who was not affiliated with a RHC or FQHC. [Soc. Sec. Act § 1888(e)(2)(A)(ii).]

Since April 1, 2000, additional items and services not included in SNF PPS payments are ambulance services furnished to an individual in conjunction with renal dialysis services, certain chemotherapy items and administration services, certain radioisotope services, and customized prosthetic devices. Separate payments are made for these services furnished during an inpatient SNF stay. [Soc. Sec. Act § 1888(e)(2)(A)(iii).] Ambulance transports to or from a diagnostic or therapeutic site other than a physician's office or hospital (e.g., an independent diagnostic testing facility, cancer treatment center, radiation therapy center, wound care center) are considered paid at the SNF PPS rate when the beneficiary is in a Part A stay and may not be paid separately as Part B services when billed to the carrier. [*Medicare Claims Processing Manual*, CMS Pub. 100-04, Ch. 15, § 30.2.3.]

Resource Utilization Groups and Wage Index Adjustments

SNF PPS is a case-mix adjusted payment system that measures the intensity of care (*e.g.*, hours of nursing or therapy time needed per day) and services required (*e.g.*, requirement of a ventilator) for each resident and then translates it into a specific payment level.

¶839

The federal payment rate is case-mix adjusted to account for the relative resource utilization of different patients. [42 C.F.R. § 413.337; *Provider Reimbursement Manual* (PRM), Part 1, § 2832.] Patients are classified into groups using a resident classification system known as resource utilization groups version III (RUGS-III), which is a system for classifying SNF residents into mutually exclusive groups based on clinical, functional, and resource-based criteria. [42 C.F.R. § 413.333.]

The Minimum Data Set (MDS) 2.0., which is a resident assessment instrument used by SNFs to assess patient needs and create a plan of treatment, is used to classify patients into RUGs. The MDS contains a core set of screening, clinical, and functional status elements, including common definitions and coding categories, that form the basis of a comprehensive assessment. The amount reimbursed to the nursing home for care of a particular patient is adjusted for the clinical condition of the patient. SNFs must report assessments according to an assessment schedule as a condition of participation in the Medicare program. SNFs that fail to perform assessments timely are paid a default rate for the federal rate for the days of a resident's care for which they are not in compliance with this schedule. [42 C.F.R. § 413.343.]

RUG-III groups are the basis for the relative payment weights used both for standardization of the federal rates and subsequently to establish case-mix adjustments to the rates for patients with different service use. Care provided directly to, or for, a patient is represented by an index score that is based on the amount of staff time, weighted by salary levels, associated with each group.

Each RUG group is assigned an index score that represents the amount of nursing time and rehabilitation time associated with caring for patients who qualify for the group. The nursing weight includes both patient-specific time spent daily on behalf of each patient type by registered nurses, licensed practical nurses, and certified nursing assistants, as well as patient non-specific time spent by these staff members on other necessary functions such as staff education, administrative duties, and other tasks associated with maintenance of the care giving environment. For Medicare billing purposes, there is a Health Insurance Prospective Payment System rate code (HIPPS) associated with each of the RUG-III groups, and each assessment applies to specific days within a resident's SNF stay. [PRM, Part 1, § 2832.]

For fiscal year 2006, CMS has expanded the number of RUG-III groups from 44 to 53. CMS added nine new Rehabilitation plus Extensive Services groups. The adjustment was made to account for the high level of variability in non-therapy ancillary costs. CMS will start using the refined RUG-53 classification group on January 1, 2006. From the beginning of FY 2006–October 1, 2005– until December 31, 2005, it will use the 44-group RUG-III classification system. [*Final rule*, 70 FR 45026, Aug. 4, 2005.]

Wage index. The *per diem* rates paid to SNFs are adjusted by a wage index to account for geographic variation in wages. [42 C.F.R. § 413.337.] CMS uses the hospital wage index instead of a SNF-specific wage index for SNF PPS because it does not have enough reliable SNF-specific data that could be used to establish a SNF wage index at this time. [*Final rule*, 66 FR 39562, July 31, 2001; *Notice* 67 FR 49797, July 31, 2002; *Final rule*, 68 FR 46036, Aug. 4, 2003; *Notice*, 69 FR 45775, July 30, 2004.]

CMS, for FY 2006, will incorporate into SNF PPS the revised Office of Management and Budget (OMB) definitions for Metropolitan Statistical Areas, as well as the new definitions of Micropolitan Statistical Areas and Combined Statistical Areas. CMS will transition use of the OMB designations over a one-year period. [*Final rule*, 70 FR 45026, Aug. 4, 2005.]

¶839

Consolidated Billing for SNFs

The SNF PPS includes a consolidated billing provision that requires a SNF to submit consolidated Medicare claims for almost all of the services that the resident receives during the course of a covered Part A stay. (In addition, this provision places with the SNF the Medicare billing responsibility for physical and occupational therapy, and speech-language pathology services that the resident receives during a noncovered stay.) SNF consolidated billing is a comprehensive billing requirement similar to the one in effect for inpatient hospital services. As with hospital bundling, the SNF consolidated billing requirement does not apply to the services of physicians and certain other types of medical practitioners. The Benefits Improvement and Protection Act of 2000 (BIPA) (PubLNo 106-554) provided that the consolidated billing requirement is limited to services and items furnished to SNF residents in a Medicare Part A covered stay and to therapy services furnished in Part A and Part B covered stays. [Soc. Sec. Act § 1842(b)(6)(E), § 1862(a)(18).] BIPA repealed the consolidated billing requirement for Part B services (other than physical therapy, occupational therapy and speech-language therapy) furnished to SNF residents whose stays are not covered by Medicare Part A, effective January 1, 2001. In a related provision, the BBA required the use of fee schedules and uniform coding specified by the Secretary for SNF Part B bills. [Soc. Sec. Act § 1888(e)(9), (10).] Finally, certain therapy services when provided to a beneficiary in a SNF can be separately payable when performed by physicians, but are subject to SNF consolidated billing when performed by physical and occupational therapists.

Limitations on consolidated billing. CMS has clarified that hospice care (as defined in Soc. Sec. Act § 1861(dd)) is not subject to consolidated billing when a SNF resident elects to receive care under the Medicare hospice benefit. The hospice rather than the SNF assumes the overall responsibility for those care needs relating to the beneficiary's terminal condition, while the SNF itself retains responsibility only for those aspects of the beneficiary's care needs that are not related to the terminal condition. In addition, consolidated billing applies only to ambulance transportation furnished *during* the SNF stay, not to an ambulance trip that occurs at either the beginning or end of the stay. [*Interim final rule*, 63 FR 26251, May 12, 1998.]

SNF Payment Rate Updates

To account for inflation factors, payment rates are adjusted annually using a SNF market basket index. The SNF market basket was most recently revised and rebased in FY 2002 to reflect 1997 total cost data. [*Final rule*, 66 FR 39562, July 31, 2001.] Starting in FY 2004, an adjustment to the annual update of the previous fiscal year's rate is computed to account for errors in the market basket forecast in past years. The initial adjustment to the update of the previous fiscal year's rate takes into account the cumulative forecast error between fiscal years 2000 and 2002. Subsequent adjustments in succeeding fiscal years will take into account the forecast error from the most recently available fiscal year for which there is final data. [42 C.F.R. 413.337(d); *Final rule*, 68 FR 46036, Aug. 4, 2003.]

Payment rates for FY 2006. The fiscal year 2006 rates reflect an update using the full amount of the latest market basket index. The FY 2004 market basket increase factor is 3.1 percent. The existing, temporary increase in the per diem adjusted payment rates of 20 percent for certain specified RUGs (and 6.7 percent for certain others) remains in effect until January 1, 2006, when the refined RUG-53 classification system is implemented. [*Final rule*, 70 FR 45026, Aug. 4, 2005.]

CMS used the SNF market basket to adjust each per diem component of the federal rates forward to reflect cost increases occurring between the midpoint of the federal fiscal year beginning October 1, 2004, and ending September 30, 2005, and the midpoint of the federal fiscal year beginning October 1, 2005, and ending September 30, 2006, to which the payment rates apply. The payment rates for FY 2005 were updated by a factor equal to the full market basket index percentage increase to determine the payment rates for FY 2006. The rates are further adjusted by a wage index budget neutrality factor. The unadjusted rates are the same under both the 44-group RUG-III classification system and the refined RUG-53 classification system. [*Final rule*, 70 FR 45026, Aug. 4, 2005.]

The wage index adjustment is applied to the labor-related portion of the federal rate, which for 2006 is 75.922 percent of the total rate. This percentage reflects the labor-related relative importance for FY 2006. The labor-related relative importance is calculated from the SNF market basket, and approximates the labor-related portion of the total costs after taking into account historical and projected price changes between the base year and FY 2006. The relative importance figure more closely reflects the cost share weights for FY 2006 than the base year weights from the SNF market basket. [*Final rule*, 70 FR 45026, Aug. 4, 2005.]

Swing-bed Facilities

Swing-bed hospitals have agreements with the Secretary under which their inpatient hospital beds may be used for services that would be considered extended care services if provided by a SNF. Effective for cost reporting periods beginning on or after July 1, 2002, swing-bed facilities, including swing-bed rural hospitals, are reimbursed under SNF PPS. All updates to rates and wage indices that apply under SNF PPS apply to all swing-bed hospitals. Swing-bed services furnished in critical access hospitals (CAHs), however, are exempt from SNF PPS. Post-hospital SNF care furnished in CAHs will continue to be paid on a reasonable cost basis. [Soc. Sec. Act § 1888(e)(7); 42 C.F.R. § 413.114.]

Effects of Hurricanes and SNF Reimbursement

The hurricanes of 2005 disrupted the lives of many beneficiaries and healthcare providers in the Gulf Coast region. Because of the unique circumstances of the hurricane and its aftermath, CMS encouraged providers to use its website to pose particular questions related to reimbursement. [CMS Frequently Asked Questions, http://questions.cms.hhs.gov.]

Example 1:

Question: Our SNF has received beneficiaries transferred from a SNF provider affected by Hurricane Katrina. I have submitted my claims for September 2005 to Medicare and I am receiving an overlap with an August 2005 claim previously sent by the affected SNF. How can I get my September bill paid?

Answer: Receiving providers should make sure they include remarks indicating "Hurricane Katrina" on any claims affected by the disaster. The receiving provider should contact their Fiscal Intermediary (FI) for assistance with these overlap situations. FIs shall identify the overlap and develop the claim accordingly, including working with other FIs that might service the affected SNF. If the transferring provider submitted its August 2005 claim with a patient status of 30 (still patient) but the patient did not stay beyond August 2005, FIs shall adjust the claim or work with the transferring provider's servicing FI to have the claim adjusted and use an appropriate patient status code to indicate a transfer.

Example 2:

Question: Will the evacuating facility still receive payment at a RUG rate for that facility?

Answer: This will depend on the arrangement between the evacuating facility and the receiving facility. If the evacuating facility does not expect the beneficiary to return, the patient should be discharged. The receiving facility would then admit the resident and begin the Prospective Payment System Minimum Data Set (PPS MDS) cycle. If the beneficiary is expected to return to the evacuating facility within 30 days and the evacuating facility is able to complete MDS assessments both accurately and timely, the evacuating facility may continue to complete the required PPS MDS assessments and submit claims. In this instance, the evacuating facility is required to reimburse the receiving facility for the services the beneficiary receives under its care. If the evacuating facility later determines that the beneficiary will not return to its facility within the 30 day time frame or if the evacuating facility is not capable of completing MDSs accurately and timely, the facility should discharge the resident. The day prior to the discharge date is the last date the evacuating facility will be able to submit claims for reimbursement. The receiving facility would then admit the resident and begin the PPS MDS cycle. The date the person is admitted to the receiving facility is considered day 1 of the person's stay. This date will start the PPS cycle, as well as the OBRA cycle, for the receiving facility. Therefore, in order to meet Medicare and OBRA requirements, a 5-day PPS MDS must be completed with an Assessment Reference Date (ARD) of day 1 – 8 and an OBRA required admission assessment must be completed by day 14.

[¶ 841] Rehabilitation Hospitals

An inpatient rehabilitation hospital or unit is a facility that serves an inpatient population of whom at least 75 percent required intensive rehabilitation services for treatment. The general threshold for establishing the need for inpatient hospital rehabilitation services is that the patient must require and receive at least three hours a day of physical and/or occupational therapy. While most patient requiring an inpatient stay for rehabilitation need and receive at least three hours a day of physical and/or occupational therapy, there can be exceptions because individual patient's needs vary. [42 C.F.R. § 412.626.]

Patient Assessment Instrument

The IRF patient assessment instrument (IRF-PAI), is a modified version of the Uniform Data Set for medical rehabilitation (UDSmr) patient assessment instrument, commonly referred to as the "FIM" (Functional Independence Measure). Inpatient rehabilitation facilities (IRFs) are required to complete the IRF-PAI upon admission and discharge for all Part A fee-for-service patients who are already inpatients or who are admitted or discharged on or after January 1, 2002. [*Final rule*, 66 FR 41316, Aug. 7, 2001.] The IRF-PAI consists of nine sections that collect different types of information, including identification and demographic information about the patient, medical information, and information related to quality of care and basic patient safety.

Each Medicare Part A fee-for-service IRF patient must be assessed twice by an IRF clinician using the IRF-PAI. The admission assessment will be used to place a patient in a case-mix group (CMG). The discharge assessment, on the day the patient is discharged or stops receiving Medicare Part A inpatient rehabilitation services before being discharged from the hospital, will be used to determine the relative weighting factors, if applicable, associated with comorbidities. [42 C.F.R. § 412.610(c).] Patient assessment data must be computerized and electronically reported to CMS, transmitted only once and at the same time for all patient assessment data for both the admission and discharge assessment, including any interruption in stay data. [42 C.F.R. §§ 412.614(c), 412.618.]

Patient Classification

Based on the data received from the IRF-PAI each patient will be placed into a CMG. Each CMG is a functional-related group, determined by distinguishing classes of IRF patient discharges on the basis of impairment, age, comorbidities, functional capability of the patient, and other factors CMS deems appropriate to improve the explanatory power of functional independence measure-function related groups. The CMG determines the base payment rate that the IRF receives for the Medicare-covered Part A services furnished by the IRF during the beneficiary's episode of care. [42 C.F.R. § 412.620(a).]

75 Percent Rule

To be classified as an inpatient rehabilitation facility (IRF) a facility must show that, during its most recent 12-month cost reporting period, it served an inpatient population of whom at least 75 percent required intensive rehabilitation services for the treatment of one of the following conditions:

- stroke;
- spinal cord injury;
- congenital deformity;
- amputation;
- major multiple trauma;
- fracture of femur (hip fracture);
- brain injury;
- polyarthritis, including rheumatoid arthritis;
- neurological disorders, including multiple sclerosis, motor neuron diseases, polyneuropathy, muscular dystrophy, and Parkinson's disease; and/or
- burns. [42 C.F.R § 412.23(b)(2).]

CMS discovered that many IRFs did not meet these classification requirements and stopped enforcing the 75 percent rule on June 7, 2002. [*Final rule*, 69 FR 25752, May 7, 2004.]

To remedy this situation, CMS issued a *Final rule* that would give IRFs time to come into compliance with this requirement. Beginning on July 1, 2004, IRFs will have three years to become compliant with the 75 percent rule. For cost reporting periods beginning:

- on or after July 1, 2004, and before July 1, 2005, 50 percent of an IRF's patients must treated for one of the qualifying conditions,
- on or after July 1, 2005, and before July 1, 2006, 60 percent of an IRF's patients must be treated for one of the qualifying conditions,
- on or after July 1, 2006 to July 1, 2007, IRFs will need to have 65 percent of their patients being treated for a qualifying condition,
- after July 1, 2007, IRFs will need have 75 percent of their patients being treated for a qualifying condition. [*Final rule*, 69 FR 25752, May 7, 2004.]

In addition, the *Final rule* made changes to the list of qualifying conditions. Polyarthritis, including rheumatoid arthritis was removed from the list and the following items were added to the list:

(1) treating a patient who has two major weight-bearing joints with severe osteoarthritis in the general osteoarthritis standard; and

(2) a new medical condition that applies to patients who meet one of the specific criteria in 42 C.F.R. § 412.23(b)(2)(iii)(M) and who have had a knee or hip joint replacement, or both, during an acute hospitalization immediately proceeding the inpatient rehabilitation stay. [42 C.F.R. § 412.23.]

Payment Rate

The payment unit for the IRF PPS is a discharge. PPS rates encompass the inpatient operating costs and capital costs, including routine and ancillary costs, of furnishing covered rehabilitation services. The costs of bad debts, approved educational activities, outlier cases, organ acquisition costs, nonphysician anesthetist's services, direct graduate medical education, indirect medical education, and disproportionate share adjustments are not included. Payment rates are calculated using relative weights to account for variations in resource needs in CMGs. [42 C.F.R. § 412.622.]

The IRF PPS standard conversion payment amount for FY 2006 is $12,767. A market basket increase factor of 3.6 percent was applied to the FY 2005 rate of $12,958 to establish the updated per discharge payment rates. [*Final rule*, 70 FR 47880, Aug. 15, 2005.] Special provisions apply to "outlier" payments, short stay cases, and for cases that expire. [42 C.F.R. § 412.624.]

It is important to note that for cost reporting periods beginning during FY 2006, the IRF PPS is based on 100 percent of the adjusted Federal IRF prospective payment amount, updated annually. Therefore, IRFs are not impacted by the FY 2006 DRG rates for hospital inpatient prospective system that were released in *Final rule*, 70 FR 47880, August 15, 2005.

CBSA Adoption

Beginning October 1, 2005, Core Based Statistical Area (CBSA) market definitions were applied to IRFs. CBSAs were defined by the Office of Management and Budget in *Final rule*, 65 FR 82228, December 27, 2000, as "a geographic entity associated with at least one core of 10,000 or more population, plus adjacent territory that has a high degree of social and economic integration with the core as measured by commuting ties." The new CBSA designations recognize 49 new Metropolitan Statistical Areas (MSAs) and 565 Micropolitan Statistical Areas.

Transition policy. In response to public comment, CMS has decided to provide for a budget neutral one-year transition policy, for discharges occurring after October 1, 2005, and before September 30, 2006, that blends the FY 2006 MSA-based wage index and CBSA-based wage index. This transition policy is comprised of 50 percent FY 2006 MSA-based wage index data and 50 percent FY 2006 CBSA-based wage index data (both of which are based on FY 2001 hospital wage index data) for all IRFs. [*Final rule*, 70 FR 47880, 47922 Aug. 15, 2005.]

Hold harmless policy. Additionally, CMS implemented a three-year "hold harmless" policy for existing IRFs that are defined as rural under 42 C.F.R. § 412.602 during FY 2005, and are classified as urban under 42 C.F.R. § 412.602 in FY 2006, because the new designation from an MSA-based rural designation to a CBSA-based urban caused the IRF to lose the FY 2005 rural adjustment of 19.14 percent. [*Final rule*, 70 FR 47880, 47944, Aug. 15, 2005.]

One-Day Payment Window

Under IRF PPS, IRFs are subject to a one-day payment window, or the "24-hour rule," for preadmission services. In other words, outpatient diagnostic services and most nonphysician services provided during the calendar day immediately preceding the date of admission to an IRF are included in the IRF case-mix group payment. Separate payment will not be made for outpatient diagnostic services provided during the 24-hour period prior to admission to an IRF.

IRFs and hospitals reimbursed under IRF PPS are not subject to the three-day payment window for preadmission services. The three-day payment window applies only to acute inpatient hospitals paid under the inpatient prospective payment system (see ¶ 810). [*Medicare Claims Processing Manual*, Pub. 100-04, Chapter 3, § 140.2.]

Statutory History

Section 1886(j) of the Social Security Act, as added by § 4421 of the Balanced Budget Act of 1997 (BBA) (PubLNo 105-33) and as amended by § 125 of the Balanced Budget Refinement Act of 1999 (BBRA) (PubLNo 106-113) and § 305 of the Benefits Improvement and Protection Act of 2000 (BIPA) (PubLNo 106-554) authorizes the implementation of a prospective payment system (PPS) for inpatient rehabilitation facilities (IRFs). IRF PPS applies to rehabilitation hospitals and units that are exempt from PPS for inpatient hospitals and was phased in over a two-year period between October 1, 2000, and October 1, 2002. [Soc. Sec. Act § 1886(j).]

A *Final rule* published at 66 FR 41316 on August 7, 2001, established the IRF PPS, replacing the reasonable cost-based payment system. The *Final rule* was effective on January 1, 2002, for cost reporting periods beginning on or after January 1, 2002.

Although the BBA contemplated a two-year transition period for IRFs to adjust to PPS, the BBA also provided that the IRF PPS be fully implemented for cost reporting periods beginning on or after October 1, 2000. Due to the delay in implementing the IRF PPS, hospitals were paid under the blended methodology for less than two years. CMS noted that the shortened transition period was equitable because hospitals had been on notice since the BBA was enacted that IRF PPS would be fully implemented for cost reporting periods beginning on or after October 1, 2002. [*Final rule*, 66 FR 41316, 41368, Aug. 7, 2001.]

During the transition period, IRF PPS payments consisted of a hybrid of the federal prospective payment and the IRF's payment under the reasonable cost system. For cost reporting periods beginning on or after January 1, 2002, and before October 1, 2002, payment was based on 33 1/3 percent of the facility-specific payment and 66 2/3 percent of the FY 2002 adjusted federal prospective payment. For cost reporting periods beginning on or after October 1, 2002, payment is based solely on the adjusted federal prospective payment. IRFs had the option of electing payment based entirely on the adjusted federal prospective payment for cost reporting periods beginning before October 1, 2002, without regard to the transition period percentages. [42 C.F.R. § 412.626.]

[¶ 843] Long-Term Care Hospitals

Long-term care hospitals (LTCHs) are defined as hospitals that have an average inpatient length of stay greater than 25 days. These facilities generally provide extended medical and rehabilitative care for patients who are clinically complex and may suffer from multiple acute or chronic conditions. Services covered under the LTCH prospective payment system (PPS) include comprehensive rehabilitation, respiratory therapy, cancer treatment, head trauma treatment and pain management. [Soc. Sec. Act § 1886(d)(1)(B)(iv)(I).]

On August 30, 2002, CMS established a PPS for LTCHs, effective for cost reporting periods beginning on or after October 1, 2002. Congress had required that the new PPS be implemented by fiscal year 2003 as part of the Benefits Improvement and Protection Act of 1999 (BIPA) (PubLNo 106-554).

Annual Update

Until June 2003, CMS published the annual LTCH PPS update in the *Federal Register* on or before August 1 prior to the beginning of each fiscal year. In June 2003, CMS changed the effective date of the annual payment update, moving it from October 1 to July 1 of each year. This places the LTCH PPS on a different cycle from the acute care hospital inpatient PPS (IPPS) (see ¶ 810) update and facilitates more efficient use of CMS resources. Accordingly,

CMS will publish the LTCH PPS annual update in the *Federal Register* by June 1 of each year. The annual update of the long-term care diagnosis-related groups (LTC-DRGs), however, will remain linked to the annual adjustments of the IPPS diagnosis-related groups (DRGs), which become effective October 1 of each year. [42 C.F.R. § 412.535; *Final rule*, 70 FR 24208, May 6, 2005.]

Payment Methodology

Payment under the LTCH PPS is made on a per-discharge basis. Each patient case is classified according to the principal diagnosis, up to eight additional diagnoses, and up to six procedures performed during the stay, as well as age, sex, and discharge status of the patient. The patient's case is classified into one of approximately 518 LTC-DRGs. The LTC-DRGs were developed based on CMS' DRGs under the IPPS (see ¶ 810). [42 C.F.R. § 412.513.]

The LTCH PPS provides for a single payment rate for both operating and capital costs, without regard to urban or rural location, to be phased-in over a five-year period. LTCH's can elect, however, to be paid immediately at 100 percent of the federal rate at the start of any cost reporting period during the five-year transition period. [42 C.F.R. § 412.533(c).]

One-Day Payment Window

LTCHs and hospitals reimbursed under the LTCH PPS are not subject to the three-day payment window for preadmission services that applies to acute care inpatient hospitals under IPPS (see ¶ 810). Under the three-day payment window rule (also known as the 72 hour payment window rule), outpatient diagnostic services and most non-physician services provided during the three calendar days immediately preceding the date of admission or during an inpatient stay are included in the IPPS DRG payment. [42 C.F.R. § 412.2(c)(5).]

LTCHs under the LTCH PPS, however, are subject to a one-day payment window, or the 24-hour rule, for preadmission services. In other words, outpatient diagnostic services and most nonphysician services provided during the calendar day immediately preceding the date of admission to an LTCH are included in the LTC-DRG payment. Separate payment will not be made for outpatient diagnostic services or nonphysician services provided during the 24-hour period prior to admission to an LTCH. The one-day payment window rule only applies if the services are diagnostic and furnished in connection with the principal diagnosis that requires the beneficiary to be admitted as an inpatient. [*Program Memorandum*, No. A-03-008, Feb. 3, 2003.]

Outlier Payments

For unusually costly cases, LTCH's under the LTCH PPS receive increased payment. The LTCH PPS outlier policy is modeled after the IPPS outlier policy. The key distinction between the LTCH outlier policy and the IPPS outlier policy is that LTCH's can receive outlier payments for a case that has:

    (1) unusually high costs that exceed the typical cost for an LTC-DRG (referred to as a "high-cost outlier"),

    (2) a length of stay that is considerably shorter than the average length of stay for an LTC-DRG (referred to as a "short-stay outlier"),

    (3) both unusually high costs and a considerably shorter than average length of stay for an LTC-DRG. [42 C.F.R. § 412.525; 42 C.F.R. § 412.529.]

High-cost outliers. A high-cost outlier under the LTCH PPS is a case with unusually high costs that exceed the typical cost for an LTC-DRG. CMS provides for an additional payment to an LTCH if its estimated costs for a given case exceed the LTC-DRG payment plus a fixed-loss amount. The fixed-loss amount for fiscal year 2006 beginning on July 1, 2005, is $10,501. The additional payment for high-cost outlier cases is equal to 80 percent of the difference between the estimated cost of the case and the outlier threshold. [42 C.F.R. § 412.525; *Final rule*, 70 FR 24194, May 6, 2005.]

Short-stay outliers. A short-stay outlier under the LTCH PPS is a discharge with a length of stay in an LTCH that is up to and including five-sixths of the geometric average length of stay for each LTC-DRG. In other words, a short-stay outlier is an adjustment to the federal payment rate for LTCH stays that are considerably shorter than the average length of stay for an LTC-DRG. The adjustment allows Medicare to pay less for cases that did not receive a full episode of care at the LTCH, and should not be reimbursed at the full LTC-DRG payment rate. [42 C.F.R. § 412.529.]

A short stay outlier payment may be triggered when an LTCH patient:

(1) is discharged to another facility,

(2) is discharged to his or her home,

(3) expires within the first several days of admission to the LTCH, or

(4) benefits expire during the LTCH stay.

Cases that qualify as both short-stay and high-cost outliers. When the estimated cost of a short-stay outlier case exceeds the high-cost outlier threshold the short-stay outlier case also qualifies as a high-cost outlier case. For short-stay outlier cases, the outlier threshold is determined by adding the fixed-loss amount to the applicable short-stay outlier payment for the LTC-DRG, not the full LTC-DRG payment. [42 C.F.R. §§ 412.525, 412.529.]

LTCH Interrupted Stay Policy

Under the LTCH PPS, an interruption of stay occurs when a Medicare inpatient is transferred upon discharge to an acute care hospital, an inpatient rehabilitation facility (IRF), a skilled nursing facility (SNF) or to the patient's home if the interruption is for three days or less, for treatment or services that are not available in the LTCH and returns to the same LTCH. CMS has redefined interruption of stay into two categories, a "3 day or less interruption of stay," and a "greater than 3 day interruption of stay." [42 C.F.R. § 412.531.]

If an interruption of stay of less than three days occurs, during an episode of care, one LTCH-DRG payment is made. Accordingly, the LTCH must provide services either directly or "under arrangements" with the other provider. The LTCH is responsible for paying the other provider for the costs of services and the three days or less interruption that the patient is away are included in the patient day count. No other payment may be made by Medicare to the other provider. [42 C.F.R. § 412.531.]

A greater than three day interruption of stay is defined as a stay in an LTCH during which a Medicare inpatient is discharged from the LTCH to an acute care hospital, an IRF or a SNF for a period of greater than three days but within the applicable fixed day period before being readmitted to the same LTCH. The applicable fixed day period is:

- between 4 and 9 consecutive days for a discharge to an acute care hospital,

- between 4 and 27 consecutive days for a discharge to an IRF, and

- between 4 and 45 consecutive days for a discharge to a SNF. [42 C.F.R. § 412.531.]

For example, if an LTCH patient is discharged to an acute care hospital and is readmitted to the LTCH on any day up to and including the 9th day following the original day of discharge from the LTCH, one LTC-DRG payment will be made. If the patient is readmitted to the LTCH from the acute care hospital on the 10th day after the original discharge or later, Medicare will pay for the second admission as a separate stay with a second LTC-DRG assignment. [42 C.F.R. § 412.531.]

The interrupted stay day count begins on the day of discharge from the LTCH and continues until the 9th, 27th, or 45th day after the discharge depending on whether the patient was discharged to an acute care hospital, IRF, or SNF, respectively. If an interruption in stay occurs, the days prior to the original discharge from the LTCH will be added to the number of days following the readmission for purposes of determining the patient's total length of stay at the LTCH. [42 C.F.R. § 412.531.]

If the patient stay exceeds the total fixed-day threshold outside the LTCH at another facility before being readmitted, two separate payments would be made. One would be based on the principal diagnosis and length of stay for the first admission and the other based on the principal diagnosis and length of stay for the second admission. Depending on their lengths of stay, both stays could result in payments as short stay-outlier, a full LTC-DRG, or even a high-cost outlier. Further, if the principal diagnosis is the same for both admissions, the hospital could receive two similar payments. It is also important to note that under the existing interrupted stay policy, a separate Medicare payment is made to the intervening provider under that provider's payment system. CMS has extended for an additional year, the surgical DRG exception to the three-day or less interrupted stay policy, which was originally established for rate year 2005, to rate 2006. Under the surgical DRG exception, an acute care hospital providing care to an LTCH patient may submit a separate Medicare claim under the IPPS if the acute care discharge is for one of the surgical DRGs. [*Final rule*, 70 FR 24206, May 6, 2005.]

Outlier payments. Interrupted stays at an LTCH are subject to the short stay and high cost outlier rules. If the total number of days of a patient's stay prior to and following an interruption of stay is up to and including five-sixths of the geometric average length of stay of the LTC-DRG, CMS will make a short stay outlier payment. If the total number of days of a patient's stay prior to and following an interruption of stay exceeds five-sixths of the geometric average length of stay of the LTC-DRG, CMS will reimburse the full LTC-DRG rate.

An additional payment will be made if the patient's case qualifies for a high-cost outlier payment. When a patient has been discharged from an LTCH and subsequently is readmitted to the LTCH after the applicable fixed-day period has elapsed, the subsequent admission is treated as a new stay, even if the case falls into the same LTC-DRG. In this instance, the LTCH will receive two separate payments for treating the patient. [42 C.F.R. § 412.531.]

Transfers to co-located providers. Special payment provisions apply when an LTCH patient is transferred to a "co-located" or "onsite" facility and subsequently readmitted to the LTCH. A "co-located" or "onsite" facility is defined as a hospital or unit that occupies space in a building also used by the LTCH or occupies space in one or more buildings on the same campus. If the number of discharges and readmissions between an LTCH and a co-located provider exceeds five percent of the total discharges during a cost reporting period, only one LTC-DRG payment is made to the LTCH for all such discharges and readmissions. This payment policy applies to discharges before and after the five percent threshold is exceeded. [42 C.F.R. § 412.532.]

Quality Improvement Organization (QIO) Review

Quality Improvement Organizations (QIOs) review services and items provided to Medicare beneficiaries by hospital staff, physicians and other healthcare practitioners. All hospitals, including LTCHs, are required to have an agreement with a QIO as a condition of participation in the Medicare program. Every QIO either must be sponsored by a significant number of physicians actively practicing in the QIO service area, or must have available to it the services of a sufficient number of area physicians to assure adequate peer review. [*Final rule*, 67 FR 36539, May 24, 2002.]

If a QIO determines that an LTCH has persisted in violating its obligations to furnish services that are economical, medically necessary, of proper quality, and properly documented, it is required to submit a report and recommendation to the Secretary on the action that should be taken, including possible exclusion from the Medicare and Medicaid programs or assessment of a fine related to the costs of the improper services. A QIO recommendation to the Secretary for exclusion automatically becomes effective if the Secretary fails to act within a 120-day review period. [Social Security Act § 1156(a)(b).]

Any beneficiary or LTCH who is dissatisfied with a QIO initial denial determination or change as a result of an LTC-DRG validation is entitled to notice and reconsideration of the determination or change by the QIO. An initial denial determination is a determination by a QIO that healthcare services are unnecessary, unreasonable, or at an inappropriate level of care. QIOs are prohibited from publicizing payment denials without first offering the LTCH notification and opportunity for a hearing. [Social Security Act § 1154(a)(3); 42 C.F.R. §§ 478.12, 478.15, 478.16.]

For more information on QIOs, see the discussion at ¶ 710.

[¶ 845] Psychiatric Hospitals and Units

A new per diem prospective payment system (PPS) for inpatient psychiatric facilities (IPFs) has replaced the old reasonable cost basis system, effective for cost reporting periods on and after January 1, 2005. Section 124 of the Balanced Budget Refinement Act of 1999 (BBRA) (PubLNo 106-113) mandated implementation of the IPF PPS. [*Final rule*, 69 FR 66922, Nov. 15, 2004, corrected at 70 FR 16724, April 1, 2005.]

Approximately 2000 inpatient psychiatric facilities are affected by the IPF PPS, which is designed to assure appropriate payment for services to patients with severe mental illness, while providing incentives to IPFs for more efficient care of Medicare beneficiaries. The rule affects both freestanding psychiatric hospitals and certified psychiatric units in general acute care hospitals that are certified separately from the hospital and are excluded from the acute care inpatient PPS (IPPS), because they meet the requirements of 42 C.F.R. § 412.23, 42 C.F.R. § 412.25, and 42 C.F.R. § 412.27. Psychiatric units that are paid under the IPPS (see ¶ 810) are not paid under the IPF PPS. [*Final rule*, 69 FR 66922, Nov. 15, 2004, corrected at 70 FR 16724, April 1, 2005.]

The final IPF PPS rule does not apply to Veterans Administration hospitals, hospitals reimbursed by Medicare under approved state cost control systems, hospitals in demonstration projects, and non-participating hospitals furnishing emergency psychiatric care. [*Final rule*, 69 FR 66922, Nov. 15, 2004, corrected at 70 FR 16724, April 1, 2005.] Nor does it apply to psychiatric "partial hospitalization" services such as individual and group therapy, which are covered under the outpatient PPS. For a discussion of reimbursement for outpatient mental health services, see ¶ 387. For information on lifetime and "spell of illness" restrictions on inpatient psychiatric hospital coverage, see ¶ 225.

Payment Methodology

The IPF PPS rule establishes a standard per diem base rate for the period from January 1, 2005, until July 1, 2006, of $575.95 for inpatient psychiatric services provided to Medicare beneficiaries. The per diem amount reflects the average daily cost of inpatient psychiatric care, including capital-related costs. This basic rate is adjusted by many factors in the IPF PPS. [*Final rule*, 69 FR 66922, Nov. 15, 2004, corrected at 70 FR 16724, April 1, 2005.]

The IPF PPS rule provides for gradually reduced per diem rates for the days of an IPF stay. The first day of any psychiatric stay provides IPFs with the highest reimbursement due to costly admitting services; the rate is even higher for IPFs with emergency departments. The payments are adjusted downward from Day 2 through Day 22 of an IPF stay. All days after Day 21 are counted at the Day 22 rate. The lower payments are made for the subsequent days due to the system's incentive to keep patient costs down and patient days to a minimum. The per diem amount is modified by facility and patient characteristics to account for variation in patient resource use. [*Final rule*, 69 FR 66922, Nov. 15, 2004, corrected at 70 FR 16724, April 1, 2005.]

Because the tiered IPF PPS reimburses facilities at a higher rate for the first few days of a stay, CMS was concerned that there would be an incentive to discharge patients and then re-admit them to obtain higher payments. To address this concern, the *Final rule* treats patients who have been discharged from IPFs and then re-admitted to an IPF within three consecutive calendar days as having one continuous hospitalization. [*Final rule*, 69 FR 66922, Nov. 15, 2004, corrected at 70 FR 16724, April 1, 2005; 42 C.F.R. § 412.424.]

Facility Characteristics

In all PPS systems, geographic differences in labor costs affect reimbursement. The IPF PPS relies upon acute care wage data and area wage index information compiled by CMS for the inpatient hospital PPS. CMS made additional adjustments for facility characteristics because it found that: IPF facilities in rural counties have unavoidable costs averaging 17 percent higher than facilities located in metropolitan areas; psychiatric teaching facilities have 12.3 percent higher costs than other IPFs; and facilities in Alaska and Hawaii have cost-of-living needs averaging 25 percent more than those in the contiguous states. Facilities with full service emergency departments also receive rate adjustments for the first day of a patient stay under the IPF PPS, as stated above. No other facility adjustments such as disproportionate share adjustments or acute care facility adjustments are made under the IPF PPS. [*Final rule*, 69 FR 66922, Nov. 15, 2004, corrected at 70 FR 16724, April 1, 2005, 42 C.F.R. § 412.424.]

Patient Characteristics and Coding Policy

Although the Diagnostic and Statistical Manual of Mental Disorders (DSM) is a well-recognized tool for diagnostic assessment in mental health treatment, CMS requires IPFs to use the psychiatric diagnosis codes in Chapter Five ("Mental Disorder") of the International Classification of Diseases-9th Revision, Clinical Modification (ICD-9-CM) to report diagnostic information for IPF PPS. Currently, IPF claims include ICD-9-CM diagnosis coding information and the GROUPER software assigns a diagnosis-related group (DRG) based on the patient's principal ICD-9-CM diagnosis. This practice continues under the IPF PPS. [*Final rule*, 69 FR 66922, Nov. 15, 2004, corrected at 70 FR 16724, April 1, 2005.]

CMS identified 15 out of 25 DRGs with one or more principal psychiatric diagnoses for which it will make payment adjustments under the IPF PPS. The remaining 10 DRGs, including a range of nervous system disorders, gastrointestinal conditions, genital diseases, and tobacco use disorder, will not receive DRG adjustments under the IPF PPS because CMS determined that they generally do not include a psychiatric diagnosis and few, if any, of the patients with these diagnoses are admitted or treated in an IPF. CMS will make payment adjustments for 17 comorbidity categories, i.e. psychiatric diagnoses combined with other types of DRGs, to compensate IPFs for the additional expenses associated with treating patients with comorbid conditions. [*Final rule*, 69 FR 66922, Nov. 15, 2004, corrected at 70 FR 16724, April 1, 2005.]

Under the IPF PPS, there also is an outlier adjustment for particularly costly cases to protect IPFs from significant losses. CMS also found that there are increased age-related

¶845

costs for IPF patients over age 65, and so there are upwards adjustments for older patients. There also is an adjustment for administration of electroconvulsive therapy treatments that is further adjusted by a facility's wage index. Although CMS noted a three percent higher cost for female patients than male patients, the IPF PPS does not make gender-based adjustments. CMS may study this distinction further. [*Final rule*, 69 FR 66922, Nov. 15, 2004, corrected at 70 FR 16724, April 1, 2005; 42 C.F.R. § 412.424; *Proposed rule*, 68 FR 66920, Nov. 28, 2003.]

Transition Period

From January 1, 2005 through December 31, 2007, there is a transition period during which payments to IPFs are a blend of the federal per diem rate and a hospital-specific amount based on the IPF's current Tax Equity and Fiscal Responsibility Act of 1982 (TEFRA) (PubLNo 97-248) payment, or in other words, a blend of the PPS payment and the reasonable cost payment derived from a facility's cost report. [*Final rule*, 69 FR 66922, Nov. 15, 2004, corrected at 70 FR 16724, April 1, 2005.]

Payment during Calendar Year (CY) 2005 is 75 percent based on the TEFRA payment system and 25 percent based on the IPF PPS payment amount. During CY 2006, payment will be split 50-50, with 50 percent of the TEFRA payment amount and 50 percent of the IPF PPS payment amount. In CY 2007, payments will be based on 25 percent of the TEFRA amount and 75 percent of the IPF PPS payment amount. For cost reporting periods beginning on or after January 1, 2008, payment will be based 100 percent on the IPF PPS amount. CMS did not propose allowing an IPF to elect to be paid 100 percent of the federal rate during the transition period, as it did with previous prospective payment systems. [*Final rule*, 69 FR 66922, Nov. 15, 2004, corrected at 70 FR 16724, April 1, 2005; 42 C.F.R. § 412.426.]

The *Final rule* also provides for a "stop loss" payment during the transition period, that is, additional payments to IPFs to ensure that aggregate payments under the IPF PPS are at least 70 percent of what they would have been under the TEFRA system. [*Final rule*, 69 FR 66922, Nov. 15, 2004, corrected at 70 FR 16724, April 1, 2005; 42 C.F.R. § 412.424.]

[¶ 847] End-Stage Renal Disease

The objectives of the end-stage renal disease (ESRD) program are: (1) to assist individuals who have been diagnosed as having ESRD to receive the care they need; (2) to encourage proper distribution and effective utilization of ESRD treatment resources while maintaining or improving the quality of care; (3) to provide the flexibility necessary for the efficient delivery of appropriate care by physicians and facilities; and (4) to encourage self-dialysis or transplantation for the maximum practical number of patients who are medically, socially, and psychologically suitable candidates for such treatment. [42 C.F.R. § 405.2101].

Benefits for qualified ESRD beneficiaries include all covered Part A and Part B items and services. Thus, coverage is not limited to the items and services associated with renal disease. [Soc. Sec. Act § 1881(a).] Similarly, these beneficiaries are subject to all the usual deductible, premium, and coinsurance provisions of both parts of the Medicare law. [Soc. Sec. Act § 226A(a).] ESRD beneficiaries, however, are not eligible to enroll in a health maintenance organization (HMO) or a Medicare Advantage plan under Part C, unless the individual was diagnosed with ESRD after enrolling in an managed care plan. [42 C.F.R. § 422.50.]

Coverage Period

In the case of dialyzing patients, Medicare coverage begins with the third month after the month in which a course of renal dialysis is initiated; however, the three-month waiting period does not apply in two instances [42 C.F.R. § 406.13(e)]:

(1) In the case of an individual who participates in a self-care training program offered by a Medicare participating facility approved to provide such training (in the expectation of completing the training and entering self-dialysis), entitlement begins on the first day of the month in which the regular course of dialysis began.

(2) In the case of a transplant candidate, coverage can begin as early as the month in which the patient is hospitalized for transplantation, provided the surgery takes place in that month or in the following two months.

In the case of an individual who receives a kidney transplant, coverage normally ends 36 months after the month of the transplant. In the case of an individual who has not received a transplant, coverage normally ends 12 months after the month in which a regular course of dialysis is ended. [42 C.F.R. § 406.13(f).] If dialysis is resumed after one of these expiration dates, a new application must be submitted but there is no waiting period requirement. [42 C.F.R. § 406.13(g).]

Note that Medicare would be the secondary payer for ESRD benefits in some cases—see ¶ 639.

Dialysis Coverage

Dialysis treatments are covered in various settings: hospital inpatient, hospital outpatient, independent renal dialysis facility, or the patient's home. There are varying levels of care in the different settings. Initially, the seriously ill patient may be treated as an inpatient at a hospital. After stabilization, maintenance dialysis treatments may be rendered in an outpatient setting at either a hospital or a nonhospital facility. In a renal dialysis facility, the patient may receive extensive attention and professionals may perform all services needed in dialysis or the patient may be placed in "self-care" where only minor assistance is given by facility technical personnel. In any of the settings a patient can be taught to dialyze at home. [*Medicare Benefit Policy Manual,* Pub. 100-02, Ch. 11, § 20.]

Generally, maintenance dialysis treatments are covered on an outpatient basis. Even when maintenance peritoneal dialysis treatments extend overnight, the treatments generally are considered outpatient services. If a patient is admitted as an inpatient of a hospital because inpatient services are required, the maintenance dialysis treatments will be covered as an inpatient hospital service (see ¶ 210).

Medicare covers home dialysis equipment, all necessary supplies, and a wide range of home support services. Home dialysis includes home hemodialysis, home intermittent peritoneal dialysis, and home continuous ambulatory peritoneal dialysis. The program also covers the rental or purchase of kidney dialysis equipment for home use. This coverage includes delivery and installation service charges, as well as maintenance expenses, for the equipment. [Soc. Sec. Act § 1881(b)(8).]

Home dialysis support services also are covered by Medicare. These services include periodic monitoring of the patient's home adaptation, visits by qualified provider or facility personnel in accordance with a plan prepared and periodically reviewed by a professional team (including the individual's physician), installation and maintenance of dialysis equipment, and testing and treatment of the water. [Soc. Sec. Act § 1881(b)(9).]

Transplantation

"Transplantation service" is covered under the ESRD program. Transplantation service is a process by which (1) a kidney is excised from a live or cadaver donor, (2) the kidney is implanted in an ESRD patient, and (3) supportive care is furnished to the living donor and to the recipient following the transplant. [42 C.F.R. § 405.2102.] (The beginning and termination dates of coverage for a recipient of a transplant are discussed above.) Reimbursement for kidney transplantation surgery will be made only if the surgery is performed in a renal transplantation center approved under the regulations. [42 C.F.R. §§ 405.2100–405.2122, 405.2171, 409.18.]

The costs of care for actual or potential kidney donors also are covered fully by Medicare and include all reasonable preparatory, operation, and post-operation recovery expenses associated with the donation, without regard to the usual Medicare deductible, coinsurances, and premium payments. Payments for post-operation recovery expenses are limited, however, to the actual period of recovery. [Soc. Sec. Act § 1881(d); Pub. 100-02, Ch.11, § 80.4.]

Medicare covers immunosuppressive drugs, such as cyclosporine, furnished to an organ transplant donee for as long as needed after the date of the transplant—see ¶ 362.

Facility Reimbursement

Effective for services furnished on or after April 1, 2005, a new case-mix adjusted prospective payment system (PPS) for dialysis services has been established. It applies to services furnished by providers of services and renal dialysis facilities to individuals in a facility or at home. The case-mix is based on a limited number of patient characteristics. Use of a case-mix measure permits targeting of greater payments to facilities that treat more costly resource-intensive patients, as required by section 623(d)(1) of the Medicare Modernization Act of 2003 (MMA) (PubLNo 108-173).

The methodology for applying patient characteristic adjusters applicable to each treatment determines the case-mix adjustment that varies for each patient. Thus, an ESRD facility's average composite payment rate per treatment depends on its unique (patients) case-mix. The patient characteristic variables that are utilized in determining an individual patient's case-mix adjusted composite payment rate include (1) five age groups, (2) a low body mass index (BMI), (3) a body surface area (BSA), and (4) an adjustment for pediatric patients. Pediatric ESRD patients, defined as under the age of 18, receive a specific case-mix adjustment factor. As a result, none of the other case-mix adjustors, that is the five age groups, low BMI and BSA are applicable to pediatric ESRD patients. [*Medicare Claims Processing Manual,* Pub. 100-04, No. 477, Feb. 18, 2005.]

The composite rate regulations require CMS to publish composite payment rates in a *Federal Register* notice when CMS incorporates new cost data or wage index. These rates are updated using new program data or revising the payment methodology. Each base rate consists of a labor portion and a nonlabor portion for both hospital and independent renal facilities. When the composite payment rates are updated, a listing of the new composite payment rates is published. These rates are updated and published as needed and are used when issuing a composite payment rate to a new facility or an existing facility. [Pub. 100-04, Ch. 8, § 30.1.]

Payment calculation. CMS explained the method used to update 2006 composite rates for ESRD facilities in a final rule on the physician fee schedule. [70 FR 70 FR 70116, Nov. 21, 2005.] Medicare pays 80 percent of the composite rate reduced by any deductible or coinsurance obligations the beneficiary may have. [42 C.F.R. § 413.176.] This payment is considered Medicare's full compensation for all of the facility's per-treatment costs except for (1) bad debts, (2) costs of physicians' direct patient care services, and (3) certain "separately billable" services and drugs that are not included in the facility's composite rate. [42 C.F.R. § 413.178; Pub. 100-02, Ch. 11, §§ 30.2, 30.4.2, 50.5, 80.1.]

In addition to the composite rate, payments to facilities for self-dialysis or home dialysis training sessions is supplemented as follows: (1) $20 per training session for intermittent peritoneal dialysis, continuous cycling peritoneal dialysis (CCPD), and hemodialysis training

¶847

furnished up to three times per week; and (2) $12 per training session for continuous ambulatory peritoneal dialysis (CAPD). Only one CAPD training session per day is reimbursable, up to a maximum of 15. [*PRM*, Part 1, § 2707; *Medicare Claims Processing Manual,* Pub. 100-04, Ch. 8, § 50.8; Pub. 100-02, Ch. 11, § 60.]

Under this payment system, an ESRD facility must furnish all necessary dialysis services, equipment, and supplies. If it fails to furnish (either directly or under arrangements) any part of the items and services covered under the composite rate, then the facility cannot be paid any amount for the part of the items and services that the facility does furnish. [Pub. 100-02, Ch. 11, § 30.]

Suppliers. Suppliers who deal directly with ESRD patients instead of through an approved facility will be paid according to a single composite rate that is related to the amount that would have been payable to a hospital-based facility. Those suppliers must have written agreements with an approved provider or ESRD facility under which the supplier certifies that the provider or facility will provide the patient all self-care home dialysis support services and all other necessary dialysis services and supplies, including institutional dialysis services and supplies and emergency services. [Soc. Sec. Act §§ 1881(b)(4)(B), 1881(b)(7).]

Drugs. Payment is made for drugs furnished in independent dialysis facilities, and paid outside the composite rate. Coinsurance and deductible are applied to billed charges. Effective January 1, 2006, CMS is implementing payment of the average sales price (ASP) plus six percent for all ESRD drugs furnished by both independent and hospital-based ESRD facilities. [*Final rule,* 70 FR 70164, Nov. 21, 2005.]

The *Medicare Benefit Policy Manual,* Chapter 11 describes drugs that are part of the composite rate and when other drugs may be covered. Except for EPO and Darbepoetin Alfa (Aranesp), drugs and biologicals such as blood, may be covered in the home dialysis setting only if the "incident to a physician's services" criteria are met (that is, they are not covered under the composite rate). Normally, a physician is not in the patient's home when the drugs or biologicals are administered, and therefore, drugs and biologicals generally are not paid in the home setting. [Pub. 100-04, Ch. 8, § 60.2.]

EPO. The drug erythropoietin (Epoetin Alfa) (EPO) (see ¶ 362), which is used to combat anemia in ESRD patients, is covered by Medicare and may be included either in the facility's composite rate or in payments to the patient's physician. [Soc. Sec. Act 1861(s)(2)(O); Pub. 100-02, Ch. 11, § 90.]

For patients with chronic renal failure who are not yet on a regular course of dialysis, EPO or Aranesp administered in a hospital outpatient department is paid under the outpatient prospective payment system (OPPS). When ESRD patients come to the hospital for a medical emergency, their dialysis related anemia may also require treatment. For patients with ESRD who are on a regular course of dialysis, EPO administered in a hospital outpatient department is paid using the statutory rate for EPO given to an ESRD beneficiary and Aranesp administered in a hospital outpatient department is paid the MMA Drug Pricing File rate. [Pub. 100-04, Ch. 8, §§ 60.4.3.2, 60.7.3.2.]

Exceptions to payment rates. A facility may seek an exception to its payment rate if it experiences hardship and one of the following factors is present: (1) atypical service intensity or patient mix [42 C.F.R. § 413.184], (2) isolated essential facility [42 C.F.R. § 413.186], (3) extraordinary outside circumstances [42 C.F.R. § 413.188], (4) excess self-dialysis training costs [42 C.F.R. § 413.190], or (5) infrequent dialysis usage [42 C.F.R. § 413.192].

As provided in § 623 of the Medicare Modernization Act of 2003 (MMA) (PubLNo 108-173), the pediatric exception rates in effect on October 1, 2002, will continue in effect so long as the exception rate exceeds the facility's updated composite payment rate. A pediatric facility is a renal facility with 50 percent of its patients under 18 years old. [Soc. Sec. Act § 1881(b)(7).]

Under § 623(b)(1)(D) of MMA, CMS opened a new pediatric facility exception request window for pediatric facilities that did not have an approved exception rate as of October 1, 2002. If a pediatric ESRD facility projects on the basis of prior years cost and utilization trends that it will have an allowable cost per treatment higher than its prospective rate, the facility may request CMS approve an exception to that rate and set a higher prospective payment rate.

CMS will adjudicate these exception requests in accordance with the exception criteria contained in 42 C.F.R. § 413.180 and *Provider Reimbursement Manual* (PRM), Part I, Chapter 27. However, if the facility fails to adequately justify its pediatric exception request in accordance with regulations or program instructions, its exception request will be denied. [*Medicare Claims Processing Manual,* Pub. 100-04, No. 477, February 18, 2005.]

Effective January 1, 2006, a pediatrict ESRD facility may request an exception to its composite payment rate at any time after it has been in operation for at least 12 consecutive months. Also, a pediatric ESRD facility that has been denied an exception may immediately file another exception request. However, a subsequent exception request must address the deficiencies cited in the CMS determination letter. [42 C.F.R. 413.80(d), (k).]

Beneficiary payment choices. A beneficiary must choose whether to receive necessary home dialysis equipment, supplies, and support services directly from the facility with which the beneficiary is associated (this is called Method I), or whether to make arrangements with an independent supplier (this is called Method II). The beneficiary is required to choose one of these methods. This selection is made on Form CMS-382, "ESRD Beneficiary Selection." [Pub. 100-02, Ch. 11, § 40.]

Under Method I, the equipment, supplies, and support services are included in the facility's composite rate. Under Method II, the beneficiary may either bill Medicare directly or have the facility or supplier bill Medicare under an assignment agreement. Medicare's payment under Method II is in accordance with the usual reasonable cost or reasonable charge rules, as appropriate. Specifically, payment will be denied if any of the following conditions are met: (1) the supplier has not accepted assignment; (2) the supplies were furnished by a second supplier; (3) the monthly payment limit has been reached (see below); or (4) the claim is marked nonassigned, and the evidence clearly shows that the supplier intends not to accept assignment. [Pub. 100-02, Ch. 11, § 40.1.]

Conditions of participation. Subpart U of Part 405 of the Medicare regulations, beginning at 42 C.F.R. § 405.2100, describes the health and safety requirements that approved provider and other facilities furnishing ESRD services to beneficiaries must meet. This subpart also prescribes the role ESRD networks have in the program and establishes the mechanism by which minimal utilization rates will be promulgated and applied.

Physician Reimbursement

Physicians furnish two types of services, routine professional services and administrative services in connection with ESRD treatment. Routine professional services may be paid under the initial method or monthly capitation payment (MCP). Administrative services are considered facility services and are paid as part of the facility's composite rate.

Under the MCP method, the physician is paid a set amount for each outpatient maintenance dialysis patient regardless of the volume of services provided or the location in which they are rendered. The MCP covers all physician services except (1) administration of hepatitis B vaccine, (2) services furnished by another physician under certain circumstances,

(3) inpatient hospital services (including inpatient dialysis services) provided by a physician who elects not to receive the MCP during the hospital stay, (4) surgical services (including declotting of shunts, but not including catheter insertions), and (5) physician services not related to the patient's renal condition or to a renal-related visit or session. [42 C.F.R. § 414.314(b).]

Physicians also may choose to be paid through a modified version of the "initial method" of payment, which provides for payment to the physician through the ESRD facility in the form of an "add-on" payment. Administrative and certain other services cannot be included in this method of payment, and all the physicians in a facility must elect to be paid according to this method. [42 C.F.R. § 414.313.]

Physicians are paid for providing self-dialysis training services by a flat fee of $500 (subject to deductible and coinsurance requirements—see ¶ 335) for each patient under the physician's supervision during the training course. If the training is not completed, the physician is paid $20 for each training session (25 sessions are considered a complete training course). [42 C.F.R. § 414.316; Pub. 100-04, Ch. 8, § 150.]

Inpatient dialysis services. If the patient is admitted to a hospital to receive dialysis for a reason not related to the patient's ESRD condition (for example, there was no space available in the dialysis unit), the dialysis is covered as an outpatient service. In this case, physicians' ESRD services are not paid separately because these services are covered under the physician's MCP or under the add-on to the hospital's composite rate for physicians under the initial method. [Pub. 100-04, Ch. 8, § 160.1.]

Supervision or direction of a dialysis treatment by a physician does not ordinarily meet the requirements for physicians' services and is not paid for as such under the Medicare physician fee schedule. On the other hand, physicians are responsible for the medical care and treatment of the dialysis patient and that care is paid under the fee schedule. Physicians' services furnished on non-dialysis days are paid under the same rules as any other physicians' services when non-renal related services are furnished. Renal-related services also may be paid if the physician chooses to prorate the MCP payment. Generally, these services are the physicians' hospital visits and are paid as such. The Medicare physician fee schedule is described at ¶ 820. [Pub. 100-04, Ch. 8, § 160.2.]

Transplants. Surgeons performing renal transplants are paid on a comprehensive payment basis, subject to the deductible and the coinsurance, that covers all surgical services in connection with a renal transplant, including preoperative and postoperative surgical care and for immunosuppressant therapy supervised by the attending transplant surgeon, for 60 days. Medically necessary services rendered after that period are reimbursed under the physician fee schedule. [42 C.F.R. § 414.320.]

Payment for physician services to a live donor provided in connection with a kidney donation to an entitled beneficiary is made at 100 percent of the allowed amount. These services include the donor's preoperative surgical care, kidney excision inpatient stay and any subsequent related postoperative period. There is no deductible or coinsurance charged for services furnished to live donors. The Part B claim includes the name, address, and health insurance number of the recipient as well as the name and address of the live donor. [Pub. 100-02, Ch. 11, § 80.4.]

¶847

Chapter 9—CLAIMS, PAYMENTS, AND APPEALS

[¶ 900] Claims and Appeals

Medicare defines a claim as a filing from a provider, supplier or beneficiary that includes or refers to a beneficiary's request for Medicare payment and furnishes the Medicare contractor with sufficient information to determine whether payment of Medicare benefits is due and to determine the amount of payment. Inpatient or institutional claims are always filed by the provider. Physicians and suppliers file on behalf of the beneficiary if they have accepted assignment (see ¶ 903). [42 C.F.R. § 424.5(a)(5), (6).]

A claim is a written submission by or on behalf of a beneficiary, which indicates a desire to claim payment from the Medicare program in connection with medical services of a specified nature furnished to the beneficiary. The claim must contain sufficient identifying information about the beneficiary to allow any missing information to be obtained through routine methods, such as a file check, microfilm reference, mail or telephone contact based on an address or telephone number in the file. Under Part A, a claim must be submitted on a claim form. Under Part B, a claim can be any writing submitted by or on behalf of the beneficiary. When the writing is not submitted on a claim form, there must be enough information about the nature of the medical or other health service to enable the contractor with claims processing jurisdiction to determine that the service was furnished by a physician or supplier. [*Medicare Claims Processing Manual*, Pub. 100-04, Ch. 1, § 50.1.7.]

Submission of Claims

For an eligible provider of services to receive payment from Medicare for services furnished to a beneficiary under either Part A or Part B, a written request for payment must be signed by the individual who receives the services, or by the individual's representative when it is impracticable for the individual to do so. The name of the incompetent person should be shown on the signature line of the Request for Medicare Payment (or equivalent authorization retained in the file), followed by "by" and the signature and address of the requestor. The requestor, other than a representative payee, should attach a statement to the Request for Medicare Payment explaining his or her relationship to the beneficiary and the reason the beneficiary cannot sign. In addition, the claim must be timely filed with the appropriate contractor for payment to be made by Medicare. [Soc. Sec. Act § § 1814(a)(1), 1835(a)(1); Pub. 100-04, Ch. 1, § § 50.1.3, 50.1.7.]

CCH Note: Between October 1, 2005, and October 1, 2011, Medicare administrative contractors (MACs) will assume all functions of intermediaries and carriers, including: determining the amount of Medicare payments to providers and suppliers; making payments; providing education and outreach to beneficiaries, providers and suppliers; and providing technical assistance. [Soc. Sec. Act § 1874A.] See ¶ 705 for more information on the role of MACs.

Under Part A, the claim forms contain either (1) a signature line incorporating the patient's request for payment of benefits, authorization to release information, and assignment of benefits; or (2) a statement that these requirements have been met and are on file with the provider. There are two forms, the Request for Payment, Form CMS-1490, and the Health Insurance Claim, Form CMS-1450. Form CMS-1450 does not contain an actual line for the patient's signature. Therefore, the billing form itself cannot be used as a request for payment. Requests for payment must be obtained and retained in the provider's records and available for carrier and intermediary inspection if requested. Under Part B, the request for payment normally is made on Form CMS-1500 (the "Health Insurance Claim Form" that is identical to forms used by other health insurance plans in addition to Medicare). If the items or services are furnished by a participating provider of services, the request usually is made on Form CMS-1450. If the claim is for ambulance services, Form CMS-1491 is used.

Under Part A, if at all practicable, the beneficiary should sign the request at the time of admission or start of care. In certain circumstances, it would be impracticable for an individual to sign the request for payment when admitted to a hospital or skilled nursing facility (SNF) (for example, if the patient is unconscious, incompetent, in great pain, or otherwise in such a condition that the patient should not be asked to transact any business). In these situations, the patient's representative payee (*i.e.*, a person designated by the Social Security Administration to receive monthly benefits on the patient's behalf), a relative, a legal guardian, a representative of an institution (other than the provider) usually responsible for the patient's care, or a representative of a governmental entity providing welfare assistance should, if present at time of admission or start of services, be asked and permitted to sign on the patient's behalf. [Pub. 100-04, Ch. 1, § 50.1.3.]

With certain outpatient diagnostic services, the hospital need not attempt to obtain the patient's signature. This is the situation when the physician sends a specimen (*e.g.*, blood or urine sample) to a laboratory of a participating hospital for analysis. The patient does not go to the hospital himself, but the tests are billed through the hospital. The hospital may sign on behalf of the patient and should note in its records that the patient was not physically present for the tests. This does not apply in cases in which the patient actually goes to the hospital or SNF laboratory for tests and the provider fails to obtain the patient's signature while the individual is there. [Pub. 100-04, Ch. 1, § 50.1.3.]

Medicare beneficiaries who are entitled to benefits under the fee-for-service hospital insurance program (Part A) and enrolled in the supplementary medical insurance program (Part B) may elect to enroll instead in a Medicare Advantage plan under Part C. Payments to such plans are not subject to the same requirements for submitting claims for payment and appeals that apply to services provided under Parts A and B. The Medicare Modernization Act of 2003 (MMA) (PubLNo 108-173) replaced Medicare Advantage plans with Medicare Advantage plans effective January 1, 2006. For a detailed discussion of payment under Part C, see Chapter 4.

Time Limits

In general, the time limit on submitting the request for payment and claim for payment is the close of the calendar year after the year in which the services were furnished. For services furnished in the first nine months of the year, claims must be submitted to the contractor on or before December 31 of the following year. For services furnished in the last three months of a calendar year, claims must be submitted to the contractor on or before December 31 of the second year following the year services were furnished. For purposes of the time limit for submitting claims, services furnished in the last three months of a calendar year are considered to have been furnished in the next year. [42 C.F.R. § 424.44(a).]

Example • • •

Patty underwent surgery in August 2005. The beneficiary (or the individual performing the surgery, if the right to claim payment has been assigned) must file a claim for payment for such services on or before December 31, 2006. If the surgery had been performed in October 2005, the claim would not have to be filed until December 31, 2007.

When a claim is not filed due to an error by the government or one of its agents—for example, due to misinformation from an official source or delay in the establishment of

¶900

Claims, Payments, and Appeals

entitlement—the time for filing a claim will be extended through the last day of the sixth calendar month following the month in which the error is corrected. [42 C.F.R. § 424.44(b).]

Prompt Payment of Claims

Contractors are required to pay not less than 95 percent of all "clean claims" within 30 days after the clean claims are received. A clean claim is a claim for which payment is not made on a periodic interim payment basis and that has no defect, impropriety, or particular circumstance requiring special treatment that prevents timely payment from being made. [Soc. Sec. Act §§ 1816(c)(2), 1842(c)(2); Pub. 100-04, Ch. 1, § 80.2.]

If a clean claim payment is not issued, mailed, or otherwise transmitted within the specified time period, the government will be required to pay interest on the amount of payment it should have made, beginning with the day after the required payment date and ending on the date on which the payment is made. [Soc. Sec. Act §§ 1816(c)(2)(C), 1842(c)(2)(C).]

Contractors are prohibited from paying electronic claims within 13 days after their receipt. As an incentive to encourage healthcare providers to submit claims electronically, this prohibition on payment is expanded to 26 days for all other claims. [Soc. Sec. Act §§ 1816(c)(3), 1842(c)(3).]

[¶ 902] Part A Benefit Claims

The claim containing a request for payment (see ¶ 900) for Part A benefits is submitted to the contractor by the hospital, skilled nursing facility, home health agency, hospice, or other provider. As discussed at ¶ 730, the provider may charge the beneficiary separately for applicable deductible and coinsurance amounts as well as for any extra services requested by the beneficiary.

When the provider knows or believes that no Medicare payment will be made because the service or item is excluded from coverage or because of the lack of medical necessity, the provider must notify the beneficiary in writing using an Advance Beneficiary Notice (ABN) (see ¶ 821). Beneficiaries select one of several billing options they prefer in the face of the provider's anticipation that Medicare will not cover a service. If the beneficiary signs a request for payment using the ABN, the provider is required to submit a claim. [*Medicare Claims Processing Manual*, Pub. 100-04, Ch. 1, § 60.4.1.] When notified that Medicare is likely not to pay the claim, the beneficiary becomes fully responsible for payment. [Pub. 100-04, Ch. 30, § 50.]

The contractor processes the claim and either approves or denies it. The results of the contractor's action are sent to the beneficiary in the form of a Medicare Summary Notice (MSN). The MSN explains which charges were allowed, any deductible or coinsurance amount, what Medicare paid on the claim and why. It also will explain various features of the Medicare program of interest to the beneficiary. If the claim is denied in whole or in part, the MSN provides the procedures for an appeal (see ¶ 920 and ¶ 930). The beneficiary is responsible for any applicable deductible or coinsurance (for Part A, see ¶ 220–¶ 222). [Pub. 100-04, Ch. 21, § 10.]

[¶ 903] Part B Benefit Claims

When services covered under Part B are furnished by a physician, practitioner or durable medical equipment supplier or outpatient facility (physician or supplier), the supplier or the beneficiary may submit a claim for payment. Payment may be made to the beneficiary directly if the physician does not accept assignment. Payment may be made to the physician or supplier, if the physician or supplier has accepted assignment (see below). If payment is made to a physician or supplier that is entitled to receive payment on the beneficiary's behalf

¶903

(see ¶ 330), the beneficiary is responsible for any applicable deductible or coinsurance requirements (see ¶ 335). The contractor sends the beneficiary a Medicare Summary Notice (MSN) that indicates the services claimed, the services allowed, and the amount paid by Medicare. The MSN also specifies the beneficiary's deductible and coinsurance responsibilities. [*Medicare Claims Processing Manual*, Pub. 100-04, Ch. 21, § 10.]

Payment to Beneficiary

When *payment is made to the beneficiary*, a claim may be submitted to the carrier by the physician or supplier furnishing the services on Form CMS-1500 (CMS-1491 in the case of ambulance services). The patient is responsible for paying the doctor or supplier, and Medicare pays the beneficiary directly. Because the physician or supplier has not accepted Medicare payment (has not accepted assignment, see below), the physician or supplier is not limited to billing the beneficiary only the amount that is covered under Medicare. The beneficiary may incur greater out-of-pocket expenses than what he or she would have incurred based on what the Medicare program allows. To protect patients from excessive charges Medicare imposes an upper limit, called the "limiting charge," on how much a physician or supplier may charge a beneficiary when payment is made directly from Medicare to the beneficiary (see ¶ 821). [Soc. Sec. Act § § 1848(g)(1), (2).]

Physicians and suppliers are required to file with Medicare all payment claims for items and services they provide to beneficiaries. They are not allowed to charge the patient for this service. [Soc. Sec. Act § 1848(g)(4).]

"Assignment"

When *payment is made to the physician or supplier* under "assignment," the beneficiary authorizes Medicare to pay the doctor or supplier directly. If the beneficiary wishes to assign the right to benefits in this manner, the beneficiary can do so only if the physician or supplier agrees to this method (see ¶ 831). By accepting assignment, the physician or supplier agrees to accept the amount allowed for the items or services under Part B (which pays 80 percent of the allowed amount of the claim—see ¶ 335) as the full charge and to charge the beneficiary no more than the remaining 20 percent and any unmet deductible. Although the payment in this case is made to the physician or supplier, the beneficiary receives a notice showing how much Medicare has allowed and how much it has paid. [Soc. Sec. Act § 1842(b)(3)(B)(ii).]

The Secretary is required to maintain a toll-free telephone number through which beneficiaries may obtain the names, addresses, specialties, and telephone numbers of physicians and suppliers who are in the "participation program" (see ¶ 833). [Soc. Sec. Act § 1842(h)(2).] Furthermore, when beneficiaries submit unassigned claims for Part B benefits, contractors are required to include in their MSNs a reminder that there are physicians and suppliers who are in the participation program and who have promised to accept assignment for all the Medicare services they provide. Contractors also must include in their MSNs the toll-free telephone number described above, as well as information concerning the limiting charge restriction when it has been exceeded. [Soc. Sec. Act § 1842(h)(7).]

Certification and Recertification

Medicare requires, as a condition of coverage, that the physician who ordered the services certify on the claim form that the services were medically necessary and, over a period of time, recertify that the services continue to be required. Nurse practitioners or clinical nurse specialists, working in collaboration with a physician, also are permitted to certify and recertify the need for post-hospital extended care services. [42 C.F.R.

§ 424.10(a).] In the case of services furnished by an institutional provider, the provider is responsible for obtaining the physician certifications. [42 C.F.R. § 424.11.]

[¶ 906] Overpayments and Underpayments

An individual overpayment is an incorrect payment for provider or physician services. Examples of individual overpayment cases include: (1) payment for provider, supplier or physician services after benefits have been exhausted, or when the individual was not entitled to benefits; (2) incorrect application of the deductible or coinsurance; (3) payment for noncovered items and services, including medically unnecessary services or custodial care furnished an individual; (4) payment based on a charge that exceeds the reasonable charge; (5) duplicate processing of charges or claims; (6) payment to a physician on a non-assigned claim or to a beneficiary on an assigned claim (payment made to wrong payee); (7) primary payment for items or services for which another entity is the primary payer; and (8) payment for items or services rendered during a period of non-entitlement. [*Medicare Financial Management Manual*, Pub. 100-06, Ch. 3, § 10.2.]

When Medicare pays for noncovered services or it pays too much for covered services, the program ordinarily will attempt to recover the amount of the overpayment. The contractor determines whether the provider, physician, or beneficiary is liable for the overpayment. Most intermediary payments for provider services are made to providers on behalf of the beneficiaries who received the services. If the overpayment is made to the provider, physician, or supplier, that party is liable for the repayment unless the intermediary or carrier determines that the overpaid party was *without fault* with respect to the overpayment. [Pub. 100-06, Ch. 3, § 70; *Program Integrity Manual*, Pub. 100-08, Ch. 3, §§ 3.8, 3.8.1.]

If the contractor determines that the provider, physician, or supplier was without fault, the beneficiary then becomes liable even though the beneficiary was without fault because the law provides that any Medicare payment made for a beneficiary's benefit will be considered as a payment to the beneficiary, even if the actual payment is received by someone other than the beneficiary. If payment is made directly to the beneficiary, liability always lies with the beneficiary unless recovery is waived under the limitation of liability provision. [Soc. Sec. Act § 1870; Pub. 100-06, Ch. 3, § 70.]

Although a beneficiary is technically *liable* for repayment of the overpayments, the beneficiary's lack of fault may lead the Secretary to waive liability, as discussed below. Furthermore, recovery of the overpayment may not be pursued if the amount involved is too small or if to attempt recovery from a without-fault beneficiary would (1) defeat the purpose of the Social Security and Medicare programs by causing financial hardship for the beneficiary or (2) be against equity and good conscience. [Soc. Sec. Act § 1870(c); Pub. 100-06, Ch. 3, § 70.3.]

In a recovery action, the Secretary will make the proper adjustment by (1) decreasing any Social Security (or Railroad Retirement) benefits to which the individual is entitled, (2) requiring the individual or his estate to refund the amount in excess of the correct amount, (3) decreasing any Social Security payments to the estate of the individual or to any other person on the basis of the wages and self-employment income (or compensation) that were the basis of the payments to the individual, or (4) applying any combination of these adjustments. [Soc. Sec. Act § 1870(b).]

If an individual who is overpaid dies, a recovery action may be initiated, as necessary, against any other individual who is receiving cash Social Security benefits on the same earnings record as the deceased overpaid beneficiary. A survivor of the deceased overpaid beneficiary who is liable for repayment of a Medicare overpayment may qualify for waiver of recovery of the overpaid amount if the survivor is without fault and if recovery would defeat the purposes of the Social Security Act or would be against equity and good conscience. [Soc. Sec. Act §§ 1870(b), (c).]

Limitation on Collection of Overpayments

After three years have expired, it will be presumed, in the absence of evidence to the contrary, that the provider or other person was "without fault" with respect to an overpayment and under such circumstances no collection will be attempted. The Secretary also is authorized to make the presumption before the three years have expired (but not before one year) if to do so would be consistent with the objectives of the Medicare program. [Soc. Sec. Act §§ 1870(b)–(c).]

The law also requires that, when collection of a beneficiary overpayment is made from a provider (or physicians or other persons who have accepted assignments), the provider and physician or others are prohibited, after three years, from charging beneficiaries for services found by the Secretary to be medically unnecessary or custodial in nature, in the absence of fault on the part of the individual who received the services. Again, the Secretary is authorized to make the presumption before the three years have expired (but not before one year) if to do so would be consistent with the objectives of the Medicare program. [Soc. Sec. Act §§ 1842(b)(3)(B)(ii), 1866(a)(1)(B).]

Payments on Behalf of a Deceased Beneficiary

When a person enrolled in Part B dies after receiving covered services for which reimbursement is due but before reimbursement has been completed, and the bill for the services has been paid by someone other than the deceased, the benefits will be paid to the person who paid the bill. If there is no such person, or if the deceased beneficiary paid for the services before death, the benefit will be paid to the legal representative of the deceased beneficiary's estate, if any. If there is no legal representative, benefits will be paid according to the order specified in the law. [Soc. Sec. Act § 1870(e).]

If a person enrolled in Part B dies after receiving covered services for which payment can be made "on his behalf" (see ¶ 330), but before payment for these services was made, and no assignment of the right to payment was made, payment of the amount otherwise due from Medicare will be made (1) to the physician or other person who furnished the services, provided the physician or other furnisher of services agrees to accept the Medicare-approved charge as the full charge for the services, or (2) to the person who has agreed to assume the legal obligation to make payment of the services, if the physician or other person who furnished the services does not agree to accept the Medicare-approved charge as the full charge. Payment in the latter case is made on the basis of submission of an itemized bill. The amount of payment is subject to the conditions applicable to the deceased individual who received the services. [Soc. Sec. Act § 1870(f).]

Interest Charges on Overpayments and Underpayments

When a final determination is made that a provider of services under Part A or a physician or supplier that has accepted assignment under Part B has received an overpayment or underpayment from Medicare, and payment of the excess or deficit is not made within 30 days of the determination, interest charges will be applied to the balance due. The interest rate on overpayments is determined in accordance with regulations promulgated by the Secretary of the Treasury and is the higher of the private consumer rate or the current value of fund rates prevailing on the date of final determination. Beginning with final determinations dated on or after October, 1, 2004, no interest will be assessed for a period of less than 30 days, meaning that no interest is paid for days 1 to 30, and interest for only the first 30 days is paid for days 31 to 60. This is a change to CMS' policy of paying a full 30-day

¶906

interest for any partial 30-day period. [Soc. Sec. Act §§ 1815(d), 1833(j); 42 C.F.R. § 405.378; *Final rule*, 69 FR 45604, July 30, 2004.]

NHSC Scholarship Program: Collection of Past-Due Loans

Individuals who have become delinquent in paying student loans owed to the U.S. government under the National Health Service Corps scholarship program, the Physician Shortage Area Scholarship Program, or the Health Education Assistance Loan Program are required to enter into an agreement with Medicare whereby their Medicare services will be provided only on an assignment basis and under which deductions will be made from Medicare payments due them to reduce the amount of their outstanding loans. [Soc. Sec. Act § 1892(a)(1), (a)(2).]

If an individual refuses to enter into such an agreement, or if the individual breaches the agreement, the individual will be excluded immediately from participation in the Medicare program until the past-due amounts have been repaid. In addition, the U.S. Attorney General is required to commence an action immediately to recover the full amount of the past-due obligation. [Soc. Sec. Act § 1892(a)(3).]

Guarantee of Payment to Hospitals

If a hospital has acted reasonably and in good faith in assuming that an individual was entitled to have payment made for inpatient hospital services, the hospital can receive payment for services furnished to the individual prior to notifying the patient that the hospital had reason to believe that the individual was not entitled to payment for inpatient hospitalization, even though the individual was not entitled to have payment made because all of the days of entitlement to inpatient hospital services in the spell of illness had been used up. The guarantee of payment provisions extend to inpatient services furnished to individuals who have exhausted their eligibility for inpatient hospital services but does not extend to individuals who have no coverage for other reasons, for example, an individual who is not entitled under hospital insurance or whose entitlement has been terminated. To receive Medicare payment in such cases, the hospital must refund any payment already obtained from the individual, or paid on the individual's behalf, with respect to the services involved. Payment cannot be made if the hospital has received prior notification that all days of entitlement have been used up, and, in any event, may not be continued beyond the sixth day after the day of admission to the hospital (excluding Saturdays, Sundays, and legal holidays). [Soc. Sec. Act § 1814(e); *Medicare Benefit Policy Manual*, Pub. 100-02, Ch. 5, § 10.1.]

[¶ 908] Waiver of Liability

When services that Medicare does not cover are provided in good faith to Medicare beneficiaries, there is a forgiveness provision in the law that allows Medicare to pay for those noncovered services. Depending on the circumstances, Medicare can forgive (waive liability) for the beneficiary, the provider, the physician or supplier. [Soc. Sec. Act § 1879(a).]

The claims payment and beneficiary indemnification provisions of the limitation on liability provision are applicable only to claims for beneficiary items or services submitted by providers, or by suppliers (which includes physicians or other practitioners, or an entity other than a provider that furnishes health care services under Medicare) that have taken assignment, and only to claims for services that are denied for the following statutory reasons:

(1) when the services are found not to be reasonable and necessary (see ¶ 601);

(2) when the beneficiary receives only custodial care (see ¶ 625);

(3) when home health services are determined to be noncovered because the beneficiary was not "homebound" (see ¶ 250) or did not require "intermittent" skilled nursing care (see ¶ 251);

(4) when hospice services (see ¶ 270) are determined to be noncovered because the beneficiary was found not to be "terminally ill;"

(5) when payment for inpatient hospital services or extended care services may not be made under Part A on behalf of an individual entitled to benefits solely because of an unintentional, inadvertent, or erroneous action with respect to the transfer of the individual from a hospital or skilled nursing facility that meets the statutory requirements by the provider of services acting in good faith in accordance with the advice of a utilization review committee, quality control and peer review organization, or fiscal intermediary, or on the basis of a clearly erroneous administrative decision by a provider of services; and

(6) when the beneficiary receives items or services furnished by an entity or individual excluded from the Medicare program because of program abuses (see ¶ 720).

[Soc. Sec. Act §§ 1862(a)(1), 1862(a)(9), 1879(e), 1879(g); *Medicare Claims Processing Manual*, Pub. 100-04, Ch. 30, §§ 20, 20.1.1.]

Waiver of Beneficiary Liability

Whenever a Medicare claim is disallowed, the ultimate liability for paying for the services falls on the beneficiary. Because in many cases the beneficiary is not likely to know that the services would not be covered, however, the law contains a provision that would "waive" the beneficiary's liability to pay for the services. [Soc. Sec. Act § 1879.]

The waiver of liability provision provides that the beneficiary will not have to pay for noncovered services if the beneficiary did not know, and did not have reason to know, that the services were not covered.

If the beneficiary's liability for the services is waived by the contractor, liability shifts either to the government or to the provider—depending upon whether the provider utilized due care in applying Medicare policy in its dealings with the beneficiary and the government. [Soc. Sec. Act § 1879(a), (b); 42 C.F.R. § 411.402; Pub. 100-04, Ch. 30, §§ 30.1-30.2; *Financial Management Manual*, Pub. 100-06, Ch. 3, § 70.1.]

Waiver of Provider Liability

When a provider furnishes services that are not covered, it normally is not entitled to Medicare payment for those services. As in the case with beneficiaries (see above), however, special allowances are made when claims are denied because the services were found (1) not to be reasonable and necessary, (2) to constitute custodial care, (3) in the case of home health services, to be rendered to a beneficiary who was not "homebound" or who did not require "intermittent" skilled nursing care, or (4) in the case of hospice services, to be rendered to a beneficiary who was not "terminally ill." A provider's liability is waived in these situations if the provider did not know or could not have been reasonably expected to know that the services were not covered. [Soc. Sec. Act § 1879(a); Pub. 100-04, Ch. 30, § 30.2; Pub. 100-06, Ch. 3, §§ 90, 90.1.]

Waiver of Physician/Supplier Liability

In deciding whether a physician or supplier knew or could have been expected to have known that items or services provided were not reasonable and necessary, the physician or supplier's allegation that he or she did not know and could not reasonably have been expected to know, will be acceptable evidence for waiver of liability in the absence of evidence to the contrary. A physician's or supplier's liability will not be waived for noncovered services, however, unless the physician or supplier accepted assignment (¶ 831) for the services. [42 C.F.R. § 411.400(a); Pub. 100-04, Ch. 30, § 30.2; Pub. 100-06, Ch. 3, §§ 70.3, 90.]

Erroneous Transfers of Hospital or SNF Patients

If a hospital or skilled nursing facility patient requiring a higher level of medical care is unintentionally, inadvertently, or erroneously transferred to a lower level of care by the provider—acting in good faith in accordance with the advice of a utilization review committee, quality improvement organization (QIO), intermediary, or on the basis of a clearly erroneous administrative decision by the provider—payment nevertheless can be made for the medically required higher level of care. This situation can arise when a hospital transfers a patient to a part of its facility that ordinarily is not covered by Medicare (*e.g.*, a part designated by the hospital as a non-skilled intermediate care nursing facility), while the patient still requires inpatient hospital services. To keep the beneficiary from bearing the adverse consequences resulting from erroneous judgments as to the appropriate level of care the beneficiary required—a judgment the beneficiary is in no position to influence—the Secretary is permitted to make payment in these cases. [Soc. Sec. Act § 1879(e).]

Determination of Liability

The decision to waive liability is made by the contractor or QIO (see ¶ 710) in the case of providers, physicians, and suppliers, and by CMS or the QIO in the case of beneficiaries. Under the waiver of liability, there are three outcomes: the government can be liable, the provider can be held liable, or the beneficiary can be held liable.

First, if both the provider and the beneficiary exercised due care (that is, they did not know, and had no reason to know, that noncovered services were involved), the liability shifts to the government, and payment will be made as though covered services had been furnished. In making such a payment, however, Medicare will put the provider and beneficiary on notice that the service was noncovered and that, in any subsequent cases involving similar situations and further stays or treatments (or similar types of cases in the instance of the provider), CMS will consider that the provider and beneficiary have had knowledge that payment would not be made. Therefore, the government's liability is progressively limited. [Soc. Sec. Act § 1879(a); Pub. 100-04, Ch. 30, § 20.]

Second, if the provider did not exercise due care, but there was good faith on the part of the beneficiary, liability will shift to the provider. The provider can appeal the intermediary's decision as to coverage of the services and whether it exercised due care. If the provider received reimbursement from the beneficiary, the program will indemnify the beneficiary (subject to deductibles and coinsurance). Medicare treats the indemnification as an overpayment against the provider and recoups the amount of the payment through a setoff against any amounts otherwise payable to the provider. [Soc. Sec. Act § 1879(b), (d); Pub. 100-04, Ch. 30, § 20.]

Finally, if the beneficiary was aware, or should have been aware, that the services were not covered, liability will remain with the beneficiary, and the provider can either exercise its rights under state law to collect for the services furnished or appeal the determination through the Medicare appeals process. In cases when expenses have been incurred for clearly noncovered services, such as routine physical checkups, eyeglasses or eye examinations to determine the refractive state of the eyes, hearing aids or examinations, routine dental services, or immunizations (except as allowed for pneumococcal, influenza, and hepatitis B vaccines and their administration [Soc. Sec. Act § 1861(s)(10)]), a presumption is made that the beneficiary and the provider were aware, or should have been aware, that the services were not covered. [Soc. Sec. Act § 1879(c), (d); Pub. 100-04, Ch. 30, §§ 20.2, 20.2.1, 20.2.2.]

[¶ 920] Beneficiary Appeals

The discussion that follows relates to beneficiary appeals under Parts A and B. Effective for items and services furnished on or after December 8, 2003, if a beneficiary dies before assigning appeal rights and there is no other party available to appeal such a determination, the Secretary must permit a provider or supplier to appeal a payment denial by a Medicare contractor. [Soc. Sec. Act § 1870(h).] For beneficiaries that have enrolled in Medicare Advantage (formerly Medicare+Choice) plans, specific requirements have been established with respect to administrative determinations, reconsiderations, appeals, and judicial review. These requirements are outlined at ¶ 403.

Medicare Entitlement and Enrollment

Any individual dissatisfied with the government's determination as to whether he or she is *entitled to* or *enrolled in* Medicare is entitled to reconsideration of the decision and to a hearing in the same manner provided for Social Security (or Railroad Retirement) benefit claims and to judicial review of the final decision after a hearing.

Written notice of the government's determination that an individual is not eligible for Medicare is mailed to the individual at his or her last known address. The claimant (or his representative) may request a reconsideration of this determination by letter or on a special form available at any district Social Security office. The request for a reconsideration should be in writing and filed at a district office within 60 days from the date of receipt of the original adverse determination. The reconsidered determination will be sent to the claimant in writing and will inform him of his further appeal rights. [20 C.F.R. §§ 404.904, 404.909.]

In appeals proceedings, the beneficiary can represent himself or herself, or be represented by a personal representative, an attorney, or the provider, physician, or supplier that furnished the services. A provider, physician, or supplier cannot represent a beneficiary, however, if there is a conflict of interest under the waiver of liability provision (see ¶ 908)— *i.e.*, if there is a question as to who knew or had reason to know that the services would not be covered. A provider, physician, or supplier cannot impose any financial liability on the beneficiary in connection with such a representation. [Soc. Act § 1869(b)(1)(B).]

Beneficiary Coverage and Payment Appeals

The Benefits Improvement and Protection Act of 2000 (BIPA) (PubLNo 106-554) established a uniform process for all Part A and Part B appeals, including a new level of appeal for Part A claims. Under the new uniform appeals process, there are four levels of administrative appeals. The first level of appeal is a redetermination made by the contractor (intermediary or carrier). The second administrative appeal, a "reconsideration," is conducted by a new entity, the qualified independent contractor (QIC). The third level of appeal is to an administrative law judge (ALJ) and finally, a review by the Medicare Appeals Council. All intermediary redeterminations became subject to QIC reconsiderations beginning May 1, 2005, and beginning January 1, 2006, appeals of carrier redeterminations were subject to QIC reconsiderations, which replace the carrier hearing. The new ALJ rules are in effect for all appeals that come through the QICs. [*Interim final rule*, 70 FR 11420, March 8, 2005.]

Benefit notices. As mandated by § 933 of the Medicare Modernization Act of 2003 (MMA) (PubLNo 108-173), when an initial determination or redetermination results in a denial of a claim for benefits, a notice must be provided in printed form and written in a manner that the beneficiary can understand. The notice must include the reasons for the determination or redetermination; the procedures for obtaining additional information concerning the determination or redetermination; and notification of the right to appeal with instructions on how to initiate an appeal. The person provided the notice may obtain, on request, information on the specific provision of the policy, manual, or regulation used in making the determination or redetermination. [Soc. Sec. Act § 1869(a)(4)-(5).]

Initial determinations. The "initial determination" of whether services are covered and how much Medicare will pay is made by an insurance company under contract with the Medicare program to process and pay claims. In the case of Part A services, the administering insurance company is called an intermediary; in the case of Part B claims, it is called a carrier. [Soc. Sec. Act § 1869(a)(1); 42 C.F.R. §§ 405.704, 405.803(a).] As required by § 911 of the MMA, however, beginning October 1, 2005, through October 2011, intermediaries and carriers will begin to be replaced with Medicare administrative contractors (MACs). MACs will assume the functions of intermediaries and carriers, including determining the amount of Medicare payments to providers and suppliers and making the payments. Unlike intermediaries and carriers, MACs do not have to be insurance companies. References to fiscal intermediaries and carriers have been removed from Medicare laws and replaced by MACs. During the transition period, references to MACs may include intermediaries and carriers. [Soc. Sec. Act § 1874A.]

Redeterminations. If there is a dispute over a contractor's initial determination, the beneficiary, the beneficiary's representative, or the provider, physician, or supplier that provided the services can appeal by asking for a "redetermination." Prior to October 1, 2004, the first level appeal was referred to as a "reconsideration" by the intermediary or a "review determination" by the carrier. [Pub. 100-06, Transmittal No. 55, Oct. 8, 2004.]

Effective for intermediary initial determinations issued on or after May 1, 2005, and carrier initial determinations issued on or after January 1, 2006, (1) a request for redetermination must be filed in writing with the contractor indicated on the notice of redetermination, and (2) a written statement request that is not made on a standard form is accepted if it contains the same required elements. [42 C.F.R. § 405.944(b).] CMS eliminated alternative locations, including the Social Security Administration, for the filing of appeals. In addition, although previously Part B requests for review could be made by telephone, under the new claims appeal process, CMS eliminated telephone requests to provide a reliable record of the request and encourage the submission of evidence to support the request. [*Interim final rule*, 70 FR 11420, 11436, March 8, 2005.] The request for redetermination must be filed within 120 calendar days after receipt of an initial determination (presumed to be five days after the date of the notice) for initial determinations dated October 1, 2002, or later. [42 C.F.R. § 405.942(a).] Contractors are required to process all redeterminations within 60 days, unless the contractor grants the appellant an extension to the 60-day filing deadline. [42 C.F.R. § 405.950.]

Qualified independent contractor reconsiderations. Section 521 of BIPA revised the Medicare appeals process to provide for a new reviewing entity referred to as a QIC, which provides a second level of appeal, referred to as a reconsideration, for a denied claim for payment. The reconsideration represents an additional level of appeal of claims under Part A and replaces the Part B carrier hearing level of appeal. [Soc. Sec. Act § 1869(b)(1)(A) and (c).] A reconsideration can only be conducted after the contractor has conducted a "redetermination" of the initial determination.

A request for reconsideration must be in writing, must be filed with the QIC indicated on the notice of redetermination, and should be on a standard CMS form. It must contain certain required elements, such as the beneficiary's name, Medicare health insurance claim number, and the specific services and/or items for which the reconsideration is being requested, and must be filed within 180 calendar days after receipt of a the notice of redetermination (presumed to be five days after the date of the notice). [42 C.F.R. §§ 405.942(a), 405.964.] Beneficiary-appellants may submit documentation that was specified

¶920

as missing in the notice of redetermination at any time during a pending appeal without the need for good cause; however, this exception does not apply to beneficiaries who are represented by providers or suppliers. [42 C.F.R. § 405.966.] QICs must complete their reconsiderations within 60 days of receiving a timely filed request. [42 C.F.R. § 405.970.] Note, however, that when a party submits additional evidence after filing the request for redetermination, the QIC's 60-day decisionmaking time frame is automatically extended by up to 14 calendar days for each submission. [42 C.F.R. § 405.966(b).] The QIC's reconsideration decision must be in writing and must include a detailed explanation of the decision as well as a discussion of the pertinent facts and applicable regulations applied in making the decision. [42 C.F.R. § 405.976.]

ALJ review. The third level of appeal, which follows a QIC reconsideration, is to an administrative law judge (ALJ). The amount in controversy must reach the threshold amount, which must be $100 or more. [42 C.F.R. § 405.1008(a).] Beginning in 2005, as required by § 940 of the MMA, the minimum amount in controversy for hearings or judicial review will be increased by the percentage increase in the medical care component of the consumer price index for urban consumers for July 2003 to the July preceding the year involved. The amount will be rounded to the nearest multiple of $10. [Soc. Sec. Act §§ 1869(b)(1)(E), (E)(iii).] To help expedite the adjudication of appealed claims, pursuant to the MMA, the Social Security Administration transferred the ALJ function to HHS as of October 1, 2005.

The ALJ conducts the hearing. At the hearing the beneficiary and/or representatives may appear in person, examine the evidence used in making the determination or decision under review, and present and question witnesses. Beneficiaries, except those represented by suppliers or providers, also may submit new evidence. In addition, CMS or its contractor may enter an appeal at the ALJ level as a party unless an unrepresented beneficiary brings the appeal. CMS will have all the rights of a party, including the right to call witnesses, submit additional evidence within the time frame specified by the ALJ, and seek review of a decision adverse to CMS. [42 C.F.R. § 405.1012.]

Under BIPA, ALJs are bound by all national coverage determinations whether based on Soc. Sec. Act § 1862(a)(1) or on other grounds, as well as the Medicare Act, applicable regulations, and CMS rulings. [42 C.F.R. § 405.1063.] ALJ also must give deference to non-binding CMS and contractor policies such as local coverage determinations, local medical review policies, manual instructions and program memoranda, but a party can request that an ALJ disregard the policy. [42 C.F.R. § 405.992.] The ALJ will issue a decision based on the hearing record. If the beneficiary or his or her representative waives the right to appear at the hearing, the ALJ will make a decision based on the evidence that is in the file and any new evidence that may have been submitted for consideration.

The notice of the ALJ's decision must be in writing in a manner that is understood by the beneficiary and must include: (1) the specific reasons for the determination (including, to the extent appropriate, a summary of the clinical or scientific evidence used in making the determination); (2) the procedures for obtaining additional information concerning the decision; and (3) notification of the right to appeal the decision and instructions on how to initiate the appeal. [42 C.F.R. § 405.1046.] The ALJ must issue a decision, dismissal order, or remand to the QIC within 90 days of when the request for hearing is received by the entity specified in the QIC's notice of reconsideration. [42 C.F.R. § 405.1016.]

Medicare Appeals Council review. If the parties are dissatisfied with results of the ALJ hearing, they are entitled to a hearing before the Medicare Appeals Council (MAC) of the Departmental Appeals Board (DAB). Under the former regulations, a MAC considered several factors when deciding whether to grant a request for review. Under BIPA, however, a

MAC may no longer "deny" review, nor may it consider ALJ decisions under a substantial evidence standard. [*Proposed rule,* 67 FR 69311, Nov. 25, 2002.] Instead, a MAC conducts a new review of an ALJ decision. The appellant must file the request for review within 60 days. [42 C.F.R. §405.1102(a).] In addition, any time within 60 days after the date of an ALJ decision or dismissal, the MAC may decide on its own motion to review the ALJ's action. CMS or any of its contractors may refer a case to the MAC for it to consider reviewing under this authority any time within 60 days of an ALJ's decision or dismissal. [42 C.F.R. §405.1110(a).]A party does not have the right to an in person hearing before a MAC, and the MAC limits its review to the evidence contained in the record of the proceedings before the ALJ. A provider, supplier, or beneficiary represented by a provider or supplier may submit new evidence related to issues previously considered by the QIC if the provider, supplier, or beneficiary represented by a provider or supplier had good cause for presenting it for the first time at the MAC level. If good cause does not exist, the MAC may not consider the evidence nor may it remand the issue to an ALJ. [42 C.F.R. §405.1122(a); *Interim final rule,* 70 FR 11420, March 8, 2005.]

A beneficiary, provider, or supplier may obtain expedited access to judicial review when a review entity determines that the MAC does not have the authority to decide the question of law or regulation relevant to the matters in controversy. The party that requested the hearing and the Secretary must agree that the only factor precluding a favorable determination is a statutory provision that the individual alleges to be unconstitutional, or a regulation, national coverage determination or CMS ruling that is invalid. This agreement constitutes a waiver by all parties with respect to the need to pursue the remaining steps in the administrative process. [42 C.F.R. §405.990(a).]

Escalation. The deadline for a contractor to make a redetermination is 60 days, and QICs must complete their reconsiderations within 60 days of receiving a timely filed request. [42 C.F.R. §§405.95, 405.970.] MACs and ALJs must issue a decision within 90 days. [42 C.F.R. §405.1016.] If, however, the QIC, MAC, or ALJ does not issue its decision within the deadline, the parties may escalate the case to the next level of appeal. [42 C.F.R. §§405.970, 405.1104, 405.1132.] Escalation affects the next level's deadlines for making a decision. For example, although the decisionmaking deadline for the MAC is generally 90 days, if a case is escalated from the ALJ to the MAC, the MAC must complete its action within 180 days of the receipt for escalation. [42 C.F.R. §405.1100(d).]

Expedited appeals of provider service terminations. Effective July 1, 2005, expedited determination and reconsideration procedures are available to beneficiaries when a provider informs them of a decision that Medicare coverage of their provider services is about to end. BIPA amended Soc. Sec. Act §1869(b)(1)(F) to require the Secretary to establish a process by which a beneficiary may obtain an expedited determination in response to the termination of provider services to determine whether these services should end. Quality improvement organizations (QIOs) conduct the expedited determination, and QICs conduct the expedited reconsideration. [42 C.F.R. §§405.1200, 405.1202, 405.1204.]

Appointment of representatives. A party may appoint any individual, including an attorney, to act as his or her representative in dealing with the contractor. A representative may be appointed at any point in the appeals process. A representative may help the party during the processing of a claim or claims and any subsequent appeal. To file an appeal, the representative must file a copy of the Appointment of Representative form or other written instrument with the appeal request. The representation is valid for the duration of an individual's appeal of an initial determination. If the initial determination involves a Medicare Secondary Payer recovery, an appointment signed in connection with the party's efforts to

¶920

make a claim for third party payment is valid for the duration of any later appeal. [42 C.F.R. § 405.910; *Medicare Claims Processing Manual,* Pub. 100-04, Ch. 29, § 60.5.1.]

Judicial review. If the amount in controversy meets the threshold, which is at least $1,000 ($2,000 for QIO appeals), and all of the above administrative remedies have been exhausted, judicial review is available. [Soc. Sec. Act § § 1155, 1869(b)(1)(E).]

Overview of Parts A and B Claims Appeals Under the Prior Process

Under the process in place for appeals of all intermediary redeterminations issued before May 1, 2005, a request for redetermination was required to be in writing and to express disagreement with the initial determination. Under the process in place for appeals of carrier redeterminations issued before January 1, 2006, a request for redetermination could be made in writing. Written requests under Part A and Part B had to be filed at the Social Security Administration, CMS or the intermediary or carrier office. Under Part B, a request for review also could be made by telephone to the number designated for this purpose by the carrier. [42 C.F.R. § § 405.710, 405.711, 405.807.] For initial determinations dated October 1, 2002, or later, the request for redetermination was required to be made within 120 days after the receipt of the initial determination for Part A. For Part B, initial determinations dated between October 1, 2002, and December 31, 2002, the time limit for a request for review was six months. Prior to this time frame, the time limit for request for review was 60 days for Part A and six months for Part B. [*Program Memorandum*, Transmittal No. AB-02-111, July 31, 2002.] There was no minimum amount in controversy for a review or reconsideration of an initial determination. [42 C.F.R. § § 405.710, 405.711, 405.807; Pub. 100-04, Ch. 29, § § 30.7, 30.8.]

Part B telephone reviews. Under the previous process, beneficiaries, providers, and suppliers could request a review of the carrier's initial determination by telephone, and the carrier could conduct the review by telephone, if possible. Whether a request for review was made by telephone or was conducted and completed as a telephone review depended on the issues and the complexity of the matters involved. [42 C.F.R. § 405.807; Pub. 100-04, Ch. 29, § 60.12.]

Hearing officer hearings. Under the previous process, if dissatisfied with the review determination, Part B claimants could request a hearing by a carrier hearing officer (HO) (formerly known as a "fair hearing") if the amount in controversy was at least $100. This was an additional appeal level under Part B; there was no parallel level of appeal under Part A. This second level for a Part B appeal, however, was eliminated and replaced by a reconsideration by QICs. [Soc. Sec. Act § 1842(b)(3)(C); 42 C.F.R. § § 405.817, 405.821; Pub. 100-04, Ch. 29, § 60.13.]

The HO hearing was the second level of appeal, available after an initial review determination. The hearing process gave a dissatisfied party an opportunity to present the reasons for his or her dissatisfaction and to receive a new decision based on all the evidence developed at the hearing. A party to a review determination was entitled to a hearing if a written request was filed timely and if the amount remaining in controversy at the time the request was filed was $100 or more. The request for a HO hearing had to be made within six months of the date of the notice of the review determination or revised initial or review determination. [Pub. 100-04, Ch. 29, § § 60.13, 60.13.2.]

QIO Reconsiderations

A Medicare beneficiary, provider, or healthcare practitioner who is dissatisfied with a determination by a QIO is entitled to a reconsideration of the determination. QIOs make determinations related to (1) reasonableness, medical necessity (including the need for using assistants at cataract surgery), and appropriateness of the services furnished or proposed to be furnished (for example, whether treatment was appropriate for the condition); (2) appropriateness of the setting in which the services were, or are proposed, to be furnished; and (3) financial liablity for the services. [*Quality Improvement Organization Manual*, Pub. 100-10, Ch. 7, § 7410.]

If the beneficiary has been found liable for payment by the QIO, the beneficiary may obtain a reconsideration of the liability determination. If the provider or practitioner has been found liable, or the beneficiary has been found liable but does not pursue a reconsideration on the issue of knowledge (see waiver of liability discussion at ¶ 908), the provider or practitioner may obtain a reconsideration of the liability determination. If the practitioner has been found liable and the beneficiary has been found not liable, or the beneficiary has been found liable but does not pursue a reconsideration on the issue of knowledge, the practitioner may ask for a reconsideration on the issue that neither the beneficiary nor the practitioner knew and could not have known that the services denied were not covered under Medicare Part B. [Pub. 100-10, Ch. 7, § 7410.]

A beneficiary may request a reconsideration by submitting a timely written request to the QIO, a Social Security Administration district office, or a Railroad Retirement Board Office (if the party is a railroad retirement beneficiary). A provider or practitioner may request a reconsideration by writing to the QIO. A timely request is submitted within 60 calendar days after receipt of the initial denial notice Receipt of the notice is assumed to be within five days of the date of the initial notice if absent proof to the contrary. [Pub. 100-10, Ch. 7, § 7410.] If the result is adverse to the beneficiary and the amount in controversy is $200 or more, the beneficiary is entitled to a review by the Secretary. [Soc. Sec. Act § 1155.]

NCD and LCD Appeals

The term "national coverage determination" means a determination by the Secretary with respect to whether a particular item or service is covered under the Medicare program (see ¶ 390), but does not include a determination of what code, if any, is assigned to a particular item or service covered or a determination with respect to the amount of payment made for a particular item or service so covered. The term "local coverage determination" (LCD) means a determination by a contractor under Part A or Part B, concerning whether a particular item or service is covered on an intermediary- or carrier-wide basis in accordance with § 1862(a)(1)(A). [Soc. Sec. Act § 1869(f)(1)(B) and (f)(2)(B).]

CMS established an appeals process for NCDs and LCDs. Effective December 8, 2003, beneficiaries who qualify as aggrieved parties can use this process to challenge NCDs and LCDs. An aggrieved party is defined as a Medicare beneficiary who is entitled to benefits under Part A, enrolled under Part B, or both (including an individual enrolled in fee-for-service Medicare, in a Medicare Advantage plan, or in another Medicare managed care plan), and is in need of coverage for a service that is the subject of an applicable LCD (in the relevant jurisdiction) or an NCD as documented by the beneficiary's treating physician. An aggrieved party includes a beneficiary who received a service, but whose claim for the service was denied. The rule allows the beneficiary to file a complaint following the procedures under 42 C.F.R. § 426.400 for an LCD or § 426.500 for an NCD. The right to challenge NCDs and LCDs has been made distinct from the existing appeal rights that beneficiaries have for appealing Medicare claims. [*Final rule*, 68 FR 63692, Nov. 7, 2003.]

There are two avenues of appeals for LCDs and NCDs: reconsideration and review. The main difference between an LCD/NCD review and an LCD/NCD reconsideration is the avenue an individual chooses to take to initiate a change to a coverage policy and who may initiate the review. The reconsideration process allows any individual, not just an aggrieved party, to submit new evidence to an expert for reconsideration of an LCD or NCD. The review process permits only an "aggrieved party" to file a complaint to initiate the review of an LCD or NCD.

Review of an LCD or NCD requires examination of an entire policy or specific provisions, not just one claim denial. Therefore, such reviews may lead to changes that impact other beneficiaries if the policies are found to be unreasonable. A beneficiary may elect to pursue a claims denial through the claims appeal process, seek review of an LCD or NCD, or both. [Soc. Sec. Act §§ 1869(f)(1), (2); 42 C.F.R. § 426.100, et seq.; *Final rule,* 68 FR 63692, Nov. 7, 2003.]

Mediation for disputes related to LCDs. Effective December 8, 2003, CMS is required to establish a mediation process using a physician trained in mediation and employed by CMS. The mediator mediates in disputes between groups representing providers of services, suppliers, and the medical director for a Medicare administrative contractor whenever the regional administrator involved determines that there was a systematic pattern and a large volume of complaints from such groups regarding decisions of the director or there is a complaint from the co-chair of the advisory committee of that contractor to the regional administrator regarding the dispute. [MMA § 940A; Soc. Sec. Act § 1869(i).]

[¶ 930] Provider Appeals

Pursuant to an interim final rule that established a uniform process for Part A and B claims appeals, Medicare providers and suppliers may now file administrative appeals of initial determinations to the same extent as beneficiaries. [42 C.F.R. § 405.906(a).] Previously, providers could appeal Medicare determinations when the determination involved a finding that: (1) the item or service was not covered because it constituted custodial care, was not reasonable or necessary, or for certain other reasons; and (2) the provider knew or reasonably could be expected to know that the item or service was not covered under Medicare. [*Interim final rule,* 70 FR 11420, March 8, 2005.]

Redeterminations. If there is a dispute over a contractor's initial determination, the provider that provided the services can appeal by asking for a "redetermination." Prior to October 1, 2004, the first level appeal was referred to as a "reconsideration" by the intermediary or a "review determination" by the carrier. [*Financial Management Manual,* Pub. 100-06, Transmittal No. 55, Oct. 8, 2004.]

Qualified independent contractor reconsiderations. A new reviewing entity referred to as a qualified independent contractor (QIC) provides a second level appeal, referred to as a reconsideration, for a denied claim for payment. The reconsideration represents an additional level of appeal of claims under Part A and replaces the Part B carrier hearing level of appeal. [Soc. Sec. Act § 1869(b)(1)(A) and (c).]

ALJ review. Providers, physicians, and suppliers that are dissatisfied with a QIC reconsideration may appeal to an administrative law judge (ALJ) if the amount in controversy reaches the threshold amount, which must be $100 or more. Under the Benefits Improvement and Protection Act of 2000 (PubLNo 106-554) (BIPA), ALJs are bound by all national coverage determinations, the Medicare Act, applicable regulations, and CMS rulings, and must give deference to non-binding CMS and contractor policies such as local coverage determinations, local medical review policies, manual instructions and program memoranda. [42 C.F.R. § 405.1063.] In addition, to help expedite the adjudication of appealed claims, the MMA mandated that the Social Security Administration transfer the ALJ function to HHS as of October 1, 2005.

MAC review. Upon receipt of an adverse ALJ decision, a dissatisfied provider may ask for administrative review by the Medicare Appeals Council (MAC) (the MAC is part of the Departmental Board of Appeals). Under the former regulations, a MAC considered several factors when deciding whether to grant a request for review. Under BIPA, however, a MAC may no longer "deny" review, nor may it consider ALJ decisions under a substantial evidence standard. [*Proposed rule,* 67 FR 69311, Nov. 25, 2002.] Instead, a MAC conducts a new review of an ALJ decision. In addition, a provider, supplier, or beneficiary represented by a provider or supplier may submit new evidence related to issues previously considered by the QIC if the provider, supplier, or beneficiary represented by a provider or supplier had good cause for presenting it for the first time at the MAC level. If good cause does not exist, the MAC may not consider the evidence nor may it remand the issue to an ALJ. [42 C.F.R. § 405.1122(c).]

Escalation. The deadline for a contractor to make a redetermination is 60 days, and QICs must complete their reconsiderations within 60 days of receiving a timely filed request. [42 C.F.R. §§ 405.95, 405.970.] MACs and ALJs must issue a decision within 90 days. [42 C.F.R. § 405.1016.] If, however, the QIC, MAC, or ALJ does not issue its decision within the deadline, the parties may escalate the case to the next level of appeal. [42 C.F.R. §§ 405.970, 405.1104, 405.1132.] Escalation affects the next level's deadlines for making a decision. For example, although the decisionmaking deadline for the MAC is generally 90 days, if a case is escalated from the ALJ to the MAC, the MAC must complete its action within 180 days of the receipt for escalation. [42 C.F.R. § 405.1100(d).]

Assignment of appeal rights. A beneficiary may assign appeal rights to a provider or supplier when the provider or supplier furnished the item or service to the beneficiary but was not a party to the initial determination. The assignment of appeal rights must: (1) be executed using a CMS standard form; (2) be in writing and signed by both the beneficiary assigning his or her appeal rights and by the assignee; (3) indicate the item or service for which the assignment of appeal rights is authorized; and (4) be submitted at the same time as the request for redetermination or other appeal is filed. In addition, the assignee must waive the right to collect payment for the item or service for which the assignment of appeal rights is made. If the beneficiary revokes the assignment, the waiver of the right to collect payment nevertheless remains valid. The waiver also remains in effect regardless of the outcome of the appeal decision. [42 C.F.R. § 405.912.]

Nonparticipating providers and suppliers. In addition, nonparticipating providers and suppliers who are not considered parties to the initial determination may appeal an initial determination relating to the services they rendered to a beneficiary who later dies if there is no other party available to appeal the determination. [42 C.F.R. § 405.906(c).]

Overview of Parts A and B Claims Appeals Under the Prior Process

Before May 1, 2005, when Medicare providers and suppliers were given the right to file administrative appeals of initial determinations to the same extent as beneficiaries, providers could appeal Medicare determinations when the determination involved a finding that: (1) the item or service was not covered because it constituted custodial care, was not reasonable or necessary, or for certain other reasons; and (2) the provider knew or reasonably could be expected to know that the item or service was not covered under Medicare. [42 C.F.R. § 405.704; *Interim final rule,* 70 FR 11420, March 8, 2005.] A provider could initiate an appeal only if the ultimate liability rested with it and the beneficiary did not exercise his appeal rights.

ALJ review of intermediary redetermination. Under the process in place for appeals of all intermediary redeterminations issued before May 1, 2005, there were three levels of administrative appeals for Part A before an appeal could be made to federal court: a redetermination (referred to as a "reconsideration" before October 1, 2004) by an intermediary, a review by an ALJ, and a review by the Medicare Appeals Council of the Departmental Appeals Board. If

¶930

a provider, supplier, beneficiary or representative of the beneficiary who had liability for payment was dissatisfied with the initial determination, a request for redetermination could be made. [42 C.F.R. § 405.710.]

If still dissatisfied and the amount in controversy met a threshold of $100 or more, the provider, supplier or beneficiary had the right to a hearing before an ALJ and, if still dissatisfied, could appeal to the MAC. If the amount at issue was less than $100, no additional hearing was provided. If the amount at issue met a threshold of $1,000 or more, the provider, supplier or beneficiary had the right to judicial review of the Secretary's final decision. [42 C.F.R. §§ 405.720, 405.730.]

Fair hearing and ALJ review. Under the process in place for appeals of all carrier redeterminations issued before January 1, 2006, if the provider remained dissatisfied with a carrier's decision and the amount in controversy was $100, the provider could request a non-adversarial hearing before a carrier hearing officer. [42 C.F.R. §§ 405.815, 405.821.] After the hearing, if the amount in controversy was $500 or more for initial determinations made on or before September 30, 2002, or $100 or more for initial determinations made on or after October 1, 2002, the provider could file a written request for a hearing before an ALJ within 60 days after the receipt of the notice of the carrier hearing decision. [Soc. Sec. Act § 1869; 42 C.F.R. §§ 405.815, 405.855.]

Administrative Review of Disputed Cost Reports

Section 1878 of the Social Security Act and its implementing regulations (42 C.F.R. § 405.1801, *et seq.*) give providers of services and other entities, such as health maintenance organizations, the right to request a hearing on disputed cost reports submitted to their contractors. A hospital and certain other providers that participate in the Medicare program are required to submit an annual accounting of the costs they incur to operate their facilities, including direct patient costs for Medicare and non-Medicare patients and operating costs such as depreciation, capital-related costs, and other expenses. The cost report is the vehicle for reporting costs and income to CMS. Hospitals specifically may receive additional reimbursement from Medicare for costs they incur related to (1) medical education if it is a teaching hospital, (2) treating a disproportionately large share of low income and poverty level individuals, and (3) Medicare bad debts that are a result of uncollectible deductibles and coinsurance due from beneficiaries.

When the amount in controversy is $1,000 or more, but less than $10,000, a dissatisfied provider or other entity may request an intermediary hearing. [42 C.F.R. § 405.1809(b)(2).] If a provider disagrees with the intermediary hearing officer's interpretation of the law, regulations, rulings, or general instructions relied on in the decision, it may request a review of the decision by a special review officer of CMS. CMS also may review an intermediary hearing officer's decision on its own motion. [*Provider Reimbursement Manual*, Part 1, § 2917.]

Any provider of services that has filed a timely cost report may appeal an adverse final decision of the intermediary to the Provider Reimbursement Review Board (PRRB) if the amount at issue is $10,000 or more. The appeal must be filed within 180 days after notice of the intermediary's final determination is received. In addition, groups of providers may appeal adverse final decisions of the intermediary to the PRRB when the matters at issue share a common question of fact or law and the total amount in controversy, in the aggregate, is $50,000 or more. Providers also may appeal to the PRRB on a late cost report decision by the intermediary if the amount involved is $10,000 or more. Implementation of the intermediary's determinations will not be suspended pending the PRRB's decision. The Secretary may elect to review a decision of the PRRB. [Soc. Sec. Act § 1878(a)-(b).]

¶930

Judicial review. If, within 60 days after notification to the provider of the PRRB's decision, the Secretary reverses, affirms, or modifies the PRRB's decision, judicial review is available. The provider also has the right to judicial review of any final decision of the PRRB. When judicial review is sought, the amount in controversy is subject to annual interest beginning on the first day of the first month that begins after the 180-day period following the notice of the intermediary's final determination. [Soc. Sec. Act §§ 1878(f)(1), (2).]

Providers also have the right to obtain judicial review of any action of the intermediary involving a question of law or regulations relevant to the matters in controversy, whenever the PRRB determines (on its own motion or at the request of the provider) that it is without authority to decide the question, by a civil action commenced within 60 days after notification of the determination is received. [Soc. Sec. Act § 1878(f)(1).]

Provider Status Determinations

Contractors make initial determinations with respect to whether a provider or supplier meets the conditions for participation or coverage in the Medicare program. Adverse decisions may be appealed to an ALJ and the DAB. Only providers, however, have the right to judicial review of an adverse decision; suppliers do not. [Soc. Sec. Act § 1866(h); 42 C.F.R. § 498.5.]

42 C.F.R. Part 498 contains the determinations and appeals procedures applicable to these and other status determinations.

Appeals Concerning Suspensions and Fines

The law contains provisions, discussed at ¶ 720, granting the Secretary authority to exclude or impose sanctions upon entities or individuals from participation in the Medicare program if they are determined to have committed certain program abuses. This authority has been delegated to the HHS Inspector General. An excluded entity or individual is entitled to reasonable notice of an opportunity for hearing by the Secretary and to judicial review of the Secretary's final decision. [Soc. Sec. Act § 1128(f).]

Any person adversely affected by a determination of the Secretary with respect to the imposition of a civil money penalty may obtain review of the determination in the U.S. Court of Appeals (see ¶ 720). [Soc. Sec. Act § 1128A(e).]

Topical Index

→ *References are to paragraph numbers*

A

Accommodations . . . 211; 232
Actual charge limits on physicians and suppliers . . . 821
Administration of program . . . 700-707
Admission
. day of . . . 224; 243
. denial of, based on ability to pay prohibited . . . 730
. dumping patients prohibited . . . 730
Advance beneficiary notices . . . 267; 730
Advance directives—see Living wills
Advisory opinions . . . 720
Age 65, attainment of . . . 200; 201; 300
Agreements—see Provider participation agreements
Aides, home health . . . 254
Alcoholism treatments . . . 214
Aliens . . . 201; 203; 300
Ambulance service . . . 355
Ambulatory payment classification (APC) groups . . . 837
Ambulatory surgical center (ASC) services . . . 386
Amount in controversy (appeal rights) . . . 920
Ancillary services, inpatient . . . 361
Anesthesiology services . . . 340; 366; 820
Anti-dumping law . . . 730
Antigens . . . 362
Appeals—see Claims and appeals
Appliances . . . 213
Applications . . . 200; 310
Artificial legs, arms, and eyes . . . 358
Assignment method of payment . . . 831; 903
. participating physician and supplier program . . . 833
. penalty for violation of assignment agreement . . . 720
Assignment of claims
. agreements . . . 831
. participation program for physicians and suppliers . . . 833
Assistants-at-surgery . . . 654; 820
Automobile insurance . . . 638

B

Beneficiaries
. disability . . . 204
. end-stage renal disease . . . 847
. retirement . . . 201
Biologicals—see Drugs and biologicals
Blood deductible . . . 223; 238; 335; 730
Bone mass measurement tests . . . 369
Braces . . . 358
Bribes . . . 720

C

Canadian hospitals . . . 227
Cancer
. drugs . . . 362
. screening tests . . . 369
Carriers . . . 705; 903; 920
Cataracts
. coverage of treatment . . . 619
. intraocular lenses—see Intraocular lenses
. prosthetic lenses . . . 357
. surgery assistants, exclusion of payment for . . . 654
Certificate of medical necessity . . . 356
Certification and recertification . . . 903
Certified Registered Nurse Anesthetist (CRNA) . . . 350; 351; 366; 635; 826
CHAMPUS and CHAMPVA . . . 607
Charges
. by relatives . . . 631
. limits on permissible charges
. . by physicians and suppliers . . . 821; 831; 833
. . by providers . . . 730
. refund of . . . 821
Chemical dependency . . . 214
Chiropractor . . . 340
Christian Science sanatoria . . . 228
Civil money penalties . . . 720
Claims and appeals
. court review . . . 920
. entitlement to benefits . . . 920
. . assignment of claims . . . 831; 903
. exclusion from program participation . . . 720
. general . . . 900; 920
. judicial review . . . 920
. Medicare Advantage . . . 411
. overpayments and underpayments . . . 906
. Part A claims . . . 902; 920
. Part B claims . . . 903; 920
. prompt payment requirements . . . 900
. PROs—see Quality Improvement Organizations (QIOs)
. reimbursement appeals by providers . . . 930
. time limits on claims . . . 900
. waiver of liability . . . 908
Clinical laboratories . . . 214; 335; 827
Clinical trials
. routine costs . . . 601; 630
Coinsurance—see Deductibles and coinsurance
Colorectal cancer screening tests . . . 369
Colostomy bags and supplies . . . 357
Community health centers
. deductibles and coinsurance . . . 335
. examinations and checkups, routine . . . 619
. government entity, services paid for by . . . 607
. legal obligation to pay . . . 604
. mental health services . . . 387
. Part B coverage . . . 382

COM

Comprehensive outpatient rehabilitation facility (CORF) services . . . 385

Conditional payments . . . 636

Conditions of participation—see Provider participation agreements

Consumer protection
. access to care . . . 402
. appeals and grievances . . . 403
. "gag clause" prohibition . . . 411
. medical records privacy . . . 409
. Medigap protections . . . 740
. sanctions . . . 720

Contact lenses . . . 357

Coordinated care plans . . . 400
. preferred provider organizations . . . 400
. provider-sponsored organizations . . . 400; 407

Coordination of benefits . . . 639

Cosmetic surgery . . . 628

Court review—see Claims and appeals

Coverage period
. Part A . . . 201-206
. Part B . . . 313
. Part C . . . 401
. hospice benefit period . . . 270

Covered services—see also Hospital insurance benefits, Supplementary medical insurance benefits, Exclusions from Coverage
. national coverage decisions . . . 390

Crimes, conviction of—see also Fraud and abuse
. Medicare eligibility, effect on . . . 201; 300

Custodial care
. exclusion of . . . 625
. hospice care . . . 270
. nursing homes . . . 244
. waiver of liability . . . 908

Customary charges . . . 211; 730

D

Deductibles and coinsurance
. blood . . . 223; 238; 335; 730
. home health services . . . 250; 335; 383
. hospice services . . . 270
. inpatient hospital services . . . 220-222
. kidney transplant surgery . . . 335
. laboratory diagnostic services . . . 335; 827
. Part B benefits . . . 335
. pn(e)umococcal and influenza vaccine . . . 335
. prevention services . . . 335
. skilled nursing facility services . . . 242

Dental services
. exclusions from coverage . . . 634
. Part A coverage . . . 218
. Part B coverage . . . 340

Dentures . . . 357

Deposits and prepayment requests . . . 730

Diabetes . . . 369

Diagnosis-related group (DRG) classifications . . . 810

Diagnostic services
. clinical laboratory tests . . . 827
. coverage of
. . inpatient hospital . . . 214
. . Part B services . . . 352; 353
. . SNF . . . 239
. supervision of . . . 353
. X-rays . . . 353

Dialysis—see End-stage renal disease

Disability beneficiaries
. eligibility and coverage period . . . 204; 311
. employer group health plan coverage . . . 639

Disallowed claims, waiver of beneficiary liability . . . 908

Discharge
. day of . . . 224; 243
. prohibition on patient dumping . . . 730

Doctor—see Physicians

Drug abuse treatments . . . 214

Drugs and biologicals—see also Prescription drug benefit
. anti-emetic . . . 362
. antigens . . . 362
. blood-clotting factors . . . 362
. coverage under Part A
. . hospice . . . 270
. . hospital . . . 212
. . skilled nursing facility . . . 235
. coverage under Part B . . . 351; 362
. EPO . . . 362; 847
. exclusions . . . 644
. . home health services . . . 255
. . immunizations . . . 351; 362
. . less than effective drugs . . . 362; 644
. . purchased by patient . . . 351
. . self-administered drugs . . . 351; 362
. . vaccinations/inoculations of preventative nature . . . 351; 362
. hepatitis B vaccine . . . 362
. immunosuppressive drugs . . . 362
. influenza vaccine . . . 362
. insulin . . . 351
. oral cancer . . . 362
. osteoporosis drugs . . . 335; 362
. payment for . . . 362; 820
. pneumococcal vaccine . . . 362
. self-administration defined . . . 362
. therapy for drug and alcohol addiction . . . 214
. vaccinations . . . 362

Dumping of patients, prohibition against . . . 730

Durable medical equipment—see also Medical equipment
. certificate of medical necessity . . . 356
. coverage under Part B . . . 356
. crutches . . . 356
. home health agency, furnished by . . . 335
. oxygen . . . 356
. repairs and maintenance . . . 356
. seat lift chairs . . . 356
. supplier payment rules . . . 356
. wheelchairs . . . 356

E

Eligibility
. Part A . . . 200-206
. Part B . . . 300
. Part C . . . 401

Emergency services . . . 227

Employees covered by employer insurance . . . 639

EMTALA (Emergency Medical Treatment and Active Labor Act) . . . 730

End-stage renal disease
. coverage . . . 205; 847
. employer group health plan coverage . . . 639
. facility reimbursement . . . 847
. immunosuppressive drugs . . . 362
. kidney transplants . . . 335; 847
. physicians' charges . . . 847

Enrollment
. Part A . . . 200; 203
. Part B . . . 310-312
. Part C . . . 401

Enteral and parenteral nutrition therapy . . . 357

Entitlement to benefits
. appeals . . . 920
. Part A . . . 200-206
. Part B . . . 300

Equipment, medical—see Durable medical equipment and Medical equipment

Exclusions from coverage . . . 217; 267; 600 et seq

Exclusions from program participation . . . 646; 710; 720; 730

Extended care services—see Skilled nursing facility services

Eyeglasses, or examination for . . . 357; 619

F

Factoring . . . 831

False reporting . . . 720

Federal government employees—see Government employees

Federal provider of services . . . 607

Federally qualified health centers . . . 382

Fee schedules
. ambulances . . . 355
. clinical diagnostic laboratories . . . 827
. durable medical equipment . . . 356
. end-stage renal disease facilities and physicians . . . 847
. inpatient hospital services under PPS . . . 810
. physicians . . . 820

Flu (influenza) vaccine . . . 362

Foot care . . . 622

Foreign country, services in . . . 209; 227; 610

Fraud and abuse . . . 646; 703; 720

G

Glaucoma, examinations for . . . 369

Global surgery . . . 820

Government employees . . . 206

Government entity, services provided by . . . 607

Graduate medical education . . . 810

Guarantee of payment to hospitals . . . 906

H

Health care practitioner . . . 351
. nonphysician . . . 270; 366; 826

Health Care Quality Improvement Program (HCQIP) . . . 710

Health insurance card . . . 200; 310

Health Insurance Portability and Accountability Act (HIPAA)
. privacy of medical data . . . 715
. rights of nursing home residents . . . 248

Healthcare Integrity and Protection Data Bank (HIPDB) . . . 703; 720

Hearing aids and examinations . . . 619

Hearings and appeals—see Claims and appeals

Hemodialysis—see End-stage renal disease

Hepatitis B vaccine . . . 362

Home health agency . . . 268

Home health aides . . . 254

Home health services
. advance beneficiary notice . . . 267
. aides, home health . . . 254
. care-of-a-physician requirement . . . 250; 260
. coverage, in general . . . 250; 383
. deductible and coinsurance . . . 250
. drugs exclusion . . . 255
. durable medical equipment, deductible and coinsurance . . . 255
. episode of care . . . 835
. exclusions from coverage . . . 267
. home health advance beneficiary notices . . . 267
. homebound requirement . . . 250; 264; 351
. hospice care . . . 270
. intermittent nursing care . . . 251
. interns and residents . . . 256
. medical social services . . . 253
. medical supplies and equipment . . . 255
. OASIS . . . 266
. outpatient services . . . 257
. payment . . . 250; 383; 835
. physical, occupational, and speech therapy . . . 252
. plan of care . . . 262
. post-institutional services . . . 250
. prospective payment system . . . 835
. qualified home health agencies . . . 268
. qualifying conditions . . . 250
. residence, place of . . . 264
. skilled nursing care . . . 251
. spell of illness . . . 250
. surety bonds . . . 268
. venipuncture . . . 267
. visits . . . 266; 383

Home infusion therapy
. supplies and accessories . . . 356; 357

Hospice care
. beneficiary rights . . . 270

Hospice care—continued
. benefit period . . . 270
. physician evaluation for . . . 270
. reimbursement . . . 270

Hospital—see also Inpatient hospital services
. emergency hospital . . . 227
. participating hospital . . . 229

Hospital-based physician—see Provider-based physician

Hospital insurance benefits
. claims and appeals . . . 900; 902; 920
. coinsurance—see Deductibles and coinsurance
. deductibles—see Deductibles and coinsurance
. eligibility—see Eligibility
. entitlement—see Entitlement
. exclusions from coverage—see Exclusions
. geographical limits . . . 209
. government employees . . . 206
. home health services . . . 250
. hospice services—see Hospice care
. hospital services—see Inpatient hospital services
. nursing home services—see Skilled nursing facility services
. outpatient services . . . 257
. payment of premiums . . . 203
. plan of care . . . 262
. psychiatric services—see Inpatient psychiatric hospital services
. spell of illness . . . 210
. voluntary enrollment . . . 203

Household members, charges by . . . 631

Housekeeping services . . . 267

I

Immunizations . . . 362

Immunosuppressive drugs . . . 362

Incident to a physician's services
. defined . . . 351
. payment . . . 820

Inpatient day of care, defined . . . 224

Inpatient, defined . . . 210

Inpatient hospital services (Part A)
. accommodations . . . 211
. blood . . . 223
. Christian Science sanatoria . . . 228
. coinsurance . . . 222
. covered items and services, in general . . . 210
. days of covered care . . . 224
. deductible . . . 221
. dental services, furnished in connection with . . . 218
. diagnostic services . . . 214
. drugs and biologicals . . . 212
. duration . . . 224
. foreign countries, services in . . . 209; 227
. inpatient day, defined . . . 224
. interns and residents . . . 215; 710
. laboratory services . . . 214
. lifetime reserve days . . . 224
. limitations on coverage . . . 220-226
. nursing services . . . 217; 810
. participating hospital requirement . . . 210; 227

Inpatient hospital services (Part A)—continued
. payment . . . 800; 810; 902
. physicians' services . . . 226
. psychiatric hospital restrictions . . . 225
. qualified hospitals . . . 229
. spell of illness . . . 210
. supplies, appliances, and equipment . . . 213
. teaching physicians . . . 215
. therapeutic services . . . 214

Inpatient psychiatric hospital services . . . 225; 387

Inspector General . . . 646; 700; 720

Insurance liability
. automobile insurance . . . 638
. conditional Medicare payments . . . 636
. employer group health plan coverage . . . 639
. Medicare's responsibility for payment . . . 636-639
. Medigap insurance . . . 740
. no-fault insurance . . . 638
. partial payments by insurer . . . 636
. workers' compensation . . . 637

Interest on overpayments and underpayments . . . 906

Intermediaries . . . 705; 902; 820

Interns and residents
. graduate medical education . . . 810
. home health services . . . 256
. inpatient hospital services . . . 215
. nursing home services . . . 237
. Part B coverage . . . 340
. physicians' fee schedule . . . 820

Intraocular lenses . . . 356; 357; 619; 654

Investigational procedures . . . 601; 602

Iron lungs . . . 356

K

Kickbacks . . . 720

Kidney disease or transplant—see End-stage renal disease

L

Laboratories, payments to . . . 214; 335; 352; 827

Late discharge . . . 224

Legal obligation to pay . . . 604

Legal representative of estate . . . 906

Lifetime reserve days . . . 224

Limitations on coverage—see also Exclusions from coverage
. drugs and biologicals . . . 362; 644
. geographical . . . 209
. inpatient hospital services . . . 220-226
. nursing home services . . . 244
. Part B deductible and coinsurance . . . 335

Limiting charge . . . 821

Living wills . . . 266; 730

Loans, overdue college . . . 906

Long-term care hospitals
. prospective payment system . . . 843

M

Mammograms . . . 369
Managed care
. graduate medical education . . . 810
. Medicare Advantage . . . 400
. nursing and allied health education . . . 810
. Part C . . . 400
Meals-on-wheels . . . 267
Medicaid
. relationship to Medicare . . . 707
Medical equipment—see also Durable medical equipment . . . 213; 236; 255
Medical information
. privacy . . . 715
. . authorization, consent and notice . . . 715
Medical records, privacy of . . . 715
Medical savings accounts . . . 400
Medical social services . . . 253
Medically necessary . . . 340
Medicare administrative contractors . . . 705
Medicare Advantage . . . 400
. appeals and grievances . . . 403
. beneficiary access . . . 409
. beneficiary information . . . 409
. beneficiary notification . . . 409
. contract determinations . . . 405
. election and enrollment . . . 401
. graduate medical education . . . 810
. marketing standards . . . 409
. nursing and allied health education . . . 810
. payments to participating organizations . . . 408
. premiums . . . 407
. provider participation rules . . . 411
. quality assurance . . . 410
Medicare secondary payer—see Insurance liability
Medicare supplement (Medigap) . . . 740
Mental health coverage
. Part A coverage . . . 214
. Part B coverage . . . 387
. psychiatric hospital restrictions . . . 225
Midwife services—see Nurse midwife services

N

National coverage decisions . . . 390; 601; 602; 630
NHSC past-due scholarship loans . . . 906
Noncovered items or services, charges for . . . 730; 821; 908
Noncovered levels of care . . . 244
Nonparticipating hospitals . . . 227; 229
Nonphysician practitioners . . . 351; 356; 826
Nurse anesthetist—see Certified Registered Nurse Anesthetist (CRNA)
Nurse midwife services . . . 366; 826
Nurse practitioner, services of . . . 350; 351; 366
Nursing home services—see Skilled nursing facility services

Nursing services . . . 217; 231; 244; 251; 351
Nutrition therapy . . . 357; 369

O

Occupational therapy services—see Therapy services
Office of Inspector General . . . 700; 720
Older workers covered by employer group health plan . . . 639
Optometrists . . . 340
Organizational structure, Medicare . . . 700
Orthopedic shoes . . . 370; 622
Outcomes and Assessment Information Set (OASIS) . . . 266
Outlier cases . . . 224; 810; 835; 843
Outpatient ambulatory surgical services—see Ambulatory surgical center services
Outpatient hospital services . . . 352; 837
. prospective payment system . . . 837
Outpatient rehabilitation services . . . 352; 385
Overcharging . . . 720; 821; 831
Overpayments . . . 906
Oxygen . . . 356

P

Pap smears and pelvic exams . . . 369
Part A services—see Hospital insurance benefits
Part B services—see Supplementary medical insurance benefits
Part C services—see Medicare Advantage
Part D services—see Prescription drug benefit
Partial hospitalization services . . . 387
Participating hospital (or other provider) requirement . . . 210; 229; 230; 231; 268
Participating physician and supplier program . . . 833
Participating provider agreements—see Provider participation agreements
Pathologist services . . . 340
Patient assessment instruments
. inpatient rehabilitation facilities . . . 266; 841
Patient dumping . . . 730
Payment for services
. assignment . . . 831; 903
. charges not covered by Medicare . . . 600 et seq.; 730; 821; 831; 833; 920
. end-stage renal disease facilities . . . 847
. HMOs . . . 405
. hospitals . . . 800; 810; 837; 902
. inpatient hospital prospective payment system (PPS) . . . 810
. Medicare Advantage . . . 408
. nonphysician practitioners . . . 826
. outpatient hospital prospective payment system (OPPS) . . . 837
. physicians . . . 800; 820; 903

Payment for services—continued
. rehabilitation hospitals . . . 841
. skilled nursing facilities . . . 839
. physicians' fee schedule . . . 820
. suppliers . . . 356; 800; 820
. therapists . . . 381

Peer review organizations (PROs)—see Quality Improvement Organizations (QIOs)

Personal comfort items . . . 270; 616

Physical checkup, routine . . . 619

Physical therapy services—see Therapy services

Physician assistant, services of . . . 351; 366; 826

Physician fee schedule
. actual charge restrictions . . . 821
. annual updates . . . 820
. limiting charge . . . 821
. nonphysician practitioners . . . 826
. payment for "incident to" services and drugs . . . 820
. services determined not to be reasonable or necessary . . . 821
. site-of-service differential . . . 820

Physicians
. assistants—see Physician assistant, services of
. defined . . . 340
. fee schedule . . . 820
. "gag clause" prohibition . . . 411
. interns and residents—see Interns and residents
. participating physician program . . . 833
. payment for services . . . 270; 820; 821; 833; 903
. private non-Medicare contracts with . . . 834
. provider-based . . . 226; 270; 340; 820
. self-referral prohibitions . . . 720
. services covered . . . 226; 340; 350; 351
. teaching . . . 340; 820

Plan of care
. establishment . . . 262

Pneumococcal vaccine . . . 362

Podiatrist . . . 340

PPS—see Prospective payment systems

Premiums
. HMO . . . 407
. Part A, voluntary enrollees . . . 203
. Part B . . . 320

Prescription drug benefit (Part D)
. discount card program . . . 535
. overview . . . 500; 505
. . beneficiary protections . . . 510
. . eligibility . . . 506
. . enrollment . . . 506
. . out-of-pocket threshold . . . 505
. . premiums . . . 520
. . subsidies for low-income individuals . . . 520

Presumption of fault . . . 908

Prevention services . . . 369; 619

Prior inpatient stay requirement . . . 230

Privacy of medical data . . . 715

Private-duty nursing . . . 217

Private fee-for-service plans . . . 400

Program abuses . . . 646; 720

Prospective payment systems . . . 800; 810

Prospective payment systems—continued
. effect on use of lifetime reserve days . . . 224
. end-stage renal disease (ESRD) . . . 847
. home health services . . . 835
. hospital outpatient services . . . 837
. inpatient hospital services . . . 810
. long-term care hospitals . . . 843
. psychiatric hospitals . . . 845
. QIO review . . . 710
. rehabilitation hospitals . . . 841
. skilled nursing facilities . . . 839
. three-day payment window . . . 810

Prostate cancer tests . . . 369

Prosthetic devices and appliances . . . 357

Provider-based physicians . . . 226; 340; 820

Provider participation agreements . . . 730

Provider Reimbursement Review Board . . . 930

Provider-sponsored organizations (PSOs) . . . 412

Psychiatric hospitals
. prospective payment system . . . 845
. restrictions . . . 225

Psychiatric services . . . 225; 229; 340; 352; 387

Psychiatrist . . . 340; 352

Psychologist's services . . . 214; 340; 351; 366; 385; 826

Public retiree beneficiaries . . . 206

Q

Quality assurance
. Medicare Advantage . . . 410

Quality Improvement Organizations (QIOs) . . . 710

R

Radioactive isotope therapy . . . 354

Radiology services . . . 820

Radium therapy . . . 354

Railroad retirement beneficiaries . . . 200; 206

Reasonable and necessary services . . . 601

Reasonable charge . . . 800

Reasonable cost . . . 800; 810

Rebates . . . 720

Recovery of overpayments . . . 906

Referral prohibitions . . . 353; 720

Rehabilitation hospitals . . . 841

Rehabilitation therapy
. comprehensive outpatient rehabilitation facility (CORF) services . . . 385
. inpatient hospital services . . . 214
. non-covered levels of care . . . 244
. physical, occupational, and speech therapy services . . . 381
. rehabilitation hospitals . . . 841

Reimbursement—see Payment for services

Relatives, charges by . . . 631

Religious nonmedical health care institutions . . . 228

Requests for payment ... 900
Residents in training—see Interns and residents
Respiratory therapy ... 214
Respite care, hospices ... 270
Room and board—see Accommodations
Routine examinations ... 619
Rural health clinic services ... 382

S

Safe harbors ... 720
Screening tests—see Prevention services
Second opinions for surgery ... 340
Self-referral prohibition ... 720
Services not reasonable and necessary ... 601
Services outside the U.S. ... 610
Skilled nursing facility services
. accommodations ... 232
. blood ... 238
. coinsurance ... 242
. covered services ... 230-239
. days of covered care ... 243
. defined ... 231
. drugs and biologicals ... 235
. generally ... 230
. interns and residents-in-training ... 237
. limitations on coverage ... 244
. noncovered levels of care ... 244
. nursing care ... 230
. participating SNF requirement ... 231
. physical, occupational, and speech therapy ... 233
. prior hospitalization requirement ... 230
. prospective payment ... 839
. qualified skilled nursing facilities ... 231
. resident rights ... 248
. "skilled" nursing care requirement ... 232; 244
. supplies, appliances, and equipment ... 236
. thirty-day transfer requirement ... 230
. three-day prior hospitalization requirement ... 230
Social Security beneficiaries ... 201
Social workers ... 253; 270; 366; 385; 826
Speech pathology—see Therapy services
Spell of illness ... 210
Splints and casts ... 359
Stark law
. self-referral prohibitions ... 720
Subversive organizations and activities
. effect on Part A eligibility ... 201
. effect on Part B eligibility ... 300
Supplementary medical insurance benefits (Part B)
. ambulance services ... 355
. ambulatory surgical services ... 386
. ancillary services ... 361
. benefit claims and appeals ... 900; 903; 920; 930
. braces, artificial limbs ... 358
. Certified Registered Nurse Anesthetist (CRNA) services ... 366
   charges for—see Charges; also see Payment for services
. coinsurance—see Deductibles and coinsurance

Supplementary medical insurance benefits (Part B)—continued
. comprehensive outpatient rehabilitation facility services ... 385
. coverage period ... 313
. deductible—see Deductibles and coinsurance
. diagnostic X-ray, laboratory, and other tests ... 353
. dialysis ... 847
. drugs and biologicals ... 351; 362
. durable medical equipment ... 356
. eligibility ... 300
. enrollment ... 310-312
. exclusions—see Exclusions
. generally ... 330
. HMOs ... 400
. home health services ... 250; 383
. incident to physicians' services, services and supplies furnished ... 351
. mammograms ... 369
. medical and other health services ... 350
. mental illness services ... 387
. nurse-midwife services ... 366
. outpatient hospital services ... 352
. outpatient surgery services ... 386
. pap smears ... 369
. payment by Medicare—see Payment for services
. physicians' services ... 340
. . provider-based ... 820
. . services and supplies incident to ... 351
. premiums ... 320
. preventive services and tests ... 369
. prosthetic devices ... 357
. qualified psychologist and clinical social worker services ... 366
. rural and community health clinic services ... 382
. screening services and tests ... 369
. therapy items and services
. . occupational therapy ... 381
. . physical therapy ... 381
. . rehabilitation services ... 352; 381; 385
. . shoes, therapeutic ... 370
. . speech pathology ... 381
. . X-ray, radium, and radioactive isotope therapy ... 354
Suppliers
. DMEPOS rules ... 356
. payment for items and services—see Payment for services
Supplies and appliances—see Durable medical equipment and Medical equipment
Surgery
. ambulatory/outpatient ... 386
. assistants ... 820
. global ... 820
. inpatient hospital—see Inpatient hospital services
. kidney transplant—see End-stage renal disease
. physicians' services—see Physicians' services
. second opinions ... 340
Surgical dressings ... 359
Suspension from program participation ... 646; 710; 720; 730
"Swing beds" ... 229; 839

T

Teaching physicians ... 215; 820

Technology payments, new ... 810

Telehealth services ... 388

Termination
. Part A enrollment ... 203
. provider agreements ... 720; 730

Therapeutic shoes ... 370

Therapy services
. hospice care ... 270
. inpatient hospital ... 214
. payment for services ... 381
. physical, occupational, and speech therapy
. . home health ... 252
. . outpatient under Part B ... 381
. . skilled nursing facility ... 233
. psychologists and social workers ... 340; 366
. rehabilitation services ... 214; 352; 381
. services covered under Part B ... 340; 352; 366
. X-ray, radium, and radioactive isotope therapy under Part B ... 354

Third-party liability—see Insurance liability

Transfer agreements, SNFs ... 231

Transportation services
. ambulance ... 355
. ambulance home health exclusion ... 267

TRICARE ... 607

U

Underpayments ... 906

V

Vaccinations ... 362; 619

Veterans Administration ... 607

Visit, home health services ... 266

Voluntary Compliance Guidelines ... 720

Voluntary Part A enrollment ... 203

W

Waiver of liability ... 908

Welcome to Medicare physical ... 369

Wheelchairs—see Durable medical equipment

Workers' compensation ... 637

X

X-rays ... 353; 354

TEC